Organisation and Management

An International Approach

Dedicated to: Anjette, Jasper, Hugo and Yannick

Nick van Dam

Jos Marcus

Organisation and Management
An International Approach

Noordhoff Uitgevers Groningen | Houten

Cover design: G2K Designers, Groningen/Amsterdam
Cover illustration: Corbis

Eventuele op- en aanmerkingen over deze of andere uitgaven kunt u richten aan: Noordhoff
Uitgevers bv, Afdeling Hoger Onderwijs, Antwoordnummer 13, 9700 VB Groningen,
e-mail: info@noordhoff.nl

1 2 3 4 5 / 13 12 11 10 09

ISBN 978-90-01-57704-9
NUR 801

About the authors & acknowledgements

About the authors

Nick van Dam

Nick van Dam is the Global Chief Learning Officer for Deloitte and advisor for Deloitte Consulting.

As an internationally recognized consultant and thought leader in Learning and Human Resources Development, Mr. Van Dam has written articles and has been quoted by *The Financial Times, Fortune Magazine, Business Week, Management Consulting, Learning & Training Innovations Magazine*, T+D *Magazine, Bizz Magazine*, and *The India Times*, among others.

He is a columnist for CLO *Magazine* (US) and *Intellectueel Kapitaal Magazine* (The Netherlands). He has authored and co-authored a number of books including: *Een praktijkgerichte benadering van Organisatie en Management*, 2005 (5th edition); *Change Compass*, 2001; *The e-Learning Fieldbook*, 2004; *The Business Impact of e-Learning*, 2005; *The e-Learning Fieldbook – Mandarin edition*, 2006; and 25 *Best Practices in Learning & Talent Development*, 2007.

He holds several advisory board positions including among others, The International Consortium for Executive Development and Research (ICEDR), Lexington, MA/USA, a global learning alliance of some 40 of the world's leading companies and 25 premier business schools. He is a visiting Professor at Villanova University, PA, USA.

He is founder and chairman of e-Learning for Kids Foundation, which is a global non-profit foundation (www.e-learningforkids.org), that provides schools and children around the world with free Internet-based courseware.

Dr. Van Dam is a graduate of the *Vrije Universiteit van Amsterdam*, Bachelor Degree in Economics, and holds a Master Degree in Organisation & Management from the *Universiteit van Amsterdam*. He finished his doctorate in Business Administration at *Nyenrode Business University*, Breukelen. He has lived and worked in the United States for 12 years. Since September 2006, he lives with his wife Judith and son Yannick in Hilversum, The Netherlands.

Jos Marcus

Jos Marcus has devoted his career to designing and developing new, state of the art study programmes for students in the field of Business Administration. He lectures in Marketing, Management and Accounting at the *Hogeschool* INHOLLAND and previously at the *Vrije Universiteit Amsterdam*.

He is currently responsible for the development and coordination of a new study programme called 'Economie Compact'. This study programme at bachelor level has been developed for experienced business administration professionals. Important design components of this study programme include: Action Learning, Tele-Learning and Self-Study.

Furthermore, he is co-founder and partner in Accompany, Innovative Learning Solutions which is specialized in the development of courseware including business simulations and other educational methods and tools (www.accompany.nl).

Together with Nick van Dam, he is co-author of *Een praktijkgerichte benadering van Organisatie en Management*, a book on Management with a widespread use among students at Colleges and Universities in the Netherlands. He has also co-authored the *TOPSIM Business Simulations series* in Dutch.

Drs. Marcus holds a Bachelor Degree in Economics and a Master Degree in Business Administration from the *Vrije Universiteit Amsterdam*. He lives with his wife Narda and three children Jasper, Anjette and Hugo in Wormer, The Netherlands.

Jos Marcus (left) and Nick van Dam

Liesbeth Perdeck
Liesbeth Perdeck is a psychologist. She worked in industry, for example, for the multinational company Philipp Brothers, for some ten years. She has also trained managers including those at ISBW. Currently, she works as a lecturer in Management and Corporate Strategy at the International Business and Management Studies at the *Hogeschool* INHOLLAND in Amsterdam / Diemen. She also freelances as a trainer and consultant.

Keith Medhurst
Keith Medhurst lectures in European Business Environment, Communication Skills and Business Organisation and Management at *Hogeschool* INHOLLAND in Amsterdam. Prior to this, he worked in the B2B travel industry around Europe, living in the UK, Ireland, Denmark and The Netherlands.

Acknowledgements

Nick van Dam and Jos Marcus co-operated with many others when compiling this international edition. Special thanks is due to Liesbeth Perdeck and Keith Medhurst, a wonderful pair who worked together on the translation of the main texts. Besides translating, they also helped us in various ways with ideas and support to make the project a success. Thank you! We regard them as co-authors of this book.

Furthermore, Judith Grimbergen is to be praised for her flair in writing the texts for all the inserts and Shanti Jamin for helping with translation of the main text.

Special thanks to Ageeth Bergsma and Martien Stege from Noordhoff Uitgevers, who have been of tremendous help in developing a top quality book.

Naturally, we must also mention the support we received from the homefront who made the writing of this book possible.

Finally we wish to thank those who also made contributions to the inset sections on International Management Insights.

Concise table of contents

Contents

Introduction

Nature and purpose of the book
Newspapers, magazines and television have a lot to say on subjects dealing with the ways in which organisations work. Through the globalisation of the world economy, many organisations these days work in an international setting. This book provides a broad introduction to subjects dealing with Organisation and Management in an international context. The subjects are dealt with from a theoretical point of view, but are brought to life by examples from international practice. This provides the reader with an insight into the ways in which theory is applied in practice. In addition to the traditional subjects of Organisation and Management, the book also deals with present-day developments in the subject area. The book is made more accessible by the layout, the use of words in the margin and colours, by its consistent structure and thematic construction.

Who is this book for?
The book aims at readers studying for Bachelor or Master Degrees and is a practice-based introduction to Organisation and Management. It can be used at both universities or colleges in several programmes since a basic textbook on the subject of Organisation and Management is included in the curriculum of many different courses. Moreover, it can also serve those already in employment as a useful handbook.

What is the set up of the book?
The book consists of three parts, namely:
A Organisations and their environment
B People and organisations
C Structure and organisation

Each part consists of separate chapters dealing with a number of themes. The three parts are preceded by a chapter called, 'The evolution of organisation and management thoughts' in which important schools of thought and personalities are discussed. The way in which people construct their organisations is influenced strongly by environmental factors. That is why we have chosen to take the environment as our starting point (part A). The central and vital role of people in the organisation (part B) leads us to the problems surrounding the structures of organisations (part C).

Each chapter closes with a workbook section including various questions and assignments. This means that a separate workbook is not needed. A website is available, however.

In the main text, quite a lot of space has been given to secondary texts (insets), which discuss practical examples in everyday work situations. These insets highlight both the international nature of the book as well as its theoretical basis. The insets illustrate the following subjects:

 International management insights

Business culture orientation

People-profit-planet

In the press

Advice

ICT

Figures & trends

Website
The book has its own website: *www.marcusvandam.noordhoff.nl*. When the book and website are used together they fit perfectly into problem-based and computer-based learning. The website supports the learning process and helps to make it more fun and more of a challenge. It runs parallel to the chapters in the book and includes for example:
· a supply of tests for each chapter
· a method for working with the concepts in each chapter
· different type of cases
· powerpoint presentations.

The theory, the definitions and the title of the book
There are two ways in which the theories in the subject area of Organisation and Management come about. On the one hand, they are based on experience and facts from practice. This is called induction. On the other hand, theories are based on certain suppositions from which, by a chain of logical thought, conclusions are drawn. This is what we call deduction. There is a strong interaction between the methods of induction and deduction in the construction of theory in this book (see Figure 1).

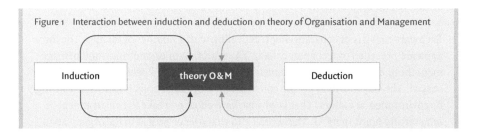

Figure 1 Interaction between induction and deduction on theory of Organisation and Management

A central theme of the book is the way in which organisations work in an international setting. But what exactly is an organisation? An organisation can be defined as: each form of human cooperation for a common purpose. This definition focuses on three characteristics of an organisation:

a it is about people who
b work together to achieve
c a certain goal.

The reason why people (= members of organisations) co-operate in an organisation is that certain goals cannot be achieved by the individual alone. Organisations are justified by the fact that (international) society needs useful and important products and services that they can supply. Consequently, an organisation is a part of (international) society, or, in other words, the environment.

The concept of 'organisation' is also used in this book to denote a company or enterprise. By company we mean an organisation that produces goods or services. An enterprise can be described as a company whose purpose is to make a profit. If we compare these two concepts then it is clear that companies are a category of organisations and that enterprises are a category of companies. Figure 2 illustrates this idea.

Figure 2   The relation between organisations, companies and enterprises

Organising is also a task or activity that puts appropriate relationships between people, means and actions in place. In other words: controlling and leading the aspects of production (work, capital and information) in such a way that the goals of the organisation are achieved.

Organising is an activity that can be carried out by one person or several. In many organisations, management is responsible for the organising. This brings us to the second concept in the title of the book: Management. We define management as the (theory of) managing an organisation. Management is made up of the people who are in charge and who lead the organisation. If we combine the definitions of organisation and management we arrive at the title of the book and the definition of the subject area of Organisation and Management: the theory of managing any form of human co-operation for a shared goal.

In closure

It has been a very enjoyable experience for us to work on this exciting project.
We hope that you value this study book and that you may apply a lot of best practices in current or future roles in organisations.

We look forward to receiving suggestions and comments which will help us to improve the next edition of this book (ho@noordhoff.nl).

December 2006, The Netherlands
Nick van Dam & Jos Marcus

1

The evolution of organisation and management thoughts

'The one exclusive sign of thorough knowledge is the power of teaching'
(Aristotle, 384–322 BC, one of the greatest Greek philosophers)

In this chapter, we will be looking at a number of important schools of thought and personalities that have had an influence on developments in the field of organisation and management.

During this chapter:
- You will become familiar with the main schools of thought in the history of organisational behaviour and personalities that have played a role during its history.
- You will gain an understanding of contemporary developments in the field of organisational behaviour.
- You will see how schools of thought and personalities are linked and understand the significance of this in relation to the structuring process within contemporary organisations.
- You will be introduced to a number of subjects that are dealt with in more detail in later chapters of the book.

Contents

1.1 Introduction

In the introduction to this book it was stated that the subject to be looked into is organisation and management. However the more widely used name for the field is much more original: organisational behaviour.

Organisational behaviour

We can define organisational behaviour as 'an interdisciplinary science that is concerned with the study of the behaviour of organisations as well as the factors that determine this behaviour, and the manner in which organisations can be directed'. When talking about behaviour in this context, we understand this to include actions and reactions within the organisations that are being studied.

This definition of organisational behaviour encompasses two aspects of the subject, namely:

Descriptive aspect
1 *A descriptive aspect.* This is a description of the behaviour of organisations, including motives and consequences.

Prescriptive aspect
2 *A prescriptive aspect.* This is advice about organisational design and the best course of action to follow.

This two-sided character can also be seen in other practical sciences, including medicine, psychology and the theory of education. However, the field of organisational behaviour is more oriented towards practical application and is more pragmatic than these in the sense that its methodology and theoretical basis is considered to be less significant than identification of the practical ramifications.

Interdisciplinary
The term 'interdisciplinary is sometimes linked with organisational behaviour, although this term is often misused. To clarify this, it is clear that organisational behaviour contains many elements that originate from other sciences. The study of organisations therefore involves many disciplines from various scientific fields. Some examples of these source fields may include business studies which comprises such topics as accounting and bookkeeping, marketing, technical sciences, information technology, behavioural science, organisational psychology, sociology, and law. If we bring together all the contributions from these fields that we need for research or project purposes, we will see that rather than an interdisciplinary approach being

Multidisciplinary
required, we are required to use a multidisciplinary approach. An interdisciplinary approach goes one step further. What we mean by this is that the various contributions from other subject areas are evaluated individually and are then used to develop a new insight, one which views the subject in its entirety. The old disciplines then cease to be recognisable in their original formats (in contrast, they remain the same in a multidisciplinary approach). This is therefore an ambitious approach. It is an ideal that is rarely reached. It is perfection. Often, even in organisational behavioural research, one does not get any further than a multidisciplinary approach.

Direction
Two other aspects of the definition of organisational behaviour are direction and effectiveness. The first of these can be described as 'targeted persuasion', or in a more specific organisational sense, the guiding activity that involves giving direction on a moment-to-moment basis when challenges take place or decisions are needed within an organisation. These directions should be aligned with a target that has been determined in advance. The processes are structured, and any development of and adaptation to the resulting structure forms an important area for management to focus on.

The extent to which such activities have succeeded is a measure of their overall

Name:	Raúl Medina Fernández
Country of origin:	Argentina
Job title:	HR Regional Director, Latin America and Caribbean
Company:	Deloitte
Company website:	www.deloitte.com
Other:	Visiting Professor IAE, Buenos Aires
Company website:	www.iae.edu.ar

What important personal qualities must people have to be successful in international work?
In my opinion, the most important quality for success in international work is to be flexible: to open our minds to understanding what drives other cultures. Another quality is to make an effort to adapt our behaviour as soon as possible to the patterns of the new culture.
Another important quality is patience. Changes in our behaviour sometimes take time to be accepted and understood by the new culture and one tends to feel frustration and isolation. If this happens, we need to analyze the reasons for any misunderstandings and then, when we have sorted things out, we should share our feelings and communicate, but now in ways that are appropriate to the local culture.

What do people need to know if they do business in your country?
People need to know that in our country, we communicate our affections, feelings and emotions very openly. At the first contact, Argentinians are likely to be friendly. They will probably kiss you even at business meetings, or if not, will offer a firm handshake or even a hug. Sometimes these physical gestures are very different from other countries' ways of relating.
Secondly, to do business in Argentina, people have to be very open in offering information about business matters and also about other activities, hobbies and family. Dinners and lunches are sometimes the best moments to discuss or define business strategies with Argentinians.

How important is the work / life balance in your country?
In general, we have a long tradition of long days at work. We work long hours and executives even take work home on the weekends. With the new young executive generation, this trend is changing and they tend to be more conscious of the work / life balance. The new generations have a good perception of the quality of life and they try to distribute their hours among work, family and sport. The influence of new neighbourhoods outside the big cities where young people choose to live is playing a very important role in this new way of living. In addition, new customs (such as coaching) are taking root. The family also plays a fundamental role in Argentine society.

What is the best way to motivate people?
The best way to motivate people is to inspire them to endorse the vision and mission of the company. No less important is to make them understand that their work, no matter what kind of work they do, contributes to the vision and mission of the company. The second point is that each person must develop in his job, both personally and professionally. We need to foster an understanding that it is important that each person be aware of the beneficial impact that their daily efforts and contribution to the job has on other people and stakeholders. Finally, leader behaviour: leaders must motivate people through their own good behaviour and integrity. If not, the vision and the inspirational messages that leaders express will not be recognized by the people.

How important is a business plan?
It is fundamental since it defines the present and describes the company's future horizons and those people needed to achieve the company's goals, vision and mission. Evaluation, rates, and balanced scorecards are the tools for monitoring the running of a company and the fulfilment of the business plan.

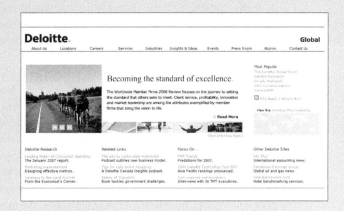

effectiveness. We expressly leave aside the matter of who should carry out the tasks: it may be the organisation's own formal management, or a consultant, a member of the advisory board, or even an employee who comes up with a suggestion during a staff meeting.

Organisational behaviour is often concerned with obtaining an overall picture of an organisation, an organisational problem or a specific project. This means that gaining an overview must become the priority, while smaller details are of secondary importance. If this were not so, one would not be able to see the wood for the trees. An organisational expert may obviously often feel less at home than a specialist in some organisational fields. You could describe him as being more a generalist than a specialist. Alternatively, we could call him a 'general specialist', perhaps warranting the criticism that is sometimes made that organisational theory is fragmented. An expert in the field might be seen as a 'Jack of all trades, and master of none'. It should not be forgotten that organisational behaviour is a young science that is still growing and developing. This is particularly evident if we realise that current debates look at a collection of approaches rather than a fixed system of knowledge and theory development. They have not yet formed a coherent whole in the way that approaches to mathematics and medicine have.

1.2   Origins of the field of study

The subject of contemporary organisational behaviour was born from the need to think in a structured manner about what to do in organisations and what goes on within them. In fact, the subject was first explored a long time ago. Back in the 4th century BC, Socrates and Plato put forward theories about leadership, task allocation and specialisation.
It was first taught as subject (although not yet in the present form) in the United States in the second half of the 19th century. After the industrial revolution, as businesses emerged and expanded, management became far more complicated and therefore required new and special skills.
One of the first persons to suggest that management was a science that could and should be learnt rather than a position awarded based on an inborn talent or inheritance was Henry Fayol (1841–1925). (See Section 1.7 for further details about his work.)

In the Netherlands, organisational behaviour was introduced as a major study at technical colleges soon after the Second World War. The subject was initially called business organisation and it had more technical content than now.
Organisational behaviour as we now know it was introduced into the Dutch higher education system during the 1960s and 70s. Other disciplines such as business studies, logistics, behavioural sciences and law were incorporated into the subject. At the same time, the idea of an interdisciplinary approach grew up. The underlying reason for this was the ever increasing complexity and size of organisations, particularly enterprises, caused by significant technical developments and general economic growth. The management of such organisations required more than simple aptitude in one of the appropriate fields or the possession of leadership skills. The need therefore arose for people who could examine aspects of the various fields and draw conclusions from them, or in other words, the managers of new businesses needed a total overview.
The initial impetus for change came from within the business world. This is why the new field of study was called business administration. Later on, other organisa-

tions saw the advantages of the approach and applied many of the new insights to their own operations.

Degree courses in business administration exist in a number of universities and colleges today. The topic is also offered as a module within other courses at universities and colleges though it is sometimes given a different label: organisational behaviour, business organisation, organisational theory, management and organisation, organisation and management or simply management.

1.3 The development of trading and the emergence of multinational enterprises

Trading between various tribes in various cross-border geographical regions has been a consistent element throughout the growth of international enterprise. The earliest examples of international trade can be found in the time of the so-called 'trade routes'. The Silk Road, one of the oldest trade routes, was set up in the 1st century BC. It connected Europe, the Middle East, and Asia, and therefore linked the large Roman and Chinese civilisations. The Silk Road ensured that commodities such as silk, fur, pottery, iron and bronze from Asia were transported to the west and exchanged for gold, other precious metals, ivory, wool and glass. This trading was mainly carried out by commission agents: middlemen who travelled a part of the route in caravans. The Silk Road went into decline as a trade route around 1400 AD. Other important commercial routes in history include the Roman trade routes (50 BC to 500 AD), the African trade routes (1000 AD to 1500 AD), the Indian maritime routes (from 800 AD), the Spanish trade routes (15th and 16th century) and the Portuguese trade routes (16th century).

The first international trading companies (or multinationals) were established with the support and financial backing of national governments who wished to support their commercial colonial policies. In 1600, the English East India Company was set up. Its prime aim was trading in East and South-East Asia as well as in India. In 1602, the Dutch East India Company (the *Vereenigde Oostindische Compagnie* – the United East Indian Company) was founded. The government of the day granted the Dutch East India Company an exclusive charter providing a complete monopoly on trade between the Republic of the Seven United Netherlands and what was then known as 'India', meaning all countries to the east of the Cape of Good Hope. During its 200 year existence, the Dutch East India Company developed into the largest company of its time, trading in such spices as cloves, nutmeg, cinnamon and pepper, and other products such as silk, tea and porcelain. The Dutch East India Company went into decline during the second half of the 18th century, primarily because of competition from the English and French. It ceased trading on 17 March 1798. Other important international trading companies were:
· The Danish East India Company (established in 1614)
· The Dutch West India Company (established in 1621)
· The French West-India Company (established in 1664)
· The Royal African Company (established in 1663)
· The Hudson's Bay Company (established in 1670)

Between the establishment of the first international trading companies and the beginning of the 20th century, the number and size of so-called multinationals hardly increased at all. However, from then on, there was a dramatic increase: from approximately 3,000 multinational businesses at the beginning of the 1900s to approximately 63,000 today. (See Figure 1.1)

Figure 1.1   Multinational enterprises 1600-2000

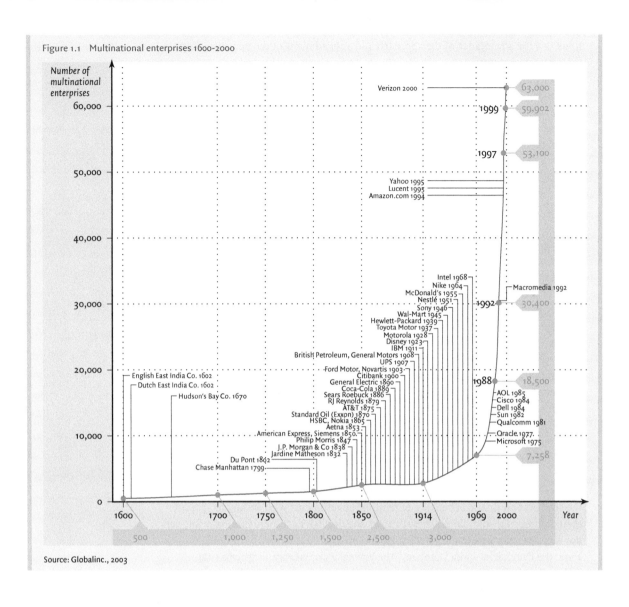

Source: Globalinc., 2003

There are a number of factors that can explain this growth pattern. Back in the 17th century, national governments exerted the main influence on trade, but this was no longer the case 300 years later on. Technological developments have also played a very important role over the past 100 years, shortening distances (transport), improving communication between people in different locations (telephone, satellite, Internet) and so on. Technology has also ensured that there is more and broader knowledge of different markets and diverse consumer groups. Enterprises have also shown themselves able to rapidly anticipate and react to global developments by making financial resources available for investments, opening offices and factories in various countries, and employing staff in many locations.

We use the term multinational enterprise for those organisations that operate internationally. Many of these enterprises have less than 250 employees yet fall into this category. Approximately 445 of the world's 500 largest businesses are in North America, Europe and Japan.

After this brief sketch of the development of trade and the birth of multinational enterprises, the rest of this chapter will be devoted to exploring the most significant schools of thought and personalities in the development of business organisation and management.

DuPont 200+ years

DuPont is one of the oldest multinationals. Eleuthère Irénée du Pont (E.I.) (1771–1834) broke new ground on July 19, 1802, establishing the company that bears his name. He had studied advanced explosives production techniques with the famous chemist, Antoine Lavoisier. He used this knowledge and his intense interest in scientific exploration – which became the hallmark of his company – to continually enhance product quality and manufacturing sophistication and efficiency. He earned a reputation for high quality, fairness and concern for workers' safety.

Early emphasis on employee safety

Safety in the workplace, a hallmark of the DuPont Company, became a major theme during the ordeals of World War I. Historically, being an explosives manufacturer had made DuPont more safety conscious than most other manufacturers. Especially significant progress in reducing accidents had been made in the years just prior to the war. However, the influx of tens of thousands of untrained workers into the munitions industry during the war created a

potential for disaster. Explosions did occur in several American plants, killing hundreds. During the war, DuPont made safety an essential and permanent part of engineering and employee relations. After the war, the new company president, Irénée du Pont, intensified the company's safety consciousness and began to award individual prizes for long accident-free performance. Irénée became a major spokesman for the growing safety movement in America generally. By the 1930s, it was established company policy for safety to be just as much a part of industry as any other operating feature (quality and quantity of finished products, efficiency, methods, etc.).
Today, DuPont operates in more than 70 countries and offers a wide range of innovative products and services for markets that include agriculture, nutrition, electronics, communications, safety and protection, home and construction, transportation and apparel.

Source: http://heritage.dupont.com

1.4   Schools of thought and personalities

Figure 1.2 places the most significant contributors in the history of organisational behaviour on a time line. These individuals often represent a particular idea or school of thought within the field of organisational behaviour. In the following sections, the schools of thought and personalities that have had the most influence on the development of organisational behaviour theory will be reviewed.

School of thought

But why are we delving into the past in this way? The reason is that these contributions still constitute part of the present theoretical framework of our field of study. Although they often originated in a different era (and might therefore be considered somewhat dated), they contain valuable elements that have a timeless character. Theoretical views and personalities of more recent times will also be discussed, and the reader might notice that many of the new theories have had their roots in the past.

The central issue has always been how best to achieve the goal through combined efforts. In addressing it, effective and coordinated division of tasks, selection of the

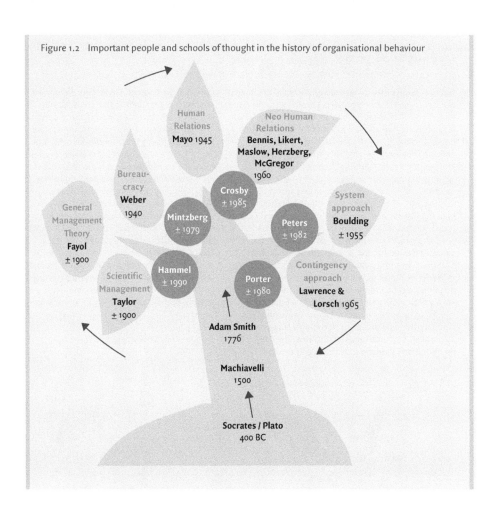

Figure 1.2 Important people and schools of thought in the history of organisational behaviour

most suitable leadership style, and utilisation of the most appropriate manner of communication play the main roles.

The contributions made by organisational behaviour gurus past and present have focussed on different aspects of organisations. Naturally, many of the theories have come from different starting points. Some theories have apparently arisen in reaction to a preceding one: it was subjected to critical examination and then called into question, or at least partly so. This produces a new explanation or approach, one which contrasts with the original idea though does not disprove the earlier contribution completely. As such, the theoretical framework of organisational behaviour has developed a rich and varied, albeit sometimes incoherent, character.

1.5   Events prior to the industrial revolution (400 BC–1900 AD)

As indicated in the previous section, notions about leadership, management and the design of organisations are, in fact, as old as mankind. Formal treatises on these topics were, however, quite rare before the twentieth century.
Nevertheless, we can find some examples in the writings of the ancient Greek philosophers such as Socrates and Plato and much later on in the work of the Italian Niccolo Machiavelli (1469–1527).[1] In his book Il Principe (The Prince) he provides numerous guidelines for rulers and other leaders. These guidelines are espe-

Niccolo Machiavelli

cially directed towards the preservation and expansion of power. They are extremely opportunistic in nature, based on pure self-interest and unscrupulously taking advantage of the situation at any opportunity. *Il Principe* represents Machiavelli's accumulated experiences as an adviser to the government and as a diplomat in Florence.

Until the second half of the 18th century, the dominant economic school of thought was mercantilism. One of its key beliefs was that the possession of bullion (gold and money) was the only measure of national wealth. The aim was therefore to export more than was imported in order to accumulate money which could be kept in reserve for times of war.

Mercantilism

Adam Smith

This view started to change in 1776 when Adam Smith (1723–1790) wrote an influential book, called *An Inquiry into the Nature and Causes of the Wealth of Nations*. Amongst other things, it put forward the notion that productive work is the source of prosperity and that effective division of labour can raise levels of productivity. With the publication of these ideas, Adam Smith rejected the principles of mercantilism completely. From this time on, management would take a more systematic approach, with much attention being paid to efficiency.

In the 18th century, pioneers developed the pressurised coal-fired steam engine, making mass production in large factories possible and replacing manufacture of products in workers' homes or in small workplaces. The explosive growth of factories attracted large numbers of workers from the countryside. As a consequence, Western society changed from an agricultural to an industrial one. In the larger cities, the growing working classes lived in poorly built workers' houses. The pay was low and living conditions miserable. This development began in England, then after 1840, it spread across Western Europe and the United States.

By the end of the 19th century, American companies had grown dramatically in response to the ever-expanding consumer market. By now, the existing controls and checks were inadequate. The division of responsibility between supervisors and staff was unclear, production standards and wages were determined subjectively and an air of unpredictability prevailed. There was hardly any planning. The managers tried to push the workers to produce as much as possible, often using harsh methods. The workers reacted in an organised way by systematically stretching out their time.

In such a situation, there was clearly a need for a more structured and systematic approach. The man who saw this and decided to do something about it was the engineer Frederick Winslow Taylor (1856–1915). With his publications and lectures, he laid the ground for what we now call scientific management.

Frederick Taylor

1.6 Frederick Taylor and scientific management (± 1900)

Frederick Taylor was the first to suggest a systematic, coherent approach to determine the manner in which factories should be organised. Rather than the manager as slave driver, it was proposed that a broader view should be adopted, allowing the manager to focus on planning, coordinating and overseeing, and checking of results.

Key elements that have grown out of Taylor's theory of management of organisations (scientific management) are:

Scientific management

1 Scientific analysis of the activities that should be carried out and the time and motion studies to be used . (The results can be used to standardise and normalise the production process and the machines and materials used.)
2 Clear division of tasks and training for the workforce so that each task and operation can be precisely identified and allocated. This results in worker routines, leading to an improvement in production.
3 Close and friendly working relationships between managers and workers being regarded as essential.
4 Managers being held responsible for seeking and analysing appropriate working methods and for creating optimum conditions for production. Formerly, this was left to the implementation phase.
5 Use of careful selection processes to obtain the best person for the job.
6 Financial rewards being given for following prescribed methods in order to reduce production costs.

Furthermore, Taylor proposed a division of front-line supervisory responsibilities within the production department into eight separate areas. Each area and its tasks was to be the sole responsibility of a particular individual:
1 Time and costing
2 Task instructions
3 Order of work
4 Work preparation and allocation
5 Maintenance
6 Quality control
7 Technical guidance
8 Personnel management

Eight-bosses system

This system has become known as the 'eight-bosses system'. Under Taylor's leadership the system worked, but it failed to become widely adopted elsewhere due to the many coordination problems and a lack of clarity for the workers.

Aside from his above theory of organisational forms, the influence of Taylor's ideas was enormous. Wherever his principles were applied, productivity shot up, and his ideas soon spread rapidly. However, the increased efficiency was rarely matched by an increase in wages or an improvement in relations with management, as Taylor had suggested should happen. The impact of such consequences, which the Charlie Chaplin film 'Modern Times' has immortalised and in which the names of Taylor and scientific management will forever be linked, was the idea of workers simply being an extension of a piece of machinery, with boring tasks, restriction of freedom and reduced job satisfaction.

Another consequence of Taylor's ideas was improvement in administration and management of production departments all over the industrial world. Administration and sales departments took their lead from production, and they were soon using similar methods in their processes. Next, sets of standards were developed, not only for production but also for materials. Planning techniques were developed and applied more than before, with accompanying improvements in control. Labour studies, job descriptions and job classification can all be traced back to Taylor's ideas. He has fundamentally changed working methods in organisations and is an important figure in the history of organisational behaviour.

Charlie Chaplin in 'Modern Times'

Henry Ford on new production methods in 1927

'A Ford car contains about five thousand parts. During our first assemblies we simply put a car together at a particular spot on the floor. When we started to make parts it was natural to create an independent factory department to make that part, but one workman usually performed all of the operations necessary to create that part, however small. The undirected worker would spend more of his time walking about for materials and tools than he did working; he received less pay because pedestrianism is not a highly paid line.

The first step forward in assembly came when we began taking the work to the men instead of the men to the work. We now have two general principles in all operations: that a man should never have to take more than one step if this can possibly be avoided, and that no man need ever bend over.

We first trialled the assembly line around about April 1, 1913. We tried it assembling the flywheel magneto. We had previously assembled the flywheel magneto in the usual method. With one workman doing a complete job he could turn out from thirty-five to forty pieces in a nine-hour day, or about twenty minutes to an assembly. What he did alone was then spread into twenty-nine operations; that cut down the assembly time to thirteen minutes, ten seconds.'

Source: Henry Ford, *Production and Prosperity (My Life and Work)*, World Library, 1927

IN THE PRESS

1.7 Henry Fayol and the general management theory (± 1900)

In Europe it was Henry Fayol (1841–1925) who first developed a coherent set of guidelines relating to the way in which organisations could manage their operations as a whole. His experiences as a manager of a mining company lead him to formulate his theory of general management, a theory which has affected entire organisations. In this respect, Fayol took a different approach to Taylor, who looked at systems primarily from the production angle. Fayol's theory was directed at organisations other than industrial enterprises. He thought that principles could be formulated that apply everywhere that people work together and that these principles should form the basis of a field of learning. His general management theory was intended to be an educational model. In it, he identified six independent management activities:

Henry Fayol

General management theory
Management activities

1 Technical
2 Commercial
3 Financial
4 Security (safeguarding people and properties)
5 Accounting
6 Directing

Activities 1 to 5 would be coordinated via activity 6 (Directing), which would consist of five tasks (see Figure 1.3):
1 *Planning.* Setting up of an action plan for the future
2 *Organising.* Structuring the organisation, its people and its resources
3 *Commanding.* Leading in a way as to ensure full participation
4 *Coordinating.* Gearing each activity to the plan
5 *Controlling.* Ensuring that the results are as planned

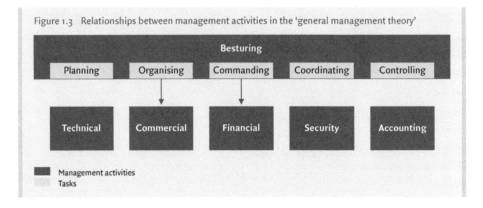

Figure 1.3   Relationships between management activities in the 'general management theory'

Unity of command

For Fayol, unity of command was the most important principle. Each employee should report to one immediate superior. Up until that time, this belief was accepted without question. It is evident in the army, where it is still the ruling principle to this day. Fayol's ideas are in agreement with this principle, a principle which clashes with Taylor's view, which broke away from convention in its functional organisational ideas and matrix structure.

Fayol's significance lies in his belief in the universal character of management and his strong support for training future managers formally in their chosen profession. His legacy includes more attention being paid to the tasks of managers.

Max Weber

1.8   Max Weber and the bureaucracy theory (± 1940)

While Taylor was focussing on manufacturing companies and Fayol on management in general, Max Weber (1864–1920) was busy studying government organisations and large businesses from a sociological perspective. According to Weber, large organisations of the day should have the following characteristics:
· Clear and definite division of tasks
· A hierarchical command structure
· Carefully defined authority and responsibilities
· Impersonal relations between officials (the position is more important than the person)
· Recruitment on the basis of ability and knowledge instead of cronyism and contacts

- Promotion and reward on the basis of objective criteria and procedures
- The execution of activities according to clearly laid down procedures
- All information, procedures and details written down, so that full control of every aspect is possible
- The power of officials, even the most senior executives, bound by documented guidelines

Weber stated that when an organisation functions according to the above characteristics, it can be termed an ideal bureaucracy. In his opinion, this was the most efficient form for an organisation to adopt as everyone in such an organisation would function coherently: like a cog in a well-oiled machine.

The 'ideal bureaucracy' is not just a description of an organisation but also a theoretical model that is helpful in the study of organisations. A number of contemporary writers in the field of organisational behaviour (writers who will be looked at more closely later on in this chapter) have also published theories in relation to such ideal types.

Ideal bureaucracy

We must see Weber's definition separate from the subsequent negative connotations that the word 'bureaucracy' has gained. It is common for us to link this word to ideas of inertia, red tape, an unending succession of pointless rules and so on. Weber's description was intended to be an objective scientific analysis of the dominant organisational form at the time. In it, he identified positive and effective qualities such as the execution of rules without personal bias, and the suitable operation of administrative tasks. He also highlighted some of the less effective, negative

How management guru C.K. Prahalad is changing the way CEOs think

Few strategic thinkers have developed as many influential global management theories over the past two decades as C.K. Prahalad.

C.K. Prahalad has a radical idea: he believes that the entrepreneurial ingenuity at work amid such poverty, where success depends on squeezing the most out of minimal resources to furnish quality products at rock-bottom prices, has cosmic implications for executives and consumers everywhere. Some of the most interesting companies of the future will come from places many executives don't even consider because they have been regarded as being too marginal. According to Prahalad, poor nations are incubating new business models and innovative uses of technology that in the coming decade will begin to transform the competitive landscape of entire global industries, from financial and telecom services to healthcare and car making. Globalisation, outsourcing, the Internet, and the spread of cheap wireless telecom are accelerating dramatic change. Few Western corporations fully harness these forces, Prahalad warns.

C.K. Prahalad's advice for executives
Think big. Set ambitious goals and then figure out how to mobilize the resources to achieve them, rather than the other way around. Most companies limit themselves because they focus primarily on what they believe they can afford.
Cater to the poor. People living in poverty, both in the US and abroad, can be immensely important

markets for consumer goods, telecom, and financial services. But they require high-quality products with appropriate technology and much lower prices.
Don't get blindsided. Some of the most innovative business models are being pioneered in developing nations. Ignore them at your peril. Competitors who use these strategies will transform your industry.
Reconsider outsourcing. Don't look at it as exporting jobs but as importing innovation. It will allow you to speed up product development, gain new technologies, slash costs, cut capital requirements, and boost flexibility.

Professor C.K. Prahalad sharing his views with the participants at a seminar in Kuala Lumpur

Source: *Business Week*, January 2006

characteristics such as inflexibility and the lack of initiative and creativity.

He saw bureaucracy as a perfect means of reaching management targets as well as an organisational form that functioned so perfectly in itself that its permanent continuation also became a target. The emphases on technical perfectionism could lead, however, to the structure being considered as more important than organisational goals, which of course would have consequences for the continuity of the organisation. Today, some of the characteristics of Weber's 'ideal bureaucratic' model are recognisable in some organisations, particularly in larger ones.

1.9   Elton Mayo and the human relations movement (± 1945)

Human relations movement

The human relations movement arose at the time when scientific management, with its associated rational approaches to managing work in organisations, was the most widely accepted organisational theory. It was against this backdrop that some research was initiated in 1927 into the influence that various levels of light in the workplace had on the performance of production workers in General Electric's plant in Hawthorne, America. In one group, light levels were raised, while in a separate control group they were kept as they were.

Hawthorne-plant

Production in the experimental group increased clearly, but to the amazement of the researchers, it also increased by approximately the same level in the control group. Then, when the lights were dimmed to a minimum level, the results showed an additional surprise, as productivity continued to rise! There was clearly a riddle here, and Elton Mayo (1880–1949) of Harvard University, was invited to find an explanation for the phenomenon.

Elton Mayo

Between 1927 and 1947 he carried out a series of experiments in order to examine the connection between improvements in working conditions (for example, shortening of the working day, increasing the number and duration of breaks, providing free soup or coffee in the morning break etc) and productivity. Each change led to an increase in production and reduction in employee fatigue. (See Figure 1.4.)

In the illumination experiments, the underlying cause for increased productivity appeared to be the increased attention that the staff were given during the experiment. Mayo proved his theory with this, and concluded that in addition to objective aspects, subjective factors such as attention, a feeling of security, belonging to a group, and appreciation had an effect on results. These subjective factors seemed

Objective aspects

Subjective factors

18

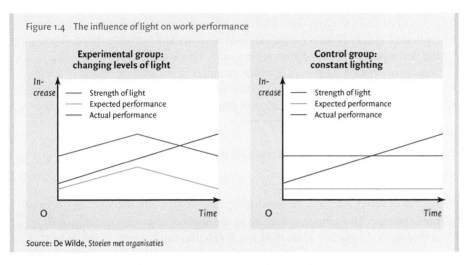

Figure 1.4 The influence of light on work performance

Experimental group: changing levels of light

Increase

— Strength of light
— Expected performance
— Actual performance

O   Time

Control group: constant lighting

Increase

— Strength of light
— Expected performance
— Actual performance

O   Time

Source: De Wilde, *Stoeien met organisaties*

even more important. According to Mayo, shared group determination exerted the greatest influence.

These thoughts – thoughts which have had a big influence on the development of organisational behaviour – were explored in his book *The Human Problems of an Industrial Civilisation* (1933).

The Hawthorne experiments generated a lot of research. A new form of management had been propagated, based on the social needs of workers in small groups. This went against the ideas of scientific management, which was strictly rational and directed exclusively towards the individual production worker.

The human relations movement is based on the assumption that happy and satisfied employees are more likely to reach their maximum potential level of performance. Management must therefore ensure good interpersonal relationships within relatively small groups. They must also give adequate attention to groups and individuals, demonstrate their appreciation, and provide sufficient responsibility and freedom to individuals. Cooperation is the key, so the possession of social skills by managers is very important. The movement's most significant contribution is the discovery of the link between human factors and organisational effectiveness.

Cooperation

1.10 Rensis Likert (and others) and the neo-human relations approach (± 1950)

The period 1950–1955 saw criticism of the ideas of the human relations movement starting to appear. Many saw it as an overly idealistic view of organisations, one that that portrayed them more as a social club, and one that would rarely if ever occur in practice. Moreover, the ideas were not supported unanimously by subsequent research results.

On the other hand, there was no desire to return to the ideas of scientific management. It was thus time for a synthesis of the two. Warren G. Bennis described the situation like this: the Taylor approach leads to 'an organisation without men' while that of the human relations movement generates 'groups of men without organisation'. He emphasized the need for a revision of the human relations approach, and from this, the term neo-human relations was born.

Warren G. Bennis

Neo-human relations

Other writers undertook to bridge the gap between the two opposing ideas, including Likert, Herzberg, McGregor, Burn and Mouton. These writers all approached the issue from an entirely individual perspective.

It was Rensis Likert (1903–1981) who first attempted to bridge the two approaches. He looked specifically at the organisational structure and internal communication, and developed the so-called linking pin model. This is a structure containing a number of overlapping groups in which members of one unit are leaders of another, meaning that the leader of one group is also a member of a higher group (a linking pin). This person not only leads one group but also ensures that there is effective communication with the higher group (see Section 9.6 for further details).

Frederick Herzberg

Another person who developed a theory in a similar direction was Frederick Herzberg.

His theory was in essence a further development of Abraham Maslow's hierarchy of needs triangle. This triangle is built up of five levels of distinctive needs, which, according to Maslow, we all try to satisfy. It can thus explain every aspect of human behaviour. Once a lower level need has been satisfied or mainly so, an individual's focus turns to the satisfaction of a need in the next level above.
In rising order, the needs are:
1. Physiological needs (eating, drinking, sleeping, sex)
2. Security and safety needs (protection, stability, regularity)
3. Love or belonging needs (friendship, family, group membership)
4. Status or esteem needs (prestige, position, success)
5. Self-actualisation needs (responsibility, personal development, making the most of one's abilities)

Rensis Likert

Maslow presented these needs in the form of a pyramid (Figure 1.5).
Although the theory has gaps and does not address every situation conclusively, it has influenced many. Herzberg, for example, applied this theory to the study of the behaviour of people in organisations. He searched for factors that strengthened motivation in staff working in organisations, as well as factors that lead to dissatisfaction. He came to the conclusion that when insufficient attention was paid to Maslow's lower level needs (physiological needs, security, and belonging), dissatisfaction arose. He went on to say that dissatisfied people could not be motivated. Recognition, self development and acceptance are, according to Herzberg, motivation strengtheners, or motivators. Significantly, an absence of motivators does not lead to dissatisfaction, but to a lack of motivation.

Abraham Maslow

Hierarchy of needs triangle

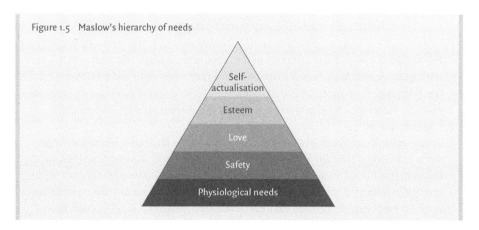

Figure 1.5   Maslow's hierarchy of needs

In his 1960 book *The human side of enterprise*, Douglas McGregor (1906–1964) presented two opposing views about 'the man in the organisation' that he named theory X and theory Y. With theory X, he outlined how most organisations at that time thought. These thoughts can be strongly linked to scientific management. With theory Y, McGregor explained his own vision about how employees in an organisation could cooperate. It should be pointed out that the X-Y theory says more about human perceptions than about the image of an organisation. Section 6.3.3 will look further at the X-Y theory.

X-Y theory

Douglas McGregor

1.11 Kenneth Boulding and the systems approach (± 1950)

After the Second World War, a number of neo-human relations supporters, including Kenneth Boulding (1910 –1993), developed a theory in which organisations were seen as a system (meaning they were viewed as a whole made up of coherent parts). According to this theory, all activities in an organisation are closely connected with each other. Another important element of the system approach is that organisations interact with the outside world (the environment).

As Figure 1.6 shows, a system (an organisation) consists of a number of subsystems (divisions) ostensibly connected with each other. When the total result of all subsystems working together is greater than the sum of their individual results, this is known as synergy.

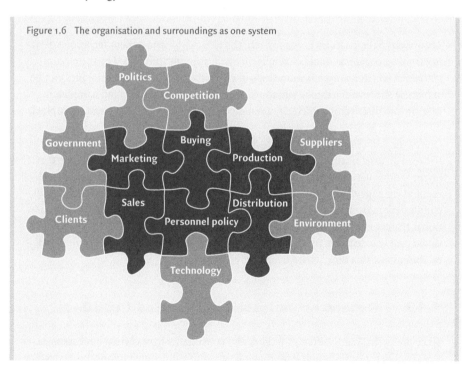

Figure 1.6   The organisation and surroundings as one system

A system (organisation) is run with the help of information that is given (feedback) to the various subsystems (divisions).

According to the systems approach, management should tackle organisational problems in a consistent way. That is to say, one should not only look at a single

Systems approach

part of the organisation when a decision is being made, but also at the effects on the total organisation. This sounds quite obvious, but frequently, local management staff try to find the perfect solution to problems in their own areas without understanding the consequences for other divisions. For example, a reduction in stock held will generate a saving in warehousing space but could lead to longer delivery times which could lose an enterprise some of its customers. This example shows the importance of using the systems approach in organisations.

1.12 Paul Lawrence, Jay Lorsch and the contingency approach (± 1965)

At the end of the 1950s, Joan Woodward published the results of an investigation into a hundred English businesses. In the investigation, she looked at the effectiveness in practice of the organisational behaviour theories of Taylor and Fayol.
The research showed that there was no connection between the extent to which an enterprise had been organised according to the rules of scientific management and its economic success. This was a sensational conclusion because up until that time it had been believed that there was 'a best way of management'.

Paul Lawrence / Jay Lorsch

Contingency

Two Americans, Paul Lawrence and Jay Lorsch, supported these findings. They carried out their own research in 1967 and came to the conclusion that to obtain optimal performance, different circumstances will require different structures, task divisions, and working methods. The concept of 'contingency' that they introduced means 'determination by situation'.

Jay Lorsch

According to the contingency approach, the choice of management technique deriving from an organisational behaviour theory is strongly influenced by the circumstances in which an organisation finds itself. Some management techniques can be extremely successful in some situations while in others, they may fail completely. The art is to discover in which circumstances which techniques can best be applied.

One of the most important elements of the contingency theory is the relationship between an organisation and its surroundings. It is of paramount importance that organisations have a clear focus on their surroundings. The contingency approach requires management to constantly be aware of how complex the interrelationships within their surroundings are and to seek the most appropriate strategy, organisational structure and so on for each situation.
In the past few decades, many new contingency studies confirming the fundamental findings of this theory have been carried out.

1.13 Recent organisational theories (1980+)

Since the 1980s, many different writers and consultants have carried out extensive studies of organisations and have then made significant contributions to the development of organisational theory. This has been of great interest to many organisations of the 90s and beyond. Many of these newly developed theories have not yet been fitted into a definitive 'school of thought'. A number of these theories and authors will be looked at briefly in the following section.

Kaizen and Toyota

One of the most important Japanese management thinkers on the topic of quality is Masaaki Imai. He published his book *Kaizen* (which stands for 'continual improvement in organisations') in 1986. He says that the best ideas for improvement can be found on the shop floor. Management should listen more for problems that crop up here. People on the shop floor are not the cause of the problem, but the source of the solution. One of the cornerstones of *Kaizen* is quality control and total quality management. This represents a development of the work carried out originally by Deming. In addition, as Imai explains in *Kaizen*, total quality control is a philosophy that will lead to continuous (i.e. not one-off) improvements in small steps over a period of time. Everybody in the organisation must be involved, from the top down. The three basis principles of *Kaizen* are:

1 The Deming wheel: plan, do, check and act
2 To measure is to know (all processes must be measured)
3 Quality should be controlled using tools such as quality circles

Quality circles are small groups of employees who voluntarily meet with each other on a regular basis to discuss problems that relate to their own work. One of the most well known businesses to have been affected by *Kaizen* is Toyota. All Toyota employees are

expected to make a significant contribution to improvements in many areas, from safety in the work-place to environmental care and productivity. These improvements are seen as the cornerstone of Toyota's success. It is worth noting that Toyota is the world's second largest car manufacturer, selling 5.9 million cars per annum in more than 160 countries.

Philip Crosby and quality control

An important recent trend in organisational behaviour relates to quality control in organisations. The founder of theories on this subject is the American W. Deming, who applied his ideas to companies for the first time after the Second World War. One of the best-known contemporary 'quality gurus' is the American Philip Crosby (1926–2001) who has developed a total quality management theory that is used extensively by companies in Japan, Europe and America. Philip Crosby was vice-president of the International Telephone and Telegraph Company where he was responsible for world-wide quality control for fourteen years. His company, Crosby Associates, is an important consultancy in the field of quality management. (www.philipcrosby.com)

For Crosby, working according to the 'zero defects' rule is crucial. This means that in organisations, one must attempt to avoid mistakes in all processes. He disregards the outdated view that quality control is only necessarily in production departments and not in the board room. Crosby believes that organisations can reduce their expenses by about 20% provided they treat quality control as number one within the work place.

Philip Crosby

Total quality management theory
'Zero defects' rule

Henry Mintzberg (b. 1939): organisational structure and strategic planning

The Canadian Henry Mintzberg stands out amongst his peers for his remarkable contributions to the fields of organisational structure, management, and strategic planning. He is Professor of Management Studies at McGill University in Montreal and a part-time professor at INSEAD In France.

Amongst the authoritative books he has written are *The Strategy Process*, *Structure in 5's*, *The Structuring of Organisations*, *Mintzberg on Management* (1991) and *The Rise and*

Henry Mintzberg

Fall of Strategic Planning (1994). He has won the McKinsey Award for the best *Harvard Business Review* article twice.

One of his most important works, *The Structuring of Organisations* (1979), can be seen as an attempt to blend the main organisational theories of how organisations ought to be structured. According to Mintzberg, the success of organisations cannot simply be explained by their choice of 'the best' organisational structure. He tells us that it is not possible to generalise about the best structure for organisations. In reality, there are many roads to success.

Mintzberg suggests that organisations should not view their qualities separately from each other, but that they should bring these together in a common form or configuration. A configuration can be seen as an 'ideal typical organisation'.

Configuration

Five basic configurations

He identified five basic configurations that he has since extended with two new forms, namely:

a The entrepreneurial (start-up) form
b The machine bureaucracy
c The professional bureaucracy
d The diversified form
e Adhocracy (innovative)
f The missionary (ideological) form
g The political form

These forms or configurations each have their strong and weak points. Depending on the prevailing environmental factors, the degree of turbulence or stability, and the goals of the organisation, certain strengths will become clear.

Although the configuration descriptions refer to 'ideal types' that in reality rarely or never occur, Mintzberg believes that the study of these is certainly still worthwhile. Because of such study, one can develop an ability to understand other organisations more quickly. A close look at the strong and weak elements within one's own organisation also has obvious value. In Chapter 9, Organisational structure and design, extensive attention is given to Mintzberg's theories of organisational structure.

In his book *The Rise and Fall of Strategic Planning* (1994), Mintzberg takes a swipe at traditional views of strategic planning. He concludes that strategy cannot be planned and that strategic planning often fails in organisations. Chapter 3 will look further at Mintzberg's views on strategic planning.

In one of his latest books, *Managers, Not MBAs* (2004), Minztzberg suggests that both management and management education are deeply troubled, but that neither can be changed without changing the other.

Mintzberg asserts that conventional MBA classrooms overemphasize the science of management while ignoring its art and denigrating its craft, leaving a distorted impression of its practice. We need to get back to a more engaging style of management, to build stronger organisations, not bloated share prices. According to Mintzberg, this calls for another approach to management education, whereby practicing managers learn from their own experience. He argues that we need to build the art and the craft back into management education, and into management itself. (www.henrymintzberg.com)

Tom Peters (b. 1942) and management principles for excellent companies
Tom Peters is a management consultant and founder of the Tom Peters Group in California. He has carried out some applied scientific research to find a set of management principles for organisational development. In 1982, he published the results of a study into 43 American enterprises that had all shown outstandingly

Tom Peters

Business lessons from world-class leaders available over the Internet

The Fifty Lessons Company uses the power of personal storytelling to capture the business lessons of world-class leaders in order to pass them on to the next generation. Experienced and respected leaders from industry, the public sector and academia are invited to contribute their most important lessons. The lessons are then fully indexed enabling Fifty Lessons to match its content directly to the strategic business learning objectives of its clients, which include corporations, public sector organisations and educators. The growing Fifty Lessons digital library already holds more than 500 individual lessons from over 100 high profile international business leaders.

Watch a lesson and visit: www.50lessons.com

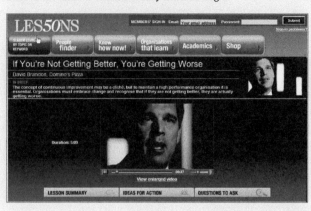

successful performance for twenty years. With his findings, he co-wrote a book with Robert Waterman called *In Search of Excellence*, which went on to sell more than four million copies.

To explain the success of the enterprises studied, which included McDonald's, Procter & Gamble, Boeing, IBM and Hewlett Packard, the researchers identified the following eight common characteristics that were found:

1 *Strong action orientation.* Although many of the examined enterprises used to make decisions in an analytical way, this did not paralyse them. The overall way of working was characterized by 'Do it, fix it, try it'.

2 *Close relationships with customers.* As an enterprise, you can learn much from your customers, and the most innovative enterprises took the best ideas for development of new products from their customers.

3 *Entrepreneurship and autonomy.* One of the most significant problems for big organisations is that they are missing what originally made them large, namely: 'innovation'. The art is to be large and at the same time able to act small. For this reason, an 'entrepreneurial climate' must be created in which employees with a lot of creativity can work on innovation. In such a culture, space must be created for the development of 'unorthodox' ideas with so much freedom that the making of mistakes is not punished.

Innovation

Entrepreneurial climate

4 *The employees are the most important source of productivity.* Enterprises that excel see their employees as a source of quality and productivity. One of the most fundamental points here is 'respect for the individual'. It is important to get the most energy and talent from employees.

5 *Hands-on, value driven.* It is of great importance that an enterprise indicates where it stands, where the enterprise is strong and what employees are proud of. All excelling enterprises seem to have clear values and take the creating of values seriously.

6 *Stick to what you know best.* Successful enterprises do not jump into areas in which they have no ability.

7 *Simple structure and lean supporting divisions.* All enterprises had a simple and clear organisational structure, i.e. not a matrix structure (see Chapter 9). Supporting staff divisions were also kept small.

8 *The structure is both centralised and decentralised.* Many enterprises that excel are run using both centralised and decentralised aspects. These enterprises control core issues from the top almost rigidly, while at the same time, divisions are given a large amount of freedom to use their entrepreneurial and innovative skills.

Recent history has shown that an enterprise that has had long-term success in the past is not guaranteed the same results in the future.
As an example, at the end of the 1980s, IBM was forced to cut its staff numbers by nearly 50%. Of critical importance is the ability of enterprises to continually keep abreast of changes in their surroundings.

In his 1987 book *Thriving on Chaos*, Tom Peters says that chaos has become the norm. Nearly every day, managers will be confronted with big changes that are linked to developments such as those in IT and telecommunications. Enterprises must show absolute flexibility in order to use chaos to meet new challenges in the market. In his book, Tom Peters gives 45 recommendations to management on how to do this. Books published by Tom Peters since 1987 include: *Liberation Management* (1992), *The Pursuit of Wow* (1994), *The Circle of Innovation* (1997), the series *The Brand You50*, *The Professional Services Firm50*, *The Project50* (1999) and *Re-Imagine* (2003) – an immediate number 1 international bestseller. (www.tompeters.com)

Peter Drucker

Peter Drucker (1909–2005) and general management
Peter Drucker is thought of by many as the 'father of all management gurus'.[2] Since 1939, he has written 35 books and his work has been translated into 24 languages, leading to publication worldwide.

Knowledge revolution

According to Drucker, following the industrial revolution and dramatic increases in productivity, we have now arrived at the knowledge revolution. Knowledge has become the critical production factor, according to Drucker. The importance of nature, labour and capital lies mainly in the limitations that they impose. Without these production factors, knowledge can produce nothing.
Drucker estimates that the number of people currently employed in traditional industry sectors such as agriculture and industry has fallen by 20 to 25%. The remaining three quarters of the workforce can be divided into three approximately equal groups, namely knowledge workers such as high-quality specialists, professionals and technicians, highly trained service providers such as sales staff, instructors and civil servants, and less trained service providers such as cleaners, drivers and administrators, whose wages often remain below other groups.

Productivity in the knowledge and services sectors
Knowledge work

Prior to 1990, management did not really direct much attention towards developments in productivity in the knowledge and services sector. Only now that the productivity revolution in the agriculture and industry sectors has come full circle can we see that an increase in productivity in the knowledge and services sectors is an absolute condition for further economic growth. A key characteristic of knowledge work is that the knowledge worker determines to a large extent the content of their job – and often without even paying much attention to productivity. Research suggests that about three quarters of the time is frittered away due to inefficient coordination or through the performance of irrelevant tasks. Productivity can be increased significantly if employees keep in mind what they are really being paid for. Anything else needs to be rejected. Other remedies suggested by Drucker for increasing productivity considerably are analyzing and restructuring of tasks, outsourcing of supporting service tasks (which promotes competition), and the forming of teams that are particularly suited to a particular type of work. According to Drucker, 'As well as there being an economic challenge to create higher productivity, there is a hidden social challenge to the dignity of (new) people with a lower education level who are employed in the services sector.

In his last book *Management Challenges for the 21st Century* (1999), Peter Drucker discusses how the new paradigms of management have changed and will continue to change our basic assumptions about the practices and principles of management. Forward-looking and forward-thinking, the management challenges of the 21st century include broad knowledge, wide practical experience, profound insight, sharp analysis, and enlightened common sense, according to Drucker.

Drucker's ability to question assumptions and see connections among disparate forces and data has made him a visionary thinker in the field of management. In *Management Challenges for the 21st Century*, he offers a head start on fundamental issues to anyone who will be working with any sort of organisation in the next century. (www.peter-drucker.com)

Michael Porter (b. 1947) and strategy

Michael Porter, a Harvard professor, has had a big influence on the development of strategic thinking and behaviour within businesses.

He is the author of 17 books and over 125 articles, and is a leading authority on competitive strategy and the competitiveness and economic development of nations, states, and regions.

Michael Porter

The value of his work, as we will see in Chapter 3, has been in the creation of structures for the implementation of analyses that lead to successful strategies. Porter was the first to monitor the link between the meaning of managerial work and its effect on the success of an enterprise. In an award-winning 1979 McKinsey article entitled 'How Competitive Forces Shape Strategy', Porter uses his Five Forces model to demonstrate how enterprises can analyse the market and their competitors' behaviour. In his first book *Competitive Strategy* (1980), Porter discusses mainly the 'what' and 'why' of strategy. The book is in its 63rd printing and has been translated into 19 languages.

His second book, *Competitive Advantage*, focusses more on the 'how' of strategy. Porter puts forward the suggestion that companies must search for their own competitive advantage. According to him, examples of competitive advantage include operating at a lower cost than a competitor, or creating 'added value' so that the buyers will pay more for the product or service.

Competitive advantage

In his book *Competitive Advantage of Nations* (1990), Porter says that countries or regions create the factors that determine whether enterprises are successful. He outlines a number of criteria that can be used by an enterprise to judge the attractiveness of a location. Again and again, Porter comes to the conclusion that an organisation's surroundings are the source of ongoing competitive advantage.

His book *On Competition* (1998) includes a series of articles on strategy and competition, including his *Harvard Business Review* article 'What is Strategy?' (1996). 'Strategy and the Internet' was published in 2001.

Michael Hammer and re-engineering of business processes

Michael Hammer is one of the most authoritative management gurus of contemporary times.

Michael Hammer

He has been a professor of computer sciences at MIT in the United States and is at present a director of his own consultancy company. Together with James Champy, he wrote the very successful book *Re-engineering the Corporation, a Manifest for Business*

Re-engineering

Michael Hammer

Revolution. In this book he argues that over the last fifty years, business has been based on three principles, namely:

1 The basic unit of work is the 'task'.
2 Simple tasks should be performed by less educated people.
3 There is a distinction between 'doers' and 'managers' (hierarchy).

In a world that changed slowly and was characterised by predictability and continuity it was understandable that these principles worked well. However, in this turbulent time with rapid technological developments and the explosion of world-wide markets, organisations are having to pay more attention to flexibility, quality, service and a reduction of overhead costs.

It is no longer appropriate to use the classic 'task-based organisation' which subdivided each process into all sorts of sub-processes that then were distributed across the whole organisation. This would obviously lead to unnecessary inertia, bureaucracy and inflexibility.

Process-orientated
Process

Hammer and Champy argue in favour of a revolution within business. At the core of this is the idea that enterprises will have to work in a process-orientated way. A process can be seen as a succession of activities that create value for the consumer. For example, when an organisation receives an order from a customer, dozens of departments will be involved. The customer has no interest in all the internal administrative and organisational processes, but is only interested in the final outcome. The process must therefore become the organisation's starting point. In a process-orientated organisation, a significant part of administrative and management supervision disappears. Simple tasks will vanish. The difference between performers and managers will become less clear. Professionals and coaches will work in new organisations. The coaches will concentrate mainly on inspiring and motivating the professionals as well as designing the work environment.

According to the authors, this new organisational approach will lead to big cost savings: between 40% and 80%. Before this can become a reality, top management needs to be convinced of the need to make this change (see Chapter 8 for further details).

Michael Hammer latest book is entitled *The Agenda: What Every Business Must Do to Dominate the Decade* (2001). The most interesting idea in *The Agenda* is that re-engineering must go beyond knocking down the internal walls that keep parts of a company from cooperating effectively. Hammer argues that companies must knock down their external walls too, so they can cooperate seamlessly with all the companies involved in making a product, from the raw material stage to the point where a customer uses it. (www. hammerandco.com)

C.K. Prahalad (b. 1941) and competition

C.K. Prahalad

Coimbatore Krishnao Prahalad was born in the town of Coimbatore in Tamil Nadu. He studied physics at the University of Madras (now Chenai), followed by work as a manager in a branch of the Union Carbide battery company, gaining management experience. He continued his education in the US, earning a PhD from Harvard. He has taught both in India and America, eventually joining the faculty of the University of Michigan's Business School, where he holds the Harvey C. Fruehauf chair of Business Administration.

At Ann Arbor he met Gary Hamel, then a young international business student. Their collaboration ultimately resulted in *Competing for the Future* (1994). This book described how management was in transition. It was moving from the old control-

and-command model towards one where managers had to find new market opportunities. Much depended on markets and the delivery of customer satisfaction. This was a riposte to the concept of business process re-engineering, which told companies to look for core competencies.

Delivery of customer satisfaction

In his most recent book (written with Venkat Ramaswamy), *The Future of Competition* (2004), Prahalad argues that companies have not made enough use of the opportunities provided by globalisation. There is an inability to realise that not only have the rules of the game changed but the role of the players has been transformed too. The 'customer' is more powerful and pro-active figure. They are no longer abstractions that have to be satisfied. Thanks to the Internet they are creative agents participating in transactions. The concept of value has also changed. It is not inherent in products or services. It cannot be instilled by producers or providers. It has to be co-created with consumers. They build this by experiencing it. The only way companies can compete successfully is through building new strategic capital.

New strategic capital

He desired a greater 'hands-on' approach to business. In 1997 he co-founded Praja ('common people' in Sanskrit), in San Diego. This Internet startup wanted to pull the Internet away from information-based content towards something more experiential. The company's fortunes were badly hit by the deflation of the tech bubble. Prahalad commented philosophically that this experience had taught him a lot.

Prahalad maintains a deep interest in the world's poor. This led him to write *The Fortune at the Bottom of the Pyramid* (2004). It stemmed from a 'long and lonely journey' to find a solution to the world's poverty. He identified the world's poor (the 'Bottom of the Pyramid' or BOP) as a potentially untapped market for companies, worth anything up to $13 trillion a year. 'The real source of market promise is not the wealthy few in the developing world, or even the emerging middle-income consumers. It is the billions of aspiring poor who are joining the market economy for the first time'. A market at the bottom of the pyramid could be co-created by multinational and domestic industry, non-governmental organisations, and most importantly the poor themselves. They would then have choice over their lives and the products they used. He pointed to Hindustan Lever's success in marketing soap powder and detergents in smaller, cheaper units. This created prosperity downstream through new distribution mechanisms. The book is accompanied by a CD ROM containing interviews with people whose lives have been improved. This has nothing to do with philanthropy. It is preferable to what has gone before. Poor people are too often patronised by certain aid agencies. He wants them to have real power in the marketplace.

Bottom of the Pyramid

The book also highlights the victimisation of the poor in some areas. In India, a 'poverty penalty' exists, where poor Indian families are forced into the arms of money-lenders charging interest rates in excess of 400 per cent.

Jim Collins and corporate culture and leadership

Jim Collins was born in Boulder, Colorado. He studied business at Stanford and stayed on the faculty after graduating. Having taught at Stanford for seven years he returned to his home town to establish what he called a 'business research laboratory'. Here he has become 'a self-employed professor who endowed his own chair and granted himself tenure'. His laboratory examines business issues and structures from a statistical standpoint. 'Others like opinions', says Collins. 'I prefer data'. His research work has involved looking at vast numbers of companies to find out what makes some good, others great, and others still downright awful. This involves a probe of how each company is managed, and the role of its CEO. This has resulted in four books, including *Good to Great* (2001).

Good to Great emerged from a simple question: can a good company become a great company? Collins and his researchers' answer was yes – but it wasn't easy. Collins started with a data set of over a thousand companies, but whittled this down to 11 that had consistently outperformed their rivals. These companies had things in common, but not what conventional B school wisdom said they should have. It was easier to see what they lacked: high profile CEOs, cutting-edge technology implementation, a business strategy or even change management. What Collins did find amongst the eleven was a common corporate culture that was big on the very out-dated concept of discipline. This was not the discipline of the martinet, but the good type – self-discipline. The companies rewarded self-disciplined people who thought in a self-disciplined way.

Types of leadership

But the difference between the good and the great was also down to different *types* of leadership. Collins says he was initially a leadership skeptic: it was too simple to pin great success or grim failure on the lapels of a leader. However this is what his data was telling him. On further investigation he identified two levels of leadership – level 5 (the great) and level 4 (the good). None of this is cast in stone, and a level 4 leader can grade up. He cites Lou Gerstner as an example: a level 4 manager at R.J. Reynolds who became a level 5 manager at IBM – though not immediately. Level 5 people have an almost heroic commitment to the company and its mission. The company gets all their emotions – there is no room or energy for self promotion. This does not mean that Level 5 managers are shrinking violets. They simply put the company before, well, everything – family, friends, and probably their health. But they are never alone. They should have a good team around them. This is their responsibility. Part of the mettle of the level 5 manager is deciding who should be on the bus and where they should sit.

There are other qualities which set the great apart from the good. These include the performance of their companies. These can be measured by financial results. Collins is a keen believer in assessing success through the company's stock price. This indicates a preference for publicly-quoted companies.

A Level 5 leader must also have the respect of other business and industry players, such as competitors. (Respect, of course, has nothing to do with liking).They should make an impact on their company, maybe their industry, that outlasts them. In his research he also looked at the identity of CEOs. Those companies who chose their chief executives from inside the organisation did better than those preferring outsiders. He suggested that outsiders are ignorant of the company they are entering at the top, with no gestation or apprenticeship period. He also suggested that outsiders lacked the capacity for commitment to a long-term relationship along with its necessary sacrifices.

A good CEO should be neither too humble nor too proud. They should not be too charismatic. They should ideally stay in the job for a minimum of seven years, as it was not possible to have any impact in a lesser time.

In his latest book *Built to Last* (2002) Collins (along with Jerry Porras) continue their analysis of visionary companies, looking at eighteen. These are united by wide-spread brand recognition, are world famous, but have been in business for more than fifty years.

Visionary companies

Collins' research stems from the corporate arena, but he reminds his readers that the lessons he puts forward are equally applicable in the non-corporate arena as well.

Kjell Nordström and Jonas Ridderstråle and changing businesses

Dr. Jonas Ridderstråle and Dr. Kjell Nordström are at the forefront of the new generation of European-based business gurus. They cut through the madness and
hyperbole surrounding the economy and their appeal is truly global. Dr.
Ridderstrale was an assistant professor at the Stockholm School of Economics and
is currently a visiting professor at Ashridge Business School in the UK.
Additionally, he acts as an advisor and consultant to a number of multinational corporations. Dr. Nordstrom is presently Associate Professor at the Institute of
International Business at the Stockholm School of Economics.

They have achieved fame amongst the ranks of management thinkers through their
books and their lectures, both of which are different. At their lectures (they prefer
to call them gigs) they appear (should that be perform?) together, dressed in black.
The similarities with the world of rock music are deliberate. Their delivery is fast
and punchy. Another flamboyant presenter, Tom Peters (a big fan) might be
described as a modern Country-and-Western performer; these guys are definitely
hard-core heavy metal artists.

Kjell Nordström

Their first book *Funky Business* (1999) caught the atmosphere of their gigs. It contained some stark and simple messages. The world of business had changed dramatically. What will work has to be different in a revolutionary way. 'Traditional
roles, jobs, skills, ways of doing things, insights, strategies, aspirations, fears and
expectations no longer count... We cannot have business as usual. We need business as unusual. We need different business, We need innovative business. We need
unpredictable business. We need surprising business. We need funky business'.
The successful organisations will be different too, unafraid of difference or creativity: they will seek emotion. The meaning of e-commerce must be changed to emotional commerce. Employees should be hired because they have some of that emotion. They can then be trained to carry out specific skills. They should be sought in
unusual ways at pop concerts even, far removed from the traditional 'milk round'.
Ideas are what will make a difference. Riches should be sought in niches wherever
they are, amongst 'homosexual dentists or pigeon-fancying lawyers'.
The workplace of the future will be Funky Inc. It 'isn't like any other company. It
thrives on the changing circumstances and unpredictability of our times'. The future
will be incoherent, dominated by movement and speed, by the imperatives of 'Move
it, move it fast, move it faster, move it now'. The strengths of an organisation will
not be core competencies but core *competents*, people whose skills and knowledge
make a difference. 'These walking monopolies will stay as long as the company
offers them something they want. When that is no longer the case they will leave'.
Today's world is a place of excess. This is the age of time and talent, both of which
are commodities. Talent will allow firms to be unique. The challenge is: how are
you make yourself more attractive, more sexy? In a world of economic Darwinism,
survival is a question of being either fit or sexy. Competition takes place using models and moods. Fitness boils down to using market imperfections to your advantage. Masters of mood exploit the imperfections of man by seducing or sedating
consumer. Excellent companies re-invent innovation.

Jonas Ridderstråle

Emotional commerce

Core competents

Their second book *Karaoke Capitalism* (2004) was never going to be a dog-eared
sequel to their earlier volume, a mere '*Funky 2*'. The two Swedes attempted to get
political and ideological, and to ask what changes we can expect to emerge from a
world dominated by super-fast and soulless machines. In places the book reads like
a manifesto, a call to the barricades. The world is undergoing change on a scale
unknown before, greater than the move from an agricultural to an industrial society

Karaoke Capitalism

that took place in Europe two hundred years ago. That took well over a century and was accompanied by major changes in behaviour and religious observance, not to mention political changes too. Individuals now have more choice than ever. The world of Karaoke capitalism is increasingly dominated by copy-cats bashing out cover versions of great originals. Only imagination, innovation and originality will place societies, organisations and individuals center-stage. The book talks about how to create capitalism with character, and how to live a fulfilling life while making a living. To develop the character of capitalism involves accepting individual responsibility. 'Look inside. Do you want to be a first-rate version of yourself or a second-rate version of someone else?'

Doing business in France

a sense of security. Nevertheless, individuality is preferable to conformity. They are reluctant to take risks, so little long-range planning is done, as the future is uncertain. One is allowed to show both positive and negative emotions in public.

Issues of equality / inequality
There is a highly stratified class system, but most people are middle class. However, there is much hostility between social groups. Superiors demand obedience from subordinates in all walks of life. Power is a basic fact of society, and leaders with the ability to unify the country or group are highly prized. Sex roles in society are fluid, and one's status is more important that one's sex.

How the French organise and process information
The French will readily accept information for the purpose of debate and may change their minds quickly, but strong ethnocentrism will not allow the acceptance of anything contrary to the cultural norm. Ideas are very important to them, and they approach knowledge from an analytical and critical perspective. They look at each situation as a unique problem and bring all their knowledge to bear on it.

What the French accept as evidence
Arguments tend to be made from an analytical, critical perspective with eloquent rhetorical wit and logic. There is a great love of debate, striving for effect rather than detail and image over facts. Feelings and faith in some ideology may become part of the rhetoric.

The basis of behaviour
Pride in their heritage sometimes makes them appear egotistical in their behaviour. Value systems in the predominant culture – how right is distinguished from wrong, good from evil, and so on – are described under the next three headings.

The locus of decision-making
The French are strongly individualistic and have a centralized authority structure that makes quick decisions possible. The relationship between the participants becomes a major variable in the decision-making process. One's self-identity is based on his or her accomplishments in the social realm. Education is the primary variable in social standing. Individual privacy is necessary in all walks of life.

Sources of anxiety reduction
The French seem to be preoccupied with status, rank, and formality. Contacts are of utmost importance. Their attachment to a public figure gives them

Ten examples of French business practices
1 The French are known for their formal and reserved nature. A casual attitude during business transactions will alienate them.
2 During negotiations, the French may make you seem to be the *demandeur* (petitioner), thus putting you in the weaker position.
3 Hierarchies are strict. Junior executives will pass a problem on to a superior. Try to cultivate high-level personal contacts.
4 Do not mistake a high-pitched voice and excited gestures for anger: they usually just mean great interest in the subject.
5 Business can be conducted during any meal, but lunch is best.
6 Respect privacy. The French close doors behind them; you should do the same. Knock and wait before entering.
7 Always shake hands when being introduced or when meeting someone, as well as when leaving. In general, the woman offers her hand first. In social settings, with friends, expect to do *les bises*, or touching cheeks and kissing in the air.
8 Find out the titles of older French people you meet, and address them in that way both during the introduction and in the course of conversation. Even simple titles like Madame should be used as you converse, whether in English or in French.
9 Do not use first names until you are told to do so. Do not be put off by the use of surnames; it does not mean that the French are unfriendly. If you speak French, use the *vous* form until you are asked to use *tu*.
10 Good gifts include books or music, as they show interest in the intellect. Bring best-sellers, especially biographies. The thicker and more complex the book, the better; simplicity is not a virtue in France.

Source: *Kiss, Bow, or Shake Hands: How to Do Business in Sixty Countries*, by Terri Morrison, Wayne A. Conaway and George A. Borden, Adams Media, 2006

Summary

Organisational behaviour is an interdisciplinary science that focusses on the study of behaviour in organisations. Key areas studied include factors that determine this behaviour, and the most effective ways of directing organisations.

The history of this field goes back to the time of Socrates and Plato. In the 1960s and 1970s, organisational behaviour as we now know it appeared in the Netherlands.

The schools of thought and personalities mentioned in this chapter have all had an influence on developments in the field of organisational behaviour. The developments are both historical and recent.

We have provided a summary of the featured personalities and schools of thought based on major characteristics and key philosophies:

- Niccolo Machiavelli (1469–1527)
- Adam Smith (1723–1790)
- Scientific management (around 1900)
- Henry Fayol (1841–1925)
- Max Weber (1864–1920)
- Human relations (around 1945)
- Neo-human relations (around 1950)
- Systems approach (around 1950)
- Contingency approach (around 1965)
- Philip Crosby (from about 1985)
- Henry Mintzberg (from about 1979)
- Tom Peters (from about 1982)
- Peter Drucker (from about 1980)
- Michael Porter (from about 1980)
- Michael Hammer (from about 1990)
- C.K. Prahalad (from about 1994)
- Jim Collins (from about 2001)
- Kjell Nordström and Jonas Ridderstråle (from about 1999)
- Power and opportunism
- Division of labour and productivity
- Production organisation and efficiency
- General management theory
- Bureaucracy and the ideal type organisation
- Informal organisation and subjectivity
- Synthesis of scientific management and human relations: the division between people and organisation
- The organisation as a system and in its interaction with its surroundings
- The application of management techniques dependent on the situation
- Quality management in organisations
- Configuration theory and seven configurations
- Management principles for outstanding companies
- Knowledge as an essential production factor
- Strategy and competitive advantage
- Re-structuring of business processes
- Competition
- Corporate culture and leadership
- Changing business

§ 1.1 Induction	The development of theories primarily derived from experience and facts gained from practical situations.
Deduction	The development of theories primarily derived from hypotheses that are subjected to further reasoning before specific conclusions are drawn.
Organisation	A group of people working together towards a common goal.
Organise	The creation of effective relationships between people, resources and operations, controlling and managing production factors in such a manner that organisational goals are reached.
The field of organisation and management	The theory of human collaboration in any form and the direction it is taking.
Management	The theory of directing an organisation.
§ 1.2 Organisational behaviour	An interdisciplinary science that is concerned with the study of the behaviour of organisations as well as the factors that influence this behaviour and the ways in which organisations can be most effectively managed.
Behaviour of organisations	The way organisations act and react.
Descriptive aspect	A description of the behaviour of organisations showing motives and consequences.
Prescriptive aspect	Advice to be followed concerning course of action and organisational design.
Interdisciplinary	Organisational behaviour contains many elements that originate from sciences such as business studies, marketing, technical sciences, behavioural science and law.
Multidisciplinary	The various contributions made by the various sciences are weighed up, compared with one another and then used to develop a new approach – one in which the subject is seen in its entirety.
Direction	Guiding the processes that take place in an organisation.
§ 1.3 Silk Road	The Silk Road was one of the oldest trade routes. It was set up in the 1st century BC and encompassed Europe, the Middle East and Asia. It linked the great Roman and Chinese civilizations.

§ 1.6 Scientific management	A systematic, coherent managerial approach relating to the manner in which production should be organised. A manager must have a broad view of his / her organisational tasks, including planning, coordinating, overseeing, and checking of results.
§ 1.7 General management theory	A coherent system of views relating to the manner in which organisations as a whole should be run. It has to do with universal principles that apply everywhere people work together.
§ 1.8 Human relations movement	The basic premise of the HR movement is that happy and satisfied employees perform better. Management must therefore give adequate attention to groups and individuals, demonstrate appreciation for appropriate behaviour, and give individuals sufficient responsibility and freedom.
Linking pin structure	The organisation consists of groups that overlap in such a way that the leader of the group is also a member of a higher group. He / she must lead the group, and also ensure good communication with the higher group.
§ 1.9 Systems approach	An approach whereby an organisation is seen as a system, i.e. a whole unit made up of coherent parts. According to this approach, all activities in organisations are closely connected to each other. The systems approach proposes that management adopt an integrated policy when tackling organisational problems.
§ 1.10 Contingency approach	Pertains to choosing the most appropriate specific management technique. The approach derives from organisational theory and is strongly influenced by the circumstances in which an organisation finds itself. The art is to discover in which circumstances certain techniques can best be applied.
§ 1.11 Configuration	Organisations should not view their qualities separately from each other but bring these together in a common form or configuration. A configuration can be seen as an 'ideal typical organisation'. The following qualities are significant: organisation members, coordination mechanisms, design parameters and situational factors.
Process	A process can be seen as a series of activities that create value for the customer.

Statements

Decide which of the following statements are correct or incorrect and give reasons for your answer.

1 Organisational behaviour is primarily a multidisciplinary science.
2 Effectiveness means a high extent of efficiency.
3 Adam Smith suggested that a division of tasks could significantly raise work productivity.
4 Unity of command means that every employee has only one immediate boss.
5 An organisation with a linking pin structure is likely to experience a lot of horizontal discussion.
6 'Theory X and Y' describes how organisations (rather than humans) are seen.
7 According to the contingency approach, certain management techniques can be very successful in some situations, whereas they will fail completely in others.
8 With reference to his seven configurations, Mintzberg has indicated how an organisation can be best structured in different situations.
9 Competitive advantage can be measured in absolute terms.
10 According to Michael Hammer, nowadays it is necessary to adopt a process-orientated work system instead of one that is based on function.

Theory questions

1 An employee has some problems and cannot meet the normal productivity standards. Describe how a manager should deal with this using the following techniques:
  a Scientific management
  b Human relations approach
  c Neo-human relations approach.
2 Give an explanation for the increase in the number of multinational businesses from approximately 3,000 at the beginning of the 20th century to approximately 63,000 at the start of the 21st century.
3 'Within organisations that are very technologically oriented, one finds more of the features of scientific management than in a service organisation'. Give your opinion on this statement and back it up with supporting arguments.
4 'An organisation that has been developed following the bureaucratic model is by definition characterised as stiff, lacking initiative and missing creativity'. Give your opinion on this statement, backing it up with supporting arguments.
5 Describe the connection between Michael Hammer's business processes restructuring theory and Michael Porter's theory of 'added value'.

 For answers see www.marcusvandam.noordhoff.nl.

Mini case study

The DHL Network – world-wide fast information

The company name DHL comes from the initials of its three founders: Adrian Dalsey, Larry Hillblom and Robert Lynn. In 1969, the three partners took a small step that would have a profound impact on the way the world does business. The founders began to send shipping documentation by air from San Francisco to Honolulu, beginning customs clearance of the ship's cargo before the actual arrival of the ship and dramatically reducing waiting time in the harbour. This idea laid the foundations for a new business sector: international air express, the fast delivery of documents and shipments by air.

DHL is the global market leader in international express, overland transport and air freight. It is also the world's number 1 in ocean freight and contract logistics. DHL offers a full range of customised solutions – from express document shipping to supply chain management.

DHL statistical details
Number of employees: around 285,000
Number of offices: around 6,500

Number of hubs, warehouses & terminals: more than 450
Number of gateways: 240
Number of aircraft: 420
Number of vehicles: 76,200
Number of countries & territories: more than 220
Shipments per year: more than 1.5 billion
Destinations covered: 120,000

In order to be able to transport the enormous volume of documents, standardization of activities and processes is needed. Only then is DHL able to deliver packages quickly and accurately to the required destinations. Furthermore, DHL aims to deliver a made-to-measure service to their customers. This might seem contradictory: 'Taylorism' and free trade seem to go quite well together in practice.

Source:
http://www.dhl.co.uk/publish/gb/en/about/history.high.html

Question

1   Do 'Taylorism' and the freedom to trade really possess conflicting characteristics?

E-mail case study

To:	Karina Thomson
Cc:	
Bcc:	
Subject:	The Royal Bank of Scotland Group

Message:

Dear Karina,

As you know, one of ABN AMRO's key activities is mortgage lending, and traditionally we have enjoyed a high market share. However, this market share has fallen during the last few years and our initial investigations suggest that the Royal Bank of Scotland Group is becoming a significant competitor within the Dutch market.

In one way or another we must improve our management procedures and adapt. But how? On behalf of the management of the mortgage department, I would like to ask you to produce a report on the Royal Bank of Scotland Group. In your investigation we'd like you use the management principles formulated by Tom Peters as a guide.

Karina, please analyse where the Royal Bank of Scotland Group stands in relation to each of the eight characteristics that make an organisation successful. We can then take a leaf from the Scottish bank's book, improving and adapting our own management processes.

Kind regards,
Piet Dankers
ABN Amro

Part A **Organisa- tions and their environment**

In this section, we will examine the ways in which organisations interact with their surroundings. Initially we will look at the environmental factors that exert an influence on organisations. Then we will look at how organisations determine their course in view of these factors. Such a strategy can sometimes lead to collaboration between various organisations.

The section 'Organisations and their environment' consists of the following chapters:

Contents

2

Environmental influences

This chapter discusses stakeholders and the environmental factors that exert an influence on organisations. The functioning of organisations is dependent on the demands and desires emanating from these two factors.

Contents

After studying this chapter:
— You will be able to identify the various environmental factors and stakeholders that exert an influence on the organisation.
— You will understand how these influences affect individual organisations.

2.1   Organisations

Organisations are part of our society, our daily lives. Our society can be regarded as the environment within which organisations work.

Environment

Parties

An organisation's environment consists of parties or stakeholders such as buyers, suppliers, competitors and financiers. These each exert an influence on organisations: they inspect the products or services of an organisation and place demands on them that must be met to a satisfactory level. Some examples of these demands are a favourable price, environmentally friendly production and packaging, good quality materials and fast delivery.

Organisations can, however, also exert an influence on these individuals and parties through means such as advertising campaigns, the provision of information, the giving of advice, the supply of products and services, and maintaining direct contact with their stakeholders.

Environmental influences

In addition to this, the organisation can be affected by those environmental influences that it does not have significant control over, but that are of high significance in the market. We include here aspects such as economic development, technological development, climate, and demographic developments. These macro factor influences are called environmental factors.

Environmental factors

Figure 2.1 shows the main stakeholder and environmental factors that exert an influence on organisations.

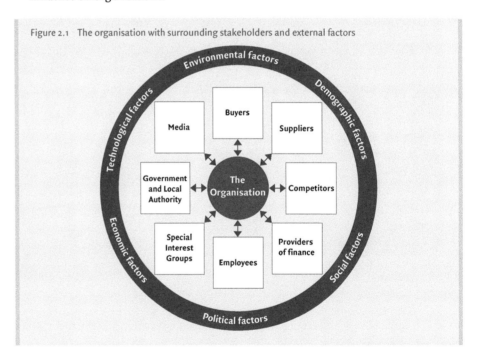

Figure 2.1   The organisation with surrounding stakeholders and external factors

Environmental influences generate circumstances that organisations must take careful account of. Many organisations find themselves confronted by extremely unstable circumstances and these have to be dealt with appropriately and effectively. This can take the form of significant changes to the products and / or services offered, or a revision of pricing strategy so as to change the pricing position within the market. It could also include changes in delivery method, the production process, organisation size and structure, the location of premises, relations with employees and so on.

Name:	Florence Plessier
Country of origin:	France
Lived in:	Singapore & France
Job title:	Executive Coach
Company:	FPEC (Europe) & Transformance Coaching & Services (Asia)
Company website:	www.transformance-coaching.com

What important personal qualities must people have to be successful in international work?
Real and genuine openness. In international environments, what we have learned to be true is not true anymore, and what we have seen work does not work anymore. Success lies on the inner belief that business is built on a win-win scenario where we truly respect each other's perspective, stakes and constraints, even if we do not really understand the values that that are the anchors. It takes real and genuine openness to want to discover each perspective and accept leaving aside your own concepts to transform two divergent ways of doing business into a common, shared culture.

What is the most important lesson that you have learned by working with people from different cultures?
I have learned to question my assumptions. When interacting with people from a different culture, the only assumption I can make is that I cannot make any. I cannot interpret body language to help me understand how people feel; I am not sure that I understand the meaning that they put behind the words that they use. There is no common past or experiences that we share that can help me predict how they will react. My instinctive interpretation of the situation will lead me astray. When I start from those assumptions, I ask questions, solicit rephrasing, test my interpretation in a respectful manner, creating trust and allowing for a deeper level of communication.

What do people need to know if they do business in your country?
The French educational system promotes and develops rationalism and argumentative skills. We are asked to approach problems and decisions with a Cartesian approach, taught to look for the flaw – in a spirit of improvement that is not always visible – and trained to find counter arguments for the sake of rhetoric. You might find people disagreeing with you when they actually would have done the same faced with a similar choice. You can count on a certain level of creativity or innovation once the rhetoric has evaporated. It might also be helpful to remember that in French culture, who you are is more important than what you do.

What is the best way to motivate people?
The best way to motivate people is to find what motivates them and to empower them to bring that motivational source to their work environment. It requires an environment of trust and openness where individuals feel that they can be authentic. Employees want an opportunity to contribute and experience the feeling of worthiness that is generated by success.

How can organisations become more effective?
I associate effectiveness with nimbleness: organisations that can re-invent themselves when there are serious changes in their environment – customer, market, competition, resources – and individual employees willing and able to shift and transform both their skill sets and their mode of operation to adjust to changing characteristics. It would probably require a capacity to create alignment very fast, processes built at a meta level with embedded flexibility, selection processes that identify adaptability to change and willingness to learn as a entry criteria, an empowered work force, on-going and permanent learning systems, to mention only a few. A 'bio' form of organisation.

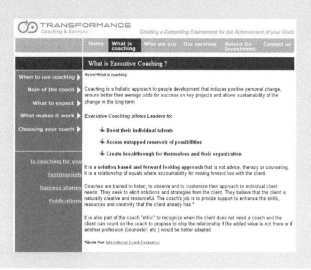

Directing an organisation by taking account of the influence of the surroundings is known as harmonisation. This chapter will look at the influences that stakeholders and environmental factors have on organisations.

2.2   Stakeholders

As already indicated in the introduction, the main direct influences on organisations are those from stakeholders and the surroundings. In this section, the influence of the following stakeholders will be discussed:
- Buyers
- Suppliers
- Competitors
- Providers of finance
- Employees
- Special interest groups
- Government and local authority institutions
- Media

Buyers

Buyers

Buyers, or consumers, are an important group as they demand products and services. The organisation gains its right to exist by satisfying these needs. The needs of the consumer often change and organisations must take such changes into account when determining the composition and features of their product range. In the last few years, many new products have arrived on the market as a result of changing buyer needs. They include new low-fat dairy products, MP3 players, hydrogen powered cars, environmentally friendly washing powders, low energy light bulbs, and new forms of mortgages and insurances.
If an organisation pays insufficient attention to changing consumer needs, the existing available products may become less popular and as a consequence, the organisation will lose customers. Customers certainly exert a powerful influence on organisations!

Suppliers

Suppliers

Each organisation uses products or services from other organisations. Thus, as a buyer, the organisation places demands on its suppliers in respect of quality, price level and delivery time. The organisation's own products and services are, after all, dependent on this. In recent years, supplier relationships have undergone great changes. Increased international competition has, for example, caused many changes in the choice of suppliers. In the past there has been a preference for local suppliers but now the trend is often to search across national borders for suppliers to do business with. Another aspect of these business-to-business relationships that deserves our attention is that buyers now want to reduce their stock held, and demand 'just-in-time' delivery from their supplier.

Competition

Competition

Almost every organisation has to deal with competition. Competitors more or less determine the amount of flexibility organisations have in the area of product features, pricing, quality, distribution channels, R&D activities, advertising budgets and so on. It is therefore of vital importance to monitor the activities of major competitors and to analyse their relative market positions.

Vespa scooters back to profitability

In 'Roman Holiday', Audrey Hepburn hitched a ride on the back of Gregory Peck's Piaggio Vespa and took in some of Rome's iconic sights. In the years after that 1953 film, the scooter itself became a global symbol of Italy and Italian design.

But in 2003, the company, based outside Pisa, found itself on the brink of default. Years of revolving-door management and millions of euros squandered on ill-conceived expansion plans had saddled Piaggio with crushing debts and left it vulnerable to competition from cheaper Asian rivals. By 2006, three years after it was bought by maverick Italian industrialist Roberto Colanninno, Piagio had returned to the black for the first time in years, opening new factories in China. Like a deft driver, Piaggio has transformed a potential wipe-out into an unlikely turnaround. After acquisition of Piaggio in 2003, Mr. Colaninno swiftly appointed a chief executive, Rocco Sabelli, who set about redesigning the factory. Previously, each assembly line could only produce certain models. Mr. Sabelli made the system more flexible so that every Piaggio scooter could be made on any assembly line. That allowed the company to easily rev up production of hot-selling models when needed.

Mr. Sabelli also injected a culture of accountability into a company where management had previously kept its distance from workers. On the first days of his job he gave his email address to every employee, demanding that even assembly-line workers let him know personally about any problems or delays. 'We knew that execution had to be our focus', says Mr. Sabelli.

Unlike the turnaround recipe applied by struggling auto makers, Mr. Colaninno didn't fire a single worker – a move which helped seduce the company's sceptical unions. Mr Calaninno based bonuses for blue collar workers and management on the same criteria: profit margins and customer satisfaction. Just as importantly, he installed air conditioning in the factory. Productivity began to increase. He also gave the company's talented engineers deadlines for projects. Piaggio returned to profitability.

Source: WSJ, June 4, 2006

Financiers

Organisations must maintain good relationships with providers of finance such as shareholders, financial institutions and the government.

Financiers

Organisations are often dependent on finance to maintain their activities, expand operations and sometimes even remain in their existing form. When providers of finance become dissatisfied with the performance or practices of an organisation, they can turn off the supply of money. This can create huge problems for the organisation and potentially pose a threat to their survival. In large enterprises, we often find that major financiers are represented in supervisory bodies such as the Board of Commissioners.

Employees

The employees of an organisation are the most important asset and can be seen as a critical success factor. The modern employee of the 21st century is more highly trained, liberated and individualistic than his predecessors. These employees will play an even greater role in product and organisational innovations as well as in quality improvement. Their support and cooperation will influence the choice of direction the organisation takes, as well as its strategies in relation to social responsibility and social policy.

Employees

Support and cooperation

In other words, employees are players in a field under siege by competitors. Employers must try to hold onto their staff using good leadership and human resources policies.

Special interest groups

This group of stakeholders includes those bodies that focus on the interests of a particular group of people. Many such groups exist. They include federations of employees and employers (for example, trades unions and the national industry confederation), consumer organisations (homeowners associations, car owners associations) and environmental activists (Greenpeace).

Government authorities

The execution of government policies is carried out through national and local government departments. These influence organisations because they keep an eye on the way that rules and legislation issued by the government are adhered to by organisations.

Some examples are controls by the police and department of trade inspectors of regulations relating to shop opening times, and checks made by the Health and Safety department in relation to working conditions within organisations.

Media

In the current information era, the media (including the Internet, newspapers, weekly magazines, television and radio) play a very important role. The attention of the media is directed at everything that takes place in society and has any meaning for individuals. Developments in the economy, politics and business are watched closely. International communication satellites ensure that we are informed almost immediately about events that take place on the other side of the world via, for example, photographs in daily newspapers and TV bulletins.

The media can have a big influence on public opinion. This has lead to many organisations setting up public relations departments which work closely with the media to update them on their current activities.

The extent to which the above-mentioned stakeholders can exercise an influence on organisations is dependent on a number of factors. Of key significance is the relative dominance that such groups have at any particular moment. With their domi-

nant position they can exert tremendous pressure on an organisation in many ways, including the withholding of funding (financiers), the stopping of deliveries (suppliers), a buyer's boycott (customers), promotional activities by other organisations in the market (competitors), placing the organisation in a very negative light (media) or industrial action such as a strike (employees).

From the above, we can see that an organisation must take care not to clash with the groups that surround it and must take careful steps to develop and maintain optimal relationships with those bodies that inhabit their immediate environment.

2.3 External factors

While external factors exert an indirect influence on organisations, organisations can only influence external factors to a limited extent. As such, external factors are crucially important in determining the success of organisations. In the sections that follow, the external factors listed here will be looked at:
- Environmental factors (Section 2.3.1)
- Technological factors (Section 2.3.2)

- Demographic factors (Section 2.3.3)
- Economic factors (Section 2.3.4)
- Political factors (Section 2.3.5)
- Social factors (Section 2.3.6).

Special interest groups protest against child labor

An estimated 246 million children are engaged in child labour around the world. Nearly 70 percent (171 million) of these children work in hazardous conditions – including working in mines, working with chemicals and pesticides in agriculture or with dangerous machinery. The vast majority of working children – about 70 per cent – work in the agriculture sector. Millions of children work under horrific circumstances: they are trafficked, forced into debt bondage or other forms of slavery, forced into prostitution and / or pornography, or recruited as child soldiers in armed conflict.
A number of organisations are protesting against child labour. They include UNICEF, Save the Children and RugMark.

RugMark is a global non-profit organisation working to end illegal child labour in the carpet industry and offer educational opportunities to children in India, Nepal, and Pakistan. It does this through loom and factory monitoring, consumer labelling, and running schools for former child workers.
RugMark recruits carpet producers and importers to make and sell carpets that are free of illegal child labour. By agreeing to adhere to RugMark's strict no child labour guidelines and by permitting random inspections of carpet looms, manufacturers receive the right to put the RUGMARK label on their carpets. The label provides the best possible assurance that children were not employed in the making of a rug. It also verifies that a portion of the carpet price is donated to the rehabilitation and education of former child weavers.
RugMark is a global program under the umbrella of RugMark International, which has registered the

RugMark name and logo as a trademark. India, Nepal, and Pakistan are the three carpet-producing countries currently participating in the RugMark program. RugMark carpets are sold in Europe and North America and are promoted through offices in the US, UK and Germany.

Source: United Nations (www.un.org) and RugMark (www.rugmark.org)

2.3.1   Environmental factors

The economic growth of the past few decades has led to an increase in the consumption of goods and services, but linked to this is also a rise in pollution of the environment and a further exhaustion of natural resources. In spite of production increases in some parts of the world, during the last twenty years, some of the main factors contributing to prosperity, including those in the areas of employment, safety and the environment, have been dealt a heavy blow.[1]

Environmental factors

Further damage to the environment is socially unacceptable and political choices that bring a halt to the pollution must be made.
Sustainable development is a term used to mean satisfying the needs of the current generation without endangering future generations but retaining the capacity to satisfy the potential needs of future generations. Prosperity can be seen as a way of measuring sustainability. Achieving this objective forms a significant task.

Some of the main environment problems include:
- Loss of biodiversity
- Climate change
- Over-exploitation of natural resources
- Health threats
- Threats to external safety
- Changes to the environment we live in

International approaches

Effective national strategies, and international approaches to the environment are needed. Many environment problems are not limited to national borders, but have a cross-border effect: for example, water, soil and air pollution. Harmonizing of international environmental standards is essential. In order to maintain a favourable and fair competitive environment for national business groups within Europe, the European Union has tried to set up a harmonized system of duties, taxes, and clear standards.

Political developments and society's changing views on the environment are exerting an obvious influence on the behaviour of organisations. During the 1960s and 1970s the environmental policies of the authorities focussed mainly on legislation, the providing of licences and the checking of companies. Present government policies also lay responsibility for the maintenance of the quality of the environment at the doors of organisations. This is not something that can simply be dealt with by practicing good public relations. Actions rather than just words are needed.

In order to carry out their responsibilities thoroughly, organisations need to tackle environmental problems in a systematic manner and integrate environmental considerations in their overall management strategy. What we are talking about here is environmental care. Included in this is the building up of understanding and the reduction of negative influences on the environment through business activities, as well as discussion with various parties from the organisation's environment. Government authorities are striving to reach a situation where organisations are take caring of their physical environment without question.

Environmental care

Environment
Strategic fields

The environment is now seen as one of the main strategic fields for attention during the coming years. The environmental challenge for organisations has three dimensions[2]:

1 *The cleaning up of present activities.* It is vital that organisations discover and monitor the effects their activities have on the environment so that they can then begin to introduce environmental care.
2 *The utilizing of new opportunities.* Organisations are able to enhance offers of future products and services by repairing past environmental damage and working to deliver new versions that have been developed using environmentally friendly processes.
3 *Working for a sustainable future.* Organisations must undergo radical changes to ensure a sustainable future. To put this into practice, management needs to develop a vision that utilises the new opportunities.

All of the organisation's departments need to play a role in working through the above-mentioned environmental challenge issues. Purchasing departments will need to seek raw materials that are less damaging to the environment and packaging that can be easily recycled. Production departments will need to develop production processes that use fewer raw materials and introduce energy-saving technologies. For marketing divisions, the challenge lies in identifying and translating the preferences of buyers for environmentally friendly products into new product specifications. Distribution divisions will need to look for ways to get their goods to

Toyota's focus on the environment

Toyota operates under a global earth charter that promotes environmental responsibility throughout their entire company. They have been leading the way in lowering emissions and improving fuel economy in gasoline powered vehicles. Toyota created the world's first mass-produced gas / electric hybrid car, and they are also at the forefront of developing tomorrow's fuel cell vehicles. Reducing greenhouse gas (GHG) emissions is one of the greatest challenges facing all automobile manufactures, and one that cuts across all life cycle stages, including design, manufacturing, sales and distribution, customer use, and end-of-life vehicle recycling.

Toyota's environmental goals include:

- Achieving top levels of fuel efficiency
- Reducing tailpipe emissions
- Introducing new hybrid electric vehicles
- Reducing energy consumption by 15 per cent

- Reducing landfill of production waste
- Reducing energy use by 15 per cent
- Promoting greener building construction
- Reducing waste
- Increasing vehicle recyclables

Source: Toyota (www.toyota.com)

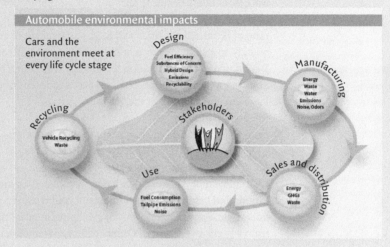

the buyers in a way that causes less harm to the environment. Financial divisions must examine and clarify the advantages of the organisation's switch to sustainability. Last but not least, legal divisions will be required to remain up to date with new legislation and environmental guidelines.

Larger organisations are being put under obvious strain by social pressure to take care of the environment. Their involvement often centres on adherence to legislation, complying with industry sector standards, obtaining environmental certification or simply improving their market image. As organisations realize that the environmental challenge they have to focus on is having a real effect on a sustainable future, they will strive for sustainability and a healthy environment.

2.3.2 Technological factors

In our knowledge-intensive Western society, technological developments are essential for the internationally competitive position of our business life. Technological developments are often called the motor of our economy. Thanks to technological development, there is continuous improvement of production methods and innovation of goods and services. A consequence of this is that the life span of existing products is becoming increasingly shorter.

Technological developments

Technological development is pre-eminently a market-driven activity. Important stimuli for technological innovation come from competition and the demand for more environmentally friendly goods and services of a higher quality with a lower cost price which can be delivered faster and more conveniently.

In the coming years, technological developments will continue at a similar pace as today. Big technological changes and successes can be expected in the areas of bio-engineering and information technology.

Bio-engineering concerns living organisms. The bio-engineering field develops

Bio-engineering

products for the food industry (yeast extracts for bread and other bakery products, beer, wine and fruit juices), the pharmaceutical industry (medicines such as penicillin and growth hormones), agriculture (genetically modified cattle), cosmetics (creams, perfumes), and the detergent sector (enzymes in washing detergents). Information technology is concerned with the application of micro-electronics and deals with the saving and adaptation of information. Information can be seen as the lifeblood of a modern organisation. Some examples of products in the field of information technology are hardware (computers, telephone exchanges etc.), software (programmes and applications), communication networks, work stations (such as PCs) and intelligent chips. The expectation is that the price-performance ratio of IT related activities will fall by 20 per cent to 30 per cent each year. Consequently, investing in information technology will become progressively cheaper. Developments in information technology will exert a big influence on all organisations in the coming years. The main consequences of this will be:

A Fundamental changes in the way work is done
B Integration of functions
C Economies of scale and changes in decision-making

A Fundamental changes in the way work is done

Communication networks are being installed to an increasing extent within organisations and between organisations and countries. A consequence of this is a reduction in 'time and distance'. As an example, financial transactions can be carried out from any city in the world. Orders can be placed directly with a producer from anywhere at any time. The same goes for booking flights. Organisations can also quickly gain access to all sorts of information through electronic data banks.

B Integration of functions

Through the expansion of communication networks, relevant information can be made available in the right form, at the right moment and in the right place. Three different categories of function integration can be identified:

1 Inside the organisation. Within an organisation, various divisions can communicate with each other and exchange information because they are connected via a local communication network.
2 Between organisations. In this case, divisions of different organisations are connected electronically with each other. For example, the purchasing department of a customer can be electronically connected with the dispatch department of a supplier.
3 Electronic markets. In this form of electronic integration there is coordination between organisations that operate in an open-market situation. For example, travel agencies can electronically search for the cheapest flight to a destination and transact business with all airlines.

Since the end of the 1990s, the Internet has been seen as the international 'electronic superhighway' and has made all public information accessible to everyone. Many businesses have developed so-called 'self-service facilities' for their customers. Online examples of this include savings, banking, cinema and theatre reservations, purchases of books, music, travel, computers and clothing.
In the Western world, the Internet has become a normal facility, with a growing number of households having a fast cable or ADSL connection. It is expected that the use of the Internet will dramatically increase over the coming years in China and India.

The Internet drives new business models

The Internet has created new business models which are having a significant impact on the competitive landscape.

Skype was founded in 2003 by Niklas Zennström and Janus Friis. Skype created a little piece of software that lets people make free calls all over the world. Skype is available in 27 languages and is used in almost every country around the world. Skype generates revenue through its premium offerings such as making and receiving calls to and from landlines and mobile phones, as well as voicemail and call forwarding.

Publish and sell your book through Internet publisher Lulu

Founded in 2002, Lulu is the web's premier independent publishing marketplace for digital do-it-yourselfers. It's the only place on the web where you can publish, sell and buy any and all things digital – books, music, comics, photographs, movies and well, you get the idea. There is no set-up fee and no minimum order to publish and sell on Lulu. They manage the online business, including printing, delivery and customer service. Customers set their own royalty for each piece of content, and at the end of each quarter, Lulu will mail them a check for the royalties their content generates.
Lulu was founded by Bob Young, who was also the co-founder of Red Hat, the world's leading open source company. Lulu believes in putting authors

and independent publishers in control of their digital content, from content creation to pricing to royalties. Lulu simply brings creative content to the world and gives our talented publishers and web visitors the venue to buy and sell independent works. Publishing through Lulu leaves control of content in the hands of the people who created it.

Share, print and store photos over the Internet with Snapfish

Snapfish is a leading online photo service with more than 24 million members and one billion unique photos stored online. We enable our members to share, print and store their most important photo memories at the lowest prices – online or off.

Source: Skype (www.skype.com), Lulu (www.lulu.com) and Snapfish (www.snapfish.org)

C Changes in economies of scale and decision-making

At the start of a new project, a lot of time is taken up appointing a new staff team. It involves discussion and the exchange of written information. With developments in information technology (communication networks in and between organisations), coordination costs can be dramatically decreased. Smaller organisations will also be able to profit from this and will therefore be able to enjoy the benefits of more flexible and lower cost production processes. Information technology leads to faster spread of information, which then generates faster decision-making.

Technological developments generally result from research carried out by universities and technical institutions as well R&D (Research & Development) departments in large businesses. A lot of resources (financial and otherwise) and effort are needed for these R&D activities. In this respect, because of their bigger capacity, *R&D activities* larger businesses thus have a clear advantage over smaller businesses. Within larger businesses, R&D expenditure can be spread across a broad range of divisions. Small and medium-sized organisations can simply not afford such expense on their own. For this reason, it is quite common for government trade and industry departments to support small and medium-sized businesses with subsidies and know-how.

The size of the R&D budget is not necessarily an indicator of how successful a business will be. The way in which technology is implemented and renewed within operations in comparison with competitor activity also plays a key role. A flexible, efficient and goal-orientated way of operating within organisations is required. Experience shows that successful implementation of new technology is rarely easy.

Problems with its introduction are often not of a technical nature, but linked to human issues.

For technological development to be successful, it is vital that technical experts know a lot about marketing and business and for marketers and business experts to understand the technical aspects.

2.3.3 Demographic factors

Demographic factors

Demographic factors are defined as the size, growth and composition of the population. These factors determine to a large extent which markets an organisation targets and which products and services they offer.

The EU is facing unprecedented demographic changes that will have a major impact on the whole of society. Figures in the Green Paper on demographic change launched by the EU Commission (2005) show that from 2005 until 2030, the EU will be short of 20.8 million (6.8 per cent) people of working age. In 2030, roughly two active people (those between 15 and 65 years of age) will have to take care of one inactive person (65+), in a situation where Europe will have 18 million children and young people fewer than today.

Demographic ageing

Europe is the first region in the world to experience demographic ageing. The populations of our neighbouring regions in Europe, Africa and the Middle East will start to age much later: their populations are much younger, with an average age of 20 years or less, compared to 35 in Europe. But China's population will age rapidly and will decline from 2025. Three different factors determine demographic ageing:

- A significant increase in life expectancy
- A significant fall in fertility
- The ageing baby-boomer generation

Average life expectancy

People are living longer and older people are enjoying better health. By 2030, the number of 'older workers' (those aged 55 to 64) will have risen by 24 million as the baby-boomers become senior citizens and the EU will have 34.7 million citizens aged over 80 (compared to 18.8 million today). Average life expectancy at 60 has risen five years since 1960 for women and nearly four years for men. By 2050, the number of people in the 80+ age group will have grown by 180 per cent.

Demographic decline

The EU's fertility rate fell to 1.48 in 2003, below the level needed to replace the population (2.1 children per woman). The paper shows that the EU's population will fall from 469.5 million in 2025 to 468.7 million in 2030. By contrast, the US population will increase by 25.6 per cent between 2000 and 2025. However, demographic decline is already here: in one third of the EU regions and in most of the regions of the new Member States the population was already falling in the late 90s. It is the result of constraints on families' choices: late access to employment, job instability, expensive housing and lack of incentives (family benefits, parental leave, child care, equal pay). Incentives of this kind can have a positive impact on the birth rate and increase employment, especially female employment, as certain countries have shown.

Between 2005 and 2030, the number of people in the 65+ age bracket will rise by 52.3 per cent (40 million), while the 15–64 age group will decrease by 6.8 per cent (20.8 million). The ratio of dependent young and old people to people of working age will increase from 49 per cent in 2005 to 66 per cent in 2030. To offset the loss of working-age people, the EU will need an employment rate of over 70 per cent.

Figure 2.2   Trends in total EU population (2005 and 2050)

Eurostat base scenario, EU25 (in thousands)	2005–2050	2005–2010	2010–2030	2030–2050
Total population	-2.1% (-9642)	+1.2% (+5444)	+1.1% (+4980)	-4.3% (-20066)
Children (0-14)	-19.4% (-14415)	-3.2% (-2391)	-8.9% (-6411)	-8.6% (-5612)
Young people (15-24)	-25.0% (-14441)	-4.3% (-2488)	-12.3% (-6815)	-10.6% (-5139)
Young adults (25-39)	-25.8% (-25683)	-4.1% (-4037)	-16.0% (-15271)	-8.0% (-6375)
Adults (40-54)	-19.5% (+4538)	+4.2% (+5024)	-10.0% (+8832)	-14.1% (-9318)
Older workers (55-64)	+8.7% (+25458)	+9.6% (+1938)	+15.5% (+22301)	-14.1% (+1219)
Elderly people (65-79)	+44.1% (+25458)	+3.4% (+1938)	+37.4% (+22301)	+1.5% (+1219)
Very elderly people (80+)	+180.5% (+34026)	+17.1% (+3229)	+57.1% (+12610)	+52.4% (+18187)

Source: Eurostat 2005

Of the six most-populated EU Member States, only the UK and France will see their populations increase between 2005 and 2050 (with the UK population projected to increase by 8 per cent and the French population by 9.6 per cent). Forecasts for Bulgaria and Romania show negative growth (-21 per cent and -11 per cent respectively by 2030), as do UN forecasts for Croatia (-19 per cent). However, the population of Turkey is set to rise by more than 19 million between 2005 and 2030 (+25 per cent). In many countries, the falling birth rates are being offset by immigration.

These demographic changes have major implications for our prosperity, living standards and relations between the generations. In Europe's recent history, there has never been a period of sustainable economic growth without population growth to create opportunities for investment and consumption. The annual rate of potential growth of Europe's GDP is projected to fall from today's 2 to 2.25 per cent to 1.5 per cent in 2015 and 1.25 per cent in 2040.

The issues are much broader than older workers and pension reform. This development will affect almost every aspect of peoples lives: for example, the way businesses operate and work is being organised, our urban planning, the design of flats, public transport, voting behaviour and the infrastructure of shopping possibilities in our cities. All age groups will be affected as people live longer and enjoy better health, the birth rate falls and the EU workforce shrinks.

There are also opportunities for organisations that focus on older generations. An increasing number of organisations are discovering that seniors (those aged between 50 and 70 years old) are an attractive target group for them. Although the household income of seniors is indeed lower than average, it would seem that the income per person in this age group is the highest of all age groups. Research indicates that seniors spend 80 per cent per person more on holidays than those in the age group 30 to 50 years. They also spend 40 per cent more on food, 16 per cent more on study and transportation, 75 per cent more in the home and 50 per cent more on personal hygiene and medical care.

Older generations

Demand for specific senior citizen products is expected to increase. In particular, products that provide security, products that increase social contact, products that promote an active and healthy life, products for leisure activity and hobbies, will all become more in demand. It is also important to think about ways of tailor-making products for this target group, including products and services such as travel (both within the country and abroad), special meals, clothing and footwear, housing, and social activities.

Because senior citizens form a highly distinctive target group, it can also be viewed as a relatively complex one, one that raises a number of difficult issues for businesses of various types. How, for example, can you let senior citizens know that there is a product for them on the market without creating too much of a distinction with

IN THE PRESS

Turning baby-boomers into boomerangs

Older workers want to retire later; companies fear they will soon be short of skills. Why can't the two get together? In January 2006 the first baby-boomers turned 60. The looming demographic cliff will see vast numbers of skilled workers dispatched from the labour force. The workforce is ageing across the rich world. Within the EU the number of workers aged between 50 and 64 will increase by 25 per cent over the next two decades, while those aged 20 to 29 will decrease by 20 per cent. In Japan, almost 20 per cent of the population is already over 65, and in the USA the number of workers aged 55 to 64 will have increased by more than half in this decade. Given that most societies are geared to retirement at around 65, companies have a looming problem of knowledge management, and some also face a shortage of expertise. Many people assume that older employees are less motivated, take more sick leave and cost more. The evidence is that many people over 65 have plenty to offer even if they are no longer at their peak. Some studies show that the over 40s are less likely to be off sick, and are more highly motivated and productive, except where great physical effort is required.

The best thing corporations can do is to make work more flexible and accommodating to grey hair. Fundamentally, baby-boomers will reinvent retire-

ment. They will 'cycle' between periods of work and leisure well beyond the age of 65. Working in retirement, once considered an oxymoron, is the new reality.

Source: *The Economist*, February, 2006

other groups or projecting an 'elderly person' image? What is the best tone to adopt when speaking to older people and should age determine communication strategy? Is it wise to develop a different strategy for the senior market?

2.3.4 Economic factors

Economic factors
Growth in national income

Economic factors play an important role in the success of organisations. Of prime significance is growth in national income. This growth generally leads to higher income for individuals, which then increases purchasing power. Those organisations that focus on the B2C (Business-to-Consumer) market will then enjoy increased turnover. Income distribution is another important factor. Changes in income distribution can have a significant effect on the size of some markets.

Income distribution

It is clear that for countries like the Netherlands, where a relatively large proportion (about 30 per cent) of national income is dependent on foreign trade, international economic developments will also play an important role. Some examples of key influencing factors are:

International economic developments

- Economic growth in other countries
- Exchange rates and currency swings
- Changes in base interest rates in other countries
- Labour costs and wages in foreign countries

These factors are likely to have a big influence on the competitive position of enterprises, and indeed, on any national economies where international trade plays a role. International economic growth exerts a major influence on developments in employment. West European businesses are being challenged by strong competi-

Employment

tion from a number of countries, including those in South East Asia. Labour costs in India and China, for example, are at present significantly lower than in the West for both highly skilled and manual work. For example, graduates from Indian Universities earn between $3,000 and $10,000 annually. Add to this the fact that transport is playing a smaller role, and we can see that there will be a shift of production to those countries that best meet future economic needs.

An important stimulus for improving the economic situation is investment in knowledge and innovation. The European Union has set itself the goal of becoming the most competitive knowledge economy in the world. To do this, it will be necessary for Member States to allocate at least 3 per cent of the EU's GNP (Gross National Product) to research and development activities. In 2004, EU spent 1.9 per cent of GDP on research and development, substantially below the 3 per cent target. However, 18 countries plan to increase R&D expenditure to an average of 2.6 per cent by 2010.

It is important to change mindsets and remove the barriers to creating and developing new businesses. Europeans lag behind Americans in this area: Europeans are more comfortable in employment than being self-employed. Yet job satisfaction is higher among those who run their own businesses. When Europeans do start new ventures, these tend to grow more slowly than their American counterparts. Barriers to innovation are a major reason. These include bureaucracy, difficulties in borrowing money to start new businesses and the high costs of obtaining patents. The European Commission is promoting action to tackle all these problems – to cut red tape, provide easier access to start-up capital and introduce a cheaper and more efficient patent system.

A far-reaching reform of Europe's innovation system is needed. The innovation gap between the European Union and its main competitors, the United States and Japan, persists, mainly in the number of patent applications, the percentage of the

China will become the largest economy by 2020

By 2020, China will narrowly outstrip the United States in GDP. The forecast uses purchasing-power parities (PPP), which strip out price differences between countries rather than market exchange rates to convert national GDPs into a common currency.

Source: Foresight 2020, Economist Intelligence Unit,

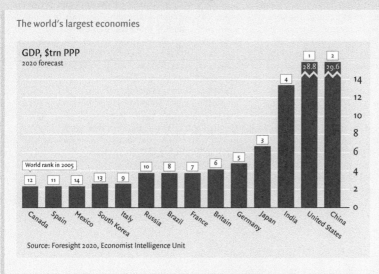

The world's largest economies

Source: Foresight 2020, Economist Intelligence Unit

population with tertiary education and ICT investments. The majority of EU Member States are addressing the strategic importance of innovation poles, networks and incubators bringing together universities, research institutions and enterprises at regional and local level in order to bridge the technology gap between regions.

International trade and globalisation

Globalisation

The past 50 years have seen exceptional growth in world trade. Merchandise exports grew on average by 6 per cent annually, and total trade in 2000 was 22 times the level of 1950. Since World War II, globalisation of trade has been driven by trade negotiation rounds, originally under the auspices of the General Agreement on Tariffs and Trade (GATT), which led to a series of agreements to remove restrictions on free trade. Globalisation can be defined as the growing economic interdependence of countries worldwide through increasing volume and variety of cross-border transactions in goods and services, freer international capital flows, and more rapid and widespread diffusion of technology.

The World Trade Organisation (WTO)

The only international organisation dealing with trade rules between nations is the World Trade Organisation (WTO). The World Trade Organisation (WTO) was established in 1995 and has more than 147 members. The WTO has been given two other fundamentally important tasks. Firstly, it has been charged with further integrating developing countries – especially the ELDCs (Economically Least Developed Countries) – in world trade and in the work of the WTO. The second task is to look at the relationship between trade and important themes such as the environment, food safety and working conditions.

A study by the World Bank found that the removal of trade barriers in developing countries would raise income by about 500 billion dollars. Furthermore, research has shown that trade liberalization since World War II has contributed to lifting billions of people out of poverty. Although the exact figure is disputed, it is accepted that the advantages of trade liberalisation are enormous.

IN THE PRESS

Deutsche Bank is moving half of its back-office jobs offshore

Deutsche Bank will have moved almost half the back-office jobs in its sales and trading operation to India by the end of next year as part of a reorganisation that has already helped boost revenues by more than $2.3 billion. The plan will triple its global markets staff offshore to nearly 2,000. The bank is also looking to increase offshore research staff from 350 to 500, more than half the current global total of 900. Deutsche's move comes as other big investment banks are also rushing to take advantage of the low cost of employing highly-educated staff in India. The moves highlight the shift in the use of offshore facilities from traditional areas such as IT support and call centres to more high-value tasks.

Deutsche Bank said the expansion in India was part of a wider reorganisation that had generated significant revenue increases and cost savings. The reor-

ganisation is designed to break down the traditional product 'silos' of debt and equity, cash and derivatives. It also reflected the changing needs of clients who are demanding more complex transactions, often involving different asset classes. The merger of functions such as securities processing between previously separate divisions had allowed some to be moved offshore more efficiently.

About 15 percent of operational staff in Deutsche's markets business are offshore and the bank plans to increase this to 40–50 per cent, mainly in Bangalore, Mumbai and Chennai, by the end of 2007. Other investments banks expanding offshore include UBS, Lehman Brothers and Credit Suisse.

Source: *The Financial Times*, March, 2006

2.3.5 Political factors

Political factors

Governmental authorities use their political powers and responsibilities to try to steer their economy in a favourable direction. For example, governments influence price levels, the distribution of income, the job market, the balance of payments and therefore economic growth.

The past years have seen an increase in the level of political influence that has been exerted on national economies from outside bodies. Within Europe, this has been brought about by the removal of borders between the Member States of the EU (European Union) in line with their goal of creating a single internal market. The unification of Europe and a shift in political power are factors which are likely to challenge organisations in the near future. When talking about unification, it should be understood that when Member States merge their national economic and political institutions to a large extent, there will be an economic union.

Economic union

In general, five forms of economic integration can be identified. Arranged according to increasing levels of integration, these are a free trade zone, a customs union, a common market, economic union and complete political and economic union.

Free trade zone

1 A free trade zone. Mutual trade agreements are entered into only by those countries that wish to participate. Each country determines their own import tariffs for products that are imported from outside the free trade zone. As a result, the trade policy for members is not harmonized. Certification of origin is therefore necessary to prevent products being imported via the country with the lowest import tariffs. An example of a free trade zone is the NAFTA (North American Free Trade Area).

2 A customs union. Here, a common trade policy is adopted. The revenue from import duty is divided between Member States using an agreed formula.

Customs union

3 A common market. This is based on a customs union with certain barriers relating to the location of production activities within the market removed.

Common market

4 Economic union. The next step includes all the above, plus the harmonisation of economic and monetary activities. This requires political and financial cooperation and the setting up of a central bank to manage the currency and interest rate across the union.

Economic union

5 Complete political and economic union. This is the situation where independent states or countries merge completely. An example of this is the formation of the United States of America.

Complete political and economic union

Within the European Union we refer to a common internal market. This common market has been based on four economic freedoms:
1 Freedom of movement of goods
2 Freedom of movement of services
3 Freedom of movement of capital
4 Freedom of movement of people

With further development of the common internal market and the formation of an economic block, Europe can improve its competitive position in relation to the other major economic power blocks of Japan, the United States and South East Asia.

The unification of Europe will have significant consequences for many organisations. It is anticipated that increased competition will put pressure on production costs, which in turn will lead to a fall in prices. Lower prices generate increased turnover, which leads to economies of scale, and possible business expansion. Larger scale production makes innovation and R&D expenditure viable, which, of course, is likely to result in the production of goods that meet customer's needs better and are easier to sell. It can be seen as a chain reaction. It is a reaction that supports the strengthening of Europe's position in relation to its competitors.

Research carried out by the European Commission suggests that for most industry sectors within a united Europe, the following consequences are expected[3]:

- A reduction of the cost price and consequently the sales price due to increased turnover and economies of scale.
- Businesses will be forced to improve efficiency in their organisation, production and distribution, because of reduced margins. That is, the sale price of products will come closer to the cost price.
- Faster adaptation and increased specialisation in different parts of Europe due to a more level playing field and transparency of costs, making comparisons easier and the identification of regional advantages clearer.
- The growth of innovation through increased interaction within an enlarged dynamic internal market.
- In the long term, European businesses are expected to have a stronger position in world markets outside the European Union.

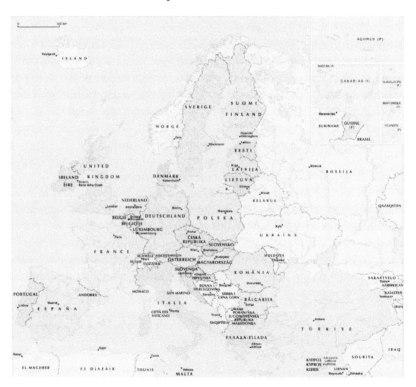

Member States of the EU (in yellow)

Obstructions

Before Europe can really see itself as a truly open internal market, a number of obstructions need to be removed[4]:

- *Physical obstructions:* customs controls with their associated paperwork as well as delays at borders.
- *Technical obstructions:* such national differences as production regulations, commercial law, and regulations designed to protect elements within the government procurement sector.
- *Financial obstructions:* differences in sales tax (VAT) rates and excise taxes that mean inspection and clearance at borders.

A separate yet significant feature of the unification of the European market is the role played by the small and medium enterprise sector (SME). By this we mean those that employ less than one hundred staff. If there are more than a hundred employees, the business is categorised as large.

Worried about your job fleeing offshore? – move to India!

One strategy is to chase it – an option a growing number of twentysomething Westerners are choosing. Sure, the trend will never make up for the thousands of positions lost back home, but for adventurous young people, a spell in a call centre in Bangalore or Bombay can help defray the costs of a grand tour of the subcontinent and beyond.

Until recently, most of the foreigners were highly paid experts from companies that were sending their work abroad, helping the new Indian team learn the processes. Those people are still coming to India, but they are joined by less-experienced ones who make little more than the rock-bottom wages paid to locals that are a key draw for multinationals. They typically earn about $350 a month and work the phones for six months to a year before they start travelling and visiting interesting places. Despite India's seemingly limitless pool of workers these workers make up for talent shortages faced by the outsourcing industry. Employers are getting choosier about the people they hire, and it's tough to train Indians to speak the kind of colloquial English, French, Spanish,

German or Dutch that customers want. The trend is also being fuelled by the changing customer base of India's outsourcing shops. Traditionally, they focussed on serving companies with customers in the US and Britain. But now they are looking to boost their business from Europe. There is even a new group of service providers in the Western world to help supply India's outsourcers with Western hires. This is called a 'reverse brain drain'.

The workers don't come only for adventure. Many have had trouble getting jobs in their native land, and India provides growth opportunities that these workers wouldn't have had in their own country. More importantly, time spent answering phones in India can also work wonders on resumes. The Indian experience looks good on their CV.

Stian Johansen (Norway), Kati Koivukangas (Finland) and Ethel Graff (Germany) are part of Tecnovate eSolutions' 30-member European team in Delhi. They work on travel processes for customers in 11 European countries.

Source: Business Week, January 2006

An important question to ask in relation to SMEs concerns the special opportunities and threats that they face in the new Europe. In many European countries SMEs operate mainly in the domestic market.

The next and obvious question is whether small and medium businesses will benefit optimally from the removal of internal borders. National enterprises that do not plan to expand into the new European market will in all probability be confronted by new competitors from elsewhere in the EU that have decided to enter the national market. In time, national SMEs will face increased competition.

As explained earlier, trade barriers are no longer permitted within the borders of the European Union. Those who export or want to export should, however, realise that the removal of trade barriers will not lead to the disappearance of cultural diversity between countries of the European Union. As such, it is also important to be aware of the cultural characteristics of a country with which one wants to do business. By understanding the main cultural characteristics, one will, in fact, already be well on the way to becoming acquainted with a country and the people who live there.

Cultural characteristics

2.3.6 Social factors

There is a societal need to try to exert an influence on organisations because of concerns about business activities and such issues as environmental responsibility, noise pollution, ethical business and employee participation (see Figure 2.3) Criticism has been levelled by various parties, including employees and local community groups. Such bodies will often use the media to gain leverage and in some case, campaigns will even lead to the introduction of new legislation.

Social factors

Figure 2.3 Organisations are a part of society, which is part of the larger environment

Organisations are a part of society. Society is, however, broader and deeper than the elements that make up an organisation. Friends, family, sport, hobbies and religion are often at least as important for individuals.

In turn, a society exists within the natural environment. The basic needs of society, such as air, food and water, come from nature, as do energy, raw materials, transport and some products. In the past, it was the natural environment that to a large extent determined how society looked. Now human activities are having an increasing influence on the natural environment.

Organisations are having to listen more and more to the wishes of society and to develop what is known as sustainable entrepreneurship.

Sustainable entrepreneurship

Sustainable entrepreneurship is a term derived from the idea of sustainable development, which was first introduced in 1987 by the Brundtland Commission, at the

Corporate social responsibility

Starbucks' commitment to social responsibility
Contributing positively to communities and the environment is so important to Starbucks that it's a guiding principle of their mission statement. Starbucks jointly fulfils this commitment with partners (employees) at all levels of the company, by getting involved together to help build stronger communities and conserve natural resources.

Mission Statement
Establish Starbucks as the premier purveyor of the finest coffee in the world and maintaining our uncompromising principles while we grow.

Guiding Principles
The following six guiding principles will help us measure the appropriateness of our decisions:
· Provide a great work environment and treat each other with respect and dignity.
· Embrace diversity as an essential component of the way we do business.
· Apply the highest standards of excellence to the purchasing, roasting and fresh delivery of our coffee.
· Develop enthusiastically satisfied customers all of the time.
· Contribute positively to our communities and our environment.
· Recognize that profitability is essential to our future success.

Sources: Starbucks (www.starbucks.com)

STARBUCKS COMMITMENT TO
SOCIAL
RESPONSIBILITY

Beyond the cup.

Highlights of Starbucks
CORPORATE SOCIAL RESPONSIBILITY

Fiscal 2005 Annual Report

request of the United Nations (UN). Businesses can make an important contribution to the sustainable development of society by adopting sustainable entrepreneurial practices. Sustainable entrepreneurship is another term for corporate social responsibility. If a company can demonstrate that its processes and procedures are socially responsible in a manner that goes further than is required by law, this will lead to an added benefit for both society and the business itself.

Sustainable entrepreneurship
Corporate social responsibility

Societal themes that are of interest to sustainable entrepreneurship can be subdivided into five areas: social, cultural, political, ethical and environmental. Topics that are a top priority for society include climate change, biodiversity, employment, economic growth, human rights, the effect industry has on the environment, child labour, extreme poverty and unequal wealth distribution.

Profit maximisation is no longer the only target, as the creation of value (including value for customers, employees, shareholders and society) is now the central issue. This is known as the stakeholder approach. Stakeholders (interested parties) are those groups of people who have an interest in the activities of the enterprise on their own behalf, on behalf of other groups of people, or on behalf of nature. As such, stakeholders can exert an influence on the direction an enterprise takes. (See Figure 2.4.)

Figure 2.4   A relationship matrix showing examples of key societal themes and stakeholders

Theme	Stakeholder											
	Customer	Supplier	Staff	Manager	Financier	Competitor	Government	Education	Media	Interest groups	Neighbours	(World) citizen
Social			Employment, part-time jobs, teleworking, child care, safety, health, well being	Employment, part-time jobs, teleworking, child care, safety, health, well being		Social covenant	Rules and regulations, employment, safety	Knowledge transfer (placements, guest lectures)	Information	Social forum information	Community groups, safety, knowledge transfer (company visits), sponsorship	Knowledge transfer (congresses, publications), sponsorship
Cultural			Sports facilities, art, language classes	Sports facilities, art, language classes					Information		Sponsorship	Sponsorship
Political	International relations	International relations		Proportional income	Opportunity to be politically active	Protection of interests	Policies for large cities, good relations with authorities	Supporting educational needs	Information	Information		
Ethical	Cause-related marketing	Supplier selection (social accountability SA8000)	Personal development, opportunity to take part in societal organisations, norms and values, minorities, discrimination	Personal development, opportunity to take part in societal organisations, norms and values, minorities, discrimination	Prospectus (financial introduction)			Information		Code of conduct, cause related marketing, idealistic adverts	Code of conduct, integration of minorities	Code of conduct
Environmental	Environmentally friendly production, hallmarks, recycling	Supplier selection (raw materials used, sustainable materials)	Energy use, waste, transport	Energy use, waste, transport	Green banking	Production chain focussed covenants	Legislation, permits, nature management	Information	Information	Information	Information	Emissions, waste management, nuisance

Businesses that permanently base decisions on sustainable policies make themselves more vulnerable to their surroundings and have to combine the needs of the business with care for man and the environment. We can refer to three dimensions: people, planet and profit. An enterprise following these 3 Ps will constantly aim to find a balance between financial results, social interest and a reduction in environment damage.

People

How successfully enterprises deal with socio-ethical issues falls under the domain of people. How does the business treat its personnel and society at large? Some of the main themes are human rights, bribery and fraud, child labour, equal treatment for men and women, diversity and discrimination, worker participation, codes of conduct and so on.

Planet

The way a business interacts with the environment in a broad sense is the domain of the planet. Some current topics that fall under this domain are environmental care, chain management, eco-efficiency, cleaner production, sustainable technological development, environmentally responsible industrial estates and so on.

Profit

Within the domain of profit, the issue is not so much the financial statistics of an enterprise but rather overall economic performance. Areas such as employment, investments in infrastructure, real estate management, political involvement, sub-contracting, and the economic effect of services and products all fall within this domain, as do sponsorship, employee participation, and where profits go to. (See Figure 2.5.)

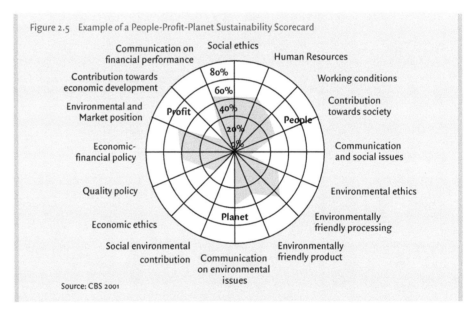

Figure 2.5   Example of a People-Profit-Planet Sustainability Scorecard

Source: CBS 2001

How can a business be sure of always making the right decisions in the area of sustainable entrepreneurship? Our ideas in this regard are still at the development stage. According to Good Company consultants, a four-step plan can help businesses make choices that lead to socially responsible commerce.

The analysis phase, a phase in which the image of the business and relevant groups of interested parties is examined and evaluated, should be followed by a strategic development phase (policy). This must be in keeping with the general direction of the enterprise. A number of critical factors need to be determined in order to specify performance indicators, and for this, the company's objectives or goals must be clarified. The next step is the execution phase. Specific projects must be started, and while doing this, it is essential that thorough and effective communication take place throughout the business. A key condition for success is sufficient attention and involvement on the part of top management: by taking their personal responsibilities seriously, and communicating meaningfully with all involved, management can increase the involvement of co-workers and other interested parties. The last phase is evaluation, and there are various ways of going about this. To determine if their social objectives have been reached or not a company can avail itself of measurements, reports, position surveys, profile sketches, self evaluation and internal group discussions. (See Figure 2.6.)

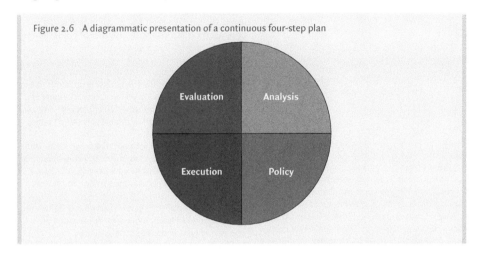

Figure 2.6 A diagrammatic presentation of a continuous four-step plan

The challenge for the present generation is to allow economic development to be linked with fair distribution of prosperity and environmental protection in such a way as to preserve the planet for future generations. It is very important that big industrial businesses support the development of sustainable business plans. By doing so they will act as role models for non-industrial sectors and for small and medium enterprises.

Protectionism

If an enterprise has decided on the perspective it wishes to operate from, it is wise to differentiate between image on the one hand and position in society on the other. The actual position an enterprise gains in society is a combination of image (how an enterprise wants to be seen) and identity (how an enterprise really is seen). The image of an enterprise is fragile and any damage suffered is not easy to repair. It is therefore best to think carefully about the position that an enterprise wishes to adopt in society. Very few enterprises manage to carry out totally unselfish policies. Most businesses end up working towards a combination of economic interests and societal needs.

Doing business in India

How Indians organise and process information
In India, information is accepted openly as long as it does not challenge religious and social structures. Rote learning and tradition mean that most thinking is associative. However, better-educated Indians think more abstractly and analytically. While universal rules of behaviour are part of the social structure, real-life situations and real-life people are nevertheless of major concern, though always viewed within the constructs of the caste system.

What Indians accept as evidence
Personal feelings form the basis for accepted truth, but a strong faith in religious ideologies is always present. The use of objective facts is less persuasive than a combination of feelings and faith.

The basis of behaviour
India has a very strong attachment to the caste system, with its social structure and all its liabilities. Value systems in the predominant culture – how right is distinguished from wrong, good from evil, and so on – are described under the next three headings.

The locus of decision-making
India is a moderately collectivistic culture in which an individual's decisions must be in harmony with the family, group, and social structure. Success and failure are often attributed to environmental factors. Friendship and kinship are more important than expertise, although diplomas and certificates are coveted. One must build a relationship with other participants in the negotiation process by discussing friends and family. Indians are generally too polite to say 'no'.

Sources of anxiety reduction
With such a strong social structure, there is little anxiety about life because one knows and accepts one's place in the society or organisation. Behaviours contrary to religious traditions are not tolerated. There is a strong sense of what Westerners call fatalism, so time is not a major source of anxiety, and passivity is a

virtue. Emotions can be shown, and assertiveness is expected.

Issues of equality / inequality
Inequality is firmly rooted in societal structures, even though there is equality under the law (though seldom enforced). The belief that there are qualitative differences between the castes is ingrained. Traditional male chauvinism is strong, and women have few privileges. The abundance of sexual symbols in society does not translate into an acceptance of public intimacy.

Ten examples of Indian business practices
1 When making business contacts, go straight to the top of the company, as all decisions are made at this level. Be prepared to establish a close personal relationship based on mutual respect and confidence.
2 Although they usually do not make decisions, middle managers do have an input. A middle manager on your side can forward your proposal. They are often more accessible and are willing to meet at any time of the day.
3 The best time of the year to visit India is between October and March, bypassing the seasons of extreme heat and monsoons.
4 Business is not conducted during religious holidays, which are numerous. Different holidays are observed throughout the many regions and states of India. As dates for these holidays change from year to year, check with the Indian Tourist Office, Consulate or Embassy before scheduling your visit.
5 Always present your business card. It is not necessary to have it translated into an Indian language.
6 Business in India is highly personal. A great amount of hospitality is associated with doing business. Tea and small talk are preludes to most business discussions.
7 The word 'no' has harsh implications in India. Evasive refusals are more common, and are considered more polite. Never directly refuse an invitation, just be vague and avoid time commitment. 'I'll try' is an acceptable refusal.
8 Indians of all ethic groups disapprove of public displays of affection between people of the opposite sex. Do not touch (except in handshaking, hugging, or kissing in greeting).
9 Gifts are not opened in the presence of the giver. If you receive a wrapped gift, set it aside until the giver leaves.
10 For business dress, men should wear a suit and tie, although the jacket may be removed in the summer. Businesswomen should wear conservative dresses or pantsuits. For casual wear, short-sleeved shirts and long trousers are preferred for men; shorts are acceptable only while jogging. Women must keep their upper arms, chest, back and legs covered at all times. Women who jog should wear long pants.

Source: Kiss, Bow, or Shake Hands: How to Do Business in Sixty Countries, by Terri Morrison, Wayne A. Conaway and George A. Borden, Adams Media, 2006

Summary

An organisation is affected by its business environment. Stakeholders form part of that business environment. While they exert an influence on organisations, at the same time they themselves are affected by the relationship. The environment indirectly exerts pressure on organisations but is itself only influenced to a limited extent. The stakeholders that organisations mainly have to deal with are buyers, suppliers, competition, financiers, employees, special interest groups, government institutions and the media. Environmental issues play an important role in the business environment and national policy dictates what organisations must do to care for the environment. Technological development is often seen as the motor of the economy, and advances in information technology often have a significant influence on the way organisations work. Changes in the size, composition and growth of a country's population are demographic factors that organisations will need to take into account in the years to come. Economic factors have an important effect on the success of organisations. Both national and international factors play a role here. Governments have the political responsibility to steer the economy of a country in a prudent manner. However, EU integration is having the effect that political influence and responsibility is increasingly shifting away from our national borders.

Definitions

§ 2.1 Harmonisation   The directing of an organisation taking the surroundings into consideration.

Surroundings   The local community or society, consisting of individuals and interested parties.

External factors   Environmental factors that organisations can influence to a lesser extent.

§§ 2.3.5 Customs union   A free trade zone in which a common trade policy is followed.

Economic union   Occurs when member countries transfer their economic and political sovereignty to common institutions. Economic union is a form of integration whereby monetary administration and financial policies are harmonised, as well as there being a common market.

Common market   A customs union where restrictions on production location within the market have been removed.

Political and economic union   Union where member states have joined together completely (e.g. the United States of America).

Free trade zone   A form of economic integration where mutual trade barriers have been abolished by the participating countries but trade has not been completely harmonised.

§§ 2.3.6 Sustainable business   Sustainable business derives from the notion of sustainable development. There will be an added benefit for society (as well as for the business itself) if businesses make a conscious decision to act in a socially responsible way that goes further than the law requires. Sustainable business is also known as corporate social responsibility.

Statements

Decide which of the following statements are correct or incorrect and give reasons for your answer.

1 An organisation is efficient if it reaches its targets.
2 An organisation is effective if it uses its available resources in a goal-orientated manner.
3 Management is another word for leadership.
4 It is easier for an organisation, business or enterprise to influence its external factors than its stakeholders.
5 As a consequence of developments in information technology, the manner in which work is performed will change fundamentally.
6 The development of the European Union has meant that there has been a shift in political power and responsibility to outside national borders.
7 Social factors relate to society in the broadest sense of the word.
8 Sustainable business is also known as socially responsible business.
9 The term 'profit' refers solely to the venture's financial performance (rather than to the broad economic picture).
10 One of the primary reasons for setting up the WTO was to promote the inclusion of developing countries – especially the 'least developed' countries – in world trade.

Theory questions

1 a Both stakeholders and external factors exercise an influence on organisations. What is the difference?
  b Why is recognition of this difference important?
2 Political choices and changing opinions in society in respect of the environmental problem have an effect on the behaviour of organisations. Give a few examples of the changing behaviour of organisations in this area.
3 Why can we consider technological development to be the motor of our economy?
4 Explain how a united Europe gives European businesses a stronger competitive position on the world market.
5 Name five social themes that are of interest to sustainable business.

Practical assignment

Identify an organisation in your neighbourhood where you would like to work or at least get some work experience. Alternatively, find an organisation that you find interesting or where a friend or relative works. The information needed to complete this task can be obtained via the Internet or an interview.

1 Analyse which stakeholders and surrounding factors exert an influence on this organisation, then turn the roles around and see how the organisation exerts an influence on them.
2 Explain what these influences consist of and how powerful they are.
3 Brainstorm future developments: what is the effect of these influences likely to be five years from now?
4 How should the organisation prepare for these changes, or react to them?

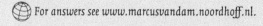 For answers see www.marcusvandam.noordhoff.nl.

Mini case study

Siemens: a cleaner future

For Siemens, innovation is on the one hand the development of new products while on the other, it is the combining of technologies to reach innovative total solutions. In the areas of mobility, health and energy, Siemens sees itself as having the potential to make a big impact.

Siemens is the world leader in the development of solid oxide fuel cells (SOFC). In this process, electricity is not created by burning, but is generated directly and without serious consequences for the environment.

SOFC is a promising technological development that will compete in the future with potential develop-ments in internal combustion engines (cars, buses) and batteries (laptops, mobile telephones).

The main advantages of the fuel cell is its conside-rably lower emissions and longer battery life span. The Siemens group was established in Berlin and Munich. Approximately 400,000 people work at Siemens world-wide. Business is transacted in around 190 countries. Two thirds of Siemens' trade comes from products that have been developed in the last 5 years.

Source: Siemens (www.siemens.com) February 2006

Questions

1 Give reasons why Siemens would want to enter the market for sustainable energy generation.

2 Is providing innovative solutions for sustainable energy development an example of sustain-able business? Give reasons for your answer.

3 What influence are stakeholders and surrounding factors likely to have on product develop-ment at Siemens?

E-mail case study

To:	Piere Dupont
Cc:	
Bcc:	
Subject:	Carrefour:Poland as an interesting market?

Message:

Dear Pierre,

During the past few months, we in the 'Internationalisation' Taskforce have often discussed the possibility of entering the Polish market with our own supermarket formula. Poland's domestic market is growing rapidly and consumer spending in the food segment is increasing significantly. The economic and demographic indicators are fine – they are not the problem. What we lack, however, is an understanding of the political and cultural scene. What issues do we need to be aware of in particular? What is the long term prognosis for political stabili-ty and the future of foreign investments? What are the features of normal business transac-tions and customer interaction? These are just three questions....

Pierre, we'd like you to make a quick sketch (in the form of a list) of the main political and cultural issues that we need to address if we decide whether to enter the Polish market.

Then we will look at the question of how to access this market.

Could you get one or two A4 sheets to us within two weeks?

Kind regards,

Sabine Durant
Chairman Carrefour Internationalisation Taskforce

3

Strategic management

This chapter deals with the way organisations attune to their environment. This process is known as strategic management. We will examine the classical approach to strategic management in some detail and will also take a look at some more contemporary views.

Contents

After studying this chapter
- You will have become familiar with the main strategic management concepts.
- You will be able to differentiate between the various phases of the classical strategic management process.
- You will be able to see how strategic management and the implementation of strategies in organisations are linked.
- You will be aware of recent developments within strategic management and understand their significance.
- You will understand the way strategic management is shaped by the business world.
- You will understand the importance of a good information system.

3.1   The strategic management process

In Chapter 2 we saw how various external parties and factors affect an organisation. The survival of organisations is highly dependent on how they cope with these external influences.

Strategic management

How organisations attune to the environment is an outcome of the process of strategic management. Strategic management is the process of careful consideration of appropriate responses to the environment as well as maintenance of standards and development of the skills required for the inclusion of possible changes to strategy.[1] As the definition shows, it is a process that involves management determining the strategy. The word 'strategy' is relatively old and is derived from the Greek word 'strategos', meaning the art or the skills of the military commander. There are many definitions of strategy. It can be defined as a plan that states what an organisation needs to do to reach its goals. Planning is one of the main tasks of management.

Strategy

In this chapter, we will cover two different approaches to strategic management. In the first approach, known as the classical school, strategic management is synonymous with strategic planning. In this approach, strategic planning is used by an enterprise to find a balance between the resources, the strengths and the weaknesses of the enterprise on the one hand, and the opportunities and threats in the environment on the other. One of the main founders of this school is Igor Ansoff, who made a significant contribution with his 1965 book *Corporate Strategy*. Michael Porter is another important pioneer, building on this theory in the 1980s and 1990s. In his book *The Rise and fall of Strategic Planning*, Henry Mintzberg made critical comments about the classical approach to strategic management.

Classical school
Strategic planning

The views of Mintzberg can be recognised in the second modern approach to strategic management. Gary Hamel and C. K. Prahalad were important founders of this school. According to this new approach, strategic management is synonymous with strategic thinking. An organisation that thinks strategically is capable of putting its vision into practice. It is argued that quantitative, analytical models are no longer adequate in dealing with the present turbulent environment.

Second modern approach

Nowadays, almost every organisation is facing the challenge of strategically reorienting itself within this turbulent environment. It can choose between a number of schools of strategic management.

3.2   The classical approach to strategic management

In the classical school of strategic management the main issue is the positioning of the organisation in relation to the environment. This is done by first analysing the strong and weak areas of the organisation and subsequently by scanning the environment of the organisation for possible opportunities and threats. Then a particular strategy for identifying the organisation's aims must be chosen, followed by the making of plans for implementing the strategy within the organisation.

Environment

The process of strategic management consists of three phases:
1   Situational analysis (Section 3.3)
2   Strategy formation (Section 3.4)

Name:	Niels Thestrup
Country of origin:	Denmark
Lived in:	Denmark, Germany and USA
Job title:	Regional Director, Europe for Danisco Food Ingredients
Company name:	Danisco
Company website:	www.danisco.com

What is the most important lesson you have learned from working with people from different cultures?

Be yourself, be flexible and respect different views. There is no single answer to complicated business deals, and the number of potential answers will increase according to the number of different cultures participating. The people you visit in the foreign country will usually know that you have a different background and you may look different, so they will expect you to be different. Learning small things like saying 'thank you', 'good day' and 'goodbye' in their language, as well as gestures (such as taking your hand to your chest after greeting, as happens in certain Asian countries) will be positively accepted. However, trying to adapt and behave exactly like the local people can send a negative signal as it will not seem at all natural.

How are major decisions made in your country?

Consensus and compromise-type decisions are employed for the major issues. The manager makes sure he / she 'sells the idea' and everybody is supportive (or in the worst case, neutral) before making public the final and official decision. Informal discussions with the relevant parties are done separately or in smaller meetings, which gives the decision maker a more nuanced view. The process creates room for possible compromises which will establish a broader support base for the decision maker. A final and typically larger meeting is held to present the conclusion / decision, and at this point the decision maker knows that he will get the support needed. This process is typical of cultures that pay less respect to authority and of highly educated business environments.

How important is the work / life balance in your country?

This is important. A balanced work / leisure life creates a balanced person, to the long term benefit of both parties. It is similar to the Chinese yin / yang, where the proper balance between two opposites (in this case, work and leisure) leads to a complete and balanced person who has good working skills as well as good people skills. Such a person will also typically be more respected by employees and will be seen as being a leader of a group or department.

What is the role of emotional intelligence in your job?

Very important. High emotional intelligence is a sign of a deep understanding and respect for social interactions, which in general are more important to achievement in an international environment due to the complexities of cultures. Strong emotional intelligence combined with good negotiation skills are important personal skills for a successful international business career.

How important is a business plan?

Less important. Business plans in terms of numbers are good guidelines, but the process of making business plans should be simple and not take up significant resources as they typically do. Qualitative milestones or accountability aligned with the overall strategy of the company or business is more important. In many companies, business plans are typically started four to six months before the start of the new financial year and the processes are typically bottom-up – building the plans from customer and production to business unit to corporate. Some of the assumptions behind business plans made four to six months before the start of the financial year can easily change and many of the details typically requested are not as important as the resources being used.

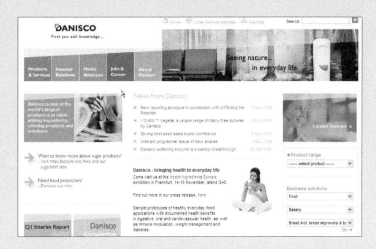

3 Planning and implementation (Section 3.5)

These phases are represented in Figure 3.1.

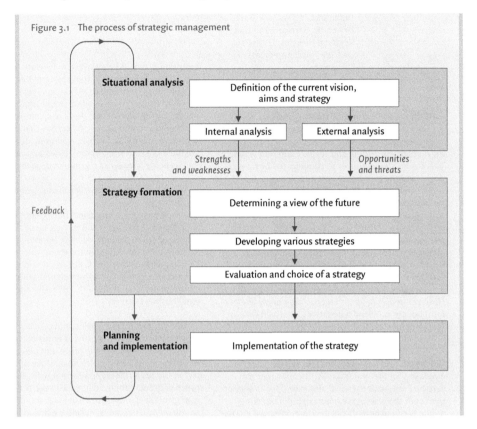

Figure 3.1 The process of strategic management

The figure shows that strategic management is a dynamic and cyclical process. It includes feedback from the planning phase and implementation in the situational analysis phase. All of the phases will be discussed in the following section.

3.3 Situational analysis

Situational analysis

The first phase of strategic management is known as situational analysis. It is also called the strategic audit or SWOT analysis (Strengths – Weaknesses – Opportunities – Threats). The situational analysis focusses on determining the current profile of the organisation while taking into account its external environment. The situational analysis consists of:

· A definition of the current vision, aims and strategy (Section 3.3.1)
· An internal analysis (Section 3.3.2)
· An external analysis (Section 3.3.3)

Figure 3.2 shows the situational analysis as part of the process of strategic management.

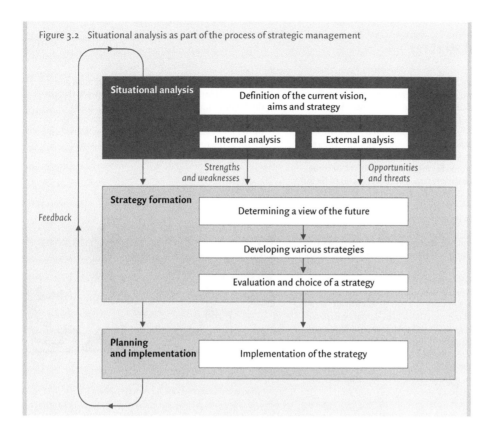

Figure 3.2 Situational analysis as part of the process of strategic management

3.3.1 Definition of the current vision, aims and strategy

The first phase of the situational analysis aims at gaining a insight into the organisation's existing situation, defining its current vision, aims and strategy.

In an ideal situation, these three elements would have already been defined and made clear to everybody. In reality, however, the definition is often insufficient or the members of an organisation interpret the elements differently.

The first element that needs to be made clear is the vision held by management. A vision is a general idea or representation of the future of the organisation and usually consists of a mission statement and principles. (See Figure 3.3.)

Vision

Vision as management tool

McKinsey Consultants developed their so-called 7-S model to analyse the role of vision as a management tool. (See Figure 3.4.)

The 7-S model consists of seven management factors that are interdependent, of equal importance and closely connected:

7-S model

1 *Structure.* This relates to the way elements within the organisation relate to each other: to the organisational framework, to the distribution of tasks and so on. According to McKinsey, the structure of an organisation can be temporarily changed (for example, by setting up project groups) without changing the basic structure of an organisation.

2 *Systems.* This refers to information and communication systems, formal as well as informal, within the organisation.

3 *Managerial style.* This relates to the characteristic behavioural patterns of the top managers of the enterprise. Management style exerts a big influence on the culture of the organisation.

Samurai strategy

The Japanese martial arts successfully developed and implemented strategies centuries ago. Miyamoto Musashi, born in 1584, is one of the best-known samurais. By the age of thirty he had won more than sixty fights and everyone considered him to be invincible. This was why he decided to dedicate the rest of his life to perfecting his strategy. Just before he died he wrote a guide for those who wished to become acquainted with strategy. This book, entitled *Go Rin No Sho* ('The Book of the Five Rings'), is used by many business people today. They apply the same principles to their business as were used in the old Japanese martial arts.

The book explains strategy in five chapters: earth, water, fire, wind and the void. The following advice is offered:

- Earth: know the smallest and the biggest things, the most superficial and the most deep.
- Water: by knowing one thing, you will know ten thousand things. (The way to defeat one man is the same as that used to defeat ten million people. A strategist makes big things out of small things, like making a big Buddha by first making a small model.)
- Fire: train night and day in order to be able to make fast decisions.
- Wind: know old traditions, modern traditions and family traditions. (It is hard to know yourself if you don't know others. All roads have side paths.)
- The void: the way of nature is the way of strategy. (If you appreciate the power of nature and are aware of the rhythm of the situation, you will be able to defeat the enemy in a natural way.)

Source: Miyamoto Musashi, *The Book of Five Rings*

Figure 3.3 Elements of an organisation

Vision	=	Mission	+	Principles

Figure 3.4 7-S model

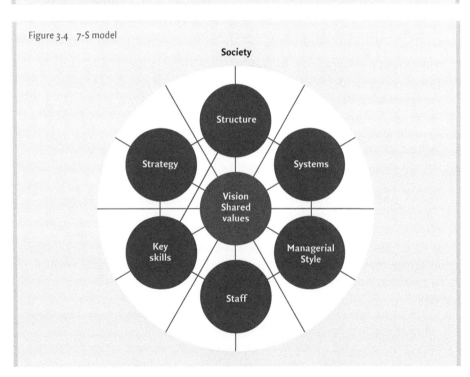

4 *Staff.* This focusses on the way the organisation pays attention to its human resources.
5 *Key skills.* These are those capabilities of individuals or the whole organisation that make it stand out and by which it can distinguish itself from its competitors.
6 *Strategies.* These are laid down in the plan that shows what the organisation needs to do in order to reach its goals.
7 *Shared values.* This is the vision.

At the core of McKinsey's model is vision. This management instrument is the link and provides the direction for the remaining factors. As an operational management tool, vision can affect operational management in the following ways:
· By motivating employees
· By focusing the attention of the employees on relevant activities
· By creating a framework that shows employees how tasks should be done and how these tasks fit into the bigger picture

The degree to which the organisation succeeds in utilising a more effective management strategy depends on the existing vision and how this is communicated. (See Figure 3.5.)

The mission statement of an organisation is a description of their product-market combinations and can be an indication of the way the organisation makes use of its structural competitive advantage.

Principles relate to the norms and values of the organisation and they can be compared with society's norms and values. The following could be aspects of an organisation's principles: *Principles*
· Quality first
· Customer first
· Reliability and honesty
· Our employees are reliable and honest
· Our employees are our strength

Mission, strategy and business principles

ING Mission Statement
'Setting the standard in helping our customers manage their financial future'

Strategy
We are a customer-orientated company with a clear organisation and a strategy which is founded on value-based management. We have a strong position in mature markets where we want to generate further growth through proper execution of our business fundamentals (such as customer satisfaction and managing costs, risk and our reputation) and we focus on growth in retirement services, direct banking and life insurance in developing markets. That way we try to offer our shareholders a higher return than our peers can average.

ING Business Principles
As a global provider of financial products and services, ING plays an important role in society. In order to fulfil this role it needs to maintain the confidence of its customers, shareholders, employees, and other stakeholders by acting with professionalism and integrity.

The ING Group attaches paramount importance to upholding its reputation, and the ING Business Principles play an important role in this respect. ING expects the highest levels of integrity from its employees, regardless of their position in the organisation.
· We are committed to our integrity
· We aim for an above-average return
· We are open and clear
· We promote sustainable development and respect human rights
· We respect each other
· We are involved in the communities we operate in

Source: ING Group 2006 (www.ing.com)

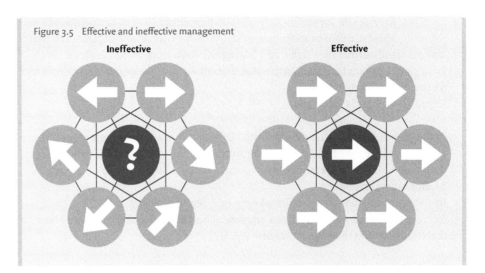

Figure 3.5 Effective and ineffective management

Ineffective

Effective

- A focus on personal self awareness
- We contribute to society

As each organisation uses the words 'mission' and 'principles' in its own way, the distinction between these terms might not always be clear. It is important for the process of strategic management, however, that these elements be recognisable and expressed in the vision of the organisation.

Organisational goals

Organisational goals

The way organisational goals are defined is based on organisation's vision. These goals show the relationship between the organisation, the environment, and employees. Naturally, the content is influenced by the organisation's stakeholders. In particular, the providers of finance (e.g. the shareholders) have a very important voice in the matter.

Organisational goals often relate to one or more of the following subjects:

1 *Balance of interests.* 'We are a reliable partner to our customers, shareholders, staff and suppliers.'
2 *Profitability.* 'We aim to make our products and services profitable for our customers and for ourselves.'
3 *Quality.* 'We always produce perfect products and are there when our customers need us.'
4 *Effectivity and efficiency.* 'We encourage our staff to contribute to the setting of targets and the planning of how they can best be achieved.'
5 *Image.* 'We are a leading supplier of products and services.'
6 *Code of conduct.* 'We work in a disciplined manner and keep our word.'

In these times of enormous and rapid change, an awareness of organisational goals is an essential and important point of reference for those who are working on strategic plans. Having such an awareness will prevents a situation where the content of the organisational strategy is determined by ad hoc decisions. 'If you don't know where you're going, any road will take you there.'

Strategies

Chosen strategies

After the organisational goals have been scrutinised, the chosen strategies are examined. It is important to check the degree to which these strategies can achieve the

Nokia's Code of Conduct

Nokia has always recognised that its own long-term interests and those of its various stakeholders depend on compliance with the highest standards of ethical conduct and applicable law. Its Code of Conduct has been approved by Nokia's Group Executive Board and is introduced and reinforced to Nokia employees through induction, training and internal communications. The Nokia Values are embedded in this Code, and without exception, every Nokia employee is expected to conduct himself or herself, and his or her business, in line with this Code. Stricter guidelines or more detailed instructions may be appropriate for certain regions or coun-

tries, but they should not contradict this Code. Nokia periodically reviews this Code and is committed to making changes in its content and implementation when changes or further clarification so demand.

Source: Nokia (www.nokia.com), 2006

identified goals. In other words, are the current strategies successful? Later in this chapter we will see that as part of the process of strategic management, an existing strategy can be adapted or revised totally.

3.3.2 Internal investigation as part of the situational analysis

The next step in the situational analysis is internal investigation (See Figure 3.6.)

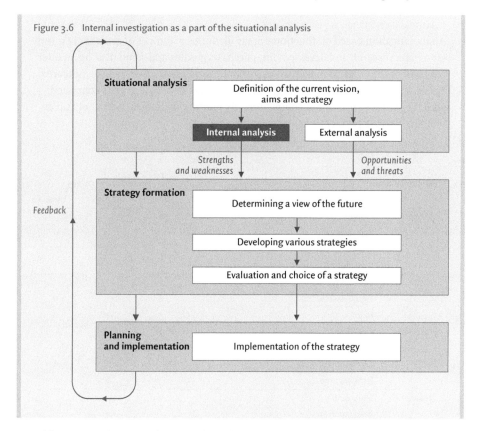

Figure 3.6   Internal investigation as a part of the situational analysis

Self-awareness is a crucial personal attribute. An insight into one's own functioning will lead to a better assessment of how feasible the options (for example, those for training or a new job) are. If you acknowledge your own strengths and weaknesses, you can correct your weaknesses and develop your strengths further.

Athletes continuoully measure their performance in order to check their progress and so that they can draw up a program with their coach in order to further improve their results. Many people tend to blame others as the cause of their problems. This also applies to organisations. Falling profits can easily be blamed on a competitor who upsets the market by introducing lower prices. One can easily forget to question one's own performance.

Internal audit

If an organisation wants to stay healthy or solve its problems, it is vital that it regularly cast a critical eye over its own operations. An investigation that focusses on the internal organisation is called an internal audit or management audit. The goal of this is to look at all internal activities and to identify the strong and weak sides of the organisation.

During this exercise, various people in the organisation need to provide a lot of information. As it is important that this information be correct, optimal commitment at every level is required.

Integral or partial approach?
An investigation into strengths and weaknesses can be carried out in either of the following ways:
1 Based on functions
2 Based on results

1 Internal investigation by functional area

Functional areas

Performance

An investigation based on functional areas identifies a number of activities of a similar nature: research and development, purchasing, sales and so on. During an internal audit of these functional areas, performance and productivity will be measured. These aspects are scored as strong, neutral or weak. The score may be compared with the scores of important competitors. By plotting the scores, we can obtain an image of relative performance. (See Figure 3.7.)

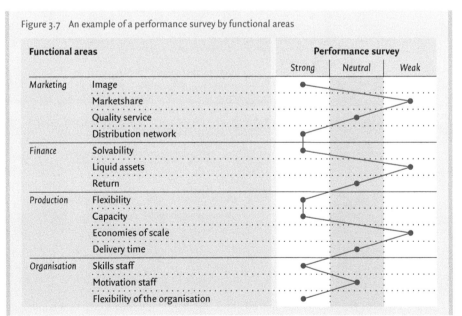

Figure 3.7 An example of a performance survey by functional areas

The information necessary for the assessment can be obtained by internal research, market research or customer research. In many organisations, account managers are required to regularly go over survey questionnaires with their customers in which the customer assesses the supplier's performance.

Not all aspects are equally important for the commercial success of an organisation. This is why the relative importance of each aspect is determined after the assessment, and the results are then weighed to give a balanced overview.

The term 'partial' or 'singular' approach describes a situation when an internal audit only investigates a limited number of functional areas within an organisation. The risk inherent in this approach is that the areas analysed, combined with an incorrect or incomplete definition of the problem, can lead to an incorrect impression of the situation and subsequent wrong decisions being made. When only a limited number of areas are investigated the advantage is, of course, time savings. *Partial approach*

Using the integral approach, all functional areas are investigated and the results subsequently related to each other, thus obtaining a complete picture of the organisation. Interest in the integral approach has grown lately as many problems cannot be approached in isolation. A good example of this is the logistical process within an organisation, which is likely to relate to almost every functional area. *Integral approach* *Complete picture*

2 Internal audit based on results

The second approach to internal auditing is based on results. Here, the focus is on the financial attractiveness of the various business activities. Profitability (current and potential) and the strategic perspective are both important in this approach. *Results*

Many enterprises divide related activities into organisational units. Typically, the products or services of these organisational units focus on clearly defined markets. Almost all functions are present within the unit: sales, purchases, administration, service and so on. The unit's results are also carefully monitored. One could say that such a unit is actually an autonomous enterprise within a group. These units are known as SBUs: Strategic Business Units. *Organisational units*

The word 'strategic' in this acronym correctly suggests that SBUs determine their own strategies, though they do need to fit in with the strategies of the group. In big enterprises, an SBU may hold a number of product market combinations (PMCs). A PMC is an SBU at a lower organisational level. SBUs and PMCs can be defined on the basis of products, groups of buyers, distribution channels or geographical areas. Figure 3.8 shows an example of an organisation with SBUs.

We can detect three strategic units within ABN Amro, a global bank of Dutch origin. This structure has been chosen in order to function as much as possible in a customer-oriented way. The strategic units are supported by the Corporate Centre. The three strategic units are:

1 *Wholesale clients*: this unit supplies integrated corporate banking activities and investment banking services to companies, financial institutions and governmental organisations.
2 *Consumer and commercial clients*: focusses on private individuals, large-scale enterprises and medium and small-scale businesses.
3 *Private clients and asset management*: responsible for private banking, asset management and investment funds.

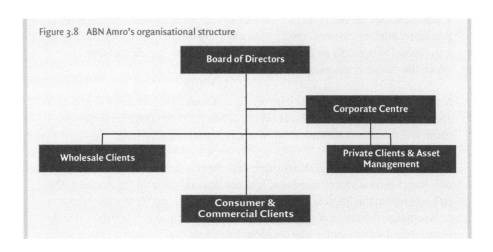
Figure 3.8 ABN Amro's organisational structure

Core activity

Many enterprises are now subdivided into a large number of SBUs. We state categorically that these SBUs should be part of the core activity of the enterprise. A core activity is an activity on which the enterprise concentrates particularly. They give the enterprise its right to exist and are responsible for its success. An example is the editing of books by Prentice Hall, a British publisher. In the coming years, an increasing number of enterprises will subdivide their structure into business units. (In Chapter 9 – Organisational structure and design – we will discuss this at length.)

Since strategic businesses units nearly always operate autonomously and in different markets, the internal audit has to focus on each individually.

Portfolio analysis

The internal audit maps all SBUs and checks whether the combination of activities is optimal. Every SBU is in a phase of the product life cycle and is thus more or less profitable. It is of great importance to determine the best way of transfering funds from one SBU to another in order to foster investment in new products. Tackling the allocation issue effectively means safeguarding the future of the enterprise. It goes without saying that a balanced portfolio of activities should be aimed for.

In a portfolio analysis, the various SBUs are categorised in a matrix and analysed according to a number of economical criteria. This analysis provides a coherent and total overview of the activities of an enterprise at a certain moment in time. A portfolio analysis can also serve to demonstrate how the enterprise and its activities have developed over a number of years.

Boston Consulting Group

The best-known and most applied approach to portfolio analysis originates from the Boston Consulting Group (BCG).
This approach addresses three aspects of the business unit, namely:
1 Turnover (expressed as the relative market share)
2 Market developments (expressed in terms of market growth)
3 Monetary flow (expressed as the cash flow: the net profit after taxes and depreciation.)

Market growth
Relative market share

With this model, the various SBUs are situated within the four-quadrant BCG matrix. Market growth is marked on the vertical axis and the relative market share (one's own market share related to the share of the largest competitor) is shown on the horizontal axis.

Heineken portfolio analyses: strong growth in the premium beer segment

World-wide beer consumption is expected to grow by 2% to 3% annually. Underlying growth forecasts for the various regions vary substantially. In the developed markets (Western Europe, the United States, Australia and Japan), the overall growth rate is forecast to be close to zero. Growth in these markets will be mainly realised in the premium / import and specialty segments, which will grow annually by about 4%, at the expense of mainstream beers. The Heineken® brand is growing at a faster pace than the premium segment itself.

In the developing regions of Central Eastern Europe, Latin America, Asia and Africa, beer consumption is growing at the solid rate of 3% to 4%. Increased beer consumption is driven by a growing population, an increase in personal income and the shift from the consumption of traditional (hard) liquors towards beer. Mainstream beers are showing the strongest growth here, while segments like the higher priced

premium and specialty brands offer potential in the long term. Russia is Heineken's largest beer market by volume. Heineken targets a market share of 20 percent in about 5 to 6 years through organic volume growth.

Source: Heineken (www.heineken.com), 2006

Within the matrix, the SBUs are represented by circles whose size corresponds to their volume of turnover within the organisation. Figure 3.9 shows data (referred to below) within such a BCG Matrix.

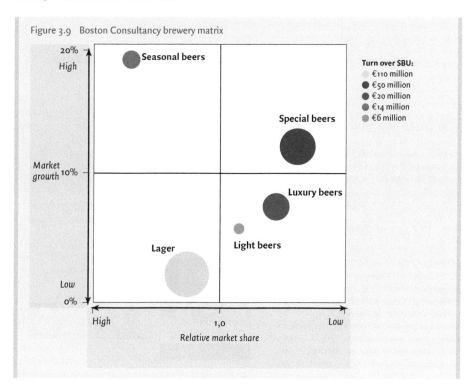

Figure 3.9   Boston Consultancy brewery matrix

To take an example, a brewery has identified the following strategic business units, each with their turnover and market share (see Table 3.1).

Tabel 3.1 A brewery's SBUs

SBU	Turnover	Market growth	Market share	Market share biggest competitor	Relative market share
Lager (mainstream)	110	0 − 1 %	25 %	20 %	25 : 20 = 1,25
Special beers (speciality)	50	10 − 13 %	10 %	25 %	10 : 25 = 0,4
Luxury beers (premium)	20	5 − 7 %	5 %	10 %	5 : 10 = 0,5
Seasonal beers	14	18 − 20 %	35 %	20 %	35 : 20 = 1,75
Light beers	6	3 − 6 %	5 %	7 %	5 : 7 = 0,71

Cash flow

The third aspect of the BCG Matrix is development of the monetary flow (or the cash flow) of the various SBUs. An SBU generates money or needs money for investment, depending on the position of the SBU in the matrix. In order to be able to fund investments, the enterprise should strive for a balanced distribution of the various businesses in the matrix. The portfolio analysis of the BCG is based on the following principles:

1 There is a positive relationship between the size of the relative market share and the amount of the cash flow. The larger the relative market share is, the larger the cash flow. This can be explained in terms of the 'experience effect' and / or economies of scale. With a large relative market share, the costs per product will come down as more experience than competitors have is acquired, resulting in more efficient deployment of staff and resources.

2 There is a negative relationship between the development of a market and the amount of cash flow. In the case of substantial market growth, the enterprise needs to invest heavily in the SBU. This will diminish the size of the cash flow. In a stable or shrinking market, hardly any money will be invested in the activity. This leads to the creation of a relatively high cash flow.

3 There is a negative relationship between the development of relative market share and the volume of cash flow. In order to increase the relative market share, a lot of money needs to be invested in the SBU.

4 Market growth decreases as the business moves ahead in its product lifecycle.

IN THE PRESS

Yahoo's 'Question Mark' strategy: tuning in to TV and mobile

Yahoo unveiled a bid to plant its services on new devices well beyond the PC, to use the TV and mobile phone to reach consumers. The services will be called Yahoo! Go.

Users of the new TV service who connect their sets to a PC, for instance, will be able to use a remote control to browse their personal digital photo collections, access Yahoo's Internet video search services or call up films and TV shows.

A version of Yahoo! Go for mobile phones and handsets made by Nokia will have access to Yahoo's instant messaging, e-mail services and Internet search. They will also automatically upload photos from the handset to a Yahoo Internet service.

A third version of the Go-branded Internet service for PCs will bring direct access to some Yahoo services without requiring users to open an Internet browser. The move echoes efforts by Google to plant its own desktop software on more PCs. Such efforts have assumed greater urgency as Microsoft prepares to launch its Windows Vista operating system, which

will integrate Internet searches into many desktop functions.

Functionality of Yahoo TV

Source: *The Financial Times,* January 2006

Based on the development of market growth, the relative market share and the cash flow, the BCG identifies four categories (as shown in Figure 3.10).

a *Question mark.* These SBUs are characterised by a high market growth and a relatively low market share. This yields a large negative cash flow. Question marks may turn out to be tomorrow's 'stars'.

Question mark

b *Star.* These SBUs have a high market growth as well as a high relative market share. They yield a negative or restricted positive cash flow. The high market growth will probably lead to an increase in competition.

Star

c *Cash cow.* This is where profit is being made. These SBUs have low market growth but a high relative market share and a large positive cash flow.

Cash cow

d *Dog.* These SBUs beg the question of whether – and if so, when – these activities need to be stopped. Dogs have low growth as well as a low relative market share. They generate a negative cash flow or a restricted positive cash flow.

Dog

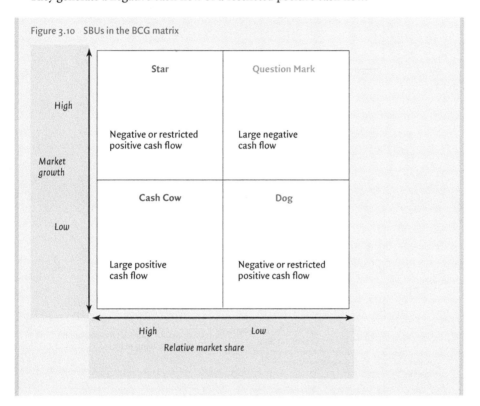

Figure 3.10 SBUs in the BCG matrix

Based on this division, we can identify the following investment strategies:

a *Dog:* Disinvest.
b *Star:* Protect and invest more
c *Question mark:* Invest or disinvest.
d *Cash cow:* Invest to keep the market share up to standard.

In Figure 3.11, the investment strategy for the various SBUs is given by means of a dotted arrow. This shows that the cash flow coming from the cash cow is invested specifically in the question mark and star SBUs. The ideal development of SBUs within the matrix is indicated by a linear arrow.

The position of an SBU in the Boston Consultancy Matrix is significant for the marketing instruments of product, price, promotion and distribution. Strategies can be

Figure 3.11   Development of the cashflow and SBU

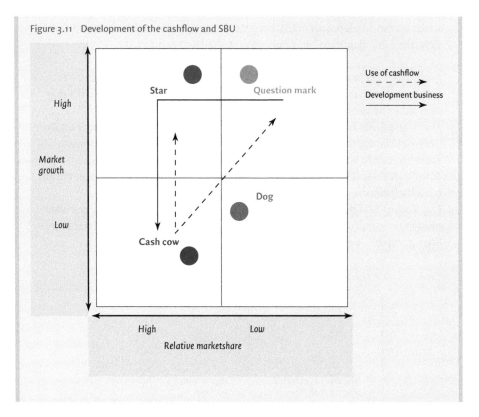

Figure 3.12   Strategies per marketinginstrument: BCG matrix

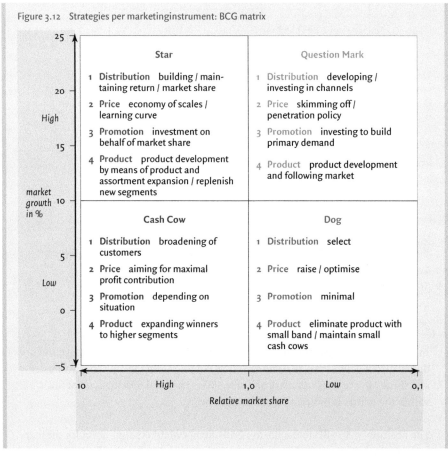

determined per instrument: for example, by the raising or lowering of the price or the expanding or shrinking of distribution channels.

Figure 3.12 shows strategies for the individual marketing instruments in each quadrant.

Portfolio management

Different portfolio matrices will be developed depending on the kind of enterprise and type of activity. Where management applies this technique for analysis, it is called portfolio management. We can identify the following phases of portfolio management:

1 Reflecting the portfolio of activities in the matrix.
2 Analyzing the portfolio. This relates to the balanced structure of the portfolio, the vision of the future and the question of whether the various activities (SBUs) can be funded, now and in the future.
3 Choosing a strategy for the SBU. As a result of the analysis, a choice must be made for the desired development of SBUs within the portfolio. (See Figure 3.13.)

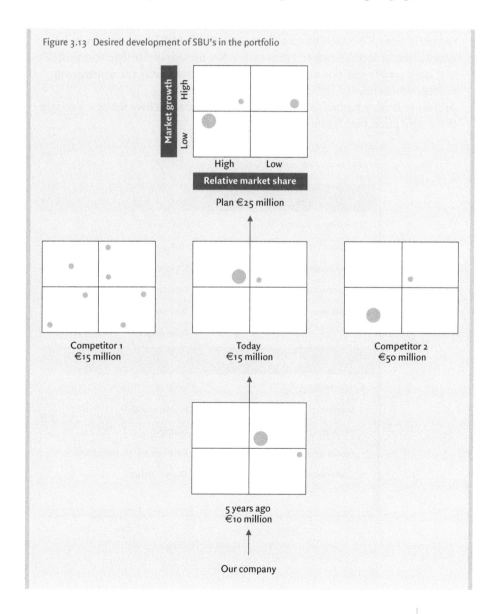

Figure 3.13 Desired development of SBU's in the portfolio

The organisation and management need to meet specific requirements in order to be able to apply the portfolio technique successfully. We discuss these requirements below.

Organisation

Organisational unit

In practice, a business cannot always be compared to an organisational unit such as a division or a department. However, information supply and management reports are tailored to the needs of organisational units. This is why it is often difficult to obtain strategic information that is applicable to one particular business.

If a business belongs to more than one organisational unit, responsibility for the business is also shared. This is an important reason for placing businesses as much possible under one organisational unit. Furthermore, financial reporting needs to be adjusted to the needs of individual SBUs. Another important issue is the (timely) availability and validity of information needed for the portfolio analysis. Often, the various information systems are not connected sufficiently, so that a lot of data has to be inputted again, increasing the chance of errors occurring.

Management

Competencies and the responsibilities

Another portfolio management problem has to do with to the competencies and the responsibilities of business unit managers. Managers of SBUs with a cash cow business will not be inclined to invest their cash in businesses outside their responsibility. A manager of a question mark business will need funds badly and will urge top management to transfer the money in from other areas.

In order to develop businesses successfully, it is important to have the right manager in the right place. (See Figure 3.14.)

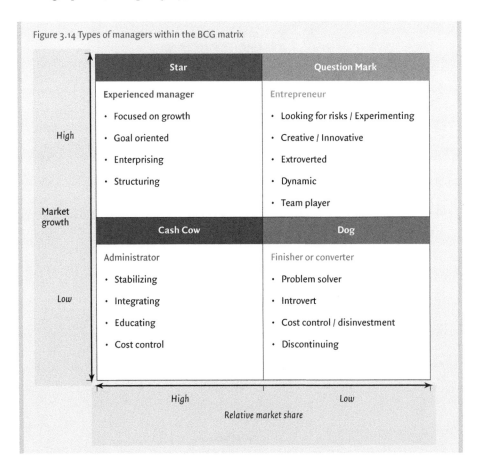

Figure 3.14 Types of managers within the BCG matrix

Managers come in different shapes and forms. Their skills and mentality will vary, and they will range from genuine entrepreneurs who do not mind taking risks and look for businesses they can build up from scratch (pioneers) to managers who avoid risks as much as possible and aim to consolidate their existing business (administrators). In general, a dog business requires a manager who takes care of reorganising and downsizing, whereas a question mark-business requires a pioneer.

To close, we will offer some critical comments on the BCG Matrix. Firstly, the BCG model is obviously a growth model. Market growth is considered high when it is 10% or more, meaning that the majority of businesses fall into the category of dogs. This can have a stigmatising effect and one consequence might be that profitable activities are ignored and possibly needlessly restructured.
Another issue is that investment of cash cow earnings might result in the cash cows themselves being neglected. By using the money for further investments in cash cows, various possibilities could be exploited.

Lastly, the importance of a relatively high market share is debatable. Until recently, only big organisations had the privilege of a large market share. However, they are known for their relatively high fixed costs. There are many examples of organisations that make a decent living with a relatively small market share, since they can take advantage of lower labour costs, accommodation expenses and marketing budgets.

In order to apply the BCG model correctly, it needs to be adapted to the industry as well as to the enterprise.

The BCG Matrix criticised[2]

Since its development in the 1970s, the Boston Consultancy Group (BCG) matrix has acquired the universal meaning it was meant to gain when it was drawn up. With the help of the matrix it is theoretically possible to compose an ideal product portfolio for any arbitrary producer. Then, ideally, an organisation will maintain sufficient cash cows to finance the development of stars and question marks, without losing sight of a healthy dividend for the shareholders. A company can thus maintain its long-term position in the competitive battlefield of business. Despite its success, the matrix has not been beyond criticism during the course of time. The first point of criticism is obvious: the risk that the qualifications are dealt with much too rigidly. The boundaries between the quadrants are actually relatively fluid. For example, it is not unlikely for certain dog products to yield attractive profits and cash cows to fail to generate the promised benefits. This flaw in the model is rooted in the assumptions that form the basis of the model. For example, the relative market share need not predict the competitive position of a product adequately. Product differentiation, market segmentation or barriers of entry for new entering producers may influence the market strongly.

3.3.3 External research as part of the situational analysis

The environment of many organisations is quite turbulent: a reason for thorough and ongoing alertness.
External research involves developments in the external environment being mapped out and translated into possible opportunities and threats for the organisation. External research is part of the situational analysis and can be done at the same time as the internal audit. (See Figure 3.15.)

Like the internal audit, external research can be carried out by a combination of employees and external professionals. It should result in identification of the main opportunities and threats to the organisation.

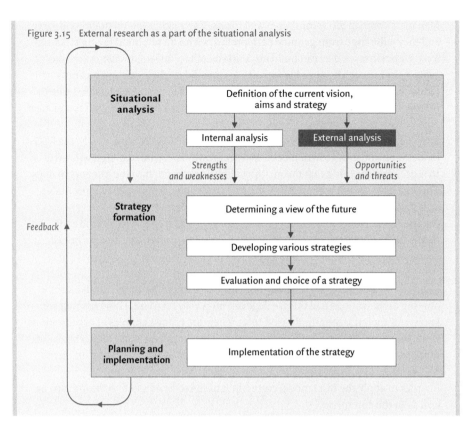

Figure 3.15 External research as a part of the situational analysis

Situational analysis

Definition of the current vision, aims and strategy

Internal analysis

External analysis

Strengths and weaknesses

Opportunities and threats

Strategy formation

Determining a view of the future

Developing various strategies

Evaluation and choice of a strategy

Feedback

Planning and implementation

Implementation of the strategy

Interconnections

External components

External investigation concerns the environment of the organisation. This environment consists of a number of parties and external factors. The basic aim of external research is to discover the interconnections between the various parties and factors, which is more than simply revealing the individual influence of each element. It is also important to realise that the influence of each party and factor will differ per organisation. To obtain a good understanding of this, it is necessary to structure the external components (parties and factors). We often find particular groupings and hierarchies of the external components within such a structure. Figure 3.16 shows the external components.

Internal environment
The internal environment relates to the organisation itself and is mostly determined by the chosen organisational structure, procedures, communication structures and staff quality.
An organisation that wants to be effectively attuned to the external environment

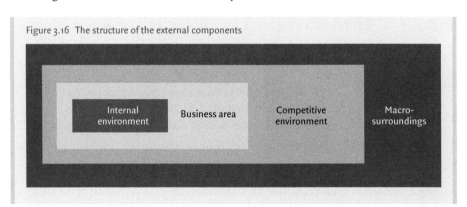

Figure 3.16 The structure of the external components

Internal environment

Business area

Competitive environment

Macro-surroundings

must be structured in a way that fits with the environment. In other words, the external environment dictates the design of the organisation. Important success factors are decisiveness, flexibility and the effectiveness of the organisation. Some examples of opportunities and threats to the internal environment are:

a *Opportunities / strengths*
   − Availability of high-quality staff
   − High level of automation
b *Threats / Weaknesses*
   − Bureaucratic organisation
   − Lack of 'entrepreneurship'

Internal environment research (the internal audit) was discussed in Section 3.3.2.

Business areas
An organisation performs individual tasks within a broader arena and this gives each organisation a certain function within the wider process. The specific tasks carried out by an organisation are also influenced by the tasks of the other organisations. Figure 3.17 shows the business area of various organisations within a supply chain.

Tasks

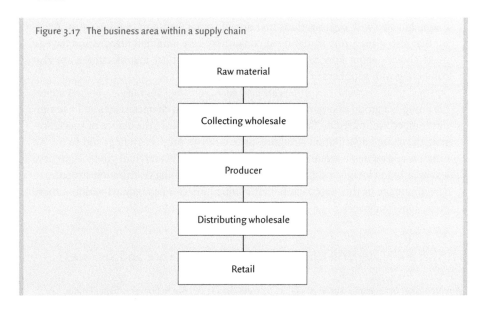

Figure 3.17 The business area within a supply chain

Raw material

Collecting wholesale

Producer

Distributing wholesale

Retail

Since the activities of organisations change constantly, the tasks of the enterprise may also change. Environmental research focusses on the mapping out of the business area of an organisation. Some examples of the opportunities and threats facing hospitals are:
· *Opportunities:* hospitals will have to perform a great number of new tasks due to the aging of the population.
· *Threats:* the rising costs of health care may lead hospitals to decide to stop performing certain tasks.

Competitive environment
The third part of the external research concerns the competitive environment. Organisations are influenced by competitors. To understand the opportunities and threats coming from the competitive environment, the following questions need to be answered:

Competitive environment

A Who are our competitors?

B What information about our competitors do we need?

C How intense is competition?

D What competitive advantages do we have that allow us to make our mark on the various markets?

A *Who are our competitors?*

We need to define the industrial sector in order to determine our competitors. An industrial sector is a group of enterprises that produce similar products, often based on a similar technology. Similar products are products that are interchangeable in the eyes of the buyers. There are two ways of identifying competitors in an industrial sector:

1 *Customer-oriented approach:* competitors are determined from the perspective of the potential buyer. The buyer (or potential buyer) must make choices in his spending behaviour. He / she not only has a choice of similar products from various companies but has to choose between different sorts of products. In general, organisations tend to identify their competitors at a product level. Particular Renault cars are in competition with particular Honda cars. However, possible competitors can also be found at other levels. Car manufacturers might consider their products as means of transportation. Consequently they do not only have to compete with other car manufacturers, but also with organisations that provide other transport opportunities. A factor that also plays a role is that most consumers have a limited income and have to make choices about how to spend it. This means that car manufacturers are also competing with suppliers of other consumer goods.

Strategic group

2 *Strategic group approach: competitors are determined according to strategic groups.* A strategic group is a group of organisations that have common characteristics and use similar competitive strategies. Some strategic group criteria are the degree of specialisation, the chosen distribution structure, price strategy, product strategy and so on. An example of a strategic group in the car market is the BMW and Audi group. Both have a similar brand image, a similar price strategy and a similar distribution structure. The advantage of this approach is that competitors can be analysed within a more consistent framework.

Competitive analyses: Will China beat India in software and services?

China's ambition is set to become a global power in software and services and so match its pre-eminence in manufacturing. While China is the world's top location for contracting out manufacturing, it has just $2 billion of the outsourced services market. But China has plenty of potential. Its workers are well educated in basic computing and mathematics. They may lack creativity, but they are disciplined and readily trained, making them better at tedious jobs than most Indians are. This suits the BPO business. These are repetitive, rules-based tasks which you can train an army of people to do, and are not tasks that require innovation. This needs millions of low-cost workers, and China has them. India used to be cheaper, but salaries for graduates, engineers and programmers have been climbing fast and staff turnover at IT companies can reach 30% to 40% a year. Throw in China's superior infrastructure, tax breaks and strong support from the state, plus the desire of multinational companies to spread risk away from India.

Yet China is still five to ten years behind India, say most observers. It has two big disadvantages. First, although many Chinese can read English, they speak and write it badly. What's more, few Chinese engineering and computer graduates are as good as their qualifications suggest. Meanwhile, fears about piracy of intellectual property – more rampant in China than India – will constrain growth. Though foreign companies in China say that copying sophisticated IT processes is difficult and can be thwarted by relatively simple safeguards, the perception that sensitive business information is at risk is likely to slow development. All this suggests that, for the moment, China is likely to capture an increasing share of low-level BPO tasks, such as data entry, form processing and software testing, while India continues to dominate higher-value functions, such as research and design, which require greater creativity and language skills.

Source: *The Economist*, May 2006

B What information about our competitors do we need?

We need to answer a number of additional questions in order to answer this main one:

- What are the present and the past strategies of our competitors?
- What are the strengths and weaknesses of our competitors?
- How big and profitable is each competitor?
- What is the organisational culture of each competitor like?

Based on this information, so-called reaction profiles can be created, which can be used to answer the following questions:

- What strategic decisions are the competitors mostly likely to take?
- What are the weaknesses of the competitors and how vulnerable are they?
- What reactions can be expected from our competitors?

C How intense is competition?

The attractiveness of an industry is determined mainly by long-term profitability, and this profitability depends on the intensity of competition. To a large extent this intensity depends on two factors:

Intensity

1 *Structural factors.* For instance, the degree of concentration and the possibilities of entering the sector. Entrance possibilities depend on such factors as economies of scale, product differentiation, the required level of investment and the possibilities of entry into the existing distribution channels.
2 *Strategic factors.* For instance, the readiness to cooperate and the degree of uncertainty about the strategies of competitors.

D What competitive advantages do we have that allow us to make our mark on the various markets?

It is important to identify how strongly the organisation can profile itself against competitors. The advantage may be based on costs, image or unique product features. The larger the applicable competitive advantage, the less vulnerable the organisation will be.

Competitive advantages

Competitive analysis according to Porter

Michael Porter, a professor at the Harvard Business School, made an important contribution to the development of strategic management. He analysed the competitive environment according to the industry to which an enterprise belonged. He identified five competitive forces within an industry. These forces determine the structure and the profitability of the industry. Figure 3.18 shows the five competitive forces:

Competitive analysis

1 New entrants
2 Buyers
3 Substitutes
4 Suppliers
5 Competitors.

1 New entrants

New entrants to the sector try to gain market share at the expense of present suppliers. Pressure could be put on prices or present supplier costs could be forced up (e.g. extra marketing expenses). This may decrease the average profit in the industry. The threat of new entrants depends on barriers to entry. Some examples of barriers are the need for economies of scale, brand awareness, required investment, entrance to distribution channels, and government policies. The entrance of new enterprises within an industry may cause changes to the strategies of the other enterprises in the industry.

New entrants

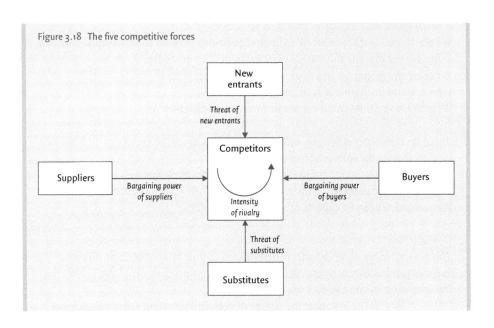

Figure 3.18 The five competitive forces

Buyers

2 Buyers
Buyers play competitors against each other and, in doing so, try to reduce prices. The power of the buyers depends, amongst other factors, on the availability of information, the costs of transfer to other competitors, the number of available alternative suppliers and the purchase volume of the buyers. When the buyers have a strong position, the average profit in the industry will be low and vice versa. A possible enterprise strategy is focussing on buyers with little power.

Substitutes

3 Substitutes
Enterprises within an industrial sector will compete with other industrial sectors if these produce substitute products. The presence of a few substitutes has the same effect as high entrance barriers: that is, a higher average output. As such, enterprises should be aware of the price-quality ratio of substitutes, the tendency of buyers to substitute and the costs of changeover to substitutes.
In the event of threats from substitutes, enterprises can react by changing the price-quality ratio of their own products.

Suppliers

4 Suppliers
Since suppliers determine the purchase price of a product, they exert a big influence on the average output. The power of suppliers depends on the presence of substitutes, the importance of the supplied product and the concentration of suppliers. There are only a few ways that enterprises can exert an influence on the power of suppliers.

5 Competitors
Within any industry, enterprises compete with each other because they want to improve their individual position. The intensity of competition depends on the number and the variety of competitors, market growth in the industry, withdrawal thresholds and cost levels.

Macro-surroundings
The last component of the environment consists of six external factors:
1 Environment factors
2 Technological factors

3 Demographic factors
4 Economic factors
5 Political factors
6 Social factors

These influencing factors have been discussed in Chapter 2.

3.4 Strategy formation

After a situation analysis, the next step is strategy formation. Strategy formation is a part of the process of strategic management (see Figure 3.19), and consists of three phases:

Strategy formation

1 Determining a view of the future (Section 3.4.1)
2 Developing various strategies (Section 3.4.2)
3 Evaluation and choice of a strategy (Section 3.4.3)

Section 3.4.4 will discuss strategy formation according to Porter.

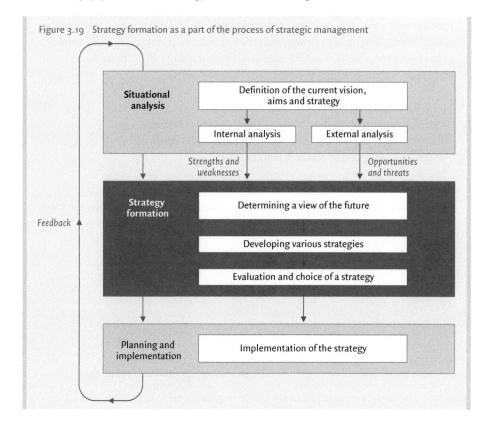

Figure 3.19   Strategy formation as a part of the process of strategic management

3.4.1   Strategy formation: determining a view of the future

The first phase of strategy formation involves an image of the future of the organisation being sketched. In particular, we need to check whether the chosen objectives can be achieved in the future by using the present strategy. This can be predicted on the basis of a situation analysis. If it seems that the objectives cannot be met completely by using the present strategy, either the strategy or the objectives must be adjusted to fill the gap between what is desired and what is reality.

Image of the future

This difference between desirability and reality will occur more often if an organisation operates in fast-changing surroundings or if competition is strong. Furthermore, the objectives might be too ambitious, or the present strategy unsuitable for the desired objectives.

3.4.2 Strategy formation: development of different strategies

Strategy

If the present strategy fails to reach the goals, other strategies should be developed: for example, developing new products, entering new markets, choosing other sales channels, increasing efficiency or collaborating with a new partner. In short, a strategy determines the options for the optimal functioning of the organisation. Strategies have the following characteristics:

- They have a medium and a long-term time span
- They are related to the organisation as a whole
- They create opportunities to promote new investments

Strategic planning

What type of strategic planning takes place depends heavily on the type and the size of the organisation, the characteristics of the industry in question, the quality of management and the knowledge of suitable methods and techniques. Organisations should select strategies in keeping with their specific circumstances. With a multitude of possible strategies available, to assist with making a final choice some initial evaluation is desirable.

The following three categories will be discussed:

1 Strategies dependent on the market share of the organisation
2 Strategies dependent on the extent of turbulence in the environment
3 Expansion strategies (the product-market matrix)

Strategies dependent on the market share of the organisation
Organisations exhibit clear differences in their market share. On this basis the following types of organisations can be identified:

A Market leaders

Challengers

B Challengers

The truth about strategy

It has not been fashionable recently for chief executives to offer grand strategic visions. Growth and profitability are the market's immediate priorities, driven by the demands of impatient hedge funds and institutions. Who has time for strategy when 'execution' is all that really matters?
'Decisions have to be taken fast but that does not spell the end of strategy', argues Joseph Bowler, a professor at the Harvard Business School. 'Companies need to adapt and change quicker, and have an approach that makes such changes easier. But the lead for that has to come from the top. The truth is, strategy is back – and it never really went away'.

Other insights
- Strategy emerges gradually and perhaps is fully understood only in retrospect
- Strategy can be formed from the bottom up, as well as from the top down.
- Henry Mintzberg on strategy: 'Strategy doesn't only have to position, it has to inspire. So an uninspiring strategy is really no strategy at all'.
- John Kay on strategy: 'Strategy is a synonym for expensive. A strategic investment means "we are going to lose a lot of money on this investment" and strategic acquisition means "we are paying more for this company than it is worth"'.

Source: TheFinancial Times March 6, 2006

C Followers

D Specialists

Each of these types have their own specific competition strategies, which are explained below.

A Market leaders

These organisations have the largest market share and are function as a beacon to other organisations. Market leaders aim to:

Market leaders

- Increase the total market
- Defend their own market share
- Expand their market share

There are various ways of reaching these objectives. The total market can be increased by increasing by the number of users, by stimulating current users to increase their consumption, or by attracting new users. To defend their market share, organisations could choose from the following competitive strategies:

a *Position strengthening*. A 'stronghold' can be built around the product by giving it unique features, low pricing, a high distribution density or powerful advertising.

b *Attacking the flanks*. The rationale that attack is the best form of defence is another way of attacking a competitor. The market leader will try to discourage attacks from competitors by using directional marketing.

c *Enhancing mobility*. Positions can also be defended by increasing the mobility of the enterprise and by creating options to move activities to other markets.

These competitive strategies can also be used if the market leader attempts to increase its market share.

B Challengers

The aim of these organisations is to become market leaders. They may use the following competition strategies to do this:

Challengers

- Attack the market leader head on
- Attack the market leader from the side
- Hedge the market leader in
- Attack the market leader via an indirect path
- Use a guerrilla strategy

In head-on attacks, the challenger fights the market leader with those marketing instruments that work well for the market leader itself. The attack will focus on the strong rather than the weak points of the market leader. The outcome of this fight will depend mainly on the power and the stamina of the competitors.

Head-on attacks

With an attack from the flanks, the challenger uses marketing instruments or other strong points that its own organisation has but which are less developed in the market leader's organisation.

Attack from the flanks

If the challenger chooses to hedge the market leader in it will attack the market leader on a lot of fronts using various marketing instruments. They may include attacks via better products, lower prices, increased distribution points and more advertising activity.

Hedge the market

The challenger can also attack the market leader via a side path: entering markets where the market leader is not operating. The final goal is to build new strongholds via new markets and / or new products.

A guerrilla strategy aims at destroying the balance of the market leader by means of

Guerrilla strategy

short attacks from different points: by lowering of prices and intensive promotion campaigns, for example.

C Followers

Followers

Not all organisations strive to become market leaders. Since the market leader will be more powerful in a number of fields, an attack has little chance of success in most situations. The follower can, however, use competitive strategies. Every follower can give his product or service a special feature to retain customers or obtain a share of new customers. There are three competitive strategies that market followers can avail themselves of:

1 Imitating the strategy of the market leader as closely as possible. The market follower copies the market leader in activities such as segmentation and the use of marketing mix instruments (price, product, promotion and place).
2 Imitating the strategy of the market leader but at a certain remove. The follower may adopt a certain degree of differentiation in some areas.
3 Mimicking the administration of the market leader in certain areas, but in other areas, the follower uses its own strategies.

Studies show that the profitability of the follower can approximate that of the market leader. This may be explained by the fact that the follower does not need to invest significant resources in basic research in the way market leaders often have to. Instead, a follower can invest in further research and development.

D Specialists

Specialists

Specialists are organisations that focus on small niches of the market. They are active in parts of the market that are out of reach for other organisations because of their special character.

Ideally, such a specialised part of the market has the following characteristics:

- It is a niche market.
- It is large enough to be profitable.
- It has growth potential.
- It lies outside the field of interest of larger organisations in the market.
- It has the ability and means to operate effectively in the specialised part.
- It is able to survive a potential attack from large organisations by means of customer goodwill.

The power of these types of organisations is derived from their specialisation. Many kinds of specialisation are possible: for example, geographical specialisation (e.g. operating only in particular regions) and product specialisation (e.g. high-quality products only).

Strategies for a turbulent environment

Turbulent environment

Today, enterprises are operating in a turbulent environment, characterised by:

- Various variables undergoing change at an increasing rate
- Greater mutual dependence of all sorts of phenomena
- Developments having an increasingly autonomous character

The prediction of future developments becomes more difficult in a turbulent environment. Predictions have a high degree of uncertainty. Instead of predicting, it is therefore much more meaningful to identify an organisation's vulnerable factors. One way of doing this is via a susceptibility analysis.

When vulnerable factors in an organisation are detected, it is important to deter-

Investing in ICT is only the beginning

Investment in ICT is not the reason the US is developing faster than the European Union. It is how ICT is used. In a recent report ('Reaping the benefits of ICT'), the Economist Intelligence Unit (EIU) tries to explain the difference between the development of productivity in the US and Europe, using the perspective of big investment in IT. ICT development started earlier in the US, so it seems logical that there the benefits will be reaped earlier. But that does not explain everything. The EIU assumes that the gap in the growth of productivity will continue in the coming years unless the European Union makes a number of important adjustments. ICT investment as such is only one of the factors that determine growth. The research done by the EIU shows that the entrepreneurial climate of a country is at least as important. On the organisational level, management skills, R&D and access to venture capital play a decisive role.

The Netherlands is one of the countries that have the potential to join the leading group: the country has a well-developed ICT infrastructure, competitive markets and a good entrepreneurial climate. However, the Netherlands still needs to work on training and education in ICT skills as the Dutch score below the European average on these points.
Among the factors that determine the success of ICT investments, managerial ability to deal with ICT in the right way is the most important. A survey conducted by the EIU amongst European managers shows that lack of cooperation between general managers and IT managers is seen as the main barrier to maximising ICT advantages. Contemporary managers need to be aware of the impact of ICT on the company and they need to possess the skills to transform the company.

The ICT development matrix

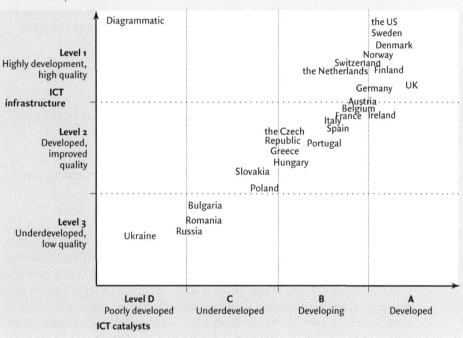

Source: *Het Financieele Dagblad*, 25 June 2004

mine how to deal with them in their own terms. In other words, the organisation must try to solve its vulnerability issues with help of turbulent situation strategies. For this purpose, the organisation has the choice of four strategies:

1 Immunisation
2 Adaptation
3 Manipulation
4 Innovation

1 Immunisation

The first and obvious way of protecting oneself in areas of vulnerability is to make oneself impervious to attack. A possible option is diversification: for example, penetrating new markets with new products, primarily looking for relationships in a new business area and / or new production techniques (concentric diversification). If there is no longer any relationship with existing markets and / or products we call this 'conglomeration forming'.

The main motive for diversifying is to spread the risks, making the organisation less sensitive to changes in the environment. In practice, diversification has a number of drawbacks:

- After diversification, organisations might find themselves with parts that are scarcely connected. This will hamper positive synergy and increase bureaucracy.
- Diversification should be the last option used to escape from a weak competitive position. Diversification can only be successful when the enterprise holds a powerful position.
- The key goal of diversification – spreading the risks – is seen mostly in financial terms, without considering interactions between new and existing activities.

2 Adaptation

This strategy relates to the ability of the organisation to adapt itself to changing circumstances, or in other words, its flexibility. The organisation can be flexible in many areas, including the following:

- Products
- Production processes
- Organisational structure
- Financing
- Information retrieval systems

An increase in the adaptability of organisations can be gained by decentralisation: that is, by using smaller organisational units with shorter decision-making processes and communication lines.

3 Manipulation

Manipulation can be defined as the full or partial recovery of earlier loss of influential power. As mentioned before, a characteristic of a turbulent environment is the increasing autonomy of developments: organisations increasingly unable to control what is happening. Trying to win back part of the lost ground is an obvious strategy. Since control over developments is a consequence of concentration of economic power, other organisations will obviously follow suit. Economic power can be recovered by internal growth and by coalition formation: collaboration with other organisations (see also Chapter 4). A consequence of coalition formation is that organisations will have to give up part of their autonomy in order to reach consensus in the area of policy.

4 Innovation

To react adequately to change, both a certain degree of flexibility and innovation are required. As with flexibility, the organzation can be innovative in many organisational aspects. They include:

- Production techniques
- Organisational structure
- Distribution
- Communication
- Information retrieval

Innovation: Apple teams up with Ford, General Motors & Mazda to deliver seamless iPod integration

Apple has teamed up with Ford Motor Company, General Motors and Mazda to deliver seamless iPod® integration across the majority of their brands and models, making it easy for iPod users to enjoy and control their iPod's high-quality sound through their car's stereo system.

iPod offerings for Ford, General Motors and Mazda provide drivers with outstanding sound quality while charging the iPod and conveniently storing the iPod in the glove compartment. Seamless iPod integration also allows drivers to use their car's multifunction controls to select their music using artist, album, playlist or shuffle songs, as well as to skip easily between tracks and playlists. Apple ignited the personal computer revolution in the 1970s with the Apple II and reinvented the personal computer in the 1980s with the Macintosh.

Today, Apple continues to lead the industry in innovation with its award-winning desktop and notebook computers, OS X operating system, and iLife and professional applications. Apple is also spearheading the digital music revolution with its iPod portable music players and iTunes online music store.

Source: Apple (www.apple.com), 2006

Where technical innovation is concerned, organisations have to choose between buying a new product or developing it themselves. Both have their benefits and drawbacks. Buying a new product can be cheaper and the introduction time is short. But by developing your own innovations you will stay ahead, which favours profitability.

Technical innovation

Expansion strategies (the product-market matrix)

Organisations have two growth possibilities:

1. New products can be developed.
2. New markets can be entered.

Expansion strategies

When the two dimensions are combined, a product-market matrix (Ansoff) arises (Figure 3.20).

Figure 3.20 Ansoff's product-market matrix

		Product	
		Existing	New
Market	Existing	Market penetration	Product development
	New	Market development	Diversification

Market penetration

Market penetration occurs when an organisation increases its market share in an existing market with its existing product. The market needs to be a growth market and the organisation needs to have a competitive advantage.

Market penetration

Product development

Product development

Product development is the development of new products while continuing to operate in the existing market.

Market development

Market development

New markets for existing products can be developed: for example, a restaurant opening a takeaway service. Another option is the selling of existing products in foreign markets.

Diversification

Diversification

Diversification refers to organisational growth by developing new products and selling these in new markets.

3.4.3   Strategy formation: evaluation and choice of a strategy

After the strategies have been set out, an organisation will make some preliminary choices. These strategies will then be evaluated in terms of their medium-term prospects. An increasingly frequent method for this evaluation is the scenario method. Scenarios can be considered as being 'qualitatively tested pictures of the future'. Figure 3.21 illustrates the concept of the scenario method.

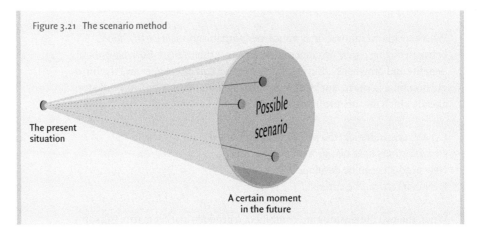

Figure 3.21   The scenario method

Scenario method

In the scenario method the development of a number of factors are predicted in the medium term (the picture of the future). The factors to be considered include competition, prices, market growth, legislation with regard to the environment and economic growth. Uncertainty and complexity increase with the time span of the predictions. This explains the 'fish-trap' structure of the illustration mentioned. All possible scenarios can take place between the outer limits. Some advantages of the scenario method are:

1 The feasibility of strategies can be tested using future projections
2 Extra options can be created by means of scenario methods
3 Scenarios can support decision-making processes relating to choice of strategies

Decision rules

For the choice of a final strategy, a number of criteria should be formulated. These 'decision rules' are again rooted in the objectives of the organisation. The chosen strategy must be in accordance with the organisation's capabilities.

Organisations and their environment

3.4.4 Strategy formation according to Porter

Since Michael Porter's theory attaches great importance to the supply chain, we will start with a theoretical introduction to the production chain.

Strategy formation in the production chain

In determining what strategy to adopt, it is important to look at one's own position in the production chain and study possible developments, such as position and horizontal or vertical growth possibilities.

A particular product travels through various production chain phases: from inception to consumer. A production chain details the participants and links that are present during the development of a particular product. An example of a production chain is given in Figure 3.22.

Production chain

Figure 3.22   A production chain

Each link or horizontal layer in the production chain represents an industrial sector. The horizontal layer contains organisations that perform the same or a similar function in the development of variations on a particular product. Within an industrial sector, groups of organisations (branches) not only use the same production or distribution techniques, but also supply largely the same products. Retailers and the food branch are examples of this. We can identify two groups of strategies.

Industrial sector

Branche

Strategies within a production chain

A particular organisation may be active within different parts of the production chain. This is known as integration. If it involves a preceding link, we call this backward integration, while a future link is termed forward integration. An example of backward integration is a retailer that also has a wholesale businesses.

The opposite of integration is differentiation: to take an example, a coffee manufacturer deciding to sell his coffee plantations to another organisation.

Integration
Backward integration
Forward integration
Differentiation

Strategies that are implemented between different production chains

An enterprise may also perform activities within another industrial sector (parallelisation). An example is a petrol station also starting up a small supermarket. We also call this industry blurring. The opposite is specialisation: an organisation removing an activity within the same horizontal layer of the production chain. This can take place both within the same branch and within the industrial sector. An example is a clothing store specialising in clothing for large people. The various strategies are illustrated in Figure 3.23. It is based on an organisation that does not form part of another organisation.

Parallelisation

Specialisation

Porter asserts that when formulating a competitive strategy, it is important to take account of the enterprise's business environment (its industrial sector and branch). Depending on the industrial sector analysis, two viable strategies are available:

Figure 3.23   Production chain and possible strategies

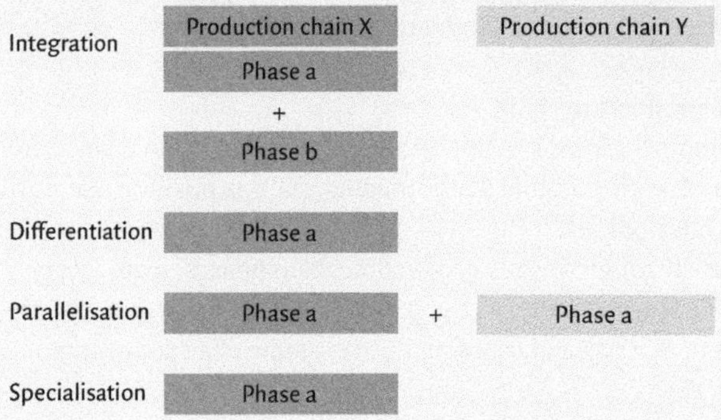

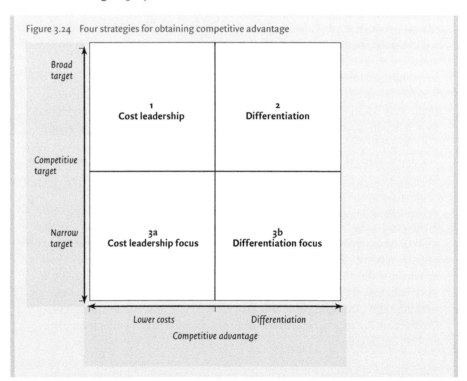

Integration

	Production chain X		Production chain Y
Phase a		
+		
Phase b		

Differentiation — Phase a

Parallelisation — Phase a + Phase a

Specialisation — Phase a

a An undifferentiated strategy. Such a strategy deals especially with the development and launching of a product at a cost that is as low as possible while guaranteeing good quality.

b A differentiated strategy. The emphasis in this strategy is on obtaining a competitive advantage by directing activities towards the specific requirements of the customer.

Competitive range

Both strategies can be made more situation-specific by including the element of competitive range. A competive range is a determination of exactly which groups of buyers an enterprise is focussed on, and how marketing instruments should be used. The competition range may be broad or narrow.

Four different strategies that an enterprise can use to obtain a competitive advantage are shown in Figure 3.24.

Figure 3.24   Four strategies for obtaining competitive advantage

Broad target

1
Cost leadership

2
Differentiation

Competitive target

Narrow target

3a
Cost leadership focus

3b
Differentiation focus

Lower costs   Differentiation
Competitive advantage

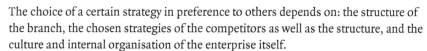

How to survive in the international market[3]

- Be strict with yourself! Ensure ongoing innovation and make high demands on your organisation and suppliers.
- Acknowledge your competitors! Keep a close watch on their activities.
- Be alert! By monitoring signals at an early stage, you will have the advantage of being able to take the initiative.

- Improve the national competitive environment. Enterprises should cooperate with customers, suppliers and distributors in order to help them to improve and strengthen their competitive position.
- Do not neglect your home market.
- Carefully select your business location

The choice of a certain strategy in preference to others depends on: the structure of the branch, the chosen strategies of the competitors as well as the structure, and the culture and internal organisation of the enterprise itself.

Porter does not recommend one strategy in particular: all strategies have their advantages. It is, however, most important that a clear choice is made for a particular strategy.

3.5   Planning and implementation

We come now to the last and possibly the most important phase of strategic management: planning and implementation. (See Figure 3.25.)

Planning and implementation

We will deal firstly with the planning process and then consider how to implement strategies in organisations.

Figure 3.25   Planning and implementation as a part of the process of strategic management

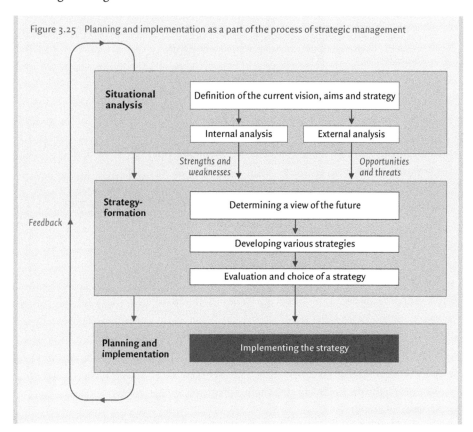

At a time when flexibility and alertness are increasingly important to the continuance of organisations, one may be inclined to assume that cutting out all planning is the best and most rapid way of reacting to opportunities and threats emanating from the environment. At least one is not tied to a certain course of action. On closer inspection, however, such a course has the following disadvantages:

1 The organisation will have less knowledge of its handicaps and future risks.
2 Future opportunities cannot be systematic explored or prepared for. With bigger and more complex organisations, it will be more difficult to keep day-to-day business in order and to react appropriately to stimuli from the environment.

Organisations have an optimal size: beyond a certain limit they will react quickly and efficiently only if the planning procedures are well oiled. Where this limit lies depends on the nature of the industry and the capacities of the top manager. In other words, at some time, planning will necessary. In most industrial sectors, the most effective term for strategic planning has come down from five or six years to two or three. This is a consequence of the faster pace of changes within the environment.

3.5.1   Planning cycles

The output of strategic management consists of a strategy or a plan. Implementation of a strategy involves translating it to shorter time frames and lower hierarchical levels. A cyclical process – the planning cycle (see Figure 3.26) – arises from this.

Cyclical process

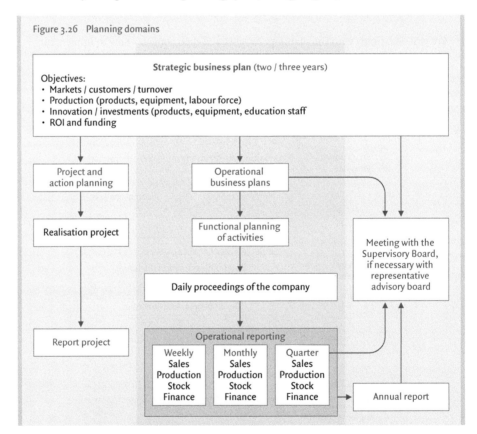

Figure 3.26   Planning domains

We can identify the following steps in this process:

1 Strategic planning
2 Operational planning
3 Function-specific planning

Starbucks' strategy: a small step from mocha to movies

With barely one movie under its belt, Starbucks is moving aggressively toward expanding its involvement in the entertainment business, seeking movies and books to promote in the hope of duplicating the success it has had with music. The retail coffee giant is to announce that it has signed an agreement with the William Morris Agency to find more movie and book projects to market.

Starbucks doesn't have the intention of financing movies, or being traditional investors in movie projects. Instead, it will selectively link the Starbucks brand with certain kinds of movies and books in the belief that Starbucks customers trust the company to, in essence, choose their entertainment for them. They want to see their name associated with the kind of music, literature, and movies of which people will say,

'I am glad Starbucks brought this to the marketplace.' Starbucks has found itself in an entertainment evolution, trying to find a way to expand Starbucks outside the four walls of the store. The reason it works is that they are a trusted brand. They have 6 million people a day in their stores, and those people trust Starbucks and what Starbucks is selling to them. Starbucks is aiming to extend the reach of its brand, but it is also trying to achieve something more ephemeral: enhancing the experience of being in Starbucks stores. It is more than just coffee, it is a human connection. In terms of content, the linkage is to that aspiration. They want to add texture to the brand, and value to the experiment.

Source: *The New York Times*, May 1, 2006

1 Strategic planning

This is high-level planning, the outcome of strategic management as described in previous parts of this chapter. Some relevant questions to ask are:

Strategic planning

· What objectives do we want to reach within two to three years as regards product-market combinations, growth, volume of trade, profit and market share?
· How do we hope to do this in terms of timing, required investments, financing, organisation, personnel and data systems?

These issues need to be looked at yearly or per quarter. It might be sensible to appoint separate study groups for some activities. They can work through the various issues, coordinate matters and report back to top management. Among other things, this might be appropriate for courses of action that:

· Involve a number of different functional areas
· Are large in scale and of great importance to the organisation
· Are new for the organisation

To take some examples:

· Product development and market introduction
· Information planning and computerisation projects
· Quality campaigns

Strategic planning should covers a period of two to three years, but should be reassessed each year, or even more frequently if changing circumstances demand it.

2 Operational planning

The goals to be reached should be identified in the strategic plan and reassessed each year in terms of expenses and yields, sale and production quantities, investments, supplies, staff planning and so on.

Operational planning

The plan will result in an annual budget in which production or sales quantities are indicated by sector together with linked costs and staff members responsible for execution of the plan. The budget is thus coupled to a degree of delegation to lower managerial levels. In order to reach their targets, these managers need to have sufficient competency and means at their disposal.

An operational plan should be worked out in detail each quarter, month or week depending on the industrial sector and size of the organisation.

3 Function-specific planning

The operational plan should be adapted to the various functional divisions for daily activities. Some examples of these activities are:

- Monthly and weekly production planning and programming
- Timetable planning for production teams
- Liquidity planning
- Recruitment and selection procedure planning

An appropriate reporting system is vital if a planning system is to function well. This should give feedback for each phase in the cycle, comparing actual results with those aimed at. The information should be available in time for any adjustment needed.

Such an approach will give rise to a continuous cycle of planning and reporting, forcing the organisation to look systematically and in a structured way at the direction it is going and to maintain this course in daily reality, while leaving room for possible adaptations.

Planning systems are often implemented when the executive manager becomes preoccupied by daily operational concerns. It is useful to start with operational planning and follow this by function-specific planning. If this is successful, management will have time for further explansion of the organisation: that is, for activities at a strategic level.

3.5.2   From planning to introduction

Development and choice of the right strategy is the basis of successful management, and if not brought into practice, all will have been for nothing. And all too often is this the case.

Research has shown that many managers are dissatisfied with strategic management.[4] More than 50% of the time it is how it is done that is the source of the dissatisfaction. Strategic management is often seen as a dual system, consisting of the development of a strategy and its introduction. But it should be considered as one integrated process: after all, a strategy is only as good as how it is implemented.

Problems

Some of the main problems surrounding strategic management are:

a *Insufficient commitment on the part of management and employees.* If the strategy is dictated by top management there is a risk that it will be insufficiently recognisable to the staff and therefore not supported by the organisation. As a result, implementing it could be delayed or hampered. Another reason for lack of commitment may be that employees have experienced some earlier strategies that were not successful. Additionally, employee commitment will diminish if management makes frequent and fast changes. It is especially important to let staff participate in the development of strategies when organisations become flatter. Employees often have relevant knowledge about the market and the customers.

b *Insufficient knowledge of and preparation for the process of strategic management.* To be able to participate in strategic management it is important for everybody to have professional skills. Participants who are unfamiliar with this process and / or its theoretical basis will only participate in a limited way. In other words, the quality of strategic management is largely dependent on the quality of the 'input' to this process.

c *Insufficiently explained strategy.* If the process of implementing strategic management stops after formulation of its objectives, it will have little value. All steps should be explained clearly and succinctly so that they are understood by all in the organisation.

d *Insufficient support from data systems.* Analysis of the market, competitors, and its own position depends on the possession of current and correct information. Use has to be made of one's own data systems, and the quality of these is often poor, especially where the availability of information is concerned. Organisations often rely on various information systems, but these are rarely connected with each other. This makes manual operations necessary for obtaining the required information.

e *The influence of a rapidly changing environment.* An organisation's environment can change so quickly (for example, new players entering the market, government legislation, price reductions, and reorganisations) that any decisions made in response to these changes will have an important effect on the organisation and its process of strategic management.

Solutions

Some solutions to the problems described above are:

1 Provide good training, education and preparation of all those who involved.
2 Form teams of employees from different divisions and let them work on strategic plans.
3 Develop detailed plans of action that are realistic and supported.
4 Develop integrated data systems.
5 Build flexible systems to make fast changes easy.

The strategic plan that top management ultimately adopts should not deviate too much from the recommendations of various staff members. If it does, enthusiasm will quickly evaporate.

From planning to action = execution!

After a long, stellar career with General Electric, Larry Bossidy has transformed AlliedSignal into one of the world's most admired companies and was named CEO of the year in 1998 by *Chief Executive* magazine. Accomplishments such as 31 consecutive quarters of earnings-per-share growth of 13 per cent or more didn't just happen; they resulted from the consistent practice of the discipline of execution: understanding how to link together people, strategy, and operations, the three core processes of every business. Leading these processes is the real job of running a business, not formulating a 'vision' and leaving the work of carrying it out to others. In their book *Execution*, Larry Bossidy and Ram Charan show the importance of being deeply and passionately engaged in an organisation and why robust dialogues about people, strategy, and operations result in a business based on intellectual honesty and realism. The leader's most important job – selecting and appraising people – is one that should never be dele-gated. As a CEO, Larry Bossidy personally makes the calls to check references for key hires. Why? With the right people in the right jobs, there's a leadership gene pool that conceives and selects strategies that can be executed. People then work together to create a strategy building block by building block, a strategy in sync with the realities of the marketplace, the economy, and competitors. Once the right people and strategy are in place, they are then linked to an operating process that results in the implementation of specific programs and actions and that assigns accountability. This kind of effective operating process goes way beyond the typical budget exercise that looks into a rearview mirror to set its goals. It puts reality behind the numbers and is where the rubber meets the road. Putting an execution culture in place is hard, but losing it is easy.

Source: Ram Charan 2006 (www.ram-charan.com)

ADVICE

3.6　Critical observations about the classic approach to strategic management

In the previous Sections, we dealt in detail with the classic approach to strategic management. It should be clear why this strategic management process is seen as a strategic planning process.

In his book *The Rise and Fall or Strategic Planning*, Henry Mintzberg considers the possibilities and limits of strategic planning. In the book he shows himself not to be an advocate of abolishing strategic planning either partially or completely. Instead, he shows its possibilities and limitations.

Firstly, Mintzberg gives his definition of a strategy. He takes the matter further than we did at the beginning of this chapter. Strategy is not only a plan, but also a 'pattern of actions'. The plan can be seen as the intended strategy. The ultimate strategy is a combination of the 'intended strategy' and a number of unexpected actions, thereby becoming more dynamic (see also Figure 3.27).

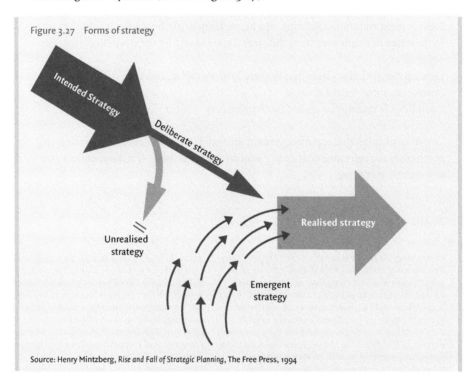

Figure 3.27　Forms of strategy

Source: Henry Mintzberg, *Rise and Fall of Strategic Planning*, The Free Press, 1994

Mintzberg has a lot of difficulty with the concept of strategic planning. As he sees it, planning strategy cannot actually even *be* planned. The development of strategies is a creative activity. Its characteristic is its combination of original and unique elements, which give rise to new strategies. According to Mintzberg, the importance of planning lies mainly in the formalising of decision-making.

Supporters of the classic approach to strategic planning are mistaken in thinking that the future can be predicted and that strategic management can be formalised (as indicated in the previous sections). Creativity would be suppressed by the compulsive urge to formalise, leading to insufficient room for the development of alternative strategies. In such a situation, alternatives would only be allowed within the framework fixed formally.

Another of the problems of strategic planning is that planning and implementation are carried out by various different people within the organisation. This could lead to problems.

Mintzberg claims that formalisation of strategic planning in artificial-intelligence systems has failed, as human intuition is difficult to replace.

Despite all this criticism Mintzberg agrees that strategic planning has an important function. It can make an important contribution to the development of a strategy. But strategic planning should be seen from another perspective. The focus is on the learning capability of the enterprise and the influence of the vision held by its employees. Furthermore, Mintzberg supports the integration of analysis (planning) and intuition (view and creativity).

The next section will deal with an up-to-date approach to strategic management in line with some of the ideas of Mintzberg.

3.7 Strategic management in perspective

Those who have followed the competitive position of enterprises in the past years will have certainly seen that major shifts have been taken place. In particular, new enterprises that are in competition with established businesses have arisen, although they have fewer financial means, a smaller market share, limited technological knowledge and often a less well known name.

Competitive position

Research has shown that the success of these enterprises cannot be explained sufficiently from known factors such as large market share, size of the enterprise, available know-how, geographical spread of activities and production in low cost countries. It seems therefore that the classic model of strategic management, where strategic management is synonymous with strategic planning, needs revising. In the approach to strategic management outlined in the sections to come, the emphasis will be on strategic thinking within organisations. Strategic thinking is demonstrated whenever organisations have a vision to share and to put into practice, highlighting the capability of the enterprise to adapt.

Strategic thinking

3.7.1 Hamel and Prahalad's strategy model

At the core of Hamel and Prahalad's strategy model is 'strategic intent': an obsessive desire within the organisation to become the market leader within a period of ten years, give or take some. However, there may well be a gap between the aspirations of the enterprise and its available means. The closing of this gap will become the main objective (Figure 3.28).

Strategic intent

To be effective, the strategic intent must inform the daily activities of enterprises. Some characteristics of strategic intent are:
· Consistency with the objectives of the enterprise
· An expression of the collective will
· The radiation of a winner mentality
· Activities within the organisation take their cue from it

Compared to a mission statement, a strategic intent is more specific and more directive of activities within the enterprise. Some examples of firms that have a clear strategic intent are:
· *Coca-Cola*: 'To put a Coke within arm's reach of every consumer in the world'.

Figure 3.28 Why do great companies fail?

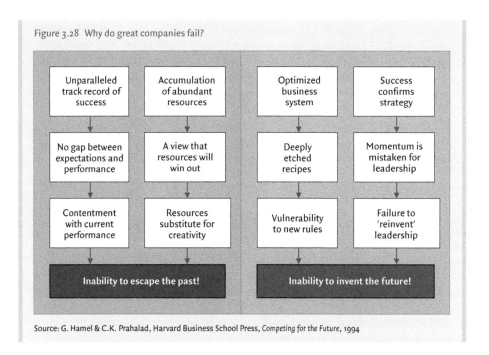

Source: G. Hamel & C.K. Prahalad, Harvard Business School Press, *Competing for the Future*, 1994

- *Honda*: 'To be a second Henry Ford'.
- *Procter & Gamble*: 'Progress was never made by standard people'.

Corporate challenges

To translate the strategic intent into practice in the short term, objectives (corporate challenges) should be determined for a period of one to three years. The strategic intent can be seen as a marathon run and corporate challenges as sprints.

A second important aspect of this model of strategy formation is that it aims consciously at a mismatch between the aspirations of the enterprise and its available

Strategy as Stretch

means, the so-called Strategy as Stretch. The emphasis lies on an ambition to reach the goal (Figure 3.29).

Figure 3.29 Strategic management model

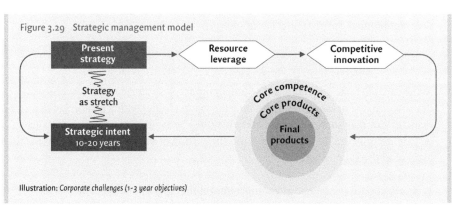

Illustration: *Corporate challenges (1-3 year objectives)*

The notion of strategy as stretch forms one of the most fundamental differences with the classic approach of strategic management. Prahalad and Hamel point out that enterprises that aim at a balance between the environment and the enterprise will only make marginal changes. The traditional concept of strategic management will result in a status quo enterprise. Only by intentionally creating such a gap will the enterprise be forced to use all its creativity, to make decisive innovations and force vital changes. The entire organisation must be convinced that this is the right way and should have a winner's mentality: reach the goal.

Organisations and their environment

Such an ambitious objective can be reached only by:

A Applying the available means more effectively (resource leverage)
B Being more inventive than competitors (competitive innovation)
C Seeing the enterprise as a portfolio of core competencies that should be developed instead of a portfolio of product-market combinations

These three methods will now be explained.

A   Applying the available means more effectively (resource leverage)

If the available resources needed to reach an ambitious objective are insufficient, they should be made more productive. Some ways of doing this are:

Resource leverage

1 *Concentrating the means on the strategic intent.* Many resources are lost unnecessarily on administrative tasks and / or are spread out over a large number of activities that are often not of strategic interest.
2 *Integrate resources and experiences.* This can be done by collaboration with other enterprises and / or by creating a mentality which focusses on learning potential.
3 *Look for additions from other available means.* Resources from the past can often be applied to the development of new products.
4 *Conserve the means for other purposes.* Available knowledge can be applied to different products. Honda keeps its knowledge of motors up to date by using it on cars, motorcycles, chain saws, motorboats, snow scooters etc.
5 *Earn back the investment made as soon as possible.* This is only possible if the resources have contributed to the development of successful products.

B   Being more inventive than competitors (competitive innovation)

This second method of implementing a strategic intent involves taking a fresh look at products, markets, competition and the use of resources. The market leaders need to be challenged by enterprises that are taking a different approach to work. Developing one business after another (competitive space) and doing this quickly and more intensively, will leave the competitors behind.

Competitive innovation

In this respect one needs to have a profound understanding of the needs and lifestyles of the customers of today and tomorrow. When putting new products on the market, merely listening to the wishes of the buyer is not enough. A few decades ago there was no need for CD players, Walkmans and so on. The point is that consumers have to be led to where they want to go without them realising that they are being led. Traditional market research has clearly failed in this respect. Only enterprises that succeed in creating really new markets and dominating them will be successful.

C   Seeing the enterprise as a portfolio of core competencies that should be developed instead of a portfolio of product-market combinations

The third method of developing a strategic intent is to consider the enterprise as a set of core competencies. This is a collective learning process that coordinates different production skills and integrates production possibilities.

Core competencies

A core competency has four aspects:

1 Technology (hard and software)
2 Collective learning (at different levels and functions)
3 Uniqueness (for customers and competition)
4 Varied application (for different target groups and markets).

Some examples of core competencies are:
· Sony's ability to miniaturise

Exploiting a core competency with Sony

In successfully exploiting its miniaturisation core competency, Sony has integrated:

1 Technological aspects (small batteries, microprocessors)
2 Ergonomic aspects (functionality, user-friendliness)
3 Life style aspects (aesthetics, design, fashion)

This requires intensive cooperation and coordination between the various departments and individuals.

Source: Sony (www.sony.com), 2004

- Philips' laser disk expertise
- Swatch's product designs
- Coca-Cola's unique distribution concept

Core products

Core competencies give rise to core products or components that increase the value of the end products. Core products form a link between the core competencies and the final products (Figure 3.30). Future competition could take place on all three levels. It is therefore important that an enterprise be strong on all levels.

Figure 3.30   Relationship between core competence, core product and final product

The long-term success of enterprises depends on their capacity to develop core competencies quickly and to produce products that perhaps do not even exist yet and do so at a low cost. It is only when an enterprise views itself as the sum of its core competencies instead of its product-market combinations that new horizons will be discovered. An enterprise specialising in semiconductors and displays will start to see products such as watches, calculators, mini-televisions and so on in a new light.

Working on core competencies demands an entirely new type of organisation. High value will be placed on commitment, communication and the willingness of staff to function outside their own division.

Last but not least, enterprises should detail and document their core competencies in a 'strategic architecture', a blue print for the future. In this, the links between consumer needs and the core competencies that need to be developed, as well as the technologies needed, can be identified.

Strategic architecture

3.8 Strategic management and Business Intelligence

Good information benefits the process of strategic management. For some considerable time, organisations have been confronted with a rapidly changing environment (both internal and external), demanding quick reaction. Decisions have to be made faster on both the strategic and on the tactical and operational levels.

For good decisions, adequate management information and analysis are indispensable. An increasing number of organisations are consequently using Business Intelligence.

Business Intelligence can be defined as all those activities linked to information, analysis and IT that contribute to effective and efficient decision-making.

Business Intelligence

In a modern organisation, Business Intelligence involves various parts of the organisation. Within Business Intelligence, an information value chain is present, a process depicted in Figure 3.31.

Information value chain

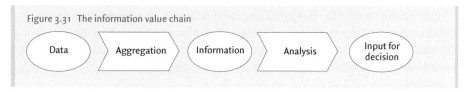

Figure 3.31 The information value chain

The chain operates in two directions:
1. From left to right, producing information.
2. From right to left, translating the information needs of the customer into appropriate definitions and sources.

It is important for management to define what kind of information is needed. Information needs form the basis of the information value chain. The information needs of an organisation can be included in a so-called information plan. An information plan can be described as a plan that documents the vision the organisation's management has in terms of improvement and expansion of the information service, as well as implementation priorities. The information plan derives directly from the general organisation strategy.

Information plan

We will now discuss the various parts of the information value chain:
· Data
· Aggregation and integration
· Information
· Analysis and interpretation
· The position of Business Intelligence in the organisation.

Data

Data deals with sources. These can take two forms: internal and external sources. Internal sources are customer files and transaction data bases such as:

Internal sources

· An energy provider's consumption data
· A telecommunication business's call data
· A bank's transaction data

Such data is often stored in large data bases (production systems). The data will have been designed to support the primary processes. Problems may arise if it is used to extract management information. Some examples of external sources are data purchased to enrich one's own data or customer profiles, which can be obtained by market research.

External sources

While internal sources are often managed in an IT environment, external sources are found mostly in marketing departments.

Aggregation and integration

Aggregation

To convert data into information requires a process of aggregation and integration. In this sense, aggregation consists of summarising rough data to enhance analysis and interpretation. Consistent definitions are important to the process of aggregation. For instance, the term 'turnover' may be understood differently to the way it was used in the original data. But the commissioning party or buyer of information will use only one definition. The correct definitions should be defined beforehand and must be maintained.

Integration

Integration consists of the mixing and connecting of data from various sources to obtain added value: for example, the combining of data from a call centre with invoice data to optimise the call centre's operations.

Information

Information portfolio

Information lies halfway along the value chain, where all information products become available for further analysis (the information portfolio) and must be managed actively to guarantee quality. New portfolio elements are being added all the time, while older ones seldom disappear. This diminishes the clarity of the available reports.

Analysis and interpretation

Skills

Information obtain via the previous step has to be connected with knowledge and skills. Knowledge is obtained from specialists in the area concerned. They have the skills to analyse the information and to draw conclusions. Important consultancy skills are required, including the ability to handle statistics, as well as 'softer' skills such as organising good brainstorming sessions or using interview techniques effectively. All these are needed to uncover the real needs of the buyer.

If all of the previous steps are taken, the input needed for a decision will be present. This, however, lies outside the scope of Business Intelligence, as it is the responsibility of the decision-maker.

The position of Business Intelligence in the organisation

The maturity of Business Intelligence within an organisation can often be deduced from where Business Intelligence within that organisation is situated.

The best place for a Business Intelligence team is within the business, directly linked to those who are responsible for profit and loss. They are the ones who are able to estimate the value of Business Intelligence for their job. The second best position is within the finance department. Although this department is focussed on the financial side of the business, the finance department is traditionally well aware of the importance of good information.

The most usual yet not immediately obvious position for Business Intelligence is within the IT department. Organisations that are not yet acquainted with modern information systems consider Business Intelligence to be a purely technological field and therefore locate it within their IT division. Such divisions are mostly dominated by the 'T' of technology while with Business Intelligence, technological features are in a supporting, not leading, position.

In the next chapter we will look at the background of a decision that emanates from the process of strategic management, namely, collaboration between organisations.

Doing business in the USA

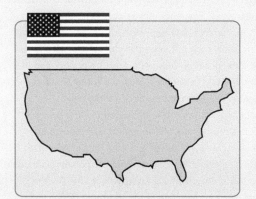

How US citizens organise and process information

The culture of the United States is highly ethnocentric. It is very analytical, and concepts are abstracted quickly. Innovation often takes precedence over tradition. The universal rule is preferred and company policy is followed regardless of who is doing the negotiating.

What US citizens accept as evidence

In negotiations, points are made via objective facts. These are sometimes biased by faith in the ideologies of democracy, capitalism, and consumerism, but seldom by the subjective feelings of the participants.

The basis of behaviour

It is often said that Judeo-Christian values are the basis for behaviour in the United States. However, these seem to be eroding and being replaced by egocentrism and ethnocentrism. Value systems in the predominant culture – how right is distinguished from wrong, good from evil, and so on – are described under the next three headings.

The locus of decision-making

Although the United States is probably the most individualistic of all cultures, each person becomes a replaceable cog in the wheel of any organisation. There is a high self, as opposed to other, orientation emphasising individual initiative and achievement. People from the US do not find it difficult to say 'no'. The individual has a life of his or her own that is generally private and not to be discussed in business negotiations.

Sources of anxiety reduction

There is a low anxiety about life, as external structures and science provide answers to all important questions and isolate one from life. There is anxiety about deadlines and results, because recognition of one's work is the greatest reward. The work ethic is very strong: one lives to work, or so it seems. There are established rules for everything, and experts are relied upon at all levels.

Issues of equality / inequality

There is structured inequality in the roles people take, but personal equality is guaranteed by law. There is considerable ethnic and social bias against some minorities. Competition is a rule of life, but there is a strong feeling of the interdependency of roles. Excellence and decisiveness are prized characteristics. Material progress is more important than humanistic progress. Traditional sex roles are changing rapidly, but women are still fighting for equality in pay and power.

Ten examples of US business practices

1 While knowing the right people and having a lot of contacts in an industry is valuable, for a salesperson, it is not seen as being as important as a good sales history.
2 The 'bottom line' (financial issues), new technology, and short-term rewards are the normal focus of negotiations.
3 US executives begin talking about business after a brief exchange of small talk, whether in the office, at a restaurant, or even at home.
4 Until you know a person well, avoid discussing religion, money, politics, or other controversial subjects (e.g., abortion, race, or sex discrimination).
5 Most business people have business cards, but these cards are not exchanged unless you want to contact the person later.
6 Business meetings are often held over lunch. This usually begins at 12.00 noon and ends at 2.00 p.m. Lunch is usually relatively light, as work continues directly afterward. Business breakfasts are common, and can start as early as 7.00 a.m.
7 The greeting 'How are you?' is not an inquiry about your health. The best response is a short one, such as 'Fine, thanks'.
8 The standard space between you and your conversation partner should be about 70 centimetres. Most US executives would be uncomfortable standing closer than that.
9 Business gifts are discouraged by law, since gifts can attract tax deductions.
10 In cities, conservative business attire is best. In rural areas and small towns, clothing is less formal and less fashionable. When not working, dress casually. You may see people dressed in torn clothing or in short pants and shirts without sleeves.

Source: Kiss, Bow, or Shake Hands: How to Do Business in Sixty Countries, by Terri Morrison, Wayne A. Conaway and George A. Borden, Adams Media, 2006

Summary

In order to survive, organisations depend strongly on how they attune to external influences. Strategic management is concerned with this process of attunement. In the classical approach to strategic management, the issue is to find a balance between the resources, strengths and weaknesses of the enterprise on one hand and the opportunities and threats emanating from the environment on the other. A lot of attention needs to be given to implementation of strategies.

Critics state that the classical approach is outdated in the rapidly changing environment that many organisations find themselves part of. Mintzberg states that strategy is not only a plan, but also a pattern of actions. According to Mintzberg, strategies cannot be planned: on the contrary, developing strategies is a creative activity. Recent approaches to strategic management focus on strategic thinking. Organisations can be described as thinking strategically if they are able to share and put into practice a vision which draws on the learning capacity of the organisation.

Information plays a crucial role in the process of strategic management. An increasing number of organisations are turning to Business Intelligence. Business Intelligence is an aspect of the information value chain.

Definitions

§ 3.1 Strategic management

Strategic management is about appropriate attunement to the environment as well as maintenance of standards and development of the skills required for the inclusion of possible changes in the strategy.

Strategy

A plan that states what an organisation intends to do to reach its goals.

§ 3.3 Situational analysis

An analysis that focusses on determining the current profile of the organisation while taking into account its external environment.

Vision

A general idea or representation of the future of the organisation.

Mission

A description of the product-market combinations and the way the organisation aims at obtaining a structural competitive advantage with these.

Principles

Principles relate to the norms and values of the organisation.

Organisational goals

Organisational goals show the relationship between the organisation, the environment, and employees.

§§ 3.3.2 Internal investigation

The goal of internal investigation is to look at all the internal activities and to identify the strong and weak sides of the organisation.

Core activity

A core activity is one of the activities on which the enterprise particularly concentrates. It provides the enterprise with its right to exist and its success.

Portfolio analysis

The various SBUs are categorised within a matrix and analysed according to a number of economical criteria.

§§ 3.3.3 External research

External research maps out opportunities and threats within the environment.

Strategic group

A strategic group is a group of organisations that have common characteristics and that use similar competitive strategies.

§§ 3.4.3 Scenario method

The scenario method provides predictions of how a number of factors will develop in the medium term.

§§ 3.4.4 Production chain

A production chain shows the participants and links that contribute to the development of a particular product.

Industrial sector	Each link or horizontal layer of the production chain represents an industrial sector. These horizontal layers contain organisations that serve the same or a similar function in the development of variations on a particular product.
Branch	Branches are groups of organisations within an industrial sector that not only use the same production or distribution techniques but also supply largely the same products.
§§ 3.5.1 Strategic planning	High-level planning that delivers the results of strategic management.
Operational planning	The goals as identified in the strategic plan are worked out over a period of a year in terms of expenses and yields, sale and production quantities, investments, supplies, formation planning etc.
§§ 3.7.1 Strategic intent	The development of an obsession.
Corporate challenges	Strategic intent translated into the short term (one to three years).
Core competencies	A collective learning process that coordinates different production skills and integrates production possibilities.
Core products	Products or components that increase the value of the final products.
Strategic architecture	A blueprint for the future wherein the links between consumer needs and the core competencies that need to be developed, as well as the technologies needed, can be identified.
§ 3.8 Business Intelligence	All activities linked to information, analysis and IT that contribute to effective and efficient decision-making.
Information value chain	A process whereby information is produced and the information needs of the customer are translated into appropriate definitions and sources.
Information plan	A plan that documents the vision of management where it relates to the improvement and expansion of information services, as well as implementation priorities.

Statements

Indicate whether the following statements are correct or incorrect. Explain your reasons.

1 The vision of an enterprise may have a general character. Organisational goals, however, should be formulated in such a way as to be operational and measurable.
2 One of the basic assumptions of the BCG matrix is a negative relationship between the size of the relative market share and the extent of the cash flow.
3 The competitive environment needs to be analysed in order to obtain an understanding of the opportunities and threats coming from this environment.
4 Differential competitive advantages can be deduced from the organisational structure.
5 Porter states that in order to formulate a competitive strategy, it is important to see the enterprise in relation to the environment.
6 Internal and external research results should determine the basis for formulating strategies.
7 According to Mintzberg, a strategy cannot be planned.
8 Core competencies consist of technology, collective learning and various applications.
9 Strategic management is wholly dependent on the availability of reliable information.
10 An information plan should be derived directly from the general organisational strategy.

Theory questions

1 How do vision, objectives and strategy relate to one another?
2 One of the core activities of strategic management is the so-called SWOT analysis.
   a What is meant by this concept?
   b How important is it to view an enterprise's strengths and weaknesses in terms of the opportunities and threats from the environment?
   c In what way is the structure of the organisation likely to be reflected in the SWOT analysis?
3 We can position a number of SBUs within the BCG matrix.
   a What are the names of these SBUs?
   b What conclusions can be drawn from the matrix on the next page? Include in your answer the notions of dogs, stars, question marks, cash cows, investing and disinvesting.
4 Planning makes sense, even in very turbulent times. Give three reasons why.
5 a What is meant by Business Intelligence?
   b Why are an increasing number of organisations starting a Business Intelligence department?

 For answers see www.marcusvandam.noordhoff.nl.

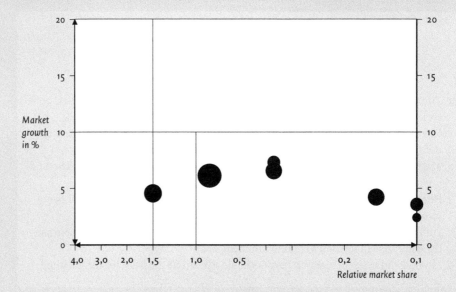

Mini case study

Plantronics

In 1969 it was a Plantronics headset that passed on the historical first words from the moon: 'That's one small step for man, one giant leap for mankind'. Plantronics Inc. introduced the first lightweight communications headset in 1962 and is today the world's leading designer, manufacturer and marketer of lightweight communications headset products. Plantronics headsets are widely used in many Fortune 500 corporations and have been featured in numerous films and high-profile events. Plantronics offers mobile headsets to address the cordless and mobile phone market, next-generation computer audio headset products for computer applications and corded and cordless headsets and systems for the office, small office / home office and contact centres.

Plantronics is a publicly held company (NYSE: PLT) based in Santa Cruz, California with offices in 19 countries, including major facilities in Mexico, Tennessee, England and the Netherlands. Plantronics products are sold and supported through a worldwide network of authorised Plantronics partners, and are available through retail and consumer electronics stores.

The world-wide use of head sets is increasing rapidly with more and more customers demanding products with excellent audio quality and sophisticated design.

Source: www.plantronics.com, February 2006

Questions

1 Strategies depend on the organisation's market share. Based on the different market shares, we can identify various types of organisations.

   a Using this perspective, how would you characterise Plantronics as an organisation?

   b The type of organisation influences the strategy chosen. Does this apply to Plantronics?

2 SBUs can be positioned within the BCG matrix in four ways, dependent on the development of market growth and the relative market share. Where would you position the SBU that focusses on products of excellent audio quality and sophisticated design for the final consumer?

E-mail case study

To:	Susan Gibson
Cc:	
Bcc:	
Subject:	Moleyfeather Private Bankers: competitive analysis

Dear Susan,

It's again time for the annual Moleyfeather Private Bankers' strategic planning process. Our last external research took place two years ago. The market and recent developments cannot be called very stable. We were very pleased with your previous research, so we'd like to ask you to do it again.

This time, please concentrate on a competitive analysis. As you know, we specialise in private banking in this country (in fact, it is our only activity here). We have a clear focus. There are other private bankers within the domestic market, but also other financial organisations who do private banking in addition to other activities. We would like you to provide an answer to the following four questions:

- Who are our competitors (two or three most important)
- What are their strategies, strengths and weaknesses?
- How intense is competition?
- What are their differential competitive advantages?

Susan, please keep it brief and to the point!

Success and regards,

Wolfgang Schneider

4

Collaboration

This chapter looks at the various ways in which organisations collaborate, their motives for doing so and the advantages and disadvantages of collaboration. It also looks at the problems experienced by many organisations when they merge or take over other organisations.

Contents

After studying this chapter
- You will understand the main reasons for collaborating.
- You will have become acquainted with the various forms of alliances, partnerships and other forms of collaboration between both competitive and uncompetitive organisations.
- You will have an insight into how organisations participate in collaborative ventures.
- You will be aware of the various issues involved in mergers and takeovers.

4.1 Types of collaboration

Collaboration is fashionable. More than ever before, companies are choosing to work with each other at both national and international levels. The decision to engage in some form of collaboration should be a strategic one (see Chapter 3). Some examples of strategic issues that can be tackled via collaborative activities are[1]:

Collaborative activities

- Competition: enterprises may try to decrease the number of competitors within their industrial sector through collaboration. This constitutes a horizontal form of collaboration.
- Risk-reduction: enterprises may try to reduce their risks by spreading them over a number of different businesses via collaborative ventures.
- The creation of specific enterprise areas: one enterprise donates its powers of innovation to a collaborative venture while another enterprise donates its major sales channels.
- The removal of specific barriers: if an enterprise wants to introduce its products into a foreign market, collaboration with a local enterprise in that foreign country can be an effective strategy.

Globalisation of knowledge

One explanation for the big increase in collaboration is the globalisation of knowledge.[2]

In the past, the main reason for working together was to gain scale advantages (a production issue). A future trend that is now becoming increasingly visible is collaboration in order to exchange and develop knowledge (a knowledge issue). It is prompted by the fact that knowledge is becoming more global and a growing number of countries are making a contribution to new knowledge development. Collaboration is easy. A lot of forms of knowledge are easy to transmit. Knowledge can easily be shared and can therefore be globally available (via books etc.). Having the edge over competitors in the area of knowledge generates a powerful competitive advantage. Developing knowledge together with a partner organisation is therefore beneficial, though it has to be remembered that while most knowledge can be transmitted, some forms cannot be.

Knowledge comes about through complex social relationships: for example, via teams of people from organisations that are working jointly. Individual organisations may not have the resources to undertake such developments alone.

4.1.1 Ways that organisations can work together

Collaboration can take many forms. The main ones are[3]:

- Strategic alliances and trade cooperatives
- Joint ventures
- Mergers and acquisitions
- Outsourcing
- Licensing and franchising

Strategic alliances and trade cooperatives

Strategic alliance

The term 'strategic alliance' refers to two or more different enterprises entering into an agreement to work together without creating a new legal entity. Both businesses continue to exist as independent enterprises. The enterprises will work together in particular areas, sharing knowledge, resources and skills with each other. The goal of such a collaboration is to generate new knowledge, new products and / or new production facilities. A trade cooperative is a cluster of interdependent organisa-

Trade cooperative

Name:	Fabien Jolly
Country of origin:	France
Country of residence:	France and USA
Job title:	Senior Director R&D
	Information Systems
Company:	Sanofi Aventis
Company website:	www.sanofi-aventis.com

What important personal qualities must people have to be successful in international work?
Working requires first and foremost the ability to communicate. Essentially, in an international environment you face two challenges. The first one is the ability to communicate in a foreign language, which I consider as something relatively easy to address through education. The second one is more complex: it is the ability to perceive, understand and then integrate in your communication the culture of your foreign partners. The culture is the mental image that we all use as a filter to interpret a situation and build a shared image. These filters are built up of behaviour patterns, values, norms and also material objects, and they differ widely from one country to another. You have, for instance, high context cultures such as China and Japan, where a large part of the message is covert and implicit as opposed to low context cultures like Germany and the United States where the message is overt and explicit. Not being able to adapt your communication to a different filter will distort the message and result in communication failure. Becoming familiar with a different culture is not easy to do. It requires first of all patience and also two important personal qualities: a genuine intellectual curiosity in learning from others and above everything else, respect for other civilizations, countries, histories and people.

How do you prepare yourself for a business meeting with people from a different culture?
To avoid mistakes that could cause an immediate breakdown in communication you need to have a basic idea of the cultural backgrounds of those attending the meeting, though you should not 'over-prepare' for such a meeting. Culture is a matter of thousands of nuances and details and you will not become familiar with it by reading a book in the plane before the meeting. You will learn it over time, through your own experiences, and the only tools that you need are respect and sharp attention so you can learn from the various situations. That being said, you should prepare for the meeting from a technical point of view. If you attend a negotiation meeting in the Middle East, for instance, you need to learn how people typically negotiate there. For instance, you have to know that relationships there focus on long-term relationships, so you must take time to establish contact before starting any business discussion. You could establish contact in a restaurant, for example.

Describe your own management style
Peter Drucker has identified the question 'What is right for the enterprise?' as one of the most pertinent questions that any executive can ask. I personally refer back to this as a guide each time I make a decision.
The answer being established, a large part of my job is to get an organisation to execute the company strategy. To do so, I firstly use my emotional intelligence to build a team and create a positive, trust-based and fun environment. Then I communicate with passion what we are trying to accomplish, why it is important and how it connects with the overall strategy of the company. I believe that each employee, whatever his or her level, should be familiar with the company's business model, and what the firm is after and why.
The team having been formed, united and motivated, I empower each individual within his area of responsibility as much as possible.

tions working together to reach a joint target. Section 4.4 looks further at trade cooperatives.

Joint ventures

Joint venture

We talk of a joint venture when two or more different companies jointly set up a subsidiary in order to develop special joint activities on the basis of equal management responsibility. In most cases, each parent enterprise will own 50% of the subsidiary. Consequently, parent companies will have access to each other's knowledge, are not required to use as many resources as normal, and can share any risks with each other.

Mergers and acquisitions

Merger
Acquisition
Takeover

A merger is the most far-reaching form of collaboration. Mergers involve two comparable enterprises joining together. In contrast, an acquisition or takeover involves one enterprise completely running its activities to fit in with the objectives and plans of another. The acquisition purchase is made via a favourable or hostile bid. These forms of collaboration are looked into further in Section 4.5.

IN THE PRESS

Disney acquires Pixar

At the start of 2006, Disney acquired Pixar for $7.4 billion (6 billion euros) in a bid to revive the animation department that is not only its heritage but also the engine of its businesses – from theme parks to consumer products.

Wall Street analysts have focussed on what role Steve Jobs, Pixar's founder and chief executive of Apple Computer, might play at Disney. He could be instrumental as the media company attempts to sell its films and television programmes through new digital devices, such as Apple's video iPod.

Yet the essential figure in the deal may be Mr Lasseter, who has been given the creative keys to the Magic Kingdom and is being asked to restore inspiration to a pioneering company that has lost its way. For Mr. Lasseter, who began his career at Disney and then went on to become the creative force behind Pixar's Animation's unprecedented run of hits, from 'Toy Story' to 'Finding Nemo' and 'The Incredibles', this is a triumphant return.

Mr Lasseter studied at the California Institute of the Arts, a Disney founded school near LA. In the late 1970s, animation was a dying business. The turning point in his career came when he saw 'Tron', one of earliest examples of computer animation. In 1983, he bolted for Pixar, a fledging studio that Mr Jobs had founded in northern California. The studio's breakthrough came with the 1995 'Toy Story', the first full-length computer-generated film. Audiences were dazzled by Pixar's technology, but Mr Lasseter has always pointed to the value of good storytelling. Part of his success also rests on his unusual blend of artistic sensibility and big-time movie producer toughness.

For a time, Disney thrived in Mr Lasseter's absence. Animated musicals such as 'Lion King', 'The Little Mermaid' and 'Beauty and the Beast' took in more than $1billion and fuelled a renaissance at the company. But that formula soon became stale and follow-ups such as 'Aladdin' and 'Hercules' disappointed. Meanwhile, talent began leaving Disney for Pixar and DreamWorks Animation. The release of 'Chicken Little' in 1995, the studio's first full-length film made entirely using computer animation, seemed to confirm that a company once synonymous with animation was now an also-ran in the field.

As Mr. Lasseter and others seek to restore the Magic Kingdom's lustre, they face a number of challenges. They will have to nurture Pixar's creative spark within a much larger corporate parent. There is also new competition, with Sony, Fox and Paramount crowding into animation along with studios from as far as India and Singapore. And he will have to satisfy the expectations of those who have waited so long for his return.

Source: *Financial Times*, January 2006, Pixar (www.pixar.com)

Outsourcing

Outsourcing, or subcontracting, falls into a special category of working together. As production increases in scale, enterprises have to focus more on their core activities. The result is that organisations are farming out particular activities to other enterprises. Outsourcing is looked at further in Section 4.3.2.

Licensing and franchising

A licence allows an enterprise's products to be made by another enterprise in exchange for a fee. A good example is Coca-Cola. They give companies in foreign countries the right to produce Coca-Cola drinks under licence.

Franchising is a specific form of licensing that is found primarily in retail businesses. By entering into a franchise agreement, the franchisee (a shopkeeper) agrees to follow the standard guidelines of the franchiser. This will determine such issues as store design, purchasing, sales promotions, marketing, pricing policies and the range of products on offer. McDonald's is an example of this. Franchising is looked at further in Section 4.3.2.

The above forms of collaboration vary in their degree of intensiveness. Figure 4.1 classifies the various forms.

Outsourcing
Subcontracting

Licence

Franchising

Degree of intensiveness

Figure 4.1 Intensity of various forms of collaboration

Moderate		Collaboration	Intense
Flexible arrangements	Contractual relationships	Pooling of assets	Integration
· Networks · Strategic alliances	· Outsourcing · Licensing · Franchises	· Joint ventures	· Acquisitions · Mergers

Source: Peter Thuis, *Toegepaste organisatiekunde*, Wolters-Noordhoff, 3rd edition, 2003

4.1.2 International collaboration

The previously mentioned forms of collaboration can be examined in the light of internationalisation of businesses. We shall firstly look at each phase of internationalisation and then discuss international organisations in general.

Phases of internationalisation

How are enterprises likely to pursue the path of internationalisation? They will often follow these three phases[4]:

1 The export and / or import-orientated phase
2 The representative phase
3 The phase of entering into some form of collaboration

1 The export and / or import-orientated phase

During the first phase, an enterprise selects products that are made in their own country and can be sold in a foreign country. Essentially, this phase represents a simple geographical expansion of the sales territory. Enterprises that have already saturated their domestic market with their products can expand further by exporting. It often happens that these companies also find products made in the foreign country that they start to sell in their home country.

Export and / or import-orientated phase

2 The representative phase

An enterprise will have entered phase two when it makes a representative arrangement for the purposes of expanding within a foreign market.

During this phase, the organisation will expand beyond simple export activity, without going so far as to base employees permanently in the foreign country. The representative company – the company looking after the organisation's interests – will be visited regularly. Interest in making products overseas starts to develop during this phase.

3 The phase of engaging in some form of collaboration

During the third phase, the enterprise decides to enter into a collaborative agreement with a foreign enterprise. This agreement can take a variety of forms. The form that is chosen should be the one that is the most efficient and most effective in the specific circumstances. If, for example, the main activity is producing products, a licensing system is likely to be most successful. If the joint development of knowledge is the key, then a strategic alliance or a joint venture is more appropriate. Alternatively, if a decision is made to keep everything within the hands of the parent company, a foreign subsidiary enterprise needs to be set up.

The above phases are shown diagrammatically in Figure 4.2.

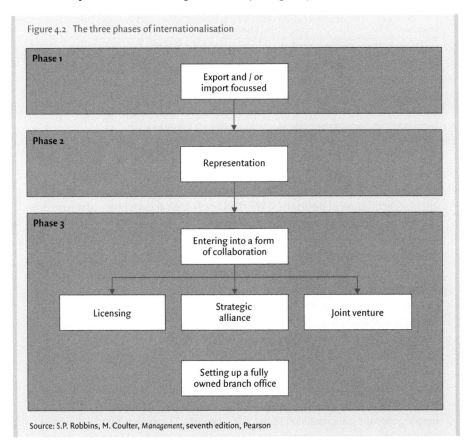

Figure 4.2 The three phases of internationalisation

Source: S.P. Robbins, M. Coulter, *Management*, seventh edition, Pearson

Basic forms of international organisations

Enterprises that operate internationally must consider how all their activities are organized and are related to each other. Which strategic point of view is vital here? In creating a useful perspective, the following two areas should be explored:

1 The extent of local differentiation of activities (low or high)

2 The extent of world-wide integration of activities (low or high)

Extent of local differentiation
Extent of world-wide integration

If we combine these two dimensions with each other, four basic forms of international organisation will arise. Figure 4.3 shows these in diagram form.

Basic forms of international organisation

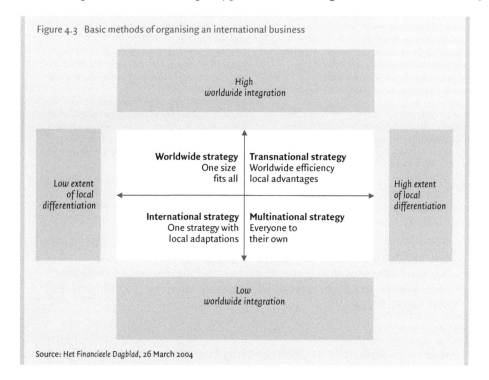

Figure 4.3 Basic methods of organising an international business

Source: *Het Financieele Dagblad*, 26 March 2004

For many years, European businesses have been choosing to pursue a multinational strategy whereby each part of the international business remains autonomous. Each country and region is seen as being unique and therefore responsible for its own success and organisation of certain activities. As such, each of the various countries and regions will pursue its own strategies, with responsibility for operations and results falling on various parts of the business. The role of head office will mainly be one of coordination. In practice, this form of organisation will be found to have some disadvantages:

Multinational strategy
Autonomous

· Relatively few possibilities for making economies of scale

· 'Mini empires' may start to appear in some countries or regions

Enterprises that have applied a long-term multinational strategy include Ahold and Shell. After recent bookkeeping scandals and misinformation incidents, such businesses are reviewing their organisational format.

Many European companies are seriously considering switching from a multinational to a transnational strategy. Such a decision to go for worldwide integration of all the company's components can bring about the benefits of worldwide efficiency. It will entail greater emphasis on centralisation and control.

Transnational strategy
Worldwide integration

Nevertheless, many European enterprises remain committed to maintaining a high extent of local differentiation.

In other parts of the world, when organisations decide to organize their operations internationally they often choose other options. Japanese companies generally select a global organisational format whereby centralised strategies are adopted in all

Global organisational format
Centralised strategies

How to navigate a global merger

1 Begin globally, then regionally.
   A primary goal of an international merger is to maximize global performance. The performance of the collective company should take priority over individual regional objectives.
2 Customize and execute locally.
   While much of the planning can be conducted at the global and regional levels, implementation should be on an individual county basis.
3 Work within a matrix, designating local resources to fill gaps.
   A matrix project structure is often the most effective option. Global mergers require clear communication channels to increase the likelihood of country-specific issues and dependencies being quickly identified and resolved.
4 Manage by exception.
   While global and regional leaders focus on the larger issues, country work teams can focus on the details. Bringing about full implementation is a matter for country management, as is making sure that all local integration issues are identified.
5 'Early and frequent' communication means planning even earlier.
   Frequent communication throughout the merger integration process may be one of the most important things a company can do to help preserve the value of the deal.
6 Address local cultures and customs.
   Begin by thoroughly analysing the cultural challenges in each country. Learn how they conduct business, make decisions, and communicate. Then apply these insights to help create a more robust integration plan.

Source: Deloitte Research 2006

No local differentiation
International strategy
Local differences

countries and regions. The result will be a single strategy where no account is taken of local differentiation.

American enterprises often choose an international strategy. Such organisations prefer a central strategy, but in contrast to Japanese enterprises, local differences often remain in existance.

4.2   Alliances: motivating factors and the keys to success

In this section, we will look at the various motives behind alliances and to what they attribute their success.

4.2.1   Collaboration: what are the motives?

There may be various motives for developing inter-company strategic alliances. Figure 4.4 shows these diagrammatically.[5]

Defence

We use the term 'defence' when the goal of collaboration is the protection of the market leader's core activity in order to secure the future competitive position. An example of a defensive strategy is IBM's developing of specific software applications for large customers.

Remain

If the activity of the enterprise is not part of its core activities though the enterprise is still the market leader, the goal of collaboration should be to remain in this position: a defensive strategy, therefore.

Catching up

When it is not the defence of the core activity but a strengthening of the competitive position that is the goal, this is known as 'catching up'. This is an offensive strategy. It is linked to the core activity of the enterprise but only as a market follower.

Restructuring

Another offensive strategy involves the setting up of a collaborative agreement: a strategy known as restructuring. Such an arrangement indicates that the enterprise is a follower in specific activities rather than occupying a leading position in the market. The restructuring might go so far that these activities are subsequently disposed of.

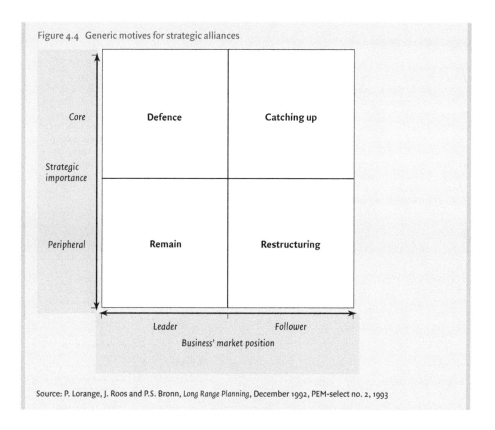

Figure 4.4 Generic motives for strategic alliances

	Leader	Follower
Core	Defence	Catching up
Peripheral	Remain	Restructuring

Strategic importance

Business' market position

Source: P. Lorange, J. Roos and P.S. Bronn, *Long Range Planning*, December 1992, PEM-select no. 2, 1993

There are many reasons for collaborating. They can be listed under three headings:

1 *Cost-orientated collaboration.* Here, the principal purpose is to reduce costs. This kind of arrangement has particular relevance for day-to-day activities within the enterprise.

2 *Position-orientated collaboration.* This is especially linked to the expansion of existing markets or the tapping of new markets and the acquisition of a particular position within a market.

3 *Knowledge-directed collaboration.* The principal purpose is to learn about each other's capacities and expertise. This usually concerns knowledge that is related to the core competencies of the enterprise.

Cost-orientated collaboration

Position-orientated collaboration

Knowledge-directed collaboration

4.2.2 Reasons behind successful collaboration

If enterprises work together they will both bring something into the arrangement: for example, production capacity, product know-how, distribution possibilities and knowledge of specific markets. It is important that both organisations benefit from this, creating a joint lead over competitors without either having to give away their most commercially sensitive knowledge and skills to the partner organisation. It would seem that in many Western enterprises, more is being given away than got back.[6]

As a form of collaboration, outsourcing of production often leads to a situation where the outsourcing company can economise on capital investments and budgets for product design and research. After some time though, a dependent relationship can develop since the partner controls both product development and production. Meanwhile, the partner will have learned a lot about the wishes of the final buyer and gained valuable experience in product development. The introduction of a competing product on the partner's own market may quickly follow, and its success is

Philips' new workplace

Over the last eighty years, Philips has expanded to become the largest foreign business in China. All divisions of the multinational have set up factories in the country and the number is growing fast. In total, Philips employs around sixty thousand people in China.

The first production activities in China date back to the 1970s. Television set parts were imported, assembled and sold. The next step took place when it became possible enter a joint venture. The Chinese were in need of knowledge and foreign currency,

both of which they could gain by exporting. China is now becoming a 'normal country', and it is experiencing accelerated growth due to its entry into the World Trade Organisation (WTO). Barriers are being swept aside as China adapts its laws and rules. Nevertheless, Philips still has sixty thousand people working directly and indirectly for them in ten locations, plus another three thousand employees in Hong Kong.

Philips' activities in China

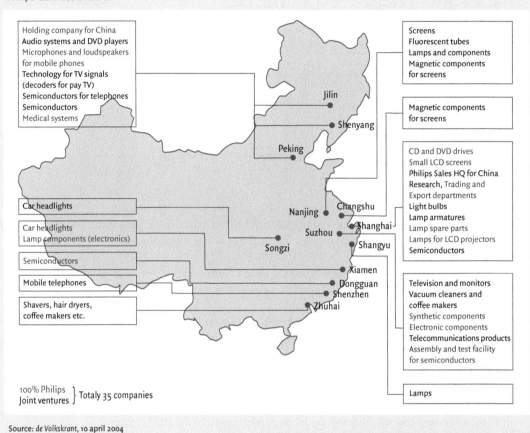

Source: *de Volkskrant*, 10 april 2004

pretty much guaranteed. The competitive strength of the outsourcing company will obviously be diminished.

We may conclude from this that collaboration can bring with it a large number of advantages, but that caution is still wise. There is a real danger of one party becoming a victim of the collaboration in the long term.

Some critical success factors that should be taken into account when entering into a collaboration arrangement are as follows:

· Cultural differences must be dealt with carefully. When people from different countries or continents start working together it is not unusual for cultural differences on three levels to arise: in addition to national culture differences, there will also be differences in business cultures and in personal cultures.

- The form of collaboration that provides the best 'fit' should be chosen. Management of enterprises can be influenced by trends. Strategic alliances are 'in'. It is very important to remain focussed on the real reasons for the collaboration and its goals. Less rigid and more operational collaboration is frequently a much better alternative than a spectacularly set up strategic arrangement.
- Impressive advantages written down on paper rarely materialise. The Chinese have a telling proverb about this subject: 'Those who walk softly will go far'. Avoid a lot of emphasis being given to form rather than content.

In evaluating the success of a collaborative arrangement between enterprises it is worth looking at the competitive potential: the organisation's ability to develop skills which form the basis for the development of a future generation of products. In most enterprises, product quality is an important indicator of future competitive success.

Competitive potential

4.3 Collaboration between competitors and partners

There is a difference between collaborative ventures involving organisations that are in competition with each other, and a situation where organisations have products or services that complement each other. However, both types – collaboration between potentially competitive and between non-competitive organisations – can be described as a network.

Difference between collaborative ventures

Network

4.3.1 Collaboration between competitors

At first glance, it might seem rather strange to see competitors working together with each other. Yet this has happened quite a lot recently. Some of the reasons for this are:

a Independent product development is prohibitively expensive
b To penetrate new (that is, unexplored) markets
c To increase production efficiency while also improving quality control

In particular, the high-tech and automobile industries have had a tradition of collaboration between competitive enterprises. This is especially so between European and Asian companies.[7]

Tradition

The collaborative agreement is likely to be useful if the following four questions can all be answered in the affirmative by both parties[8]:

1 *Are the strategies complementary?* A collaborative venture will have a high chance of success if both partners follow a complementary strategy and the objectives of both partners complement each other.
2 *Is collaboration vitally important for both parties?* The greater the interest in collaboration and in the extent to which each side is willing to invest in working together, the more time both sides will contribute to the process in order to ensure that the plans are really carried out.
3 *Will both parties become dependent on each other through collaboration?* Developing mutual dependency on each other is often the price that must be paid for working together. At the same time, there is a benefit in reinforcing the competitive position of both sides against outside competitors.

Nokia and Sanyo plan a joint venture for CDMA handsets

Nokia, the world's biggest maker of mobile hand-sets, and Sanyo, the troubled Japanese electronics group, are set to combine their CDMA mobile hand-set business in an effort to strengthen their position in the market. CDMA is the main rival to GSM, the world's most popular wireless technology and most widely used in the US, Japan, India, Latin America, Korea and China.

Sanyo is expected to take a controlling stake in the venture, which will combine the Japanese company's strength in mid- and high-end handsets with Nokia's focus on cheaper CDMA phones.

While Nokia is the biggest maker of GSM handsets, the Finnish operator has failed to replicate that success in DCMA.

The joint venture, which echoes the creation of Sony Ericsson in 2001, highlights the impact of fierce competition and rising development costs in the sector.

Source: *The Financial Times, February 2005*

4 *Can both parties grow as a result of collaboration?* A key goal of collaboration is the strengthening of the competitive position. When trade and growth are more likely to increase with collaboration than without it, the chance of the arrangement being a success will increase.

4.3.2 Collaboration between non-competitive organisations

Organisations that are not in competition with each other can combine their strengths by entering into a collaborative arrangement. The following three types of arrangement will now be explored:

1 Collaboration in retailing
2 Public-private collaboration
3 Outsourcing

Collaboration in retailing

Collaboration in retailing

During recent years, large retail stores and franchisers have grown in strength at the cost of small enterprises. Small entrepreneurs who want to survive in the long term must consider joining forces with others for their purchases of stocks and supplies. Such an arrangement will lead to the potential double advantages of lower purchase prices (a large-scale advantage) and local customer orientation (a small-scale advantage). Such collaboration, however, will always mean that part of the small enterprise's autonomy must be surrendered. How much needs to be given up depends on the form of collaboration that is chosen. In the section below, we will discuss collaborative forms that range from large franchise organisations to small buyers' cooperatives.

Buyers' cooperatives

Buyers' cooperative

A buyers' cooperative is a fairly traditional arrangement whereby retailers of similar products work together in order to obtain a number of advantages. Participating in a buyers' cooperative has special significance when a retailer wishes to take advantage of a full service package offered by a service provider or trade association.

Full service package

Such a full service package can include joint marketing and advertising campaigns, sales consulting, sales technique advice, store design, automation and administration support. In addition, the entrepreneur receives a purchase discount and is offered special finance and payment terms. The content of a full service package can vary, and entrepreneurs are able to select the elements they wish to take advantage of. The entrepreneur will thus retain a considerable amount of freedom of choice.

Franchising

Franchising is another type of collaboration. It involves a franchiser and a franchisee (the shopkeeper). Within a franchise agreement, the franchisee is strictly bound to standard guidelines that relate to store design, purchase, sales promotion, marketing, price politics and product range. The standard guidelines are laid down by the franchiser in a contract. The franchiser may be a manufacturer, a large merchant or a retailer. The franchisee pays an amount of money to the franchiser in exchange for the rights to use the retail model. In general, the fee is made up of a percentage of the turnover. The franchisee is self-employed. For both parties, the franchise system has many advantages.

Franchising

For franchisees, the advantages are:
· They can take advantage of the national image of the chain.
· They can benefit from the services of the franchiser (including product range and advertising).
· There is less risk because the retail formula is an established one.
· They only need focus on one thing: sales.

For franchisers, the advantages are:
· Only moderate investment is required to expand a chain of stores, which means relatively rapid expansion is possible.
· As franchisees are self-employed, their motivation is likely to be high.

Collaborating via a franchise agreement works well in practice and offers small entrepreneurs good future prospects. In short, the franchise system combines the advantages of a large business with those of a small one.

In practice, it has been shown that franchising is an effective way of competing with the large voluntary retail chains in which all retail locations are owned by one enterprise. The success of franchising is also demonstrated by the fact that these large retail chains have also started using the franchise system. Traditional chain stores such as Ahold and HEMA (a Dutch department store with outlets in the Netherlands, Belgium and Germany) now include some franchisees. The previously mentioned buyers' cooperatives are also increasingly following the franchising model. A well-known example of a purely franchise business is McDonald's.

Effective way of competing

Chain stores

The aforementioned forms of collaboration can be regarded as being successful as soon as the common objectives stipulated at the outset are reached (for example, when combined purchasing ensures a stronger position similar to that experienced by a larger business).
Some other forms of collaboration within the retail sector are:
· Collaboration between Interflora florists whereby a consumer can get flowers delivered to any address
· Collaboration between a bar and a brewery whereby the brewery not only supplies the drink, but also provides financial support in decorating the interior of the bar.
· Collaboration between a petrol station and an oil company in relation to the various oil distribution networks.
· Collaboration between a computer hardware manufacturer and a software company leading to the installation of complementary programs on computers.

Public-private collaboration
Collaboration between local or national government authorities and the business world is frequent in many different areas, including[9]:

Public-private collaboration

IN THE PRESS

IKEA's successful franchise business model fuels global growth

IKEA constantly seeks market expansion, and grants new franchises to markets / territories according to a detailed expansion plan. Franchises are granted only to organisations and / or individuals that can secure a strong market position and market penetration in the given territory. To qualify as an IKEA franchisee, applicants must have thorough retail experience combined with extensive local market knowledge. Potential IKEA franchisees must also be able to clearly document their full understanding of and commitment to the IKEA concept, and their financial

strength and potential. As well as this, they must have well-located sites for the retail activity.
IKEA provides IKEA franchisees with the support they need to operate the IKEA Concept. They do this on a on-going basis.
Opening an IKEA operation requires considerable investment which is entirely at the expense of the IKEA franchisee. The first store in China (in Shanghai) was opened in 1998.

Source: IKEA (www.ikea.com), 2006

- Urban renewal
- Infrastructure projects
- Environmental projects
- Education

Financial and social in nature

The two most important reasons for this type of collaboration are financial and social in nature. Government authorities have too limited financial and staff resources to engage in a lot of projects. The business world has an interest in profitable investment projects.

Social benefit

Government authorities aim to secure maximum social benefit. Consequently, projects need to be completed as quickly as possible, and to the highest quality standards. The advantage to the business world may consist of an acceleration of procedures as a consequence of working together with public bodies. Greater larger involvement of a public authority in the project will make this possible. In addition, for a private sector business, working along with public institutions will reduce the financial risks involved. The authorities will look carefully into the viability of the project, and will keep the investment risks as low as possible. Take the example of a situation where a private sector company is instructed by a local authority to clear some chemically polluted ground. The local authority will be keen to see this work carried out properly and quickly. The private sector company will be attracted by the financial potential of the project. The local authority will not place any obstacles in the way of getting the job done. In short, the official machinery will be inclined to be obliging towards the private sector organisation.

Obviously, not all public-private joint ventures will be successful. Some government authority activities are being privatised to improve them and to make them more manageable. As a consequence, collaboration with other organisations will become simpler and the financial rationale for new investments clearer. A more effective and efficient system for anticipating social changes will also have been created.

Privatise

Outsourcing

Outsourcing can be seen as a form of collaboration between organisations. With increasing expansion, many organisations are focussing more on their core activities.[10] As a result, a number of activities will cease, while others will be outsourced to other organisations. It is not uncommon for those non-core tasks that were performed by supporting departments to be outsourced as these departments create significant indirect costs and it is often difficult to identify the link between the costs and the primary activities of the organisation. An example of outsourcing of supporting activities is the contracting out of parts of the personnel and accounting activities within an organisation.

Outsourcing
Core activities

Indirect costs

Another problem is that the quality of the services provided by a company's own supporting departments is difficult to measure objectively. But quality of service is a key consideration when looking at the question of whether to carry out future projects in-house, as opposed to contracting them out. One important aspect of quality is the correct and timely delivery of services.

Quality

It is likely that in the future, medium and small-sized business will outsource a part of their supporting activities, especially in the area of specialised services. In general, we can expect to see this trend in organisation and automation consultancies, catering services, marketing research and development and training of personnel.

Another important business trend that goes hand in hand with outsourcing is offshoring. Offshoring can be defined as relocation of business processes from one country to another. This includes business process such as production, manufacturing, or services.

Offshoring can take the form of either production offshoring or services offshoring. After its accession to the World Trade Organisation, China emerged as a prominent destination for production offshoring. Since technical progress in telecommunications has improved opportunities for trade in services, India has became a leading country in this domain, though many parts of the world are now emerging as offshore destinations. Newly emerging countries for offshoring include Vietnam, Bangladesh, the Philippines, the Russian Federation, Rumania and Mexico.

The economic rationale is cost reduction. If people can use their skills more cheaply than others they will have a comparative advantage. The theory is that countries should freely trade those items that cost them least to produce.

Five offshore practices that pay off

What are the pitfalls to avoid when outsourcing? What are the best practices to follow? Corporations have run into trouble as they have shifted jobs offshore. But they have persisted, since the process is so crucial to corporate success.

1   Go offshore for the right reasons. Despite the lure of lower costs and the promise of big gains in efficiency and innovation, it may make no sense at all to go offshore. Can you boost efficiency and competitiveness by shaking up operations or improving technology at home? What is the risk of a damaging backlash from your customers or community?

2   Choose your model carefully. As you develop your strategy, weigh up whether you should set up your own subsidiary offshore – known as a 'captive' operation – or contract with outside specialists.

3   Get your people on board. Keep in mind that employees and middle managers can make your bold move happen – or stop you in your tracks.

4   Be prepared to invest time and effort. 80% of companies cite cost-cutting as the main reason for outsourcing. But you will not save as much after the initial year unless you are prepared to invest serious management time and effort. Investing heavily in teaching your contractors English language skills and giving intensive training in business practices are the keys to becoming successful in your offshore adventure. Regular meetings between operational managers and their offshore counterparts are needed, as well as quality control once the offshore project is up and running. Often, what is lacking in offshore partners is a lot of deep process knowledge.

5   Treat your partners as equals. While working with offshore partners can be scary at first, the gains will be greater if you regard them as equals. Make them feel part of the team. If you treat these suppliers as you would a repair shop – telling them exactly what to do and how to do it – things will not go well. Let them work together for a period so that they learn how to their work efficiently and you will get the maximum payoff.

Source: *Business Week*, January 2006

How far can we go with outsourcing?

For decades it has been usual for organisations to pursue a strategy of concentrating on their core activities while outsourcing all the rest as much as possible. The question now is how far they should go in that direction. If we reach a situation where everybody is contracting out everything, the business will obviously grind to a halt. An optimal amount of outsourcing must exist, but when is that point reached?

In the 1980s, Michael Porter wrote books about competition in which he suggested that organisations were better off if they concentrated on doing single activities well. Since then an increasing number of companies are focussing on their own core activities, and as a result, more tasks are being outsourced. The results are clear: an increasing proportion of sales turnover. Core activities are not fixed but can change over time, sometimes quite dramatically. For example, in 1865, the Finnish company Nokia started out as a producer of paper, but it is now one of the largest producers of mobile telephones. It is not always clear which activities are core ones and which are not, and this factor supports the notion that an organisation's core activities are liable to change. If a company adapts too slowly to changed circumstances and fails to define new core activities, it risks going out of business. Building maintenance, guarding the premises, catering and health, and safety at work services are not core activities and so many businesses contract these out.

The motives for outsourcing can be summarised as follows:

1   *Costs*: if subcontractors can carry out tasks at a lower price, there will be an opportunity to reduce costs.

2   *Capital*: outsourcing makes it possible to save either on capital expenditure or to use the funds for investment in core activities.

3   *Knowledge*: the utilizing of a subcontractor's knowledge is a real way of raising quality.

4   *Capacity*: by calling in subcontractors, the organisation can react more rapidly to changes in the market.

With growing knowledge and advancing technical developments, outsourcing will increasingly be used to meet the need for specialization. Specialization is primarily the province of our core activities. As such, we can identify three motives for outsourcing:

1 *Flexibility*: the organisation must be flexible enough to react to market fluctuations.
2 *Specialisation*: the organisation must be able to use the best expertise and production techniques and so reach the highest possible quality.
3 *Expense reduction*: the previous two features must come at the lowest possible cost.

While flexibility is essential, continuity is just as important. We need both: being flexible allows us to follow market trends and so maintain market share, while continuity is necessary to ensure volume of trade and level of staffing. Although outsourcing often looks like a convenient option, employment commitments may make this impossible. Personnel cannot be dismissed without financial repercussions. Severance packages and work unrest can cancel out any advantage gained. A compromise solution may involve the transferring of personnel or the selling off of complete parts of the organisation. In such situations, however, rights acquired earlier can still play a role. Flexibility is especially necessary in cyclical industry sectors. Fluctuations in market demand can be dealt with as smoothly as possible by making the suppliers responsible for as much risk as possible. There are organisations that take a maximum of 80% of required staff on permanent contracts, while hiring the remainder via temporary job agencies. If sales fall, production can be adjusted quickly to match the trend. If the economy grows and demand rises, one takes on extra personnel.

Quality requires specialist knowledge and techniques. Not even large organisations have all the specialist knowledge they need in-house (whether legal, financial, technical, marketing etc), so they have to buy these services in. As knowledge continues to expand this trend will continue and the hiring in of external experts will increase. However, having one's own in-house services has a number of advantages. For example, a company's own personnel office will carry the advantages of trust, availability and accessibility. Internal personnel services generally perform better (for example, when it comes to the management of sick leave and reintegration).

There are some medium-sized enterprises that have managed to command an exceptionally favourable market position and achieve strong trading results while keeping as much work as they possibly can within their own companies. The volume of business that they buy in amounts on average to less than 50%. This is surprisingly low for modern industrial businesses. These companies have remained independent in the fields of production, research and development. They are able to develop unique tools and techniques via their own management processes and can therefore create value at an early stage that surpasses that created via the end product. They can thus achieve remarkable quality standards. Such companies will probably have sacrificed large-scale production (that would have been within reach with subcontracting) to their belief that quality is more important than cost.

Outsourcing HR 'may not be the best way to cut costs'

Outsourcing HR may not deliver the quick cost-cutting that people imagine, according to experts. At a recent People Management round table, Philip Vernon, principal at Mercer Human Resource Consulting, said that he warned HR directors that if you want to save 20 per cent a year, outsourcing may not be the quickest and best way to get there.

In a large organisation, HR may represent only 3 per cent of total costs. With the risks involved, saving 20 per cent of 3 per cent may not be the best option for the CEO and finance director. Marika Whitfield, HRO business manager at Northgate HR Outsourcing,

said potential clients were more interested in adding value than cost saving. And Debbie Sallis, HR director for Combat Air Defence Systems at BAE Systems, said her firm's support for outsourcing (through a joint venture with Xchanging) was now about effectiveness rather than efficiency, although cost drove the business agenda at the start.

Vernon insisted that he felt cost-cutting was still the primary reason for outsourcing HR.

Source: People Management, February 2006

4.4 Collaboration in trade cooperatives

Network of organisations

Collaboration may be seen as participation in a network of organisations. It has already been stated that a network is a cluster of interdependent organisations that combine resources in some manner in order to reach a particular target.[11] As such, a

Active interaction

network involves active interaction between organisations (or parts of them), with the intention of gaining the benefits of positive synergy. A network exists irrespective of any competitive relationship between its participants. Gaining the full benefit of a network arrangement is dependent on the manner in which the individual participants operate and influence the direction within the network.

Networks are attracting more attention because of the increase of two kinds of phenomena:

1 Strategic behaviour
2 Technology

Strategic behaviour

1 Strategic behaviour

We have already noted that collaboration is becoming increasing popular. It has been shown that in real life, organisations cannot function independently of each other. This applies equally to sections of organisations. The challenges posed by efficiency and effectiveness, force individual organisations to enter particular relationships, such as those involving distribution, research and development, and production. It is striking how many organisations are now joining such networks. The result is a rich tapestry of different organisations and components.

2 Technology

Technology

The changes that have taken place within manufacturing companies constitute striking evidence of recent changes in technology. Technological changes are causing goods and services to be produced in a different way, and thus the requirements placed on physical surroundings are also changing.

The globalisation of knowledge and rapid development in information technology has facilitated flexible exchange of business activities. Successful performance in markets today means higher requirements for organisations in the future. Specialist knowledge is therefore indispensable. With organisations focussing increasingly on their core activities and technology being applied in an increasing number of ways to the solving of problems, survival now depends on participation in networks. The following sum this up:

Siemens and GE to cooperate over ship containers

General Electric and Siemens, the largest conglomerates in the US and Europe respectively, have launched their first direct cooperative venture in an effort to prevent terrorists tampering with ship containers.

The security initiative aims to equip most container traffic with devices that register when they have been opened. Siemens will market the product in Europe, and later in India, Australia, New Zealand and Africa. Mitsubishi is already partnered with GE for sales in Japan and potentially other parts of Asia. Although the actual device will cost only a few hundred dollars, the more profitable part of the business will be the service fees garnered for monitoring whether they have been tampered with. The development of a reliable and low-cost tracking service had presented a surprisingly difficult technical challenge.

Source: *The Financial Times*, January 2006

IN THE PRESS

- The pace of technological development is accelerating all the time.
- Developmental and production processes are increasingly capital-intensive.
- Products are being offered in ever-increasing diversity.
- The life cycle of products is becoming increasingly shorter.
- Development costs are growing at an increasing rate.
- New technology means that unexpected market / product combinations can be met at short notice. How viable these are is, however, dependent on how unique they are.

In summary we can conclude that the commercial risks involved in business activities will continue to increase.

Organisations and their divisions can expect to experience significant pressure as they try to operate within a competitive world. Participating in networks offers advantages in such a situation. Within the network, the strengths of organisations can be used to full advantage. Joining a network can have an added value for individual organisations. However, it will also have certain repercussions, including the control that can be exerted over particular business processes.

Being part of a network can carry the following advantages for an organisation:
- More technological possibilities
- More products or variations on them
- Better products
- Accessibility to more markets
- Better market position
- Better production processes.

Being part of a network

We can identify eight basic types of network. They clearly demonstrate the various goals of collaboration and are listed in rising degree of intensiveness[12]:

Eight basic types

1 Joint improvement of secondary processes in areas such as logistics and quality. This is achieved by carefully attuning information, organisation, planning and control needs to each other.
2 Joint projects in relation to the primary activities of production, research and development, and sales.
3 Collaboration in marketing and sales activities such as marketing research, pricing and promotion.
4 Joint acquisition of knowledge, people and means: for example, joint training courses and purchases.
5 Vertical collaboration in production. In such a situation, production activities are geared to successive links in the business chain.

6 Horizontal collaboration in production. The aim here is to produce goods jointly. Individual organisations produce components that together form the end product. Research is not done jointly.

Co-makership

7 Co-makership – a collaborative form in which, in contrast to the previous examples, research and development processes are also carried out jointly. This form of collaboration is vertically structured.

8 Horizontal collaboration which also involves working together on research and development, but this time with a horizontal connection. The partners both have the task of developing and producing a product.

It can be concluded that networks go through a number of phases and that these are comparable to those of the product's lifespan. Organisations start off becoming aware that there are possibilities for collaboration. This is called the awareness phase. The exploration stage sees the creation of a network. The expansion stage sees further expansion of the network. The commitment stage represents the network's strongest phase. However, most networks are temporary in nature. The reasons for its existence disappear, and thus the network is dissolved: the dissolution phase.

Awareness phase

Expansion
Commitment
Dissolution

4.5 Mergers and acquisitions

Large scale mergers

Large scale mergers and acquisitions are currently taking place within all sectors of industry. Indications are that this trend will continue in the future.

After some introductory remarks about mergers and acquisitions, this section will look at the following in greater detail:
· The motives behind mergers and acquisitions
· Acquisition price and price calculation
· Problems associated with mergers and acquisitions;
· The next step after the merger

As the terms 'merger' and 'acquisition' are used in a similar context, it is wise to take a moment to define the meaning of each.

Merger

Acquisition

A merger is a form of collaboration and joining together of enterprises by which they completely abolish their economic and legal individuality and in which the partners join forces to determine what the joint goals are and how they will be reached. The term 'acquisition' is used when one or more of the parties takes sole responsibility on behalf of all partners in the new venture for the venture's objectives and strategies for reaching the objectives. It is only the partner that has been taken over that will lose its autonomy. Sometimes they will not relinquish their autonomy voluntarily. Figure 4.5 shows the following various merger and acquisition methods.[13]

1 In this situation (two partners: A and B), A is able to purchase shares in B. It can either pay in cash or in its own shares.
2 Partners A and B put their shares into a joint holding company. They do so in exchange for shares in C.
3 Partners A and B create a new subsidiary (D). A's and B's assets are put into D in exchange for shares.
4 A and B have now started to acquire the character of a holding company.

Figure 4.5   Explanation of merger and acquisition methods

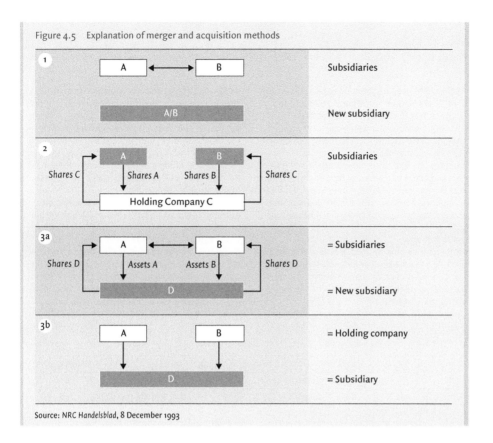

Source: NRC Handelsblad, 8 December 1993

4.5.1   The motives behind mergers and acquisitions

With an eye to a growing European market, many organisations are considering a strategic reorientation. Many companies have become stronger in the European market by determining which of their activities are core ones, thereafter increasing their growth via mergers and acquisitions. These organisations hope that by gaining a larger market share, they will then increase their profits. Some will try to do this by creating economies of scale and slimming down supporting or staff divisions. One way of doing this is by improving productivity and cash flow. As the consumer market is not expanding dramatically, the only way to grow would seem to be via acquisition purchases or mergers.

Strategic reorientation

The organisation's competitive position also plays a very important role. If a market leader enters a new market, its competitors are likely to seriously consider doing the same. Enterprises need to reduce the chance of a competitor seeing a chance that they have missed. Of course, it is always possible for the market leader to make a mistake: lurking competitors will then be misled.

Competitive position

Synergy is also identified by many enterprises as a motive for a merger or acquisition. Where there is synergy, organisations will complement or strengthen each other through features such as joint expertise or the creation of economies of scale (the $1 + 1 = 3$ effect).

Synergy

In addition to commercial motives, personal interests can play a role in a merger or acquisition. A larger enterprise will often mean greater prestige for management and sometimes an increased remuneration package. Naturally, the larger the enterprise becomes, the smaller the chances of it being taken over.

Mergers and acquisitions in the financial services industry

Banks the world over are scrambling to become larger, whether via organic growth or via mergers and acquisitions. It is the banks themselves that are volatile, shifting shapes and strategies as furiously as their regulators will allow them in their efforts to win markets and market share.

For example, in Japan three new 'megabanks' have eaten 11 old banks and are now digesting them; in Central Europe foreigners have bought or built 80% of the top local banks since the fall of communism. In America, the ten biggest commercial banks control 49% of the country's banking assets, up from 29% a decade ago.

One argument commonly used in favour of mergers (in banking as in many other industries) is the pursuit of economies of scale in areas such as procurement, systems, operations, research and marketing. Another argument for mergers is based on

economies of scope: the proposition that related lines of business under the same ownership or management can share resources and create opportunities for one another. A third reason for banks to pursue growth through mergers and acquisitions is managerial ambition. Chief executives want the gratification of running a bigger company, or the fear that their own company will be taken over unless they grab another one first.

'Bigness' may also have benefits not easily captured in studies of financial performance. One is the ability to place strategic bets on future markets such as China without putting the whole bank at risk. Another is regulatory capture. The bigger the bank, the more likely its home-country regulators and legislators will be to take its interest into account when drafting new rules, and the more likely they will be to judge it 'too big to fail' in the event of a crisis.

How the mighty have grown, World's top ten banks by assets*, $bn

2004		1995		1985	
UBS	1,533	Deutsche Bank	503	Citicorp	167
Citigroup	1,484	Sanwa Bank	501	Dai-Ichi Kangyo Bank	158
Mizuho Financial Group	1,296	Sumitomo Bank	500	Fuji Bank	142
HSBC	1,277	Dai-Ichi Kangyo Bank	499	Sumitomo Bank	135
Crédit Agricole	1,243	Fuji Bank	487	Mitsubishi Bank	133
BNP Paribas	1,234	Sakura Bank	478	Banque N. de Paris	123
JPMorgan Chase	1,157	Mitsubishi Bank	475	Sanwa Bank	123
Deutsche Bank	1,144	Norinchukin Bank	430	Crédit Agricole	123
Royal Bank of Scotland	1,119	Crédit Agricole	386	BankAmerica	115
Bank of America	1,110	ICBC+	374	Crédit Lyonnais	111

Source: *The Banker*
*Mitsubishi-UFJ Financial Group was formed in October 2005 with assets of $1.71trn
+Industrial & Commercial Bank of China

Source: *The Economist*, May 2006

4.5.2   Acquisition price and price calculation

Acquisition prices

With the increase in the number of mergers, prices have risen. Although most acquisition prices are not published, indications are that these are between fifteen and twenty-five times the net profit. If the company being taken over has experienced a loss, there is the issue of future profits.[14] Whether the purchase price is justified is very much the issue. Prices paid are very often based on expected market developments and past sector experiences.

Returns on investment

For a business with a reasonable balance sheet, high returns on investment (ROI), an attractive strategic position and clear synergy potential, an acquisition purchase price of twenty times the net profit can be justified.[15] The price is often dependent on the manner in which the takeover purchase comes about. Once in a while, large

Battle

acquisitions are the result of a tough battle between different enterprises. Smaller acquisitions often take place in relative quiet and there is therefore more time to

Mergers and acquisitions
Deal value by target country, 2005, $trn

Country	Value	Number of deals
United States	1,17	7,548
Britain		2,646
Japan		2,535
Germany		947
France		1,215
Canada		1,014
Spain		527
Italy		660
China		1,695
Australia		1,184
Netherlands		679
Russia		426
Denmark		279
Turkey		102
Sweden		520

0   0.1   0.2   0.3   Number of deals

Source: *The Economist / Dealogic 2006*

negotiate the details. A shortage of takeover purchasers will obviously have an important effect on the asking price.

Some industrial sectors may only have a few potential candidates for takeover, and yet the prices will still go up and the size of the average business will increase. It would seem that an acquisition price greater than ten times the net annual profit can only be justified when there are very favourable prospects for profit.

4.5.3 Problems associated with mergers and acquisitions

Mergers and acquisitions are not always as successful as we once thought. It appears that approximately 40% of new mergers fail to get off the ground, while half of the acquisitions are overturned within six years. Nor do the expected advantages of a merger always measure up against the disadvantages. In fact, a large number of intended mergers do not materialise. Because very large companies arise as a result of mergers and there is consequently less competition, management might fall into the trap of becoming complacent.[16] Scale advantages disappear when a company reaches a size at which growth generates more problems than benefits because efficiency improvements have already been instigated.

Scale advantages

It is worth taking a moment to consider some of the main problems associated with mergers and acquisitions. One of the biggest problems posed by attempts to fuse two enterprises together is the existence of different organisational cultures.[17] An

Problems

organisation can be recognized by its customs, its way of thinking, the existence of rituals and the maintenance of particular norms and values. When totally different cultures exist it is sensible to start with a joint venture, so that each part of the new organisation can gradually get to know each other. All parties will need to make some concessions and it must be understood that clinging to individual organisational cultures will stand in the way of a successful new operation as well as having a negative effect on individual prospects within the organisation. The subject of organisational culture is treated in more detail in Chapter 10.

It is vital that the management and staff of the enterprise that has been taken over be kept fully up to date. If information is not always provided and there is a lack of clarity, a vacuum will tend to be created and this is likely to have undesirable consequences. Management will become demotivated as a consequence of uncertainty about job security, position within the company, salary scaling and so on. The staff will be even less motivated and as a result, talented employees may be tempted to leave. Takeovers attract head-hunters all too frequently. It is not unusual for between 5 and 10% of the employees of a company to leave voluntarily when there is a merger or acquisition. This depends naturally on job scarcity and staff quality.

Particularly in organisations with an informal character, loss of management and staff with experience and knowledge can have disastrous consequences. Filling the resulting vacancies with new staff and managers can be very costly as a lot of recent experience and knowledge will not have been written down, and so is very difficult to transfer.

Lastly, expectations in relation to the merger may be overly optimistic from both a quantitative and a qualitative point of view, especially if major results are expected within a short time.

The above-mentioned common problems must be taken seriously when considering a merger or acquisition. The chances of a successful merger or acquisition are increased when:

a A strategic plan exists in which the objectives of the enterprise are clearly stated and the strategy for reaching these objectives is explained.

Differences in business culture are often the biggest obstacle during a merger

Most companies seriously underestimate differences in organisational cultures during a merger or acquisition. As a result, the anticipated results often fail to materialise. Integration problems can arise because culture differences are not given adequate attention. This is one of the findings from a investigation by Right Management Consultants, who surveyed 156 businesses in Europe, North America, Asia and Australia with a turnover of at least five hundred million euros.

Companies going through a merger or acquisition are still overly preoccupied with financial issues. Other areas will need extra attention. Even though more talented personnel are staying with their employer compared with five years ago, the human aspects of an acquisition are frequently shoved to one side.

HR managers must concentrate on the selection of new managerial staff for the new organisation, as suitable candidates will not necessarily come from the enterprises that merge. They must also prevent any arrogance developing in the acquiring company as that could endanger the success of the integration process. Sufficient attention must be paid to the middle layers of the organisations. Middle management can contribute significantly to the harmonisation of business cultures, as well as to the creation of value, saving in costs, and overall growth.

Source: P&O actueel, April 2004

b Management leads the process properly and keeps staff well informed of developments.

c The process is supported by a thorough and well-thought-through plan.

d An accurate financial and feasibility analysis has been carried out in advance, identifying expected short, medium and long-term results.

4.5.4 After the merger

Once the merger contract or memorandum of collaboration has been signed, it is time to start with implementation. A number of necessary tasks must be systematically carried out in each part of the business. Management plays a central and guiding role in this. Figure 4.6 shows a number of business areas that will require attention. A practical first step to take is setting up task forces for each different part of the business for the purpose of creating an integrated plan for the entire operation. We will now look at those activities that should be undertaken in each business unit.

Implementation

Task forces

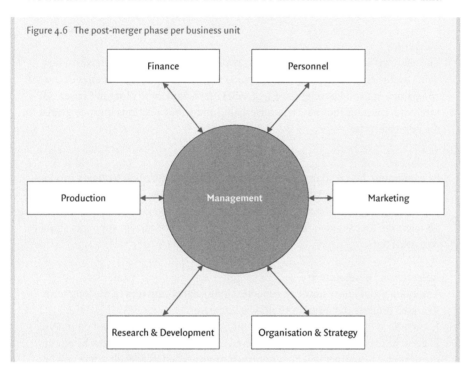

Figure 4.6 The post-merger phase per business unit

Organisation and strategy

As already mentioned, a clear strategy must be drawn up as soon as possible and communicated to those inside the organisation as well as to external interested parties such as customers, shareholders, and competitors. From here on, it should be clear what the objectives of the enterprise are, which products will be launched on which markets, what the competitive advantages are and what the plans for the short and medium term are.

Strategy

The next step is the new structure, with the most important positions identified and filled. The progress and the results of the various task forces can be negatively influenced if an extended period of uncertainty occurs.

The danger of individual's own interests taking priority over those of the enterprise should not be ignored. Finally, all bookkeeping procedures should be matched and contracts harmonised.

Finance

Financial reporting

It is important that financial reporting procedures throughout the various parts of the new organisation be brought into line with each other quickly so that it is possible to keep abreast of the overall results of the new enterprise. The integration of different automations systems can be a complicated, time-consuming and costly matter. Attention must be given to planning procedures and distribution of budgets.

Personnel

Harmonise job functions and conditions of employment

On the personnel side, steps should be taken to harmonise job functions and conditions of employment. Then it is necessary to look at any duplication that may have occurred as a result of the merger or acquisition. If there are too many staff members it will be necessary to transfer some employees or let some go, and these may require support and assistance.

The various personnel functions in the new organisation (such as recruitment and selection, evaluating and rewarding, career planning and training) must also be geared to each other (see also Chapter 5).

Marketing

Own image

The new organisation must develop its own image. This should begin with a new name for the enterprise. Frequently, a name is chosen in which the names of the old companies can still be recognised (e.g. ABN Amro Bank or JP Morgan Chase). All external communications such as advertising and public relations must be geared to the new enterprise.

External communications

Production

Production facilities

By combining their resources, organisations can make use of each other's production facilities. These must be examined carefully to see how they can be matched with each other. Additionally, purchasing of materials and goods can be combined. To select the best supplier for the future, a comparison of current suppliers should be carried out.

Research and development

The exchange of know-how can generate significant advantages in the long term. Research projects that overlap should be integrated.

Post-merger phase

If too little attention is paid to the post-merger phase, productivity and output are likely to be disappointing. As a result, even more time and energy must be put into the project. The merger will then not reach its target and as a result, there will be more sorrow than pleasure.

Doing business in Poland

How Poles organise and process information

Polish culture has always been open to information from the West. Since the demise of Communism, many aspects of education in Poland have been in a state of flux. Poles are abstract thinkers, processing information conceptually and analytically. Nevertheless, they value relationships as much as rules.

What Poles accept as evidence

In Poland, truth rests more on objective facts than on the subjective feelings of the moment. Faith in ideologies that may change one's perspective of the truth is changing, shifting from the ideologies of the Communist party to those of nationalism and democracy.

The basis of behaviour

Since the fall of the Iron Curtain and the rise of democracy, Polish value systems are increasingly being influenced by those of the West. Value systems in the predominant culture – how right is distinguished from wrong, good from evil, and so on – are described under the next three headings

The locus of decision-making

As freedom and privatisation becomes a part of life, more decision-making responsibility is being placed on the shoulders of the individual. There is a strong sense of individualism and democracy, plus a belief that all citizens should influence the way that society is governed. The individual may frequently transfer decision-making responsibility to the group as a whole or to a consensus of privileged individuals.

Sources of anxiety reduction

Post-Communist freedom is perceived as threatening most of the structures the Poles have depended upon for stability and security. However, since most Poles are Catholics, the church is a significant factor in filling this need. Polish Catholicism has been described as emotional and traditional, and the Poles are considered the most devout of all European Catholics. Strong extended family ties also help to give structure and security.

Issues of equality / inequality

The removal of Communist party control has allowed resentment over inequality to surface. Internal disputes over power and control have arisen. Poland has a homogenous population and the drive for power is evident at all levels of society, including the government and industry. The drive for power is threatening to undermine humanitarian belief in equality. There is some disjunction between private and public morality. Although Poland is a male-dominated society, hiding one's emotions is not felt to be necessary. Traditionally, there is sensitivity to the feelings of others: intentions, feelings, and opinions are openly expressed.

Ten examples of Polish business practices

1. The Polish working day starts early. Appointments at 8.00 a.m. are not unusual.
2. It is difficult to predict how long it will take to negotiate a business deal. Nowadays, if the government is involved, you can expect negotiations to proceed slowly. On the other hand, some of Poland's entrepreneurs are anxious to move quickly.
3. Bring plenty of business cards and give one out to everyone you meet.
4. Proposals, reports, and promotional materials should be translated into Polish. If graphics are included in this material, make sure that they are well done and neatly printed. Poland has long had some of the best graphic artists in the world.
5. If possible, keep the conversation away from politics. Food, sports, and sightseeing are good topics to bring up.
6. Business lunches and dinners are popular, but breakfast meetings are virtually unknown in Poland.
7. Despite having to go to work early, Poles love to stay up late, talking and drinking. Leaving early may insult them, so be prepared for a long night.
8. Shake hands when you meet a Pole and when you take your leave. Be sure to shake hands when you are introduced to someone for the first time.
9. A foreign gift is appropriate the first time you meet a Polish businessman. Liquor (anything except vodka) is a good choice.
10. Business dress is suits and ties for men, dresses for women. Colours tend to be conservative.

Source: Kiss, Bow, or Shake Hands: How to Do Business in Sixty Countries, by Terri Morrison, Wayne A. Conaway and George A. Borden, Adams Media, 2006

Summary

A growing number of organisations are signing cooperative agreements, and these have a variety of goals. In the future, agreements
are most likely to be made for reasons of creating knowledge.
Collaboration may be sought for offensive or defensive reasons and
may take many different forms. Some of the main ones are strategic
alliances, joint ventures, mergers and acquisitions, outsourcing, licensing and franchising. Success can be measured by increase in competitive position. Cooperative agreements can take place between competitive or non-competitive parties. Where the latter is concerned, a distinction needs to be made between collaboration in the retail sector,
public-private collaboration and subcontracting. Where there is a cluster of dependent organisations that have joined forces, this is
described as a trade cooperative. Cooperatives are particularly significant in the areas of strategic behaviour and technology. Cooperatives
can take eight different forms, each with its own level of intensiveness.
The recent trend in mergers and acquisitions is not likely to end soon
as global competition is on the rise and increasingly exerting pressure.
Synergy is often cited as a motive for these. Mergers and acquisitions
are often not as successful as expected. Some of the biggest problems faced relate to culture, personnel and expectations. A lot of
attention needs to be paid to the implementation phase that follows
the merger.

Definitions

§ 4.1 Strategic alliance A term used to describe two or more different enterprises entering into an agreement to work together.

Trade cooperative A cluster of interdependent organisations that work together to reach a joint target.

Joint venture Two or more different companies that have jointly set up a subsidiary enterprise on the basis of equal management responsibility and in order to develop special joint activities.

Merger Two comparable enterprises joining together in such a way as to completely abolish their former economic and legal individuality and in which the partners join forces to determine what the joint goals are and how they will be reached.

Acquisition When one or more of the parties takes sole responsibility for the new venture's objectives and strategies on behalf of all the other partners in the venture.

Outsourcing The farming out of certain activities to other enterprises.

Licensing One enterprise allowing its products to be made by another enterprise in exchange for a fee.

Multinational strategy A strategy whereby each part of an international business remains autonomous.

Transnational strategy A strategy chosen when the company wants worldwide integration of all the company's components, with the aim of bringing about the benefits of world-wide efficiency.

Worldwide strategy A single world-wide organisational format which implements centralised strategies in all countries and regions without allowing local differences.

International strategy A centralized strategy but in contrast to the world-wide version, local differences are often allowed to exist.

§§ 4.2.2 Competitive potential The capacity an organisation has to develop those skills that will form the basis for developing a future generation of products.

§§ 4.3.2 Buyers' cooperative An arrangement whereby retailers of similar products collaborate in order to obtain a number of advantages.

Franchising Involves a franchiser and a franchisee (the shopkeeper). Within a franchise agreement, the franchisee is strictly bound to standard guidelines that relate to store design, purchase, sale promotion, marketing, price politics and product range. The franchisee pays an amount of money to the franchiser in exchange for the rights to use the retail model. Both parties remain independent enterprises.

§§ 4.5.1 Synergy

Organizations complementing or strengthening each other because they have combined certain features, such as their expertise (also called the 1 + 1 = 3 effect).

§§ 4.5.2 National competition authority

National competition authorities prevent the formation of cartels and reduce abuse of economically dominant positions as well as ensuring that mergers and acquisitions do not create anti-competitive situations. Their goal is an effective competitive environment that is good for consumers and the business world.

Statements

Decide whether the following statements are correct or incorrect and give reasons for your answers.

1 The big increase in strategic alliances is mainly due to the globalisation of knowledge.
2 The primary aim of collaboration is to try to spread the risks.
3 A strategic alliance is entered into when two or more enterprises decide to work together on the basis of an agreement.
4 A trans-national strategy is chosen in order to gain a considerable amount of freedom to select components world-wide. It is aimed especially at creating local bonds.
5 A franchise agreement obliges the franchisee to conform strictly to uniform guidelines in relation to store design, purchase, sales promotion and marketing, pricing policies and range of stock.
6 A cooperative involves active interaction between organisations (or sections of them), with the aim of gaining the benefits of synergy.
7 Because organisations are focussing increasingly on their core activities while trying to implement technology in increasingly unique ways, their survival depends on joining cooperatives.
8 A merger is a fusion of enterprises in which the merger partner suffers a loss of autonomy.
9 Competitive potential is the capacity an organisation has to develop those skills that underpin the development of a new generation of products.
10 One of the biggest problems confronting merging enterprises is the existence of different organisational cultures. They can even vary per division.

Theory questions

1 Explain why entering into a collaboration agreement is strategic in nature.
2 Give three reasons why organisations are increasingly outsourcing activities.
3 Collaboration in organisational networks has increased due to many factors, including technological change. Explain why.
4 Mergers and acquisitions are often unsuccessful.
   a Describe the various problem areas.
   b How can the success rate of a merger or acquisitions be increased?

 For answers see www.marcusvandam.noordhoff.nl.

Mini case study

Collaborating companies increase competition

Collaboration intensifies competition. That seems contradictory. After all, the more companies work together, the less they are in competition with each other. In practice, however, we see that this is not so, and for two reasons.

The first reason is that the majority of alliances are 'offensive': newly created capabilities are directed towards new products, services and processes with which the alliance can enter into competitive situations. Only a minority of alliances aim to decrease competition, divide markets or fix prices.

Secondly, some new forms of competition are associated with alliances: co-opetition, competition between alliance groups and competition between alliances and other parties.

Co-opetition – a combination of collaboration and competition – is what happens when companies work together while at the same time competing with each other. European chip manufacturers work together on research projects, while at the same time competing with each other via their current products.

Another form of co-opetition takes the form of businesses working together with partners that are in competition with each other. Hewlett Packard works just as closely with Microsoft as with competitor Redhat. Both partners are therefore in competition for the attention of Hewlett Packard.

A third form of co-opetition takes the form of a company training a partner followed by the partner setting up business on an independent basis. The Dutch supermarket chain parent Ahold once supplied Shell with products for their Shell shops. Shell copied the pattern, broke off relations with Ahold and is now Ahold's competitor.

The second new form is competition between alliance groups. The best-known example is that of the three airline alliances of Star Alliance, One World and Skyteam (including Air France-KLM). In this situation, there is less competition at an individual operator level, but more at the level of the alliances. Competition can be quite tough.

The third form of competition is between alliances of a similar organisational format. In the mobile telephone sector, Vodafone is the largest European player. Two alliance groups have evolved that are in competition with Vodafone in trying to offer an even larger geographical coverage than Vodafone does. Smaller businesses can decide to work together like this, counterbalancing a dominant player. The dominant player is thus confronted by an adversary that must be contended with. This demonstrates, therefore, that collaboration leads to more competition.

Source: Ard-Pieter de Man, www.financieeldagblad.nl, 30 June 2004

Question

1 The above text suggests that entering into collaborative agreements does not limit competition, but instead intensifies it. Explain why you agree or disagree with the text above. Give reasons for your choice.

E-mail case study

To:	Philip Johnson
Cc:	
Bcc:	
Subject:	Fly Globe Span: reasons for collaboration

Message:

Dear Philip,

During our last management team meeting, we made the decision to enter into an airline alliance. Our Scottish airline, Fly Globe Span, is certainly a fast growing airline, but its long-term survival will be better guaranteed within such an alliance of airlines. An alliance that we have our eye on is the Skyteam alliance.

Before we enter discussions we would like to ask you to carry out a brief investigation into the following three questions:

1 What were the key reasons for this alliance?

2   What do the various airlines want to get out of the alliance?

3   How is the alliance structured?

Philip, would you get back to me with answers to the above questions within a week? I think that a lot of information can be found on the Internet.

Kind regards,

Brian McLand

Notes part A

Chapter 1
1 De Wilde, F.H.P., *Stoeien met Organisaties*, Samsom, Alphen aan den Rijn.
2 From an interview with P. Drucker, *NRC Handelsblad*, March 29, 1994, Ferry Versteeg.

Chapter 2
1 Conclusions from the conference by IMSA in co operation with 'Ministerie van VROM en Platform Duurzame Ontwikkeling', *NRC Handelsblad*, January 27, 1994.
2 Hutchinson, C., 'Corporate Strategy and the Environment', in: *Long Range Planning*, August 1992.
3 From: *Select*, October 1990.
4 From: *Select*, October 1990.

Chapter 3
1 After: Keuning, D. and Eppink, D.J., *Management & Organisatie, theorie en toepasssing*, Stenfert Kroese, Houten, 1996.
2 Research NIB, FEM, September 1989 / 34.
3 *Rendement*, November 1992.
4 Gray, D.H., 'Gebruik en misbruik van strategische planning', in: *Harvard Holland Review*, Autumn 1986.

Chapter 4
1 Badaracco, J.L., *The Knowledge Link, how Firms compete through strategic alliances*, Harvard Business School Press, Boston, 1991.
2 Badaracco, J.L., *The Knowledge Link, how firms compete through strategic alliances*, Harvard Business School Press, Boston, 1991.
3 Thuis, P., *Toegepaste organisatiekunde*, Wolters-Noordhoff, Groningen, 2003.
4 Robbins, S.P. and Coulter, M., *Management*, Pearson.
5 P. Lorange, Roos, J. and Bronn, P.S., 'Long Range Planning', December 1992, from: PEM-select, No. 2, 1993.
6 R.B. Reich and Mankin, E.D., 'Joint Ventures with Japan Give Away our Future', *Harvard Business Review*, March / April 1986.
7 Hamel, C., Dos, Y.L., Prahalad, C.H., 'Profiteren van samenwerking met de concurrent', *Harvard Holland Review*, Winter 1990.
8 Crijns, H., *De durf om te ondernemen anno 2001*, www.ktnobrief.be

9 Ster, W. van de, and Wissen, P. van, *Marketing in de Detailhandel*, Wolters-Noordhoff, Groningen, 1983.

10 Kouwenhoven, drs. V., 'Publieke Private samenwerking stoelt op wederzijds vertrouwen', *Binnenlands Bestuur Management*, No. 2, 1989.

11 Van Gils, 1987.

12 Boekema, F.W.M., and Kamann, D.J.F., *Sociaal-economische netwerken*, Wolters-Noordhoff, Groningen, 1989.

13 Hartog, prof. dr., (e.a.), *Encyclopedie van de economie*, Elsevier, Amsterdam, 1973.

14 *Het Financieele Dagblad*, January 31, 1989.

15 Interview with drs. A.J. de Vries, from: ELAN, March 1990.

16 Schoot, drs. ir. E.J. van der, 'Postfusiefase meestal zwaar onderschat', *Het Financieele Dagblad*, October 18, 1988.

17 'Snuffel eerst goed aan uw fusiepartner', FEM, February 1990.

Part B **People and organisations**

In the previous section, we described an organisation as a means of human cooperation towards a common purpose. People determine whether an organisation will achieve its purposes. People play the principal role in every organisation. In this section, this role will be viewed from various angles. The section 'People and organisations' consists of the following chapters:

Contents

5

Individual and teams

'People believe gladly what they want to believe'.
(Caesar, Gaius Julius, 100–44 BC, Roman general and statesman)

Within organisations, people are the most important production factor. It is people who determine the degree of success an organisation is able to achieve. Within organisations, people have to cooperate to achieve goals. As such, this chapter will focus attention not only on humans as individuals, but also as part of a group.

Contents

This chapter will:
- Make you aware of the importance of individuals and groups to an organisation
- Acquaint you with some general concepts relating to the individual, including motivation and personality
- Make you aware of some specific concepts relating to the individual, including emotional intelligence, overloading and core qualities
- Make you aware of some general concepts relating to groups/teams, such as various kinds of groups and their various characteristics
- Make you aware of some specific concepts relating to groups, such as team management and organisational conflicts.

5.1   People in organisations

In the introduction to this book, an organisation was defined as 'each form of human cooperation for a common purpose'. This definition highlights the fact that cooperation between people is a feature of an organisation. For many organisations, the human effort that goes into activities is crucial to the survival of the organisation. This applies not only to the strategic level, but also to the tactical and operational levels. In this chapter, the focus is on the people who 'inhabit' organisations. A large part of their active life takes place within organisations. What motivates them? In what terms can we describe their behaviour within organisations? How can management within organisations encourage a particular type of behaviour? The purpose of this chapter is to give an insight into individual and group behaviour, including how to predict and influence it.

People in organisations can be considered from various perspectives. This chapter will focus on them at the level of the individual and of the group. As regards the former, attention will be given initially to general concepts such as motivation, personality and attitude. In addition, the following specific subjects will be treated:
- Motivation
- Emotional intelligence
- Overloading, stress, stress prevention and burnout
- Intuition and creativity
- Core qualities

Group behaviour will then be handled. Within organisations, people operate nearly always in groups. Apart from their individual tasks, they also form part of a group or various different groups. Organisational goals are largely realised by appropriate forms of cooperation. This part of the chapter will deal initially with general structural definitions such as what a group is, what kinds of groups exist and what their characteristics are. Then more specific issues will follow:
- Team management and characteristics of successful teams
- Organisational conflict

5.2   Motivation

Organisations prefer to attract motivated employees. Motivated people are good at their job and therefore add extra value to the organisation. But what is motivation? The word 'motivation' comes from the Latin word 'movere', meaning 'moving'.

Motivation

Motivation is what gets us moving. Motivation can be described as the inner readiness of a person to perform certain actions.

Chapter 1 briefly described some general theories of motivation: those of Abraham Maslow (the need for hierarchy), Elton May (human relations movement), Frederick Herzberg (revisionism) and Douglas McGregor (theory X and Y).

The distinction between work-related motivation and non-work-related motivation (see also Section 9.2.1) is a crucial aspect of the concept:

Motivation intrinsic to the job

- *Motivation intrinsic to the job.* Motivation intrinsic to the job is motivation that derives from the work itself. People who are motivated in such a sense see their job as a challenge. For these people, work is an important part of their life. If we translate this motivation to Maslow's need for hierarchy we will arrive at more fundamental needs: the need for acknowledgement and self-fulfilment. Bearing responsibility, expansion of skills and living up to performance expectations constitute important motivating factors. Work-related motivation would seem to provide long-term stimulation.

Name:	Vladimir Turin
Job title:	Director of Research & Development
Country of origin:	Russia
Company:	Quest Software
Company website:	www.quest.com

What important personal qualities must people have to be successful in international work?
It may sound trivial, but I would emphasise language and communication skills over anything else. And not just a 'TOEFL' level of knowledge, but ability to communicate on an interpersonal level. Ability to hear what was said and, more importantly, what wasn't.

What do people need to know to do business in your country?
In Russia, personal relationships are paramount. Personal means exactly that: a relationship that cannot really be developed over the phone or by two to three visits a year. If you are not ready to invest in a locally-based native speaker representative, maybe you're not yet ready for the local market.
In Russia, the boss is expected to behave like a personal friend with his or her subordinates. It is normal to call an employee at home after 8.00 PM to discuss business because this way the employee feels connected to you personally. Management by walking around is a popular management style here. The boss is expected to know everything and be able to help any subordinate on the spot.
One important aspect to consider is the difference in conflict resolution styles. A foreigner should be prepared to engage in confrontational disputes. The typical withdrawal style, frequently seen in US or Canada, doesn't come over well here.

What is the best way to motivate people?
Above all, give people an interesting job. While this may be true for any other country, in Russia it frequently forms a substantial part of the overall compensation package. The feeling of personal involvement is a goal in its own right, even if it is not supported by any financial benefits.

Describe one important trend in organisation and management
The job market is getting highly competitive. A few years ago, finding 'ready to use' talent was easy – the only issue was the right compensation. These days companies are focussing increasingly on access to internal education and non-monetary compensation to build and retain the workforce.

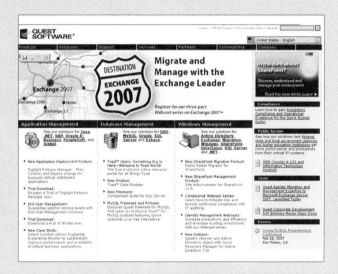

FIGURES & TRENDS

Global drivers for employee engagement

Highly performing enterprises have employees who are highly engaged and show a high level of commitment. The engagement and commitment matrix pro- vide an objective assessment of the degree and commitment and engagement among different groups of employees.

Engagement and Commitment Matrix

	Impact on Time	Impact on Work	Impact on Product / services	Identity of employee
Engagement & commitment	Limitless	High output and flexibility	Innovation and improvement	Goal identity
Cooperation	Limited extension of hours	Output data	Learning Seeking	Welcome change
Compliance	Clock watching	Have to bargain to obtain effort	Skills remain static	Critical, joking
Discordance	Time wasting	Additional pay	Fiddle around	Resist change
Withdrawal	Absence	More for same	Pilfering	Negative, contentious
Hostility	Terminations	Sabotage	Theft	Confrontational, solidarity

Research by Towers Perrin (2006) has identified 5 top drivers for employee engagement globally:
1 Opportunities to learn and develop new skills
2 Improvement of capabilities and skills over the last year
3 Reputation of the organisation as a good employer
4 Input into decision-making in one's own department
5 Organisation focusses on customer satisfaction

Source: PricewaterhouseCoopers, *Key Trends in Human Capital* (2006) / Towers Perrin, World at Work (2006)

Motivation extrinsic to the job

- *Motivation extrinsic to the job.* Motivation of this type does not derive from the work itself. It derives from items extrinsic to the job such as work circumstances, rewards, emoluments and status. These are the job's 'perks', so to speak. People whose motivation is extrinsic to the job have a pragmatic attitude to their work. In practice, such a form of motivation is short term.

Many new theories of motivation have developed from the original ones. These theories consider motivation from certain perspectives and give further insights into particular aspects of motivation. Three of these theories will be considered: Alderfer's theory, McLelland's theory and Vroom's expectancy theory.

5.2.1   Alderfer's theory

Maslow discussed five needs. Alderfer's theory (1969) identifies a more limited number of needs:

Existential needs

- *Existential needs.* These concern material security, corresponding to the physiological needs and security of Maslow.

Relational needs

- *Relational needs.* These concern good relationships with other people. Social acceptance, appreciation and acknowledgement are important. Translated into Maslow's terms, these are the need for acceptance and the need for acknowledgement.

Growth needs

- *Growth needs.* These needs are directed towards personal growth and self-fulfilment and equate to Maslow's main need within the pyramid, the need for self-fulfilment.

In its simplified form, this is known as the ERG theory (the abbreviation standing for the three groups of needs). While the theory strongly resembles that of Maslow, there are some significant differences.

Alderfer needs are not hierarchical. Maslow believed that satisfied needs no longer form effective stimuli. Alderfer is of the opinion that various different needs can be in operation simultaneously. Not only this, but there is no question of a fixed order. He also introduces a new element: the frustration-regression hypothesis. By this he means that a need on a lower level will become more significant if higher-level needs are frustrated or are not feasible. But Alderfer has the same opinion as far as deprivation of needs is concerned: he too believes that people are prompted into action if they experience a deficiency (that is, a deprivation of their needs).

Frustration-regression hypothesis

5.2.2   McLelland's theory

Maslow and Alderfer assume that everyone's needs are fixed and thus are innate. McLelland has a different opinion: needs are learnt. He believes that in the first years of a human life a personal need profile is developed. During the development of this personal profile, a particular need becomes dominant. With further development of life this functions as a 'steering' instrument. McLelland identifies three needs profiles (1971):

1 *Performance need.* This need is directed toward providing a good performance. The person looks for challenges, both during work and in other activities.
2 *Power need.* This is a need to obtain influence and control over people.
3 *Affiliation need.* This mainly concerns the building up of good relationships.

Performance need

Power need

Affiliation need

Research has shown that one can indeed discern a dominant need within the needs profile. At the start of the 1980s, Kotter and Kolb investigated higher and lower management and hypothetical dominant needs. The investigation showed that within higher management, performance and power needs were particularly dominant, but that lower management chiefly possessed an affiliation need.
McLelland is of the opinion that acquisition of a needs profile takes place mainly during the first years of a life. It does not change after that stage. Other researchers do not endorse this. They believe that the needs profile can develop further during life, dependent on situations and experiences: the needs profile is situation-dependent.

McLelland's theory could have particular significance if used to determine the kind of needs profile required in order to effectively carry out particular functions within organisations. For a salesperson, is the performance need particularly essential? For an account manager's private banking, is the affiliation need most important? The dominant need profile could form an important criterion in selection procedures or assessment of employees.

5.2.3   Vroom's expectancy theory

For his approach to motivation, Victor Vroom has chosen another perspective: a process orientation. A process-oriented motivational theory deals with the issue of the motivational processes of employees and attempts to explain why these processes take the form they do. Gaining an insight into this will enable motivation to be influenced.
Vroom assumes that an employee will act to achieve a certain goal. For Vroom it is not important what the real motivation is. Expectancy theory (1964) states that an employee is inclined to act in particular way based on the expectation that his action will have a particular outcome. The motivational process is comprised of three variables or steps:

Process-oriented motivational theory

Expectancy theory

Temps happier than permanent staff

Temporary workers are happier and healthier than permanent employees, according to new European research. A study of 642 staff from 19 organisations in the UK, ranging from factory workers to professionals, showed that temporary workers were half as likely as permanent employees to say that work caused them anxiety. The study is part of European Union research across seven countries, involving more than 5000 workers. The results were similar in all countries.

Temporary workers were more satisfied with their jobs and less likely to experience work overload. Yet they were almost twice as likely to feel job insecurity and nearly half as likely to be on their preferred con-tract of employment. These surprise findings could be because temporary workers had more healthy exchanges with employers than their permanent counterparts. More attention should be given to the experiences of permanent workers. Continuing to improve the quality of jobs in general and increasing the number of healthy relationships between workers and employers could be necessary. Permanent workers were more likely to feel that the psychological contract with their employer had been violated, which would have an adverse impact on their well-being.

Source: People Management, January 2006

Expectancy

1 *Expectancy.* This variable indicates how effort relates to performance. How does the employee estimate what is required for his or her efforts to produce the desired performance?

Instrumentality

2 *Instrumentality.* This variable indicates how performance and reward are related. Will a good performance indeed yield rewards to the employee?

Valence

3 *Valence.* This variable indicates the attractiveness of the reward.

The motivational process is shown in Figure 5.1.

According to the expectation theory, an employee will perform better:

- The greater the chance of good results in his / her estimation
- The greater the chance of he / she obtaining certain rewards
- The higher the rewards

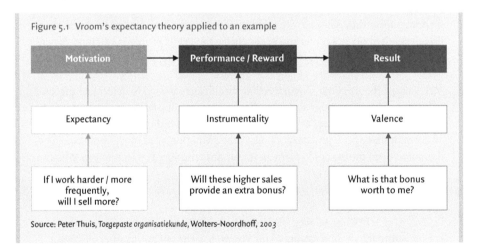

Figure 5.1 Vroom's expectancy theory applied to an example

Source: Peter Thuis, *Toegepaste organisatiekunde*, Wolters-Noordhoff, 2003

According to the expectancy theory, the extent of motivation can be expressed by the following equation:

Extent of motivation = expectancy × instrumentality × valence

It is important to realise that these variables cannot be seen as being separate from each other. Instead, they form a trinity. Managers wanting to exert an influence on the employee must therefore keep the entire picture in mind.

5.3 Personality

When we talk about a person we usually have a picture of that person in our mind. We may describe him using concepts such as 'persevering' or 'difficult to work with' or 'somewhat volatile'. What we are in fact doing is characterizing that person: summarizing his or her character by attaching labels based on our experiences of the person or on what we have heard about him. We also have an image of the behaviour that belongs to a certain personality. This behavioural image allows us to explain or predict his or her behaviour.

An individual can be defined as a combination of psychological characteristics that are characteristic of that person. Just as with motivation, people will usually look at personality from various angles. It is particularly important for organisations to have knowledge in this respect, because the characteristics of the person and the characteristics of his or function must match each other.

Individual

Researchers have developed many different personality models. In this section we will focus on three of these models:
1 The Enneagram (Section 5.3.1)
2 The Myers-Briggs Type Indicator (Section 5.3.2)
3 The Big Five model (Section 5.3.3)

5.3.1   Enneagram

The Enneagram is an ancient model. The word is Greek and the components 'enneas' and 'gramma', mean respectively 'nine' and ' what has been written'. The model is used to describe the human personality and to explain behaviour. In the sixties and seventies of the previous century, psychologists in the USA adapted the model to fit our times. The Enneagram is shown as a nine-pointed figure within a circle. Each point represents a type of personality (Figure 5.2).

Enneagram

According to the Enneagram, every person has one basic type of personality, and this personality is not subject to change. However, while the basic type will remain unaltered, one can develop it by expanding on it and giving it depth.
A description of the nine personalities is given below.

How to make your mark in a new job

Do your homework. You have done a great deal of research to get the job offer. Keep digging. Absorb the company's literature, spending time absorbing the language of the organisation.

Begin by focussing on people. In your first two weeks of the new job your first strategy is to listen, learn and ask intelligent questions.

Hit the ground running. Learn cultural codes quickly, particularly how much should be confirmed in writing and how decisions are made. Work out the cycle of routine activities. Learn as much as you can about procedures and standards.

Watch your step. Be careful if you are tempted to suggest new ideas and working methods at this stage. Try not to criticise the way the job is already

done. You might be able to make some tentative suggestions about methods that you have used. Better still, show some respect and enthusiasm for what you find rather than challenging everything from day one!

Get networking. Sit next to new colleagues every day at lunch. Seize opportunities to visit other departments and branches. Show interest in your new colleagues' jobs and problems, and show you are impressed by what they do.

Look for quick wins. Decide (or seek permission) to implement two or three changes that are low on cost and high on imagination.

Source: People Management, March 2006

ADVICE

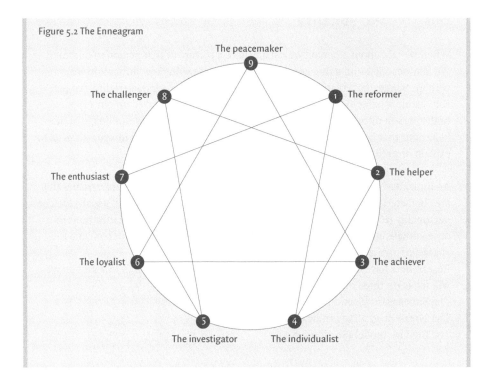

Figure 5.2 The Enneagram

The peacemaker 9
The challenger 8
The reformer 1
The enthusiast 7
The helper 2
The loyalist 6
The achiever 3
The investigator 5
The individualist 4

The nine personality types

1 The reformer
- is good at evaluating
- believes in corroborating things in a responsible and rational way
- is critical when phrasing questions, especially those concerning definitions and underlying principles
- is good at reasoning, arguing and discussing
- surveys the consequences of words and actions
- is irritated by people who pretend to be experts
- does not want to make mistakes and is afraid to make them
- does not like self-satisfaction in colleagues
- is particularly annoyed by ignorance, nonchalance and stupidity
- has difficulty with emotional expression

2 The helper
- is spontaneous and expresses what bothers him
- senses what others need
- has social skills
- has ready access to his emotions
- is personally committed and brings depth into important personal relations
- finds it hard to limit his helpfulness
- finds it hard to recognise and respect the borders of others
- finds it hard to put a lid on his or her emotional explosions
- pays a lot of attention to the needs of others and sometimes not enough to his own
- needs to be mindful of not seeking too much appreciation

3 The achiever
- success is important: the sky is the limit
- has will power, where there's a will, there's a way
- is effective and efficient, the fastest way is the best, irrespective of the consequences
- is good at realizing goals
- can reduce complexity to simplicity
- senses what is 'in' and what potential that has, and can anticipate this well
- has a positive way of speaking, thinking and acting and has a dynamic and energetic appearance
- believes that something has value if it is useful
- cannot stand failure
- finds it hard to acknowledge when things are not going well

4 The individualist
- feels compassion is important in this world
- has a sense of aesthetics: things must be beautiful
- authenticity is important
- can analyse well and sees the problem quickly
- has a rich imagination and ethical vision
- is alternately introverted and extroverted
- talks with intense expression in his / her words and gestures
- does not like superficial contacts or small talk
- has a creative way of life
- is not always capable of sketching a positive self-image

5 The investigator
- is detached, does not mind other people's business
- values self-determination highly: it is up to me to decide whether to share something private with others
- values being autonomous
- can go deeply into certain subjects
- acquires expertise patiently
- is good at being alone
- is good at putting order into complex matters
- is discreet and can keep a secret
- cannot stand dependence

6 The loyalist
- loyalty is very valuable: you have to keep your appointments
- practical applicability is important: you have to know what you can do with it
- finds strength important: in this society, you have to be strong
- is punctual when executing tasks
- can detect mistakes well
- has a talent for designing structure and procedures; looks for concrete solutions
- high tempo of thinking, mostly also of acting and speaking
- can quickly scan the environment to locate what is happening, who is where and what is wrong
- finds it hard to make mistakes
- finds it hard to admit his shortcomings

7 The enthusiast
- find the world fascinating
- functions less well when he / she is not enthusiastic
- is attracted to the extraordinary and finds the ordinary too restricting
- is versatile and sees many ways of approaching things
- sees various options and is not easily caught out
- is a fluent speaker and a fascinating narrator
- can generate ideas
- opens up new horizons, focusses on possibilities, sees potential, develops a new vision easily
- has trouble with routine, limitations, measures, seriousness and borders
- talks a lot about emotions but rarely shows them

8 The challenger
- the result is important
- is direct: to postpone something is to renounce it
- needs a challenge
- has will power: if I want something, I get it done
- is a natural leader: delegates well
- is good at detecting the weak spot of another
- is a witty speaker with humour
- is protective: stands up for himself and friends
- has respect for opponents that dare to resist and fight him
- does not want to be emotionally vulnerable

9 The peacemaker
- values solidarity and unity in the group
- strives for harmony, balance and equilibrium
- feels unpleasant when the atmosphere is not good
- believes that people are equal: basically, every human being is equally important
- believes in the goodness of human beings: there is something good in everyone
- is helpful, caring and attentive, knows how to be impartial
- is a patient and usually also a hard worker, is versatile and sees things in perspective
- is usually kind-hearted and those around find that he / she radiates peace, is slow to anger
- has trouble with conflicts in which he is personally involved
- finds it hard to say 'no' and show his limits

According to the Enneagram, humans intuit the world in three ways: via thinking, feeling and instinct. These three intuitions are related to body parts:

1. thinking   → the head
2. feeling   → the heart
3. instinctive   → the belly.

While every person makes use of all three ways of intuiting the world, one is dominant in the basic type. From these intuitions follow the nine personality types. Without slipping into caricatures this comes down to:

- The personality types 5, 6 and 7 are focussed on the head. The have a strong tendency to think and their basic emotion is fear.
- The personality types 2, 3 and 4 are focussed on the heart. These types have a strong tendency to feel. Relationships and the opinions of others are important for them. The basic emotion of these personality types is shame.
- The personality types 1, 8 and 9 are focussed on the belly. They are directed to the 'being' of things and themselves. They have a strong urge to show their importance, their significance. People of this type quickly feel guilty. Their basic emotion is anger.

How useful is the Enneagram? In the first place, the Enneagram offers the possibility of getting an insight into one's self. Which type am I? What are my personality characteristics, what are my strengths? How could I develop my basic type further and how can I become more aware of my less pleasant sides? Which leadership style fits my type? Where are the stress pitfalls? The Enneagram can be used for such situations and applied on an individual basis.

There are also other ways of using the model. It is a good instrument for relationships with others. When you work together you are confronted with people who are likely to have another basic type. Just being aware of this is already a step in the direction of improved communication and cooperation. It also constitutes a good tool for managers. What types are successful in particular functions? What types need to be represented in a team in order to realise its goals? The Enneagram also offers way of coaching employees and of obtaining better insight when directing people.

See Table 5.1 for an overview of the nine personality types and their specific characteristics.

Table 5.1 The nine personality types and their specific characteristics

Type	Good at	What gets in the way	Leadership style	Growth challenge
Type 1 The reformer	Reasoning, evaluating	Fear of making mistakes	Deliberate, well-argued, correct, demanding	Type 7 More easy-going, allowing humour, joy as a goal in itself
Type 2 The helper	Empathy, emotional expression	Needing to be liked	Emotional, wants to receive explicit appreciation. Not a typical leader	Type 4 Genuinely sensing the other's pain
Type 3 The achiever	Results-oriented, enthusiasm	Having to score	Positive, dynamic, the end justifies the means	Type 6 More loyal, more critical
Type 4 The individualist	Ethical vision, rich imagination	Seeing another's misery	Not very structured, not a leader by nature	Type 1 More rational
Type 5 The investigator	Specialisation, discretion	Invasion of one's privacy	Focussed on content, not a leader by nature	Type 8 Standing out more
Type 6 The loyalist	Solving problems	Not being in command of a situation	Based on rules and procedures, loyal, finds it hard to delegate	Type 9 More relaxed, having more faith in the environment
Type 7 The enthusiast	Generating ideas	Limitation of freedom	Loose, no strong need to lead	Type 5 Holding back, more discrimination
Type 8 The challenger	Removing obstacles, delegating	Own weakness	Natural leader, confident, impatient	Type 2 More empathic, more emotional expression
Type 9 The peacemaker	Maintaining harmony, mediating	Conflict, saying no	Reassuring, uniting, not always clear	Type 3 More purposeful, more assertive

Source: www.intermediair.nl

5.3.2 Myers-Briggs Type Indicator[1]

A model that is frequently applied is the Myers-Briggs Type Indicator (1980). The psychiatrist Carl Jung laid the basis for this model around 1920. B. Myers and K. Briggs used his results to develop the model further. The model can be used to estimate a person's personality. It is based on the assumption that individual preferences exist. Differences in individual behaviour can be largely explained in terms of these preferences, which are as follows:

Myers-Briggs Type Indicator

1 Social interaction: extravert   or   introvert
2 Data collection: sensing   or   intuitive
3 Decision-making: thinking   or   feeling
4 Styles of decision-making: judging   or   perceiving.

People will exhibit a preference for one of each of these alternatives, choosing either the former or the latter. It needs to be stressed that one preference is no better then another.

We will now explain what the various options imply. Myers and Briggs abbreviated them to the first letter of the word.

1 Social interaction or 'uploading':
- Extravert / extraversion (E): the individual prefers to derive his or her energy from the outer world, such as from activities, people and objects. He or she is directed to action and experience and he is broadly oriented.
- Introvert / introversion (I): the individual prefers to derive his or her energy from the inner world, including thoughts, feelings and ideas. He or she is shyer and more withdrawn and prefers to concentrate on a limited number of subjects.

Uploading

2 Data collection or 'observing':
- Feeling / sensing (S): the individual prefers to concentrate on information obtained by connections, patrons and meanings.
- Instinctively / intuition (N): the individual prefers to concentrate on information obtained by the five senses and practical applications.

Observing

3 Decision-making or 'deciding':
- Rational / thinking (T): the individual prefers to make decisions based on logic and an objective analysis. He / she is not influenced by emotions of others.
- Sensitively / feeling (F): the individual prefers to take in consideration what is important for people. He / she takes the wishes of others into consideration and strives to obtain harmony.

Deciding

4 Styles of decision-making or 'living':

- Judge / judging (J): the individual prefers a planned, organised way of life. He / she has a clear purpose and is directed to it.
- Observant / perceiving (P): the individual prefers a flexible, spontaneous approach and keeps all options open. He is flexible and adapts easily.

The answers people select to a variety of questions will make it clear what positions this person will adopt on these four scales. There are eight possible positions. If we combine go these positions, sixteen types arise.

To take an example, someone may be a INFJ-type. An INFJ-type is introverted, intuitive, sensitive and judging.[2] He / she is stable, scrupulous and takes pity on others. He / she is persevering, original and does what is necessary or wanted. He / she is respected because of his / her integrity.

This indicator can also be used to explain individual behaviour and for personal development, team building, communication improvement and coaching.

5.3.3   The Big Five model[3]

Finally, we will briefly describe the Big Five model. This model was developed in the 1990s. From 1980 onward, a lot of research went into reaching a scientifically acceptable division of personality qualities. Combining many different studies finally resulted in five personality factors, the so-called 'Big Five of the personality' (see Table 5.2).

Table 5.2 The five dimensions of the Big Five model

Big Five dimension	Factors
Open (O)	• original, artistic • creative, curious • investigating, critical • contemplative, abstract • unconventional, broad
Conscientious (C)	• systematic • orderly, punctual • efficient • thorough, meticulous • persistent, strong-willed
Extroverted (E)	• expressive, talkative • exhibitionistic • straightforward, uncomplicated • dominant, assertive • self-assured, firm • active, energetic • proactive, intense
Agreeable (A)	• helpful, tolerant • friendly, sympathetic • modest, mild • discreet, courteous • flexible, interested • cooperative, good-natured • adapts to others • easygoing
Stable (S)	• quiet, imperturbable • calm, relaxed • level-headed • well-balanced, stable • independent • autonomous

Source: Prof.dr. P.G.W. Jansen, *Organisatie en Mensen*, Uitgeverij H. Nelissen, Baarn, 1996

It is also called the OCEAN model, according to the first letters of the five dimensions of the model, where stability is replaced by neuroticism.

The Big Five model provides a framework of concepts relating to general personality qualities. Individuals will obtain various scores within these dimensions, giving an insight into the personality of the person in question.

How do the Big Five dimensions and working behaviour / work performances relate to each other? Do particular scores based on personality characteristics affect a person's work performance? Research shows such a connection exists. A number of examples are shown in Table 5.3.

Table 5.3 Relationship between Big Five dimensions and working behaviour / performance

Dimension	Suitable for	Explanation
Open	• learning form training courses • management	Prepared to acknowledge one's own mistakes and willingness to try out new behaviour are important factors for learning.
Conscientious	• all professions • all job criteria (promotion, performance, learning from training courses etc.)	A sense of order and performance motivation will turn out to be important for work effectiveness.
Extrovert	• management • commerce	There is a positive connection between extroversion and sales results
Agreeable	• function performance	Being agreeable is seen as being very important. Agreeable people make things happen and hold things together.

Source: Prof.dr. P.G.W. Jansen, *Organisatie en Mensen*, Uitgeverij H. Nelissen, 1996

5.4   Attitude

The final individual concept to be discussed is manner or attitude. An attitude is a relatively consistent response to particular circumstances. These circumstances can vary: they may be a person, a situation, an object, an organisation and so on. Everyone has a certain attitude with respect to particular circumstances.
Experiences in the past give rise to attitudes. These experiences may have occurred in childhood, during study, in the groups to which you belong and of course, to work-related experiences. Formation of attitudes takes place throughout one's entire life and can change under particular circumstances. Attitudes are therefore not a matter of hereditary.
Interestingly, attitude and behaviour have much in common. If someone has a particular attitude to a certain subject, he or she will also act accordingly. It is useful for organisations to be aware of what gives rise to a certain attitude as well as how that attitude will affect behaviour. Insight into this can be helpful in guiding and coaching as well as in selecting employees. Unwanted behaviour can be analysed and by giving the person an insight into the origins of his or her attitudes, possibly corrected.

Attitude

A person's attitude may be affected by three aspects.
1 *Cognitive aspect.* The cognitive aspect concerns knowledge. A person refers to various sources (including personal experience) to obtain information about a subject.

Cognitive aspect

2 *Affective aspect.* The affective aspect has to do with feelings or emotions. Feelings exert a strong influence on people's attitudes. In fact, attitudes are primarily formed via this aspect.

Affective aspect

Motivation a management challenge

Keeping 'ideas people' inspired may require ingenuity on the part of their supervisors, according to a survey from the Creative Group. When asked to name their biggest challenge, nearly one third (30%) of executives cited motivating employees. Finding qualified staff came in as a close second (28%). Training ranked third on the list: 14% of executives reported it as a management obstacle.

Source: The creative group (www.thecreativegroup.com), 2006

Behavioural aspect

3 *Behavioural aspect.* Information and emotions will tend to manifest themselves in particular behaviour.

5.5   Motivating people

This section will deal with issues relating to the methods that organisations and / or managers use to motivate their employees. We will deal not only with financial incentives but also with how tasks are formulated and objectives stated.

5.5.1   Motivating by means of financial incentives

That financial incentives increase motivation is an accepted fact. However, research has shown that it is mainly effective in the short term and a higher income is not the prime motive. A challenging job and personal development are usually more motivational. However, financial incentives keep people on the move. Financial incentives are rewards for performance: the employee will receive a wage increase in proportion to the extent that he / she provides the agreed performance. Performance rewarding is an example of motivation that is extraneous to the job (see Section 5.2).

Financial incentives

It is essential to strike a good balance between the performance to be furnished and the rewards provided in return. This is not just a matter that concerns the organisation and the individual employee, but increasingly also a social problem. At what level should the financial incentives provided to executives be fixed? When are such motivational methods socially justified? Many organisations have developed performance rewarding criteria not only for the top level of management, but also for other employees at many other levels of the organisation. Performance rewarding is usually tied to a certain basic salary. A variable reward is then paid on top of this basic salary.

Highest Paid CEOs

Europe			United States		
Company	Name CEO	Compensation	Company	Name CEO	Compensation
1 L'Oreal	Owen Jones	$32 Million	1 IAC / Interactive	Barry Diller	$295Million
2 Novartis	Daniel Vasella	$20 Million	2 Capital One	Richard Fairbank	$249Million
3 Axa	Henri de Castries	$13.8Million	3 Babors industries	Eugene Isenberg	$203 Million

Source: Fortune Magazine (www.fortune.com), 2006

Organisational characteristics that matter to job seekers

	Characteristic	%
1	Offers challenging and interesting work	60%
2	Recognises and rewards accomplishments	58%
3	Provides an opportunity for fast career growth and advancement	44%
4	Is financially strong	42%
5	Is people oriented	42%
6	Offers flexible work arrangements	41%
7	Is innovative	33%
8	Is approachable	27%
9	Fosters a team-oriented environment	27%
10	Is a global company	26%

Source: Accenture, 2006

Financial incentives can take many forms. The most frequent are:

- *Bonuses.* A once-only payment for an agreed performance. A bonus may also be awarded if a particular contribution has been made.   *Bonuses*
- *Profit sharing.* This is a payment in the form of a percentage of the obtained net profit in a certain year. The height of the sum depends on the net profit obtained and consists of a percentage of it.   *Profit sharing*
- *Shares-option arrangement.* This is a payment in the form of shares. The employee has the right to buy shares for a fixed price in the future.   *Shares-option arrangement*

5.5.2 Motivation by means of task design

While financial incentives constitute an example of motivation extraneous to the job, motivation of employees via the job itself is an example of motivation that is intrinsic to the job. Research has shown that employees whose motives are intrinsic to their job obtain a high degree of satisfaction from their job. To provide work-based motivation involves compiling a range of duties attuned to the needs of a specific employee. The employee will view his or her job as a challenge to which he or she gradually adapts. The tasks to be performed can be made attractive in three ways:

- *Task enrichment.* Elements of a qualitatively higher level are added to the range of duties.   *Task enrichment*
- *Task enlargement.* Elements of a qualitatively equal level are added to the range of duties.   *Task enlargement*
- *Task rotation.* Employees rotate the tasks they perform.   *Task rotation*

The subject of task design is treated further in Chapter 9 (Section 9.2).

5.5.3 Motivating by setting high objectives

A good way to motivate people is to require optimal performance of duties. To do so is to call on the best the individual can offer. Motivation via the setting of high objectives is known as the theory of objectives. The theory of objectives involves agreeing on specific objectives in order to improve performance.   *Theory of objectives*

Not all agreed-on high objectives will lead to motivated employees. To do so the objectives must satisfy a number of conditions. They are[4]:

- The objectives should be high but realistic.
- The objectives should be specified.
- The objectives should be accepted by the employees.
- There has to be regular feedback on progress.

Include 'flow' in your job!

What would happen if the best moments of your life happened at the office? That would be 'flow', and thanks to the American psychologist Mihaly Csikzentmihalyi, more and more businesses want to know about it.

Csikzentmihalyi describes flow as a condition of heightened focus, productivity and happiness that we all intuitively understand and hunger for. In the last few years, many major companies have realised that being able to control and harness this feeling is the holy grail for any manager, or even any individual, seeking a more productive and satisfying work experience.

How can companies get the best out of their workers or create more compelling connections with their customers? Without flow, there is no creativity, and creativity is a requirement, not a frill. Exceptionally creative people reported the greatest sense of well-being while pursuing challenging activities.

In a flow state, people engage so completely in what they are doing that they lose track of time. All sense of self recedes. At the same time, they are pushing themselves beyond their limits and developing new abilities. The best moments usually occur when a person's body or mind is stretched to capacity. People become more self-confident, capable, and sensitive. The experience becomes 'autotelic', meaning that the activity actually becomes its own reward. To improve life, one must improve the quality of experience. A state of flow has the advantage that it enables people to escape the state of distraction, depression and dispiritedness that constantly threaten them. So flow, flow, flow.....

Source: *Fast Company*, December 2005

SMART principle

The SMART principle is an aid that can be used to formulate objectives. The SMART principle indicates what conditions should be met for the desired objective:

- *Specific (S)*. The purpose must be described as concretely as possible. The purpose should not be liable to different interpretations and must not be formulated in terms that are too general.
- *Measurable (M)*. The purpose must be formulated quantitatively. If the purpose has been formulated quantitatively it will be controllable. These must be some kind of standard.
- *Acceptable (A)*. The purpose has to be accepted by the person or persons that have to realise the goals.
- *Realistic (R)*. Realisation of the goal should be done with an acceptable amount of effort. The goal must be challenging but not impossible to reach.
- *Time-fixed (T)*. The goal must be reached within an agreed period.

An example of a SMART objective is increasing the volume of trade of product X by 5% measured in euros in the Netherlands in 2008.

5.6   Emotional intelligence

While a high IQ, some extra studies or specific technical knowledge are important, this is not all that is needed. Emotional intelligence (EQ) is just as important as or even more important than IQ. Emotional intelligence is more general in character than merely the capacity to understand other people and to deal with others in an appropriate way. It also concerns one's own personal emotions. Dealing with one's own emotions rather than excluding them makes it easier to assess a tense situation and to control an imminent conflict.

Emotional intelligence

A general definition of the concept of emotional intelligence is 'a series of non-cognitive capacities, competencies and skills that influence an individual's success and his or her ability to meet demands and counter environmental pressure'. The five main EQ qualities are[5]:

1 *Self-awareness.* People with a high EQ are conscious of their feelings.
2 *Emotional control.* People with a high EQ are positive about their own qualities and are not easily dismissed.
3 *Self-motivation.* People with a high EQ are able to deal with things in the longer term.
4 *Empathy.* People with a high EQ are good in interpreting the feelings of others.
5 *Social skills.* People with a high EQ can deal equally well with both familiar figures and strangers.

The concept of emotional intelligence became well known after the publication in 1995 of *Emotional Intelligence* by the psychologist and Harvard instructor Daniel Golemen. His book *Working with Emotional Intelligence* (1998) served to increase familiarity with the concept.

Emotional intelligence is an ability that exerts a big influence on every aspect of our functioning, and thus on personal and social success (see Table 5.4).

Table 5.4 Five components of emotional intelligence

Component	Definition	Characteristic
Self-awareness	• The capacity to recognise and understand your moods, feelings and motives as well as their effects on others.	• Self-confidence. • Realistic self-assessment. • Sense of humour and relativity
Emotional control	• The ability to control destructive impulses or emotions or to redirect them.	• Reliable and honest • Can handle unclear situations • Open to change
Self-motivation	• A passionate desire to work for non-financial reasons or status. • The tendency to put a lot of energy and persistence into realising goals.	• Strongly competitive spirit. • Optimism, even when facing failure. • Strongly committed to the organisation.
Empathy	• The ability to understand what drives others on the emotional level. • The ability to treat others with sensitivity	• Experienced in encouraging and retaining talent. • Cross-cultural sensitivity. • Experienced in delivering services to clients and customers.
Social skills	• Skilled at managing relationships and to build networks. • The ability to identify common interests.	• Effective in complementing changes. • The ability to influence others. • Experienced in the development and management of teams

Source: Daniel Goleman, *Working with Emotional Intelligence*, Bantam Books, 1998

5.7 Overloading, stress and stress prevention and burnout

An employee is strongly psychologically influenced by experiences and events occurring during work. Work penetrates into the private lives and leisure activities of the employee. Negative emotions have an especially great influence on one's private life. Employees who are not happy during work will often not be happy in their private lives either, regardless of how long they spend at home or on holidays. Strikingly, while work-related emotions nearly always have an effect on one's private life, the opposite is less likely to hold. During work, little thought is given to family or holidays, though major private problems may influence the quality of one's work.

We will now deal with the topics of overloading, stress, stress prevention and burnout.

5.7.1 Overloading

Overloading can take four different forms, namely:

Emotional overloading

1 *Emotional overloading.* This factor has the biggest influence on private life. Concerns, problems and feelings of satisfaction or pleasure are taken home. The mood there is determined by the positive or negative experiences of the past working day.

Physical overloading

2 *Physical overloading.* After a busy and strenuous day, the employee comes home tired. His / her only interest is in food, TV or sleep. He / she does not have the physical strength or time for a lively private life.

Attitude and behaviour overloading

3 *Attitude and behaviour overloading.* The views and behaviour exhibited in the employee's life are strongly related to social experiences during work. An employee with a job which requires much strength and has little space for showing feelings will have trouble showing feelings of attachment and tenderness at home.

Existential overloading

4 *Existential overloading.* People who are dissatisfied with their job will encounter psychological problems more than others. A failed career may cause a deep depression which extends to all aspects of life.

Long-term tension makes employees insensitive to events in their private lives and will diminish their ability to enjoy things when they are not at work.
Emotional outlets such as feelings of enjoyment, sorrow, rage and pleasure are suppressed. Psychological withdrawal is also typical (as the French say: 'Il n'est pas disponible').

FIGURES & TRENDS

Working hours

In most rich countries, the average worker spends much less time at work now than in the early 1990s. In Japan the number of hours has dropped by 6.5% since 1994. The decline is slowing in Germany, where hours even increased a little from 2003 to 2004. The OECD cautions against comparing how hard different countries work, because one nation's figures are not comparable with another's.

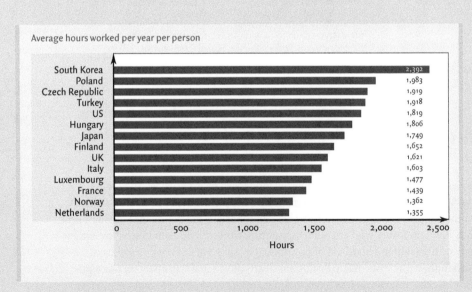

Average hours worked per year per person

Country	Hours
South Korea	2,392
Poland	1,983
Czech Republic	1,919
Turkey	1,918
US	1,819
Hungary	1,806
Japan	1,749
Finland	1,652
UK	1,621
Italy	1,603
Luxembourg	1,477
France	1,439
Norway	1,362
Netherlands	1,355

Source: *The Economist*, July 2006

5.7.2 Stress

Stress is the main cause of overloading. A distinction can be made between stress as a condition and stress as part and parcel of a process. By stress as a condition we mean the psychological and physical situation that arises when demands are made of a person which he or she cannot satisfy. Process-related stress can be seen as the physical, psychological and social changes that are connected with stress as a condition.

Stress as a condition

Process-related stress

The so-called Michigan model sums up the consequences. This model depicts a number of stages that stress progresses through (see Figure 5.3). In it the influence of stress on the health of a person is described as a chain of events. Job requirements and threats to the job may lead to feelings of stress that then cause physical and psychological reactions and eventually have a negative effect on the health. Personal and environmental factors may decrease or increase the problems.

Michigan model

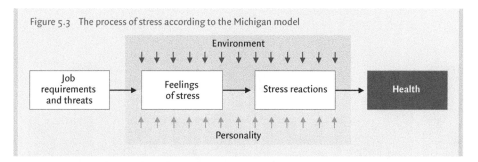

Figure 5.3 The process of stress according to the Michigan model

Personality factors can be subdivided into:
· Effect-increasing factors such as excessive and aggressive fixation on the job and a need to alienate oneself from other people
· Effect-increasing factors such as good social contacts, self-confidence, flexibility and a good physical condition

The environmental factors are:
· Physical working conditions
· Ergonomic factors
· Safety risks
· Work and leisure times
· Travel times and circumstances
· Private circumstances.

There are, however, a number of factors will cause stress with degree of high certainty and which are characteristic of the work situation though are not connected to the personality or to environmental factors:

a Problems at work that have occurred for a long time or recur regularly (e.g. when a person realises that he cannot perform his task well).

b Problems at work with important consequences for the individual's performance within the organisation and from which he is unable to withdraw (e.g. not being aware of volume of trade and profit objectives for which he / she is responsible).

c A psychologically burdening work situation that is not easy to change (e.g. having to collaborate with a colleague with whom one has great difficulty).

d Problems at work that radiate to other functional areas such as the situation at home (e.g. job uncertainty, uncertainty about the future).

Shell: our approach to safety

The safety of employees is of paramount importance. Our business principles include a commitment to provide employees with good and safe working conditions. They also set out specific requirements for Health, Safety and the Environment (HSE). Our goal is for all our staff and contractors to return home safely every day.

Commitment and Standard

We manage employee safety as part of our overall approach to HSE. Our HSE Commitment and Standard, adopted in 1997, includes a commitment 'to pursue the goal of no harm to people'. They are supported by a Group Procedure for a Management System, which includes requirements to:

- assess risks, implement measures to control them and to recover in the event of control failure
- have emergency response procedures in place that are tested regularly
- investigate and report serious incidents and near-misses so we can learn from them and help prevent similar incidents
- conduct audits to review and verify the effectiveness of the management system

All Shell companies, contractors and joint ventures we control are required to manage safety in line with our HSE Standard.

Source: Shell (www.shell.com), 2006

But not all stress is disastrous. According to Selye, a Canadian endocrinologist who made a lifetime study of stress, complete freedom from stress equates to death. A distinction also needs to be made between positive and negative stress, where positive stress may even strengthen the manager and invigorate him. Positive stress is also known as 'positive tension' in the literature.

Research has shown that stress at work is caused mainly by:
- Time pressure
- Long working days
- Too much work
- Personal relationships
- Employee quality

5.7.3   Stress prevention

Given the frequent occurrence of stress amongst employees and the possibility of
serious consequences, it is important to look at ways of reducing or even preventing
stress at work.

Three different approaches to stress prevention or reduction can be identified,
namely the organisational approach, the individual problem-solving approach and
stress treatment and stress management.

The organisational approach

The organisational approach involves making changes to the job or more successful
attuning of the employee to the job. The changes may take various forms:
· Changing of the organisational structure
· Changing of the reward structure
· Clarifying the expectations that the organisation has of the employee
· Improving individual opportunities and changing work demands
· Training of management in human-directed leadership
· Improvement of communication
· Provision of personnel facilities (child care, a social worker)

In general, organisational approaches fall within in the area of social management.

The individual-directed approach

This approach focusses on the individual and aims at increasing problem-solving
capacity and the ability of the employee to cope with the work burden. It puts an
emphasis on the organising of training programmes that are directed at:
· Acting in a purposeful way
· Assertiveness
· Cooperation
· Time management
· Acting to solve problems
· Dealing with conflict
· Social skills

Handling and management of stress

Individual stress management is aimed at decreasing a person's susceptibility to
stress, not at solving the problems that cause the stress. This approach cannot be
considered separately from the individual-directed approach. It overlaps or combines with it.

Stress-management techniques are based on scientific stress research. Research has
shown that stress can be countered by good social support, a capacity to put things
into perspective, self-confidence and physical relaxation. The following techniques
are utilised:
· Techniques for the learning of physical relaxation (e.g. meditation).
· Techniques for improving the physical condition (e.g. company fitness, jogging).
  Enterprise fitness is care of the physical and spiritual health of an organisation's
  employees. Participating in company fitness may have a favourable influence on sickness absence, work output and business culture. Physical exertion relieves the body
  and the mind and reduces stress elsewhere. In Japan and the United States, company
  fitness forms part of the company's strategy for improving business culture.
· Systematic desensitisation. This is a technique based on the experience that sensitivity to tension is decreased when it is offered bit by bit and increased gradually.
· Cognitive structuring. With the help of this technique, people are taught to look real-

istically at the requirements and possibilities.
- Techniques for increasing social support. Improving social skills makes people more prepared to fall back on each other in times of need.

Research in Dutch companies has shown that these three approaches are used in combination with each other in the prevention of stress.

Employees stay fit at Nike

'At Nike EMEA headquarters we work hard, play hard'. It's an old adage, but we believe that you will perform better in the workplace if you have the opportunity to perform on the track, the field, the court and the gym. We would not be the world's leading sportswear brand if we did not.
The facilities at the EMEA (European, Middle East and Africa) Headquarters defy comparison. Whether you want to compete, get fit, or simply have fun there is something for you. And it's not just the obvious things like football, track, and basketball. We have a fully equipped gym offering classes. Under supervision of professional trainers, Nike employees can work out during days and weekends. We have an employee store where you can buy products at a substantial discount, and a superb cafeteria offering healthy food (and the odd treat).

Source: Nike (www.nike.com), 2006

5.7.4 Burnout[6]

Burnout

Burnout can be seen as a specific form of stress. Burnout may occur after some time in occupations where the contact between people is frequent and intensive. Burnout is difficult to describe because it has so many guises. An often used definition is the following: a psychological problem of emotional exhaustion, self-alienation and a feeling of decreasing competence. Someone who had suffered from burnout once described it as follows: 'Burnout is a neglected situation of overstrain that has been going on for a long time. It manifests itself in various complaints in the physical, psychological, emotional, cognitive and social areas'. The definition given includes three core concepts of burnout:

Emotional exhaustion

1 *Emotional exhaustion.* An important characteristic of burnout is loss of energy and a feeling that the emotional reserves are exhausted. It is accompanied by feelings of frustration and sadness because those suffering from burnout realise that they cannot continue to give themselves fully or to accept responsibility in the same way as they had done before.

Depersonalisation

2 *Depersonalisation.* Sufferers have a tendency to consider people as objects rather than individuals. This attitude is often accompanied by a negative and cynical attitude towards employees and the job.

Feelings of decreasing competence

3 *Feelings of decreasing competence.* There is a tendency for sufferers to judge themselves in a negative way. They have a feeling of performing less well and of being less successful in their work. They have a negative self-image.

Burnout differs from stress in that if the causes of the stress are taken away, one can quickly recover and regain one's balance, while with burnout the symptoms remain. Burnout is the product of an accumulation of stress factors and frustrations over a long term, usually years.

What causes burnout? It is too simplistic to assume that burnout is related solely to the job itself. It has various causes. They can be divided into three groups: work-related causes, personality related causes and organisation-related causes.

Work-related causes

The causes of work-related burnout are:

- *Interpersonal contact.* Burnout that occurs when the job requires direct and intensive contact with other people, sometimes in emotionally loaded circumstances.
- *Role conflicts.* Burnout that occurs when there are different (and often contradictory) expectations about the division of roles between employees.
- *Role ambiguity.* Burnout related to lack of clarity about the employee's role and how to fill it.
- *Job overloading.* This may take the form of either qualitative or quantitative job overloading. With qualitative overloading the person often finds the work too difficult and has the feeling of missing some of the skills required to do the job efficiently. Quantitative overloading occurs if there is too much work and if the person has the feeling of not being able to complete the tasks within the time available.

Personality related causes

The following personality related characteristics may cause a burnout:

- *Biographical.* Some people are more susceptible to burnout than others. Burnout occurs mainly in the beginning and middle stages of one's career. People who are single, who have no children, who are highly educated or are female have a higher risk of burning out.
- *High expectations.* Expectations (personal and within the organisation) about position and personal suitability may contribute to a burnout.
- *Career progression.* People who are successful in their careers are less sensitive to burnout.
- *Social support.* There is a relationship between social support and burnout. The chance of a burnout increases the less support there is. Help and support from colleagues and the top manager directly responsible, as well as the opportunity to develop and put skills to use play a big role in avoiding burnout.

Organisation-related causes

Apart from the quantity of work, the chance of a burnout is much larger with increasing frequency and intensity of contact, especially in situations without positive feedback. Individuals need affirmation and clarity from their clients and their organisations.

Finally we shall look at the Job Demand-Control model of Kasarek (1979). His model relates job demands to control. Job Demands have to do with the quantity and the level of difficulty of the work. Control has to do with the extent to which an employee can decide how to execute his or her duties: for example, how quickly he / she carries out the work activities. Other aspects that may play a role in this respect are the influence and control that an employee (or executive) has on his work or on that of others (see Figure 5.4).

The model suggests that in principle, job demands should cause no problems. The risk of stress and burnout arising will increase only if large job demands are accompanied by little control. A high level of tension will build up, and in a situation where an executive carries responsibility for certain affairs but cannot actually influence or control them, this will cause stress, especially if the executive's superior also exerts a lot of pressure to achieve results.
High job demands combined with large control will give rise to a positive situation. Because the employee can do something about the situation causing the stress, he or she will experience the tension as being of a positive kind.

Interpersonal contact

Role conflicts

Role ambiguity

Job overloading

Biographical

High expectations

Career progression

Social support

Job Demand-Control model
Job demands
Control

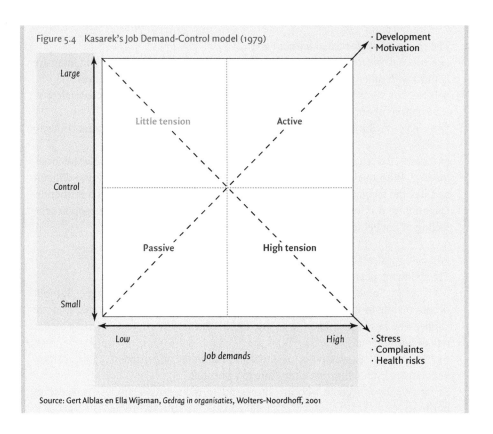

Figure 5.4 Kasarek's Job Demand-Control model (1979)

Source: Gert Alblas en Ella Wijsman, *Gedrag in organisaties*, Wolters-Noordhoff, 2001

5.8   Intuition and creativity

This section will deal with intuition and creativity within organisations. We will also describe how creativity in organisations can be encouraged and organised.

5.8.1   Intuition

Intuition

Intuition is often mentioned as a key to success. Intuition is knowledge obtained via non-logical ways of thinking. Intuition can be described as an immediate awareness of the truth of the matter not based on thinking in concepts or reasoning. A characteristic of intuition is that connections are made between certain entities, leading to a conclusion or idea and skipping a number of logical steps. Intuition is often a premonition, a knowing without knowing why.

Intuition appears to play an important role in scientific breakthroughs. As Albert Einstein stated, 'there are often no logical roads leading to particular laws: they are inspired only by intuition based on the instinctive insight of experiences'. He called his theory of relativity the best discovery of his life.

Many executives in the business world agree that intuition plays a very important role in how they manage. It is not always possible to model decision-making processes, and inner feelings are often decisive in the final decision. Moreover, intuition can play an important role in the creation of ideas, the choice of alternative strategies and the acceptance of new employees.

The interest that the business world is increasingly attaching to intuition is evident in the fact that it forms part of training sessions for higher management.

Sparking creativity at Ferrari

Ferrari is best known for its cutting-edge cars. Less well-known are its creative approaches to creativity. Four years ago they launched a program called Formula Uomo that combines the creation of an architecturally pleasing and healthy work environment with the development of some unusual training and wellness programs. It is a way to link employees' well-being and personal growth with company performance. Staff members can have an English or German breakfast, lunch or tea. Having multilingual employees is good for Ferrari.

They also run a program called Creativity Club that is designed to get the employees' 'creative juices' flowing. There are six programs where employees meet various types of artists and can attend classes where these artists teach their skills. The goal is for the employees to learn about how artists generate ideas and solutions. In these sessions, all levels of the company mix comfortably and get to know one another. These events were designed to activate people's deep, individual creativity –something that traditional training activities rarely do. The hope is that the employees will make links between the inspiration they get and their professional activities at Ferrari. Ferrari wants to let the creativity metaphor work at the level of their unconscious.

Source: *Harvard Business Review*, April 2006

5.8.2 Creativity

Creativity

Just like intuition, creativity is indispensable within a modern organisation. According to Picasso, the famous painter, creativity is destructive but in a positive sense. By this he means that creativity demolishes old views, insights, opinions or feelings in order to create something new. We can describe creativity as a way of thinking that produces new ideas and new solutions.

Figure 5.5 shows that without creativity, innovation is impossible.

In areas where figures and rationality provide insufficient information for the development of new products (such as new planes and cars) creativity is crucial to decision-making. The creative process consists of three steps:

1 Generation of ideas
2 Screening
3 Implementation

1 Generation of ideas

There are many ways of generating ideas: for example, brainstorming, synectics, lateral thinking, day-dreaming and the COCD technique. The first three examples will be dealt with in Chapter 7, which deals with decision-making.

The COCD technique has nothing to do with decision-making. This technique was developed by the Belgian Center for the Development of Thinking Creatively. According to the theory, the human mind thinks in patterns which give rise to a chain reaction. It is a process of moving from one certainty to another rather than from one truth to another. If the basis is wrong, the certainties that emerge will not be reliable ones, with disastrous results.

COCD technique

What the COCD theory boils down to is that people can be encouraged to be creative by learning how to build onto their initial premises and thus develop a new kind of logic. According to Prof. R. de Bruyn of the University of Antwerp, the instruments used by COCD include:

· Searching continuously for more possible alternatives.
· Taking an arbitrary idea and drawing connections between this idea and the problem.
· Looking for obvious ideas and eliminating these in order to develop new views.
· Isolating the problem by considering the case from a part of the whole.
· Sketching the problem three times, eliminating one particular dimension on the fourth occasion and looking at the consequences.

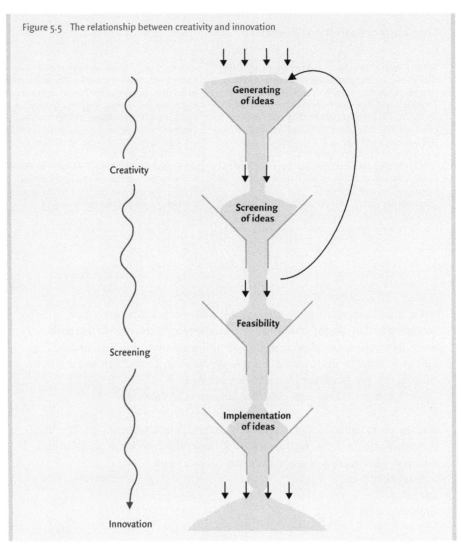
Figure 5.5 The relationship between creativity and innovation

2 Screening

Screening involves first 'filtering' ideas and then testing them for commercial feasibility. Ideas can be screened in various ways. They include:

a *Clustering of ideas.* With this method, all available ideas are written on separate pieces of paper and subsequently put on a table or a wall. Then the ideas are divided into as many categories as possible. This will produce a number of manageable groups. Each group will now have become a higher level idea.

b *Setting up hurdles.* This involves the use of increasingly more challenging criteria which an idea must satisfy in order to pass the filter. It is important for everybody to agree with the chosen hurdles as well as with the order in which these are placed.

c *Weighing up of ideas.* Every aspect of an idea is assigned a value. This allows them to be compared with each other and selected.

d *Speculating.* If information is minimal and a decision has to be made quickly, this method might be chosen. The general knowledge and intuition of the decision-maker are important factors when using this method.

3 Implementation

After the ideas have been screened, they can be implemented: innovative solutions such as new products, services or methods are put into practice.

New creativity drives Disney!

At the beginning of 2006 Disney acquired Pixar for $7.4bn (6 bn euro) in a bid to revive the animation department that is not only its heritage but also the engine of its businesses – from theme parks to consumer products. Wall Street analysts have focussed on what role Steve Jobs, Pixar's founder and chief executive of Apple Computer, might play at Disney. Yet the essential figure in the deal may be Mr Lasseter, who has been given the creative keys to the Magic Kingdom and is being asked to restore inspiration to a pioneering company that has lost its way. For Mr Lasseter, who began his career at Disney and then went on to become the creative force behind Pixar's Animation's unprecedented run of hits, from 'Toy Story' to 'Finding Nemo' and 'The Incredibles', this is a triumphant return.

Mr Lasseter studied at the California Institute of the Arts, a Disney-founded school near LA. In the late 1970s, animation was a dying business. The turning point in his career came when he saw 'Tron', one of earliest examples of computer animation. In 1983, he bolted for Pixar, a fledging studio that Mr Jobs had founded in northern California. The studio's breakthrough came with the 1995 'Toy Story', the first full-length computer-generated film. While audiences were dazzled by Pixar's technology, Mr Lasseter has always pointed to the value of good storytelling.

The Disney acquisition of Pixar provided a unique opportunity to make Disney / Pixar movies available on Apple's iPod.

Meanwhile, talent began leaving Disney for Pixar and DreamWorks Animation. The release of 'Chicken Little' in 1995, the studio's first full-length film made entirely using computer animation, seemed to confirm that a company once synonymous with animation was now an also-ran in the field. As Mr Lasseter and others seek to restore the Magic Kingdom's lustre, they face a number of challenges. They will have to nurture Pixar's creative spark within a much larger corporate parent. 'Pixar studios is exactly what Disney used to be. Thankfully, it will be soon that way again', said one animator, all but certain of a fairytale ending.

Source: *Financial Times*, January 2006

Organisation of creativity

Although everyone admits that having creative managers and employees is of vital importance to the continuity of an organisation, many big organisations seem to unintentionally slowing down the development of their employees, and with this their potential to be innovative. While companies pay a lot of attention to increasing productivity and quality, creativity is barely promoted. But creativity is the very factor needed to promote productivity. It can do the following:

Organisation of creativity

· Improve the quality of solutions to organisational problems
· Indicate how to be profitably innovative
· Motivate people
· Bring personal skills to a higher level
· Act as a catalyst to group performance

Creative managers have means at their disposition to stimulate and enhance the innovative mentality, and with this also the performance of both the organisation and the employees. Figure 5.6 shows how creativity can be organised. The following expands on this.

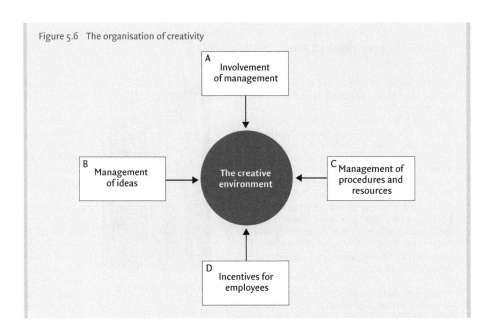

Figure 5.6 The organisation of creativity

A Involvement of top management. The involvement and support of top management is crucial to organising creativity in the organisation as a whole. Their commitment will become visible in the form of making budgets available for organised creativity and showing interest in ideas via active participation and evaluation of creativity in its concrete realisation.

B Management of ideas. This involves not only developing methods for stimulating the creation of ideas, but also having a positive attitude towards this. This will come to expression in the establishment of a creative climate.
The following are some of the ways that one can consider: using a suggestion box system, registering and evaluating ideas systematically or raking together all sorts of 'odd' ideas. Avoid slating brand new ideas.

C Management of procedures and resources. The development of administrative aids such as planning methods, follow-up methods, building networks of experts and creating databases of ideas is central to this.

D Stimuli for employees. Employees can be encouraged to be creative in the following ways:
· Giving them access to information (e.g. literature, conferences, seminars)
· Making budgets available
· Making time for developing creative ideas available to them
· Letting them travel
· Giving them support in their research

5.9   Core quadrants[7]

In the training world, 'core quadrants' is a frequently used instrument. It is a method developed in order to obtain an insight into an individual's strengths and weaknesses, their challenges and so on. The idea behind it is that people cannot be changed in more than superficial ways. Their personal characteristics can be changed to a limited extent only. It is preferable to make people conscious of how they can develop further.

This instrument was developed by Ofman (1992) and gives an insight in a person's essential qualities: their 'core' qualities. Some examples of core qualities are a capacity for empathy, carefulness and decisiveness.

Essential qualities

A core quality is a positive quality. Sometimes it is hidden: only latently present. Everybody has a number of core qualities, though they differ from person to person. Each core quality has, however, also its pitfalls, its challenges and the things that provoke a sort of 'allergic reaction':

- *Pitfalls.* Each core quality has its dark side. The dark side represents an overdeveloped core quality. The core quality of flexibility can overdevelop into changeability, decisiveness into pushiness.

Pitfalls

- *Challenge.* A challenge is the polar opposite of a pitfall and poses the problem of how to keep core quality pure. In the case of the core quality of flexibility (whose pitfall is changeability) the challenge is a sense of order. The challenge can be seen as the component that holds the core quality in balance.

Challenge

- *Allergy.* An 'allergy' represents a challenge that has gone too far. The challenge can be seen as what an individual strives for. If this striving is overdeveloped it changes into an 'allergic reaction'. With the core quality of flexibility, there will be an allergic reaction to rigidity. Rigidity represents a surplus of the challenge to develop a sense of order.

Allergy

The four elements discussed can be shown in quadrant form. Figure 5.7 shows the quadrant of the core quality of flexibility.

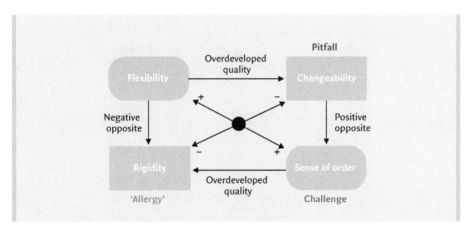

The 'core quadrants' instrument can be used as an aid to individual development and as an aid to problems with working with others.

Aid to individual development

The core quadrants can aid self-examination in various ways. They include the following:

- *The instrument can give an insight into a person's strong points.* When choosing a career, knowing one's strong points can be crucially important.
- *The instrument can give an insight into a person's behaviour.* It is consequently used during performance interviews. It can explain why people react in a certain way to situations or to the behaviour of other persons.
- *The instrument can be used as an aid to a person's development.* Certain situations can be simulated (by means of role-playing, for example) and behaviour then analysed. Appropriate behaviour models for future situations can then be developed.

Many activities take place within a collaborative context. When one works with others, one is confronted with the core qualities, pitfalls, challenges and 'allergies' of others. Since our behaviour is partly determined by the behaviour of others, core quadrants can serve a useful function. They can explain both one's own behaviour and that of others. During interactions with each other all kinds of mechanisms come into play that may hamper cooperation. If a situation occurs where somebody's pitfall corresponds to with someone else's allergy, a conflict may arise. They can be regarded as two negative positions. Insight into the mechanism of this situation can be very enlightening.

To sum up, the core quadrants developed out of an individual perspective. In the training world, it is an instrument that is used frequently. It can also be used at the organisational level. Why do certain branches of organisations behave the way they do? Why do they react in a certain manner to the behaviour of other divisions? What kind of mechanism determines the typical reaction of a sales division or a production division?

Figure 5.8 shows two other examples of core quadrants.

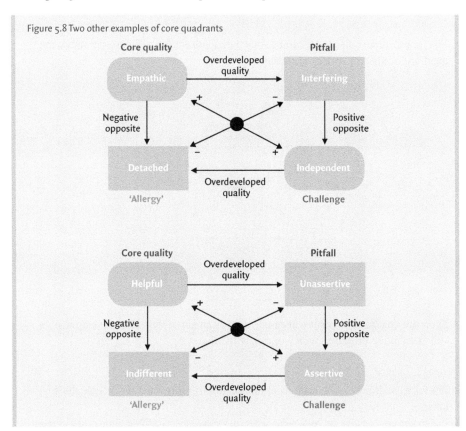

Figure 5.8 Two other examples of core quadrants

5.10   Individual tests

Sections 5.1 up to and including 5.9 have dealt with various basic concepts of individual behaviour and explaining, analysing or predicting it. They have given an insight into the theories that have been put forward. We may also wish to know what motivates us as individuals. What are my personal characteristics? To what extent do I have emotional intelligence? What is my degree of sensitivity to stress? It is outside the scope of this book to include tests. However, tests are readily available via the Internet, including tests relating to:

- IQ
- EQ
- The Big Five model
- The Enneagram
- The Myers-Briggs Indicator
- Stress

The possibilities are virtually unlimited. Other interesting tests include:

- The style of learning test
- Belbin
- Personal effectiveness
- Styles of management.

Tests are easy to find on the Internet.

5.11   Groups and teams

Being active within an organisation means working with other employees. In definitions of an organisation collaboration is always mentioned: every kind of collaboration towards a common purpose. Goal-oriented and appropriate collaboration is an important aspect of successful organisations. This part of the chapter will consider the phenomenon of collaboration from various viewpoints.

A group is formed when two or more persons collaborate consciously in order to realise certain objectives. An interaction takes place as they realise that they need each other to achieve their purpose. Taking this definition of a group will make it apparent that organisations are made up of many active groups. They may include projects, committees, brainstorming sessions and management teams. Branches may be considered as being a group. Groups form the binding factor within organisations.

Group

Teams: myths about diversity

Myth	Reality
1 Diversity is divisive	1 If properly explained by management, diversity can bring a unifying esprit to the company's effort.
2 There is a single business case for diversity.	2 Each company has its own business case study
3 The hardest part of diversity is recruitment.	3 The hardest part of creating a diverse workforce is retention of that workforce.
4 Diversity means lowering of standards.	4 Diversity can bring out the best performance in anyone.
5 If the CEO is on board, diversity will succeed.	5 If the rest of the top management is not committed as well, diversity will fail.

Source: Fortune (www.fortune.com), 2005

FIGURES & TRENDS

Different sorts of teams

Various types of teams may be found within modern organisations. They will differ according to type of task, the factors that impel or hinder learning and the behaviour that is required from the members. We can identify at least six different sorts of teams, defined according to two parameters:
1 Stable or new / changing tasks
2 Stable or new / changing membership

This is shown in the following figure.

Types of teams within an organisation

Stable tasks

	Stable team	Cabin crew
Stable membership	Virtual team (club)	New / changing membership
	Attack team	Evolutionary team
	Development alliance	

New / changing tasks

- Stable teams. These teams perform the same tasks or variations on it for a longer period, with a relatively stable crew. Two examples are a production line and a sales agency.
- Attack teams. These teams have usually been set up to do one-off tasks within a short time. The members usually come from other teams.
- Evolutionary teams. These teams handle long-term projects such as the development of a new product. The team membership is relatively instable as the members will come and go, depending on the phase of the project.

- Cabin crews. The members of these teams rarely come together: sometimes only once. Although the task stays the same and has to be done consistently, the team membership often changes (just as with the cabin crew of an airplane).
- Development alliances. These teams consist of two or more people who agree to exchange learning experiences such as off-line mentoring.
- Virtual teams. These teams are generally not recognised formally. The members work together on an ad hoc basis, having mutually understood goals.

Source: Management Executive, January / February 2004

We can categorise groups in various ways. The most obvious division is formal groups versus informal groups and virtual teams.

Formal and informal groups

Formal group

We denote a group as a formal one when it has a place within the structure of the organisation. This formal group can have a permanent or a temporary character. An example of a formal permanent group in an organisation is a management team. A formal temporary group could be a study group responsible for a computerisation project. When the project is completed the group is dissolved. A formal temporary group is also called a taskforce.

Informal groups

Besides formal groups, informal groups are also present in organisations. These are groups outside the structure of the organisations. Employees may choose to form a group themselves. These groups are mostly based on friendship and / or common interests. The importance of informal groups should not be underestimated. Communication between people in informal groups can be important for the development of policies and the execution of all kinds of activities as well as fort strengthening common standards and values in an organisation.

Horizontal, vertical and mixed groups

When the group members derive from the same hierarchical level of the organisation we are dealing with a horizontal group. Horizontal groups can be active at various hierarchical levels of the organisation. An important purpose of a horizontal group is the reaching of harmony and the coordination of particular activities.

Horizontal group

We denote a group as a vertical one when the group members originate from different hierarchical levels of an organisation. The purpose of a vertical group is usually to be found in the domain of communication. A combination of a horizontal and a vertical group is known as a mixed group.

Vertical group

Horizontal, vertical and mixed groups can be present as formal or as informal groups within an organisation.

Mixed group

These are traditional kinds of groups. Those characteristics are rather more out of the ordinary include:
- Virtual groups or teams
- Autonomously operating teams

Virtual teams

To an increasing extent, organisations have employees who are active in different countries. With large multinational organisations, the countries may be distributed over the entire world. With so many borders, collaboration is a special problem in this type of organisation. Modern information and communication technology means that there are new opportunities for this type of organisation. Collaboration no longer means meeting physically: members can now 'meet' each other via the digital highway. This can take place in different ways. Conference calls, and seeing each other 'live' by means of a 'video conference'. Exchange of information and communication can take place via a digital platform. A virtual team is also known as an electronic group network.

Virtual team

Collaboration in virtual teams means that organisations can save considerably on expenses and still reach the organisation's goals. It should not be forgotten that besides the technical problems of virtual teams, other problems can also play a role in virtual teams. The very fact that virtual teams often bring together people from different continents means that the composition of the team is an important issue too. A multiplicity of cultures might be present in a virtual team. This may hamper collaboration.

To see and experience each other physically remains important, even with new technology. Many organisations choose to arrange meetings with each other not only virtually but also physically (though these meetings are likely to be infrequent).

Geert Hofstede developed a model for obtaining an insight into the cultural differences between various countries. Cultural aspects obviously exert a lot of influence on behaviour, and organisations are no exception. Within the model, a culture is described in terms of the following five parameters:

1 *Power distance.* This is the extent to which power distance within organisations is tolerated by society. This acceptance varies according to society. Some societies tolerate a large power distance, while others prefer a small power distance as their basis. The relationship between executives and employees will be viewed differently.

Power distance

Figure 5.9   The cultural dimensions power distance and individual or collective attitude in picture

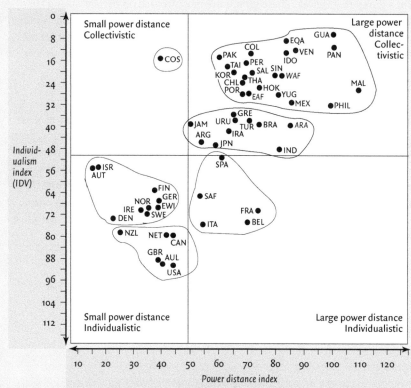

Abbreviation	Country name
ARA	Arab countries (Egypt, Iraq, Kuwait, Lebanon, Saudi Arabia, United Arab Emirates
ARG	Argentina
AUL	Australia
AUT	Austria
BEL	Belgium
BRA	Brazil
CAN	Canada
CHL	Chile
COL	Colombia
COS	Costa Rica
DEN	Denmark
EAF	East Africa (Ethiopia, Kenya, Tanzania, Zambia)
EQA	Ecuador
FIN	Finland
FRA	France
GBR	Great Britain
GER	Germany
GRE	Greece
GUA	Guatemala
HOK	Hong Kong
IDO	Indonesia
IND	India
IRA	Iran
IRE	Ireland
ISR	Israel

Abbreviation	Country name
ITA	Italy
JAM	Jamaica
JPN	Japan
KOR	South Korea
MAL	Malaysia
MEX	Mexico
NET	The Netherlands
NOR	Norway
NZL	New Zealand
PAK	Pakistan
PAN	Panama
PER	Peru
PHI	The Philippines
POR	Portugal
SAF	South Africa
SAL	Salvador
SIN	Singapore
SPA	Spain
SWE	Sweden
SWI	Switzerland
TAI	Taiwan
THA	Thailand
TUR	Turkey
URU	Uruguay
USA	United States
VEN	Venezuela
WAF	West Africa (Ghana, Nigeria, Sierra Leone)
YUG	Yugoslavia

Source: G. Hofstede, *Allemaal andersdenkenden*, ed. Contact, 2002

Virtual teams

Virtual teams are making a strong entry. A virtual team is a group of people who work together electronically to execute a collective project. E-mail, voicemail, videoconferencing, and other electronic modes are at their command. The various participants may come from different parts of the world. While physical contact between the participants of the virtual team will naturally remain important, it will only occur periodically.

What is the best way of assembling a virtual team? There are a number of important initial considerations to take into account:

1 Identify the team sponsors, the parties concerned and the supporters.
2 Develop a 'charter' describing the reasons for, the tasks of, and the goals of the project. One can best do this during a meeting where the different parties are physically present.
3 Select the team's participants. Teams usually consist of different kinds of participants: core staff members who work on the project regularly, and additional staff members who give support and advice, and consent to certain project activities.
4 Introduce the participants. Make clear why they have been selected for the project in question, introduce them to each other, make it possible for their questions to be answered and ensure good communication.
5 Summon a team orientation session. This is a very important initial activity. Meeting physically preceding the project will have a highly positive effect on the virtual team's results. Knowing each other and working on teambuilding will enhance the outcomes.
6 Make work arrangements. It is important to make arrangements about how certain matters (such as file structures, software being used, and who delivers what, how, and when etc) will be handled.

Source: *Mastering Virtual Teams: Strategies, Tools, and Techniques That Succeed*, D. Duarte and N. T. Snyder

2 *Avoidance of uncertainty.* The world around us is changing rapidly. Organisations as well as society at large are being confronted with these changes. Not every societal group reacts in same way to these changes. For one group, the variability of life constitutes a challenge; others will prefer to avoid change. A group with a high avoidance of uncertainty will have difficulties with risk-taking.

Avoidance of uncertainty

3 *Individual or collective attitude.* This has to do with the social structure within a societal group. A society with strong social and cultural values will help each other and show loyalty. This implies a collective attitude. In a society where the individual plays a major role, there will be a weaker social structure. A loose social structure implies an individual attitude.

Individual or collective attitude

4 *Masculine or feminine attitude.* Some societies value masculine qualities such as determination, toughness, the possession of material things and prosperity. Other societies attach much more value to relationships and the welfare of its people.

Masculine or feminine attitude

5 *Long or short-term orientation.* This aspect measures the extent to which societies retain their traditional values, are directed to immediate results and attach value to social obligations. A society that does this to a great extent is short-term directed. Long-term directed societies prefer to modernise traditions and to comply with social obligations within limits. A society of this type will place an emphasis on economy, perseverance and purposefulness. This dimension is sometimes called 'Confucian Dynamics'.

Long or short-term orientation

Hofstede investigated many countries in terms of these five dimensions. Figure 5.9 lists fifty countries and positions them within country groups according to the parameters of Power Distance and Individual or Collective Attitude.

A comparison of the countries shows considerable differences in attitude. An insight into the differences will enhance cooperation between the cultures. Culture will be discussed in more detail in Chapter 10.

Self-governing teams

Self-governing teams (also called autonomously working teams) are very much on the ascendant.

Traditional teams are known as functional teams and are composed of an executive and employees who are responsible to the executive. In self-governing teams, a group of employees is responsible for the activities to a certain degree. This group of employees makes the decisions necessary for carrying out the activities. These decisions concern both operations and management. In traditional teams, management tasks are reserved for the executive.

A self-governing team has to satisfy the following characteristics[8]:

· There has to be fixed group of employees who work together and are responsible as a team for all the tangible activities needed to supply a product or service to an internal or external customer.
· The team must be able to manage itself to a certain extent and to take responsibility for the tasks to be carried out, based on a common purpose.
· In order to do this, the team must have relevant information at its disposal and the necessary abilities and aids. The team has the authority to make independent decisions in relation to work.

Self-governing teams are not new. In Britain they were already active in the mines in 1950 and were jointly responsible for the entire process of mining coal.
The difference between a functional team and a self-governing team is shown diagrammatically in Figure 5.10.

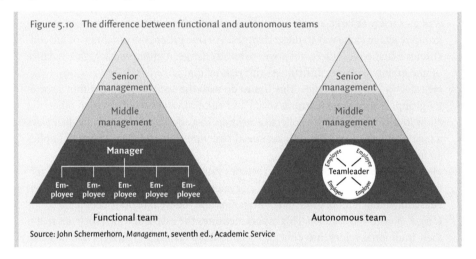

Figure 5.10   The difference between functional and autonomous teams

Source: John Schermerhorn, *Management*, seventh ed., Academic Service

By using self-governing teams to organise the activities, various different purposes can be reached. These purposes cover the following areas:

· *Management.* Making management more efficient and effective. Research has shown that self-governing teams can raise productivity as well as improving flexibility and customer service.

· *Quality of the work.* This concerns the employees themselves. Team work requires active involvement of the team members. People become increasingly willing to view their activities in terms of the team's common purpose. Team members are not only responsible for their own tasks, but also for the results achieved by the team as a whole. Self-governing teams often rotate their tasks. This gives the employees the opportunity to learn how to perform each other's tasks, thereby increasing the opportunities for further development.

· *Learning organisation.* With self-governing teams a situation will arise where more use is made of creativity and the learning capacity of the employees then is the case with functional teams, in which everybody is responsible is for his or her specific task only. Creativity and the learning capacity of the employees are important elements for organisations in a strongly variable environment.

5.12   Characteristics of groups

In this section we will deal with the specific characteristics of groups or teams, including the stages of group development, group cohesion and group standards. The objective is to give more insight into group processes.

Stages of group development
We all have experience in working in groups. If we are introduced to a group for the first time or assume a position within an existing group, we will perceive big differences in atmosphere and working style. Research has shown that groups develop throughout a number of stages. A well-known model is that of Caple. It deals with the stages of development of new groups working together intensively for a certain time. Their collaboration is thus temporary in nature. Caple observed five stages during the development of such groups:

1 *Formation of the group.* The group members have just met. During this period, the members get to know and understand each other. There is uncertainty within the group and the group members try to become acquainted with the rules and the purpose of the joint effort. During this stage, the group can be characterised as 'a collection of individuals'. *Formation of the group*

2 *Conflict within the group.* After some time the group members will start to show their true colours. Conflict situations will arise. Group members will operate in accordance with their own specific knowledge and insights and try to impose these on the activities and functioning of the team. Within the group, small subgroups who are in conflict with each other may be formed. This is known as 'clique formation'. This stage is important in the development of the group, because it eventually gives clarity about each other's contributions, position, opinions, approach and so on. The foundations are laid for a certain degree of group cohesion. During this stage, the group can be characterised as 'a starting group'. *Conflict within the group*

3 *Standardisation within the group.* In order to achieve its goals, a certain amount of unity must exist within in the group. While Stage 2 focussed on differences between the group members, during this stage, agreement within the group is sought and the members are more willing to make compromises. Their dealings with each other are more 'adult'. During this stage, the group can be characterised as 'an advanced group'. *Standardisation within the group*

4 *Group performance.* During this stage, everything is directed towards the joint effort needed to deliver a good performance. Effective team work is now imperative. The group is busy organising and performing their activities in such a way as to fulfil the purpose as optimally as possible. Conflicts may occur, but now they will tend to exert a positive influence on the final result. During this stage, the group can be characterised as 'an effective group'. *Group performance*

5 *Ending the group.* The purpose of the collaboration has been achieved. Group members will feel pride in what they have achieved. The group will often find a way to mark the end of their collaboration and to say goodbye. For some group members will be an emotional time; others will look back on it as mainly an instructive and interesting experience. *Ending the group*

It must be mentioned that the stages just described represent the standard. In actual fact, some groups do not even get to Stage 3, having already been dissolved or reconstituted, with some members leaving and others coming. If Stage 3 is not passed satisfactorily, this may diminish the results achieved via the joint effort. It may also cause scepticism about working together and such a feeling may run into the next project.

Group cohesion

An important aspect of a group is its cohesiveness. Group cohesion is the degree of mutual relationship within the group. The performance of a group is strongly dependent on mutual relationships. Solidarity and team spirit are an important characteristics of group cohesion. There is a relationship between cohesion and group productivity. This relationship is shown in Figure 5.11.

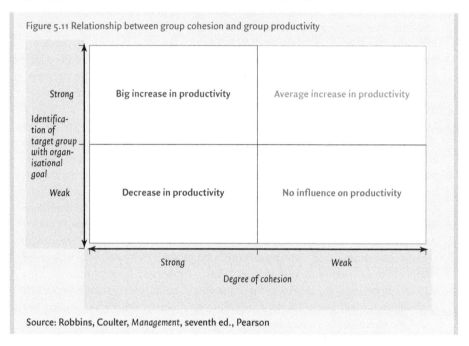

Figure 5.11 Relationship between group cohesion and group productivity

Source: Robbins, Coulter, *Management*, seventh ed., Pearson

'Group think' is especially characteristic of group cohesion. Group think is the tendency of groups to loose their capacity for objective judgement. This occurs especially in teams which are highly cohesive. Group members may become less critical toward each other, which will have an adverse effect on group functioning.

In view of this one may ask whether large groups perform better then small groups. Some general findings are given below:
· When fast results are required, small groups are more effective.
· The contribution of each member shows up better in small groups and there is less adopting of the opinions of others.
· Group members who contribute a lot to the group will also have also a big influence on the final result.
· The input of individual group members usually remains at the same level. Those who exert a big influence will continue to do so during the course of time.

Group standards

How should we deal with other? What kind of behaviour is acceptable and what is not? As a member of a group we are confronted with these questions at home, among friends and at work. Group standards will develop according to the extent of group cohesion. The greater the cohesion within a group, the more discussion there will be about group standards. Group standards can differ between groups. Group standards develop spontaneously. The following is an example of a group standard: 'We will always address each other with 'Mr' and Mrs / Ms' and we will always shake hands on meeting'.

Group standards can affect many situations, including mutual relationships, loyalty, the way that conflict is dealt with, contact with other branches and so on. Group standards are unwritten rules that determine group behaviour within a group. They indicate what behaviour is desired in particular situations. Groups standards are not comparable to formal rules within an organisation.

Group standards

Executives can make an important contribution to the development of desired group standards. An executive may, for example:

· Reward desired behaviour and punish unwanted behaviour
· Provide training sessions and promote team building
· Set a good example him or herself
· Select new employees on behavioural criteria
· Make standards debatable and talk about such matters with each other
· Show that the desired behaviour has advantages

5.13 Team management and characteristics of successful teams

Purposeful and efficient teamwork depends on a clear awareness of the various roles that need to be fulfilled within a team and the conditions needed to ensure purposeful and efficient team functioning.

Team members cannot be expected to perform every task, and the best results are obtained by effective division of roles. This is the secret of team management. The goals of team management are to create teams and delimit and divide the tasks within them in such a way as to optimise the results of the joint collaboration. In addition to fulfilling a functional and professional role, team members also have to fulfil a team role. One's professional ability, which is a function of one's position, is demonstrated via one's professional role. One's place within the organisational hierarchy is what is on show when one fulfils one's organisational role. These character roles are complementary: the one balances out the other. Management of team roles is based on three principles:

Team management

Professional role
Organisational role

1 Each role represents a quality.
2 People are naturally capable of successfully fulfilling two or three roles.
3 Group roles must be well divided and as much as possible in keeping with the team member's natural character.

In fact, the following key players must be present within every team: doers, thinkers, go-getters and people with feeling.

We will now examine team roles and team conditions.

Team roles

To obtain the best results from group efforts depends not only on the composition of the team. The conditions under which the team members and the team have to function are also important. How can we ensure effective execution of tasks? It is a complex matter and one that is affected by many different factors. The following roles must be filled for the work performed by the team to be effective:

Team roles

1 *The coordinator.* Organises and manages the activities of the team by using all the potential present in the team.
2 *The shaper.* Gives form and content to the activities of the team.
3 *The innovator.* The main source of innovation and new team ideas.
4 *The evaluator.* Analyses ideas and proposals, evaluates their usability and practical applicability in relation to the objectives of the team.
5 *The contact.* Examines external possibilities and makes contacts that may be useful for the team.
6 *The team worker.* Improves the performances of the individual team members.
7 *The organiser.* Converts general concepts and strategies into practical tasks and activities, and then ensures systematic execution.
8 *The quality guard.* Ensures that the team improves its efforts and that the task is completed.

Figure 5.12 illustrates these 8 roles. Individual team members are capable of filling more than one team role. This will depend on the main purpose of each role.

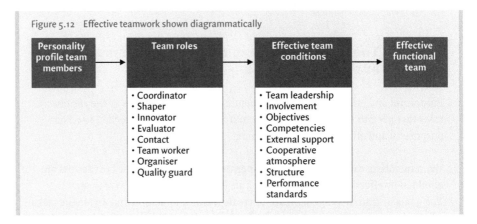

Figure 5.12 Effective teamwork shown diagrammatically

Personality profile team members	Team roles	Effective team conditions	Effective functional team
	• Coordinator • Shaper • Innovator • Evaluator • Contact • Team worker • Organiser • Quality guard	• Team leadership • Involvement • Objectives • Competencies • External support • Cooperative atmosphere • Structure • Performance standards	

Team conditions

Subsequently, attention must be paid to the team conditions needed for effective execution of the team roles. The following are some examples of team conditions:
1 Clear and vitally important objectives
2 A purposeful communication structure: the information system must not produce a superabundance of data (which would make it difficult to oversee matters) but those statistics needed to run the enterprise
3 Competent team members, both in terms of technical and of team skills
4 Identification with and involvement in the team
5 A cooperative atmosphere
6 The maintenance of performance standards
7 External support and acknowledgement
8 Leadership based on vision.

In this section on team management, we have considered team roles and team conditions. The question is how to get the best results from group work. Much research has been done into the effectiveness of working in groups. There is no doubt that effective group work has a positive influence on the enterprise's results. It has been established that an effective team has the following characteristics[9]:

- Clear objectives to which everybody is committed
- Coherence and unanimity
- Acceptance and acknowledgement of each other's cultural differences, plus mutual regard and insight
- A broad basis for trust between team members
- The capacity to solve problems and internal conflicts effectively
- The capacity to learn collectively from experiences
- Team members who know their own style
- A balance between on the one hand a number of different personalities and on the other the required abilities, divided equally among all team members
- Knowledge and acceptance of one's own team role and the team roles of the other team members
- Harmony between team role and the individual team members' functions
- A harmonious atmosphere at work in which people respect and trust each other, listen to each other and give each other useful feedback
- Open communication, with relevant information at everybody's disposal
- Ongoing training of the team members

5.14   Organisational conflict

Within organisations, situations may arise where the goals, interests, standards and values of individual employees or of groups of employees are incompatible with each other. If this means that individual employees or groups of employees are unable to reach their own objectives the situation can be described as one of organisational conflict.

Organisational conflict

Because organisational conflicts occur regularly, it is important for managers to be able to cope with them. Conflict within organisations has consequences for their performance and in extreme cases the survival of the organisation may be threatened. The relationship between organisational conflict and level of performance is shown in diagram form in Figure 5.13.

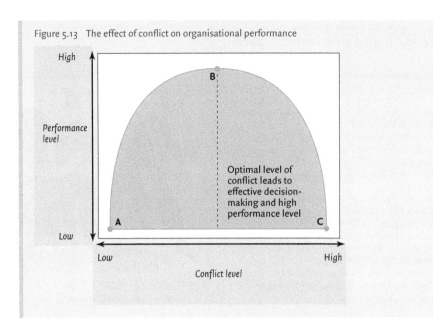

Figure 5.13 The effect of conflict on organisational performance

Figure 5.13 indicates that in the absence of conflict, performance is not necessarily optimal (situation A in the figure). This can be attributed to the employees (either as a group or individually) being insufficiently challenged to get the best out of the situation. Differences of opinion mean more discussion and hence better decisions. A certain degree of critical appreciation of each other is essential for making the right decisions (situation B). If there is too much conflict and those involved are only interested in pursuing their own purposes or playing political games, then the result will obviously be a negative influence on the performance of the organisation (situation C).

It can be concluded that organisational conflict has a certain function and should therefore not be avoided for the sake of doing so. To control conflict, it the important to have an insight into the various types and sources of conflict.

IN THE PRESS

Sources of frustration

Career bottleneck   The baby boom generation is a big one, with a lot of people competing for too few leadership positions in organisations that have been shedding layers of hierarchy. Next to job security, this is one of the biggest concerns of managers in their forties and fifties.

Work / life tension   Mid-career workers are sandwiched between commitments to children and parents, often at the same time that their work responsibilities are peaking.

Lengthening horizons   Those who are not accumulating sufficient wealth for retirement face the prospect of having to work many more years. Many of today's mid-career employees have been lavish spenders and sparse savers.

Skills obsolescence   Some struggle to adjust to new ways of working and managing in the information economy. Some hope that merely time or diligence will get them promoted into better and higher-paying jobs when what they most need is upgraded skills.

Disillusionment with employer   This includes insecurity and distrust following waves of downsizing, as well as resentment over the enormous compensation gaps between top executives and almost every other employee.

Burnout   People who have been career-driven for 20 or more years are stretched and stressed, find their work unexciting or repetitive, and are running low on energy and the ability to cope.

Career disappointment   The roles employees play and the impact of their work fail to measure up to their youthful ideals and ambitions.

Source: *Harvard Business Review*, March 2006

We can identify the following types of organisational conflict (see also Figure 5.14):
· Interpersonal conflict (such as conflict between individual employees)
· Conflict within groups (such as that within a department)
· Conflict between groups (for example, a conflict between the marketing and production departments)
· Conflict between organisational unities such as branches

Figure 5.14 Different types of organisational conflicts

Sources of organisational conflict

The following may cause conflict within organisations:
· *Irreconcilable purposes and time frames.* Conflict may arise if the employees derive from organisational entities (such as different departments, committees or branches) which have different purposes and different time frames.
· *Overlapping responsibilities.* Conflict may arise if the various employees or organisational entities feel that they are entitled to claim responsibility for the same activities or tasks.
· *Task dependence.* Conflict may arise if employees or organisational unities become involved in activities for which they are jointly responsible.
· *Different assessment and reward systems.* Conflict may occur if employees or organisational unities are assessed and / or rewarded differently.
· *Scarce resources.* Employees or organisational unities having to compete for scarce resources such as financial means and staff may create conflict.
· *Different status.* Difference in status between employees or organisational unities may become a source of conflict.

Figure 5.15 shows this in diagram form.

Managers have a duty to address and rectify organisational conflict between employees or organisational unities. A successful end to the conflict is only possible when employees or organisational unities are willing to compromise in order to be able to work together. Managers are able to give direction to this process by using conflict management techniques. Conflicts are easier to resolve if the various parties have an insight into what has motivated the other's point of view. Conflict will then become an issue for discussion. Other possible techniques include rotation of tasks, allotting temporary tasks to enable greater insight into the problems, transferring employees, and if the matter is no longer under control and no other solution can be found, dissolving the team.

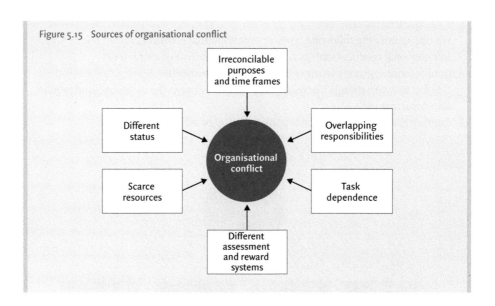

Figure 5.15 Sources of organisational conflict

Doing business in the United Kingdom

How the English organise and process information

The English are generally closed to outside information on most issues. They will participate in debates but are not easily moved from their perspectives. They are quite analytical and process information in an abstractive manner. They will appeal to laws or rules rather than looking at problems in a subjective manner. Company policy is followed regardless of who is doing the negotiating.

What the English accept as evidence

Objective facts are the only valid source of truth. Little credence is given to the feelings one has about an issue. Faith in few if any ideologies will influence decisions. They are the masters of understatement.

The basis for behaviour

The following three sections identify the value systems in the predominant culture: their methods of dividing right from wrong, good from evil, and so on.

The locus of decision-making

The English are highly individualistic, taking responsibility for their decisions, but always within the framework of the family, group, or organisation. Individual initiative and achievement are emphasised, resulting in strong individual leadership. They do not find it difficult to say 'no'. The individual has a right to his or her private life, and this should not be discussed in business negotiations. Friendships are few and specific.

Sources of anxiety reduction

There are established rules for everything, and this gives a sense of stability to life. Well-entrenched external structures (law, government, organisations) help to insulate them from life. They are very time-oriented, and anxiety is felt over deadlines and results. Emotions are not be shown in public; the phrase 'keep a stiff upper lip' says it all.

Issues of equality / inequality

There is an inherent trust in the roles people play (but not necessarily in the people) within the social or business system, and a strong feeling of the interdependency of these roles. There are necessarily inequalities in these roles, though people are assumed to be guaranteed equality under the law. There is some bias against ethnic groups. There is a high need for success, and decisions are made slowly and deliberately. Women have a great deal of equality in both pay and power.

Ten examples of English business power

1 The business hierarchy is as follows: the managing director (CEO in the US), the deputy (corporate vice president to US executives), the divisional officers, the deputy directors, and finally, the managers.
2 The English are normally more interested in short-term results than in the long-term future.
3 After a meeting, be sure to leave detailed data with your English partners.
4 The English do not often reveal excitement or other emotions; try to keep yours restrained as well. They also traditionally underplay dangerous situations.
5 Avoid the hard sell: don't push them into making a decision.
6 The English do not consider themselves European. This is vital when discussing issues to do with European Union.
7 While the English are often self-critical, visitors should avoid criticising their ways. Similarly, if they share their complaints with you, remain impartial.
8 If you go out after work, do not bring up the subject of work unless your English associates do, otherwise, you will be considered a bore.
9 Conversation partners maintain a wide physical space.
10 Gifts are not part of doing business in England. Rather than giving gifts, it is preferable to invite your hosts out for a meal or a show.

Source: *Kiss, Bow, or Shake Hands: How to Do Business in Sixty Countries*, by Terri Morrison, Wayne A. Conaway and George A. Borden, Adams Media, 2006.

Summary

This chapter has discussed employees both from an individual and a group perspective. At the individual level, general concepts of motivation, personality and attitude were examined. Motivation can be defined as an individual's inner readiness to engage in certain activities. Work-related motivation relates to the work itself; non-work-related motivation to the rewards derived from work. Three theories of motivation were discussed: those of Alderfer and McLelland, and Vroom's expectancy theory. Within organisations people can be motivated by means of financial incentives, task design and high targets.

An individual can be defined as the combination of characteristics that typify that person. Three models were discussed: the Enneagram, the Myers-Briggs Type Indicator and the Big Five model.

An attitude is a relatively stable position in relation to a certain subject. A lot of attention was given to overloading, stress and burnout. A distinction needs to be made between stress as a condition and stress as part and parcel of a process. Stress in the latter sense can be viewed as being the physical, psychological and social changes that are connected with stress as a condition. The Michigan model summarises a number of the phases of stress. Burnout is a specific form of stress and it can be described as a psychological condition of emotional exhaustion, self-alienation and a sense of decreasing competence. Some attention was given to emotional intelligence, intuition, creativity and the 'core quadrants', all of which can give an insight into a person's qualities, weaknesses, challenges and so on.

A group was defined, and various sorts of groups and their characteristics described. A group can be defined as two or more people who have chosen to work together in order to realise certain goals. Groups may take various forms: formal and informal, horizontal, vertical and mixed groups, virtual teams and autonomous teams. Two ways of typifying groups were discussed: phases of group development and group cohesion.

Team management involves team-building and dividing and defining tasks in such a way as to achieve the best results. Various roles are represented in teams: eight were described. Lastly, organisational conflict was discussed. When the goals, interests, norms and values of individual employees or groups of employees are incompatible with each other and when this results into individuals or groups not being able to realise their goals, this can be described as organisational conflict.

Definitions

§ 5.2 Motivation	The inner readiness of a person to perform certain actions.
Intrinsic work motivation	Motivation that relates to the work itself. People see their work as a challenge
Extrinsic work motivation	Motivation that is not intrinsically related to the work itself but to other factors.
§§ 5.2.1 Existential needs	Needs associated with material secutity.
Relational needs	Needs associated with good relationships with others.
Growth needs	Needs relating to personal growth and development.
§§ 5.2.2 Performance need	The desire to deliver a good performance.
Power need	The desire to influence and control other people.
Affiliation need	The desire to establish good relationships.
§§ 5.2.3 Process-oriented motivation theory	Theory dealing with the issue of the motivational processes of employees which attempts to explain why these processes take the form they do.
Expectancy theory	The inclination of an employee to act in a certain way based on his / her expectation that these activities will lead to a particular outcome.
§ 5.3 Personality	A combination of psychological characteristics that typify a person.
§ 5.4 Attitude	A relatively fixed opinion on a subject.
§ 5.5 Performance rewarding	An increase in salary based on the contribution made by the employees towards agreed performance targets.
§ 5.6 Emotional intelligence	A series of non-cognitive abilities and skills which influence a person's likelihood to succeed and help the individual to deal with the challenges and pressures emanating from their surroundings.
§§ 5.7.2 The state of stress	The psychological and physical situation that arises when a person cannot meet the set requirements.
Process-related stress	The physical, psychological and social changes that are connected with stress as a condition.

§§ 5.7.3 Dealing with stress and stress management	Aims to make an individual more stress-resistant rather than resolving the problems that initially caused the stress.
§§ 5.7.4 Burnout	A psychological process of emotional exhaustion, self-alienation and a growing sense of decreasing ability. Burnout is a result of continual and excessive strain which has been neglected for a long time.
§ 5.8 Intuition	Knowledge obtained via non-logical ways of thinking.
Creativity	The banishing of old opinions, views, thoughts or feelings followed by the production of something new.
Innovation	Solutions put into practice in the form of new products, services or processes.
§ 5.9 Core qualities	Positive qualities that form an essential part of a person, such as a capacity for empathy, carefulness or decisiveness.
§ 5.11 Group	Two or more people who have chosen to work together in order to realise certain goals.
Virtual teams	An electronically linked group which does not need to meet in the flesh in order to work together since teamwork is now possible via the digital highway.
Self-managing teams	An autonomous team which takes responsibility for all their own activities to a significant degree.
§ 5.12 Group cohesiveness	A sense of solidarity and team spirit within a group.
Group thought	The tendency of group members to lose their critical ability.
Group norms	The unwritten rules that determine how members behave within a group. They indicate how members are expected to behave in particular situations.
§ 5.13 Team management	The creation of teams followed by the defining and allocating of tasks in such a way as to obtain optimal results.
§ 5.14 Organisational conflict	Organisational situations in which the goals, interests, norms and values of individuals or groups of employees are incompatible with each other. When this results in individuals or groups not being able to reach their goals, it is termed organisational conflict.

Statements

Decide whether the following statements are correct or incorrect and give reasons for your answers.

1 Work-related motivation has to do with the rewards obtained for doing work.
2 EQ is less important than IQ.
3 Kasarek's model shows that a big workload does not necessarily lead to burnout.
4 Creativity goes hand-in-hand with the destruction of old notions or ideas.
5 'Core quadrants' is not an instrument for use in situations where people work together.
6 Multicultural cooperation is usually not an issue with virtual teams.
7 According to Hofstede, a collective attitude entails a small power distance.
8 A functional team is a team that consists of a manager and her / his immediate subordinates.
9 Group thinking has to do with feelings of solidarity and team spirit.
10 Organisational conflict will arise if employees (either individually or in groups) cannot realise their objectives.

Theory questions

1 a What is the difference between motivation intrinsic to the job and that extrinsic to the job?
  b Which motivation would an employer prefer and why?
2 How can a dominant profile, as described by McLelland, be an important criterion in a selection procedure?
3 How can the Enneagram be useful in the work situation?
4 What is the difference between stress and burnout?
5 a To what uses can Hofstede's five dimensions be put?
  b Explain these dimensions.

Practical assignment

According to Caple, group development goes through five phases. What are they?
1 Describe Caple's model using additional information from the Internet and other sources.
2 Take a group which you are part of or have been in the past. It may be a project group, a department, a company committee or a sports group. Give a short history of the group. Who are / were the members? When did the group start and what was its goal? What problems did the group encounter and have they been resolved? If so, how? You can do this on your own or together with other group members.
3 Using Caple's model, describe your group's phases of development. Was there (for example) any initial uncertainty and did the members examine the situation? How did the group acquire cohesion and was there any forming of cliques? What about conflict? Did the group reach phase three? Was the teamwork effective and did the team achieve its goals?
4 For each phase described under C, indicate its positive and negative contributions to the development of the group.

 For answers see *www.marcusvandam.noordhoff.nl.*

CHAPTER 5 | *Individual and teams*   **211**

Mini case study

EXERCISES

Sadet and Ersin and stress

Sadet, Ersin and Ebru are a young family. Sadet and Ersin are both in their early thirties and Ebru is their five-year-old daughter. Both parents work four days a week: Ersin as a composer and audio engineer in a sound studio that mainly composes sounds for TV commercials, and Sadet as accounts and project manager with a communication design bureau. Lately, both have been suffering from stress. Ersin, who is calm by nature and does not easily become agitated, is nevertheless often tense because of the situation at his work. The company is small and the owner / director, Gizem Marmara, is often away on acquisition and customer visits. When he is away he doesn't want to be disturbed and he expects Ersin to take over. This is quite a responsibility for Ersin and it also means that he cannot finish his own work. On his return, Gizam wants to discuss in great depth what has happened during his absence. Often, he reverses decisions Ersin has made and that gives Ersin the feeling that he has worked for nothing. This annoys Ersin, but he finds it difficult to discuss it with Gizam. Gizam is short-tempered and also often stressed as the business is not going particularly well. Sales are declining in spite of his efforts to acquire more customers and orders. Ersin often has a headache when he comes home. He should work out at the gym more, but where can he find the time? Fortunately, he enjoys being with his family; and when he is playing with Ebru or discussing the day

with Sadet, his stress vanishes into thin air. Once a week he spends an evening out with his friends and that also helps.

Sadet also has her problems. She is a bit of a fidget, and on top of that she has a very busy life. There have been cutbacks in the company she works for, and in her department three people are having to do the work that was previously done by five people. Sadet is not really enjoying her job anymore, but it is difficult to find something else. The situation with her child is also stressful. Both she and Ersin spend one working day taking care of him; the other three days he is at the day nursery. The nursery is at quite a distance and it is Sadet's task to bring and collect Ebru as Ersin often has to work overtime when Gizem is not there. So for three days a week, she really has to leave her office at five thirty, pray there will be no traffic jams, collect Ebru, race home and do the cooking, except when Ersin is home earlier and has already started in the kitchen. Lately, they have been ordering a pizza or buying a meal at a Turkish take-away: expensive and not particularly healthy. After such a busy day, Sadet often has problems falling asleep. Unfortunately, they cannot afford to work less since they really need the money for the mortgage. But she goes swimming once a week with a friend and she also relaxes completely when she spends time with Ebru, or when the three of them go out for the weekend.

Questions

1 Which forms of overloading are evident in this case?

2 a Analyse Sadet and Ersin in terms of stress-creating factors according to the Michigan model (effect reinforcing and protecting personality factors, environmental factors, characteristics of the work situation).

   b Based on this analysis, what conclusions could you draw in relation to Sadet and Ersin and the stress they are suffering?

3 Based on your conclusions, to your mind, what possibilities for stress prevention and reduction are available?

4 Are Sadet and Ersin running the risk of burnout in your opinion?

5 To what extent can Kasarek's model be applied to the work situations of Sadet and Ersin? Can you give any recommendations?

E-mail case study

To:	Gunter Schach
Cc:	
Bcc:	
Subject:	Conflict and Core Quadrants

Message:

Dear Gunter,

I need your advice as I have a problem with a colleague.

You know me well, so you know that I am a flexible, creative and enthusiastic being. OK, I know I can also be too casual and I sometimes don't finish what I have started and I can create an almighty mess. I have a new colleague called Heike. Things are not really going well between us. She does her work very well but she's fairly inflexible. Everything has to go according to plan. Just look at her desk and cupboard: all strictly aligned.

Some days ago I took a letter home that belonged to her (by accident, of course). It had somehow got caught up in my papers and so Heike couldn't find it. She panicked like nothing else!!! When I got home in the evening I found that I had the letter in the stuff that I had brought home. The next morning I returned it to her, with apologies. She went mad and screamed at me that I was a loafer without a sense of responsibility and a total scatterbrain. Unfortunately, I couldn't control myself and became very angry, too. I told her she was a rigid control freak...

Gunther, what do you make of all this? Where do those core quadrants fit in? How can I avoid a conflict like this ever happening again? I'd love to get some advice from you.

Best regards,

Hanna Schondorf

6

Management

This chapter focusses on how managers do their job and under what conditions. Several levels of management and styles of leadership will be discussed, including the manager as a person. Ethics and information will also be considered.

Contents

After studying this chapter:
—   You will be aware of the main concepts of management.
—   You will have become familiar with the main tasks of management.
—   You will be able to identify various leadership styles.
—   You will have gained an understanding of how managers run an organisation.
—   You will be able to recognise aspects of the manager as a person.
—   You will have become more aware of the connection between management, ethics and information.

6.1 The manager

Managers and others in positions of authority impinge on our lives, whether we be an employee or a purchaser of products and services. Newspapers frequently highlight connections between a manager's behaviour and the ensuing success of an organisation. Saturday news editions are packed with advertisements for financially attractive jobs under the heading of 'manager'. A large number of papers on management are published weekly, and magazine articles covering management are always in great demand.

Manager

A manager may be characterised as a person who can stimulate and direct the behaviour of other people within an organisation.[1] A manager will usually be responsible for the financial results of a division or department via his or her direction of groups of employees.

While this may suggest that it is the employees rather than their managers who do the work, in reality, many managers are workaholics, working on average more than fifty hours per week. Research has shown that many managers spend even more time than this on their work, even when they not actually working, since they are continually mentally occupied with their job. Their preoccupation with the job extends to the hours they spend with their families in the evening and other times (though this is a phenomenon not, of course, restricted to managers!).

Management/leadership to the organisation
Management team

Management is that group of people responsible for providing leadership to the organisation. The job may often involve a number of people who are frequently referred to as 'the management team'.
Within such a team we often see specialists representing the various functional departments of an organisation, such as Purchasing and Sales, Finance, Production, Personnel and Auditing. In the business world, divisional managers or managers of business units are frequently also members of a management team. Within government organisations, heads of departments may participate as team members.
There is an obvious interest in management courses and training institutions, varying from one-day seminars to complete studies that might last many years. This is indicative of a position in management being attractive from a financial perspective, both at the local as well as the international level.

6.2 The manager within the organisation

A distinction should be made between the level of the managerial activity and those activities themselves.

Management levels
Within a growing organisation a need may arise to separate operational control from leadership. This situation will give rise to the development of a number of levels at which managers are required to coach their employees. The number of levels of hierarchical control will depend heavily on the size of the organisation, the degree of specialisation and the type of organisation and policy.

Number of levels

There are three main management levels within an organisation's hierarchy: top management, middle management and first line management. It is the responsibility of the senior level to provide leadership for the organisation; middle management directs the activities of operational levels, including the lower management

Top management
Middle management

Name:	Sushant Buttan
Country of origin:	India
Lived in:	India and USA
Job title:	Senior Vice President, former CEO for Maximize Learning
Company:	Techbooks (www.techbooks.com)

What important personal qualities must people have to be successful in international work?

I would classify these personal qualities under the following:

• **Ability to embrace change** – International work involves working in different cultures, a new country, new rules of business and most importantly, dealing with change. I grew up in an Indian environment and was used to dealing with people in a certain way and that was the way I thought the world functioned... until I made my first business trip out of the country. I would not say that the experience was a rude awakening. However, I was definitely in denial for the initial few months, thinking that I knew everything that needed to be known, and didn't make a major effort to learn about the country's systems, culture or sensitivities.

• **Spirit of adventure** – While many may question this, a spirit of adventure is a key attribute for success in international work. We spend our lives in our cocoons and safe havens and international work requires us to venture out into new lands. At the risk of making it sound like the Wizard of Oz, the truth is that there will be many moments of uncertainty while we navigate international business situations. How we respond to these situations is the difference between success and failure. If you initially gear yourself to the idea that this is going to be an adventure, your curiosity to explore will propel you through many a tough situation.

How do you deal with people who resist change in the workplace?

Where change is concerned, there are three types of people in the workplace: types A, B and C.

Type A personalities are those people who are the first to embrace change. These people are generally optimistic and positively minded in their personal lives as well as at work. They are 'always look on the bright side of life' types. This group forms 30% of the crowd.

Type B personalities are those that are 'fence sitters', people who cannot make up their mind for themselves and constantly need someone to help them do so. They are followers, and will follow and sway in any direction depending on who is leading them. This group forms 50 to 60% of the crowd.

Type C personalities are the ones that get up every morning heaving a big sigh. These people are perpetually depressed about life and how unfair the world is to them. There is an innate sense of negativity and 'Doomsday thinking', in their approach to life: they are people who never look on the bright side of life. Fortunately, this group is usually no greater that 5% of the crowd.

My approach has been to use evangelists from the Type A group to convince the Type B personalities to embrace change, to offer ongoing change management training to the entire group and to weed out the Type C personality people. While this may sound brutal, it is time-tested and saves everyone a lot of trouble. There is just no winning with this Type C group and it is best to let them go.

What is the most important lesson that you have learned from working with people from different cultures?

Never take people for granted! That is definitely the most important business lesson I have learned. I have faced many embarrassing situations when I have addressed people in a certain way or responded in a certain way. For example, I met with a senior executive called Mary Jane Stanton. Conventionally, I am used to the concept of first, middle and last name. My continued addressing her as Mary annoyed her, and I later learned that she should have been addressed as Mary Jane and not just Mary. The fact that I never bothered to ask her about how she liked to be addressed was taking this for granted. While this may sound insignificant or trivial, it is one of the many simplistic ways that you can take people for granted and find yourself in an embarrassing situation. Try saying your own name out in a combination of your first and middle name or some other combination and you will see what I mean... then imagine someone who you do business with, constantly addressing you in that peculiar manner.

First line management

level (especially within large enterprises). First line includes heads of departments or group managers, who are located between the operational levels and the middle management level. Within a modern flat organisation there is far less need for multiple tiers of management as less distinction is made between the lower and middle levels of management.

Policy forming tasks

Executing tasks

The two main functions of management are policy forming and executing tasks. Policy forming includes diagnosis, prediction, planning and organising activities. The executing of tasks relates mainly to the delegation of activities and the supervision and motivating of employees.

As Figure 6.1 shows, the activities of the top managerial layer consist of the carrying out of policy forming tasks. Middle management is involved in both policy forming and executing tasks. Goals formulated by top management are translated by middle management into tasks of a more operational type to be performed by the various divisions or departments within the organisation. Responsibility for the tasks that have been set by middle management will then shift to the lower management teams.

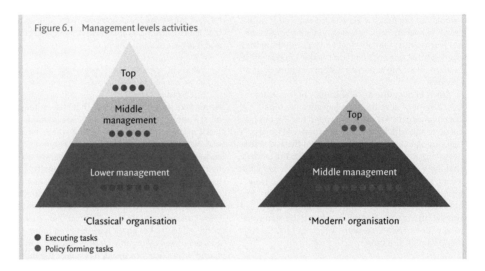

Figure 6.1   Management levels activities

Managerial activities

We can make a distinction here between the two main management groups: functional and general managers.

Functional manager

The responsibilities of a functional manager relate to the management and performance of a single main activity within an organisation. Employees are coached by this manager to focus on this task only. Purchasing managers and marketing managers are two examples of functional managers.

General manager

A general manager, on the other hand, may be made responsible for all the activities within a certain part of the organisation. Amongst other areas, he might be held responsible for the production, marketing and finances of the organisation. The business unit manager or the divisional manager are two examples of managers with general managerial duties.

Within those activities performed by management a number of trends have recently become visible:

Flattening

· Organisational structures are becoming increasingly flatter through the assimila-

Redefining Leadership

Just over a decade ago, Steve Jobs was considered a has-been whose singular achievement was co-founding Apple Computer back in the 1970s. Now, given the astounding success of Apple and Pixar, he's setting a new bar for how to manage a Digital Age corporation:

Strategy. Jobs is an obsessive perfectionist who insists on having total control over the most minute product details. That was considered hopelessly idealistic in the lean years as Microsoft and its partners trounced Apple with cheaper PCs. Now, as music, movies and photography go digital, consumers want elegant, simple devices.

Leadership. At Apple, micromanagement is not a dirty word. While Jobs relies heavily on his execs, he's astonishingly hands-on in his areas of expertise. He can demand miniscule changes in product designs, rehearse for hours to perfect his famous product intro presentations, and work at length with reporters on stories he chooses to be involved with.

Innovation. Other CEOs may focus on finance or sales. Jobs spends most of his time trying to come up with the next blockbuster product. Think iPod and iTunes. As a tech pioneer, he doesn't have to depend on lieutenants for technology smarts or product taste.

Marketing. Yet Apple has consistently stood out for aspirational ads with a heavy dose of counterculture rebellion. The 'Think Different' series featured John Lennon, Rosa Parks, and Pablo Picasso. The message is this: if you dream of changing the world, we want to help you do it. Jobs even had a hand in writing the copy.

Culture. Elitism has its advantages. Since founding Apple with engineer Stephen Wozniak, Jobs has believed that small teams of top talent will outperform better-funded big ones. He'd rather have all his creatives working together than save a few bucks by outsourcing such work overseas.

Source: *Business Week*, February 2006

tion of lower and middle management levels. Consequently, the number of management levels and the number managers has also fallen.

- The task of the manager is increasingly changing from the classical, directive leadership style to more of a coaching and guiding of employees style.
- There has been a shift away from the recruiting of functional managers to the development of more general managers in the workplace. This has been caused by the subdivision of organisations into more autonomous business units (for example, when a unit is made responsible for all activities directed towards a certain product-market combination, with the policy-making tasks becoming the responsibility of middle management. A key priority for top management is then to create the required conditions (as the specific and necessary know-how is found in the functionality of a business unit or division), which makes adaptations in a changing environment quicker to perform.

Business units

We will return to the first two tendencies in Sections 6.2.3 and 6.3.

6.2.1 The manager's tasks

The main function of the manager is to direct employees and manage the resources under his or her control and so meet the organisation's requirements. The manager will spend his time performing three important roles which originate from this function (see Figure 6.2). A role is defined as an expected behavioural pattern or an

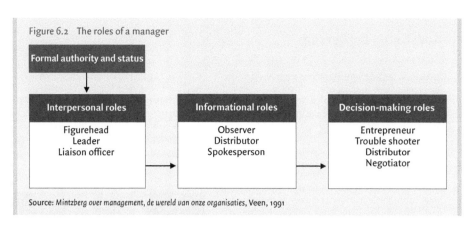

Figure 6.2   The roles of a manager

Formal authority and status		

Interpersonal roles	Informational roles	Decision-making roles
Figurehead	Observer	Entrepreneur
Leader	Distributor	Trouble shooter
Liaison officer	Spokesperson	Distributor
		Negotiator

Source: *Mintzberg over management, de wereld van onze organisaties*, Veen, 1991

organised collection of behaviours that are identified as belonging to a particular position.[2]

The three roles of a manager are:
A The interpersonal role
B The informational role
C The decision-making role

A   The interpersonal role

Interpersonal role

A manager gives guidance to employees and is responsible for the results and professionalism of the unit, often using formal and informal networks to build relationships with team members both inside and outside the organisational work environment. The main aspects of this role are:
- Being a figurehead
- Being a leader
- Being a liaison officer

This last role includes the making of contacts from outside one's own organisational unit. These contacts constitute a distinct externally-directed information system and are used during the daily activities of the unit.

B   The informational role

Informational role

A manager needs to be informed of any changes within the organisation that will affect the operational results of the division. The manager will share this information with both organisation members and other interested parties from outside the organisation. To be able to react quickly within a changing environment requires accurate information, and thus imformation is increasingly important. The main informational roles are:
- Being an observer
- Being a disseminator of information
- Being a spokesperson

C   The decision-making role

Decision-making role

As the person in charge of a business unit, a manager is responsible for implementing policy. He or she will make decisions by using all available information, the contacts that have been maintained and the specific circumstances of his or her unit (its external opportunities and threats weighed up against its internal weaknesses and strengths). A manager needs to continually evaluate situations in order to achieve the required objectives. He or she will need to make optimal use of the

staff and resources that are available. In order to make the right decisions in such a complex situation, managers must be able to rely on their staff. The following are aspects of the decision-making role:
- The entrepreneur
- The trouble shooter
- The provider of resources
- The negotiator

These suggest that a manager spends a lot of his time communicating with people both inside and outside the organisation.

Communicating

As the activities of a manager are varied, a manager needs to be competent in many areas. Figure 6.3 illustrates the manager's main tasks. For each individual function, the time that each task consumes will also differ. The span of a manager's control can be limited to a smaller number of management task requirements.

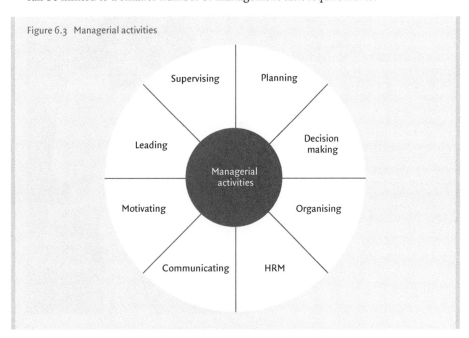

Figure 6.3 Managerial activities

6.2.2 Top managers

The job title of a person who heads a large business has recently undergone a number of changes. Not long ago the most senior manager was known as the director; later on he or she preferred to be known as a manager. With an increase in the number of line and staff managers, this term has been somewhat devalued. Nowadays, the chairmen of the board or the director wishes to be known as the top executive and to be regarded as an entrepreneur.

Director

Despite considerable decentralisation of competencies, a top manager in an organisation is the main motivator and initiator of the enterprise in its present modern form. Moreover, top managers often serve as symbols or figureheads to their teams. They are held responsible and accountable for the future successes or failures of the organisations they lead. As such, the role of top manager requires specialist qualities. A top manager needs to inspire his employees by showing creativity, enthusiasm and an open mind. Their behaviour and values must be impeccable from an ethical point of view. Last but not least, a top manager should be able to behave and think like a politician, both within and outside his professional workplace.

Top manager

Symbol

Managing from a virtual office

The 52-year-old Mr Green runs what might be called a virtual company. Accenture has no operational headquarters and no formal branches. The chief financial officer lives in Silicon Valley. The chief technologist is based in Germany and the head of human resources is in Chicago. And the firm's thousands of management and technology consultants are constantly on the go, often reviewing projects and negotiating new contracts in clients' offices or working temporarily in offices that Accenture leases in more than 100 locations around the world.

As companies move jobs around the world, managers are increasingly supervising out-of-sight employees. There are some difficulties to this approach. With participants scattered across time zones, scheduling phone conferences can trigger conflicts over whose sleep will be interrupted. And some matters, especially sensitive personnel issues, require a personal visit – no matter the distance. Another challenge: weathering constant jet lag. Overall, Accenture executives say virtual management works for them: none of the overhead costs of having headquarters, and spending time with clients cements relationships.

Technology helps keep a virtual company on track. Through the internal website, the employees log in every day to record where they are working. They get access to their files, email and phone messages. They share documents and financial data with other executives. Many companies are following Accenture's management mode.

Source: *Wall Street Journal*, June 2006

6.2.3   Middle management

The largest group of managers – the middle management level – is the level immediately below the top management level. This level usually consists of division managers, assistant directors and heads of departments. The main importance of middle management lies in its skilful execution of general tasks and in providing coaching for the operational levels of management.

Some of the main tasks undertaken by middle managers are:

Middle management

- Organising and directing activities in general
- Making operational decisions
- Passing information from the top down and the bottom up
- Planning
- Organising activities
- Motivating employees
- Maintaining internal and external contacts
- Reporting
- Generating business

A characteristic of the middle management level is that their daily workload has more to do with policy-making than it does the execution of tasks. The current trend of employing middle managers in a decentralised and more authoritative role is considered a main feature of this trend. It has resulted in middle management having an increasingly greater say in managing the operations of an organisation's business activities. Middle management collaboration is therefore crucial within organisations when changes have to be carried out. New projects generated by top management are then introduced by middle management to employees in terms that are more straightforward and easily grasped, and that are aimed at inspiring further achievement through greater effort. A quality of good middle management is the ability to achieve an adequate balance between the level of satisfaction required by both top management levels and staff. In view of the many tasks and increased responsibility placed on middle managers, one could say that increasingly higher demands and expectations are today common requirements of this level.

Policy-making tasks

The development today of increasingly flatter hierarchical structures within organisations has resulted in many large organisations shedding superfluous levels of bureaucratic management. The organisational requirements for flatter hierarchical structures have adversely affected opportunities for promotion available to middle managers today. Potential middle managers are forced to compete harder to access the remaining management positions now available. As a result of increased competition, organisations are forced to provide more flexible working conditions for their employees. The simplification of an organisation's structure has had the added benefit of increased business effectiveness. Within Dutch society, this is exemplified by a modern model which emphasises strong levels of individualism together with small increments in power distance. This flattening of organisational structures will, of course, have further consequences for changes in management style,
budgeting policies and personnel management. We will come back to this later in Section 6.3.3.

Flatter hierarchical structures within organisations

Restricted promotion from middle to higher management has also been seen as one consequence of flatter organisational structures. In order to give people new challenges and to promote further business effectiveness, greater use of staff horizontally transferring between various business positions will become more widespread.

Horizontally transferring

In the future, it seems likely that the demise of more traditional business activities such as planning and control will lead to these roles eventually being phased out and the workload taken over by computers. As a consequence, some middle management roles will become less important or disappear entirely, meaning ever-increasing demands on a reduced middle management staff.
The educational levels of employees will continue to rise to meet the higher standards required, and as a consequence, current management leadership styles will be challenged. Demands made by an organisation's top management for increasingly better performance by their middle management level will result in those middle management staff becoming indistinguishable from the category of entrepreneurial staff.

Wanted: successful top managers

The longer the search for the competencies and characteristics associated with the successful manager, the more it resembles a quest for an illusory quality. The world around us is too complex to draw up a standard profile, or so it seems. Success is largely determined by situations, which is why standardisation hardly ever stands up to strict scientific testing. In the meanwhile, however, a recipe for a successful top manager has been partly created. A set of skills (shown in the following model) has gradually been defined. It highlights individuality, commitment to people and commitment to the organisation.

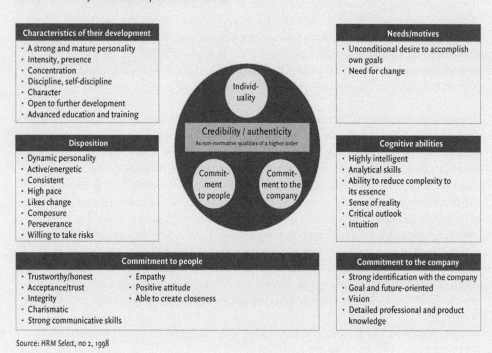

Characteristics of their development
- A strong and mature personality
- Intensity, presence
- Concentration
- Discipline, self-discipline
- Character
- Open to further development
- Advanced education and training

Disposition
- Dynamic personality
- Active/energetic
- Consistent
- High pace
- Likes change
- Composure
- Perseverance
- Willing to take risks

Needs/motives
- Unconditional desire to accomplish own goals
- Need for change

Cognitive abilities
- Highly intelligent
- Analytical skills
- Ability to reduce complexity to its essence
- Sense of reality
- Critical outlook
- Intuition

Individuality

Credibility / authenticity
As non-normative qualities of a higher order

Commitment to people

Commitment to the company

Commitment to people
- Trustworthy/honest
- Acceptance/trust
- Integrity
- Charismatic
- Strong communicative skills
- Empathy
- Positive attitude
- Able to create closeness

Commitment to the company
- Strong identification with the company
- Goal and future-oriented
- Vision
- Detailed professional and product knowledge

Source: *HRM Select*, no 2, 1998

6.2.4   Managers in government

Administrative and political factors

Managing board
Top management

Managers within government require different skills from managers within the business world. In governmental management functions, the administrative and political factors are of greater significance. Management positions within government fall roughly into those associated with the managing board and those at the top management level. In general, the managing board is responsible for making new policy decisions, and top management for putting the policies into practice. This is changing, however, as responsibilities and competencies are increasingly being delegated to top management. This affects internal policy, with top management needing to inspire and to motivate staff in the implementation of those policies.

Top ministerial officials

As well as their job requirements, the managerial problems faced by top ministerial officials and central government bodies differ in type from those of managers working within the market sector. This is caused by a number of factors:
- The government is not part of a market-oriented organisation. Activities are not determined in a direct way by the buyer of the service, but by the decisions of parliament, regional government or city councils.
- Services delivered by government and the cost of delivering those services have an

unstable character as they are produced within a political and administrative decision-making process that is constantly changing.

- Within government, the influence of financial results on management is less clear than within the market sector, since the financial position of a business is more transparent.
- A government has additional requirements and duties not found within the market sector: for example, the principle of good governance, the acceptance and prioritising of certain duties of care to special groups and transparency of administration.

As such, top government managers require additional skills in order to effectively carry out their main duties:

1 Managers must have an understanding of the social and administrative ramifications of the democratic process.
2 Managers must be able to deal appropriately in areas of conflicting interests.
3 Managers should have a very thorough knowledge of their area of business.

The management profiles of semi-governmental organisations such as municipalities, health care, social work and education are increasingly similar to those within the business world, tending to be more independent both in policy as well as financial decision-making. The supplier-customer model has come to the fore much more strongly.

Moreover, managerial positions are often filled by individuals with specific management training rather than specialists in particular fields. In the field of health care, there is a call for those with a business, administrative or economic background.

6.3 The manager as a director of others

As previously mentioned, it is a manager's task to direct the activities of others. Henri Fayol (see also Chapter 1) identified a number of activities in this area:

- Planning
- Organising
- Being in command
- Coordinating
- Controlling

6.3.1 Managers and power

The aim of leadership is to help direct an organisation in the realisation of its goals. Power – the ability to influence the behaviour of employees – is an import feature of leadership. Two important aspects of power are therefore:

1 Sources of power
2 Power relationships

Sources of power

A manager's authority will depend on the way he manages the power he has been given. The extent of one's authority depends on how well it is accepted or how legitimate it is seen as being. Organisations recognise that employees are entitled to exercise the power that is linked to their position.

Apart from position, a manager has various other sources from which he or she can tap to exercise power. French and Raven identified five sources of power that can be used either positively or negatively. These power sources are:

1 *Reward power.* This is the capacity to influence somebody's behaviour by reward. The

Authority

Sources of power

Reward power

Woman underrepresented in leadership roles

Work-life balance tensions, combined with stereotypes and gender-biased pay and evaluation systems continue to hold women back in the job market. Women account for just 32% of managers. Only 10% of members of boards and 3% of CEOs of larger EU enterprises are women. Additionally, in the EU, women earn 15% less than men and progress has been slow in closing gender gaps with men, according to a 2006 European Commission report. The 2006 'Report on equality between women and men' calls on EU countries to provide better ways to help women deal with home and work pressures. The report found that difficulty in managing a work / life balance means that many women are leaving the labour market. At 55.7%, their employment rate is 15% lower than that of men. Women who do work are often confined to a limited number of sectors — more than 40% work in education, health or public administration, compared to less than 20% of men. Part-time work accounts for over 32% of women's jobs, but just over 7% for men. Women earn 15% less than men partly because they are concentrated in lower paid professions. On the positive side, the report found that more than 75% of new jobs created in the EU in the last five years have been filled by women.

The report invites EU Member States to help both men and women to balance work and private life through such things as more and better childcare, innovative and adaptable working arrangements or better equality policies. It also urges them to reduce employment and pay differences between men and women.

Sources: OECD 2005 and website European Union, 2006.

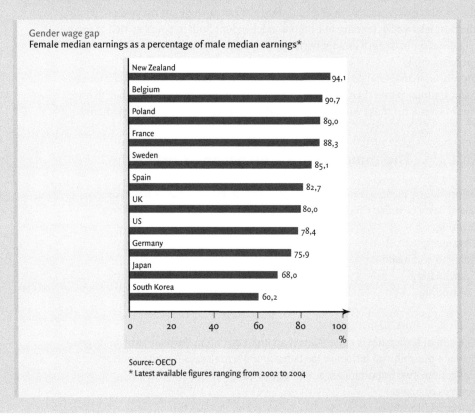

Gender wage gap
Female median earnings as a percentage of male median earnings*

Source: OECD
* Latest available figures ranging from 2002 to 2004

reward is thus an instrument for encouraging particular behaviour.

Coercive power

2 *Coercive power.* This is the ability to influence somebody's behaviour by punishment: the opposite of reward power. Here, the options are to prevent or to fight specific behaviour. What it boils down to is obtaining a minimum level of achievement by force.

Legitimate power

3 *Legitimate power.* The employee accepts it as normal that, within certain limits, the manager is entitled to exert an influence on behaviour.

Expert power

4 *Expert power.* This is the capacity to influence somebody's behaviour by specific and relevant knowledge. The power is based on the manager's expertise.

Characteristics and levels of power

IN THE PRESS

Power has four characteristics:

1 Support from a group. It is a fairy tale that top managers can always fall back on a team. Everyone knows that so-called top teams rarely function as a real team because of the pressure of other priorities, the strong desire to hold on to individual responsibility, or just because of pride. The supervisory board often turns out to be a faithful ally.

2 Symbols. These are the bait that attract managers: a secretary, a room furnished according to one's own taste, VIP treatment and media attention.

3 Charisma. This is an enticing characteristic.

4 Vision. Vision is the rarest of all top manager qualities. The boardroom is full of self-made men – generals who send the troops to the field, street fighters who do not mind doing some slapping,

mediators who try to keep everyone on board – but very few visionaries.

Power exists at various levels:
- The power to influence. This is the lowest level of power. The restructuring of an organisation is relatively simple.
- The power to control processes. These are more difficult to control.
- The power to change thoughts: scenarios and innovations which are not obvious but can have a big impact.
- The power to influence the entire working and living environment. Creating an atmosphere in which people feel energetic and happy.

Source: Intermediair, September 1998

5 *Referent power.* This is the capacity to influence somebody's behaviour based on prestige or on admiration for the manager. In the eyes of the employees the manager possesses a certain charisma.

Referent power

These five sources of power are either linked to the position or to the personality of the manager.[3]

Power linked to position
An organisation assigns managers certain tasks. To carry these out, a manager has power linked to his position at his disposal. A manager can use these power resources to stimulate or discourage certain types of behaviour:
- *Physical resources.* These concern indirect resources: for example, the design of offices and facilities for employees.

Physical resources

- *Economic resources.* These concern all kinds of financial arrangements.

Economic resources

- *Information.* The slogan 'Knowledge is Power' is a familiar one. Access or denial of access to certain sources of information can influence the preconceptions or the opinions of the employees.

Information

Power linked to personality
The two resources of power linked to the personality of a manager are:
1 *Expertise or knowledge.* This kind of power has already been discussed earlier in this section.

Expertise or knowledge

2 *Interpersonal resources.* This concerns the way a manager handles his employees and will depend on his character and modus operandi.

Interpersonal resources

If applied positively, power can lead to success in management. The limits within which a manager is permitted to make decisions are fixed. Decision-making power is necessary for an organisation to reach its targets. Two models are relevant in this connection: the harmony model and the faction model.

The harmony model supposes that members and / or divisions of an organisation have the same interests. There is a balance of power and consequently the manager does not have to do much to coordinate his or her staff. In the faction model, however, such harmony is assumed to be lacking. The employees or divisions may have

Harmony model

Faction model

conflicting interests, and the manager has to use his power to achieve the organisation's goals. The faction model comes closer to reality and makes the need for power in organisations far more obvious. However, in practice, the power at a manager's disposal will fall somewhere between the two models. The nature of a manager's power will depend on ways that it is used and on how the employees react.

Power relationships

A relationship between two people is always one of power, whether at work or in a private setting. One person is considered by the other to be either less or more powerful. These power relationships both guide our behaviour and determine how dependent one person is on another. Power relationships can have one of three basic formats[4]:

1 Equal
2 Unequal: high versus low
3 Unequal: high versus middle versus low.

Figure 6.4 shows these basic formats diagrammatically.

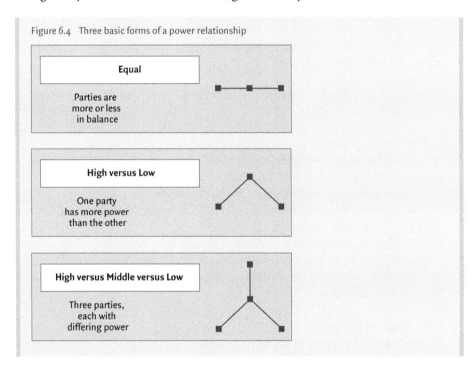

Figure 6.4 Three basic forms of a power relationship

Equal

Parties are more or less in balance

High versus Low

One party has more power than the other

High versus Middle versus Low

Three parties, each with differing power

These power relationships influence the various behaviours of the people concerned. One should be aware of their presence within organisations and try to neutralise the disadvantages inherent in them by highlighting one aspect or reducing others.

1 Equal

Equal

A balance of power is the basis here. Such power relationships will appear in a situation where there is a tendency to compete with one other. In an extreme case, the contacts will remain at a formal level. In a situation where an employee concentrates on his or her own work and pays little attention to the organisation as a whole, this can lead to an imbalance between the functions of the organisation. To avoid such a problem, it will be necessary for:

- The parties to be brought more in line with each other
- The parties to be trained in negotiating skills, with the issue being seen as more important than personalities.
- Emphasis to be laid on the common interest of the organisation and on the feeling of being a part of a group (the 'we' feeling). This will strengthen mutual dependency and encourage cooperation rather than competition.
- The dividing line between each other's work is clearly defined in respect of tasks and responsibilities as well as competencies.

2 High versus low

In this form of power relationship there is a hierarchical relationship between the various parties. This may lead to a situation where the higher-ranking person wishes to increase his or her power over a subordinate but the subordinate wants to maintain or even increase his or her autonomy. The two parties can use various mechanisms to help increase their power. To avoid a lack of motivation and resistance to change, a manager may adopt various methods of control: *High versus low*

- Adapting a leadership style, emphasising mutual interdependence in the power relationship, and taking on the role of coach.
- Enhanced participation in the decision-making process. The power relationship will then be viewed as more normal and legitimate.
- Avoiding a personal display of power. Increased use of procedures and various other methods such as 'management by objectives'.
- Delegating responsibility and accompanying competencies, thus stimulating motivation. The employee will become more independent, thereby increasing his or her sense of responsibility.

3 High versus middle versus low

In this power relationship, the position occupied by middle management is a relevant factor. Such a relationship may lead to a conflict of loyalties, to uncertainty about where the responsibility lies and to stress, as there may be situations of conflict with both the upper and the lower levels. There are two ways of avoiding such conflict. Either the power relationship is kept as it is and any adverse developments are evaded or counteracted, or the power relationship is ended. *High versus middle versus low*

To keep the relationships in equilibrium depends on improvement in communication (especially in terms of the quality of information exchanged) and better delineation of functions. The position of middle management should be clearly defined in terms of expectations, goals and priorities. If one chooses to change the power relationship, one option is to flatten the organisational structure. This will reduce the number of functions and the number of conflicts. The remaining functions can be extended, which will also make them more attractive.

6.3.2   Leadership

In order to achieve the goals of the organisation, the leader should possess a number of specialist qualities. Aptitude and training are important, but life experience also appears to have a great influence on the quality of leadership. A leader is expected to support employees in helping them fulfil their tasks in as meaningful and as pleasant a way as possible. Success will make them more loyal to their leader. A true leader: *Qualities*

- Attracts supporters without needing to be coerced
- Demonstrates an ability to fulfil the wishes of followers
- Is an expert

ADVICE

Leadership lessons from the former CEO of Intel

Andy Grove arrived in the US in 1957 and by the late 1960s he had earned a Ph.D. in chemical engineering at Berkeley. He joined Fairchild Semiconductor, birthplace of the integrated circuit. When colleagues Robert Noyce and Gordon Moore quit to start Intel, Grove declared that he was coming too. In 1968 he became in charge of operations. He succeeded where others didn't, in part by approaching management as a discipline unto itself. He became famous for his 'imminent failure' theory that there is a growth rate at which everybody fails and the whole situation results in chaos. Your job as a highest-level manager is to identify the maximum growth rate at which the wholesale failure phenomenon begins. Andy Grove's biggest tumble from the learning curve began in 1994. Thomas Nicely, a mathematician, spotted inconsistencies in the way Intel's latest Pentium chip performed a rare, complex scientific

calculation. Intel engineers knew about the bug but deemed it too insignificant to report. The discussion became a tempest and soon IBM announced it was suspending shipments of its Pentium-based computers. It was a moment when Grove should have switched into observer mode. He didn't. The uproar grew and Grove was forced to adopt a no-question-asked replacement policy and to apologise to customers. The apology was not very gracious, but Intel had decided to indulge their irrationality. Intel had become a marketing company with the slogan 'Intel Inside'. In branding, a customer's subjective reality, even if confused, becomes your objective reality. The learning experience was more expensive than most: the Pentium recall required a $475 million write-down.

Source: *Fortune*, December 2005

Leadership

Leadership is not something that can be imposed. A manager can only maintain the role of leadership by proving to be the superior person with the best methodology.

A leader has the power to determine the developments of an organisation in collaboration with his or her subordinates. A true leader will not have direction determined by chance. Real leaders have specific qualities that distinguish them from others. Some of these qualities are innate, others may be learnt. A study dealing with charismatic leaders showed that the relationship between the leader and his employees had these following qualities:

· A leader is considered by his employees (followers) in some ways to be superhuman
· Employees do not question the opinion of the leader
· Employees follow their leader unconditionally
· Employees will give a leader complete emotional support

According to Charles de Gaulle, leadership is characterised by 'the eagerness to undertake big things and the determination to bring them to a good end'. He added that 'the effective leader has to be well informed about the details of specific circumstances, he should not think in abstract or vague general theories and should have more self-confidence then his rivals'. Other historical examples of great leaders are Napoleon, Winston Churchill and Eisenhower.

The task of the leader becomes simpler after being accepted and valued by employees. Real loyalty has to be won. If a manager bases the daily activities on the rules mentioned above, a good foundation for successful cooperation will have been laid.

6.3.3 Leadership styles

Leadership style

A leadership style is shaped by its methods and attitudes towards it and has certain features. A complete integrated theory about leadership does not exist: each existing theory deals with various aspects of leadership. For example, in the scientific management theory, the emphasis lies on task-directed leadership, but the human relations movement focusses more on a human-directed leadership style.
The following theories of leadership styles will be discussed:

1 Classifying leadership according to the participation of the employee and his / her ability to make decisions
2 X-Y theory
3 Leadership diagram
4 The 3-dimensional leadership model
5 Situational leadership
6 Situation-dependent leadership
7 Transformational leadership
8 Self-leading style

1 Classifying leadership according to the participation of the employee and his / her ability to make decisions

Based on this criterion, three basic styles can be identified:
A Authoritarian leadership
B Democratic leadership
C Participating leadership

Source: Harvard Business Review, May / June 1998

A Authoritarian leadership

A leader gives orders to employees concerning their work and the way they should behave. Power is used to establish authority. There is a strict hierarchy between the leader and subordinates. There is no space for participation or discussion. All deci-

Authoritarian leadership

sions are made by the leader himself, who has access to all the required competencies. There may be person-to-person control and the leader will be strongly focussed on results.

B Democratic leadership

In contrast to an authoritarian style of leadership, group participation is the normal procedure here and leadership therefore becomes a function of the group. Members of the organisation are thus involved in the management of the organisation or department. The leader coordinates the group decision-making process. A drawback of this type of leadership is that it might also give rise to indecision and ineffectiveness.

C Participating leadership

This type of leadership is situated between the authoritarian and democratic styles. The leader retains responsibility for the manner in which the tasks of his department are carried out. Members of the organisation are asked to participate in discussions, and to inform and advise their leader. The final decisions are made by the leader after the consultation process with employees has concluded.
The relationship between power and these three leadership styles is shown diagrammatically in Figure 6.5.

Figure 6.5 The relationship between power and leadership styles

	Power influence		
	Authoritarian	Participating	Democratic
Goal	Submission	Co-responsibility	Determination
Via	Sanctions	Effort and insight	Group experience
Relationship	X-theory	Y-theory	Y-theory

Source: Marcel Pieterman, *De middle manager in confrontatie met de praktijk, de middle manager en zijn organisatie*

The advantages and disadvantages of these styles are:
- In the short term, authoritarian leadership may lead to the best performance from employees.
- With an authoritarian leadership style, employees become more dependent on the leader.
- With participating and democratic leadership styles:
  - employees are better motivated and will show greater initiative
  - employees work more independently
  - there is less aggression within the group
  - team work will improve

Although the advantages of democratic and participating leadership are clear, one should not assume that these styles are always preferable to an authoritarian leadership style. In times of crisis, authoritarian leadership can be more effective, with many decisions being made quicker.

Leadership competencies at 3M

The global HR team at 3M has isolated twelve competencies and defined them in terms of leadership at a general management level.

Basic

1 Ethics and integrity. Shows unconditional integrity and commitment to the corporate conditions, human resources statutes and the professional behaviour codes of 3M.
2 Intellectual capacity. Absorbs information quickly, appreciates the complexity of issues, is critical, and has a sense of reality. Is able to deal with diverse, complex and paradoxical situations. Communicates clearly, concisely and comprehensibly.
3 Maturity and judgment. Shows resilience and balanced judgment in relation to problems at a business or corporate level

Essential

4 Customer orientation. Is continuously working towards the creation of superior value for 3M's customers and ensures that each interaction is a pleasant one.
5 Staff development. Selects and retains an excellent work force within an environment that appreciates diversity and respects autonomy. Stimulates a continuous learning process and develops himself / herself and encourages others to do so in order to reach their maximum potential.
6 Inspiring others. Has a positive influence on the behaviour of others. Motivates them to aim for personal satisfaction and worthwhile accomplishments by setting clear goals in a spirit of cooperation.
7 Healthy commercial orientation. Identifies and creates growth opportunities at the product, market and geographical levels. At the same time, achieves positive results in the short term.

Visionary

8 Global perspective. Has a knowledge of global markets as well as the capacities and resources of 3M, and operates with these in mind. Practices global leadership and behaves respectfully in multicultural environments to the benefit of 3M.
9 Vision and strategy. Creates and communicates a customer-oriented vision that is geared to the corporate level and that makes sure that all employees pursue a common goal.
10 Cherishes innovation. Creates and supports an environment that promotes experimentation, rewards risks, stimulates curiosity and scrutinises the status quo critically in a free and open way and without pre-judgment.
11 Develops alliances. Develops and improves favourable mutual relationships and networks (both internal and external) which deliver a multitude of possibilities for 3M.
12 Keeps the organisation at the cutting edge. Knows, respects and strengthens the culture and the assets of 3M.

Source: *HRM Select*, January 2001

---

2   X-Y theory

In his book *The Human Side of Enterprise*, Douglas McGregor (a revisionist) relates leadership style to the leader's views of his or her subordinates and what motivates them. Under the name 'X-Y theory' McGregor identifies two opposite viewpoints within the human mentality. The X theory assumes that a human being:

X theory

· Is lazy and dislikes working
· Cannot and does not want to think
· Has to be forced to perform tasks and is interested only in money
· Does not want to accept responsibility and prefers to be led

The Y theory, on the other hand, assumes that a human being:

Y theory

· Is eager to work and considers it a natural process
· Is inventive, creative and has imagination
· Achieves more when development is made possible and when rewarded in an immaterial way. Money is not the only incentive.
· Is prepared to accept responsibility

The leadership style resulting from theory X is characterised by no feedback, submission, compulsion, control and punishment. It is an authoritarian leadership style. If the leader bases his actions on the assumptions of theory X he or she runs the risk of never making any progress. Employees working with an authoritarian type leader will eventually demonstrate the very behaviour described by theory X. By contrast, the leadership style resulting from theory Y will show features such as participation, discussion, opportunities for development of the employee, encouragement and reward. This is a form known as participating or democratic leadership.

Nowadays, with the achieving of organisational goals gaining in importance, it is important to have a leadership style based on theory Y's assumptions. Neglecting the needs of employees can lead to a situation where organisational members will try to satisfy those needs outside the organisation. For example, they may actively participate in boards or clubs, or put their other talents to use in their hobbies. In time, these employees will lose interest in the organisation and function only at a minimum level. Employees will not want to accept responsibility and will resist changes. This could result in an unnecessary loss of talent and may ultimately harm the organisation. The comment should be made that not all members of the organisation will want to (or are able to) accept responsibility to any great extent.

3 The leadership grid

Leaderschip grid

In their book *The Leadership Grid*, Robert Blake and Jane Mouton (two revisionists, see Chapter 1) developed a grid which shows a large number of different leadership styles. (See Figure 6.6.)

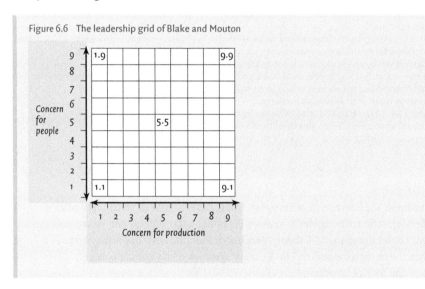

Figure 6.6   The leadership grid of Blake and Mouton

Task orientation

Relationship orientation

This model is based on their assumption that a leadership style will have two dimensions: concern for production or a task orientation, and concern for people or a relationship orientation. The diagram shows the degree to which a manager focusses on these dimensions. Blake and Mouton used their model to develop five different leadership styles:

Impoverished management
- Style 1.1 (Impoverished management). This style is characterised by low concern for production and low concern for people.

Authority-compliance management
- Style 9.1 (Authority-compliance management). This is a very directive style which focusses on production rather than people.

Country club management
- Style 1.9 (Country club management). This 'social club' style is characterised by a high concern for the welfare of the employee and little attention for production.

Middle-of-the-road management
- Style 5.5 (Middle-of-the-road management). Concern for production and people is balanced.

Team management
- Style 9.9 (Team management). High concern for both production and people leads to a high level of efficiency, a good atmosphere within the group and strong team work.

In practice, style 9.9 seems to provide the best results with the fewest undesirable side effects.

Figure 6.7 compares these different leadership styles from five perspectives. The value of the leadership grid is that it projects the different styles that a manager can adapt. Most managers employ different styles of which one is prominent. Depending on the situation, a manager will change consciously or unconsciously to another style.

Figure 6.7 Comparison of different leadership styles

Dimension	Leadership style				
	1.1	9.1	1.9	5.5	9.9
Productivity	Small	High	Small	Moderate	High
Communication	Superficial	One-Way	Intense	Considerate	Open
Attitude towards employees	Hardly involved	Directing	Positive	Listening	Pleasant
Motivation	Hardly	By punishment and fear	Strong	Moderate	Very strong
Attitude towards mistakes	Indifference	Ignoring	None	Solving	Removing causes

4 The three-dimensional model of leadership

William Reddin added a third dimension to the leadership grid of Blake and Mouton, namely *effectiveness*.

Effectiveness

The three dimensions in the model of Reddin are:
1 Attention to people
2 Attention to production or the task
3 Effectiveness

Based on the two-dimensional model of Blake and Mouton, Reddin developed four basic leadership styles (see Figure 6.8):

1 *The relational style.* This style is applied by managers who communicate regularly and at length with their employees. Such a manager is receptive to all that goes on with their employees and possesses good social skills.

Relational style

2 *The integrating style.* The manager gears his activities to other managers, making less use of power but more use of various other kinds of motivational techniques.

Integrating style

3 *The non-involved style.* The manager attaches value to procedures, guidelines, methods and systems. These mainly concern routine affairs that need to be assigned and executed according to specific instructions.

Non-involved style

4 *The dedicated style.* The manager is often a specialist who directs subordinates that have to do a large amount of work within a short time frame. This style often has the features of autocracy and absolute power.

Dedicated style

In Reddin's opinion, the integration style (style 9.9 of Blake and Mouton) is not always the most effective style as the degree of effectiveness will depend on the situation of the leader and his employees. According to Reddin, managers need to possess certain qualities in order to be effective in various situations:

- *Style awareness.* A manager is aware of different styles and is able to evaluate them.
- *Situational sensitivity.* A manager is able to assess and evaluate situations.
- *Style flexibility.* The capacity to adapt one's leadership style to a changing situation.

Style awareness
Situational sensitivity
Style flexibility

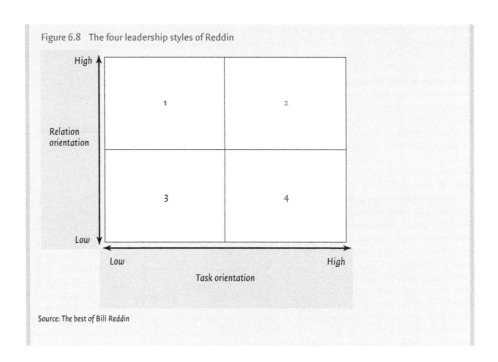

Figure 6.8 The four leadership styles of Reddin

High

Relation
orientation

Low

Low   High

Task orientation

Source: The best of Bill Reddin

• *A talent for change.* The skill to change in any given situation in such a way that the situation can be managed more effectively.

An analysis of a situation will indicate which leadership style is likely to be the most effective. Figure 6.9 shows how these different types of managers will evolve as they apply leadership styles with varying degrees of effectiveness. The essence of this model is that it suggests that the manager should match his leadership style to situational demands.

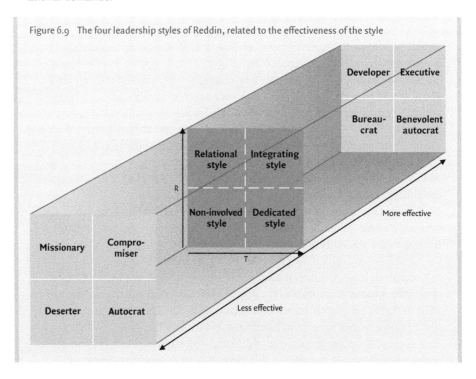

Figure 6.9 The four leadership styles of Reddin, related to the effectiveness of the style

5 Situational leadership

Effective leadership will depend on many factors. Practice has shown that effective managers possess various qualities and that to obtain optimal results, different situations require different leadership styles. This leads to the conclusion that no single effective leadership style exists. This is why further research is particularly focussed on isolating factors that influence the effectiveness of a style in specific situations. This approach is also known as the 'contingency approach'. The factors that influence effective leadership styles are shown in Figure 6.10.

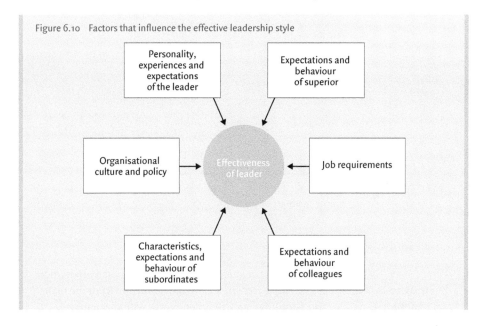

Figure 6.10   Factors that influence the effective leadership style

Hersey and Blanchard as well as Reddin and Fiedler are exponents of this approach. Paul Hersey and Kenneth Blanchard's approach is known as situational leadership. Successful implementation of this leadership style will depend on various factors, including the level of expertise the employee possesses to carry out the required business tasks, or his / her 'task maturity'. Hersey and Blanchard define task maturity as the ability to carry out a certain task and the willingness to take on that task together with the level of corresponding responsibility it entails. The extent to which an employee demonstrates task maturity is thus determined by two main criteria:

Situational leadership

Task maturity

1 The ability of the employee (training, experience etc.)
2 The willingness of the employee to accept responsibility (curiosity, self-confidence etc.)

An employee can be scored and assessed according to his or her individual acceptance level in performing a task. Hersey and Blanchard identified four levels of task maturity:

1 Unable and unwilling / insecure (M1)
2 Unable and willing / motivated (M2)
3 Able and unwilling / insecure (M3)
4 Able and willing / motivated (M4)

Here, a specific leadership style is linked to each of the four levels of task maturity. Using this method, two main features relating to direction (task orientation) and support (relational orientation) can be analysed. Task orientation entails the manager giving certain directions to an employee in relation to the execution of various

Task orientation

tasks. This itself is based on the ability of the employee to perform those tasks. Relational orientation concerns the level of support the manager will need to provide. This implies other aspects such as an achievement orientation and responsibility (see Figure 6.11). Figure 6.11 expands on leadership styles.

Relational orientation

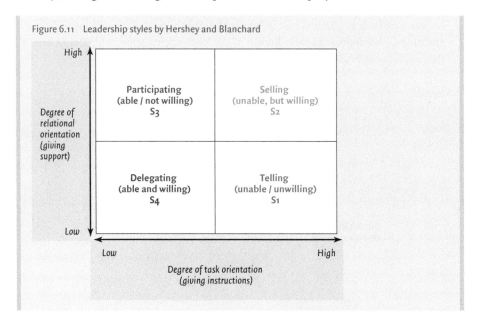

Figure 6.11   Leadership styles by Hershey and Blanchard

Participating

- *Participating.* This leadership style is characterised by a strong relational orientation but weak task orientation. The employee will receive little direction from the manager but a lot of support. Decision-making will occur jointly, with the manager encouraging the employee in the completion of the required activities.

Selling

- *Selling.* This style is characterised by a strong emphasis on both the directional and support dimensions. The employee will be given a lot of direction as well as a lot of support in the execution of the tasks.

Delegating

- *Delegating.* This style scores low in both dimensions, with the manager giving little direction and support to the employee in respect of completing a certain task and delegating the accompanying responsibility to that employee. The employee will thus be acting autonomously in the execution of those tasks.

Telling

- *Telling.* The employee will be given a lot of instructions but little in the way of support. This leadership style scores high on task orientation, but low in relational orientation.

The essence of Hersey and Blanchard's approach is that it treats leadership style in relation to the employee's level of task maturity. Hersey and Blanchard call their model a development model, as employees pass through a number of phases (see Figure 6.12). It is the manager's task to stimulate the emplyee's task maturity. As such, a manager needs to be aware of the maturity of his or her employees and be able to encourage their development. It is also important that a manager be able to adapt his or her behaviour to various new situations and not be limited by a preference or style.

If a leadership style fails to fit the level of task maturity required of an employee, that employee might start developing his or her skills in the wrong direction. The result may be activation of various defence mechanisms on the part of the employee as he or she may feel singled out for unfair criticism. When the employee's level of task maturity has increased to a more acceptable level, the manager should then adapt the management style to this new behaviour. The manager should also be very aware of differences in task maturity between employees. The manager will

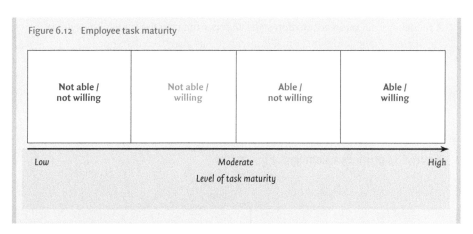

Figure 6.12 Employee task maturity

Not able / not willing	Not able / willing	Able / not willing	Able / willing

Low   Moderate   High

Level of task maturity

ultimately delegate certain tasks to the employees, which in turn will allow the manager to take on additional new tasks. This development is shown in Figure 6.13.

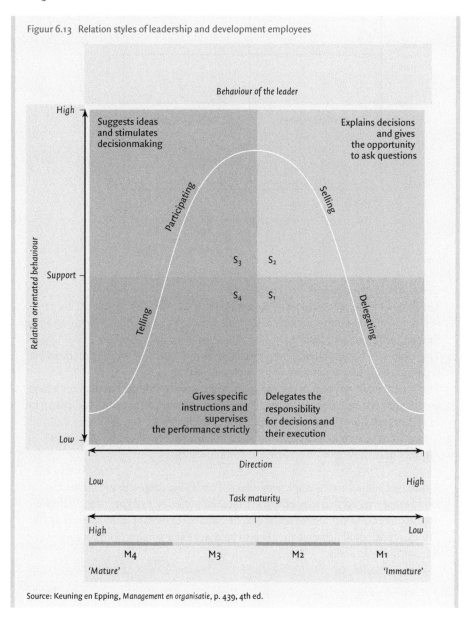

Figuur 6.13 Relation styles of leadership and development employees

Source: Keuning en Epping, *Management en organisatie*, p. 439, 4th ed.

Leadership acquisition style

A model of leadership acquisition styles that is similar to the leadership styles of Hersey and Blanchard (situational leadership) has also been developed.

The style of leadership acquisition will depend on the following three factors:
1 The situation
2 The ability of the receiver
3 The willingness of the receiver

Figure 6.14 provides a summary of this model.

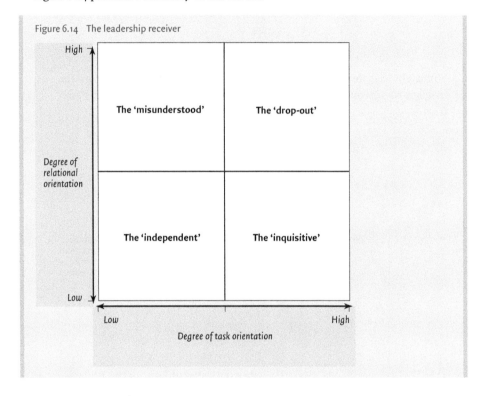

Figure 6.14   The leadership receiver

The four leadership acquisition styles:

Inquisitive acquirer

1 The inquisitive acquirer will want to develop both knowledge and skills. This person is self-motivated in approach and inquisitive, wanting to know everything about the task as quickly as possible.

'Drop-out' acquirer

2 The 'drop-out' acquirer needs both instructions and support. This person lacks the required ability and is not yet willing to execute tasks.

'Misunderstood' acquirer

3 The 'misunderstood' acquirer does not need many instructions, but requires a large amount of acknowledgement. This receiver is reasonably capable and will have a lot of ideas about how things could be performed better.

Independent acquirer

4 The independent acquirer is very capable and has a lot of self-confidence. This acquirer likes to be given high levels of responsibility.

A manager should coach employees who fall under the drop-out and misunderstood categories so that they can evolve into the preferred category of the independent acquirer. The drop-out should also be coached to develop assertiveness skills. The misunderstood acquirer should also be coached to develop both communication and attitude skills.[5]

6 Contingency leadership models

Fiedler has made an important contribution to the theory of leadership. Fiedler stated that it is difficult for managers to change their leadership style, especially when the situation is itself unfavourable. His model links the decisiveness of the manager and the situation in which the team works. The manager's decisiveness is influenced by personal qualities and the favourability of the situation in the eyes of the leader. The team can only perform well when the manager is attuned to the situation or visa versa. Fiedler measures effectiveness in quite a simple way: the extent to which you are judged by the person with whom you have to work positively or negatively.

Contingency leadership model

Leadership situation

Fiedler also identifies three aspects of the leadership situation which will affect success in implementing a certain leadership style:

1 The leader-member relationship and the leader-group relationship. (To what degree is the relationship based on mutual trust?)
2 The task structure: both the size and nature of the task given to the group. (What are the objectives? Is it a routine job? Might unexpected problems arise?)
3 The position of power of the manager. (How far does the manager's power extend?)

Based on these three aspects, Fiedler constructed eight situations and indicated matching effective styles (as shown in Figure 6.15). This model emphasises that managers should adapt their management style to the various situation types.

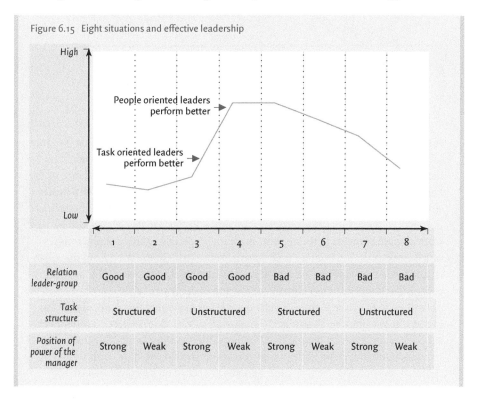

Figure 6.15 Eight situations and effective leadership

	1	2	3	4	5	6	7	8
Relation leader-group	Good	Good	Good	Good	Bad	Bad	Bad	Bad
Task structure	Structured		Unstructured		Structured		Unstructured	
Position of power of the manager	Strong	Weak	Strong	Weak	Strong	Weak	Strong	Weak

Two examples of situations that will require an adapted leadership style are:
A An organisation in which professionals are active
B An organisation in a certain phase of its development

A   An organisation in which professionals are active

Increasingly, managers are having to deal with professionals whose educational level is higher than that of the organisation's employees. Professionals can be described as people who use their intelligence, know-how, expertise, experience and problem-solving skills in a creative and relatively independent way in order to realise the goals of the organisation and by implementing efficient management skills. A professional person of this kind can be compared to a person whose abilities have been shaped by advanced academic training and who belong to the higher vocational professions: the architect, consultant, lawyer, economist, sociologist, physicist and so on.

Knowledge is also an important weapon in the competitive business arena. Product life cycles are increasing becoming shorter while investment in R&D, production facilities and marketing is increasing, thereby also increasing the importance of knowledge skills and consequently the work of professionals. Some regard professionals as difficult to manage. Their loyalty is more often to their specialist occupation than to the organisation that employs them. Professionals are regarded by many as perfectionists in the application of their specialist skills but regarding office work more as a hobby. Professionals like to work in isolation from the organisation since they have an aversion to management methods. As such, managing professionals will require a certain culture and management style.

According to Mintzberg, the difficulty involved in managing this group lies in the fact that they cannot be controlled by imposing rules and procedures. Professionals experience and expect a natural freedom in relation to their work. This freedom is fed by a number of views and opinions that professionals hold. According to research, the opinions held by professionals are based on seven viewpoints[6]:

1 The right to be exempted from management decisions if they do not comply with their own norms and values.
2 The desired management style is an absence of being managed.
3 The professional must be able to critically appraise the manager.
4 The professional must be able to work in isolation from management practices.
5 Any conclusions based on professional skill should be given priority over management's own conclusions.

6 The professional owns the work he produces.
7 Any information given to a professional must be clear, consistent and true.

Based on research and experience, M. Weggeman, a consultant at Twijnstra Gudde, a Dutch consultancy firm, formulated six propositions. These aim to describe the specific style a leader should adapt when working with professionals.[7]

1 The manager should translate the organisational goals into group goals in consultation with the group. Agreement should be reached between these group goals and personal goals.
2 The success of the group leader is mainly determined by his capacity to:
   – Select professionals with the required level of skills to work in existing teams
   – Create productive positions for professionals with particular potential
3 The manager should not use rules, procedures and data systems to lead professionals, but should pay particular attention to clearly defining the desired results.
4 Professionals that aspire to management positions because they consider these positions more attractive or 'higher' than their own are probably not functioning at the optimum desired level. This reduces their chance of acceptance into a future management position and will also increase their tendency to become averse to rules and procedures.
5 Of all the tasks, managers of professionals should be given more freedom to delegate interesting, challenging and difficult problems to their employees. If the most interesting tasks are completed by a manager rather than employees, we cannot expect much esprit the corps to develop between management and staff.
6 A manager should find a balance between flexibility and efficiency within the department. Plans and activities should be carefully arranged in consultation with the group.

B   *An organisation in a certain phase of its development*
Organisational theory describes the phases of development of an organisation, the first phase being the pioneer phase and the last the maturity phase. A manager should tailor his leadership style to the phase the organisation is currently in. It may be possible to typify this phase of development in terms of the nature or direction of strategy chosen by the organisation. Certain types of managers will match certain phases of development (see Table 6.1)[8]. Managers may be typified using a certain number of behavioural characteristics. See Figure 6.16.

Table 6.1   *Development phase and types of managers*

	Strategic direction	Type of manager
1	explosive growth	pioneer
2	expansion	strategist
3	continuous growth	steady stayer
4	consolidation	administrator
5	antiskid strategy	frugal manager
6	cut back / trimming down	persevering diplomat

7   **Transformational leadership**
Organisations that have to contend with big changes which have to be carried out quickly require a special kind of leader, namely a transformational leader. Interest in this specific type of leadership style has increased strongly during recent years. The notion of transformation in the business world is seen as emanating from the so-called New Age movement. This movement was based on the premise that we are on the eve of a major revolution that will ultimately bring about an entirely new

New Age movement

Figure 6.16 The relationship between development phase and management style[9]

Development phase organisation	Type of manager	Behavioural characteristics				
		Conformity	Sociableness	Activity	Competitive spirit	Way of thinking
Explosive growth	Pioneer	Very flexible, very creative, divergent	Very extroverted, a lot of flair and glamour, but driven by circumstances, solitary and suspicious	Hyperactive, agitated, anticipating, uncontrolled	Stormy, daredevil, looking for challenges, motivated by uniqueness	Intuitive, irrational, fragmentary, original, divergent
Expansion	Strategist	Adapting non-conformist, creative, structured towards the new	Selectieve extroversion, forms groups of favourites	Energetic, responds to weak signals, nervous, some degree of self control	Increasing sphere of influence, calculated risks	Cross-border vision, generalist, rational
Continuous growth	Steady stayer	Strictly structured according to timetable, security	Aimable, teamworker, keeping the grip, keeping it nice	Goal-oriented, stable, by agreement	Balanced growth, getting satisfaction by controlling the situation	Thorough, systematic, depth, specialist
Consolidation	Administrator	Reproductive, routine, obedient	Introverted, coaching	Stable-static, via procedures, expectant, 'yes, but'	Maintaining status quo, defending territory	Thorough and conformist vision, linked to previous situations
Antiskid strategy	Frugal manager	Bureaucratic, dogmatic, rigid	Directive, procedural	Laissez-faire, doing what needs to be done, little initiative	Reactive behaviour, external incentives	Legalistic, conservative
Cutting back, skimming down	Persevering diplomat	Maximal flexibility within accepted limitations	Attentive, human, considerate, decisive, inspiring trust, responding to emotions	Steady, persevering but flexible	Strategically more oriented on the long term, goal-oriented in the short term but also well balanced efforts	Thorough, systematic, depth, specialist

culture. The key to this culture is a new way of thinking and perception. Some key words relating to transformational leaders are awareness, insight, creativity, harmony, spirituality and intuition. As we move towards the new age, individual transformation has a prominent place. Only a person with a 'new' awareness will be able to contribute in a meaningful way to the new era.

Oganisational transformation

Around 1982, a number of business people became inspired by New Age notions. This gave rise to conferences built around the notion of the transformational process of management within organisations, with participants encouraged to exchange their experiences. Over the years, organisational transformation – an accompanying process that grew out of individual changes in management – has lead to radical changes within organisations.

Organizational transformation can be characterised as follows:
1 Its onset is sudden: a particular event such as a merger or a new management or organisational structure prompts it.
2 The old structure disappears totally and a new one takes its place. The transitional process is not gradual. For example, a new production process which completely replaces the old one is introduced.

Leadership development at IBM: an interview with CEO Sam Palmisano

Why is leadership such a hot topic at this moment?

The world has changed. Strategies are increasingly tending to be based on intellectual property and human innovation. In the old days, your assets and your capital dictated success. That may still be true for some industries. You still have the Big Three automotive companies, for example. But the world has changed so much. It's not who has the most assets or the best capital structure. It's about having an innovative strategy. That competitive advantage is not being encouraged in people – not in their thoughts, their ideas or their creativity. That's different to the way it was before. Networking and the Internet mean that you can form horizontal structures. I no longer have to have the biggest manufacturing rate. Because we're the largest, I can rely on Asian manufacturers in our supply chain and create $6 billion in savings.(...)

How to retain talent on a global basis

It's a luxury that we have access to top talent from all over the world. One way you retain that talent is by giving them an opportunity to become the future leaders of the IBM Corporation. Not just the future leader in Japan, or India or China or what have you. You have to give them the opportunity to advance all the way through the ranks. We want to be your employer as long as you contribute and buy into our values over the long term. You can go all the way in IBM. We try to instill the fact that we want to be representative of the communities we work in all over the world. We reach out to diversity. Again, this lends itself to the process. To be more than value statement, to make it a reality, you have to reach out in your development and hiring. We've done all kind of studies. It takes a long time to become an executive at IBM, but it's no different to the average: it's about 17 years.

Source: *New York Times*, 2006

3 There is a complete change of awareness on the part of the organisational members. For example, a governmental organisation might change their centralised control system with employees being given individual responsibility for the quality of their work in the new system.

Transformations within organisations can take place at two levels: at the individual or at the collective level. These levels also apply to the structural and cultural dimensions. Figure 6.17 shows that the transformational process always starts with an individual and ends with a change in the organisational structure. If one wishes to change an organisation one should always start with the people in that organisation.

Individual / collective level
Structural / cultural dimension

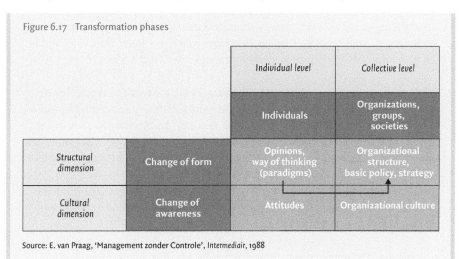

Figure 6.17   Transformation phases

Source: E. van Praag, 'Management zonder Controle', *Intermediair*, 1988

Management that is engaged in organisational transformation is termed transformation management. Its purpose can be defined as 'enhancing the ability to function well in a situation of turbulent social transition characterised by a high degree of complexity and an enormous velocity of change'.[10] The form and consequences of

Transformation management

transformation management within organisations will depend strongly on the individuals involved.

According to transformation theory, a leader must possess a number of specific qualities including[11]:

- The ability to anticipate change: in a continuously changing environment the leader must have a visionary outlook.
- Vision: the leader must be able to direct organisational members to new goals and challenges, generated either individually or as a team.
- A leader must take a broader scale of factors into account, including economic, spiritual, aesthetic and psychological factors. Moreover, a leader should turn these into collective goals.
- A leader shares the power with his or her employees.
- A leader must have a large degree of self-knowledge and be aware of his or her own goals and motives as well as those of the employees.

8 Self leadership

Coach

In many ways, this approach is similar to the approach whereby the manager becomes the coach. In this viewpoint, a manager is not considered superior to his or her employees but as being on their level. The main tasks of a manager are to stimulate employees and make it possible for them to function optimally. The current trend within organisations to limit their number of management levels was discussed earlier. This development is also accompanied by adding levels of competency to lower organisational levels, taking over responsibility for the formation and results of business units. This requires a new management style, characterised

Horizontal management style

as a horizontal management style. Within this process the planning, organising, checking and coordinating is mainly done by autonomous units. With employees becoming better trained and more mature in the performance of their tasks, a manager must be able to create an atmosphere that encourages the change by developing, training, delegating and creating the necessary facilities. This is a strongly interactive role and requires managers to prove their leadership skills in order to promote better levels of communication with staff members. Research has shown that organisations today are demanding a high level of ability from their staff.[12] In assessing employee performance, managers use criteria such as responsibility, commitment and creativity. Employees are expected to complete their work and to be both loyal and disciplined in all their dealings. (See Figure 6.18.)

If we compare the changing needs of a manager with the needs of employees we will see an emphasis on appreciation, respect and self-realisation. Physiological and social needs are not as crucial. The 'higher' needs as described by Maslow in his pyramid may sometimes be the same for managers and employees. They will share a mutual interest in such things as equality, respect and attention, and it is in these areas that a basis for working together should be sought.

Communicative skills are also of crucial importance to a manager. The employee must be given all due attention. Outcomes relating to new leadership styles are shown in Figure 6.19 which will now be further explained.

a *The manager.* The manager should have an open style of communication and be attentive to employees, stimulating their motivation and commitment. This can have far-reaching consequences for autonomy within organisations and delegation of responsibility. A lot of emphasis should be placed on team-building with managers selected according to their capacity to cultivate a sense of belonging.

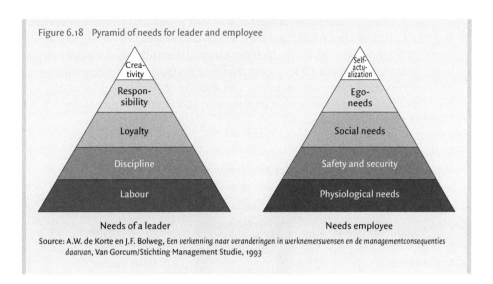

Figure 6.18   Pyramid of needs for leader and employee

Needs of a leader

- Crea-tivity
- Respon-sibility
- Loyalty
- Discipline
- Labour

Needs employee

- Self-actu-alization
- Ego-needs
- Social needs
- Safety and security
- Physiological needs

Source: A.W. de Korte en J.F. Bolweg, *Een verkenning naar veranderingen in werknemerswensen en de managementconsequenties daarvan*, Van Gorcum/Stichting Management Studie, 1993

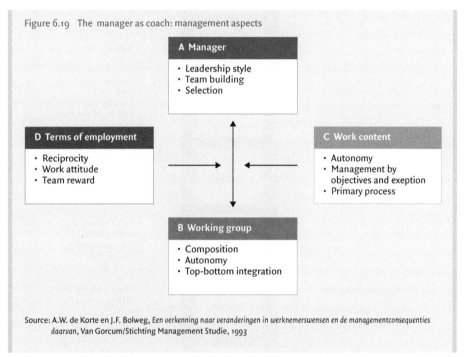

Figure 6.19   The manager as coach: management aspects

A Manager
- Leadership style
- Team building
- Selection

D Terms of employment
- Reciprocity
- Work attitude
- Team reward

C Work content
- Autonomy
- Management by objectives and exeption
- Primary process

B Working group
- Composition
- Autonomy
- Top-bottom integration

Source: A.W. de Korte en J.F. Bolweg, *Een verkenning naar veranderingen in werknemerswensen en de managementconsequenties daarvan*, Van Gorcum/Stichting Management Studie, 1993

b *Work groups.* A lot of emphasis is placed on the functioning of the group and its composition. A group that functions well is said to have strong mutual bonds. Such a group will have a large degree of autonomy, with the manager providing support in areas such as facilities and training. Employees are integrated within the organisation via the work group, which equates to integration between the top and the bottom levels of the organisation.

c *Work content.* There is a striving towards autonomy in executing activities and this is allied with management support. 'Management by objectives' is a management technique that encourages such an approach, as is 'management by exception'. With the former, individual or departmental objectives are determined, and with the latter, only predetermined deviations from targets are raised with the manager. All of the activities are related to the primary processes of an organisation and any changes within these primary activities will mean the formulation of new work contents.

d *Terms of employment.* Their personal lifestyle is at least as important for employees as is their job. To adapt to a changing culture, organisations need to provide greater flexibility for their work force. This includes adapting the terms and conditions of employment to an individual's needs and requirements (part-time working hours and career-based criteria). Seen in terms of its ability to attract high-quality staff, this is one of an organisation's most important areas. The various types of rewards need to be linked to performance.

9 Survey leadership styles

Various theories of leadership styles are shown in Figure 6.20.

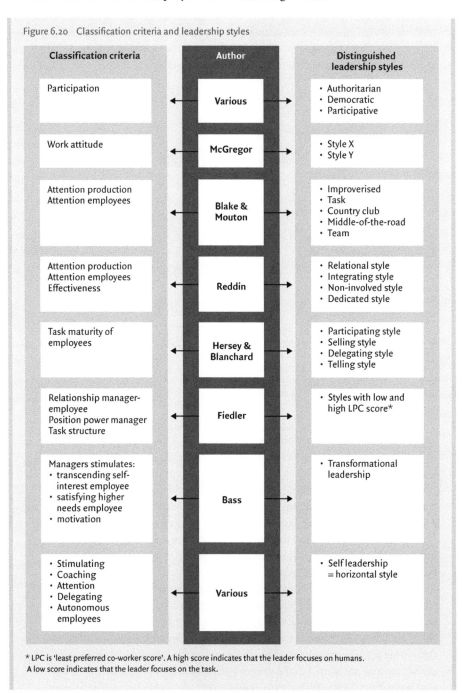

Figure 6.20 Classification criteria and leadership styles

Classification criteria	Author	Distinguished leadership styles
Participation	Various	• Authoritarian • Democratic • Participative
Work attitude	McGregor	• Style X • Style Y
Attention production Attention employees	Blake & Mouton	• Improverised • Task • Country club • Middle-of-the-road • Team
Attention production Attention employees Effectiveness	Reddin	• Relational style • Integrating style • Non-involved style • Dedicated style
Task maturity of employees	Hersey & Blanchard	• Participating style • Selling style • Delegating style • Telling style
Relationship manager-employee Position power manager Task structure	Fiedler	• Styles with low and high LPC score*
Managers stimulates: • transcending self-interest employee • satisfying higher needs employee • motivation	Bass	• Transformational leadership
• Stimulating • Coaching • Attention • Delegating • Autonomous employees	Various	• Self leadership = horizontal style

* LPC is 'least preferred co-worker score'. A high score indicates that the leader focuses on humans. A low score indicates that the leader focuses on the task.

In practice, the chosen leadership style will depend on various factors:

· Organisational culture (is the culture based on a formal or an informal style?)
· Size of organisation (within small businesses, the employees know one another and are more aware of what is happening in and around the enterprise)
· The nature of the work (routine or varied, simple or complex)
· The level of education of employees compared to management (lower versus higher education)
· Social tendencies (is democratisation within the organisation being carried too far?)
· Scarcity in the labour market of a particular skill (if the employee does not like the leadership style he / she might look for work elsewhere)

6.3.4 The international manager

Mergers and joint business ventures mean that organisations are confronted with various different types of leadership style. Unsuccessful mergers and joint ventures are evidence that these differences can cause great problems within the workplace. In this section, we will first discuss the differences in leadership styles from one European country to another and then we will look at ways of achieving success and and resolving difficulties in intercultural management.

The EU research paper *Culture and Management* came up with the following findings:
The Netherlands. Dutch organisations are in general fairly flat and flexible in their hierarchies. The Dutch leadership model is reflected in business cultures. The boss is often considered to be 'one of us'. When setting personal targets, job security, independence and a sense of duty are important considerations for the manager. A manager is expected to be an expert in the area for which he / she is responsible and he or she is expected to take risks. Managers are inclined to short-term decision-making and their decsions are made reactively and intuitively.

France. In France, managers are strict and authoritarian in style. Their subordinates are used to being led. Respect is based mainly on the leader's competence level. The French attach great importance to a person's expertise and experience level. For French managers, self-development, competence, wealth and being accepted by work colleagues are important personal targets. The decisions they eventually make are often intuitive and made in reaction to specific short-term issues.

Germany. Germans seek strong and convincing leaders. High positions in management are viewed with respect and awe. A manager will often have a somewhat detached relationship with a subordinate. Managers expect obedience from their subordinates, and they in turn require clear instructions from their leader. Achievement and realising one's ambitions are important, with self-development, prosperity and independence also scoring high on their list of priorities.

Spain. The Spanish manager is a kind autocrat, steadfast in approach and with clarity and courage being the most important qualities. Rules, procedures and a formal hierarchy are all subordinate to loyalty. The most important characteristic of the Spanish leadership style is commitment. Decisions are often made intuitively by the manager and any decision-making by the group constitutes an adverse reflection on management style. Being supportive of others, pursuing self-development, prestige and a sense of duty are important managerial attributes.

Global management culture?

Average leadership and thinking styles differ around the world according to a research report which was published in the *Harvard Business School Review* (2006). The database which was used for global research included a sample of more than 180,000 managers and executives on four continents. By comparing Europe, Asia, and Latin America, researchers hoped to isolate the cultural impact on leadership and thinking styles. The differences identified focussed on styles dominant at the various levels of management. For instance, entry-level Asian managers generally score higher than managers from other regions in terms of decisive leadership style; Latin Americans stand out for their increasingly flexible thinking style the more their career progresses. But when the researchers looked inside each region, comparing people with others in the same region only, they were amazed to see the same basic progression in both leadership and thinking styles. Additionally, they noticed a transition point where style profiles do a flip around the middle management levels. And despite differences in degree, by and large the styles followed the same trajectory across all four continents. (See also the next page.)

Source: Harvard Business Review, February 2006

Great Britain. Honesty in relationships is very important. This is demonstrated in particular in communication and decision-making that is participative and open in style. People have trust in the capacity of others. The well-known British reserve in personal contacts results in a more detached relationship style. This is also why British managers and their subordinates often appeal to rules and procedures, thus avoiding unnecessary risk-taking. Important personal targets are job security and the pursuit of pleasure and wealth.

What will make you successful as a manager in an international context? There is no simple answer to this question. Depending on the culture, people will have different ideas on leadership style and the bearing of responsibility. Fons Trompenaars, an author who has researched intercultural management, considers that there is no such thing as the 'Ten Commandments' of the successful international manager, as cultural differences vary too greatly. However, his research did reveal rules for success and potential issues ('communication jammers'). Intercultural communication plays an important role here.

Rules for success
Intercultural communication

Rules for success[13]

According to Fons Trompenaars, the rules for success are:

- *Know yourself.* Everybody communicates with others on the basis of a particular attitude, a prejudice or an opinion. In order to be able to communicate successfully in an international context it is very important to be aware of one's style of communication.
- *Take the physical and human setting into account.* Each culture has its local customs and it is very important to be able to adapt to these customs. Having a knowledge of these things can mean the difference between success and failure.
- *Try to understand different communication systems.* It is important to find some common ground (such as language) when doing business. Language is strongly related to culture. There are advantages to being able to speak the local language since the culture is entrenched in language.
- *Develop empathy.* Be receptive to other cultures. An interest in other cultures and what motivates people can be of crucial significance.

Communication jammers

Communication plays an important role in the international context. While it is important to be aware of the factors that can contribute to success, being aware of the factors likely to detract from it – the 'communication jammers' – will also con-

Communication jammers

International leadership styles

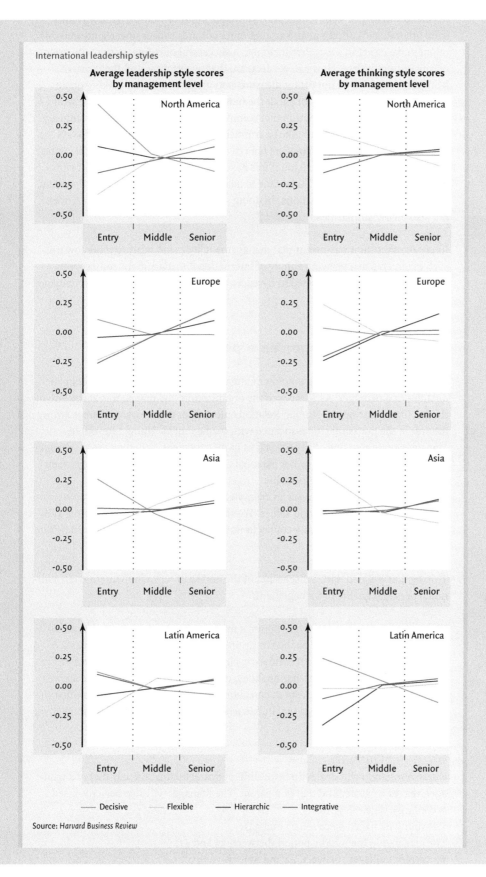

Average leadership style scores by management level

North America

Europe

Asia

Latin America

Average thinking style scores by management level

North America

Europe

Asia

Latin America

— Decisive   ⋯ Flexible   — Hierarchic   — Integrative

Source: *Harvard Business Review*

tribute to a manager's effectiveness. Jamming of communication usually results from ignorance. Working in and around other cultures causes uncertainty and this might make us act in a way detrimental to a successful outcome, even to the extent of causing a nuisance. How can we decrease that uncertainty, and the threat of being a nuisance? One important measure is to prepare well when taking on an international job, reading a lot about the new culture and talking to people who have been there or worked within that community. Learning to speak the language a little is also important. Try to take in as much of the culture as possible, always asking for extra information. Managers tend to act fast, but in another cultural context this could mean a wrong decision if it is based on incorrect assessments of situations, the culture and so on. Take time to adapt and learn how things are done and how you should handle situations. In doing so, focus not only on the differences but also on the similarities.

Internationalisation has meant that management styles are gearing more towards each other. Due to a growing supply of international management courses, the future manager can be expected to have less trouble interacting with other management cultures.

6.4 The manager as a person

Personal qualities
In recent years an increasing amount of attention has been given to the personal qualities of a manager. As a leader of the organisation, the manager is at the hub of things. Just as during the Human Relations movement of the 1930s, there is strong interest in the human factor associated with management. Human Resource Management is also one of the core tasks of management. Whether a manager succeeds will depend upon his or her personal character and the interaction between professional activities and private life.

Set an example
The manager's function is to set an example. He or she will need to develop a vision that take account of norms and values. We shall look at the manager's norms and values in some depth and draw connections between relationship matters in private and professional life.

This section will end with a discussion of the notion of 'entrepreneurship', an additional personal quality of management.

With a working week of over fifty hours, a manager has less time for other activities, especially those related to the family. In the book Is the price of success too high?, the authors relate private and work circumstances after they researched 532 managers from more than 20 nationalities, 95% of which European.[14] The answer given by the authors would seem to corroborate the often made suggestion that the modern manager is a professional in business life but an amateur at home.

6.4.1 Career

Career
Our investigation will deal with three different career paths, namely that of a manager, that of a partner and that of a parent. The manager will also be scrutinised according to age categories:
- The young manager (between 27 and 34)
- The manager in the middle period (between 35 and 41)
- The senior manager (between 42 and 65)

Figure 6.21 shows the relationship between the age category of the manager and the importance attached to the various career stages.

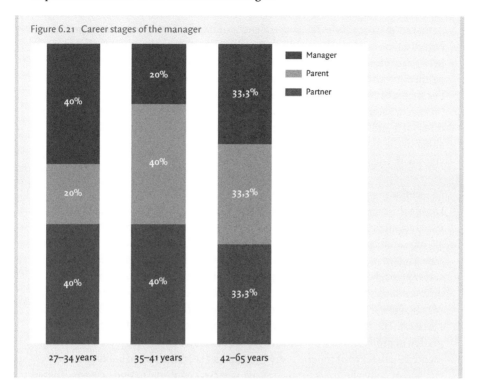

Figure 6.21 Career stages of the manager

The researchers highlight the fact that their study shows that role patterns for female managers are often comparable to these of their male colleagues. However, in trying to combine a professional and private life, the dilemmas facing woman and the conflicts they are involved in are more difficult for them than for men. Managers in the different age categories and the relationships between the various career choices are also discussed here:

The young manager (27 to 34)
A manager who falls into this category will have launched his or her career at an early age and succeeded in obtaining a managerial function. To have reached that point, the manager will have displayed considerable ambition and have invested large amounts of time and energy in his or her work. The career of the younger manager is characterised by many uncertainties and challenges. If the work is not going well and the manager feels that the chosen career path is in danger, a normal reaction will be to work even harder. However, if the work is going well, even less attention will be paid by a manager to personal and private situations, though these also require a great deal of constant effort.

It is difficult to maintain different activities at the same level. Since the career of a manager will probably be given priority, the job of parent and partner will normally take either second or third place. Even though this might cause a lot of conflict, he or she is likely to prioritise the career and have a corresponding apparent lack of sensitivity to what is happening within the marriage or other relationship. The mañana syndrome (tomorrow everything will be different) is a well-known phe-nomenon. Investment in family life will just have to wait, and even if their marriage is on the rocks, this will not necessarily lead to changes in the way managers spend their time or what receives most attention.

Mañana syndrome

The manager in the middle period (35 to 42)

The midlife crisis looms ahead during this period. During this middle period, the successful manager spends 70% to 80% of his or her energy at work. He or she will now start to worry about the consequences of this for family life. After a period of reflection, he or she will probably choose to create a more harmonious balance between professional and private life. In addition to paying greater attention to their partner and children, managers should also develop more interest in leisure activities such as sport, hobbies and intellectual interests. It is only during a crisis that the career should be given special attention. According to Evans and Bartolomé, the threat of a midlife crisis becomes real if something goes fundamentally wrong either in the job or in the relationship with partner and / or children or in relationships with friends.

The senior manager (42 to 65)

During this age category, managers start to break away from their career paths. Work remains important in this phase, but the career itself is no longer paramount. After all, most managers have already reached the top levels of their chosen career. There is now likely to be more of an equal distribution of attention over the three different career paths, with family life and children now becoming the most important area. A private evaluation of one's career now becomes important, with approximately 60% of managers in this age category more concerned with their lifestyles. Time is spent in reassessment, doubting one's own values, accomplishments and lifestyle. The integration of professional work and private life has either become firmer or more fragmented. In the case of fragmentation, a manager is unlikely to go looking for new challenges, and where it is firmer, the manager will continue to find new possibilities for personal development either within or external to the job.

Pension?

An investigation by consulting firm Twijnstra Gudde showed that only 30% of managers reach their pensionable age in good health. Of the remaining group, 40% end up claiming for a work related disability, either through private insurance or a government scheme, and 30% do not make it to pensionable age. This is why older managers should be given the opportunity to step backwards or to one side of their career ladder. Obviously, this will depend on personal circumstances and choice.

ADVICE

Avoiding a mid-career crisis

To understand and encourage career rejuvenation for your organisation's mid-career workers, answer these ten questions:

1 Who are your keepers? Besides those on the leadership track, who has the skills, experiences, attitude and adaptability you need most for the long term?
2 How many of your mid-career employees need to rejuvenate some of their skills or careers?
3 Are you employing any methods to rejuvenate mid-career workers? Which work best?
4 How freely does experience, knowledge, and talent flow in your company? Can employees move around the organisation? What's clogging the arteries?
5 How consistently do you make each job assignment work not only for overall business perform-

ance but also for individual employee growth?
6 Do you tap people for fresh assignments when their personal circumstances change (for example, when their children grow up and leave home)?
7 Do you encourage employees to change careers within your organisation?
8 Do you offer sabbaticals?
9 How often do you hire mid-career people, including workforce re-entrants?
10 Do you know which jobs are particularly suited to mid-career candidates? Which jobs do you avoid hiring them for or assigning them? What implicit biases are holding you back?

Source: *Harvard Business Review*, March 2006

Moreover, it is claimed that a manager functions at his or her best between the ages of forty and fifty. Thereafter his or her managerial qualities are likely to decrease (perhaps even quickly). It may be better to relinquish some managerial control than to keep going and endanger the stability of an organisation. This does not mean that an older person should leave the organisation: expertise can still be utilised in other ways and an older employee can still continue but with a more relaxed lifestyle. Besides permanent employment, there are other options available. They may include part-time employment or consultancy work.

6.4.2 Leisure activity

Choices about leisure activities will obviously have to be made as time is often a scarce resource for managers. One would expect managers to become very critical about how to spend their time and to manage it in an efficient way. However, interviews show that 77% of managers say that they often just 'mess around the home a bit'. Four different sorts of leisure activities can be identified:

Leisure activities

1 *Leisure activities undertaken in order to recover.* These are the above-mentioned activities of 'just messing around'. A manager does this in solitude, and in general, conversation is not appreciated.
2 *Leisure activities in order to release tension.* These are sport and other serious hobbies. Tennis, golf, swimming, skiing and sailing are popular items with Dutch managers. They provide a good outlet for built-up inner aggression and tension.
3 *Leisure activities in order to invest in private and family life.* These may be individual, parallel or joint leisure activities. Some examples of parallel activities include painting the house together, going to the movies or taking care of the garden. The presence of a partner is not essential for these activities, though other parallel activities such as having dinner together, holidaying and playing games is. It is a well-known fact that such joint activities contribute positively to 'relationship happiness'.
4 *Leisure activities for personal development.* These concern hobbies and occupations with a semi-professional character, often leading to alternative careers. They may include a study course, political involvement, music, art and writing or translating books.

Figure 6.22 shows the relationship between professional and private life, and the chosen leisure activity. For a manager, deciding on leisure activities constitutes an important choice. However, the choice is largely determined by the degree of career success. If a manager still needs to spend a large portion of his or her time and energy at work and has little time left over, this will also have an effect on his or her ability to pursue leisure activities.

6.4.3 Entrepreneurial management

Entrepreneurship could very well be the manager's most important personal quality. If the environment is very turbulent, many organisations need entrepreneurial management that is capable of tuning in to trends and developments earlier than their marketplace competitors, and then transforming these hunches into new plans. Entrepreneurship is a function of having a particular vision and a feeling for the market. It also involves some risk-taking behaviour.

Entrepreneurial management

Some characteristics of entrepreneurial managers are as follows:
· They have very energetic personalities, they are fast decision-makers and they are driven by challenges.

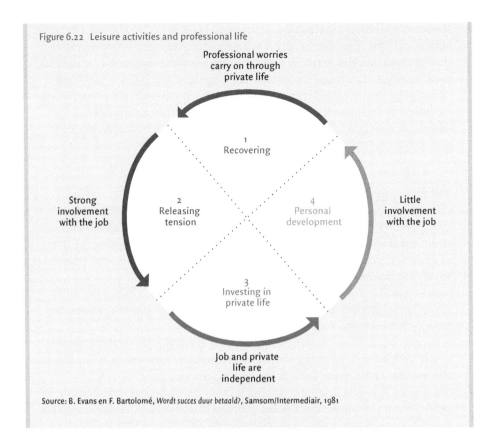

Figure 6.22 Leisure activities and professional life

Professional worries
carry on through
private life

1
Recovering

Strong
involvement
with the job

2
Releasing
tension

4
Personal
development

Little
involvement
with the job

3
Investing in
private life

Job and private
life are
independent

Source: B. Evans en F. Bartolomé, *Wordt succes duur betaald?*, Samsom/Intermediair, 1981

- Their activities are highly pioneering and inspiring. They make new plans all the time and the changes they make have a motivational effect on employees.
- They possess the ability to control and check their plans and activities.
- They are good listeners and are able to detect employee problems or frustrations quickly.
- Entrepreneurial managers usually have common sense ideas.

All entrepreneurial managers need to possess some of these characteristics. Managers who understand their own limitations and take account of these when selecting new employees will become the most accomplished managers. Managers who fail to develop such entrepreneurial qualities are more likely to opt for an unchanged policy, as this is considered to be most 'safe'. Paradoxically, in the long term, this option will become the more risky.

6.5   Management and ethics

Ethical aspects

During recent years, an increasing amount of attention has been given to the ethical aspects of entrepreneurship and management. The internal and external stakeholders of an organisation are today less interested in the fiscal performance of an enterprise. So-called 'non-commercial goals' – greater involvement in environmental issues – are playing an important role in enterprises that wish to maintain good relationships with the wider environment. Evidence for this can be found in, for example, company annual reports, which may mention ethical choices either explicitly or in passing. Issues relating to personnel policy, environmental pollution, discrimination, trade with less developed countries, tax policy, religion and so on cannot be approached solely via a profit perspective. Practical ethics involve painful

The business case for corporate citizenship

Corporate citizenship is about the contribution a company makes to society through its core business activities, its social investment and philanthropic programmes, and its engagement in public policy. The manner in which a company manages its economic, social and environmental relationships and the way it engages with its stakeholders (such as shareholders, employees, customers, business partners, governments and communities) has an impact on the company's long-term success.
A growing number of research projects and surveys highlight the links between the quality of a company's stakeholder relationships and / or its wider economic, social and environmental performance, both real and perceived, as well as the following key value drivers:
1 Reputation management
2 Risk profile and risk management
3 Employee recruitment, motivation and retention
4 Investor relationships and access to capital
5 Learning and innovation
6 Competitiveness and market positioning
7 Operational efficiency
8 Licence to operate

Corporate citizenship in action at GE
'Ecomagination' is GE's committment to imagine

and build innovative solutions that benefit customers and society at large. It is both a business strategy that drives growth at GE and a promise to contribute positively to the environment in the process.
In May 2005, GE launched its ecomagination initiative based on four commitments.
1 GE's commitment to double its investment in R&D for cleaner technologies is on track.
2 GE products and services form the basis of its ecomagination commitment, providing a solution for customers to meet the increasing challenge of running their businesses in a way that continues to minimise the environmental impact.
3 One of GE's four pledges under ecomagination is to improve the energy efficiency of its operations and reduce the company's greenhouse gas (GHG) emissions.
4 GE utilises several vehicles to engage the public, including its website, advertising, special engagements and conferences, stakeholder events and 'dreaming sessions' with customers on issues that will affect specific industries over the next 10 years.

Source: website GE, 2006 and EU, 2006

---

choices and dilemmas. A moral choice often costs more and works against the purposes of an enterprise. Despite this, many enterprises make decisions that lessen maximal profit but which represent a compromise between aiming for higher profit on the one hand and promoting socially acceptable activities on the other.

Moral choice

Many organisations have ethical goals, allow themselves to be influenced by ethical motives and position themselves clearly in relation to them. Managers at all levels often have to make decisions in which ethical issues play a part: for example, singling out those employees to be made redundant because of restructuring requirements or choosing between an employee who is single and someone who has a family to support. What choice should he or she make when the options are an individual with an indigenous background and an immigrant worker, or a female and a male applicant? Ethical aspects play a role one way or another in almost every decision a manager needs to make. The way a manager behaves or interacts with his employees will reveal something about their values, norms and ethical sense.

We can identify four ethical stances: the utilitarian stance, the individual stance, the moral stance and the egalitarian stance.

The utilitarian stance

Utilitarianism is derived from the Latin 'utilis', which means useful. The founder of utilitarianism was J. Bentham (1748–1832), a British man. According to his view, ethical decisions should be based on the outcomes and effects of the decision. The costs weighed up against the benefits is the criterion, and the best decision is that which benefits the greatest number of people. Closing a department because this is the best way to guarantee the continuity of the organisation is an example of such a decision.

Utilitarian stance

The individual stance

Individual stance

Here, the focus is on the individual. The rights and freedoms of the individual must be protected and respected. In organisations, this means that the individual and his development are of crucial importance. Decisions need to be made with the long-term interests of the individual in mind. Honesty and integrity are important aspects of this approach.

The egalitarian stance

Egalitarian stance

According to this stance, decisions are ethical when the costs and profits are divided between the interested parties and / or individuals as proportionally and impartially as possible. An organisation's policy on salary should not permit differences between employees who perform the same task or provide the same level of effort.

The moral stance

Moral stance

According to this stance, a decision is ethical when it agrees with our fundamental rights. These rights should be respected and protected when making decisions. They include the right to live freely, to receive fair treatment, to respect for one's privacy, to equality and to the freedom to express one's own opinion. The 'Universal Declaration of Human Rights' (United Nations, 1948) may serve as a moral guideline.

Ethical behaviour

To avoid becoming involved in a moral conflict, managers need to put their personal decisions and behaviours to the test, using the norms he or she has developed by living within society.[15] The ethical behaviour of an organisation is also influenced by various other factors (see Figure 6.23).

Figure 6.23   Factors influencing the ethical behaviour of organisations

Norms and values that are commonly accepted by society are thus the most influential. These behaviours concern values such as honesty, privacy, justice, social norms, habits and traditions. These cultural norms and values developed over time differ from one country and continent to another. Since an organisation forms part of society at large, ethical behaviour in organisations is determined to a large degree by that society.

Professional norms and values are also playing an increasingly important role. Groups of professionals have their own codes (physicians, accountants, consul-

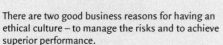

How to create an ethical culture

There are two good business reasons for having an ethical culture – to manage the risks and to achieve superior performance.
Additional research shows that companies which have principled leaders and a truly values-based culture significantly outperform those that do not.

1 Develop a collective understanding of ethics
Most companies have a set of values or principles that mention ethical behaviour, but their employees are often not aware of them. It can help to introduce an awareness of what 'ethics' actually involve and how they relate to the culture of the business.

2 Instil your values into your behaviour
From this, a practical framework can be formed, consisting of defined behaviours and practical support for those facing ethical dilemmas. This can be achieved by interviewing a cross-section of leaders to ascertain examples of the types of behaviours that underpin the values. The final step is to translate the values into behavioural descriptions that are written in the language of the business and supported by the leadership.

3 Embed the new values and behaviours
The key is to introduce a new way of thinking about ethics. Begin by raising awareness of ethical issues,

then introduce new ways of resolving ethical dilemmas. Finally, encourage teams to tackle live business issues. We use the 'Right' aid to memory: What are the rules? How do we act with integrity? What good is created? What harm is avoided? Can we be open with the truth?

4 Introduce ethics into all talent management processes
Ethical behaviour needs to be considered in every aspect of the talent life cycle, including: recruitment, performance management, succession planning and disciplinary proceedings.

5 Find out what people think
As with all corporate change, there needs to be both clear communication and a range of feedback techniques. A good method for detecting the gap between rhetoric and reality is to poll employees, customers and suppliers regularly on the defined behaviours. Where strengths are seen, they should be made known widely and individuals and teams praised for their ethical behaviour. Where corrective actions are needed, it is again important that change is seen to take place.

Source: *People Management*, February 2006

---

tants etc.). If an individual belonging to that group then deviates from these codes, he or she could be barred from it. Individual norms and values are also important and are strongly influenced or even formed via one's education or via peer groups.

6.6   Management and information

As mentioned at the beginning of this chapter, most of a manager's time is taken up by interpersonal, informational and decision-making activities. According to Mintzberg, a manager spends 40% of time on information exchange.[16] We can identify four informational roles relating to the manager. (See Figure 6.24.)

Informational roles

The 'Antenna' role entails the manager collecting as much information as possible from external sources (personal and business contacts and experts) and internal environmental sources (employees and other managers) in order to obtain as complete as possible a description of the organisation's activities. For the most part this information comes from informal personal contacts and to a lesser degree from formal channels such as memos, written reports, executive pronouncements and the company's magazine.

'Antenna' role

We need to be aware of the fact that information is not synonymous with data. Data represents facts. When those facts are transformed in such a way as to become useful to the receiver, they will have become information. Data is therefore the raw material required to provide information. A manager analyses and interprets the information received before distributing it in a particular quantity and form to other

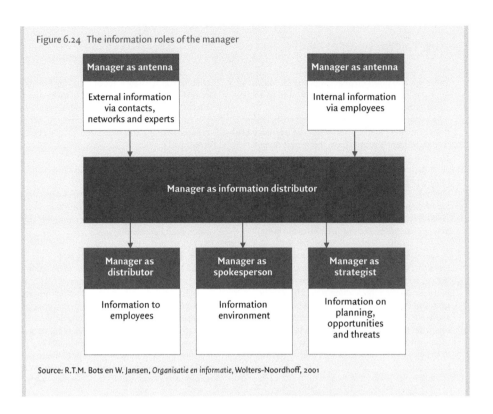

Figure 6.24 The information roles of the manager

Manager as antenna	Manager as antenna
External information via contacts, networks and experts	Internal information via employees

Manager as information distributor

Manager as distributor	Manager as spokesperson	Manager as strategist
Information to employees	Information environment	Information on planning, opportunities and threats

Source: R.T.M. Bots en W. Jansen, *Organisatie en informatie*, Wolters-Noordhoff, 2001

Information distributor

members of the organisation. As such, the manager performs the role of information distributor. Stakeholders will derive other types of information from outside the organisation: information from customers, suppliers, the press (in its role as public spokesperson) and so on. A manager also plays an important role in determining the strategy of the organisation by obtaining an overview of the organisation as a whole (in his / her role as strategist). To be able to provide leadership to the organisation and make the most appropriate decisions, a manager must have relevant, fast and future-directed information.

In general, we can identify three types of information:

Strategic information

1 *Strategic information.* This information relates to the organisation's position within the environment and often provides the basis for medium-range decisions. Information about competitors, the market and politics are some examples of such information.

Tactical and organisational information

2 *Tactical and organisational information.* This is information that relates to the internal management of the organisation and includes decisions on how to go about strategic decision-making.

Operational information

3 *Operational information.* This information concerns the primary processes in the organisation, such as production, transport, administration and sales. Decisions on how to implement tactical decisions are based on it. Production figures, cancellation and waste percentages, figures on sick leave, amount of overtime per employee and so on fall under this category.

The various types of information needed depend on the management level and the decisions made at that level. In general, the executive management level will be the first to create strategic information. Lower management levels within the organisation contribute to that information, generating information which flows to the executive levels in summary form, where it is then combined with other information and an overall view obtained.

How I work, by Bill Gates

'It's pretty incredible to look back 30 years to when Microsoft was starting and realise how work has been transformed. We are finally getting close to what is called the digital workstyle.

If you look at this office there isn't much paper in it. I have three screens, synchronised to form a single desktop. I can drag items from one to the next. The screen on the left has my list of e-mails. On the center screen is usually the specific e-mail I'm reading and responding to. And my browser is on the right-hand screen. This setup gives me the ability to glance and see what news has come in while I am working on something, and to bring up a link that's related to an e-mail and look at it while the e-mail is still in front of me.

At Microsoft, e-mail is the medium of choice. I get about 100 e-mails a day. We apply to keep it to that level.

The challenge is how to communicate effectively with e-mail. I use tools such as 'in-box rules' and search folders to mark and group messages based on their content and importance.

Staying focussed is one issue; that's the problem of information overload. The other problem is information underload. Being flooded with information doesn't mean we have the right information or that we are in touch with the right people. I deal with this by using SharePoint, a tool that creates websites for collaboration on specific projects, These sides contain plans, schedules, discussion boards, and other information. Sharepoint puts me in touch with lots of people deep in the organisation.

The one low-tech bit of equipment still in my office is my whiteboard.'

Source: *Fortune*, April 2006

As Figure 6.25 shows, top managers require tactical, organisational and operational information. The same applies to the lower management levels. With middle management becoming more involved in strategic management, this has generated a need for greater levels of strategic information.

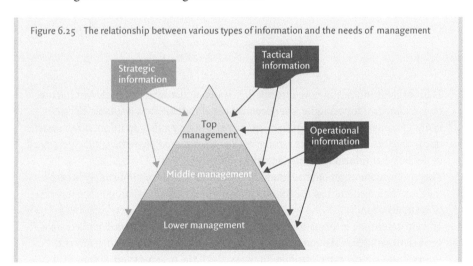

Figure 6.25   The relationship between various types of information and the needs of management

The informational need of a manager also depends on the specific management function (e.g. the sales manager needs sales figures and a production manager needs figures on manpower in relation to production lines), on the management level (top, middle, lower) and on the individual management style.

Informational need

Management information should be:

- *Recent* (information is often made available too late)
- *Reliable* (the manager has to be able to trust the details)
- *Global* (condensed, without detail but in summary format). Many people think they are presenting information when they are actually merely providing data.
- *Predictive* (when information is needed for decisions that relate to the future)

For a manager, completeness of information is often of less importance than the information criteria mentioned above. Less information on time is often better than extensive information that arrives too late.

A flexible information system can help managers fulfil their informational needs.

Information system

An information system will be composed of people, machines and activities that transform data into information that satisfies the needs of both organisational and non-organisational members. As this definition implies, almost everyone and everything within an organisation is part of the information system or acts on its behalf (e.g. telephoning people, filing, producing and distributing lists).

With increasing computerisation of organisations, the informational needs of managers will change too. Growth in technology means better information available faster, and the need for information will grow correspondingly. Supply of information however, should not be a goal in itself. It must relate to the goals of the organisational as a whole (see Figure 6.26).

Figure 6.26 The relationship between the general organisational strategy, information strategy and information planning

Many organisations still have information systems that were once relevant but are now redundant: for example, overviews on paper that are now available electronically. Organisations need to reflect on the requirements that an information system needs to meet. To maintain control over their operational processes, managers need to define what information they actually require.

The involvement of top management in determining information supply is essential. Top management has the following important tasks in relation to the information supply chain[17]:

- To help determine information strategy. Such a strategy should be derived from a

Information strategy

general organisational strategy. An information strategy should show how the information supply can contribute to the goals of the organisation. It should also specify how to go about implementing and supervising the information supply.

Various organisational functions

- To indicate the links between the various organisational functions (purchasing, sales, production, personnel, finance and other information) and their operating conditions.
- To indicate the degree of integration between the various information systems both within and outside the organisation. Since information systems are concerned with

communication, they run the risk of becoming fragmented, causing coordination problems. Many organisations have computerised administrative, production and office systems. It is up to management to decide to what extent these information systems should become integrated.

- To indicate informational needs, especially focussing on the various levels of management.

An informational advantage over others could be used as a tool for exerting an influence on decisions. If a person has specialised information, this could be used to obtain a position of power over others. Competitive relationships between mangers or departments, each trying to secure their own interests by managing the supply of information in a 'creative' way, are typical of organisations. However, personal or departmental interests are not necessarily contrary to the interests of the organisation: rivalry may lead to increased effort and alertness on the part of the organisation's staff members.

Information can be used improperly, as in the following:
- Supplying too little information in order to provide a false picture
- Presenting information in such a way that it looks more positive than is justified (e.g. by adapting the scale division within a diagram)
- Spreading information to certain departments in order to provoke certain emotions
- Withholding information in order to influence the decision-making process in either a negative or positive way
- Supplying too much information in order to delay decision-making or to cause confusion

The following chapter will deal with information in greater detail.

Doing business in Argentina

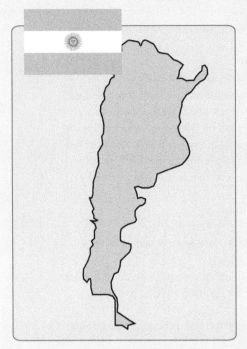

How Argentinians organise and process information

Strong European influences make Argentinians less open to discussion of new ideas than the citizens of most Latin American countries. Those with a higher education are more apt to think abstractly although associative and experiential thinking is the general rule. Strong personal relationships make Argentinians more concerned about the consequences of an action than about the action itself.

What Argentinians accept as evidence

The forces of feeling, faith and facts are in obvious conflict. Argentinians look at problems from a subjective perspective, and these feelings are usually influenced by faith in some ideology (primarily the Catholic church, a political party, or ethnocentrism). Facts are acceptable as long as they do not contradict either feeling or faith.

The basis of behaviour

While humanitarian values are strong, society is becoming more materialistic and consumerism is strong. Value systems in the predominant culture – how right is distinguished from wrong, good from evil, and so on – are described under the next three headings.

The locus of decision-making

Decisions are usually made by an individual, but they are always made with the best interest of a larger group in mind. The most honoured group is the extended family, from which one gains one's self-identity. Kinship and friendships play major roles in decision-making.

Sources of anxiety reduction

Although the older generations still derive their sense of security from the church and the extended family, the younger generation is putting more faith in the social structure. This sometimes leads to unrealistic allegiance to a strong political figure or ideology.

Issues relating to equality / inequality

Those who are in power consider themselves entitled to the privileges that come with the office. Although *machismo* is still very strong, it is being challenged on all fronts. There are now more women than men at school, and women are taking a leading role in both politics and business.

Ten examples of Argentinian business practices

1 It's wise to make your first appointment in Argentina via an enchufado – an individual who has high-level contacts in your industry segment. This person opens doors and can greatly facilitate the process of doing business.
2 Argentinian executives may put in a very long day, often lasting till 10.00 p.m. An 8.00 p.m. business meeting is not all unusual.
3 Personal relationships are far more important than corporate ones. Each time your company changes its representative, you'll be starting virtually from scratch. A new relationship must be built up before business can proceed.
4 Don't assume that each section of a contract is finalised once agreement on that section has been reached. Until the entire contract is signed, each section is subject to renegotiation.
5 As dinner does not begin until 10.00 p.m., Argentinians have tea or coffee and pastries between 4.00 p.m. and 6.00 p.m. If you're in a meeting during that time, you'll be offered something. Accept something to drink, even if you don't want it. Argentinians don't put milk in their coffee, so it probably won't be available.
6 Close male friends shake hands or embrace upon meeting; men kiss close female friends. Close female friends usually kiss each other. The full embrace (*abrazo*) may entail a hug, a handshake, and several thumps on the shoulder, ending with another handshake.
7 If a person has a title, it is important to address him or her that title followed by the surname. A Ph.D. or a physician is called *Doctor*. Teachers prefer the title *Profesor*, engineers go by *Ingeniero*, architects are *Arquitecto*, and lawyers are *Abogado*.
8 A pat on the shoulder is a sign of friendship.
9 Dress is very important for making a good impression in Argentina. Your entire wardrobe will be scrutinised.
10 As in any country, any gift given should be of high quality. If the item is produced by your corporation, the corporate name or logo should appear discreetly, not emblazoned over the whole surface.

Source: *Kiss, Bow, or Shake Hands: How to Do Business in Sixty Countries*, by Terri Morrison, Wayne A. Conaway and George A. Borden, Adams Media, 2006.

Summary

Management was defined as a group of organisational leaders whose task it is to direct the organisation. An organisation will have several management levels, each with specific managerial tasks. These tasks relate to policy development and / or execution. Managers spend most of their time communicating with people inside and outside the organisation. As a leader the manager makes use of the power available to him or her. Power was looked at in terms of two important aspects: sources of power and power relationships. The leadership style of a manager is demonstrated in the way he / she directs employees and by his / her attitude.

The following models of leadership style were discussed: leadership styles based on participation and decision-making by subordinates, X-Y theory, the leadership diagram, the three-dimensional model of leadership styles, contingency leadership models, transformational leadership and self leadership. Each theory has its own approach to leadership. In addition, each theory discusses certain aspects of leadership, which is why there is no complete theory of leadership.

Attention was also given to leadership within an international context. The interaction between a manager's professional and private life strongly influences the way he / she functions. Attention was given to entrepreneurship. Lately, there has been increased interest in the ethical aspects of entrepreneurship and management. Many organisations have goals that are influenced by ethical motives and which add to their profile. Four positions on ethics were discussed.

The role adopted by a manager when he communicates with others may take various forms. We discussed the antenna role, the role of distributor and that of spokesperson. The informational need of a manager is determined by the function, the level and the individual management style. The information supply in an organisation is not a goal as such, but derived from organisational goals.

Definitions

§ 6.1 Manager

A person who stimulates and directs the behaviour of other people within an organisation. A manager is often responsible for the financial results of a division or department and is in charge of a group of employees.

§ 6.2 Policy formulating tasks

Tasks to do with diagnosis, predicting, planning and organising.

Policy executing tasks

Tasks to do with delegating of activities and supervising and motivating employees.

§§ 6.2.1 Interpersonal role

A manager directs employees and is responsible for the processes and the results obtained using them. The manager needs to be able to maintain relationships while maintaining the processes and should promote the interests of his / her group both within and outside the organisation.

Informational role

A manager needs information in order to be able to direct the organisation. In turn, he / she communicates the information to organisational members and stakeholders outside the organisation.

Decision-making role

As director of an organisational unit, the manager is responsible for implementing policy. Using information collected and personal contacts, he / she will translate opportunities and threats from the environment and unit strengths and weaknesses into decisions.

§§ 6.3.1 Power

The ability to exercise power in order to influence employees. Power is an essential part of leadership.

§§ 6.3.2 Leadership

The ability to determine the organisation's course of development in collaboration with other employees.

§§ 6.3.3 Leadership style

The form that leadership takes and the attitude with which it is provided.

Leadership diagram

A manner of categorising style based on the apects of task and relationship orientation.

Impoverished management

Low concern for the task and low concern for relationships.

Situational leadership

Leadership style which depends on what the employee is capable of. The criterion is the degree of task maturity possessed by the employee.

Transformational leadership	Leadership during a period of major organisational change. It is a notion emanating from New Age thinking and the idea that we are on the eve of a major revolution which will ultimately bring about an entirely new culture. The key words are awareness, insight, creativity, harmony, spirituality and intuition.
§§ 6.4.3 Entrepreneurship / entrepreneurial management	Management involving the taking of risks. When the environment is very turbulent, organisations need management that is able to discern trends and developments before competitors do so. These perceptions should then be transformed into new plans based on a certain vision and a feeling for the market.
§ 6.6 Antenna role	Management with an emphasis on trying to collect as much information as possible from both the internal and external environment in order to get a complete picture of the organisation.
Information distributor	Management with an emphasis on analysing and interpreting information and then distributing it in a succinct form to other organisational members. The manager will also distribute information to stakeholders outside the organisation.
Strategist	In order to make the right decisions, the manager needs relevant, fast and future-oriented information.
Information strategy	Strategy derived from the general organisational strategy. It should show how information supply contributes to organisational goals.

Statements

Indicate whether the following statements are correct or incorrect, giving reasons for your choices.

1 The management of an organisation consists of all those people who direct others.
2 As organisations become increasingly split up into autonomous units, the tasks of middle managers will become more administrative in nature.
3 Flattening of organisations will mean a reduction in the number of hierarchical levels.
4 According to the faction model, the various parties within the organisation share the same interests.
5 Under an equal power relationship, the emergence of competitors constitutes a possible danger.
6 According to Blake and Mouton, style 9.9 on the Managerial Grid will always give the best results as long as it is applied consistently.
7 Reddin added the dimension of effectiveness to the Managerial Grid of Blake and Mouton.
8 Management styles differ sharply from one another within the various European countries.
9 Ethical behaviour in organisations is determined primarily by the norms and values of the society within which that organisation operates.
10 Information strategy shows how the supply of information can contribute to achieving organisational goals.

Theory questions

1 What is the difference between power and authority?
2 What is the relationship between flattening and power relationships?
3 According to Fiedler, what three aspects contribute to leadership success?
4 a Why is it so hard to manage professionals?
  b Give three recommendations for the management of professionals.
5 What is meant by a horizontal management style?

Practical assignment

Form groups of three to four students.
1 Study the site www.geert-hofstede.com and focus on the five dimensions of cultural differences. Go to 'Business Etiquette'. Choose three or four countries that the group finds interesting and study the general cultural differences and the business etiquette. Make an overview of your findings. Also indicate the consequences for leadership and doing business with those countries.
2 Present your findings to your class.

 For answers see www.marcusvandam.noordhoff.nl.

268 | PART B | People and organisations

Mini case study

Women bring in more

The emancipation program 'Mixed', which aims for more women at the top levels of the business world, is an initiative of the European Commission. What do companies stand to gain if they appoint more women to top positions?

According to American research, they bring in more money. This research, carried out by the Catalyst agency within Fortune 500 companies, showed that organisations with a lot of women in their top man-agement echelons perform much better. It also showed that the most successful companies have more women in top positions. According to Catalyst, business leaders nowadays are increasingly demanding more data on the link between gender diversity and profit. Diversity is one of the key drivers of creativity, innovation and inventions. Diversity stimulates creativity. Diversity is important because of the competition it creates.

Questions

1 'Diversity stimulates creativity'. Can you explain this?
2 Diversity is not only gender diversity but also diversity in terms of culture, sexual orientation, religion, education and physical condition (disabilities). Could these forms of diversity also stimulate creativity in a company? Indicate using examples whether you agree or disagree and provide reasons for your opinion.
3 Some people find it hard to deal with diversity in their work place: for example, they do not like to work together with someone of another sexual orientation, another gender or another religion. How could a company deal with this?

E-mail case study

To:	Andromeda Christofora
Cc:	
Bcc:	
Subject:	Petra property developer

Message:

Dear Andromeda,

As you know, our business is doing well. We are growing quickly and we have a great portfolio of construction projects. The future looks bright!

However, there is one negative development that we are worried about. By tradition, we are a long-established Greek construction company. But in recent years we have started an increasing number of construction projects in other European countries, including France and Spain. Some of them are very attractive developments indeed: mostly small-scale holiday parks built mainly in the Greek style (our trademark, of course). When we do such a project in France or Spain, it is managed by one of our Greek project managers who then stays in that country for a while. We hire local staff for the building process itself.

However, our Greek project managers and the local staff find it extremely hard to work together. It appears that there are all kinds of difficulties with communication. This results in projects not being carried out according to plan. The quality also leaves a lot to be desired. This is happening more and more. The profitability of our international projects is under pressure.

Andromeda, you are experienced with leadership styles within an international context. What advice can you give us? How can we can solve this problem effectively?

With kind regards,

Sebasti Sotirios

7

Decision-making

This chapter deals with the importance of decision-making in organisations. Five kinds of decision-making processes and various aspects of decision-making are discussed. The chapter ends with a description of aids and techniques.

Contents

After studying this chapter
- You will have a general understanding of decision-making in organisations.
- You will be able to identify several kinds of decision-making.
- You will be familiar with the problems that arise during each phase of rational decision-making.
- You will be familiar with and understand the factors influencing decision-making.
- You will know what kinds of aids and techniques are used in decision-making.

271

7.1 The decision-making process

People within organisations are continuously engaged in solving problems. Some will be merely be minor daily problems which are easy to solve, while others will be of vital importance for the continuity of the organisation and will demand further analysis. They may be relatively complex, involving many factors: for example, determining the organisation's direction over the coming five years, selecting those segments of the market that the company should be operational in and developing the best international strategy. For such situations, a well-devised decision-making process is of key importance.

Choices

An important aspect of decision-making is that choices have to be made. In most cases, alternatives will be available and the best one should be chosen. In order to select the best option, relevant information is needed. It follows that the decision-making process is closely related to data collection and data assimilation processes. Decisions often have to be made in situations where there is a lack of information, resulting in a certain degree of uncertainty. Decision-making is a human activity, so cooperation and creativity play an important role. A number of techniques and tools can be used to help make effective decisions.

Human activity

The context in which decisions must be made is becoming increasingly complex due to the following factors (Figure 7.1):

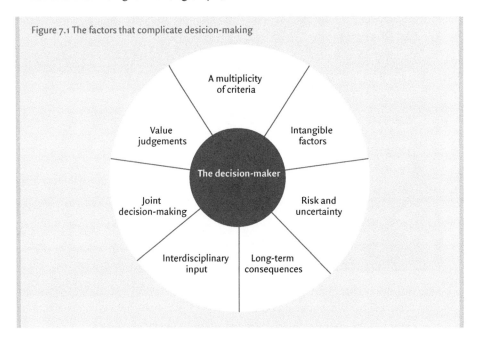

Figure 7.1 The factors that complicate desicion-making

1 *The multiplicity of criteria.* Decisions are made by various parties who often have conflicting interests and use different criteria for the same problem, thereby increasing the complexity of the problem.
2 *Interdisciplinary input.* Specialists are increasingly involved in the decision-making process. They may include those with an in-depth knowledge of technology, law, taxation and marketing. Their various skills must all play a part in reaching the final decision.
3 *Joint decision-making.* Particularly for decisions that are crucial to the future of the organisation, it is essential that they be made by a number of people representing the

Name:	William P. Corbett
Country of origin:	USA
Job title:	Global Account Manager – Business Development
Company:	Schenker Inc.
Company website:	www.schenker.com (subsidiary of Deutsche Bahn)

What important personal qualities must people have to be successful in international work?

Working internationally requires a variety of personal qualities, including but not limited to the following: patience, a friendly demeanour, resilience, persistence, and openness to and acceptance of other cultures.

Although one's task might be to bring about change within an international environment, it is important to realise that change is not always welcomed. These skills are thus critical in navigating international operations and bringing them to a successful conclusion. Didn't I mention patience and acceptance?

Those embarking on an integration of international operations, developing new markets, or just amalgamating the current home office approach and culture would have to employ all of the skills mentioned. These skills and qualities will be tested again and again far beyond anything you could possibly imagine. Take heart: with a good business plan, an aligned bonus structure and goals and a healthy blend and application of these skills, one can succeed internationally.

What is the most important lesson that you have learned from working with people from different cultures?

Understanding the culture is the critical but most intangible element of a successful international venture. Failure to recognise the cultures that are involved and how and what drives each group can spell doom, outright failure, or at least increase costs unnecessarily. One only need reflect on

some of the recent high-profile mergers and failed launches to realise how important culture is.

As I noted earlier, understanding what drives those cultures in their core beliefs and approaches to business is critical. Failure to gain such an insight will sooner or later cause an organisation considerable discord and misunderstandings and be very costly. The costs associated with culture are often not taken into account when embarking on an international venture. It is crucial to understand the culture that one is interfacing with and how it may impact on your international plans.

In order to develop a successful international operation one needs to have cultural insights. You need to be aware of the country's history and its customs. Take the German / American relationship. The concept of cultural change is one that Germans are relatively unfamiliar with. It is important to realise this. On the other hand, Americans come from a culture of possibilities and the United States is truly a melting pot of different cultures. Americans view change, evolution, and innovation as part of their very being. This should shed some light on how a merger or major development would be approached by both parties. Their World War II history means that Germans are generally reluctant to listen to anyone with a highly emotive leadership style: the steady leader is better received.

As an American and long-time employee of a German company, I have seen at first hand how culture has an impact on the flow of everyday business. Both the German and the American cultures are highly individual. Germans, for example, tend to be dogmatic and directive, and Americans are all about 'we' and 'why', and tend to be more democratic and inclusive. Germans expect orders made by senior members to be followed, never questioned: 'Just do it, don't ask why'. This is relatively unacceptable to most Americans and thus a potential source of conflict.

Despite these differences, unity can be achieved. It depends on gaining cultural understanding and blending in.

The decision-driven organisation

The defining characteristic of high-performing organisations is their ability to make good decisions and to make them happen quickly. The companies that succeed tend to follow a few clear principles:

- Some decisions matter more than others. The decisions that are crucial to building value in the business are the ones that matter the most. Some of them will be strategic decisions, but just as important are the critical operating decisions that drive the business day-to-day and are vital to effective execution. Action is the goal. Good decision-making doesn't end with a decision; it ends with implementation.
- Ambiguity is the enemy. Clear accountability is essential: who contributes input, who makes the decision, and who carries it out? Without clarity, gridlock and delay are the most likely outcomes. Clarity doesn't necessarily mean concentrating authority in a few people; it means defining who has responsibility to make decisions, who provides input, and who is charged with putting decisions into action.

- Speed and adaptability are crucial. The best decision-makers create an environment where people can come together quickly and efficiently to make the most important decisions.
- Decision roles trump the organisational chart. No one decision-making structure will be perfect for every decision. The key is to involve the right people at the right level in the right part of the organisation at the right time.
- A well-aligned organisation reinforces roles. An organisation has to reinforce the right approach to decision-making through its measures and incentives, information flows, and culture.
- Practice beats preaching. Involve the people who will live with the new decision roles in designing these roles. The very process of thinking about the new decision behaviours motivates people to adopt them.

Harvard Business Review, January 2006

various organisational functions. External expertise is sometimes called for and government departments may sometimes also want their say.

4 *Risk and uncertainty.* Markets are changing so quickly and world economic development is so unpredictable that competition can come from unexpected sources. When making decisions, it can be very hard to know what future events and changes are just around the corner. We will look at uncertainty in greater detail in 7.2.

5 *Long-term consequences.* Decisions made with a short time view (controlling expenses, for example) may have indirect long-term consequences (for example, on the competitive position of the enterprise).

6 *Value judgments.* Decisions are often made by people from various backgrounds, and on the basis of different perceptions, aspirations, norms and values. The recent growth of sustainable entrepreneurship and ethical issues have not made this any easier.

7 *Intangible factors.* To make choices as objectively as possible, factors within the process are often converted into a monetary value. However, enterprises are increasingly expected to take social factors such as sustainability, the environment and ethics into account.

7.2   Decision-making in organisations

Decisions made within organisations are about issues or problems of a varied nature, derive from a variety of situations and need to be worked on by various people or groups. If there is a significant discrepancy between what should be happening and what is actually happening, there is a problem.

Routine problems

Specific problem

Problems can be either routine or specific in character (see Figure 7.2). Common daily problems such as dealing with complaints can be handled using set procedures. More specific problems such as determining the best price for a product demand a less structured approach.

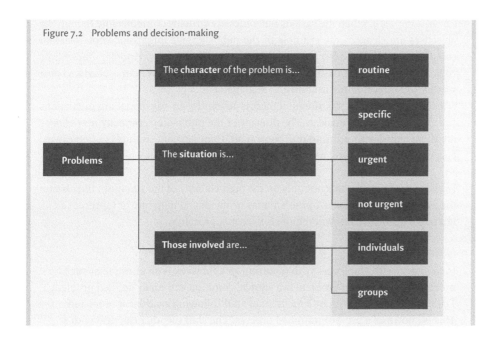

Figure 7.2 Problems and decision-making

Sometimes a quick decision is needed (for example, when a competitor lowers prices and you have to decide whether to follow suit) while in other cases more time is available and a careful assessment can be made (for example, when a new office location is needed). Both individuals and groups may be involved in the decision-making process.

An important characteristic of decision-making is that a choice has to be made between a number of alternatives. Often these alternatives are linked to unpredictable future events: for example, economic growth in South East Asia, a competitor's reaction when a new product is introduced, future wage costs.
The extent to which these future events can be predicted plays a major role in decision-making. The degree of predictability will vary. (See Figure 7.3.)

Predictability

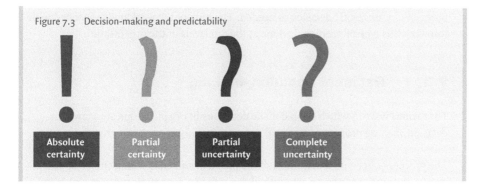

Figure 7.3 Decision-making and predictability

1 *Absolute certainty.* When the objectives and outcomes of all alternatives are known exactly: for example, when selecting a printer for this textbook, the publisher knows the precise number of copies required, the required quality and the deadline. The publisher can then invite tenders from a number of printers, and compare offers.

Absolute certainty

2 *Partial certainty.* When the objectives are clear but the exact outcome of the alternatives is unknown though to a certain extent predictable. In our example, if sale figures from the past are available a prediction can be made about the number of books likely to be sold.

Partial certainty

3 *Partial uncertainty.* When the various outcomes are virtually unpredictable though the objectives are clear. In the example of the publisher, we might not know whether competing publishers will also be bringing out new books. Another uncertainty could be the overall increase or decrease in the number of class hours scheduled next year for the subject 'Organisation and Management'.

4 *Complete uncertainty.* In this situation there is absolutely no way of making predictions and the objectives are unclear. The director of the publishing company may choose not to go ahead with printing this book at all. Complete uncertainty is often caused by a rapidly changing and turbulent environment.

Decision-making depends not only on the predictability of the situation, but also on the nature of the problem. A problem may be incidental in nature or represent an unknown quantity. They will require different approaches.

Incidental problems

How to deal with employees who reporting sick for work is an example of such a problem. An incidental problem is a simple, common and easily defined problem. The message is dealt with by a member of staff following a clear-cut procedure.

This is known as a pre-programmed process. The staff member can deal with a problem of this kind in a routine manner as the organisation will have laid down procedures, rules and guidelines.

- *Procedure.* This is a series of mutually coherent and successive steps for reacting to the problem.
- *Rule.* This is an explicit agreement about what may and may not be done.
- *Guidelines.* These provide general direction for decision-making.

Resolving such problems and bearing the workload they entail falls on the lower levels of the organisation.

Unique problems

Problems of this sort are problems new to the organisation and they occur less frequently. Typically, the information available is incomplete and unclear. An example of such a problem is how to develop a new product in the absence of pre-programmed

processes. A 'once-off' decision is needed. The bulk of the workload associated with resolving this type of problem is done at the top levels of the organisation.

7.3 Rational decision-making

The various ways in which people make decisions in organisations are known as decision-making processes. Rational decision-making is one such process.

The process starts with a definition of the problem and ends with a choice of an option. A number of phases are worked through in a systematic manner. Solutions to any problematic situation can be found using this approach. Information is collected during the course of the process and analysed. It is then used both as input and output in the decision-making process.

In order to have an effect on the process, this information should meet a number of requirements:

- It has to be relevant
- It has to be reliable
- It has to be available on time

Carsdirect: A resource for car comparison!

CarsDirect is the leading multi-brand online car-buying service, providing new and pre-owned automobiles and related products and services. As a pioneer of the direct online car buying model, CarsDirect has become the natural choice for consumers who demand objectivity, choice and upfront pricing, and for dealers who want to leverage the Internet for cost-effective incremental sales and revenue. CarsDirect offers no-haggle, upfront new car pricing to consumers. They can research, price, order, purchase, insure and finance a vehicle online via an intuitive website that offers product information for nearly every make, model and style of automobile available in the United States.

The CarsDirect Research Center gives shoppers all the tools needed to make an informed buying decision, including vehicle reviews, ratings, safety features and specifications. Customers can even simultaneously compare the specifications of competing

vehicles, or search for available manufacturer rebates and incentives on any new vehicle.

Source: www. carsdirect.com, 2006

- Its costs should be in proportion to its value
- It should be presented in a way that makes it easily viewed: that is, the lay-out, size, details and distinction between important and incidental issues should be clear.

The many possible sources of information include one's own data resources, specially commissioned and executed market research, a study of literature, external databases and consultation with suppliers and customers.

Sources of information

The following phases of the rational decision-making process can be identified (Figure 7.4):

1 Defining the problem
2 Devising of alternatives
3 Evaluation of alternatives
4 Making a choice
5 Implementing and monitoring the decision

7.3.1   Defining the problem

There are two aspects to problem definition: problem identification and problem analysis. Problem identification is the detection and determination of the problem. A problem arises when the desired situation (the norm) deviates from the actual situation, either in a positive or negative sense (Figure 7.5).

Problem definition
Problem identification

Problems arise in various ways. They may be caused by external circumstances (for example, a delay in the delivery of an order) or be a logical consequence of a management decision (for example, sales of a particular product needing to be increased by 10% within three years).

When a problem is detected, it is important to ascertain its exact character. 'A well-formulated problem is halfway to being solved', as the saying goes.

It is important to realise that not everybody is interested in identifying problems. One may be faced with problem denial and evasive behaviour. Lack of clear objectives and norms in certain fields is common in many organisations and where this is so, problems are difficult to recognise.

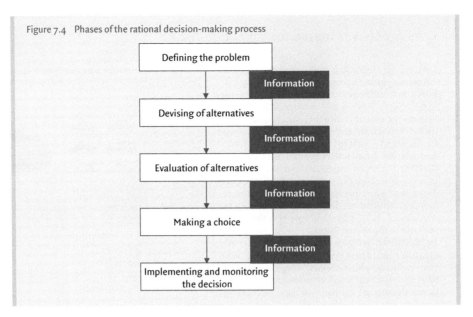

Figure 7.4 Phases of the rational decision-making process

Defining the problem

Information

Devising of alternatives

Information

Evaluation of alternatives

Information

Making a choice

Information

Implementing and monitoring
the decision

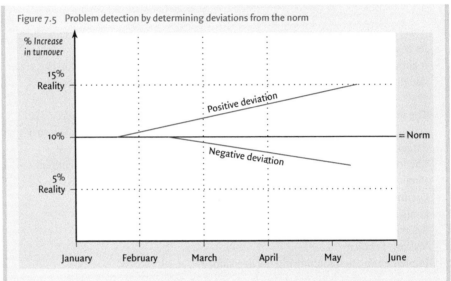

Figure 7.5 Problem detection by determining deviations from the norm

% Increase
in turnover

15%
Reality

Positive deviation

10%   = Norm

Negative deviation

5%
Reality

January   February   March   April   May   June

When a problem has been recognised, it has to be analysed. This involves searching for the real causes and consequences of the problem. Facts corroborating the existence of problem have to be found. Since they are is often based on subjective ideas about certain developments, extreme care should be taken at this stage.

During this phase of the process the following questions can be asked:
· Is the problem a minor or a major one?
· How urgent is the problem?
· What is the scope of the problem?
· How does the problem relate to other areas / divisions within and outside the organisation?
· Is the nature of the problem relational or organisational?

The gap between planning and decision-making

How executives plan:
66% of those surveyed say that their companies conduct strategic planning only at prescribed times.
67% of those surveyed say planning is done on a unit-by-unit basis.

How executives decide:
100% of those surveyed say that they make strategic decisions on an ongoing basis and without regard to the calendar.

70% of those surveyed say that they make strategic decisions on an issue-by-issue basis.

No wonder that only 11% of executives say that they are convinced that strategic planning is worth the effort!!

Source: *Harvard Business Review*, January 2006

7.3.2 Devising of alternatives

During this phase, viable alternatives capable of resolving the problem as identified during the previous phase have to be developed. Sometimes the solution will already be evident in the way the problem has been described and analysed. Sometimes the solution will not be as evident.

Devising of alternatives

How alternatives are devised will partly depend on the organisation's familiarity with the problem. If the problem is already a well-known one, a solution that was used in the past might be suitable. New problems will need the devising of as many alternatives as possible and it is important not to simply take the first option devised. Finding a lot of alternatives will place major demands on the creativity of the organisation's members (see Section 7.5.1 for more details).

Creativity

7.3.3 Evaluation of alternatives

Now that all the options have been identified, during this phase the aim is to select the best alternative. Two aspects play an important role here:

Select the best alternative

1 Criteria have to be drawn up.
2 The likely consequences of each alternative have to be assessed.

To make a wise decision will involve weighing up all the criteria. The complexity and specific nature of some problems will mean that the criteria are difficult to formulate and will not be generally applicable. However, the criteria should meet a number of requirements:

- *The criteria must be measurable.* Criteria have to be quantitative or else the testing of alternatives against criteria will become ambiguous and differences in interpretation may arise.
- *The criteria must be feasible.* It must be possible to implement the chosen option and the people who are responsible for doing this must be convinced that this is possible.
- *The criteria must fit the problem.* There must be a plausible link between the criterion and the problem. If the terms are too general, the wrong choice could be made.
- *The criteria must complement each other.* If the criteria are in contradiction with each other, a situation will arise where no final choice can be made. A compromise solution might have to be found or certain criteria prioritised over others.
- *The criteria must relate to all aspects of the alternative.* A limited number of criteria might result in certain consequences not being tested or taken into consideration. Whether a solution stands up or fails will depend on how extensively each aspect of the option is tested.

Decision-making in the European Union

Decision-making at European Union level involves various European institutions, in particular:
- The European Commission
- The European Parliament (EP)
- The Council of the European Union.

In general, it is the European Commission that proposes new legislation but it is the Council and Parliament that pass the laws. Other institutions and bodies also play a role here.

The rules and procedures for EU decision-making are laid down in treaties. Every proposal for a new European law is based on a specific treaty article, referred to as the 'legal basis' of the proposal. This determines which legislative procedure must be followed. The three main procedures are consultation, assent and co-decision.

1 Consultation. Under the consultation procedure, the Council consults Parliament as well as the European Economic and Social Committee (EESC) and the Committee of the Regions (CoR). Parliament can:
   - approve the Commission's proposal,
   - reject it,
   - or ask for amendments.

   If Parliament asks for amendments, the Commission will consider all the changes Parliament suggests. If it accepts any of these suggestions it will send the Council an amended proposal.
   The Council examines the amended proposal and either adopts it or amends it further. In this procedure, as in all others, if the Council amends a Commission proposal it must do so unanimously.

2 Assent. The Council has to obtain the European Parliament's assent before certain very important decisions are taken. The procedure is the same as in the case of consultation, except that Parliament cannot amend a proposal: it must either accept or reject it. Acceptance ('assent') requires an absolute majority vote.

3 Co-decision. This is the procedure now used for most EU law-making. Under the co-decision procedure, Parliament does not merely give its opinion: it shares legislative power equally with the Council. If Council and Parliament cannot agree on a piece of proposed legislation, it is put before a conciliation committee composed of equal numbers of Council and Parliament representatives. Once this committee has reached agreement, the text is sent once again to Parliament and the Council and it is finally adopted as law.

Modernising the system

The EU's decision-making system has evolved over half a century. But it was originally designed for a community of just six nations. The EU now has 25 member states, and its membership will increase further in the years ahead. Its decision-making system is in obvious need of simplification and streamlining. To avoid paralysis, most decisions should have to be made by 'qualified majority voting' rather than requiring every single country to agree.

Having tested all the options, the one that seems to solve the problem the best is the one to select. However, the consequences of choosing one alternative over another have to be compared. The likely effects of each option must be estimated. This involves weighing up the positive and negative aspects of each: a crucial stage of the final selection process.

Positive and negative aspects

Examining the consequences can lead to some alternatives being seen as unfeasible due to such factors as unacceptable costs.

7.3.4 Making a choice

Final choice

After the alternatives have been evaluated on the basis of the criteria, a final choice has to be made. A number of possibilities exist:
- If one of the options satisfies the criteria perfectly, this alternative should be chosen.
- If no alternative completely satisfies the criteria, either new alternatives have to be found, or the criteria have to be adjusted.
- If two or more alternatives produce the same result, further research is necessary.

A possible solution in such a situation is not only to look at the ultimate consequences of choosing a particular alternative, but also at considerations such as timing, resources and risks associated with each alternative.

A factor that may influence the choice is the degree of uncertainty. Not all of the required information may be available and predictions are only possible to a limited extent.

7.3.5 Implementing and monitoring the decision

When a particular alternative is chosen, the decision has to be translated into plans and actions. It is important that the decision have the support of the organisation. Decisions that lead to changes in the organisation may arouse a lot of resistance. This may be due to a number of reasons:

Implementing and monitoring

- *Perceptual reasons.*   An inability to imagine the new situation
- *Emotional reasons.*   Fear and uncertainty in an unknown situation
- *Cultural reasons.*   A desire to maintain existing norms, values and convictions
- *Environmental reasons.* Anxiety that management will fail to provide sufficient information and support

If these areas are not taken into account sufficiently it may appear afterwards that the choice of option was not correct.

Finally, how progress will be monitored and reported should be made clear.

Two approaches to decision-making

Not all decision-making processes are effective. Research by David A. Garvin and Michael A. Roberto, from the Harvard Business School in Boston, shows that two approaches are often used. One can best be described as 'defending' and the other as 'researching'. At first, these approaches may seem similar: a group of people making decisions. Further study, however, will show that these two approaches produce quite different results and that the 'researching' approach is the preferred method by far. This approach is an open process, focussed on the exchange of ideas and collective devising of alternatives, leading to a well-considered decision. The 'defending' approach resembles a battle of wills, though not always an intentionally engaged in battle. Those at the meeting who stand up for their own point of view may be completely blind to the argu-

ments of others. Below is a comparison of the two approaches.

	Defending	Researching
Concept	competition	cooperation
Aim of discussion	convincing and lobbying	testing and evaluating
Role of participants	spokesperson	critical thinker
Behavioural patterns	• a battle to convince others	• balanced arguments
	• defensive of one's own position	• open to alternatives
		• accept constructive criticism
Minority positions	discouraging or rejecting	developing and appreciating
Result / outcome	winners and losers	jointly owned result

7.4   Irrational decision-making

Ideal model

The rational decision-making process discussed above can be seen as an ideal model. It supposes that decisions are based on a clear problem definition with an option being chosen after careful assessment of the alternatives.

In reality, the decision-making process may be very different for the following reasons:

· Insufficient information is available.
· The rational decision-making process takes too much time.
· Only a limited amount of money is available for buying extra information.
· The decision-makers have limited capacities.
· The decision-makers have conflicting interests.
· Divergent opinions are not always tolerated.

In practice, we can identify four types of decision-making processes (Figure 7.6), namely: neo-rational, bureaucratic, political and open-ended. This classification is based on the degree of centralisation (the top-down influence of decisions), and the degree of formality (the issuing of rules).

Degree of centralisation
Degree of formality

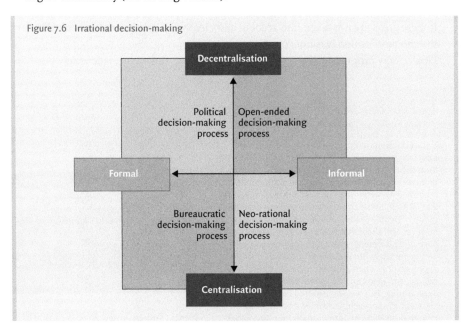

Figure 7.6   Irrational decision-making

7.4.1   The neo-rational decision-making process

Informal and centralised decision-making process

'Neo'-rational process

This process resembles the rational type discussed in Section 7.3. It is informal and centralised and in most cases only one person makes the decisions. There is no extensive prior research and the decision-maker is not impeded by a lot of rules. It is known as the 'neo'-rational process because emotional and intuitive aspects also play a role. The advantage of this decision-making process is that it is directed by one point of view and has clear targets that are acceptable to everybody. A disadvantage is that not many people are involved: there is little room for the opinion of anyone other than the central decision-maker.

Difficult decisions? Put on different hats!

Our thinking processes are quite complicated. All sorts of thoughts, emotions and reactions mingle with each other. Dr Edward de Bono has developed a simple but effective method that can help everyone to become a better thinker and therefore to make better decisions. The method is known as 'Six Thinking Hats'.[1]

De Bono has identified six different thinking styles, associating them with six hats of different colours. The categories created are:

1 White hat. White is neutral and objective and relates to objective facts and numbers.
2 Red hat. Red suggests anger, emotion and threats. The red hat provide the emotional and intuitive perspective.
3 Yellow hat. Yellow is sunny and positive. The yellow hat symbolises optimism and relates to hope as well as positive and constructive thinking.
4 Green hat. Green is the colour of grass and vegetation and it refers to growth. The green hat symbolises creativity, movement and new ideas.
5 Blue hat. Blue is the sky that is above us. The blue hat refers to the control and organisation of our thinking process.
6 Black hat. Black is dark and it has negative associations. The black hat considers the negative aspects and is the devil's advocate: why something should not be done.

The purpose of the Six Thinking Hats model is to unravel the thinking process. This is done by putting on a different hat and then 'thinking' according to the hat.

Application during a meeting
First, the problem that needs to be resolved has to be defined. Then a discussion takes place using the different perspectives (the thinking hats). After one discussion has taken place, the next hat is put on, following a certain order.
The order may be:

EDWARD DE BONO
Six Thinking Hats

An essential approach to business management from the creator of *Lateral Thinking*

1 Blue hat. How should we organise the process? In what order, in how much time, and who takes the minutes?
2 White hat. What facts and figures are available?
3 Red hat. How do we feel about the problem?
4 Yellow hat. What are the positive aspects?
5 Black hat. Where is it likely to fail or not work out?
6 Green hat. In view of the previous perspectives, what are the options?

The advantages of using the Six Thinking Hats model are as follows:
· It helps to clarify the thinking process.
· It leads to more creative thinking.
· It improves communication and decision-making.

7.4.2 The bureaucratic decision-making process

This type is characterised by decisions based on fixed rules instead of consciously made choices as is the case in the neo-rational decision-making process. Extensive use of rules, planning and controls mean that this type of process is very formal and centralised. The rules may be internal (e.g. corporate guidelines for the lay-out of advertisements) as well as external (e.g. legislation). It strong point is that experience from the past is taken into consideration and the rules are known by all so there is no ambiguity. The downside of the bureaucratic decision-making process is, however, that innovation is stifled.

Bureaucratic decision-making process

7.4.3 The political decision-making process

This process has a formal and decentralised character. The latter results from the involvement of many different parties with divergent interests. Decisions result from

Political decision-making process

negotiations and interactions between groups. The advantage of this process is that everybody has a good opportunity to influence decision-making. However, the process carries the potential for a lot of energy to be spent on internal political games, and the final result might be a stalemate or even a severely damaged organisation.

7.4.4   The open-ended decision-making process

The open-ended decision-making process has both a decentralised and an informal character. It has no clear starting and ending points. Decision-making is erratic and unpredictable. There are no clear objectives and decisions have an ad hoc character with chance playing a large role. The turbulence creates new situations to which one has to adapt constantly. Step-by-step decisions are advisable, with follow-up decisions based on new developments and information. The process is flexible and allows for corrections. There is always room for new ideas and creativity is stimulated. However, the down side is that the decisions made may not be very effective.

The types of decision-making process mentioned above rarely occur in pure form. The character of the process often depends on the situation in which it occurs. An organisation might use a neo-rational decision-making process in one situation while opting for an open-ended process in another. It is important for employees to be aware of the decision-making method so that they can determine their own position in the process.

7.5   Aspects of decision-making

Running an organisation means ongoing decision-making. To react to changes in the environment and to safeguard the continuity of the organisation these decisions must be flexible, efficient and effective. In the following sections, various aspects of decision-making that are related to these objectives will be discussed:
· Creativity
· Participation
· Meetings
· Negotiations
· Power (see Section 6.3.1)
· Styles of decision-making

7.5.1   Creativity

Since creativity can increase an organisation's competitive advantage, employee creativity should be utilised to the fullest during all phases of the decision-making process. A broad range of tools is available to free up and encourage creativity.

One widely used tool is brainstorming, a method that can be used to generate a lot of new ideas quickly. The focus is on generating these new ideas rather than evaluating them or making a selection from them.
During a brainstorming session, criticism of new ideas is discouraged as it would put others off making new suggestions of their own, thereby defeating the whole purpose of the exercise. It is important to create the sort of atmosphere in which individuals feel empowered to be creative. During a brainstorming session, initial suggestions should be used as a springboard for ideas to be developed further by others and for creating new perspectives.

Brain jogging: how to get the most from a creative session[2]

Slumped in a chair, feet and wine on the table: the ideal posture to stimulate creativity? Rubbish! The most imaginative explosions occur in a tightly structured process with hard and fast rules:

- **Delay judgment.** No judgements should be made during the creative process.
- **Lying is allowed.** Let your imagination run wild. Screaming boxes of washing powder, bears playing chess, everything is allowed.
- **Privacy from the outside world, openness inside the group.** Mutual trust is essential so that no one feels like a fool. All the mad ideas remain within the group. Not even the customer needs to know how the solution came about.
- **Space for the impossible.** Give extra attention to imaginative suggestions that seem unworkable at first: it is these ideas that stimulate thinking out of the box.
- **No hierarchy or arrogance.** Differences in position should not play a role. If a director refers to his or her position during a session, the process will stop. The group punishes this kind of remark with a black card.

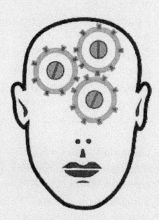

- **Criticism afterwards.** Only at the end of the session should ideas be evaluated critically according to various criteria.

Brainstorming sessions often take place at a location that is quite different from the normal working environment and the participants are often a specific group. For example, office workers might meet at a rural location, a potentially stimulating change. Brainstorming works best in small groups of 10 to 15 people. Involving people from various backgrounds will enhance the results since they will introduce new perspectives on the problem.

It must be clear to the participants what the key problem is. Experience shows that brainstorming is most effective when:

- Subjects or problems are simple in nature. The greater the complexity the more specialists are needed and this would be to the detriment of the particular nature of brainstorming sessions.
- Sufficient knowledge of the problems is available.
- The problems or subject matter are clearly defined.
- The participants are keen to suggest solutions to the problem.
- The sessions do not last longer than about an hour.

7.5.2 Participation

Many employees find a challenging job essential. It increases their motivation and motivated staff will take on all sorts of tasks and will feel more involved in helping the organisation to reach its goals. One aspect of a challenging job is the opportunity for the job holder to be included in general and work-related decisions. Employee participation combines the rights and competencies of the staff to influence the establishment, execution and control of company policy and the decisions that lead to this. Participation may be indirect (workers councils where elected staff members discuss issues) or direct (staff representatives meeting department heads to ratify employment conditions). With both, workers are able to influence decision-making in their own department, increasing their involvement during work. Within Europe, employee participation in multinational organisations occurs via a European workers council.

Participation

Works Councils

Depending on the size of the organisation and the country of origin, employee councils have:

1 A right to information: the employer is obliged to give all information needed by the council.
2 A right to be consulted: the employer is obliged to ask for advice on certain issues, usually regarding significant matters concerning the future of the organisation.
3 A decision right: the works council has the right to be part of the joint decision-making process on certain issues linked to the future of the organisation as well as management of personnel.

European Works Councils

European Works Council

A decision of the European Commission made in 1994 ('The Establishment of a European Works Council'), obliged European multinational enterprises to establish European works council. The enterprises affected are those with at least 1000 employees spread throughout the European Union, with a minimum of 150 employees in two member countries.

The function of a European works council is to inform and advise employees on cross-national issues. A council can be set up by top management or by a group of 100 employees. Representatives from the latter form a special team that meets top management to discuss key subjects such as the areas of activity of the Council and its composition, competence and term of office.

A European works council has minimum of three and maximum of 30 members and has a right to a meeting with top management at least once a year. The European guidelines have been implemented in most member countries and more than 500 works councils have been set up.

FIGURES & TRENDS

The goals / support matrix

The goals / support matrix is an effective tool for creating greater understanding and cooperation between employees. It aims to help people understand the goals of others and shows how they can support each other. They then receive support in return. The best results are achieved when this matrix is applied to new issues.

How to draw up a Goals / Support matrix:
- Draw a square on A3 paper. Form a group and go and stand next to each other.
- Add your name to A and those of your colleagues to B, C and D.
- Put your goals in section A / A – no details.
- Ask your colleagues to do the same in the sections B / B, C / C, D / D.
- Ask your colleagues how they could support you to reach your goals.
- Summarise their contributions in the sections A / B, A / C and A / D.
- Continue with each of your colleagues in the same way.
- Make sure that every one listens well and cooperates. Ask them to be critical if the ideas do not seem practical or productive.

The goals/support matrix

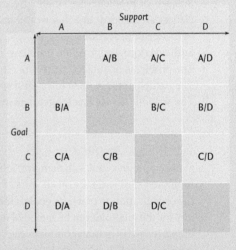

7.5.3 Meeting skills

Decisions are generally made during meetings. Nowadays, with participation considered important, meetings are essential. Quite a few organisational members will complain that they spend too much time in meetings. Meetings have a number of different functions[3]:

- *Bringing people together.* Meetings serve a social function, making its members feel that they belong to the same group.
- *Common knowledge.* A group has a larger amount of knowledge available to it than an individual. Meetings allow accumulated knowledge to be built upon and thus the generation of greater insight.
- *Working together.* A group has a greater capacity for creativity than an individual. By sharing opinions with each other, better and more efficient solutions to problems can be generated.
- *Joint involvement.* One is often more inclined to want to carry out tasks if one has been involved in the decision-making.

For a meeting to be as effective as possible, it should be structured as shown in Figure 7.7, the so-called 'fish-net model'.

Figure 7.7 The 'fish-net model' of meetings

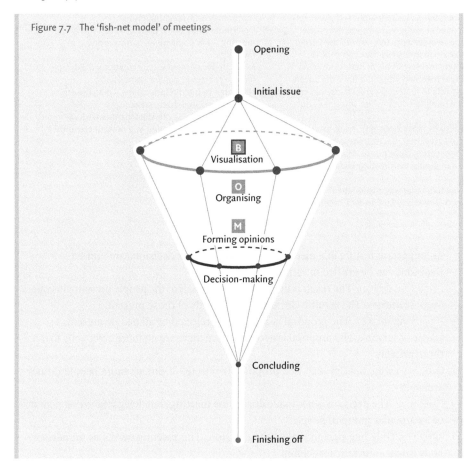

This model consists of the following steps:

1 *Opening.* Welcome, recording of attendees and absentees, verifying that everybody has received the minutes, questions and comments about the minutes, confirming finishing time of the meeting.
2 *Initial issue.* Choice of subject to be discussed.

3 Visualisation. Inventory of problems without a discussion or the use of visual aids such as a flip-chart.

4 *Organising.* Brief and succinct introduction to the subject, including goal and criteria; commencement of discussion and generation of solutions to the problem.

5 *Forming opinions.* Summarising each point, keeping discussion relevant, managing time, working purposefully, handling differences of opinion professionally.

6 *Decision-making.* The process that leads to a decision being made.

7 *Concluding.* A definitive decision is made and recorded.

8 *Finishing off.* Brief summary of the decisions made and agreements made, any other business, next meeting date.

FIGURES & TRENDS

Seven tips for great virtual international meetings

For most of us, virtual meetings are a business reality. We dial in to conference calls, click in to web meetings and participate in video conferences. And the trend worldwide is rising.

Virtual meetings are the heart of virtual work. They are the regular contractions that pump the blood that allows everything else to function. These meetings pose special challenges. Have you ever tried finding a time to meet with people from the Europe, USA and Asia? No matter what time you choose, someone will be meeting in his or her pyjamas! As well, in a virtual meeting, you don't have the advantage of being able to read non-verbal cues, and there isn't a chance to build relationships informally during breaks.

Perhaps this is why most managers, team leaders and participants feel that meeting virtually will never be as good as meeting face-to-face. Many secretly read their email during the meeting and leave feeling dissatisfied.

It doesn't have to be that way. Virtual meetings can be more effective than any face-to-face meetings.

Here are seven practical tips that can help you lead great virtual meetings.

1 Level the playing field – if one person is virtual, make everyone virtual.

2 Make the meeting progress visible – forget the video camera and invest in synchronous meeting technology and a technographer.

3 Determine what's best done in versus out of the meeting – say goodbye to status reporting in meetings!

4 Facilitate for participation – create a virtual conference table and poll for responses.

5 Take time to build relationships – plan time for non-work-related discussions.

6 Leverage technology to start the momentum before the actual meeting and make it continue well after.

7 Meet in person sometimes.

Source: www.kateharper.com, 2006

An important feature of a meeting is the way in which decisions are ratified. Decisions can be ratified in various ways:

- *Democratic decision.* The result is decided by at least half of the people present plus one.
- *Majority decision.* The result is decided by two thirds of those present.
- *Unanimous decision.* The proposal is accepted or rejected by all people present.
- *Consensus principle.* The proposal is accepted once there are no more objections to it by those present.
- *Decisions with a right of veto.* The proposal is rejected if one or more people do not accept it.
- *Delegation.* The decision is not made during the meeting, but delegated to one person or a particular group of people.
- *Authority.* Only one person makes the decision. The meeting serves as an advisory body for an autocratic leadership.

Democratic decision

Majority decision

Unanimous decision

Consensus principle

Decisions with a right of veto

Delegation

Authority

The way a decision is made influences (1) the speed of decision-making and (2) acceptance within the organisation. These two aspects are illustrated in figures 7.8 and 7.9 respectively.

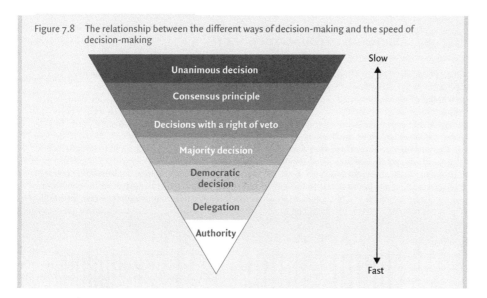

Figure 7.8 The relationship between the different ways of decision-making and the speed of decision-making

Slow

Unanimous decision

Consensus principle

Decisions with a right of veto

Majority decision

Democratic decision

Delegation

Authority

Fast

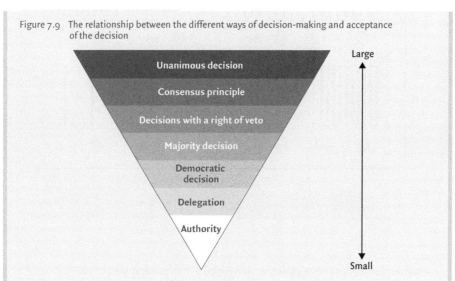

Figure 7.9 The relationship between the different ways of decision-making and acceptance of the decision

Large

Unanimous decision

Consensus principle

Decisions with a right of veto

Majority decision

Democratic decision

Delegation

Authority

Small

7.5.4   Negotiating

Like attending meetings, negotiating is a common activity that takes place when parties pursue different goals. The purpose of negotiation is to find compromises acceptable to all parties. It differs from collaboration, where the various parties have similar interests. During negotiations the parties are mutually dependent yet at the same time have different interests.

Negotiating

A distinction can be made between negotiations and negotiating manner. The latter is particularly problematic, since a decision about the position to take and the expected reaction of the opposition will need to be made in advance.

FIGURES & TRENDS

The prisoner's dilemma: to cooperate or not?[4]

The 'prisoner's dilemma' is a situation that occurs frequently during decision-making processes in which you wonder whether you should cooperate or not.

Imagine that you and your friend were caught during a bank robbery. You are locked up and interrogated separately. The interrogator informs you that if you confess to the robbery, you will be sentenced to only one years' imprisonment while your friend will be sentenced to ten years. If you both confess to the robbery, you will both be sentenced to eight years. If you both deny the robbery, you will be sentenced to

only two years' imprisonment. You have to make a decision: confess to the robbery or not!

For the lightest punishment you need to confess that you committed the crime. However, if both of you do so, you will both be sentenced to eight years. This is why it is better not to be completely focussed on your own interests but to cooperate and to both deny the crime (two years in jail).

The point of this story is this: organisational research has shown that in general, parties profit more from cooperation than from pursuing their own interests completely.

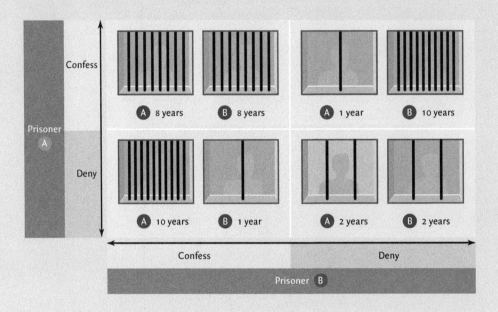

A successful method of negotiation developed by the participants of the Harvard Negotiation Project and already applied in many countries was recently developed. It is known as principled negotiating.[5]

Principled negotiating

With this method, rather having strong or weak positions, points of disagreement are judged on their merits. Principled negotiation usually produces four generally applicable pieces of advice based on the following aspects of negotiating:

1 *People.* Separate the people from the problem. It is important to avoid a situation where participants take up subjective positions and end up being too attached to an issue.

2 *Issues.* Concentrate on the issues, not on the positions. All too often, parties concentrate on the starting positions instead of the issues that are fundamental to those positions.

3 *Choices.* Create all sorts of possibilities before making a decision. All too often the creativity needed to come up with alternatives is suppressed by time pressures and the presence of opposition. In such situations it is advisable to take more time to formulate alternatives that promote common interests and reconcile conflicting ones.

4 *Criteria.* The result has to be based on objective norms. These norms should be disconnected from the personal sphere as much as possible and drawn up independently of any of the parties. By preference, use norms that are generally accepted: market values and legal precedents, for example.

7.5.5   Styles of decision-making[6]

Each person makes a decision in his or her own way. If we look at this more closely we can identify different styles, depending on the way we think and the extent to which we tolerate ambiguity. Thinking can be rational or intuitive. A rationally thinking person follows a structured way of reaching decisions. An intuitively thinking person follows a less structured but more creative way. One person might be able to make decisions in a highly obscure context and not find it difficult to deal with a lot of information at the same time. Another person may prefer to deal with the multiplicity of information in a logical way, via planning.

Way of thinking

Tolerance

If we relate our way of thinking (rational / intuitive) to tolerance of ambiguity (low / high) then four styles of decision-taking arise (Figure 7.10), namely:

Four styles of decision-taking

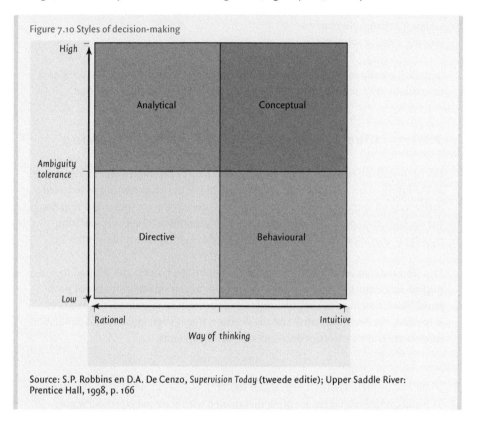

Figure 7.10 Styles of decision-making

Source: S.P. Robbins en D.A. De Cenzo, *Supervision Today* (tweede editie); Upper Saddle River: Prentice Hall, 1998, p. 166

The directive style of decision-making

People who make decisions in this way are rational and have a low tolerance of ambiguity. The characteristics of this style are that decisions are made:
- In a fast, logical and efficient way
- With a focus on the short term
- By using minimal information
- By assessing few alternatives

The directive style of decision-making

The behavioural style of decision-making

Decision-makers with a behavioural style work well with others. The characteristics of this style are:
- An interest in the achievements and suggestions of others
- Finding it important to be accepted by others
- Avoiding conflict

The behavioural style of decision-making

The analytical style of decision-making

In contrast to the directive style, there is a high tolerance of ambiguity with this style. Its characteristics are:

- Extensive use of information
- Looking at many alternatives
- Taking calculated risks
- The ability to deal with unusual circumstances and adaptability in unique situations

The conceptual style of decision-making

Individuals using this style combine an intuitive manner of thinking with a high degree of tolerance of ambiguity. The style's characteristics are:

- A focus on the long term
- Adopting a broad view of the whole problem
- Looking at many alternatives
- Finding creative solutions.

In reality, most people have a mixture of styles, some of which are more dominant than others. The same person might use a different style in a new situation.

7.6   Aids and techniques for decision-making

Decision-making is a fundamental managerial task but it is not always a simple one as the information needed is not always available. If decision-making were based exclusively on facts, one would simply enter all data in the computer and wait for the decision to appear. The manager would be superfluous. However, decision-making is also about uncertainties, which is where entrepreneurship comes in.

Decision-making techniques and decision-supporting systems can be used to simplify or accelerate the process of finding the right solutions to a number of problems. The following decision-making techniques will be discussed: the balanced scorecard, the decision matrix and the decision tree. Expert systems and simulation models are two examples of decision-supporting systems.

7.6.1   The balanced scorecard

Top and middle managers are often dissatisfied with their management reports. They are often too one-sided, not directed towards the future and not related to the strategic targets. Management reports as we know them are almost completely based on financial information, information from annual accounts or interim figures. By definition, these elements can only provide retrospective information. However, organisations need the future view. Another major drawback is that the present financial-performance indicators hardly give any information about the extent to which the strategic targets have been reached. The balanced scorecard refers not only to financial but also to non-financial indicators. They can give management a more complete and balanced picture of the results achieved. In fact, the balanced scorecard combines the financial performances with the underlying driving factors. It is a regulating and measuring system aimed at translating a strategy into concrete action. It is a compass of sorts, an instrument to help the manager reach the desired objectives.

The balanced scorecard is also:
· A support tool for formulating or reformulation of strategy (ongoing improvement)
· A tool for future-orientated management (insurance of continuity)
· An internal means of communication
· A way of integrating vision, strategy and objectives

The idea behind the balanced scorecard is simple (Figure 7.11). The organisation's performance is looked at from four different perspectives:
1 The financial perspective: how can we represent the interests of the shareholder?
2 The internal perspective: what abilities do we need?
3 The perspective of the customer: how are we judged by the customers?
4 The innovation perspective: how can we improve?

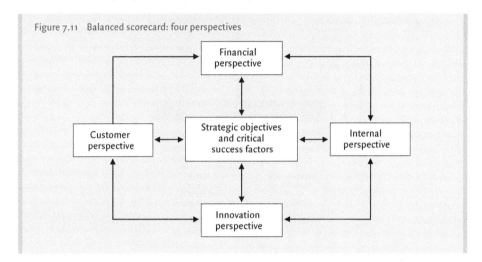

Figure 7.11   Balanced scorecard: four perspectives

Strategic objectives are translated into concrete measurements by the establishment of critical success factors. A critical success factor is a business variable that is cru- *Critical success factor* cial either to reaching a strategic goal or carrying out a key business activity. As a qualitative description of a part of the business or its strategy, it indicates those areas in which the organisation must excel if it is to be successful. Success can be seen as the extent to which the organisation reaches its strategic goals, or how well it carries out its core activities.

The critical success factors are measured by units called performance indicators, or to put it another way, performance indicators are used to measure critical success *Performance indicators* factors. These are quantitative and are expressed in numerical or percentage form.[7] (See Figure 7.12.)

Successful implementation of a balanced scorecard requires an integrated approach. It should fit in smoothly with the entire managerial process. Although it is important to involve line management closely, what often happens is that the balanced scorecard is often approached abstractly, as a tool for staff. It is, of course, essential that each organisation's balanced scorecard be custom-made.

When implementation of the balanced scorecard is problematic, the following factors are often involved[8]:
· There is an absence of a clear strategy: goals are not specific and not measurable.
· Authority and responsibility within the organisation are poorly defined.
· There is a lack of continuity in the way that process-control activities are organised

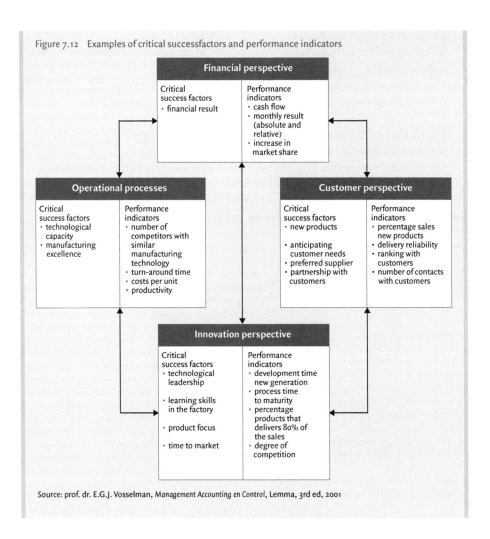

Figure 7.12 Examples of critical successfactors and performance indicators

Financial perspective

Critical success factors
· financial result

Performance indicators
· cash flow
· monthly result (absolute and relative)
· increase in market share

Operational processes

Critical success factors
· technological capacity
· manufacturing excellence

Performance indicators
· number of competitors with similar manufacturing technology
· turn-around time
· costs per unit
· productivity

Customer perspective

Critical success factors
· new products

· anticipating customer needs
· preferred supplier
· partnership with customers

Performance indicators
· percentage sales new products
· delivery reliability
· ranking with customers
· number of contacts with customers

Innovation perspective

Critical success factors
· technological leadership

· learning skills in the factory

· product focus

· time to market

Performance indicators
· development time new generation
· process time to maturity
· percentage products that delivers 80% of the sales
· degree of competition

Source: prof. dr. E.G.J. Vosselman, *Management Accounting en Control*, Lemma, 3rd ed, 2001

· Internal culture and management style have not been geared towards the use of the balanced scorecard.
· The expenses / profits relationship has not been a matter for consideration.

Value-based management

Another steering instrument has recently been developed under the name of 'value-based management' (VBM). This is a management approach used for increasing the value of the enterprise and creating shareholder value. VBM came about due to the increasing pressure exerted by shareholders and financial markets to maximise the economic value of enterprises. An increasing number of organisations have adopt-

Value-creating capacity

ed this concept. VBM requires the value-creating capacity of strategies to be judged in advance. Managers have to be aware of the long-term effects of their actions. Value-based management can be supplemented by integrating it with the balanced scorecard. The result is a value-oriented directing and measuring system known as the value-based scorecard (VBS).

7.6.2 Decision matrix

Decision matrix

A decision matrix is a method for comparing alternatives by means of weighted criteria.

The procedure is as follows:
1 Identify a number of alternatives

2 Select your evaluation criteria
3 Give each criterion a weighting factor
4 Allocate values to each criterion used for the alternatives
5 Multiply these figures by the weighting factor and calculate totals for each alternative
6 Make a choice

We shall illustrate these steps using an example. A personnel manager has to select a candidate for a commercial position in the company. After a number of interviews two candidates remain. The manager enters the data into a decision matrix. (Figure 7.13)

Figure 7.13 Decision matrix

Evaluation criteria	Candidates							
	D. Dun				I. Weiss			
	WF	× VA	= TOT		WF	× VA	= TOT	
• academic education	5	2	10		5	3	15	
• communication skills	3	1	3		3	2	6	
• job experience	2	3	6		2	1	2	
• commercial skills	4	2	8		4	2	8	
• salary wishes	2	1	2		2	3	6	
• fit in with the team	5	3	15		5	1	5	
• induction time	1	2	2		1	2	2	
total			46				44	

Decision matrices can also be used to choose a location for a branch or head office, to determine the sales price of a product, to identify market segments, and to select an organisational structure.

The advantage of this method is that alternatives can be compared quantitatively easily and quickly. A drawback is the difficulty of objectively determining the weighting factors, the criteria and their value.

7.6.3 The decision tree

A decision tree is a graphic illustration of the alternatives and consequences associated with a particular problem. The style of illustration often has a significant influence on the final choice of solution.

A decision tree is created by answering a series of questions. A 'yes' or 'no' to each

Decision tree

Decision-support software

New competitors pop up almost overnight. Risk is much more important than the current value of money. In such an environment, spreadsheet models simply do not capture the true complexities of the business situations you face.

Enterprises need a business modelling tool that takes a holistic view of the future – assessing the impact of all possible outcomes simultaneously. This requires a new set of techniques for dealing with risk and uncertainty and a new way of looking at business decisions.

DecisionPro from Vanguard Software provides a complete spectrum of proven management techniques

for you to use in dealing with risk, imperfect information, competing options, and contingency plans. These capabilities are combined with an innovative interface that closely resembles the way people think. The result is a business modelling tool where numbers are not absolute, logic is as important as equations, and models reflect strategy rather than calculations.

You can try Decision Pro by downloading the software at: www.vanguardsw.com / decisionpro / download.htm

Source: www.vanguardsw.com, 2006

question will ultimately be the best option. For example, an enterprise wants to increase profits by expanding trade volume and visualises the alternatives by means of a decision tree. (Figure 7.14.)

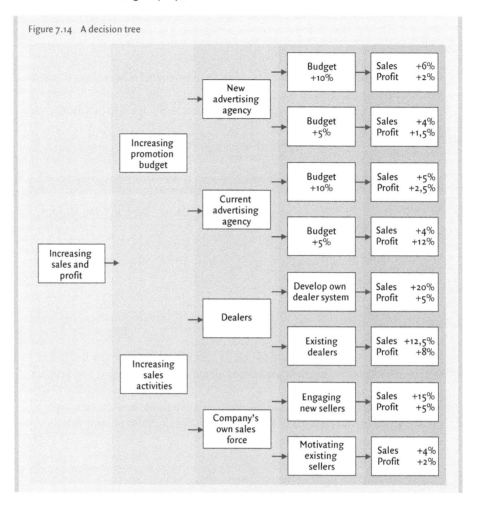

Figure 7.14   A decision tree

The decision-tree method is very suitable in situations where one wants to compare the consequences of alternative decisions in a structured way. The method is also used by medical physicians for diagnosing an illness and technical experts for locating a car defect.

7.6.4   Decision-support systems

Decision-supporting system

It goes without saying that the rapid developments in the field of computers and software are having an effect on decision-making within organisations. Information is more readily and extensively available now. Computers can even be utilised to a certain extent as a support tool in the decision-making process. A decision-supporting system is defined as a computer-based system that helps decision-makers solve problems of a non-routine nature by means of direct interaction with raw data. Expert systems and simulation models are two examples of decision-supporting systems.

Expert systems

Expert / knowledge system

Expert or knowledge systems are computerised systems that have been devised to solve problems needing specialised knowledge (expertise) in tandem with the user. An expert system consists of three parts:

1 The knowledge and experience bank (the knowledge and experience of the expert)
2 The concluding system (a reasoning mechanism using imported data for analysis and diagnosis)
3 The operating system (linking the reasoning mechanism and the user)

Expert systems contain knowledge and expert experience. The knowledge includes generally accepted facts and published information. Experience is based more on the personal opinion of the expert so will consist of rules of thumb, estimates and judgement. If a system contains only generally accepted published information it is known as a knowledge system. Expert and knowledge systems are basic applications of artificial intelligence. Their advantages lie in the fact that non-experts can use the knowledge and experience of an expert for decision-making and transferring and distribution of knowledge experiences is fast and simple. *Artificial intelligence*

It is the expert's responsibility to ensure that the required information is included in the knowledge and experience bank. He also gives advice on the structure and features within the reasoning and concluding system. The user inputs questions into the expert system and in return, gets an answer in the form of advice and an explanation of what that advice is based on. (Figure 7.15.)

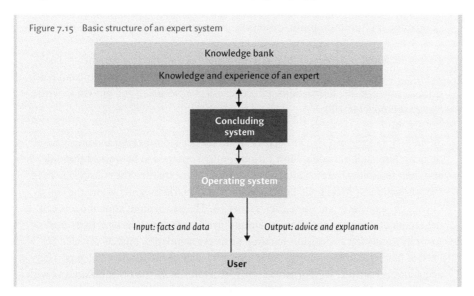

Figure 7.15   Basic structure of an expert system

It is estimated that expert systems will increasingly be used in the future for a range of decision areas including medical diagnoses, investment protection, purchasing stocks and shares, legal planning based on precedents, mortgage advice, credit acceptances and the development of industrial products.

The large-scale introduction of expert systems will, however, have an influence on the position of experts both within as well as outside the organisation (e.g. consultants and managers). After all, in our society, knowledge goes hand-in-hand with power. What are the consequences likely to be if, for example, the knowledge possessed by a lawyer or an accountant is transferred into a knowledge system? Will there be a need for these people in the future?
As we see it, much of the knowledge and experience possessed by experts cannot be replaced by expert systems, though in the future, demand for the services of experts may significantly decrease. After all, humans – in contrast to computers – are

creative and capable of combining new knowledge and experience with existing knowledge. Moreover, humans can apply their acquired experiences to any problem and switch quickly from one context to another.

Simulation models

Simulation model

The simulation model is another type of decision-support system. Simulation techniques have been used for as long as people have made plans and made decisions. Alexander the Great as strategist, Charles V as the ruler of an empire, and Henry Ford as a pioneer of an affordable car have all used the technique. Simulation is nothing more than translating as yet unknown quantities to a given situation and considering the resulting consequences. With the help of the computer, simulation has become a generally applicable management instrument. The computer simulations most commonly used in this field are known as business simulation models.

Business simulation model

A business simulation model is a software model that simulates the economic situation of a particular sector or enterprise. This is done by inputting data of various sorts into the model, including:
· Market and industry data
· Data relating to competitors
· Macro-economic data
· Company data (turnover, profit, expenses, number of staff, products, budgets, etc.)

To this are added a number of hypotheses built up using variable parameters such as price and market variations, industrial relations indices, changes to oil and gold prices, exchange rate fluctuations, effectiveness of advertising and growth in Gross National Product (GNP).

Simulation models can also be used as an aid for decision-making and policy development. Simulation models allow various policy scenarios to be worked through and their feasibility tested. Shrinkage or growth in the market, the consequences of reorganisations, product positioning in particular market segments and the consequences of a takeover are some such scenarios. The use of simulation models can help to reduce uncertainty when important investment decisions have to be made. As well as assisting in decision-making, business simulation models can also be used in management training programmes for existing and future managers. They acquaint the manager with organisational structures in all their complexity and with the effects of decisions made in different areas. Simulation training can thus promote multidisciplinary thinking, team work and an understanding of micro and macro-economic relationships. An additional advantage of simulation training is that it makes it possible to experiment with the future in complete safety.

Doing business in Germany

How Germans organise and process information
In general, Germans are not open to outside information and do not freely share information among their own organisational units. The younger generations are becoming more open. Germans are analytical and conceptual in their information processing. Team commitment is strong. They are not quick to develop friendships but their friendships are deep and lasting.

What Germans accept as evidence
Objective facts form the basis for truth. Feelings are not seen as relevant to negotiations. There is a strong faith in social democratic ideology, and this influences a German person's perceptions.

The basis of behaviour
Some differences between the value systems of what was once East and West Germany still exist. Value systems in the predominant culture – how right is distinguished from wrong, good from evil, and so on – are described under the next three headings.

The locus of decision-making
While Germans are strongly individualistic, they regard it as important to take account of cultural history when decisions are made. Decision-making is slow and involved, as peripheral concerns must be taken care of during the process. Once a decision is made, it is set in concrete. Individual privacy must be respected in all walks of life, and while personal matters should not be discussed during business negotiations, it is important to develop a personal friendship with your counterpart.

Sources of anxiety reduction
Universal rules and regulations combined with strong inner discipline give stability to life and reduce uncertainty. There is a high need for social and personal order, and low tolerance of deviant behaviour. Emotional displays are not highly regarded. Fear or scepticism about the future may breed anxiety and pessimism.

Issues relating to equality / inequality
German society is distinctly hierarchical, and organisations are no exception to the rule. While equal rights for all are guaranteed by law, they may not necessarily be practiced in the marketplace. Woman still have a strong bias to overcome, both in terms of pay and power.

Ten examples of German business practices
1 The German reputation for quality is based in part on slow and methodical planning. Every aspect of the deal you propose will be pored over by a lot of executives. Don't expect to be able to speed up this process.
2 Appointments should be made well in advance.
3 Germans also take a lot of time to establish close business relationships. Once they get to know you, they're are quite gregarious.
4 If your company has been around for many years, the date of its founding should be on your business card.
5 Privacy is very important to Germans. Doors are kept closed, both at work and at home. Always knock on a closed door and wait to be admitted.
6 Germans tend to be well-informed about politics and to have firm political opinions. They are honest and may tell you what they think of your country even if these opinions are negative.
7 Traditionally, only family members and close friends address each other by their first names. You may never establish a close enough relationship with your German colleague to get on a first-name footing.
8 German business people don't give or expect to receive expensive gifts. A gift should be of good quality but not exorbitantly expensive.
9 While customs vary in different regions of Germany, the general rule is to shake hands both upon meeting and upon departing.
10 Business dress in Germany is highly conservative. Follow the lead of your German colleague with regard to removing your jacket or tie in hot weather.

Source: Kiss, Bow, or Shake Hands: How to Do Business in Sixty Countries, by Terri Morrison, Wayne A. Conaway and George A. Borden, Adams Media, 2006

Summary

People within organisations are engaged in solving problems on an ongoing basis. These problems may be routine or specific. The way people make decisions is reflected in the decision-making processes. An important characteristic of decision-making is that alternatives have to be weighed up. They may relate to future events of a more or less predictable kind.

A rational decision-making process starts with a definition of the problem and ends by choosing an option. It is a phased and structured process, unlike irrational decision-making processes. Organisations should strive for effective and efficient decision-making. Creativity, participation, meeting skills, negotiating and decision-making style are keywords here. Certain tools can be used as an aid to decision-making. These include the balanced scorecard, decision matrix, decision tree and decision-support systems such as expert systems and simulation models.

Definitions

§ 7.2 Absolute certainty
The objectives and outcomes of all alternatives are known exactly.

Complete uncertainty
The objectives are unclear and there is absolutely no way of making predictions.

Partial uncertainty
The various outcomes are virtually unpredictable though the objectives are clear.

Partial certainty
The objectives are clear but the exact outcome of the alternatives is unknown though to a certain extent predictable.

§ 7.3 Rational decision-making process
A decision is made after the problem has been clearly stated and alternatives carefully weighed up. The process is characterised by phasing and structure.

§§ 7.4.1 Neo-rational decision-making process
A process that strongly resembles the rational type but emotional and intuitive aspects also play a role.

§§ 7.4.2 Bureaucratic decision-making process
Decisions are based on fixed rules instead of consciously made choices. The use of rules, planning and controls give this process a formal character.

§§ 7.4.3 Political decision-making process
This process has a formal and decentralised character as many different parties with divergent interests are involved. Decisions result from negotiations and interactions between groups.

§§ 7.4.4 Open-ended decision-making process
This process has a decentralised and informal character. It has no clear starting and ending point. Decision-making is an erratic and unpredictable process. There are no clear objectives and decisions have an ad hoc character, with chance playing a major role.

§§ 7.5.1 Brain-storming
The goal is to generate as many new ideas as possible rather than to evaluate them or make a selection. During a brainstorming session, criticism of new ideas is discouraged. Initial suggestions should be used as a springboard for ideas to be developed further by others.

§§ 7.5.2 Participation
The rights and competencies of staff to influence the establishment, execution and control of company policy and the decisions that lead to this.

§§ 7.5.4 Negotiating
Like meetings, a routine activity in situations where the various parties are pursuing different goals. The purpose of negotiation is to find compromises acceptable to all parties. It differs from collaboration, where the various parties have similar interests. During negotiations the parties are mutually dependent yet at the same time have different interests.

§§ 7.6.1 The balanced scorecard	A regulating and measuring system aimed at translating a strategy into concrete action. It is a compass of sorts, an instrument to help the manager reach the desired objectives.
Critical success factor	A business variable that is crucial either to reaching a strategic goal or carrying out a key business activity. As a qualitative description of a part of the business or its strategy, it indicates those areas in which the organisation must excel if it is to be successful.
Performance indicator	An indicator used to measure critical success factors. It is expressed as a number or percentage.
Value-based management	A management approach used for increasing the value of the enterprise and creating shareholder value.
§§ 7.6.4 Decision-support system	A computer-based system that helps decision-makers to solve problems of a non-routine nature by means of direct interaction with raw data.
Expert / knowledge system	A computerised system that contains specific knowledge and expertise devised to solve problems in tandem with the user.
Simulation model	A model that translates as yet unknown quantities to a given situation and considers the resulting consequences.
Business simulation model	A software model that simulates the economic situation of a particular sector or enterprise.

Statements

Indicate whether the following statements are correct or incorrect, giving reasons for your choice.

1 As decision-making is a human activity, cooperation and creativity play an important role.
2 A specific problem can only be resolved by following a precise and definite procedure.
3 When evaluating alternatives, the setting of criteria plays an important role.
4 One characteristic of the neo-rational decision-making process is that decisions are usually made by one person.
5 The drawback of participation is that it takes a lot of time and consequently contributes little to the effectiveness and efficiency of the organisation.
6 European works councils are now to be found within multinationals based in Europe.
7 Negotiating is characterised by the fact that the parties are mutually dependent yet have different interests.
8 The balanced scorecard is a regulating and measuring system aimed at translating a strategy into concrete action.
9 Value-based management aims to maximise the value of the organisation for its clients.
10 An expert or knowledge system is a computerised system containing knowledge about a particular field that a user can draw on to solve problems in that area.

Theory questions

1 What is the difference between routine problems and specific problems?
2 On which criteria is the classification of the various irrational decision-making processes based?
3 When is a multinational in Europe required to have a European works council?
4 In a meeting, a decision can be made in various ways. What is the difference between:
   · A unanimous decision and consensus
   · A majority decision and a democratic decision
   · A decision with a right of veto and decision made by an authority.
5 What are the characteristics of negotiating?

Practical assignment

1 a Develop your personal balanced scorecard (BS) (see Section 7.6.1 in the textbook). Also check the various sites on this subject.
   b For an organisation, the balanced scorecard is not only an instrument for translating a strategy into concrete action. It can also be used in other ways (see 7.6.1 in the textbook). How does this compare with your personal BS?

 For answers see www.marcusvandam.noordhoff.nl.

Mini case study

THEA

The THEA company has been going steadily downhill of late. Its markets are changing fast, competition is increasing and the owner / director of THEA has been relatively slow to react to these changes. He eventually hired an expert from a consultancy firm run by his niece. The expert recommended a series of measures. One of them involved radical cutbacks and some staff redundancies. In your department, one employee has to go. The director has asked you for a rational suggestion. Your department includes you and the following people:

- Alfred Bailey. He is 54, married, and has three children. Alfred has been working for THEA for 30 years and joined when the company was first set up. In the past his performance was excellent, though lately he has had a hard time keeping up. The technical aspects of THEA's products are changing continuously. Alfred is very enthusiastic about his new hobby: geology.
- Nora Lowry 43, single mother of two children. Nora has been working with THEA for eight years and she has turned out to be an outstanding employee.
- Jane Mitchell, 32, single, no children. Jane has worked with THEA for three years now. She is a good hard worker but her social skills could be improved: she can flare up quickly, even with customers. You have discussed this unwanted behaviour with her several times, but Jane has not changed yet.
- Tom Morgan, 27 years old, single, no children. Tom has been with THEA for two years, and in the year before that, he made a round the world trip. Tom is a motivated, talented and ambitious employee who dreams of starting his own company.

Question
1   What would you do and why?

E-mail case study

To:	Helmi Hakinnen
Cc:	
Bcc:	
Subject:	Meeting problems

Message:

Dear Helmi,

How are you? You've probably heard that I was recently promoted within our Finnish company and that I'm now the manager of a team of eight employees. All is going well, except the meetings and that's why I'm e-mailing you.

Once a week during the coffee break we discuss all kinds of items that I have written down myself during the previous week. The employees may also add suggestions. However, things are terribly chaotic during these meetings: there is discussion of what was on TV the night before, there is much interruption of each other, a lot of digression and some people say nothing at all. So we don't even get to the important stuff and then I have to make all the decisions. I know that this isn't right and that everyone should participate in the decision-making. But it's simply not happening!

You train members of organisations in meeting skills. Would you advise me on what you think is going wrong during these meetings and how I can tackle it? Maybe we could do this over dinner at my place.

Regards,

Kielo

Notes Part B

Chapter 5

1 *http: | home.iae.nl*, www.menscentraal.nl, Robbins, S. and M. Coulter, *Management*, Pearson 2006.
2 Robbins, S. and Coulter, M., *Management*, Pearson 2006.
3 www.dsz.service.rug.nl, Jansen, P.G.W. and Nelissen, *Organisatie en Mensen, Inleiding in de bedrijfspsychologie voor economen en bedrijfskundigen*, 1996.
4 Alblas, G. and Wijsman, E., *Gedrag in Organisaties*, Wolters-Noordhoff, Groningen, 2001.
5 www.goodfeeling.nl
6 www.burnin.nl
7 L. de Caluwe and Vermaak, H., *Leren Veranderen*, Kluwer, Deventer, 2002. Hogeschool van Utrecht, Michiel Scager, May 2003.
8 Tjepkema, S., *Werken, leren en leven met groepen*, 2003.
9 Rampersad, H., *Effectief Teamwork, gebaseerd op Total Performance Scorecard*, Sciptum Management, October 2002.

Chapter 6

1 Keuning, D. and Eppink, D.J., *Management & Organisatie, theorie en toepassing*, Stenfert Kroese, Houten, 1996.
2 Mintzberg, H., *Mintzberg over Management, de wereld van onze organisaties*, Veen, Utrecht, 1991.
3 Alblas, G. and Wijsman, *Gedrag in Organisaties*, Wolters-Noordhof, Groningen, 2001.
4 Stoner, *Management*, Academic Service, Schoonhoven, 1994.
5 Effting / Kint & Partners, *Personal change & growth*.
6 Pol, Van de, Messer and Wissema, in: *Holland Harvard Review*, Spring 1989, No. 18.
7 *Holland Harvard Review*, Spring 1989, No. 18.
8 *Het Financieele Dagblad*, October 12 1978.
9 Pol, Van der, Messer and Wissema, *Het Financieele Dagblad*, October 1978.
10 Praag, E. van, *Management zonder controle*, Intermediair, 1988.
11 Stoner, *Management*, Academic Service, Schoonhoven, 1994.
12 Korte, A.W. de and Bolweg, J.F., *Een verkenning naar veranderingen in werknemerswensen en de managementconsequenties daarvan*, Van Gorcum, Stichting Management Studies, Assen, 1993.
13 *www.vacature.com*, Fons Trompenaars.
14 Evans, P., and Bartolomé, F., *Wordt succes duur betaald?*, Samsom / Intermediair, Alphen aan den Rijn, 1981.

15 Robbins, S. and Coulter, M., *Management*, Practice Hall, New England, 2002.
16 Mintzberg, H., *The nature of Managerial Work*, Prentice-Hall, Englewood Cliffs, 1973.
17 Bots, R.T.M., and Jansen, W., *Organisatie en Informatie*, Wolters-Noordhoff, Groningen, 2001.

Chapter 7

1 Bono, E. de, *Six Thinking Hats*, MICA, 1985.
2 *Avanta Magazine*, May 1998.
3 Boertien & Partners, *Syllabus Vergadertechniek, theorie en praktijk*, 1980.
4 Stoner, J.A.F., *Management*, Academic Service, Schoonhoven, 1994.
5 Fisher, R., and Ury, W., *Succesvol onderhandelen, de Harvard-aanpak*, Veen, Utrecht, 1981.
6 Robbins, S. and Coulter, M., *Management*, Practice Hall, New England, 2003.
7 From: *Accountant-adviseur*, No. 4, April 2001.
8 *www.hcg.net*.

Part C Structure and organisation

Sections A and B of this book have dealt respectively with the influence of the environment and of people on organisations. This last section discusses the way organisations are managed, how they are structured and how they adjust to changes within their environment.

Contents

8

Managing organisational processes

'What you believe to be the top is a mere step.'
(Seneca, 4 BC–65 AD, Latin tragedy writer and moralist)

This chapter deals with managing
organisations. The topics examined
include the various types of business
processes and ways of carrying them
out. We will discuss logistics
management, customer relationship
management and human resources
management, as well as looking at the
tasks performed at the various levels
of the hierarchy and a number of
methods and techniques for
monitoring them.

Contents

After studying this chapter
- You will be familiar with problems that might occur when managing
  organisations.
- You will be able to identify different types of business processes.
- You will have an understanding of the way business processes are carried out
  and the impact of business processes on added value and quality.
- You will be familiar with the Human Resources Management approach.
- You will be familiar with HRM instruments: recruitment and selection, reward,
  appraisal, career development, knowledge management and outplacement.
- You will be able to distinguish between various management levels and their main
  tasks.
- You will understand the meaning of corporate governance.
- You will be familiar with a number of general management methods and
  techniques.

8.1 Managing organisational processes

Management of organisational processes

In this chapter we discuss the management of organisational processes. By this we mean leading the organisation towards the goals that have been set. These goals can only be achieved if a number of business processes (i.e. human activities) are carried out effectively. A business process is a set of organised human activities relating to the production of goods and/or services.[1] These processes can apply to both profit as well as non-profit organisations.

Business process

Some examples of business processes are purchasing, production, administration, marketing and sales. Each business process can be subdivided into sub-processes. To be sure of accomplishing its objectives, business processes need to be supervised by management. This activity is known as process control. Process control is defined as the effective management of business processes by planning, coordination and adjusting.

Process control

In this chapter, attention will be given to various types of business processes, their management, added value, quality, logistics management and customer relationship management. In addition, the various managerial levels within an organisation and their specific tasks (including corporate governance), types of organisation management and methods needed to run business processes will be discussed.

8.2 Business processes

Raw materials
Transformation

Every organisation acquires raw materials and resources (input) and transforms these into products and / or services (output). (See Figure 8.1.) This transformation process consists of a number of business processes. We will discuss input and output, followed by the transformation process.

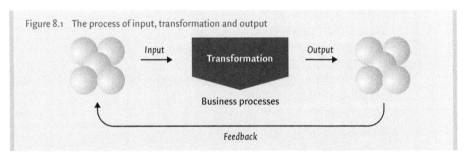

Figure 8.1 The process of input, transformation and output

Input consists of four factors. These are:
- *Labour:* people
- *Natural resources:* raw material, semi-manufactured products, energy etc
- *Capital:* money, plant and machinery
- *Information:* about competition, demographic data etc

These production factors must be bought in by organisations from specialised markets such as the labour market, the energy market and the information market (e.g. market research bureaus). After the transformation, the resulting products and / or services are sold to the customers and to other interested parties. Here, too, are various markets. Figure 8.2 shows several examples.

Name:	Rüdiger Weskamm
Country of origin:	Germany
Job title:	Business Director for Germany
Company:	Fast Lane
Company website:	www.flane.de
Prior employer:	Siemens

What do people need to know before doing business in your country?

German business culture has a well-defined and strictly observed hierarchy, with clear responsibilities and distinctions between roles and departments. Professional rank and status in Germany is generally based on an individual's achievement and expertise in a given field. Academic titles and backgrounds are important, conveying an individual's expertise and thorough knowledge of their particular area of work. In formal German business meetings it is customary for the highest-ranking person to enter the room first. However, in more informal business situations this is less important. In Germany punctuality is essential. Arriving even five or ten minutes after the appointment time is considered late and disrespectful. If running late for an appointment, it is best to notify the person. Appointments are made for most situations, and sometimes several weeks in advance.

Give an example of a mistake that foreign business people often make when doing business in your country

Do not use first names in the business environment! First names are only used with family, close friends and close colleagues. Always use last names – and appropriate titles. You will often find that colleagues who have worked together for years still maintain this level of formality.

How are decisions made in your country?

Facts are essential in decision-making and problem-solving. In business negotiations, for example, the preferred approach to successful decision-making is based on logic and analysis of information rather than on intuition and well-developed personal networks. Personal relationships play a secondary role in business dealings. The attention paid to targets to be achieved is evidenced, for example, in the precision of timetables, meeting planning and achievement of milestones. Close adherence to time schedules is also considered vital.

What kind of role does Internet play in your job?

The Internet is used for information research. In the sales area, it is used for information searches on the customer's company structure, customer products, customer needs and general customer representation on the Internet. It is also used for product and partner information, and last but not least, as a journey planner tool for airlines, trains, public transport, and map and city information.

Besides this, we use the Internet for our own communication purposes, such as the company's website, customer eMail shots, Skype, call back button, booking systems for customers, info system for suppliers, and international access to our labs. What it boils down to is that the Internet is the company's central nervous system.

What is the best way to motivate people?

For as long as I have been with Siemens, I have always found that people have to be motivated by setting targets, with support incentives and money. In fact, there should be a new rule: 'Don't only concentrate on motivation, but concentrate on not demotivating your employees!'

What sources do you use to stay on top of new developments in your profession?

All types of e-newsletters and print newspapers, a minimum of 5 customer meetings a week, visits to the annual fairs of our main partners, regular and informal meetings with employees, stakeholders, and competitors. My motto is *Be in the market – live in the market*.

Figure 8.2 The relationship between input, transformation and output

Production factors	Transformation	Service and / or product
• Labour • Natural resources • Capital • Information	*Type of organisation* • Hospitals • Universities and colleges • Municipal social services • Employment offices • Financial institutions • Publishing companies • Car industry	• Medical care • Education, research • Benefits • Jobs • Mortgages, insurances • Books, magazines • Cars

Input → *Output*

Organisations are not only judged by their products and / or services but also by the quality of other outputs:

- *labour*: employees leaving the work force (through dismissal, retirement, long-term disability)
- *natural resources*: waste, heat loss, noise, pollution, smell
- *capital*: profit, depreciation of machinery etc
- *information*: annual reports, public relations, advertising

Organisations can survive only if the production process is continuous, which depends, among other things, on the relationship with society and demand for its products.

8.2.1   Types of business processes

Three types of business processes can be identified:

1 Primary processes
2 Secondary or supporting processes
3 Administrative processes

Primary processes

Secondary processes

Administrative processes

Primary processes are all activities that contribute directly to the making of the product or service (purchasing, producing, selling and furnishing) and to the overall goal of the organisation. Secondary processes include all activities that support primary processes, such as management of personnel, finances and data systems. Administrative processes are all activities that direct the primary and secondary processes, and help to reach the organisation's goals.

ICT

Supply Chain Management at SAMSUNG

Delivering the right product to the right place at the right time and the right price is the essence of supply chain management (SCM). It is a strategy that requires system-level integration with partners, suppliers, and customers to achieve maximum performance. Samsung has implemented solutions to address each of these aspects of SCM strategy as it cuts overall lead time from manufacturing to sales. For example, the company upgraded their global Enterprise Resource Planning (ERP) solutions to support a weekly planning cycle for demand forecasting, resource management, and production planning functions for the entire global network of 32 production facilities and 49 sales subsidiaries. This upgrade is enabling them to better synchronize production and sales, a capability they expect to boost on-time delivery performance significantly.

Source: SAMSUNG (www.samsung.com), November 2006

A summary of the relationships between the primary, secondary and administrative processes is given in Figure 8.3.

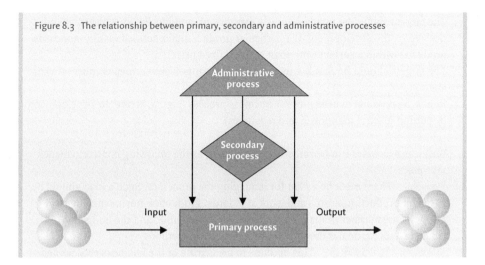

Figure 8.3 The relationship between primary, secondary and administrative processes

The tasks of administrative processes are:

a *Selection of strategy.* During this process, a vision of the future is agreed upon and a strategy is chosen. Strategies need some flexibility and should anticipate fluctuations in demand for products and services to avoid saturation of the market.

b *Planning.* To reach the goals set by the organisation, primary and secondary processes need to be coordinated. Planning the tasks carried out by staff members, the means of production and how time is scheduled increases control over the processes (see also Section 8.5).

c *Structure.* This is the setting up of a system within an organisation enabling people and resources to be utilised (see also Chapter 9).

d *Process control.* Processes can be executed in an appropriate and purposeful way by planning, measuring, comparing and adapting the business.

The relationship between the various business processes and administrative tasks is shown in Figure 8.4.

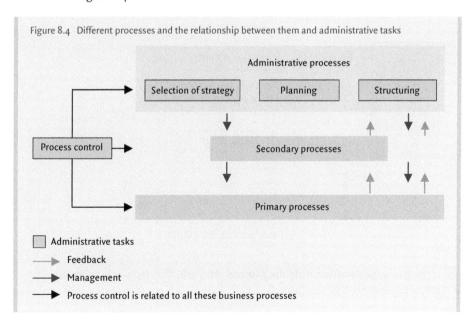

Figure 8.4 Different processes and the relationship between them and administrative tasks

8.2.2　The management of business processes

It is in the interests of the organisation for the business processes to be managed in such a way as to reach pre-set targets. Three conditions are needed for this:

1 The targets should be unambiguously formulated, and ideally, formulated quantitatively (e.g., the development of a particular product under defined quality standards, produced within a certain time span and at a fixed price).
2 The targets should be feasible (e.g., sufficient manpower and means must be available)
3 It must be possible to influence the business process (e.g., to accelerate development by putting in extra manpower and resources).

Control activities

Business processes can be run effectively as long as the following control activities take place:

- *Planning.*　There must be a plan for managing the processes. Such a plan should be based on production norms and work standards. Production norms include such things as the number of man and machine hours available, and the budget. Work standards are particular development or production methods.
- *Measuring and comparing.*　This pertains to measuring of the business process and comparing this with the norms and standards of the plan.
- *Adjustment.*　This pertains to steps that need to be taken if limitations are exceeded.

Figures 8.5 and 8.6 show management activities and the relationship between adjusting and managing tasks.

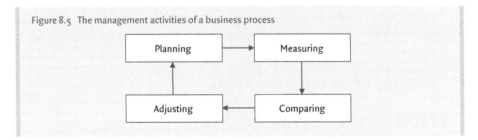

Figure 8.5　The management activities of a business process

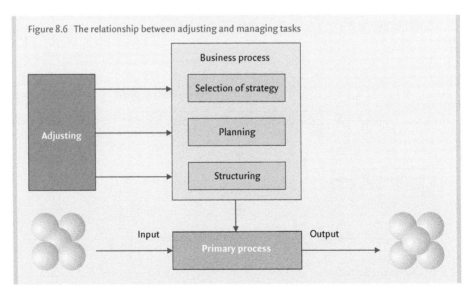

Figure 8.6　The relationship between adjusting and managing tasks

If there is some deviation from the planned standard, intervention is necessary. The following may need to be adjusted:

- *The objectives.* Are the objectives well chosen?
- *The strategy.* Have the right strategic choices been made?
- *The plans.* Is the balance between people, resources and time effective and efficient?
- *The structure.* Has the right form of organisation been chosen?
- *The primary process.* Was the process efficient?
- *The secondary process.* Has the available information been interpreted correctly?

A growing number of organisations have come to the conclusion that process control is important for obtaining a competitive advantage. Michael Hammer, an American professor of computer science (see also Chapter 1) devised an approach known as business re-engineering or business processes re-engineering. In this approach, the organisational process is not seen as a system of separately organised activities, but as a collection of core business processes that are related to each other. *Business re-engineering* *Business processes re-engineering*

A core business process consists of a number of linked activities that give extra value to the buyer. This added value can be measured using a combination of four criteria: quality, service, expenses and cycle time. These criteria enable buyers to compare products and / or services supplied by different organisations and to then make a choice. Within each organisation, some five to eight different core business processes can be identified. They can be put to use to obtain a competitive advantage. *Core business process* *Extra value*

The core business processes should be developed from the buyer's perspective. *Buyer's perspective*

The business re-engineering approach is an approach in which business processes are central. It aims at eliminating the divisions within an organisation that have arisen out of the splitting up of functions and divisions.

Traditionally, processes such as product development and order handling were split up into small parts. These parts were distributed across the various divisions of an organisation. A slow and inflexible system was the consequence. When markets are stable, such subdivisions do not constitute a risk. However, this is not the case in strongly changing markets, where flexibility, quality and service are necessary. The

New business models: a closer European continent

Low-cost airlines are opening up places that used to be beyond most people's comfort zones. Ryanair, easyJet, and nearly 40 other low-cost airlines across Europe are accomplishing what politicians in the expanding European Union couldn't: they came on strong and that allowed millions of Europeans to cross borders en masse for business and pleasure. Last year, airlines logged more than 420 million passengers on intra-European flights, an increase of some 40% from five years ago.

Jetting around Europe used to be a luxury. Now it's possible to crisscross the region for as little as $30 return – less than the fare on a taxi ride to the local airport. The trend originated in 1997 when Brussels deregulated the aviation industry, enabling discounters to get airborne. To fight back, the bigger, more established companies have been slashing their own fares. The fare wars could set the stage for an industry-wide European shakeout, but for now consumers are the big winners.

Source: Business Week, May 2006

overall results of the process rather than of the constituent parts are therefore at stake.

The aim of business re-engineering is to offer more added value to the buyer via a process orientation. Figure 8.7 shows an example of a financial institution that was obliged to review its business processes or else lose control over them when the demand for loans rose from 33,000 per annum to 300,000 per annum.

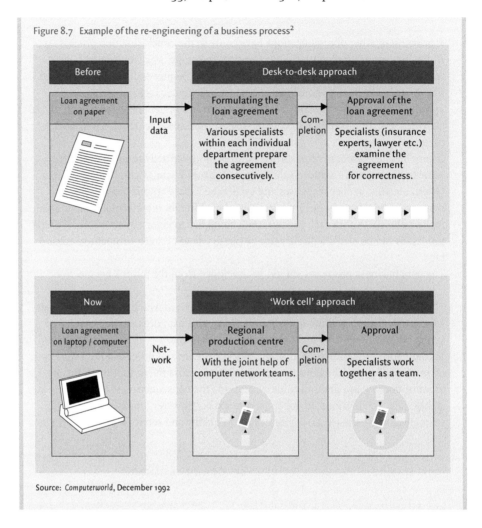

Figure 8.7 Example of the re-engineering of a business process[2]

Source: *Computerworld*, December 1992

Business re-engineering is not new. In the 1960s, the Japanese successfully organised their production processes according to this approach. At the end of the 1970s, a number of Western enterprises adopted the approach, giving it such names as Just in Time (JIT) and Total Quality Management (TQM). By importing process orientation, the results for businesses improved considerably. This result is measured in terms of the added value that products give to the buyer.

Business re-engineering influences the style of leadership used for staff. Employees are given wider tasks as well as responsibility for the end result. They are judged by their contribution to the increase in added value, and not simply by the way they perform certain tasks. In this context, coaching, motivating and stimulating become important tasks for managers. What the main task of a manager boils down to is creating an environment in which staff can function effectively.

Why manufacturers must take advantage of design advice

Cooperation between managers and designers is the key to a product's success and even to the company behind it.

The growth of interest in iconic design products such as the Apple iPod or the Toyota Prius has turned everyone into a designer. Consumers' expectations of technology have been sharpened, and as competition and the rate of product development increases, manufacturers are obliged to differentiate their models. Those that fail to get the message risk a downward path. There will most likely be a problem in the relationship between designer and management. Marketers can use their sales data, market research and focus groups as the basis of a design brief for a new product. But without imagination, the brief is likely to be retrospective and incapable of carrying the business forward. And if the design cycle takes two or three years from concept to shipment – as it typically does – the result can be market stagnation. Here are some tips for making product design work:

- Ensure that the corporate culture does not stifle innovation.
- Make product development an ongoing process.
- Improve communications between functions and select a multidisciplinary team.
- Use outside help in assessing products and services for competitiveness, ease of use and visual impact.
- Research customer attitudes, usage, needs and gaps.
- Decide on priorities: replacing unsatisfactory products, improving existing ones or defining new products.
- Appoint external designers to examine and criticise.
- Revise priorities, appoint a champion and budget for chosen new products.

Source: Financial Times, February 2006

There are five basic principles that organisations need to uphold when they implement the business re-engineering process within an organisation[3]:

1. *The customer is the centre of attention.* Everything begins and ends with the customer. He / she is the key to the entire business process, from the first contact to after-care.
2. *Business re-engineering can be applied to all business processes.* All activities are focussed on increasing added value for the customer.
3. *The improving of processes is a domestic affair.* Responsibility for this should not be shifted to suppliers, although they must be involved: business re-engineering does not stop at the gate.
4. *Business re-engineering must yield clear market results.*
5. *Business re-engineering is a phased process.*

The first step is defining of core business processes and targets. Then a plan should be formulated to adapt the chosen core processes in order to reach the intended goals. The last phase is the implementation phase. Employees must be very aware of the role they play in the entire operation and the responsibilities belonging to this role.

8.2.3 Business processes and added value

A business process adds value to raw materials or semi-manufactured articles. This added value increases an organisation's competitive power fundamentally, according to Michael Porter. He states that a competitive advantage is obtained by lowering the costs of production or by creating added value for products which the customers will pay extra for.

Competitive power

Added value

Porter's theory is based on the so-called 'value chain', comprising all activities needed to offer a product to the market. In other words, the value chain indicates the amount of added value produced by the various parts of the organisation. These different parts are coordinated by what Porter calls 'linkages'. By carefully structuring and coordinating the business processes, a competitive advantage over other suppliers arises.

Value chain

Linkages

The value chain provides a framework for the analysis of the various activities within an organisation. Within business processes, the added value comes from a combination of the costs (such as for raw materials and work) and the profit that the organisation wants to make. The value chain diagram is shown in Figure 8.8.

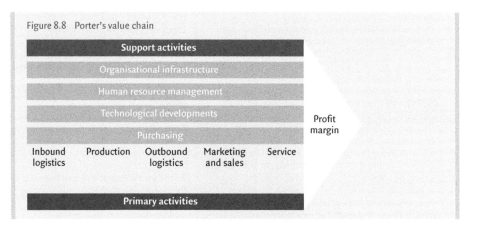

Figure 8.8 Porter's value chain

Primary activities

Within the value chain a distinction is made between primary and support activities. Primary activities are activities that add value directly to products; support activities have supporting roles. They create the conditions needed by the primary processes, thus contributing indirectly to the value of the products.

Some examples of primary activities are:

- *Inbound logistics.* Purchasing and storage of the goods needed for production.
- *Operations (production).* Transformation of the purchased goods into products (packaging included).
- *Outbound logistics.* Distribution of the products to the buyers (making up orders, transport and storage).
- *Marketing and sales.* Stimulating the demand for a product (promotion campaigns, advertisements and sales representatives).
- *Service.* Keeping up or increasing product value with customer service (installing, repairing, and training of the buyers).

Support activities

Some examples of support activities are:

- *Procurement.* The purchase of goods needed for the entire value chain.
- *Technological development.* Research and development of products or processes.
- *Human Resources.* Recruitment, rewarding, training and motivation of the organisation's employees.
- *Administrative infrastructure Management.* Activities performed by management and support staff, such as finance and quality control.

Information provision

According to Porter, information provision within an organisation does not belong to the primary or support activities, but occupies a central position like that of a spider in a web: it connects the separate primary and support activities. It can certainly help to increase competitive advantage.

Organisations can obtain a competitive advantage by structuring and coordinating the business processes in the value chain in a particular way. The invention of a new production process (a supporting activity) can add more efficiency to production (a primary activity), lowering the costs of a product considerably.

According to Porter, competitive advantage can be obtained in three ways.

Figure 8.9 Competitive advantage via improved internal organisation[4]

Success factor	Competitive capacity		
	Low	Middle	High
Product position			
Quality			
Functionality			
Price			
Market position			
Distribution channels			
Market share			
Internal organisation			
Productivity			
Running time			
Flexibility			

●——● Enterprise A
●——● Enterprise B

1 The first strategy is to run your operations against the lowest costs. For this it is important to know the effects of particular activities or factors. The so-called 'cost-drivers' must be traced and analysed. A change in structure or coordination can lead to considerable cost savings. *Lowest costs*

2 The second strategy is based on product differentiation. The product is given unique characteristics compared with those products produced by competitors. The consumer is willing to pay extra for these new features. For the organisation it is important to structure and to coordinate the value chain in such a way that this competitive advantage can be used to gain a favourable price-quality ratio. *Differentiation*

3 Both the low cost and the differentiation strategy can be combined with a segmentation strategy (the focus strategy of Porter). The organisation can choose to address just one or a number of segments in the market. *Focus strategy*

Europe's web use overtakes newspapers

The time European consumers spend online has overtaken the hours they devote to newspapers and magazines for the first time, according to a new study. But the growth of new media is expanding total media consumption rather than simply cannibalising print and television.

Print consumption has remained static over the past two years at three hours a week, while time spent online has doubled from two to four hours. Viewers are also spending more time watching television, up from 10 hours to 12 hours a week.

The survey shows that European use of the web is still behind the rates seen in the US. A similar survey in the US found that Americans now spend 14 hours a week online – as much time as they spend watching television – and just three hours reading print. The rapid spread of fast broadband connections across Europe is likely to accelerate the trend. The average time spent online by broadband customers in Europe was seven hours a week, compared to just two hours a week for those using dial-up connections.

The fact that Internet consumption has passed print consumption is an important landmark in the establishment of the Internet in Europe. The shift in the balance of power will increasingly shape content distribution strategies, advertising spending allocation and communication strategies.

Source: Financial Times, October 2006

8.2.4 Business processes and quality

Many enterprises pay attention to quality management in the area of business processes. Quality management is that aspect of management that falls under quality strategy and is implemented by management as a whole. *Quality management*

While quality is a much used term, it can be defined in different ways. Traditionally, it has been associated with the technical specifications of a product, with the degree of quality determined by a number of scores representing measurements of technical specifications. A high score is indicative of a high-quality product. Such a definition of quality is referred to as technological quality.

Technological quality

Relative quality

The so-called relative quality[5] is that which is directed to the needs of the buyer and the competitive position. Here, quality is judged from the market perspective (a marketing approach) and the product is assessed in terms of a number of individual qualities, differing in value according to customer needs and the product's uses. Quality is defined as the degree of satisfaction experienced by the target group. In addition to technical aspects, a number of other aspects play a role, including delivery time, after-sales service and design.

Total quality management

Implementing relative quality requires a different organisational approach to that for technological quality and is known as total quality management.[6] This is a system aimed at achieving the desired level of quality with minimal expenses. Total quality management integrates and performs all quality-related activities and makes decisions that influence quality, irrespective of position within the organisation. (See Figure 8.10.)

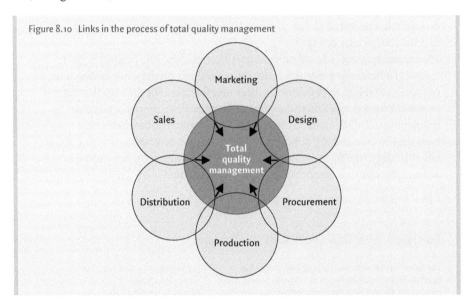

Figure 8.10 Links in the process of total quality management

Total quality management should therefore:
- Form part of the general policy of an enterprise
- Include all phases of the production process, from market analysis to delivery and after-sales service
- Be adopted by all levels of the organisation, from top management down to the work floor

Total quality management is often abbreviated to TQM. Four important reasons for quality control are:

1 *Increasing competition.* Many enterprises have witnessed decreased growth in their traditional consumer markets while competition from outside has gradually increased. The increasing globalisation of the market has only added to the overall effect. To be successful depends mainly on selling products with a very favourable price / quality ratio.

Quality is king at Porsche

More than 70% of all Porsches ever built are still on the road today. This record value speaks for itself. To give you maximum security when buying a Porsche, all vehicles within the Porsche Approved Certified Pre-owned Car Program must pass a demanding quality inspection. An obligatory checklist with over 100 quality criteria is used for this purpose. This way you can rest assured that your pre-owned Porsche is in perfect condition, both technically and visually.

Source: www.porsche.com, November 2006

**Porsche Approved
Certified Pre-Owned**
Limited Warranty

2 *Increasing buyer awareness of quality.* Buyers are increasingly better informed about the characteristics of products and so are demanding higher quality.

3 *The costs of quality.* The costs associated with making high quality products constitute an important part of the cost price. These expenses can be broken down into costs associated with the prevention of errors during the production process, such as control expenses and non-quality costs and repairs. Such non-quality expenses can make up 20% of the cost price of products. The problem is that in many businesses, these quality costs are insufficiently taken account of in the price calculations. The costs associated with the prevention of poor quality will initially be high, but will thereafter go down.

4 *Changes in legislation.* Organisations are increasingly being held legally responsible for the delivery of inferior products, with financial penalties also rising.

While quality programmes should always focus on the customer, in reality, such programmes often only concentrate on improvements to business processes. However, it is the customer who ultimately determines the quality, as market success is a consequence of customer decisions. As such, quality programmes should be in line with customer needs.

Quality programmes

To achieve this, the customer's needs must be identified and integrated within the production processes. Figure 8.11 shows how this can increase the market share. This figure also demonstrates that quality has both active and passive effects. For example, through mouth-to-mouth advertising new customers will be attracted to the organisation, while existing customers will remain faithful.

Quality is guarded by certification of quality programmes, by ISO certification and by the Six Sigma system.

Certification of quality programmes

A quality programme forms the basis for quality care, and includes organisational structure, responsibilities, procedures and supply. When a quality programme

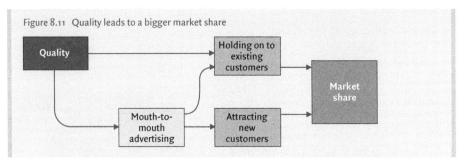

Figure 8.11 Quality leads to a bigger market share

Certificate

meets the standards and requirements of an external authority it is awarded a certificate. Gaining quality certification is important for an organisation for a number of reasons:[7]

- In a market where quality demands are increasing, the buyer gains a feeling of security and trust from products that are quality certified.
- European unification has lead to an increase in competition on certain markets. An internationally recognised quality certificate can improve an enterprise's market position.
- New international and national legislation has been introduced in relation to product liability. Manufacturers can be held responsible for any damage caused by their products. The possession of a quality certificate may limit the size of any claim for damages and insurance companies sometimes have an input concerning demands in this respect.

ISO certification

International Organisation for
Standardisation
ISO

In 1987, the European Commission decided to introduce international quality standards that originated from the International Organisation for Standardisation (ISO). The Dutch version of the standard is known as NEN-ISO, while the Flemish version is BIN-ISO. Some requirements for this standard are:

- Management must set up the quality system together with a description of objectives.
- Competencies and responsibilities should be determined with quality principles in mind.
- Educated staff should be attracted and given training in relation to quality systems and processes.

IN THE PRESS

Caterpillar's CEO on the need for International Quality Standards

'Caterpillar supports the ISO goal of one standard, one test accepted globally', says Jim Owens, Chairman and Chief Executive Officer of Caterpillar Inc.

'This approach offers a level field of competition across the world, so that companies can compete based on the value they can offer customers no matter where in the world those customers may live and do business', he tells ISO Focus.

Owens goes on to affirm his appreciation of how ISO standards help reduce non-tariff barriers to trade, whilst making industry more efficient. 'It is not economical to develop products to meet different requirements in each country', he says. 'Thus, the ISO standards are very valuable for promoting global requirements to minimise the time and costs of

developing and testing new products'.

International Standards also bring a great many benefits to new technology, Owens emphasises:

'Standards help establish acceptance criteria and test methods for the introduction of new technology. Particularly in the safety area, International Standards provide performance criteria that can be used as a baseline for adopting new innovations and technology'.

As the world's leading manufacturer of construction and mining equipment, diesel and natural gas engines and industrial gas turbines, with 300 facilities in more than 40 countries, Caterpillar is committed to developing and promoting ISO standards.

Source: www. iso.org, November 2006

- Quality should be measured during all phases of the production process.
- The monitoring process should be organised so as to correct mistakes and prevent them reoccurring in the future.

In general, ISO standards put more emphasis on processes than on results. The ISO certificate is a minimum requirement for many organisations and indicates a basic level, just as a driving licence indicates the basic ability to drive. In time, the quality system (or driver's ability) develops further.

A description of the quality system has to be made when an organisation decides to apply for ISO certification. This description should include a quality manual, thus *Quality manual* providing the possibility of checking the quality system against the ISO standards. (Figure 8.12.)

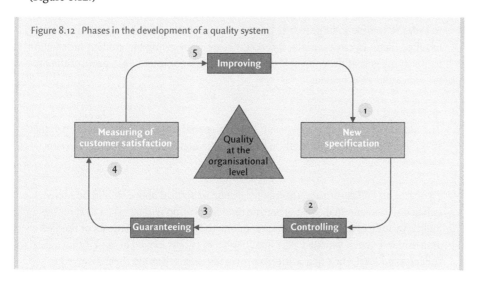

Figure 8.12 Phases in the development of a quality system

It can be seen from this figure that a quality system develops in phases. To illustrate how these phases work, an example – a commercial training centre – will be looked at in detail.

Documentation of specifications
Initially, product specifications should be determined, keeping in mind the requirements of the customer. In this example, the specifications are the course timetable, the nature and amount of course material, the educational level and experience of the teacher, the assessment methods for testing the students, and so on.

Determining the business processes
Next, the business processes needed to deliver the products are identified. It is important to cover only the essential features. In the example, the following processes are regarded as the main ones:
- Appointing the instructors
- Developing the course material
- Delivery of courses
- Quality checking of the courses

Quality control
The maximum attainable quality is ultimately determined by the choice of specifications and business processes. Achieving the desired quality standards depends on

Quality control

quality control. This in turn can be defined as the operational tools (e.g. a fishbone diagram) and activities that are needed to meet the quality requirements. In our case, this could include defining the contents of the course following feedback discussions with students, or preparing and testing the course material beforehand.

Quality standards

Quality standards

If a quality system has been introduced, it is important to ensure that the system continues to meet the required levels. This should be done using quality standards. Included in these are all planned and systematic checks necessary to verify that the product comes up to standard. In other words, quality standards underpin quality control. In the example, we would need to fully investigate the quality system.

Monitoring and customer focus

In order to be able to improve the quality of products and services it is important to monitor them. In our example, this could be done by giving out student satisfaction forms at the end of the course. Students could then comment on aspects of the programme, and give feedback.

Implementing improvements

The monitoring of quality may result in updates to the specifications of the product. In the example, this could result in better course material or extra IT facilities in class.

Audit

To obtain an ISO certificate, the quality system described above should be established and documented. Next, a certification institution will be asked to carry out an audit. An audit is an examination intended to judge if all requirements of the ISO standard have been satisfied. The quality system is first looked at, and if this meets the required level, the organisation's processes themselves are then observed to see if they match what has been written down.

Six Sigma[8]

Six Sigma is a quality system that has been intensively developed over the last few years. ISO-certified enterprises pay a lot of attention to the quality of products, services and processes. However, practice shows that ISO-certified enterprises regularly deliver bad quality.

China Compulsory Certification Mark

China uses the China Compulsory Certification Mark (CCC) before exporting to or selling on the Chinese market. Products not meeting the CCC requirements may be held at the border by Chinese customs and will be subject to other penalties.

The Import Commodity Inspection: Chinese law provides that all goods included on a published Inspection List, or subject to inspection pursuant to other laws and regulations, or subject to the terms of the foreign trade contract, must be inspected prior to importation, sale, or use in China. In addition, safety licensing and other regulations also apply to importation of medicines, foodstuffs, animal and plant products, and mechanical and electronic products.

Chinese buyers or their purchasing agents must register for inspection at the port of arrival. The inspection undertaken by local commodity inspection authorities includes product quality, technical specifications, quantity, weight, packaging, and safety requirements. The standard of inspection is based upon compulsory Chinese national standards, domestic trade standards, or in their absence, the standards stipulated in the purchase or sale contract.

Source: www.fedex.com, November 2006

Six Sigma, which originated in America, was developed in 1987 by Motorola. The programme is based on the customers and their wishes, and has a strong quantitative focus. After it was proved to be a success with Motorola, other American multinationals such as American Express, Ford, Citibank and General Electric started using it. An increasing number of enterprises (including the Dutch multinational Philips) now work with Six Sigma. It is a quality system that can be used for the production of goods and of services. The popularity of Six Sigma is based on the fact that it not only leads to quality improvement but also to cost reduction.

Quantitative focus

Six Sigma can be defined as a comprehensive and flexible system that enables the organisation to achieve maximum and sustainable success. This is due to:
· Constantly keeping a close watch on customer needs
· Rigorous use of facts, data and statistical analyses
· Thorough attention being paid to the management, improvement and innovation of business processes

Six Sigma

Sigma is the Greek letter σ, used in statistics to indicate standard deviation, which indicates the degree of variation. Levels of quality vary during production. Many business processes are measured to have a 3σ-level, which is equivalent to a 6.7% deviation or defect percentage. Enterprises that work with Six Sigma are very ambitious in terms of the quality standards they consider acceptable (i.e. their Six Sigma level). The goal of the system is to have a maximum of 3.4% deviation per million items. Six Sigma aims to achieve the smallest possible variation / deviation in a process.

Standard deviation

This is accomplished by the setting up of Six Sigma improvement projects. A Six Sigma project with the label (DMAIC) has the following five phases:
1 Define
2 Measure
3 Analyse
4 Improve
5 Control

1 Define

Define

The objectives of the project are defined during this phase. It is also necessary to determine exactly what the project is about and what the limits are. Determining objectives is not only about defining the criteria for the required quality. It is also necessary to examine those issues that influence the target quality.

2 Measure

Measure

This phase mainly concerns the gathering of information about the current status of the quality process. The process is mapped with the help of flow charts and diagrams. Measuring is very important with Six Sigma. How many mistakes are being made? What are the chances of the process running smoothly? What risks are involved in the process? This information is all recorded statistically. During this phase it is important to obtain reliable information. Consideration should be given to the selection of measuring instruments and the ways in which they are used.

3 Analyse

Analyse

This phase is about obtaining in-depth knowledge of and insights into the process. This in-depth knowledge and insight is needed later to generate cost reduction and / or quality improvement. Knowledge is gained by analysing the information by means of statistical techniques such as standard deviation, contingency tables, and regression and correlation analysis. Methods and techniques from other disciplines are also used, including systems development and project management.

4 Improve

The aim during this phase is developing the most effective process. By simulation and experimentation, an attempt is made to design the activities within the process as optimally as possible. This is based on the acquired knowledge of, and insights into, the process.

5 Control

It is not enough to simply determine the best possible process. The results need to be monitored. During the control process, the results of the improvement phase are evaluated and examined. Without this control, it is not inconceivable that the old procedures are reverted to and that much that has been learnt is not applied.

Six Sigma takes a specific approach towards projects and the roles of project members. Six Sigma projects must be carried out by employees who are completely involved with the area of activity in their daily work. These employees are called 'black-belts' and they need to be trained in statistical techniques. They also need to know how to run projects. 'Black-belts' are supported by 'green-belts', who provide input from the shop floor. Lastly, there are the so-called 'champions'. It is their task to monitor the progress of the project. They must also ensure that the 'black-belts' deal with the issues from the perspective of the organisation.

8.2.5   Logistics management

To control business processes involves quite a number of logistic issues, including supply volume and ways of reducing delivery time or the time it takes customers to place an order. Logistics is about the flow of goods and / or services within the business chain. Logistical management deals with the planning and controlling of these flows plus the corresponding information stream.

Logistical management is also of increasing importance in general service and health care. The Dutch insurance company Centraal Beheer forms a good example. In this company, insurance can be ordered by telephone, without having to go through an agent. 'Patient logistics' is increasingly common in the health care sector.

Since the foundation of the European Union, the possibility has arisen of delivering products quickly from a factory in one member country to a customer in another member country without having to go via a wholesale trader's warehouse. In the near future, all organisations are likely to improve their logistics management with a view to lowering costs and improving services, and therefore increase their overall performance. Logistics management (business logistics) has two focal points:

1 Material management
2 Physical distribution management

Material management includes all logistical activities from the supply of raw material to the final product. Physical distribution management includes all logistical activities from the completion of the product to delivery to the buyer. Figure 8.13 shows the relationship between these activities.

As each organisation fulfils certain tasks in the business chain, it has to deal with various logistical problems, depending on its place in this process. In relation to

Six Sigma: reduction in the number of rejected batches in a production company

A manufacturing company in the medical sector had a problem. The production department was sometimes not able to make the products to specification. When this happened, Quality Control then had to reject the whole production batch. The root cause of the problem was not known, and so a Six Sigma project aimed at resolving the situation got under way. The primary aim (target): the current level of 1.75 rejected batches per week (2.3%, i.e. 3.5 sigma) had to be reduced by 10%, resulting in a score of at least 4.3 sigma.

Three improvement teams were set up. Each team was made up of machine operators plus one employee from each of the following departments: Technical Services, Manufacturing Engineering and R&D. The project was facilitated by a consultant plus an internal black-belt trainee.

- Team 1: Optimisation of equipment
- Team 2: Optimisation of manufacturing procedures
- Team 3: Optimisation of tooling and materials.

The project time scale was:
2 months to start the improvement teams and to make an inventory of the current situation (operational strategy, customer requirements, general data on production).
7 months to resolve all aspects of the problems using the CASE (DMAIC) method.

The issues were
1 Better climate control within the production room
2 Prevention of product contamination
3 Implementation of detailed manufacturing procedures
4 Improvement in the maintenance of equipment and tools
5 Optimisation of the design of equipment and tooling
6 Training of operators and exchange of Best Practices

The goal was accomplished in 27 weeks. The problem of rejected batches was resolved: there were no rejects in the last 20 project weeks. These 20 weeks were used to refine the procedures and guarantee the results. Ultimately, the level of rejected batches was reduced from 3.5 sigma to more than 4.7 sigma.

Rejected batches

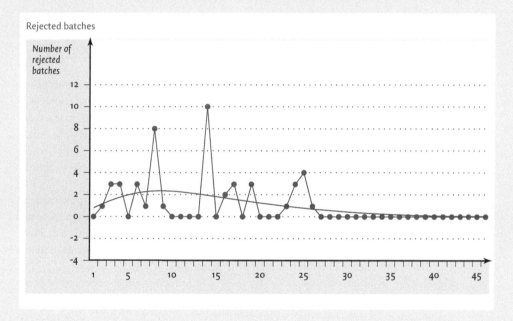

Source: www.aimingbetter.nl

material management, organisations need to make decisions with particular regard to the following[9]:
- Planning and control of the production process
- Stock control of raw materials and semi-manufactured products
- Transport and storing of raw materials and semi-manufactured products. In physical distribution, it is important that the goods be available at the right place and

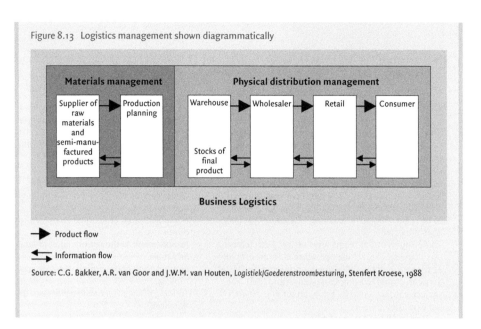

Figure 8.13 Logistics management shown diagrammatically

Source: C.G. Bakker, A.R. van Goor and J.W.M. van Houten, *Logistiek/Goederenstroombesturing*, Stenfert Kroese, 1988

time. Decision-making in this area is mainly concerned with:
· Stock control of the end product
· Warehouse management
· Transport control and distribution planning

Well-executed logistics management may increase competitive advantage by, for example, reducing purchase prices, making production capacity flexible, more effective use of machines and shorter delivery times.

Research has shown that customers' choice of suppliers depends not only on price, but to a large extent on delivery time and reliability, service and personal contacts. When considering these advantages, the relationship between logistics, marketing, financing and development of products and processes should also be kept in mind.

Strategies

In order to maximise the advantages of logistics management it is crucial to coordinate the different activities. Theoretically, four strategies are possible[10]:

1 *Building in margins.* Lowering the performance level will produce surplus capacity. Accurate coordination of the activities will no longer be necessary, though there will be a drawback in that costs will increase and products may become hard to market.
2 *The creation of autonomous units.* This will make the divisions of the organisation less dependent of each other, but decrease the advantages of scale.
3 *Investing in vertical data information systems.* Coordination will be enhanced by better availability of information.
4 *Introducing a lateral structure.* This will enable decisions to be made at lower levels where the relevant information is available.

Radio Frequency Identification

The flow of goods and data play an important role in logistics management. A well-known method is the use of bar codes or its improved successor, the Radio Frequency Identification (RFID) which has many advantages compared to the bar-code. The RFID uses radio signals for transmitting over longer distances. It is based on a system consisting of two parts, a 'tag' and a write / read unit. The tag has a chip and an antenna. The components can be miniaturised by current technological developments.

Structure and organisation

Dutch Auction Company Sends Flowers via RFID

Dutch flower auction company FloraHolland sells flowers to about 250 horticultural traders daily at its Naaldwijk facility. Now the worldwide cooperative of flower and plant growers, which announced to have plans to merge with global horticultural vendor Bloemenveiling Aalsmeer, is embarking on several RFID projects to move flowers more efficiently, and to gain more data about its products and their movements as they pass through the facility.

It's a tall order–the Naaldwijk facility, one of the largest commercial warehouses in Europe, is the size of 100 soccer fields. Trucks begin arriving at the 1-million-square-foot facility at 4 a.m. every day, where employees use tractors and trolleys to handle incoming shipments. Time is of the essence, as flowers must be on their way to buyers within a few hours of their arrival.

For the past four years, FloraHolland has utilized several RFID systems. One of that systems includes several loop antennas embedded in the floor to monitor when tractors pulling trolleys of flowers arrive at the auction floor. These antennas interrogate the Texas Instruments ISO 18000 134.2 KHz passive tag embedded in each passing trolley. The cooperative brings traders daily onto its auction floor, and more than 100,000 trolleys of flowers are moved from one location to another for selling and shipping. The buyers subsequently sell the product to retailers throughout the world. Data about the trolley number and the products on it are displayed on an LED screen on the auction floor, alerting buyers as to which products are heading to auction.

Source: www.rfidjournal.com, November 2006

Technological developments have also brought down the price of RFID, which has allowed significantly broader application of the system. RFID has many applications, such as:

- Tracking & tracing
- Product protection (e.g. against theft)
- Identification in unfavourable surroundings (heat, liquid and noise)
- Logistical activities within the distribution chain
- Quality control

In summary, RIFD can be applied more widely than barcodes and it will be used widely in the future. It make better control of logistical activities possible and it can reduce costs.[11]

8.2.6 Customer Relationship Management

Customer Relationship Management takes the relationship with the customer as its basis, rather than the product or business process. From a strategic point of view, the organisation tries to gain competitive advantage by concentrating more fully on the needs of the customer. Customer Relationship Management is an approach for building, keeping and extending relationships with individual customers, thus creating value for both customer and enterprise.[12]

Customer Relationship Management

Some customer groups are more valuable to an organisation than others. An organisation's customer groups can be represented via a pyramid diagram, classified by turnover. Research has shown that irrespective of size, branch or locality, companies follow the following pattern[13]:

Pyramid diagram

- Top customers   1%
- Big customers   4%
- Medium-sized customers   15%
- Small customers   80%

                                 100%

Research has also shown a pattern within each a customer category, indicating contribution to turnover and related expenses. This can be summarised as follows:

- 90% of the turnover comes from existing customers (Figure 8.14).
- 80% of the turnover comes from 20% of the customers (Figure 8.15).
- 150% of the profit is generated by the same 20% of customers. The remaining 80% actually contribute towards a loss (Figure 8.16).
- 30% of the existing customers have a strong potential for volume growth.

Based on their position in the customer pyramid, specific activities can be developed for the various segments.

The purpose of Customer Relationship Management[14]

Competition is increasing and market growth is slowing down. Product life cycles are also decreasing. Gaining an advantage through a larger scale of production not longer seems feasible. Information and communication technologies enable customer groups to be identified and their buying behaviours increasingly better anticipated. This development has been encouraged by new media such as the Internet. Customers now have the opportunity to make their individual wishes clear to organisations. The new technologies give organisations extensive possibilities for collecting, storing and handling information about their customers. By anticipating the individual wishes of the customers, it is possible to develop commitment towards the enterprise. Customer loyalty will be the result, with the customer providing a sustainable competitive advantage. Customer loyalty is a reflection of the quality of the relationship between organisation and customer. On one hand, it indicates the added value for the customer; on the other it has a strong link with current and future profit potential.

Loyalty

The architecture of Customer Relationship Management[15]

Customer Relationship Management is structured to encompass five areas, each tightly related to each other (Figure 8.17):

Contact Management

1 *Contact Management* This deals with the communication between customer and enterprise, including a balanced distribution policy and contact management.

Customer Management

2 *Customer Management* This deals with the relationship with the customer and allied developments such as acquisition, retention and expansion of the customer base.

Data Management

3 *Data Management* This has to do with the collection, analysis and distribution of information. Security and privacy constitute special points of interest.

Operational Management

4 *Operational Management* This has to do with the fulfilling of the customer's needs and support of the primary activities. There is a strong connection between production, research & development, human resource management, financing and logistics.

Strategy

5 *Strategy* Strategy is at the heart of Customer Relationship Management since it forms a stimulus for the other four areas.

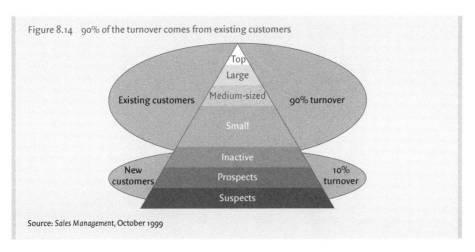

Figure 8.14   90% of the turnover comes from existing customers

Top
Large
Medium-sized
Small
Inactive
Prospects
Suspects

Existing customers   90% turnover

New customers   10% turnover

Source: *Sales Management*, October 1999

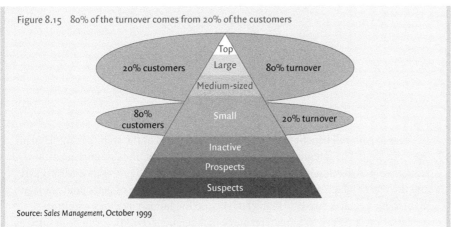

Figure 8.15   80% of the turnover comes from 20% of the customers

Top
Large
Medium-sized
Small
Inactive
Prospects
Suspects

20% customers   80% turnover

80% customers   20% turnover

Source: *Sales Management*, October 1999

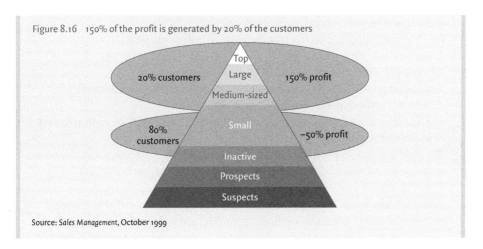

Figure 8.16   150% of the profit is generated by 20% of the customers

Top
Large
Medium-sized
Small
Inactive
Prospects
Suspects

20% customers   150% profit

80% customers   –50% profit

Source: *Sales Management*, October 1999

8.2.7   Human resource management

Organisations are being confronted with new developments that are manifesting themselves at a quicker rate and with more intensity than in the past: technological developments, globalisation, changing market circumstances, demographic, socio-cultural and political developments. These developments have important consequences for the organisation's human resources and are leading to new and tougher demands on organisations, where flexibility and manoeuvrability are now of particular importance.

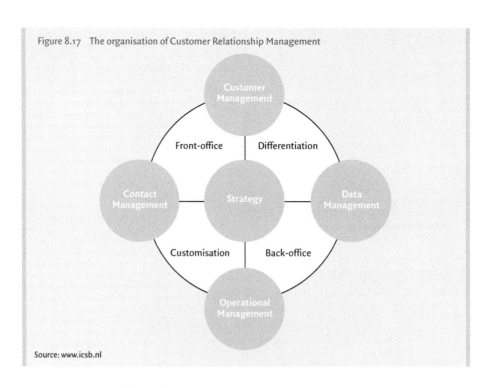

Figure 8.17   The organisation of Customer Relationship Management

Customer
Management

Front-office   Differentiation

Contact
Management

Strategy

Data
Management

Customisation   Back-office

Operational
Management

Source: www.icsb.nl

In order to gain full benefit from the skills and abilities of the staff, personnel management should be integrated into strategic management, thus prompting a close relationship to develop between the way an organisation adapts to its environment and the way in which a personnel strategy emerges. The type of personnel management that integrates strategic management and the human qualities within an organisation is known as human resource management (HRM). It can be defined as all standards and values relating to an organisation's employees and the translation of these into techniques and methods that optimise the use of existing human qualities and their contribution towards the goals of the organisation.

Human resource management

The main aspects of human resource management are:
· Acknowledgement by top management of the importance of the human factor
· The conviction that human qualities can be used better
· The understanding that the qualities and motivation of the staff are critical factors in implementing the organisation's strategy
· The need to apply systems and tools in a professional and systematic way, focussing on using the human qualities in order to arrive at the organisation's goals

Personnel management within an organisation consists of the following aspects: recruitment and selection, rewarding, appraisal, career planning, knowledge management and management of staff departures. A characteristic aspect of HRM is that these personnel aspects are integrated within the strategic management of the organisation, as shown in Figure 8.18.

Strategic personnel management

HRM thus constitutes an important organisational function, and consequently top management must take responsibility for strategic personnel management. An employee's immediate boss is responsible for implementing this policy. It is their task to stimulate and coach their employees so that they can develop optimally. Appraisal, training plans and guidance during poor health are clear-cut tasks for management, with the HRM department mainly playing a supporting and advisory role.

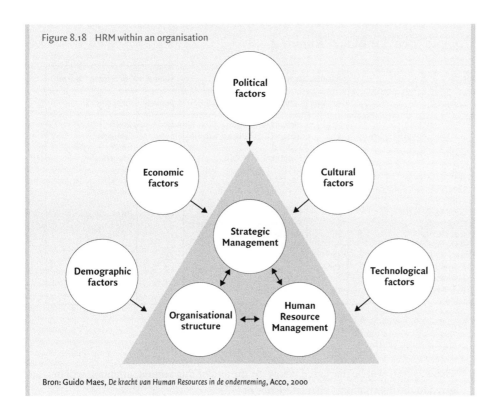

Figure 8.18 HRM within an organisation

Bron: Guido Maes, *De kracht van Human Resources in de onderneming*, Acco, 2000

The organisation's personnel will typically undergo a process of entering, passing through and exiting the organisation. The following figure (Figure 8.19) expands on the steps.

Entering

Passing through

Exiting

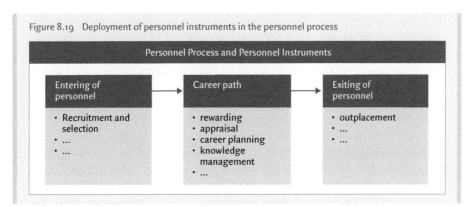

Figure 8.19 Deployment of personnel instruments in the personnel process

The following section will deal with the following personnel instruments in greater detail:
- Recruitment and selection
- Rewarding
- Appraisal
- Career planning
- Knowledge management
- Learning and development
- Management development
- Outplacement

Pan European Ideal Employer Ranking

MBA Students		Business Students		Engineering & Science Students	
Ranking	Company	Ranking	Company	Ranking	Company
1	McKinsey & Co.	1	McKinsey & Co.	1	IBM
2	Boston Consulting Group	2	Boston Consulting Group	2	Siemens
3	Bain & Co.	3	L'Oreal	3	BMW
4	BMW	4	Procter & Gamble	4	Porsche
5	Apple	5	BMW	5	Sony
6	Goldman Sachs	6	Porsche	6	Ferrari
7	LVMH Moet Hennessy Louis Vuitton	7	European Central Bank	7	Microsoft
8	General Electric	8	JPMorgan	8	Intel
9	Citygroup	9	Price Waterhouse Coopers	9	EADS
10	Coca-Cola	10	Nestle	10	Nokia
11	Booz Allen Hamilton	11	IKEA	11	Audi
12	BP	12	Goldman Sachs	12	Philips
13	L'Oreal	13	Ferrari	13	Shell
14	Johnson & Johnson	14	Coca-Cola	14	General Electric
15	A.T. Kearney	15	Unilever	15	McKinsey & Co.

Source: Universum Communications, Study 2006

These aspects will be discussed below. At the end of this section, attention will be given to the international characteristics of HRM.

Recruitment and selection

Recruitment and selection

Since an organisation is a group of people who collaborate jointly, the quality of the organisation depends to a large extent on staff quality. Functions have been subject to a great deal of change, and selection is increasingly directed more toward careers than towards specific jobs. It is not surprising that many organisations have painstakingly set up procedures for the recruitment and selection of personnel.

Internal procedure

External procedure

The organisation initially needs to decide whether it will look for candidates inside or outside the company. Many organisations have a policy of undertaking an internal procedure first. If this does not fill the vacancy, an external procedure will get underway. The recruitment of internal candidates has the advantage of successful internal candidates being granted a desirable promotion or transfer.

Selection should take place as soon as the recruitment period has expired and the chosen candidate allocated a specific post. It is important to maintain a good balance between the person, the job and the organisation. The company and job demands on the applicant should be made explicit. The following items should be included: terms of employment, date of entrance, notice period, job description, location, probation period, competition clause, duty of confidentiality and perks (e.g. telephone and study expense allowances).

During the weeks that follow the appointment of the new employee, it is important to ensure that he / she is worked into the job. Many organisations appoint a mentor for the new employee. However, time pressures often mean that lip service is paid to support and counselling.

Rewarding

Reward

The relationship between performance and reward is important as there is an interaction between these activities. The issue is which performance elements should be recognised in the reward.

There are various ways of addressing this issue, and they have led to several different reward systems. While some systems use financial incentives to translate the relationship between performance and payment, others link such factors as degree of responsibility to the financial incentives. To ensure that the balance is right when such a system is being structured, we need to pay attention to two basic factors that influence the reward:

1 The work that the person does (appreciation of the task)
2 The way that this person is doing the work (appreciation of performance)

1 The work that a person does

The purpose of job evaluation is to arrive at a fair salary for the work done. To do this requires analysis and a description of the jobs within an organisation and how they are graded. The result should be an objective method for salary calculation (a evaluation system). As well as being used for the systematic assessment and justification of the salary structure, such a method can also be used for personnel appraisal, career planning, recruitment and selection, and structuring (or restructuring) of the organisation.

Job evaluation

The point of departure of a job evaluation system is the way the organisation and the jobs need to be structured. The organisational and subsequent goals (such as sector and department goals) form the structure within which the jobs form part. The system should, however, be flexible enough to allow for any adaptation to future developments in the market that may be necessary. This is why the organisation should keep the system completely up to date. Various tools for job evaluation have been developed, the most well-known being:

1 *The ranking method*   A number of main jobs with existing salaries are identified. The position and the salary for other jobs are derived from these main jobs

The ranking method

2 *The factor-comparison method*   In this method, a number of key factors within a job are identified and linked to salary scales in similar positions in outside organisations. The frame of reference is therefore not entirely internal, but is based on market rates. A description of these key factors is used for comparison with and adaptation of other jobs.

The factor-comparison method

3 *The classification method*   So-called task classes are determined and defined. The various classes are grouped around standard jobs with a known salary range. These standard jobs can be based on internal and external points of reference. The other job descriptions are then compared with these standard jobs and put into a certain task class.

The classification method

4 *The points plan*   Each job is divided into factors that are evaluated separately by means of a weighing coefficient. By multiplying each factor with its coefficient, a total grade is obtained. This determines the value of the job.

The points plan

2 The way that a person does his / her work

Two methods may be used to determine the reward:

1 *The market value method*   The reward is determined by asking what the employee could earn within another organisation. With this system, the reward is not a policy matter and there will be a lack of coherence between the various salaries. This method is often applied by small and medium-sized organisations. Rewards can also be checked with employer or employees organisations.

The market value method

2 *The systematic method*   In contrast to the market value method, this system aims for a certain structure in the reward system. The goal is the development of a systematic salary structure for all staff, containing logical and effective differentiations. This means that the rewards are both competitive from an external point of view and internally acceptable. Large organisations in particular use this method.

The systematic method

Rewards: thinking outside of the box

Years of research have focussed on designing successful reward programs that keep employees productive and engaged, yet one critical audience – the line manager – has often been overlooked, according to a new book, The Manager's Guide to Rewards (2006).

While many organisations focus heavily on monetary rewards for motivating employees, the book points to the significant impact of intangible incentives such as job design, career development and the work climate of the organisation. It identifies the most successful managers as those who recognise and use a variety of tools to reward employees – from linking specific performance measures and bigger organisational goals, to recognising and rewarding valuable employee contributions, to clearly defining job roles. Hay Group research (2006) has shown that up to 30% of variance in business results can be explained by differences in the work climate created by the manager.

Despite the fact that compensation is one of the most controllable forms of expenditure an employer makes – up to 70% of the total costs – less than 20% of organisations report using a formal Return on Investment (ROI) analysis for making decisions, according to the book. While there may be evaluations on specific pieces of the reward system, such as benefits or training costs, there is often no one accountable for assessing the total investment in terms of its human capital.

'Most companies view compensation as a cost to minimise on their balance sheet instead of a long-term investment that needs to be optimised', said Doug Jensen. 'As the competition for talent intensifies, it will become increasingly important for companies to accept the investment viewpoint and look beyond traditional compensation vehicles to attract and retain employees'.

Source: www.haygroup.com, November 2006

Appraisal

Staff performance is appraised on a daily basis. Whether someone has the potential for promotion, should be considered for a salary raise or should be made a permanent staff member are appraisal issues. Helping the employee to gain an insight into his / her own performance and providing guidelines for special issues are also matters for appraisal. An appraisal should indicate strengths and weaknesses and provide guidelines for further development.

An appraisal of such a kind shows the concern of the organisation for the performance of the individual employee.

Appraisals generally involve the activities of discussing, interpreting and weighing up the ability of the person in question, as well as making agreements for the near future. Naturally, a high level of objectivity should be aimed at.

Appraisal interview

Performance review

An appraisal interview should not be confused with a performance review. Such an interview is based on the participants being equals, not on their hierarchical position, as is the case with an assessment interview. The purpose of the performance review is to discuss how the tasks are carried out and to make arrangements for the future: for a coaching interview, for example. One or more performance reviews are often held before the assessment interview takes place.

A traditional assessment interview purports to give the employee feedback on the way he / she is functioning, as seen by the manager. The manager often has little information on what the employee is really doing. The employee is the only one who knows this. Rarely is sufficient information available from the employees' own surroundings. There is consequently a need for feedback that is objective, systematic and independent. The so-called 360-degree feedback method was devised to fill this purpose.

360-degree feedback method

With this method, evaluations of the employee in question are collected from a number of people, including colleagues, employees from various departments and sometimes from customers. The employee also assesses his / her own performance. The collected information is then compared to the manager's own viewpoint. The data can be discussed between manager and employee either as part of the yearly assessment or in any other suitable situation. This method gives a more balanced and reliable image of reality than a one-sided appraisal by the manager. (See Figure 8.20.)

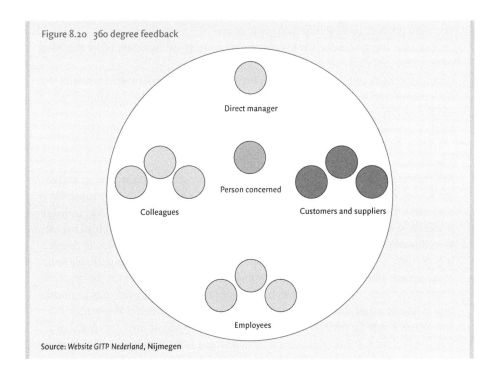

Figure 8.20   360 degree feedback

Direct manager

Person concerned

Colleagues

Customers and suppliers

Employees

Source: *Website GITP Nederland, Nijmegen*

Career planning

For an organisation to be flexible, its staffing must be mobile. Staying in the same job for years is not desirable: the changes an organisation normally has to deal with make this impossible. As mentioned previously, people are not usually recruited for the job as such, but for a career, and thus the employee must have the potential to do various jobs in the future. Career planning is an important part of HRM. Organisations often support employee career planning by offering coaching and training. Career planning policy depends on the answers to the following questions:

· What is the organisation's vision of employee career planning? (Who is responsible, and to what degree is the organisation capable and willing to offer support?)
· What is the future demand for staff likely to be like?
· How do the individual employees view their own career plans?

Career planning

Employees who want to develop within a particular job or who want to be considered for promotion need to develop certain competencies. Competencies are the knowledge, the skills and the attitudes possessed by the employee:

· *Knowledge*: what the employee knows or is familiar with.
· *Skills*: what enables the employee to act
· *Attitudes*: the point of view and the mentality in the spirit of which the employee acts (for example, he / she might be particularly results-oriented).

Competencies

Competency management is looking at competencies from an organisational level: translating the core competencies of the organisation into the necessary knowledge, skills and attitudes possessed by the employees. The developing, assessing and rewarding of employees can be managed on the basis of these core competencies. It is of vital importance for the organisation to recognise its core competencies as these make it possible to obtain competitive advantages. These core competencies should form the guiding principle in setting up competency profiles for individuals or groups of staff. A competency profile is a group of competencies structured according to accomplishments and roles.

Competency management

Competency profile

The main goals of competency management are:
- Performance improvement: the organisational strategy is implemented by clarifying what is expected from the employees
- Consistent HRM: optimal coordination between the various personnel activities
- Maximising staff loyalty to the organisation by supplying good opportunities for further development
- Flexible deployment of staff by moving away from the notion of fixed tasks

Knowledge management

In a rapidly changing society, knowledge has become an important production factor. Knowledge is the ability a person has to execute a certain task. This capability is obtained with the help of information, experience, skills and attitude. A knowledge worker is someone who needs to keep on learning in order to perform his / her job. Seen this way, almost everyone is a knowledge worker to a greater or lesser degree. It is the task of management to systematically deploy the knowledge available to it. Management also determines what new knowledge is needed to reach the organisation's goals. Every organisation has large amounts of data, knowledge and information at its command, but it is often difficult to locate it. Successful knowledge enterprises create an environment and a culture where people are encouraged to learn and to share knowledge. This is what learning organisations do. These are organisations which are constantly increasing their ability to create their own future. Knowledge management is directed at the achievement of a high return for the knowledge input. This applies to learning results as well as financial results. Learning results mean that the employee is able to successfully apply what he has learnt. It is profitable for an organisation if this investment in learning can be used to do such things as developing new services. The knowledge value chain is a central issue when managing knowledge. (See Figure 8.21.)

Knowledge

Knowledge management
Financial results
Learning results

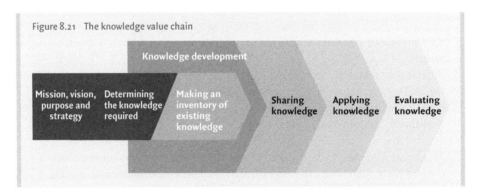

Figure 8.21   The knowledge value chain

Figure 8.21 shows that the various elements of the knowledge value chain are related to the mission, the vision, the goals and the strategy of the organisation. Knowledge development always starts with determining the required knowledge and making an inventory of existing knowledge. The main issue of knowledge management is how to obtain, innovate, distribute and use knowledge in order to create a new competitive advantage.

We will now consider training policy, training courses and their quality, and management development.

Developing professionals to satisfy growing demand in China

Despite a population of 1.3 billion, a growing number of global companies are experiencing significant difficulty attracting and retaining talent in mainland China. Leading companies are responding to this challenge by providing their staff with extensive learning and development opportunities.

The growth of the Chinese economy has resulted in a booming demand for people in professional and managerial jobs. McKinsey estimates that China will need to produce about 75,000 globally capable executives over the next five years. Most companies working in China are narrowing the talent gap by:
- Sourcing Chinese candidates who have studied abroad
- Expanding expatriate programs for experienced professionals (a relatively expensive option that will not be adequate in the long term)
- Recruiting talent from elite Chinese universities: Tsinghua University, for example, launched an MBA program in 1991, the first to do so.
- Targeting experienced people from other global *Fortune 500* companies
- Acquiring local Chinese companies

As demand for talent outstrips supply, turnover rates have jumped to more than 30 percent in a number of companies. Compensation is also increasing at a steady pace, closing the gap that formerly existed compared to compensation in other Asian countries. Benefits are becoming a tool for aiding retention, again increasing the total cost to the company. Instead of just focussing on recruiting and replacing talent, companies will need to pursue a strategy of employee retention initiatives. This is cost-effective (the cost of a replacement may be one-and-a-half to three times the annual salary) and will become a differentiator in attracting new talent. One key retention strategy that is working particularly well in China is providing best-in-class learning and development opportunities. Ideally, the retention strategy should link this growth and development with career development and performance management practices.

Source: *CLO Magazine*, 2006

Learning & Development

An important aspect of knowledge management is the learning and development strategy, which is the responsibility of line management. Line management also has final responsibility for the entire process of selection, promotion, reward, learning and coaching of employees. Professional staff departments such as Learning and Development may support line management by taking on these activities, as may external experts. Line management often has insufficient time and lacks the expertise to do it alone.

Learning and development strategy

E-learning (any form of learning that uses a computer network for distribution, interaction and facilitation) is playing an increasingly large role in these activities. A network may consist of the Internet, intranet or extranet. Some characteristics of e-learning courses are as follows:

E-learning

- *Any time.* The subject matter is always accessible (24 / 7).
- *Any path.* The pathway of learning is determined by the student.
- *Any pace.* The tempo of learning is determined by the student.
- *Any place.* The student can follow his / her course from any connected location.

Many enterprises offer an extensive curriculum of e-learning courses. These started as IT courses, but now almost any conceivable course is offered in an e-learning format, and they are often even available in different languages.

E-learning courses enable employees to use their time more flexibly. A variety of courses allows for better preparation for new jobs and encourages knowledge development in a 'just-in-time' manner which fits better with the needs of adult learners. In addition, knowledge can be built up worldwide and much more quickly. E-learning also cuts costs considerably by reducing travel and accommodation expenses as well as the other costs associated with having a trainer.

Quality of learning programs

A course can be judged as being successful if the acquired knowledge can be applied appropriately to the work situation. The attending of courses is becoming less of an optional activity, and an increasing number of organisations use tests at the end of the course to measure the effectiveness of the acquired knowledge and skills.

Need for a certain course

The inclusion of someone in a course often depends on the wants and needs associated with the knowledge and skills in question. The selection of a particular course to satisfy a want should not be based on knowledge directly related to the employee's present position, but on what might be useful in a future position. In contrast, the need for a certain course should be linked to the contents of the current job: a word processing course needed by a secretary forms a good example. A specific course may be needed to carry out one job and desired for another. The word processing course could be desired by an administrator.

FIGURES & TRENDS

Learning & development is the number 1 driver of employee engagement globally

Towers Perrin's annual global workforce study identifies only 14% of employees as highly engaged in their job. The correlation between engagement and business performance is now widely acknowledged and so the leadership agenda has moved towards HOW to engage employees. Arguably, competitive advantage will only be achieved by improving levels of employee engagement. The top drivers for employee engagement globally are:

1 Opportunities to learn and develop new skills
2 Improvement of one's own capabilities and skills over last year
3 Reputation of the organisation as a good employer
4 Input into decision-making in one's own department
5 An organisation that focusses on customer satisfaction

Source: www.towersperrin.com, 2006

Management Development

Courses

Finally, we will briefly address the issue of courses specially for future managers. Organisations need to pay attention to management development (MD) since qualified managers constitute a critical success factor for the organisation's future. An MD programme also serves as an excellent selection tool for future managers. Job rotation will provide a clear and consistent picture of who the so-called high potentials (those with the potential to go far in career terms) are.

Management development

Management development is not only a form of training. It is also:
- a process of systematically balancing the needs and potential of employees
- which results in the creation of an individual career plan and activities associated with this
- aimed at ensuring ongoing and appropriate job performance both from managers and specialists as well as creating optimal developmental possibilities for staff.

MD deals demonstrably with the systematic integration of both organisational interests and those of employees. However, experience has shown that there are a number of problems associated with MD:
- Only very large organisations can afford MD. They will have sufficient positions for job rotation and the resources to monitor and correct mistakes.
- Currently, organisations are getting rid of entire managerial layers, thereby reducing the number of opportunities for career advancement considerably.
- Uncertainty about the future has made career planning almost impossible. It is

unrealistic to look too far into the future, meaning that only short-term career steps can be contemplated.

- Decentralisation is a feature of a growing number of organisations. Specific products are being made for specific markets by specialised business units. This is hampering the training of those with general skills and diminishing mobility between units.
- The practice of selecting high potential individuals has become almost impossible. Effective criteria are difficult to find and there is no certainty that individuals will develop in the right direction.

Outplacement

In the preceding sections we dealt with the appointment and development of personnel. Now we will discuss the coaching of employees who are leaving the organisation. The main reasons for leaving the organisation are:

- Retirement
- End of a temporary contract
- Long-term illness
- A conflict
- A new job

Developments of all kinds – automation, for example, and its subsequent effect of reducing employee numbers – may force employees to leave the organisation. The ensuing problems can be dealt with by outplacement, an instrument for coaching employees in the event of forced redundancy. Outplacement should include appropriate help for individual employees or groups of employees in finding a suitable new job or future direction. The help should be provided by professional counsellors who are authorised by the organisation. Most organisations delegate these activities to specialised bureaus, which means less risk of a conflict of interests than when support is provided internally, since in such a situation the organisation is both employer and counsellor. Employers may also have insufficient information about the job market and how to go about applying for job. Their information and contact networks may also be inadequate to the purpose.

Outplacement

International Human Resources Management

Many organisations operate internationally and consequently it is essential that they
have a global strategy for developing and managing their human resources
International HRM should start with developing a global understanding of the
global economy and its consequences for the organisation. This understanding
should not be limited to the local business sector but should also include global
and local competitors and customers.

In view of the fact that there is a shortage of talent (and as more baby boomers
retire, the problem will only become worse), global Human Resources leaders
should also develop a strategy to source, attract and retain talent globally.

Successful international HRM depends on:
· Top management realising that international HRM is of crucial importance. HRM
  should be deeply integrated into the core activities of the organisation.
· The enterprise's international strategy being linked to the goals of international
  HRM
· A good mix between on-the-job training and off the job courses. These courses are
  necessary to gain 'economies of skills'.

To be successful internationally, organisations need to realise that business largely
revolves around people.

8.3 Hierarchical levels and specific tasks

An organisation can be described as any form of human collaboration that shares a
common goal. An organisation's management has the task of achieving the organisation's goals. These goals will be achieved if the organisational processes are executed in an effective and efficient way. In most organisations, the work cannot be
done by a single person, which is why activities have to be delegated. This leads to a
division between management and operations as well as the creation of a hierarchy
within the organisation.

The larger the organisation, the greater the number of hierarchical layers. In concrete terms, these will be the various managerial and the operational levels. Each
level will have own specific role, a role which contributes towards the organisational goals. (Figure 8.22.)

Top management mainly deals with strategic decisions, while the more junior staff
are responsible for decisions relating to operational processes. Middle management
is located between these levels, so occupies a pivotal position. This management
level is mainly involved with organisational decisions. It translates strategic decisions into operational decisions. It fulfils more of an executing function compared
to top management, while it fulfils a directing function in relation to the first line
management.

The flattening of organisations and the introduction of business units and subsidiaries is changing the tasks of middle management. Since they have to determine
the strategy of the organisational unit, middle management that directs these business units (or subsidiaries) has to take on strategic tasks in addition to their organisational tasks. Sections 8.3.1, 8.3.2 and 8.3.3 address the main tasks of the various
management units within an organisation.

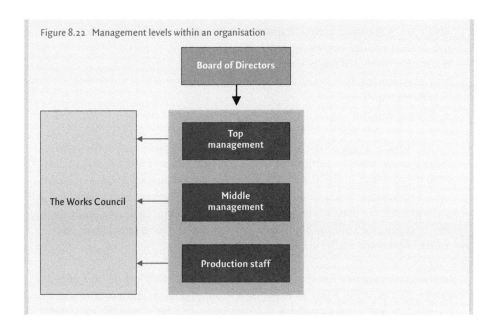
Figure 8.22 Management levels within an organisation

In Section 8.3.4, two important trends that many organisations are confronted with will be discussed. They are social entrepreneurship and corporate governance.

8.3.1 The Board of Directors

As well as paying attention to general developments within the organisation, an organisation's supervisory board also has to supervise the activities of top management. The Board should have the interests of the entire organisation at heart and not focus on the specific interests of one group of stakeholders within or outside the organisation, such as employees or shareholders, at the expense of others. The Board is not involved in the actual management of the company, as this is the task of top management. The Board needs an assortment of skills – financial, legal, marketing and so on – in order to carry out its tasks. This means that the board's composition is often quite diverse. Whether a supervisory board or simply a board of directors is necessary depends both on the size of the organisation and its location. There are many differences between the various countries and their legal requirements.

Supervise the activities of top management

In general terms, there are two models for supervisory boards. In the Anglo-Saxon model, also known as 'one-tier' system, there is no strict separation between management and supervision. British and American enterprises have a mixed top level, comprising of both executives and non-executives. This model assumes the dominant position of financiers.
In the Rhineland model, or two-tier system, there is a strict division between management and supervision. In this system, the supervisory board needs to consider all the different interests of the various stakeholders. According to this model, profit is not the only goal of the enterprise, as business also has a significant social role to play. This model is used in Germany and the Netherlands.

8.3.2 Top management

The main task of top management is the formulation of policy. (See Section 6.2.2 for further top management tasks.) Various forms of management can be identified

Formulation of policy

Forms of management

within an organisation, each differing from each other in terms of composition, task division and decision-making. The main forms are:
- Management vested in one person
- Joint management
  - Collegial structure
  - Alliance structure

Management vested in one person

With management vested in one person, that one person possesses all the decision-making power. Such a situation can arise either when there is just one manager, or when the chairman of the board of management has the final say in decision-making. The advantage of this form of management is that it generates fast decision-making. There are potential disadvantages in that important issues are only considered by one person, continuity could be at risk at times of long-term illness, and management could easily become overburdened.

Joint management

Joint management or a board of management is characterised by a division of tasks between, for example, a general manager, a financial director and a commercial director. The additional knowledge and experience available within this structure allows for any necessary corrections to be made by common consultation, thus safeguarding continuity and preventing overburdening. On the other hand, decision-making may be slow, and major differences of opinion can arise between the board members.

Collegial responsibility

Alliance structure

Decision-making may be collegial or alliance-based. With collegial responsibility decisions are made by consensus. All board members need to agree, so there is equal power of decision. The board members are collectively responsible for the success of the enterprise as a whole and not merely for a specific part. In an alliance structure, the directors have both individual and collective decision-making power. We see this structure mainly in large organisations where expertise is required in certain areas. In addition to their individual decision-making power in a specific area, the directors share collective decision-making power in more general matters. (See Figure 8.23.)

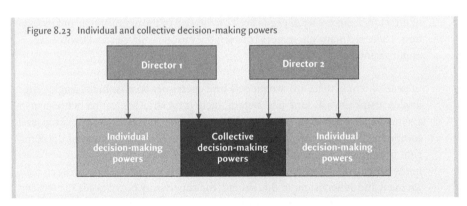

Figure 8.23   Individual and collective decision-making powers

Below is an example of the alliance structure within a legal organisation.
Individual decision-making power:
- Director 1: International law
- Director 2: Corporate law
- Director 3: Criminal law

Collective decision-making powers apply in respect of:
- Financial affairs
- Promotional activities
- Investments

8.3.3 Middle management

The task of middle management is to implement out the general policy as laid down by top management. Middle managers also direct a number of operational staff. Using the policies issued by top management, middle managers generate policy guidelines for their own departments. They then translate these guidelines into fixed plans, supervise the completion of the tasks and evaluate the results, and report back to top management with these results. Middle managers also perform their own individual tasks. What these tasks actually consist of is currently in a state of flux. The real added value of a middle manager is likely to come to lie in their entrepreneurial flair. For further details about middle management, see Section 6.2.3.

Middle management

Supervise

Individual tasks

8.3.4 Operational staff

Operational staff are responsible for the actual transformation process. Input (labour, natural resources, capital and information) undergoes a transformational process and becomes output (products or services). This level is the level of primary processes that contribute directly to the creation of a product or service. Secondary processes support the efficient and effective running of the primary processes. Managing processes direct the primary and secondary processes. Operational staff are mainly concerned with operational tasks. The main managerial activities relate to operational decision-making and include supervising and adjusting activities.

Operational tasks

8.3.5 Corporate social responsibility (CSR) and corporate governance

In recent years we have seen a world-wide trend towards socially responsible enterprises. What role should business play in our society and how much responsibility should it bear? Society is increasingly expecting companies to be open about their business activities and for the consequences to be transparent, not only in terms of financial information but also in terms of the environmental consequences and the social issues involved. The purpose of an enterprise is increasingly seen as not merely profit-making or profit maximisation. Businesses derive their right to exist not merely from the amount of profit they make but from how they function within a network of economic, ecological and social factors.

Socially responsible enterprises

Transparency in business is becoming both an internal matter (how responsibly the business treats its employees) as well an external matter (how responsibly the business treats its shareholders, banks and insurance companies, suppliers, authorities and people living in the neighbourhood). From this viewpoint an enterprise can be considered to be a collection of stakeholders.

Some specific areas of corporate behaviour are regulated by law, including employee participation in works councils (see Section 7.5.2) and financial reporting via external annual accounts.

Corporations support Kids Foundation to promote free learning around the world

A number of organisations, including IBM, Deloitte, Gallup, General Motors, Harvard Business School Publishing, Saba, Skillsoft, and Save The Children, support the e-Learning For Kids Foundation (www.e-learningforkids.org) as part of their Corporate Social Responsibility.

E-Learning For Kids provides free course material via the Internet for children aged 5–12. The subject areas include language skills, maths, science, keyboard navigation, and health and life skills.

Source: e-learningforkids.org, 2006

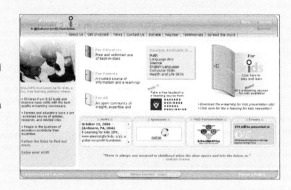

Corporate governance in the Netherlands

Corporate governance

Corporate governance is defined as a system for the directing and managing of enterprises in which transparency and justification are considered to be the main characteristics of good reporting. Corporate governance is decent entrepreneurial management that makes justified choices based on political, social, economical and ethical considerations.

Decent entrepreneurial management

Peters Committee

In 1997, the so-called Peters Committee formulated forty recommendations for proper direction, effective management and accountability. The reasons for these recommendations were:

· Diminished trust caused by a number of accounting scandals
· Some bad stock market developments revealing ill-planned or overly aggressive takeover policies and financial management
· An increase in the number of shareholders and people with investment pensions demanding an increase in transparency and reporting

Tabaksblat Committee

However, at the global level, ideas were changing, and many companies chose to ignore the recommendations made by the Peters Committee. The Dutch government then decided to commission the Tabaksblat Committee, named after Morris Tabaksblat, a former chairman of the Board of Directors of Unilever.

Code for Dutch Corporate Governance

On 1 July 2003 the Tabaksblat Committee published a code for Dutch Corporate Governance. Various experts from the worlds of business, science, accountancy, institutional investors, private shareholders and the stock market have served on this committee. The code came into operation on 1 January 2004. It calls for enterprises themselves to take the initiative, and if unsuccessful, for the government to regulate special issues by law. The code is intended for enterprises that are quoted on the stock exchange and it is based on the 'comply or explain' principle. Enterprises which do not follow the code either fully or in part are required to explain why.

Comply or explain

Some of the recommendations of the Tabaksblat Committee include the following:

· Shareholders should exert more influence on executive salary levels.
· Share options possessed by executives may only be cashed when certain performance levels have been reached. Shares obtained as a performance bonus must be retained until the end of the employment contract.
· The severance pay for executives should not exceed twice their annual salary.
· The maximum number of directorships is five per person. A business manager may serve as a director on a maximum of two other boards.

PEOPLE-PROFIT-PLANET

Championing sustainable development through corporate social responsibility

Companies today must accept and discharge the growing responsibility they have towards the various stakeholders. This responsibility should cover several domains, including governance, ethical behaviour, sustainable development, environmental impact, trading and employment practices, workplace management, and community involvement. Sustainable business practices are essential to maintaining competitive advantage in the long term. Although governments, businesses and organisations define sustainability and corporate social responsibility (CSR) in different ways, we find the figure below useful in that it encompasses the broad range of issues involved. Today, sustainability covers all activities from charitable and community involvement to legally-obliged compliance with environmental or social norms – with a growing range of voluntary business practices in between.

Source: Deloitte Magazine, July 2006

- Directors must be able to understand and evaluate the enterprise's key policies in broad terms.
- Shareholders should be able to dismiss poorly performing managers or directors more easily or reject nominations.
- Decisions about important acquisitions or buy-outs should be approved by the shareholders.
- Shareholders should have the right to question accountants about the accuracy of the annual accounts.
- Enterprises quoted on the stock exchange must draw up regulations for investments by managers and directors. Share transactions entered into by Dutch enterprises quoted on the stock exchange must be reported to the compliance officer.
- Former managers of an enterprise cannot take up a position as chairman in the Board of that enterprise.

Corporate governance in other countries
It is not only the Netherlands that has drawn up codes for corporate governance. The United States, Great Britain and Germany have also developed rules of conduct for enterprises in their own jurisdictions.

United States
In the United States, the code is known as the Sarbanes-Oxley Act. In contrast with the Netherlands, this code is a law. An important part of this law is the obligation for the chair and the financial members of the board to declare in writing that their accounts are correct. If at a later stage this turns out to be incorrect, they can be prosecuted, with long custodial sentences as possible punishments. They might also face disqualification: a ban on taking up a similar job for a number of years. In the Netherlands, the department of trade can use the 'mismanagement' label to brand the manager or director. Formally, a similar punishment is possible, but as yet, no prison sentences have been handed out.

Sarbanes-Oxley Act
Law

Disqualification

Great Britain

Combined Code

In Great Britain, the code is known as the Combined Code. It is one of the London stock exchange's requirements. Just as in the Dutch code, the principle of 'comply or explain' is applied.

Germany

Corporate Governance Kodex

The German Corporate Governance Kodex is mainly aimed at the relationship between a company's management and the Supervisory Board, half of which is appointed in line with the recommendations made by the employees of the enterprise. Compared to the codes in the Netherlands, the United States and Britain, the German code is considered somewhat restricted.

Since many enterprises operate internationally, they often have to meet the requirements of different corporate governance codes. For example, Dutch enterprises listed on the American stock exchange need to comply with the Dutch as well the American corporate governance codes.

In the past, attempts have been made to establish a single international code. In 1999, the Organisation for Economic Cooperation and Development (OECD) drafted their 'Principles of Corporate Governance' and the European Commission is also preparing an international code. This faces many obstacles, however, since commercial laws in the member countries differ from one another. Cultural and political differences also play a role.

Principles of Corporate Governance

8.3.6   The works council

The works council does not actually form part of the organisation's usual management levels. Its members are elected directly by the employees of the organisation. The works council influences decision-making within the organisation (see Section 7.5.2).

PEOPLE-PROFIT-PLANET

Governance: good company, best practice

In his book Keeping Better Company, Jonathan Charkman sets out to compare and assess corporate governance systems in the US, Japan, Germany, France and the UK. Since Enron, the US corporate sector has had to wrestle with the Sarbanes-Oxley Act. In Japan, the crucial governance role played by the banks is unravelling, as are the cross-shareholdings that cemented the business and governance arrangements. In Europe, there has been new legislation at both the European Union and the national levels, while new governance codes have proliferated.

The picture that emerges across the five countries is one of slow progress towards convergence on something that approximates the Anglo-American model. In the US, accountancy, audit and federal laws and regulations are directed primarily at making securities markets work more efficiently, whereas the UK model puts more emphasis on the stewardship role

of shareholders while denying chief executives the imperial status enjoyed by so many of their US counterparts. Japan now has smaller boards, a growing component of independent directors and a law that permits board committees instead of the peculiarly Japanese corporate auditors known as kansayaku. In Germany, there are doubts whether governance reforms have worked.

In all the countries, definitions of independence in relation to directors remain problematic. The verdict is that the country's entrepreneurial spirit remains intact. But a system that places so much emphasis on immediate values and where stock options and other equity rewards encourage many chief executives to take a pathological interest in the share price may be at a competitive disadvantage to others with a long-term focus.

Source: The Financial Times, January 2006

8.4   Types of organisational management[16]

No two organisations are managed in the same way. A small organisation is managed differently from a large one. There are also demonstrable differences between the management of a manufacturing company, a service provider and a governmental institution.

The way an organisation is managed depends to a large extent on its environment and its employees. These two factors help us to identify the following patterns of organisational management:

- *Bureaucracy.*   In bureaucratic organisations, power is mainly concentrated at the top of the organisation. At lower levels there is little latitude, and few opportunities for taking the initiative. Procedures and orders are important. A bureaucratic management form is appropriate in a stable environment with compliant employees. *Bureaucracy*

- *Entrepreneur.*   When organisations are in a pioneering phase the entrepreneurs and their personalities play an important role. They are the central figures in an organisation that does not yet have much structure and is informal in character. This form is ideal in a simple but dynamic environment, with compliant employees able to cope with chaotic situations. *Entrepreneur*

- *Coalition.*   In this kind of organisation, as much allowance as possible is made for the requirements of both the internal and the external parties. Such an organisation will have many different types of consultative bodies, and they will be interconnected. This form works well in turbulent environments with socially skilled staff. *Coalition*

- *Atomic.*   Atomic organisations are formed from basically unrelated parts such as divisions or business units. The absence of rigid management and consultation is characteristic of these organisations. Each unit has a high degree of independence. This type of organisation is suitable for professional employees in a reasonably protected environment. *Atomic*

The four organisational types (Figure 8.24) demonstrate global divisions which are useful for the purposes of comparison.

Figure 8.24   Patterns of organisational management in relation to environment and employees

	Bureaucracy	Entrepreneur	Coalition	Atomic unit
Environment	• calm • stable • market growth	• Dynamic • simple	• 'pushy' participants • many goals	• sufficient means • honour and professional integrity
Management	• hierarchical • top-down • controlling	• young • informal	• forming of coalitions • consultation	• empowering management • laissez-faire • 'cores'
Employees	• obedient • dependent • fear	• obedient • can cope with chaos	• social skills • knowledge of power / interests	• independent • professional
Traditional examples	• the Church • business • the Army	• advertising sector • Yorin	• political parties • welfare sector	• university • research department

In practice, however, the matter is more complicated as various patterns will be represented within a single organisation. These different patterns are caused partly by developments such as greater democracy and can have the effect of some elements being incorporated into all four types, resulting in smaller differences between them. The fact that the environment is not the same for all parts of the organisation also contributes to different patterns. The environment of a production department can be seen as different to that of a research department in terms of factors such as the degree of uncertainty, the dynamics and the degree of complexity. It follows that the management of the various organisational parts should be geared to the environment of that part. The effect will be different types of management in use within a single organisation, and consequently a lack of control in policy formulation, planning and operation.

8.5 Methods used to run organisations

Method

The management of organisations sometimes involves the use of methods for clarifying and understanding the processes, thus enabling the coordination, supervision and directing of processes within the organisation to be carried out in a more efficient and effective way. A method can be defined as a well thought-out plan to accomplish a desired goal.

This section will deal with the various methods under the following headings:
1 Techniques directed towards individual employees
   – management by objective
   – management by exception
   – time management
2 Techniques directed towards the organisation as a whole
   – risk management
   – unit management
3 Techniques directed towards processes
   – project planning
   – network planning

However, these divisions are only of limited value, as the various methods cannot be viewed in complete isolation from each other.

8.5.1 Techniques directed towards individual employees

Individual's performance

A common feature of the three methods directed towards the individual is the optimisation of the individual's performance within a specific area of the organisation.

Management by objectives

Management by objectives

Management by objectives (MBO) is a method in which the manager and his / her subordinates determine the objectives for the coming period by mutual agreement as well as the results that are required at the end of that period. MBO is based on the assumption that people perform better and more happily if they:
· Know what is expected of them
· Are involved in setting these expectations and accept them as being realistic
· Have the opportunity to determine how they can fulfil these expectations in the sense that they can plan their activities themselves
· Are kept well informed about their performance, and are therefore able to learn from their own experiences

Deciding on the objectives jointly is more profitable that merely giving orders. The objectives of the organisation and the objectives of the employees need to be geared towards each another more. Doing so will increase motivation and the employees will execute their tasks in a more purposeful way. Since objectives and results are determined at every level of the organisation, the result will be better coordination between these hierarchical levels. This is why MBO sees an organisation as a hierarchy of objectives, with the lower-order objectives directed towards the next objective in the chain.

hierarchy of objectives

Practical objectives should conform to the following criteria[17]:

Practical objectives

· They should be quantitatively measurable.
· They should be specific.
· They should be results-orientated.
· They should be realistic and attainable.
· They should be have a clear and limited time frame.

MBO is essentially the determination of objectives along with the necessary competencies and responsibilities to be able to reach those objectives. The process can be broken down into eight steps (Figure 8.25):

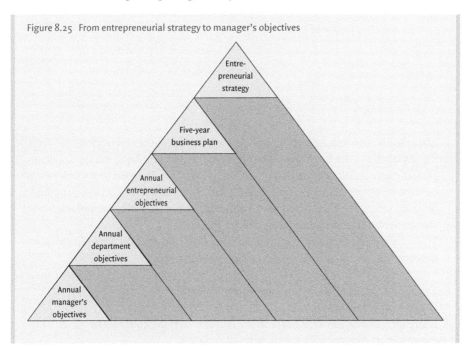

Figure 8.25 From entrepreneurial strategy to manager's objectives

Step 1 Defining responsibilities and competencies
Step 2 Determining priorities
Step 3 Selecting scales of measurement
Step 4 Determination of objectives
Step 5 Planning of actions
Step 6 A definitive arrangement
Step 7 Progress control
Step 8 Discussion of the results

In determining the objectives, two important matters should be taken account of. Only those areas that the subordinate can influence and that contribute towards effectiveness in terms of doing the task should be chosen. The objectives should also be as measurable as possible so that at the end of the period, the performance of the employee can be appraised.

CHAPTER 8 | *Managing organisational processes* | **353**

In order to appraise someone's performance, a norm is required. Formulating the objectives and norms in a quantitative way allows the measurement and the appraisal to be be more objective. After the appraisal, the process of setting objectives and results will recommence. (See Figure 8.26.)

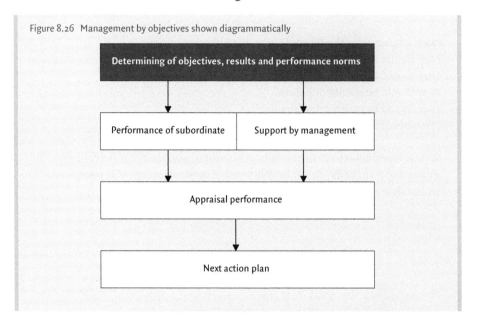

Figure 8.26 Management by objectives shown diagrammatically

After the objectives and the result have been determined, the real work starts. Both the manager and the employee have specific tasks. The employee will try to accomplish the set objectives by executing specific actions. It is the manager's task to support the employee during this process. Obstacles that block the employee should be removed where possible. Wherever possible, factors outside his / her influence should not be permitted to interrupt the employee.

MBO is a method used in many organisations. The manager, the subordinate and the organisation are all able to gain advantages from MBO.[18]

The advantages of MBO for managers are as follows:
· It motivates subordinates
· It strengthens relationships between the manager and the subordinate
· It provides a framework for coaching and support
· It forms a basis for the appraisal of employees

The advantages of MBO for subordinates are:
· The subordinate knows what is expected of him / her
· The subordinate can measure his / her own performance
· Authority and responsibilities are clearly described and defined

The advantages of MBO for the organisation are:
· The method gauges the effectiveness of managers
· It focusses the activities of a manager on what he / she should accomplish
· It simplifies the coordination of activities
· It offers objective criteria for reward
· It keeps track of the need for management development, thus providing opportunities for well-directed training and education

However, MBO has also a number of drawbacks. These impede the achievement of positive results:

- *The 'paper tiger'.* Too many changes and additions may result in a mass of paperwork, hampering real work.
- *The 'activity trap'.* Everybody starts by enthusiastically formulating the most desirable objectives they can think of. The eventual result is overburdening and the risk that even the smallest result might not be obtained.
- *The order mistake.* If too much energy is put into conforming to the objectives, proper coordination may be neglected, with adverse consequences.
- *Mutual harmony.* In this situation, employees fail to bring errors to each other's attention. It is important to maintain a critical attitude in relation to each other.
- *Timing problems.* There is a danger of results being expected in too short a time span. Essential changes can only be produced gradually.
- *Leadership problems.* MBO and the leadership style may be incompatible. MBO requires a working style with an emphasis on task performance and cooperation.[19]

Management by exception

As we have seen above (management by objectives), task division (a feature of every organisation) involves the definition of objectives to be carried out by each unit, division or person. Checks should be carried out at regular times to assess the results, and if any deviation from the agreed tasks is detected, this should be corrected. Practice has shown that this is often necessary. If doing this were solely a managerial responsibility, there would be a risk of overburdening. To avoid such a situation, a method known as 'management by exception' is frequently used.

Deviation

Management by exception

To secure good results, those responsible for the delegation of tasks (including inherent responsibilities and authority) should retain control (see Section 9.2.3). But delegation as such means that the delegator is freed from routine tasks and has time to concentrate on other task more appropriate to management. A middle manager may then take over tasks from his / her superior. Within certain limits, the middle manager is entitled to define and use specific means needed to make corrections. If these limits are exceeded, this will be seen as exceeding the limits of his / her authority. His / her superior will be informed, and the necessary action taken. But such appeals to the top manager should be avoided where possible.

Limits

Coming to grips with the time management myth

Do you feel the need to be more organised and / or more productive? Do you spend your day in a frenzy of activity and then wonder why you haven't accomplished much?

Time management skills are especially important for small business people, who often find themselves performing many different jobs during the course of a single day. The following time management tips will help you increase your productivity and stay cool and collected.

1 Realise that time management is a myth.
2 Find out where you're wasting time.
3 Create time management goals.
4 Implement a time management plan.
5 Put the time management tools to use.
6 Prioritise ruthlessly.
7 Learn to delegate and / or outsource.
8 Establish routines and stick to them as much as possible.
9 Get in the habit of setting time limits for tasks.
10 Be sure your systems are organised.
11 Don't waste time waiting.

You *can* be in control and accomplish what you want to accomplish – once you've come to grips with the time management myth and taken control of your time.

Source: www.about.com, 2006

ADVICE

Time management

The task of an organisation's managing Board is to direct its operations. Among these are time-consuming operational and ad hoc activities. But while managers complain that not enough time is left for dealing with more important problems, they are usually responsible for the problem themselves. They have failed to deal efficiently with the time available.

Pareto principle

According to the Pareto principle, 20% of the time spent gives 80% of the result. It is therefore important to be aware of what the main tasks within each job are. Neglect of these tasks may have serious consequences for the performance of the employee and the organisation.

Time priorities must be set. Activities with a high priority demand an atmosphere where concentration on the task without any disturbance is possible (Figure 8.27).

Figure 8.27 How to set priorities in time management

	Activities are:	
	Important	Not important
Urgent	• work on undisturbed • put on action list	• delegate • not spend too much time on it
Not urgent	• remove from action list • reserve time	• delegate • do between times

Priority

The degree of priority an activity is given should depend on two criteria[20]:

1 How important are the activities?
2 How urgent are the activities?

Weighing up these factors against each other will give a global impression of how best to spend one's time.

Time planning

Good time planning of activities is essential. Time planning is a way of achieving a better balance between the tasks that have to be performed and the time frames within which to perform them. The crucial thing is gaining control over one's own work processes. Keeping a record of the time spent on various activities is a useful way of getting an insight into one's own successes and simplifying priority assessment in the future.

Time wasting

To improve time planning, both the factors that lead to time wasting as well as those that promote good results should be scrutinised. Time wasting is especially prevalent if[21]:

- There are many disturbances and interruptions.
- The activities are not fully completed.
- Activities are postponed.
- Two or more activities are performed simultaneously.
- Energy is not used economically.
- The activities are poorly organised.

Improve results

To improve results it is advisable to[22]:

1 Create an inventory of the activities that make up a particular task and distribute this inventory among the members of the unit in question.

Structure and organisation

2 Formulate concrete targets and deadlines.
3 Set up long-term plans.
4 Translate these long-term plans into monthly, weekly and daily plans.
5 Decide which activities can be delegated.
6 Take a step back from your daily activities and consider the needs of future targets.

It is important to balance daily activities between the time available for your own job (controllable time) and the time set by others (dependent time). (See Figure 8.28.)

Controllable time
Dependent time

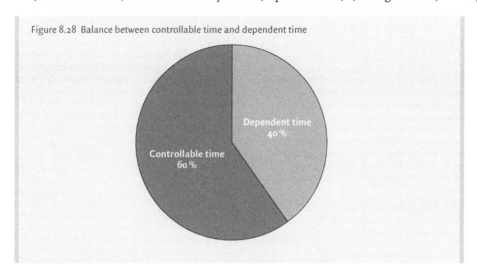

Figure 8.28 Balance between controllable time and dependent time

Many managers claim that they are 'governed by their agenda', and not enough time is left for their own activities. Such situations will eventually create problems, and a critical look at time management will become necessary.
The daily distribution of activities also needs attention. The amount of personal energy available is limited and changes during the course of the day. It is important to schedule daily tasks in a way that agrees with the specific demands of the person in question (see Figure 8.29).

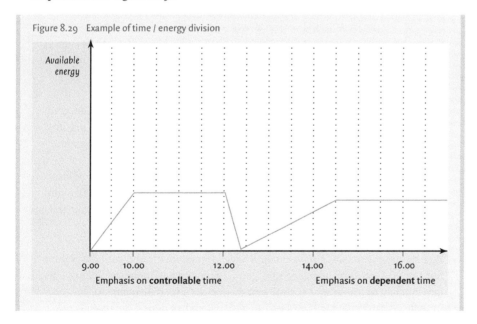

Figure 8.29 Example of time / energy division

Hierarchy of tasks

If you have many tasks to do, it is advisable to prioritise them, creating a task 'hierarchy'.
- A tasks. These tasks are both important and urgent and they need immediate execution. You cannot leave them waiting and you should attend to at least some of them every day.
- B tasks. These tasks are either important but not urgent, or they need to be done urgently although it would not be a disaster if they were not since they are not particularly important. In general, one's daily time is mainly taken up by B tasks.
- C tasks. As the lowest tasks in the hierarchy, these are the routine tasks that demand a minimum of concentration and are neither urgent nor important. These tasks can wait and if there is no time to do them, let them be.

It is important to spread the various tasks over the day. This is more effective than trying to finish a certain type of task. It allows moments of heavy concentration (A and B) to be alternated with moments of less effort (C).
The task hierarchy is not a rigid structure: tasks may change in importance because of extra information coming in or unexpected events occurring. To take an example: you need to hand in a report to your director the day after tomorrow. If she is brought down with the flu, your report will suddenly become less urgent.
Another point is that dividing tasks up will not diminish their priority. You might sometimes be overwhelmed by the amount of work that confronts you. At such a moment it is convenient to make an overview of the various deadlines. Just doing this will already have a therapeutic effect, and it will also give you a broad overview that automatically generates solutions. If such an overview doesn't give any solace, you will need to drop some of your C and B tasks. This method is especially important for people who are always fully occupied. Taking a moment to check your activities and to plan your tasks has a psychological effect: it makes you feel as if everything is under control.

Source: www.vacature.com

It has also been found that with a full attention span, an individual can deal simultaneously with up to six different tasks. Such concentration on the job should not be diminished by brooding over other unfinished activities.
The 'Personal Efficiency Program' (developed by the Institute for Business Technology) formulated the crux of the matter in just three words: 'Do it now!' By doing things now, a work habit is developed which gives more time to think about the main problems.

8.5.2 Techniques directed towards the organisation as a whole

Organisation-directed methods

For improved organisational functioning, organisation-directed methods such as risk and unit management can be used.

Risk management

Entrepreneurship is not free from risk. Commercial premises could be damaged heavily by fire, the computer system could fail, and the sales of a certain product might be very disappointing. Risks can be divided into two categories: dynamic risks and static risks.

Dynamic risk

Dynamic (speculative or entrepreneurial) risks can result in either profit or loss (e.g. the introduction of a new product or investment in a new enterprise). Static risks (pure risks) have only negative consequences (e.g. fire, flood or criminal damage). We will deal solely with static risks at this point.

Static risks

To a certain extent, static risks can be avoided by systematic and periodic evaluations of the risks threatening people, goods, activities and interests, followed by the development of procedures to deal with these risks (risk management).[23]

Risk management

Initially, risk management involves categorising and analysing the risks. A risk management plan is then set up for the biggest risks. Risk management is a common activity in most organisations. It puts a demand on all members to adopt an attitude of responsibility towards minimising risks. The activities that form part of risk minimisation must, of course, be managed and the necessary expertise should be delegated to specialists or an equipped department. To that extent, risk management resembles the marketing activities that an organisation undertakes. The goal of risk management is to avoid disturbances from identifiable risks and to ensure that the objectives of the enterprise remain attainable. We have seen that primary processes contribute to reaching the goal. Managing these processes includes the management of inherent risks. Risk management is shown diagrammatically in Figure 8.30. As a general rule, by managing risk, continuity is guaranteed.

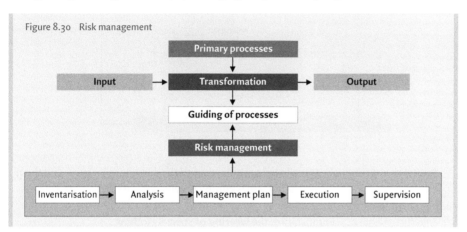

Figure 8.30   Risk management

Figure 8.31 surveys the various kinds of risks.

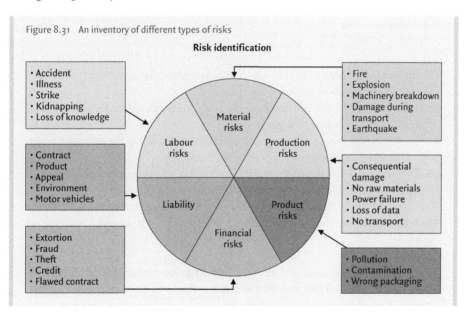

Figure 8.31   An inventory of different types of risks

Risk management has to be planned and Figure 8.32 shows that it is important for the organisation to know what kind of risks there are and what methods are available for dealing with them.

Risks that are a characteristic of the type of organisation will remain. To deal with these, options for special financing or services should be considered.

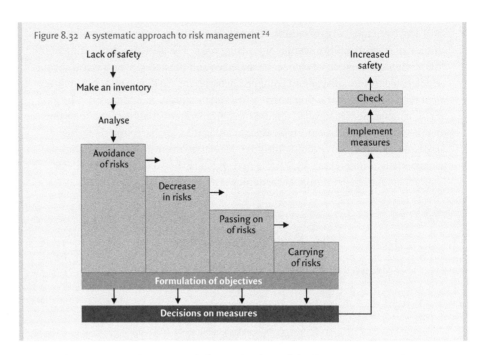

Figure 8.32 A systematic approach to risk management [24]

Several measures can be taken to help avoid risks and the damage associated with them:
- *Preventive measures.* The purpose here is complete avoidance of risk (e.g. safeguarding of equipment).
- *Protective measures.* For instance, the wearing of special clothing.
- *Reduction measures.* The purpose here is to diminish the damage (e.g. by setting up a first aid centre).
- *Repair measures.* The purpose here is to limit the repercussions of the damage.
- *Training and instruction of staff.*
- *Planning of maintenance activities.*

The measures that need to be taken each require a particular investment, and this can vary according to the degree of complexity.

Risks may vary in the damage they have the potential to cause. The following defines damage according to degree:

1 *Trivial damage.* Very minor damage that can be repaired within the existing budget.
2 *Small damage.* Damage that occurs relatively frequently.
3 *Medium-sized damage.* Damage low in frequency but whose impact is relatively great though not posing a threat to the survival of the organisation.
4 *Large-scale damage.* Damage that occurs rarely, but whose consequences are severe. The continuity of the enterprise is seriously threatened and it may even be forced to close down.

Knowledge of the frequency and amount of damage is necessary for deciding what risk should be handled first and what measures should be taken to avoid or reduce its effect. Only then will it be possible to set up a management plan, and rank the risks according to their importance.

Frequency and the extent of the damage

The relationship between the frequency and the extent of the damage is illustrated in Figure 8.33.

Some examples are:
- *Category 1:* broken windows
- *Category 2:* storm damage

Figure 8.33 Relationship between frequency and extent of damage

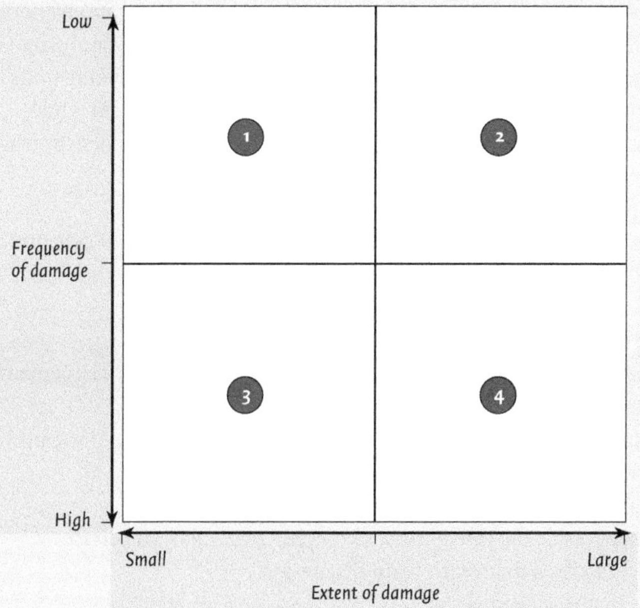

- *Category 3:* theft from stores
- *Category 4:* fire

Category 1 damage can generally be dealt with by the organisation itself. Damage that falls under categories 2 and 4 is usually covered by insurance, and therefore not paid for by the organisation. The amount of insurance cover bought is a question of weighing up profits against expenses. The uninsured risk left is then born by the organisation. Damage that falls under category 3 attracts a lot of attention and is dealt with using special measures. This sort of damage has to be dealt with by the enterprise itself.

IN THE PRESS

Managing risk today is not what it used to be

Technological innovation, globalisation, complex regulation and increased accountability at the top management and board levels have all combined to significantly change the landscape of risk management today. Managing risk has become increasingly complex due to the new 'Network Economy' and the emerging risks of e-business from online security to customer privacy. The complexity also comes from the:

- Increasing need for knowledge of local laws and customs
- Evolution of trading markets
- Pervasive nature of information technologies
- Higher accountability standards for boards of directors and top executives
- Unprecedented complexity of the regulatory environment, pressing firms for better risk reporting and more integrated and comprehensive risk management
- Shortage of skilled personnel

To help the market cope, new positions, tools, rules and even language have been created. New executive positions such as chief risk officer, chief security officer and chief privacy officer have been created. There also has been a proliferation of risk management software and other technology solutions as well as new regulations making certain risk management practices relating to security, privacy, operations, compliance and economic exposures mandatory. Indeed, the term 'enterprise risk management' (ERM) has become part of the general business vocabulary.

Source: www.deloitte.com , 2006

Unit management

Markets are rarely static, especially in the areas of consumer behaviour and technology. As a consequence, organisations may need to change their strategy and structure often. Structural changes may include increasing the autonomy of some units to some extent, thus enabling them to adapt to the changing environment while still benefiting from the facilities of the organisation as a whole. The goal here is to improve the competitive position by reacting quickly.

Adapt to the changing environment

Unit management

An organisational form that is currently enjoying some interest is unit management. This is a management method directed towards a policy of decentralisation within the organisation.[25]

The conditions for successful unit management are[26]:
- Short reporting lines (fewer levels between top management and unit management)
- Each unit having its own goals to fulfil
- Units having a high degree of autonomy in respect of the primary functions (purchasing, sales, production, etc.)
- A well-set-up management data system
- Exclusive support services or the freedom to use certain external staff services
- Personal definitions of jobs a matter for team discussion
- The power to make major decisions
- A common code of behaviour (or culture) for the entire organisation

Semi-independent units

Units can be described as semi-independent when they behave in similar ways to independent enterprises. They have been dealt with already in the section on the portfolio model of the Boston Consulting Group (3.3.2), where these units were referred to as business units or product-market combinations.

Since the unit remains part of the organisation, it shares the advantages of the larger organisation. Such advantages may include shared sales teams, use of common grounds and buildings, exchange of experience, and so on.

Unit management thus combines the advantages of small-unit autonomy and the advantages of a larger organisation. (See Figure 8.34.)

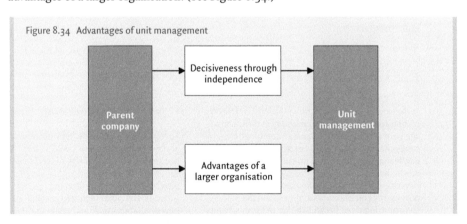

Figure 8.34 Advantages of unit management

Autonomy / mutual dependence

Unit management is characterised by both a large degree of autonomy and by mutual dependence. As these units have been established to have more autonomy, they could conceivably compete with each other to a certain extent. To avoid this demands a strong corporate culture with the organisation as a whole. There will also be situations where the units need to cooperate with each other. The culture of the units should consequently be in line with the culture of the organisation. The organisation as a whole must remain governable. To do so makes special demands on both the unit's management and on top management. The unit manager should have general skills rather than specialist ones. He / she is responsible for the unit as a whole. Just like any other head of a commercial concern, he / she has to make decisions and must be able motivate his team to ensure good performance.

The top management level must be completely willing to grant autonomy. The advantages of unit management can only be fully enjoyed when responsibilities and authorities are truly delegated. If this is only partially done, ambiguity will occur, causing conflict and discouragement. Decentralising carries the advantage to top management of allowing it concentrate on responsibilities of a more general and strategic nature.

The disadvantages of unit management are as follows[27]:
- There may be diminished efficiency as the tasks are duplicated in every unit.
- Coherence between the units may lessen as each unit may consider itself to be an independent enterprise.
- Short-term interests may prevail over the long-term view.
- The image of a single coherent organisation may become blurred

8.5.3 Process-oriented methods

Process-oriented methods focus on the control of specific organisational processes and projects. Firstly, we will look at project planning. This method is used for processes whereby employees from various departments work together on a temporary basis in order to find solutions for particular problems. Network planning is a technique that can be used within project planning. It shows the relationships between the various project activities.

Project planning

When an organisation wants to develop new activities such as the development of a new IT system or a new product, a project-oriented approach is, in general, preferable. The distinguishing feature of such activities is that the solutions cannot come from a single department or specialist. The problem needs to be addressed from various angles.

For coordination's sake, a specific project group that is responsible for a particular problem is set up within the existing organisational structure. The members of this group represent all departments and / or areas of expertise needed for the project, and could be recruited from various levels of the organisation. The cultural differences between these levels could lead to problems within the group: the members may speak a different language, so to speak, or be unfamiliar with the approaches used. In the context of the project they will be required to work together as equals while in other situations they might encounter each other on a different footing. Group members must be able to accept this inconsistency.

A project-oriented approach is often used in situations where:
- Involvement of various functional areas is required
- A one-off goal needs to be accomplished

A project has a temporary character. Upon completion, the project's findings must be incorporated into the main organisation. A project is characterised by various phases (see Figure 8.35)[28]:

Process-oriented methods

Project planning

Network planning

CHAPTER 8 | *Managing organisational processes* | **363**

- *Phase 1*. During this phase, the project is set up and the necessary conditions and authorities are drawn up. Decisions are also made about the employees that need to participate in the project.
- *Phase 2*. The project and its members are introduced to the organisation. This phase should not be underestimated. Underlining the importance of the project and the creation of broad support are important conditions for reaching a good final result. This is why management should support and encourage all aspects of the project.
- *Phase 3*. The group works towards achieving the project's goals during this phase.
- *Phase 4*. The project results are incorporated into the organisation and become a permanent feature of that organisation. Former project members might be made responsible for this process.

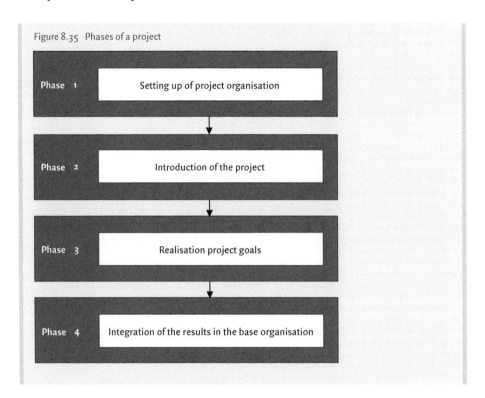

Figure 8.35 Phases of a project

Phase 1 — Setting up of project organisation

Phase 2 — Introduction of the project

Phase 3 — Realisation project goals

Phase 4 — Integration of the results in the base organisation

Chapter 9 will discuss the organisational aspects of project planning further.

Network planning

Network planning

Network planning is used to control large, one-off activities such as assembling an aeroplane, building a house, or developing a new payment system. During the course of time, various techniques for network planning have been developed, each with their own characteristics. In general, each technique operates from the same basis. We will focus here on the Critical Path Method (CPM).

Critical Path Method

Network planning can be used for any project of a temporary nature and combines a number of tasks. It provides an overview of the project as a whole and details the sometimes complex relationships between the various activities that constitute the project. Network planning aims to obtain an understanding of the project's running time. This will lead to better control of the project (see Figures 8.36 and 8.37).

Aim of network planning

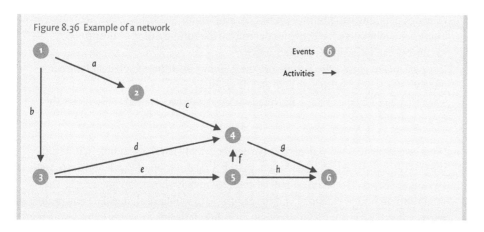

Figure 8.36 Example of a network

Events ⑥

Activities →

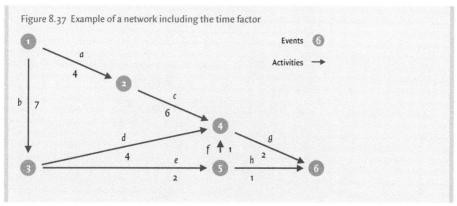

Figure 8.37 Example of a network including the time factor

Events ⑥

Activities →

In order to set up a network plan, several steps need to be taken[29]:
- Step 1: *structural analysis.* What tasks or activities need to be carried out? What relationships between tasks need to be determined? The logical sequence of the project stages then needs to be determined.
- Step 2: *chronological analysis.* The duration of the various elements needs to be estimated.

As soon as the structural and chronological aspects of the project have been determined, the times needed for each individual element are added up and the project's running time estimated. Figure 8.38 shows the longest possible running time.

Running time

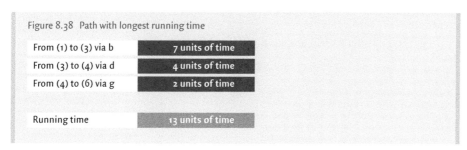

Figure 8.38 Path with longest running time

From (1) to (3) via b	7 units of time
From (3) to (4) via d	4 units of time
From (4) to (6) via g	2 units of time
Running time	13 units of time

The other running times will be shorter, as the calculations demonstrate. The running time that gives the earliest possible moment for the project to be finished is known as the critical path. This path shows the minimum time needed to complete the project. Any delay to the activities on this path will delay the project as a whole.

Critical path

Network planning can improve project control when:
- There is insight into what activities determine the running time of the project.
- Resources can be assigned to each activity.
- It is possible to check whether the project is going according to plan and the consequences of delay occurring are also clearly visible.
- The role played by the various activities within the project is clear. This allows for better coordination.

What consequences will a delay to a particular activity have? Assuming that during the project, activity E is delayed by 4 days, the total duration of E will now be 6 days (see Figure 8.39). The changed critical running time is shown in Figure 8.40. The total running time is extended and the critical path will have changed. If this problem is spotted early on, the project managers might decide to assign extra resources to activity E so that the original running time can still be maintained. The costs and benefits of assigning extra resources need to be carefully considered.

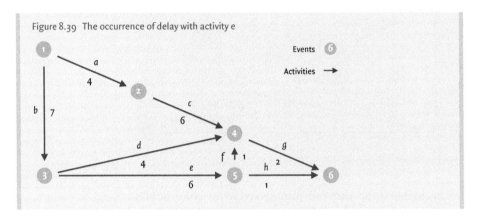

Figure 8.39 The occurrence of delay with activity e

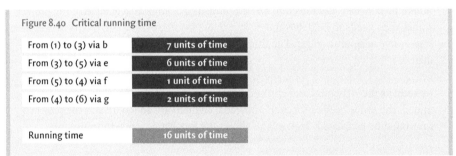

Figure 8.40 Critical running time

From (1) to (3) via b	7 units of time
From (3) to (5) via e	6 units of time
From (5) to (4) via f	1 unit of time
From (4) to (6) via g	2 units of time
Running time	16 units of time

In the next chapter we will discuss the design of organisations.

Doing business in Denmark

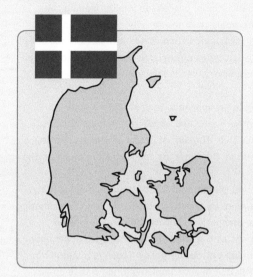

Sources of anxiety reduction

Life's uncertainties are accepted, and anxiety is reduced by a strong social welfare system – the government is there to serve the people. Though individualistic, most Danes are resigned to a high-tax social welfare state in which there is little distinction available through individual accomplishments. Young people are encouraged to mature early and to develop a strong self-image by taking risks.

Issues of equality / inequality

Denmark is basically a middle-class society, with family needs as the central issue of social policy and governmental intervention. Danes strive to minimise social differences, so there is very little evidence of poverty or wealth, although they do exist. Nationalism transcends social differences, and in a largely homogeneous population, ethnic differences are accepted. In this society, well-off husbands and wives share responsibility for child care.

How Danes organise and process information

The Danes are a proud people who tend to be satisfied with their own accomplishments and thus do not need (and are not open to) information or help from others. Their education is moving away from rote learning and toward the application of abstractive, conceptual thinking. They tend to follow universalistic rules of behaviour rather than react to particular situations.

What Danes accept as evidence

Truth is centred in a faith in the ideology of social welfare, with objective facts used to prove a point. Subjective feelings do not play a part in negotiation processes.

The basis of behaviour

Denmark is a social welfare state in which the quality of life and environmental issues are given top priority. Value systems in the predominant culture – how right is distinguished from wrong, good from evil, and so on – are described under the next three headings.

The locus of decision-making

Danes have a strong belief in individual decisions within the social welfare system. There is a strong self-orientation, but with an obligation to help those who are not able to help themselves. There is an emphasis on individual initiative and achievement, with one's ability being more important than one's station in life. The dignity and worth of the individual is emphasised, along with the right to a private life and opinions.

Ten examples of Danish business practices

1 The Danes tend to get down to business right away, with a minimum of small talk.
2 Danes are relatively informal. You can introduce yourself to the executive with whom you have an appointment rather than expecting the secretary to introduce you.
3 Be prepared to give detailed briefings since Danes are relatively meticulous.
4 Danes are often quite frank and direct but do not intend any offence.
5 Avoid making any comments that could be regarded as personal. Even complimenting someone on his or her clothes may be taken as too invasive!
6 Danes are very tolerant, and it is not advisable to criticise other people or systems.
7 Toasts in Denmark can be quite formal. Never toast your host or anyone senior to you in rank or age until he or she has toasted you first. Never start drinking until the host has said the traditional toasting word, *skoal*.
8 It is common to rise when being introduced to someone, and to shake hands with both men and women. Handshakes are firm but brief. When greeting a couple, it is customary to shake hands with the woman first.
9 Gifts are not required in a business relationship.
10 Conservative dress will always be appropriate: Danish casual attire is still conservative, although jeans that are clean and pressed will be seen.

Source: *Kiss, Bow, or Shake Hands: How to Do Business in Sixty Countries*, by Terri Morrison, Wayne A. Conaway and George A. Borden, Adams Media, 2006

Summary

The management of organisational processes implies leading the organisation towards the goals that are set. These goals can be achieved when a number of business processes are carried out effectively and efficiently. Various types of business processes can be identified in an organisation: primary, secondary and administrative processes.

Business Re-engineering is an approach that considers business processes to be the central issue, and so strives to eliminate the splitting up of an organisation. The aim of Business Re-engineering is to offer more added value to the buyer by concentrating more on the process.

Porter's value chain shows the amount of added value produced by each part of an organisation. By carefully structuring and coordinating the business processes, competitive advantage can be created.

Quality management refers to the whole of the management function that determines and carries out quality policy. There is a distinction between technical and relative quality. Implementing relative quality requires internal quality management. This quality management integrates and directs all activities and decisions that influence quality. Important reasons for the increasing interest in quality control are growing competition, increasing buyer awareness of quality, the costs of poor quality and changes in legislation. Six Sigma is a quality system that is growing significantly. It uses a quantitative (statistical) approach.

Customer Relationship Management is an approach for building, keeping and extending relationships with individual customers, thus creating added value for both customer and enterprise.

Human Resource Management aims at an integrated approach between strategic management and the human qualities in an organisation. In this way, the traditional personnel instruments are integrated into organisational policy. The instruments being discussed concern inflow, through flow and outflow of employees.

The separation between management and operation creates hierarchy in organisations, which can be seen in the various management levels. Each level has specific tasks. Special attention is now given to corporate governance. Society places more and more demands on enterprises to justify their business activities and their consequences in a transparent way.

Various methods are used to manage organisations in order to clarify and understand management processes. Individual methods (management by objectives, management by exception, time management), organisational methods (risk and unit management) and process oriented methods (project planning) are all discussed in this chapter.

Definitions

§8.1 Management of organisational processes
Leading the organisation towards the goals that have been set.

Business process
A set of organised human activities relating to the production of goods and / or services

§§8.2.1 Primary processes
All activities that contribute directly to the making of the product.

Secondary processes
All activities that support the primary process.

Administrative processes
All activities that direct the primary and secondary processes and help to reach the organisation's goals.

Control activities
The goal-orientated implementation of business processes.

§§8.2.2 Core business process
A number of linked activities that give extra value to the buyer.

§§8.2.3 Value Chain
All activities needed to offer a product to the market. The value chain indicates the amount of value added by the various parts of the organisation to the whole.

Primary activities
Activities that add value directly to products.

Support activities
Activities that create conditions required by the primary processes, thus contributing indirectly to the value of the products.

§§8.2.4 Quality management
That management function that determines and carries out quality policy.

Total Quality Management
A system aimed at reaching the desired level of quality at minimum cost. It integrates and performs all quality-related activities and makes decisions that influence quality, irrespective of position within the organisation.

§§8.2.5 Logistics management
Deals with the planning and control of the flow of goods and / or services within the supply chain plus the corresponding information stream.

§§8.2.6 Customer Relationship Management
An approach aimed at building, keeping and extending relationships with individual customers, thus creating value for both customer and enterprise.

§§8.2.7 Human Resource Management
All standards and values relating to an organisation's employees and the translation of these into techniques and methods that optimise the use of existing human qualities and their contribution towards the goals of the organisation.

Competency management	The translation of the core competencies of the organisation into the necessary knowledge, skills and attitudes possessed by employees. The development, assessing and rewarding of employees is based on these core competencies.
Knowledge management	Management that aims for a high return on knowledge input. This includes learning results as well as financial results. The central issue of knowledge management is how to obtain, innovate, distribute and use knowledge in order to create a new competitive advantage.
Management Development	The process of systematically balancing the needs and potential of employees.
§ 8.3 Hierarchy	A graded separation between management and operations caused by the need to delegate activities within the organisation.
Management levels	The various hierarchical levels within an organisation.
§§8.3.1 Two tier system	A system with a strict division between the management of an organisation and supervision (the Rhineland model).
One tier system	A system without a strict separation between management and supervision (the Anglo-Saxon model).
§§8.3.5 Social responsibility	Seeing the purpose of an enterprise as not just profit making or profit maximisation. Businesses should derive their right to exist not merely from the amount of profit they make but from how they function within a network of economic, ecological and social factors.
Corporate governance	A system for the directing and managing of enterprises in which transparency and justification are considered to be the main characteristics of good reporting. Corporate governance means decent entrepreneurial management that makes justified choices based on political, social, economical and ethical considerations.
§§8.5.1 Management by Objectives	A method in which the manager and subordinate determine the objectives for the coming period by mutual agreement and agree on the results required at the end of that period.
Management by Exception	Within certain limits, the middle manager is entitled to define and use specific means needed to make corrections. If these limits are exceeded, this will be seen as exceeding the limits of his / her authority. His / her superior will be informed and the necessary action taken.
§§8.5.2 Risk management	The management of static risk within organisations. The aim is to minimise the potential effects of identifiable risk and to ensure that the objectives of the organisation remain attainable.

Unit management	A way of managing by pursuing a policy of decentralisation within the organisation.
§§8.5.3 Project planning	A method used for processes whereby employees from various departments work together on a temporary basis in order to find solutions for particular problems.

Statements

Indicate whether the following statements are correct or incorrect, giving reasons for your choice.

1 Management is the process of directing the organisation towards set goals.
2 Primary processes consist to a large degree of those activities that direct secondary and administrative processes.
3 A core business process is a group of linked activities that add customer value.
4 Porter's value chain can be seen as a modern way of representing the development of goods along the production and marketing chain.
5 Total Quality Management refers to the relative as well as the technical quality of products.
6 With Customer Relationship Management, the customer is considered to constitute a sustainable competitive advantage.
7 To determine how much priority an activity should be given, one merely has to estimate the urgency of that activity.
8 The aim of risk management is to be in a situation where the organisation can reach its goals while not being adversely affected by risks and their consequences.
9 Human Resource Management should be integrated into strategic management so as to utilise the qualities possessed by the members of an organisation to their fullest
10 The various elements of the knowledge value chain relate to the mission, the vision, the goals and the strategy of the organisation.

Theory questions

1 Take an organisation of your choice and identify the primary, secondary and administrative processes within that organisation.
2 Porter's theory is based on the value chain.
   a What are the similarities between Porter's theory and Hammer's theory of business process re-engineering?
   b Indicate how secondary activities can add value indirectly to products and / or services.
   c What is the significance of information in Porter's theory?
   d How can information add value to products and / or services?

3 a What forms of decision-making exist within senior management teams?
   b What are the advantages and disadvantages of these forms of decision-making?
4 What are the similarities between Management by Objectives and Management by Exception?
5 The Tabaksblat Code was introduced in the Netherlands on January the 1st, 2004.
   a List five recommendations contained in the Code.
   b What are the key differences between the Dutch code for corporate governance and the Sarbanes Oxley Act in the USA?

Practical assignment

The institute where you are studying or perhaps the business in which you are working part-time will probably have at one management level.
1 Describe the hierarchical levels and what they are composed of.
2 How are the tasks divided and how are decisions made?
3 What is your opinion about the effectiveness of this division and the way decisions are made?
4 Give your opinion, supported by reasons, of the management of the organisation and its effectiveness.

 For answers see www.marcusvandam.noordhoff.nl.

Cost-benefit analysis of theft prevention

In recent years a steady increase in theft has been noticed at Riu Hotels & Resorts. The recently appointed Risk Manager has been asked to set up an in-depth investigation into all aspects of theft prevention.

For several years the hotel group has used the services of a security organisation. The insurance premium, which has a policy excess, has gone up as the number of thefts has increased.

Research has come up with a number of recommendations, including one in particular that needs further exploration. There are indications that the majority of thefts have occurred because someone is using forged or stolen keys to open guest room doors. Experience has shown that a key card is safer to lock up rooms. The key card is a plastic card that is re-programmed when it is issued to guests as they check in to the hotel. In effect, it has the same functionality as changing of the locks, which used to be a somewhat costly affair.

One hotel that is felt to be representative of the whole group is chosen for a trial run. The costs for the necessary materials amount to €60,000. Their life span is estimated to be six years. The advantages of the system are varied, and include factors such as a decrease in the number of thefts and a possible reduction in the insurance premium.

These are the estimated savings generated by the adoption of the new system:

Year	Amount (in euros)
1	6,000
2	12,000
3	18,000
4	24,000
5	30,000
6	36,000

The increase in savings each year is due to the measures having a variety of beneficial effects.

At the same time that the budget proposal is submitted, a second bid for funding is made. The building needs new modern, energy saving heating and lighting equipment. The costs of installation and equipment are estimated at €60,000. The equipment will need to be replaced after five years. It will lead to the following savings in energy costs:

Year	Amount (in euros)
1	30,000
2	21,000
3	12,000
4	9,000
5	6,000

The directors of the hotel group are willing to make funds available for only one of the projects. The manager responsible for the second proposal states: 'The estimated savings are very subjective and moreover, the hotel group is insured against theft. That is what we pay premiums for!' Both managers are asked to prepare a presentation.

Source: *Corporate Risk Management*, G.C.A. Dickson, Whitherby, London.

Questions

1 How does the theft prevention plan relate to the primary process of the hotel group?
2 Is the theft prevention plan aimed at static or dynamic risks, or at both? Give reasons for your answer.
3 Describe the theft prevention plan using the systematic approach to the process of risk control.
4 Describe some aspects that the Risk Manager should include in his presentation.
5 Produce a financial analysis of the projects.

E-mail case study

To:	Ambrus Sipo
Cc:	
Bcc:	
Subject:	Business processes and added value

Message:

Dear Ambrus,

It is now two years since we worked together in a company in the beautiful Hungarian capital of Budapest. It was a nice project to work on and we had a great time there. You have started your own company now and I imagine that securing new orders isn't always easy.

I think I have an interesting and worthwhile assignment for you. As you know, I'm currently working with a large industrial organisation in Poland. My department wants to gain an insight into business processes and their added value. We have chosen to follow Porter's model, especially the concept of the value chain and the link with competitive advantages. Before we start investigating, we would like to commission a report looking at a large industrial organisation in the EU.

We'd like to ask you to produce this report. You can select any European company. Based on the information you can obtain about the organisation, we'd like an answer to the following questions:

- What are their competitive advantages and where do they derive from?
- Which organisational units are responsible for them?
- What role does information supply play in this regard?
- What coordination mechanisms are in use?
- What are the organisation's primary and secondary processes?
- What are the competitive advantages of the chosen strategies?

Ambrus, please keep the research concise and concentrate on the main factors. I'd like to receive the report in two weeks.

Good luck and regards,

Dorika Soros

Organisational structure and design

'As soon as you've reached the top, there's no where else to go but down'.
(Seneca, 4 BC–65 AD, Latin tragedy writer and moralist)

This chapter will look at the structuring of organisations. The main focus will be on the division and coordination of tasks, organisational systems, and communication and consultation structures.

Contents

After studying this chapter:
- You will be aware of the relationship between managing company processes and key structuring issues.
- You will have a knowledge of and insight into the division and coordination of tasks in organisations.
- You will have become aware of the various organisational systems.
- You will have a knowledge of communication and consultation structures.

9.1   Organising activities

The management of company processes was examined in Chapter 8. We firstly looked at the various company processes in an organisational context. Then we investigated the way in which company processes are monitored. We concluded with an investigation of some methods of giving direction to see if they could be applied to the management processes.

In this chapter we will continue this line of exploration. After an insight has been obtained into the various company processes within the organisation and into the management of those processes, it is important to consider how all those activities can best be organised. To implement and manage company processes requires a *External factors* high level of efficiency and goal awareness. On the one hand, external factors that affect the organisation should be taken into account and any adjustments necessary made, depending on the choice of strategic management process (discussed in Chapter 3). By setting strategic objectives, the organisation is plotting the general direction of the route towards achieving the desired goals. On the other hand, inter- *Internal factors* nal factors involving individual staff members, machines and other tools must be taken into account, with day-to-day operations being given all due attention. These need to be utilised in such a way as to support each other.[1] Of particular importance are the start-up processes and the managing of daily operations.

The internal and external factors that influence the organising of activities are illustrated in Figure 9.1.

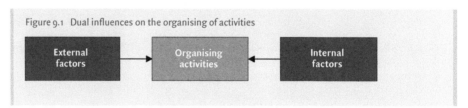

Figure 9.1 Dual influences on the organising of activities

Because organising is situation-bound, we can safely say that there is no one best way of going about it. In each set of circumstances, one must look for a solution that *Structuring* matches the situation. Structuring involves the creation of an organisational structure in which people and resources are optimally utilised to reach the organisation's objectives. Finding the ideal arrangement will require adjustments at both the exter *Organisational structure* nal and internal levels. An organisational structure defines tasks, competencies, and responsibility and sets out the pattern of relationships between positions. When designing an organisational structure, not only should the organic form be considered but also the staff structure.

The organic structure
Wherever people work together towards particular goals, the tasks need to be divided between the various departments of the organisation. Groups to carry out certain *Organic structure* functions must be formed: the organic structure.

A coordination mechanism must then be added to ensure that all the divided tasks and roles match each other. Designing a framework in which people are optimally occupied is consequently just as much an issue of task division as it is of coordination.

Name:	Norman Sze
Country of origin:	China
Job title:	Managing Partner
Company:	Deloitte Consulting (Shanghai) Co. Ltd
Company website:	www.deloitte.com.cn

What must people know if they do business in China?

If you are a newcomer to China, you have to understand the communication style of the Chinese. Lesson number one is that Chinese people will never give a direct answer. They often use indirect ways of saying 'no'. You have to look for the hidden messages or thoughts in their answers. Learning how to read their minds and analysing what they really want to tell you is a most important skill.

Lesson number two is that negotiation skills are widely used in business development in China. China is a rapidly developing country with newly emerging business rules and practices. Doing business in China means negotiating for whatever you want. Since China is a big country, each Chinese city will have its own culture, style, and business rules. There are major differences between Northern and Southern China, and even major difference from one province to another.

How important is the work/life balance in your country?

Previously, we Chinese people had only seven days of annual public holidays and we had to work six days a week. Chinese people always work hard and most of us believe that work is more important than leisure. During the past five years, the government has extended the length of our national holidays and our annual leave, which may also differ from level to level within the enterprise.

Nowadays, the concept of a work/life balance is becoming increasingly popular in China, though it is mainly our public holidays and annual leave that we focus on. The quality of our personal lives is more important than ever and we are focusing our efforts on improving the quality of life of our employees. A newly married couple may request leave for a honeymoon vacation; staff may participate in outdoor activities organised by the firm and so on. We always say 'work hard, play hard'. Finding a work / life balance will ensure work quality and improve employee loyalty.

Describe one important trend in organisation and management in China

China is one of the most energetically developing countries in the world. A new trend in business organisation that is highly regarded by the management team is providing learning opportunities. Hundreds of senior management staff of Chinese state-owned enterprises (SOEs) are seeking enhanced learning opportunities to improve their knowledge. They are interested in corporate strategy, HR management, corporate governance, internal control, financial management, and much more. That's why the EMBA curriculum is 'hot' in China. The CEIBS EMBA (Chinese Europe International Business School (CEIBS), Executive MBA) has been ranked 13th worldwide. In addition, there are many types of training institutes that provide certified training in technical and management skills to business organisations.

As the various state-owned enterprises recognise the importance of training, they are becoming increasingly willing to invest in training centres to create and provide a targeted curriculum to the staff. The concept of the 'learning organisation' is already becoming an important one in China.

Personnel structure

Personnel structure

After the functions have been allocated to departments, the personnel structure needs to be determined. The personnel structure is the human dimension of the organisation's structure. In creating this structure, attention needs to be paid to:

- *Hierarchical relationships.* Who issues instructions?
- *Authority.* Who makes certain decisions?
- *Position identification.* Which employees should be allocated to which departments and what jobs will they perform?
- *Communication.* Who informs others and how?

9.2 Task division and coordination

Task division

An organisation's business processes generate activities that have to be allocated to various workers. Task division is the splitting up of activities into separate tasks that are then either assigned to individuals or to other units such as departments. This division and allocation process is especially significant the greater the number of people working within the organisation. There are many reasons why task division in organisations attracts so much attention. One reason is the desire for

Productivity

increased productivity (= number of accomplishments in a given time). Within production departments, task division has a special and significant influence on productivity. Effective task division will have a considerable effect on the costs associated with production. Effective task division also makes it easier to mechanise processes. Although still in its infancy, there is some potential at this level for the use of robots and other advanced forms of automation.

If we compare the way the various organisations allocate their tasks, we will find that there is still a demand for custom-made solutions. While the process of task

IN THE PRESS

Task division and coordination at eBay

eBay Inc. pioneers communities built on commerce, sustained by trust, and inspired by opportunity. eBay brings together millions of people every day on a local, national and international basis through an array of websites that focus on commerce, payments and communications. eBay Inc. has customers in various different business segments including eBay Marketplace, PayPal, Skype, Shopping.com, Rent.com and Online Classifieds. Their global executive management team and their respective tasks include:

- Beth Axelrod, Senior Vice President, Human Resources
- William C. Cobb, President, eBay North America
- John Donahoe, President, eBay Marketplaces
- Rajiv Dutta, President, Skype
- Michael Jacobson, Senior Vice President and General Counsel
- Jeff Jordan, President, PayPal
- Pierre Omidyar, Founder and Chairman of the Board

- Bob Swan, Senior Vice President, Finance and Chief Financial Officer
- Meg Whitman, President and CEO
- Niklas Zennström, CEO and Co-Founder, Skype

Source: ebay.com, 2006

Questions to ask when creating work positions

- Are the daily tasks reasonable ones? Is there a risk of understaffing or overloading in any area? Are the tasks evenly distributed amongst staff?
- Have any tasks been forgotten? Are there gaps anywhere?
- Is there any duplication of tasks in the various job descriptions?
- Is the organisation vulnerable because of the creation of essential specialist positions? If a particular specialist were to leave the company, would this directly endanger the continuity of operations?
- Is the coordination effective? Are positions structured in such a way that coordination problems can be kept to a minimum?
- Do any top managers have too many direct subordinates (span of control)?
- Is the organisational design flexible enough to adapt to changes without too much trouble?
- Are jobs structured in such a way that everyone can experience job satisfaction when performing their tasks?
- Does the organisation offer sufficient opportunities for development for all staff members? Has anyone been stuck in a particular job without any opportunity to develop further?
- Can the organisation be staffed efficiently? Can the job market provide enough people to service the job requirements as laid down?

Source: H. Luijk, *Taakverdeling en functievorming*

division is general in nature, allocation of tasks is more dependent on the specific situation. This process has vertical and horizontal dimensions.

9.2.1 Vertical task division

The many different tasks that are carried out inside an organisation have their own unique characteristics. A task is the 'technical' content of a function and indicates precisely what a person does: meet, consult, manage, make a call, administrate, monitor proceedings and so on. The differences between tasks are based especially on the required expertise, experience and skills. Tasks fall into various different levels. For instance, a manager's tasks do not include typing up minutes and letters. He / she is too expensive for that. Cost considerations mean that these activities are passed down to a lower hierarchical level. This process is called vertical differentiation. Tasks that are of the same level are brought together within an organisation. Where tasks are grouped according to level, it is important to ensure that the resulting collection of duties constitutes a complete and worthwhile day's work. The latter consideration is sometimes ignored when tasks are divided up. Extreme specialisation can lead to a lot of monotonous work and consequently under-stimulation and decreased job motivation. One should always take the social aspects of a job into consideration when dividing up tasks.

As a consequence of vertical differentiation, the various activities within an organisation will become hierarchical in nature. When activities are delegated to a lower level, the higher level will want to retain control over them. The higher level needs to provide guidelines governing the performance of lower-level activities.

The issue here is the managerial aspects of task division. Effective leadership means ensuring that tasks are performed consistently and according to the published guidelines. Supervision is required.

Finally, it should be noted that social aspects also play a role when an organisation allocates tasks. Society places demands on some aspects of task composition: for example, legislation in relation to working conditions (Health and Safety legislation etc.).

In summary, we can state that four factors influence the division of tasks[2]:

1 *Cost factors*. Tasks must be arranged in such a way that efficient functioning and production is possible.

Task

Vertical differentiation

Social aspects

Managerial aspects

Social aspects

Cost factors

Managerial factors	2 *Managerial factors*. The way in which tasks are structured and divided must lend itself to management of the organisation. Supervision of the various tasks and how they are executed is required.
Individual factors	3 *Individual factors*. Jobs must have a certain amount of appeal for individuals. Variety, responsibility and decision-making power all come into play.
Societal motives	4 *Societal motives*. Society makes demands that must be complied with when tasks are structured: health and safety precautions, for example.

Work structuring
The conscious consideration of technical, economic, and social aspects of working in an organisation or a division is known as work structuring. Work structuring is closely linked to the relationship that exists between the needs of staff and the targets of the organisation. Work structuring has attracted the attention of researchers for a long time, and its central themes have developed in line with changes in society and attitude. Work structuring has gone through the following phases:

Extrinsic job factors
a Initially, attention was paid to extrinsic job factors and changes in the working environment: external matters such as noise, temperature, light, music at work, humidity, and the layout of working spaces and how they are furnished. The working environment was improved by adapting those factors that were extrinsic to the job.

Intrinsic job factors
b The structure of the job itself then came under scrutiny, with special attention paid to factors intrinsic to the job. Interest during this phase focussed on:

Job enrichment
- *Job enrichment*: the addition of elements of a more meaningful and challenging nature to an individual's tasks.

Job enlargement
- *Job enlargement*: increasing the range of duties by addition of tasks of a similar level.

Job rotation
- *Job rotation*: staff movement from one job to another, with mutual exchange of jobs with colleagues.

These three forms of intrinsic work factors have in common that they can increase work satisfaction and generate better cooperation between the various layers of an organisation.

Today, greater attention is being paid to the structure of departmental units. While intrinsic work factors are involved, this is at the unit rather than the individual level. Departments are increasingly being regarded as individual units with specific tasks, authority and responsibilities being assigned to them. A department may, for example, be divided into semi-autonomous work units, each performing a set of tasks and jointly performing the department's tasks.

9.2.2 Horizontal task division

Task division
The purpose of task division is not only to identify tasks of the same level. It is also to seek coherence between the various tasks. The various components of the task must have some connection with each other. When the tasks are allocated, attention must be paid to how they are to be coordinated. Insufficient attention being paid to this will result in failure to reach a high level of efficiency or to achieve targets.

Coordination

The bringing together of certain tasks will result in the creation of functions. A function unites the common objective of those tasks that have to be performed as well as the responsibilities and authority that belong to them. Functions relate not only to individuals but also to organisational groups such teams or units.

Related tasks are initially grouped together according to an individual's position (functionalism). After that, these individual positions are regrouped to form departments (department formation).

Functionalism
Department formation

DSM retains leadership position in Dow Jones Sustainability World Index

The Dow Jones Sustainability Indexes track the performance of the leading sustainability-driven companies worldwide through a thorough assessment of these companies' economic, environmental and social performance and accounts for more than 50 general as well as industry-specific criteria in each sector. DSM has been named the worldwide sustainability leader in the chemical industry.
Sustainable development at DSM is driven by the Triple P: People, Planet and Profit approach, which devotes special attention to corporate governance and risk management, innovation, occupational health and safety as well as human capital development. In 2005 and as part of DSM's new strategy program 'Vision 2010 – Building on Strengths', the company set new environmental targets for the period

until 2010 including switching from petroleum-derived to renewable raw materials via white (or industrial) biotechnology.
'We are very pleased that we have been able to retain our top position for the third year in a row', said Peter Elverding, chairman of DSM's Managing Board. 'It is a clear recognition of our performance and transparent reporting in the field of sustainability and our ambition to be a sustainability leader in the industry. I especially welcome the attention that has been given to our efforts in white biotechnology, because DSM is of the opinion that innovation is the key to sustainable development'.

Source: www.dsm.com, 2006

The two main forms of horizontal task division are:

1 Internal differentiation
2 Internal specialisation

Internal differentiation

Internal differentiation involves searching for tasks that have something in common. Take a manufacturing company that makes furniture, for example. Various different people are responsible for performing the tasks. These tasks include designing the furniture, purchasing the materials, cutting the wood, assembling the furniture, and selling it. In this example, task division is based on the various steps of the manufacturing process rather than the product itself. Such a division of tasks is known as a functional division of tasks. The company's positions departments will be based on the various manufacturing processes. (See Figure 9.2.)

Internal differentiation

Functional division

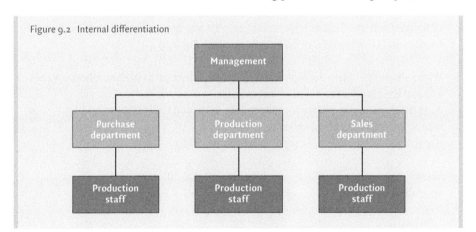

Figure 9.2 Internal differentiation

In many organisations, divisions placed directly under the executive level of management are split up again into sub-divisions. (See Figure 9.3.)
One of the dangers of internal differentiation is its potential to lose sight of the inner coherence between the various work processes. As such, it is essential to establish extra coordination mechanisms such as consultation structures and planning activities that involve the various manufacturing phases.

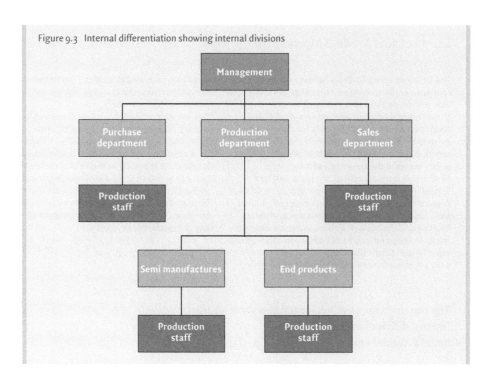

Figure 9.3 Internal differentiation showing internal divisions

Internal specialisation

Internal specialisation

Internal specialisation involves grouping the activities carried out by a unit on the basis of the end result. To take the example of the furniture manufacturer again, certain employees will focus solely on the task of making chairs, including designing them, purchasing the material for them, cutting the wood for them, assembling them and then selling them. All activities relating to chairs are brought together and the natural cohesion of the activities to be performed will remain intact. The same grouping will be used for tables and cupboards.

Product, Market, and Geographical division

Internal specialisation activities revolve not only around products. They may also be concerned with markets or buyers and geographical areas, the so-called Product, Market, and Geographical division of tasks. (See Figure 9.4.)

With a division of tasks according to any of these three criteria, the highest organisational level (under the board of directors) is:
- A *product division* (e.g. different product units A, B, and C).
- A *market division* (e.g. retail and wholesale).
- A *geographical division* (e.g. Europe, Asia, and America).

We will now look at the differences between internal differentiation and internal specialisation.

Differences

The choice between internal differentiation and internal specialisation will depend on the organisation's given situation. Small organisations almost always chose internal differentiation. As soon as a company has reached a certain size and also manufactures and sells different products, there will be some basis for internal specialisation within the organisation. In general, differentiation and specialisation carry the following advantages and disadvantages.

Figure 9.4   Internal specialisations

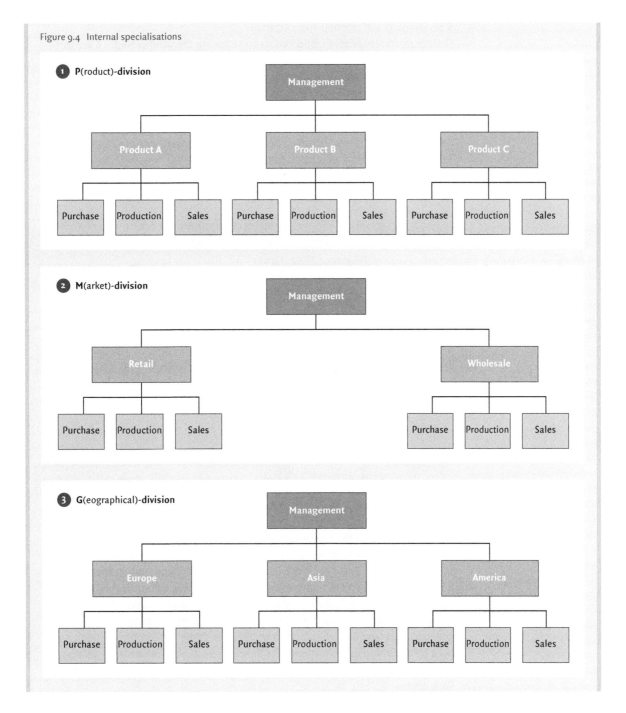

The advantages of internal differentiation:
- Efficient use of the manpower available because it can be put to use in a greater number of activities, creating greater capacity
- Higher skill levels and more efficient routines
- Greater opportunities for automation

The disadvantages of internal differentiation:
- Coordination problems due to splitting up of the work processes
- Repetition and monotony
- Little flexibility for individuals since they perform a limited number of processes each

The advantages of internal specialisation:
- Greater guarantee of efficient coordination between the various steps of the work process
- Shorter communication lines and faster problem-solving
- Less monotonous work

The disadvantages of internal specialisation:
- Less efficient use of resources as a consequence of inevitable duplication
- Reduction in expertise in relation to technical know-how
- Fragmentation of skills due to the broader range of work processes undertaken by each person.

In larger organisations, various internal specialisations might be grouped under a particular section of the organisation. (See Figure 9.5.)

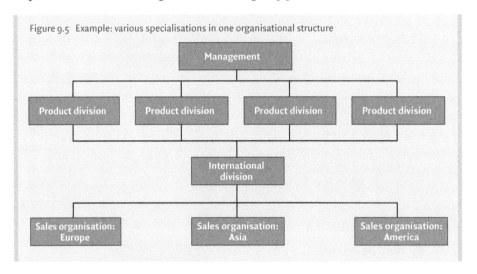

Figure 9.5 Example: various specialisations in one organisational structure

The first level under the top management level has a product-based structure. Activities below this level are split up based on geographical regions. This organisational form can be opted for if consumers in different continents are prepared to buy the same products or minor variations on them. Production can be carried out efficiently (even though these production activities will, of course, take place at different locations). After the production phase, the products are exported to those countries that have a market. Each continent has its own sales organisation.

Both methods aim at converting tasks to functions. Once the functions have been compiled, job descriptions which contain the following elements are created:
- Task content
- Authority
- Responsibilities
- Level within the organisation
- Relationships with other organisational members
- Nature of the position

Job descriptions

Filling in the above information will generate a detailed picture of the job content as well as an image of the area within which the job holder will carry out the tasks and exercise his or her authority. This demonstrates the close link between task, authority, and responsibilities. Each job comes with a certain authority to perform the task. The person in question can be held responsible for carrying out the task.

In the next section we will focus on delegation and span of control: that is, the number of subordinates that a manager can effectively manage. We will also examine organisational charts which illustrate how tasks are distributed.

9.2.3 Authority, responsibility and delegation

We have seen that by distributing tasks between individuals and departments, jobs are formed. A job consists of a combination of tasks, authority, and responsibilities. Authority is the right to make the decisions necessary to perform a task.[3]

Authority

Responsibility is both the moral obligation to perform a task to the best of your ability as well as the duty to report back concerning the progress of that task.[4]

Responsibility

By dividing work horizontally, tasks, authority and responsibility are split up across the hierarchical level of that organisation. When work is divided vertically, tasks, authority and responsibility are divided amongst the various hierarchical levels.

Dividing work horizontally
Dividing work vertically

When tasks alone are transferred without any accompanying authority or responsibility, those individuals at the lower level will simply become operators. All the decisions will be made at the higher level.

In such a situation, staff in the lower level can never be held completely responsible for the execution of their tasks, because all powers of decision are held elsewhere. The lower level staff can only be held responsible for carrying out their tasks if they are given some involvement in decision-making. When tasks with their associated authority and responsibility are handed over, this is known as task delegation. (See Figure 9.6.

Delegation

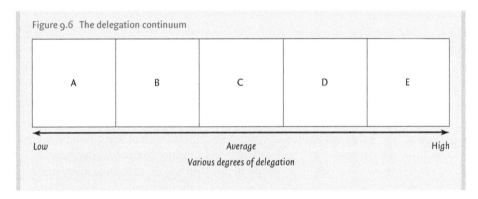

Figure 9.6 The delegation continuum

| A | B | C | D | E |

Low   Average   High
Various degrees of delegation

Delegation is rarely total. Complete absence of delegation is equally rare. However, there are degrees of delegation, as shown in Figure 9.6:

a Get the facts and report back.
b Get information and make recommendations in relation to some activities.
c Investigate and make recommendations in relation to all planned activities.
d Analyse the situation, develop and take a course of action, and report back on the results.
e Get the facts and take action.

Delegation of tasks does not always involve responsibility and authority being transferred from a higher to a lower level. What is important when delegating is that tasks, authority and responsibility remain in balance. If managers delegate, they remain responsible for the task even though they do not perform the activity themselves. A subordinate carries out the duties and the manager remains responsible for the choice of to whom and how the delegation takes place. The manager therefore retains control of the activities carried out by the subordinate.

Delegation quandary: what to do when it doesn't work?

They delegated the task according to the book. However, it's obvious that the staff member is having difficulty with it. In such a case, it's easy to choose the line of least resistance and do the job yourself or hand it over to someone else. Both may be unwise. By taking away his or her work, you will be depriving the employee of a chance to get the work done and do a good job nevertheless. By transferring the job to a colleague the member of staff will lose face and miss a chance for further growth.

It is better to check how one has delegated and how one can improve the delegation. Ask yourself the following questions:

- Were the performance standards clearly set?
- Is the employee aware of how everything works?
- Is the employee aware of how he can monitor his progress?
- Was there enough follow-up after the job was finished?

It's also important to work together with your employees until they have learnt how to perform the delegated task to a satisfactory level. The following guidelines may help:

- Talk to the individual before taking action. Take a close look together at the performance standards and explain why the work has not been accept-

able. Give specific feedback. The purpose of this conversation is to generate the feeling that you are going to get this job done together. Split the task up into main points and side issues and take over parts of the work on a temporary basis if necessary. The employee can then concentrate on his or her core responsibilities. Ask the individual involved to resolve the problems as he/she sees fit. Develop a set of procedures together with the member of staff.
- Make a clear agreement. Ensure that the required standards are understood. Make a time plan to determine when you will touch base to check progress.
- Give guidance to the employee in the carrying out of his/her tasks. Be a mentor. Be involved in such a way that the individual does not get the idea that he is constantly being supervised.
- Delegate more tasks as the performance improves. Recurring tasks can be delegated again as performance improves and the staff member gains confidence. When you delegate tasks again, explain their importance and emphasise their connection to the work previously delegated.

Source: D. Keuning, Organiseren en leiding geven, Stenfert Kroese, 2006

The extent to which tasks are delegated within an organisation will differ. The level at which decisions are made may also differ. Such factors will give an indication as to where the power in the organisation lies. If the power to make decisions is concentrated in one place (usually at the top), this suggests centralisation. In such a situation, a significant proportion of important decisions will be made high up in the organisation. There will be little delegation. In contrast, with decentralisation, the decision-making powers will be distributed over a greater number of positions, including those lower down the organisational structure. In such a situation, significant decisions will also be made at lower levels in the organisation. There will be a lot of delegation. (See Table 9.1.)

Centralisation

Decentralisation

Table 9.1 Centralisation and decentralisation continuum

	A strongly centralised organisation	A strongly decentralised organisation
How many decisions are being made at the lower levels of the organisation?	No decisions or just a few	All or almost all decisions
How important are the decisions being made at lower organisational levels?	Not very important	Very important
How many different functions (e.g. marketing, human resources, finance) count on decisions being made at lower organisational levels?	None or just a few	All or almost all functions
Does senior management check whether decisions are being made at lower levels and does it take action when needs be?	Yes, almost always	No, or virtually not

The first large-scale attempt at decentralisation took place in the 1950s in the United States and was followed a decade later in Europe. It was all about assigning at least partial independence to other organisational bodies, such as divisions, subsidiaries, and departments. In order to promote cooperation and coordination between autonomous bodies, coordinating organisations were set up with extensive support services. Soon after, there was a second wave of decentralisation, when the structure of some units became completely product or market-oriented. Within this structure, the relatively independent units operated in clearly separated product or market segments.

Staff in such units think and act independently in a professional sense, and are highly entrepreneurial (so-called 'intrapreneurs'). The parent company looks after the control and allocation of financial and human resources.

Intrapreneurs

9.2.4 Span of control

Delegation involves handing over tasks and the associated responsibility and authority to lower levels. The person who delegates the tasks retains ultimate responsibility for those tasks. To make sure that the delegated tasks are carried out as required, those who have been given the tasks must be managed. The issue here is how many subordinates a manager can effectively manage. We call this the manager's span of control. If a manager tries to direct too many subordinates, a situation will arise in which there is insufficient time to effectively direct all the activities. It will also be difficult to take a break and to look at the quality of the completed tasks. One solution to this is to appoint extra managers. This will give rise to a new hierarchical layer in the organisation, making the organisational structure taller. A large span of control for managers will cause a flatter organisational structure to develop. A small span of control will generate a steeper organisational structure. Figure 9.7 and 9.8 give an overview of a large and small span of control.

Flatter organisational structure
Steeper organisational structure

Span of control has two dimensions.
1 *The horizontal dimension.* This is the number of direct subordinates a manager supervises. It is known as span width or span breadth.
2 *The vertical dimension.* This is the number of levels affected directly or indirectly by a manager. What matters here is the degree of influence that a manager exercises over the lowest levels in the organisation (also called 'depth of control').

Depth of control

Span breadth is mainly determined by the following factors[5]:

Span breadth

- *The manager's qualities.* Dependent on the personality characteristics and the expertise of the manager as well as the time available.
- *The qualities of the employees.* What matters here are the personality characteristics and the expertise of the staff.
- *The nature of the organisation.* Dependent on the degree of delegation, the lines of communication, the attitude towards planning, task divisions, the corporate culture, and decision-making procedures in the organisation.
- *The nature of the work.* Dependent on the variety, complexity, routine, and the uniformity of the activities to be accomplished.
- *The character of the job.* The issue here is to what extent the work involves either leadership or simple execution of tasks.

Considering these factors, it can be concluded that span of control depends on the situation. If a situation arises where a manager is supervising too many subordinates, a solution can be sought on the basis of the following:

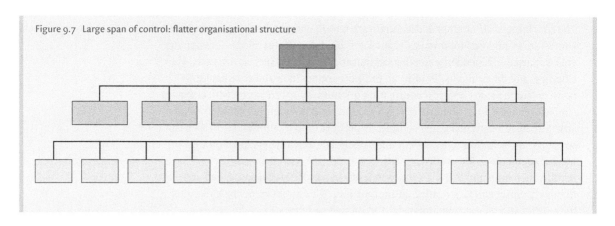

Figure 9.7 Large span of control: flatter organisational structure

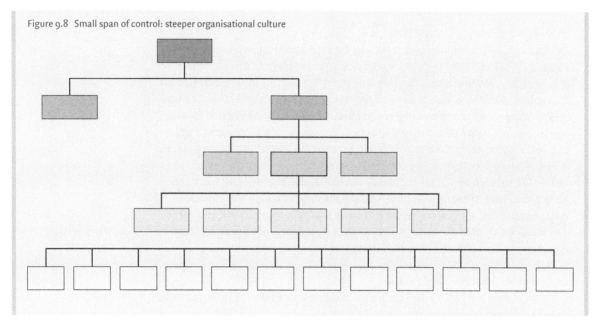

Figure 9.8 Small span of control: steeper organisational culture

- Greater delegation of tasks to a lower level, together with the accompanying responsibility and authority. The manager must retain the capacity to delegate further and to adjust the delegated tasks as necessary.

Assistant manager
- Appointing an assistant manager hierarchically below the manager, but with complete authority over subordinates in respect of general or supervisory tasks. (See Figure 9.9.)

Personal assistant
- Appointing a personal assistant (such as a secretary) to the manager to take over some routine activities. He / she will not have any supervisory authority over the manager's subordinates. (See Figure 9.10.)

- Involving other bodies in the organisation, such as support staff (see 9.3). This may result on the one hand in some of the 'brain-work' being transferred to another unit within the organisation, leaving the manager more time for managerial activities. But on the other hand, because of this, some managerial activities can be transferred from the manager to another section in the organisation, allowing more attention to be spent on policy work.

9.2.5 Organisational diagrams

Organisational diagram
An organisational diagram (also called an organisation chart) is a simplified chart of the way in which tasks are formally divided between individuals and / or depart-

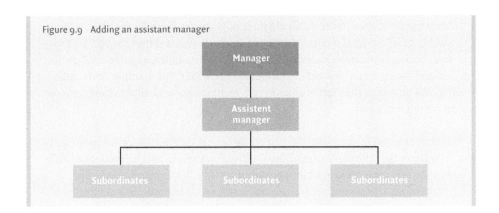

Figure 9.9   Adding an assistant manager

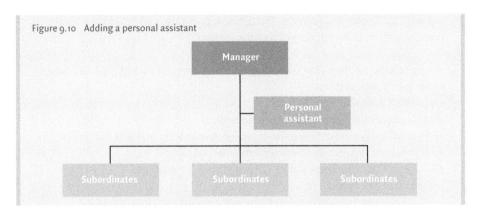

Figure 9.10   Adding a personal assistant

ments. It also shows the hierarchical relationships between individuals and divisions. We could therefore say that such a diagram is a simplified reproduction of the formal organisational structure. It is 'formal' in the sense that the task divisions, job descriptions, manuals and procedures are all written down and have an official nature. The formal organisation is the organic structure plus the staff structure. (See Figure 9.11.)

Formal organisations

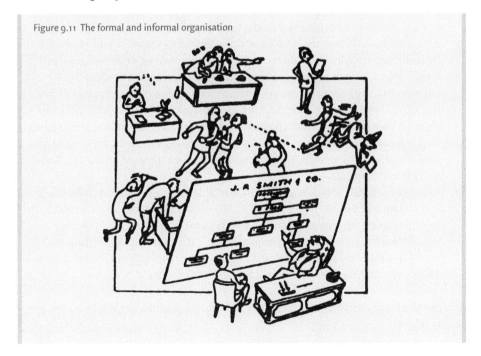

Figure 9.11 The formal and informal organisation

Other contacts, relationships and divisions of tasks occur within the organisation but do not fall under the formal organisation. Practice has shown that the formal organisation is always in a state of flux and therefore additional guidelines are necessary to support the desired organisational behaviour. For example, some rules may not fit in with the current situation while others are undesirable from a customer point of view.

Informal organisation

All activities and relationships that do not fall under the formal organisation can be included in the informal organisation. Informal organisational behaviour can influence the organisation in a positive or a negative way. When negative informal organisational behaviour occurs, the undesirable activities need to be corrected or addressed by imposing additional rules. An organisational diagram enables one to obtain an overall insight into the organisational structure and the functioning of the organisation. Tasks and function descriptions, planning, and procedures also represent part of the functioning of an organisation.

An organisational chart may take many different forms. It should provide answers to the following questions:
- From when does the diagram date?
- Has the organisational chart changed since then?
  - If so: what was the date and the nature of the changes, and why did they occur?
  - If not: has the organisation really remained stable?
- How many hierarchical levels does the organisation consist of?
- Is there a further division in:
  - main units such as departments, product units, or principal divisions?
  - departments of main units?
  - groups within departments?
  - consultation units between groups and departments?
- According to what criteria is the organisation structured (F, P, G or M structure)?

9.3 Organisational systems

An organisation can be described on the basis of number of characteristics, including organisational structure, division of tasks, authority, responsibility, power and decision-making style. Based on these characteristics, two very different organisational systems, known as mechanistic and organic systems, can be identified.

Mechanistic organisational system

A mechanistic organisational system resembles a machine in its structure and functioning to a large extent. Key features are its technical and financial efficiency. The organisation will have been set up on rational and practical grounds. It presupposes a stable business environment. With this system, changes in the business environment will rarely lead to organisational changes. As such, they are primarily effective in stable environments.

Stable environments

Organic organisational system

An organic organisational system closely resembles a living organism in the way it is structured and the way it operates. In such a system the actions of those within the organisation are crucial. The organisation serves their social needs. An organic organisational system is appropriate in a dynamic environment. The organisation is flexible in nature and capable of dealing with change. These types of organisations are only effective in environments that are subject to change.

Dynamic environment

The main characteristics of mechanistic and organic organisational systems are listed below.

The ING organisation

ING is one of the world's largest financial services companies, offering banking, insurance and asset management in over 50 countries.

ING has a two-tier board structure consisting of the Executive Board and the Supervisory Board. In ING's view, a two-tier board is the best way to ensure the right checks and balances.

The Executive Board is responsible for day-to-day management of the business and long-term strategy. The Supervisory Board is responsible for controlling management performance and advising the Executive Board. The Supervisory Board is made up exclusively of outside directors.

ING's business lines

In 2004, ING introduced a new structure of six business lines. A clear client focus and strong business logic are the key elements of this structure.

Insurance (Europe)

Operates insurance activities in the Netherlands, Belgium, Spain, Greece and Central Europe and asset-management activities in Europe. In these countries we offer life insurance with special attention to pensions. In the Netherlands and Belgium we also offer non-life insurance.

Insurance (the Americas)

Maintains insurance operations and asset-management activities in the Americas. Its retirement services, annuities and life insurances are well established in the US and it occupies a leading position in non-life insurance in Canada and Mexico. It is also active in Chile, Brazil and Peru.

Insurance (Asia/Pacific)

Maintains life insurance operations and asset/wealth management activities in Asia/Pacific. It has well-established positions in Australia, Hong Kong, Japan, Korea, Malaysia and Taiwan. The activities in China, India, and Thailand are future growth engines for ING.

Wholesale Banking

Takes care of the global wholesale banking operations. It has five divisions: Clients, Network, Products, Corporate Finance and Equity Markets, and Financial Markets. It offers a full range of products to corporations and institutions in the home markets of the Benelux countries, and elsewhere it operates a more selective and focussed client and product approach.

Retail Banking

Operates retail banking activities in the Netherlands, Belgium, Poland, Romania and India. Retail Banking also offers private banking in selected markets: for instance, in the Netherlands, Belgium, Switzerland, Luxembourg and several countries in Asia.

ING Direct

Operates direct retail-banking activities for individual clients in Australia, Canada, France, Germany, Austria, Italy, Spain, United Kingdom and the United States. The main products offered are savings and mortgages. A separate activity is ING Card, which manages a credit card portfolio within the Benelux.

Source: www.ing.com, 2006

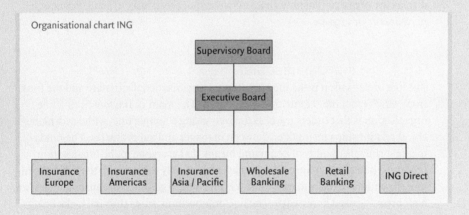

Organisational chart ING

A mechanistic organisational system

A mechanistic organisational system has the following characteristics:

- *Organisational structure.* Hierarchical in nature.
- *Division of tasks.* Every member of staff has their own tasks. Individual achievement is a priority.
- *Authority and responsibilities.* Clearly stated and must be respected.
- *Respect.* Determined by the position an individual occupies within the hierarchical structure.

- *Decision-making.* Decision-making is a matter for the top levels of the organisation and there is a minimum of consultation with or involvement of subordinates.
- *Cooperation and communication.* Employees work together according to formal hierarchical lines. Communication is one-way, namely from the top down. It is also highly formal and its contents strictly concerned with the matter in question.
- *Operating method.* Standardised and limited to set procedures.
- *Adaptability to change.* A preference for tested and reliable management principles whatever the company's circumstances.

Organic organisational system
An organic organisational structure has the following characteristics:
- *Organisational structure.* Rather than having a traditional hierarchical structure, it has horizontal working units (that is, it has a flat organisational structure).
- *Division of tasks.* Individuals have specialist tasks but execute them as a team. The focus is on team achievements.
- *Authority and responsibilities.* Authorities are broadly defined and responsibility lies with the team as well as the individual.
- *Respect.* Derives from the knowledge and skills of the individual.
- *Decision-making.* Decentralised decision-making shared by various members of the organisation. Participation and group consensus play an important role in this.
- *Cooperation and communication.* The various teams and departments work together intensively. Communication takes place from the bottom up as well from the top down. The communication channels are open so that everybody has access to relevant information.
- *Operating method.* Deviation from norms is permitted whenever necessary.
- *Adaptability to change.* The organisation adapts itself without question to changing circumstances.

In the following sections, the main organisational systems will be reviewed. They display features that illustrate characteristics that are at least to some extent either mechanistic or organic.

9.3.1   Line organisation

Line organisation

The line organisation is the most traditional organisational structure and the form from which most other structures are derived. The main characteristic of a line organisation is that orders travel exclusively along a simple line, with strict hierarchical relationships maintained between manager and subordinates. The funda-

Unity of command

mental principle of unity of command means that everyone in the organisation reports to just one manager. This manager is the only person with the authority to give the employee tasks to carry out. Within a line organisation, a manager needs to have broadly-based knowledge. The line organisation arises through tasks being passed down to lower levels as a consequence of growth or overload higher up.

The line organisation can be represented very simply (see Figure 9.12). The relationships between individuals and departments are very clear.

The advantages of a line organisation are:
- The organisational structure is simple and clear.
- The power relationships between individuals in the organisation are clear (every employee knows who his superior is).
- Tasks, authority and responsibilities can be clearly defined and allocated.

The KLM Group: its organisation

KLM Royal Dutch Airlines is an international airline operating worldwide. KLM forms the core of the KLM Group, other members being KLM cityhopper and transavia.com. Under a business model that is unique in the aviation industry, KLM merged with Air France in 2004. Under the Air France-KLM holding company, both KLM and Air France operate as network airlines: via hubs (transfer airports), they maintain a worldwide network of services to European and intercontinental destinations. KLM and Air France complement each other through the optimal alignment of their networks and through the coordination of their three core activities: passenger transport, cargo transport and aircraft maintenance. KLM works in three core areas: passenger transport, cargo transport and aircraft maintenance. But the KLM Group is bigger than that – transavia.com constitutes a fourth division, and there are a number of support services as well.

Source: www.klm.com and AMS/DS

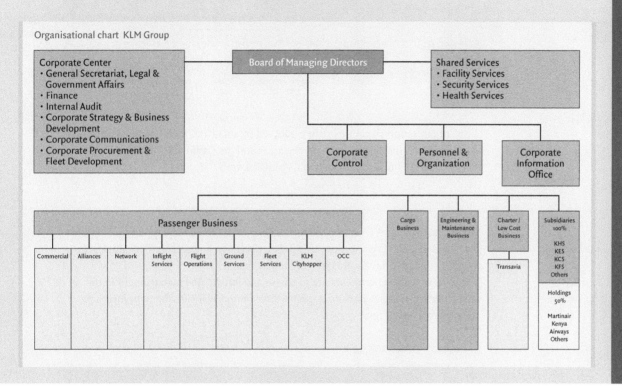

Organisational chart KLM Group

- Good supervision and control of company processes can be achieved.
- Quick decision-making is possible.
- Management and organisation costs are relatively low.

The disadvantages of a line organisation are:
- Because all communication has to go via a single line, bottlenecks may arise, resulting in delays in decisions being made.
- Management's expertise is not always sufficient to make the right decisions in all situations.
- Coordination between departments can only take place via a senior manager who is responsible for both.
- A line structure can lead to a lot of organisational levels, as managers can only supervise a limited number of people.

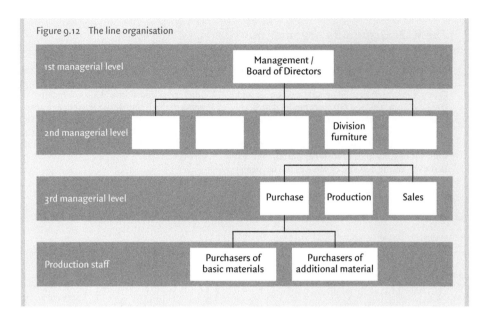
Figure 9.12 The line organisation

1st managerial level	Management / Board of Directors
2nd managerial level	Division furniture
3rd managerial level	Purchase · Production · Sales
Production staff	Purchasers of basic materials · Purchasers of additional material

A line organisation structure is often adopted by small and medium-sized business-es. In the form they had in the past, the army and the Catholic Church are good examples of the line organisation in its purest form.

9.3.2 Line and staff organisation

Line and staff organisation

Advise/inform

Where staff with specialist knowledge and expertise (so-called support staff) assist managers in a line organisation, this is described as a line and staff organisation. Support staff are often located in staff departments.

The tasks of staff departments are to advise and inform line management in the area of their expertise. They do not have direct authority over other employees or departments. (See Figure 9.13).

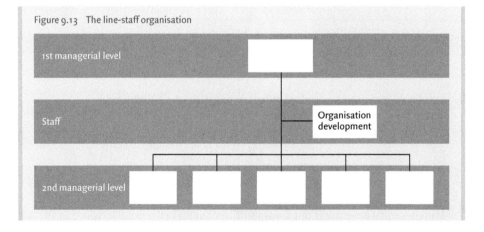
Figure 9.13 The line-staff organisation

1st managerial level	
Staff	Organisation development
2nd managerial level	

Overall responsibility remains with the line manager, who is also in charge of deci-sion-making. The staff department, on the other hand, is responsible for the quality of the advice or information that is supplied to the line manager. The advantages of a line and staff organisation are:
· Because greater expertise is available to the line manager, better decisions can be made.

Unilever to keep dual structure

Unilever, the UK-Dutch consumer goods company, said that it would keep its dual corporate structure, including separate stock listings in London and Rotterdam. The decision, which comes after Unilever replaced its dual chairman/chief executive structure with a single executive so that it could make faster decisions, disappointed investors looking for more changes to Unilever's corporate culture.

Unilever's decision differs from that of another UK-Dutch group, Royal Dutch Shell, which united its holding companies in July 2005 with a primary listing in London.

Unilever said moving to a single listing would have been disruptive and would make it more difficult for the company to arbitrage its corporate tax liabilities between the UK and the Netherlands.

Source: Financial Times, December 2005

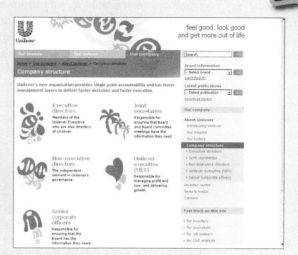

IN THE PRESS

- Involving support staff can save time and increase efficiency. The span of control of line managers can therefore be extended.
- The principle of unity of command is maintained.

The disadvantages of a line and staff organisation are:
- Because staff departments may only have a theoretical understanding of operations, they may not be aware of the practical elements of a situation.
- Given that the support staff are not responsible for the decisions made, there is more chance of slip-ups occurring within the department.
- Staff departments are inclined to expand, which increases overhead costs. As well as this, it is not always easy to determine objectively whether the contribution made by support staff has lead to better decisions being made.
- There is a chance of the line manager becoming too dependent on the staff function.

Almost every large organisation has staff departments such as Human Resources (HR), Marketing Research, and Research and Development (R&D).

9.3.3   Functional and line staff organisation

If the advice of the support staff becomes so specialised that the line official can no longer assess it, the advice will take the form of an instruction or task (such as legal advice) that has to be followed. The staff relationship will therefore develop a 'functional' character.

Functional and line staff organisation

Functional responsibility can be assigned to individuals and departments. In the event of the latter, it is termed a functional staff division. The main characteristic of a functional staff division is that part of the actual task is also executed.

Functional staff division

Because of its specialist responsibility, a functional staff division will use its position to give instructions to other departments or managers on the policy that should be followed (such as the subcontracting of certain activities), the operational method that should be followed (e.g. an administrative method) or a procedure (such as the selection of staff).

Line managers are often compelled to consult a functional staff division before making decisions that require the expertise of the functional staff division, such as advice concerning legal, automation or construction issues.

If an organisation is striving for uniformity and consistency, it is wise to give certain departments functional responsibility to do such things as setting up an hourly work monitoring system, designing forms, leaflets or brochures, purchasing computer equipment or analysing a production processes. The expertise required for these sorts of activities are often either absent from the line structure or it is difficult to coordinate such matters from the line.

In the following organisational chart, the functional relationships are indicated by a dotted line. (See Figure 9.14.)

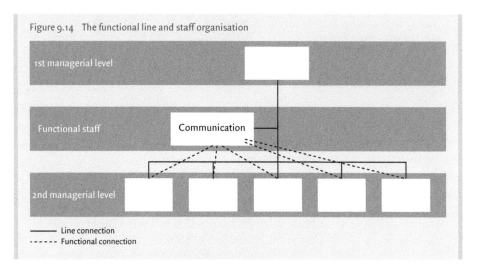

Figure 9.14   The functional line and staff organisation

1st managerial level

Functional staff   Communication

2nd managerial level

——— Line connection
- - - - Functional connection

The advantages of functional staff divisions are:
- Greater input of expertise into company processes
- Involvement of members of the functional staff department in the end result
- Uniformity and consistency in policy, guidelines and procedures

The disadvantages of functional staff divisions are:
- Employees having to deal with different managers. The principle of unity of command is abandoned, and that can lead to confusion.
- Control over the way the tasks are executed may become more difficult.

Functional staff divisions include the following: Administration, Human Resources, Finances, Secretarial support, Maintenance, Automation, Legal Matters, and Communications. Obviously, the more line managers are caught up in functional relationships with other departments, the less time they can put into their own area of activity.

9.3.4   Line-staff-committee organisation

Line-staff-committee organisation

In the previously mentioned organisational formats, all communication needs to go along 'the line'. Theoretically, this means no consultation between employees of the various departments other than that between the departmental heads. However, it is often necessary to involve other departments and their staff in business activities.

Committees or consulting bodies

Establishing committees or consulting bodies can boost cooperation between employees and departments as well as assisting the coordination of activities. Such

The management structure within the Heineken Group

Standing at the head of the Heineken Group is Heineken Holding N.V. and its Board of Directors. The management of Heineken N.V. is under the Executive Board, which has two members and is chaired by Jean-François van Boxmeer. Heineken has five operational regions: Western Europe, Central and Eastern Europe, the Americas, Africa and the Middle East, and the Asia-Pacific region. Each region is headed by a regional president. The two members of the Executive Board, the five Regional Presidents and five Group Directors together form the Executive Committee. The Executive Committee supports the development of policy and ensures the alignment and implementation of key priorities and strategies across the organisation.

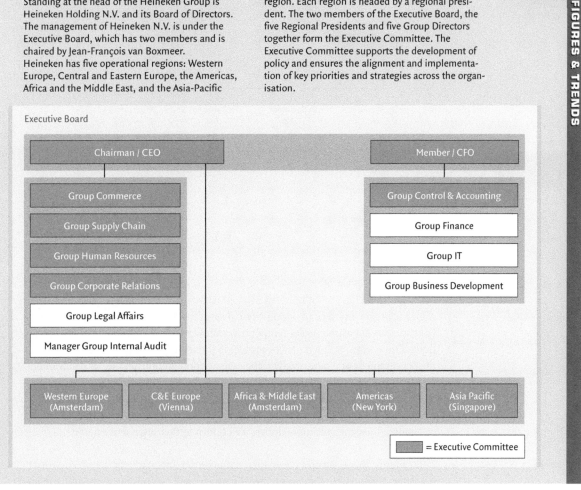

committees are set up for purely consultative purposes and have no authority to make decisions. The advice of a committee has to be approved by management. The committee structure represents a variant on the line or the line-staff (functional or otherwise) organisation.

The line-staff committee is often found in big organisations, especially those in the service sector. Figure 9.15 shows a line-staff-committee organisation. The committees are indicated separately.

The advantages of a line-staff-committee organisation are:
- Input of know-how by different experts
- Greater acceptance of decisions that have involved a group of people
- Improvement of coordination and cooperation between line and staff officials

The disadvantages of a line-staff-committee organisation are:
- Officials can hide behind a group decision, so individual responsibility may decline.
- Group decisions can be time-consuming and can slow down the decision process.

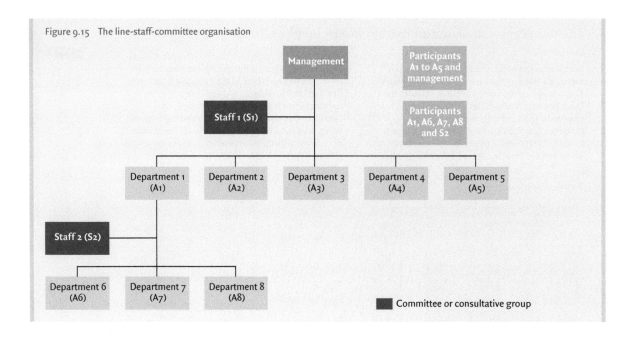

Figure 9.15 The line-staff-committee organisation

Management

Participants A1 to A5 and management

Staff 1 (S1)

Participants A1, A6, A7, A8 and S2

| Department 1 (A1) | Department 2 (A2) | Department 3 (A3) | Department 4 (A4) | Department 5 (A5) |

Staff 2 (S2)

| Department 6 (A6) | Department 7 (A7) | Department 8 (A8) |

■ Committee or consultative group

9.3.5 The matrix organisation

Matrix organisation

A matrix organisation is an organisational form in which professional specialists from various departments are temporarily transferred for a specific project over a limited time span. Some issues or problems (for example, office computerisation, the development of a new product, the construction and furnishing of a new building) may not be able to be resolved by one department only, and require the involvement of a project group. Part of the project members' working time is spent on the project and they put the rest of their hours into their normal tasks. Once the project has ended, the project team members will return to their own departments.

Project managers

This organisational form is based on the line or the line-staff organisation. Project managers responsible for completing the project will be appointed, meaning that many of the employees will be dealing with two managers: the department heads as well as the project managers. Those responsible for the project will report to a project manager. Such a format is called a 'matrix organisation' because of the way in which the lines of authority can be drawn (within a matrix – a diagram with two axes). A matrix organisation is characterised by joint authority. There needs to be a balance in the division of authority linking the interests of the project on the one hand and the requirements of the department on the other. (See Figure 9.16.)

Joint authority

The advantages of a matrix organisation are:
· The establishment of project groups means that cross-departmental tasks can be tackled.
· The existing line organisational structure can be maintained and needs specific to the organisation's leadership also met.

The disadvantages of a matrix organisation are:
· Tensions and conflicts between the project manager and department heads may occur because their interests may conflict (line managers are not always happy to release staff to set up new project teams).

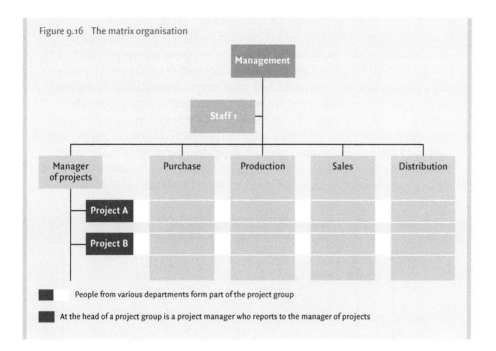

Figure 9.16   The matrix organisation

Management

Staff 1

| Manager of projects | Purchase | Production | Sales | Distribution |

Project A

Project B

■ People from various departments form part of the project group

■ At the head of a project group is a project manager who reports to the manager of projects

- Project members could take advantage of their dual roles: within the department and as project team members.
- If an individual has been busy in a project team for a long time, his contacts with his departmental colleagues and his awareness of their activities might weaken.

Figure 9.17 depicts a matrix organisation. It is an organisation whose internal specialisations fall under the following categories:
- Occupational groups
- Country desks
- Sector groups

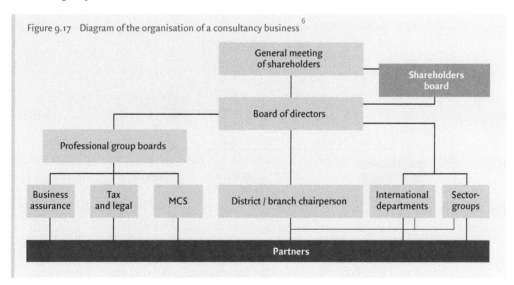

Figure 9.17   Diagram of the organisation of a consultancy business [6]

General meeting of shareholders

Shareholders board

Board of directors

Professional group boards

| Business assurance | Tax and legal | MCS | District / branch chairperson | International departments | Sector-groups |

Partners

9.3.6   Project-based organisation (PBO)

Project-based organisation

In section 9.3.5 we mentioned that in a matrix organisation, part of the line managers' authority and responsibility is assigned to the project managers. If the project management has full control and all necessary authority to run the projects, the organisation can be termed a project-based organisation. The authority of the project manager will then be equal to that of a head of department in a line organisation. Figure 9.18 compares the matrix organisation and the project-based organisation with each other. Whether the organisation can best be described as a matrix organisation or a project-based organisation will depend on the extent of the influence exerted by the line organisation and the project organisation. Another characteristic is that a project-based organisation is split up into different divisions or 'pools'. (See Figure 9.19).

Pools

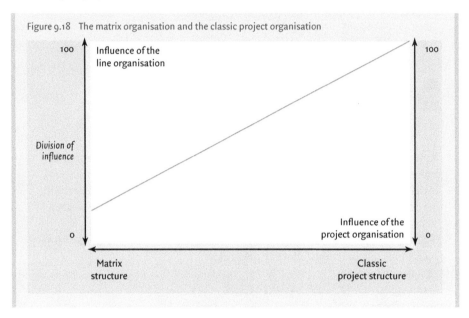

Figure 9.18   The matrix organisation and the classic project organisation

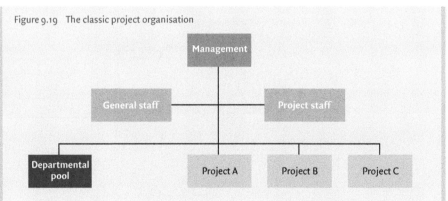

Figure 9.19   The classic project organisation

Staff from various departments are allocated to various projects. They will focus 100% percent of their time and energy on these projects. After finishing a project, these staff members will return to the departmental pool, after which they may be re-allocated to another project.

Job agencies specialising in the IT sector often have a project form of organisation, with staff from a pool being outsourced to various different projects.

The advantage of a project-based organisation is that it has a single manager, ensuring optimal functioning of those involved in the project. Its drawback is the constant shifting of its employees from one project to another, with full employment depending on the generation of new projects.

9.3.7 Internal project organisation

The last topic that we will address here is how projects can be organised internally. We will look at three variants. In practice, these are used in combination with each other. The three variants are:

1 The steering committee / working group model
2 The programme model
3 The phase model

Internal project organisation

1 The steering committee / working group model
This model of internal project organisation consists of a steering committee, a project manager and one or more working groups. The steering committee occupies the highest level in the hierarchy and is appointed by the organisation's top management.
Policy considerations with regard to certain projects will have to be approved by the steering committee. The members of a steering committee participate on an equal basis.
The steering committee is usually composed of heads of functional departments, selected on the basis of their expertise.
It is the task of the project manager to direct all aspects of a project, including the coordination, motivation, control, and monitoring of the activities of the project working groups. The project manager answers to the steering committee. The working groups are staffed by specialists and experts who take on the actual work and report to the project manager. The working groups are required to study specific problem areas and to give advice.
This model is mainly applied to organisations that sometimes carry out extensive, complex or advanced projects. (See Figure 9.20.)

Steering committee/working group model
Steering committee

Project manager

Working groups

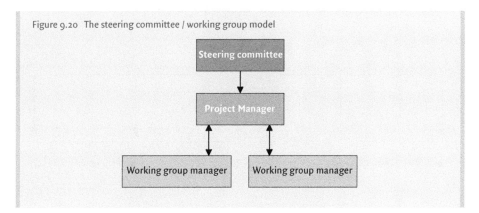

Figure 9.20 The steering committee / working group model

2 The programme model
The programme model is another option if project-based work is frequent and extensive, and complex or advanced projects are common, particularly when some parts of the projects have a close mutual connection and common features.
Such a model requires a programme manager, a location manager and a project manager. (See Figure 9.21.)

The programme model

Programme manager

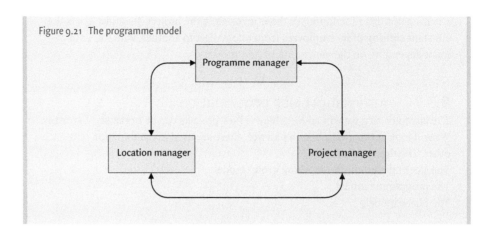

Figure 9.21 The programme model

Programme manager

Location manager

Project manager

Programme manager

The programme manager is responsible for policy coordination between the various aspects of the projects that fall within one programme and are carried out at different locations (for example, an urban renewal project).

The project manager is responsible for achieving the required project result according to agreed preconditions (for example, building a new suburb within the existing urban limits). The project manager is also jointly responsible for the operational coordination between projects that fall within a single programme.

Location manager

The location manager is responsible for the operational coordination between projects within one location or establishment (e.g. the electrical installations in a house). His / her responsibility is directed towards efficient deployment of people and resources in one location.

Phase model

3   The phase model

This model is usually applied when relatively standardised projects are regularly carried out on behalf of a certain client. Such projects are characterised by a few short-term activity phases: for example, a definition phase, a designing phase, a preparation phase, and a completion phase. At the start of each new phase the project is handed over to another team. (See Figure 9.22.)

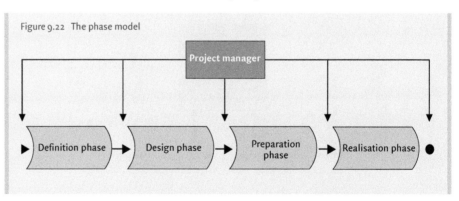

Figure 9.22 The phase model

Project manager

Definition phase → Design phase → Preparation phase → Realisation phase ●

This model has the advantage that every phase is taken care of by specialists, and there is no risk of a clash of authority. However, there is the risk of the various managers responsible for the project each having divergent opinions, and thus the potential for disagreement with the client.

9.4   Divisional organisation

In a divisional organisation, the activities and processes within a company are *Divisional organisation*
grouped around a number of related products or markets and located within divi-
sions. This organisational form is found in big, often multinational, enterprises
that produce a variety of products for various markets and are often located in a
number of different locations. (See Figure 9.23.)

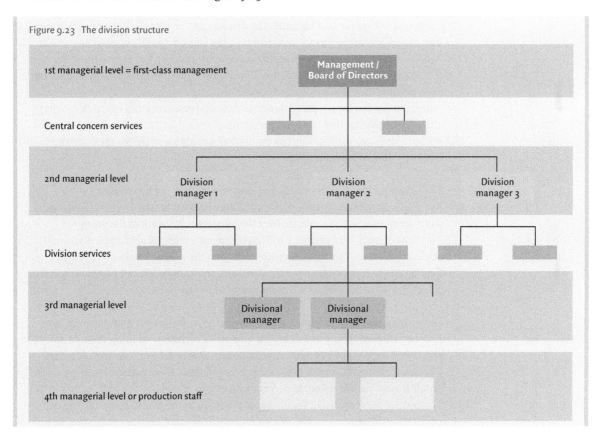

Figure 9.23 The division structure

1st managerial level = first-class management — Management / Board of Directors

Central concern services

2nd managerial level — Division manager 1 — Division manager 2 — Division manager 3

Division services

3rd managerial level — Divisional manager — Divisional manager

4th managerial level or production staff

The head of the division is the divisional director or manager. Theoretically, he / she *Divisional director*
is responsible for the strategy within that division, the way in which the division is
structured and the way in which tasks are carried out in the division.
The so-called 'group management' level is that level between the board of directors

and divisional management, and is responsible for general strategic planning, overall control, and reaching the goals of the divisions. To do this, group management uses the services of specialist staff departments, known as group services. The divisions can also consult these services. Divisions with a large degree of independence and scope will often have their own support services.

Group services

Since the divisions are completely responsible for their own achievements, management will have to give the division the necessary room to manoeuvre. The extent to which a division can remain independent of management will depend on the decisions that need to be made by the division in the future. Their powers of decision are often limited in the following areas:

· Strategic management
· Reorganisations and mergers
· Financial planning methods and procedures
· Large capital investments
· Human resources policy in relation to payment structures, selection procedures, and training

Although divisions are held responsible for generating profit they rarely have any influence over where the profit they generate goes. Management can decide to transfer any profits to divisions that are underperforming. Such a division might well become a future cash cow for the organisation (see Chapter 3).

The advantage of a divisional organisation is that the assets of a small unit can be combined with those of a big unit. The division can be regarded as a relatively small unit of a relatively big group. Other advantages of a divisional organisation are:

· A division can anticipate the wants of the customer quicker, better, and more decisively.
· A division can make use of the know-how of those group support units that are too expensive for the division alone to set up.
· A division can bid for resources (such as financial resources and research results) and people (management) within the group.
· Within a division, profitability can be used as a ready standard for measurement and evaluation of achievements.

The disadvantages of a divisional organisation include the following:

· In a division with a high level of responsibility for profits, self-interest (sometimes short-term) can take precedence over the long-term interests of the group.
· The costs of extra management and overheads as a result of setting up divisional staff support units can have a negative effect on the overall results.
· Because of the independence of the divisions, the knowledge and experience that is present in the other divisions may not be used to full advantage.

Decentralisation helps a growing company to be more flexible and more decisive. But the parent company has to keep a grip on its divisions, running them in such a way that they produce a maximum return. But what is the best way of doing that? The answer depends on external and internal factors. Theoretically, there are three possible ways for the parent to direct its divisions:

Parent company

Strategic planning

1 *The strategic planning model.* This is appropriate when the parent company focuses primarily on strategy development and places little emphasis on controlling its subsidiaries.

The strategic management

2 *The strategic management model.* This is appropriate when the parent company is mainly interested in testing and adapting strategies for its subsidiaries.

Financial management

3 *Financial management.* This is appropriate when the parent company has set itself up as an institutional investor of sorts and needs to check whether its subsidiaries meet the output requirements as laid down.

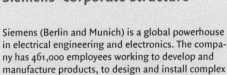

Siemens' corporate structure

Siemens (Berlin and Munich) is a global powerhouse in electrical engineering and electronics. The company has 461,000 employees working to develop and manufacture products, to design and install complex systems and projects, and to tailor a wide range of services for individual requirements. Founded more than 150 years ago, Siemens provides innovative technologies and comprehensive know-how to benefit customers in 190 countries. The main business areas include Information and Communication, Automation and Control, Power, Transportation, Medical and Lightning.

As a German stock corporation with registered offices in Berlin and Munich, Siemens is subject to German corporate law. Consequently, the company has a two-tier management and oversight structure consisting of a Managing Board and a Supervisory Board (a two-tier board structure). As the company's top management body, the Managing Board is obliged to promote the interests of the company at all times and to drive sustainable growth in company value. Its nine-member Corporate Executive Committee cooperates with the President and CEO to define overall company policies and is also

responsible for determining the company's strategic orientation, for planning and finalising the company's budget, for allocating resources, and for monitoring the executive management of each group. The Managing Board also prepares the company's quarterly reports, the annual stand-alone financial statements of Siemens AG and the Consolidated Financial Statements of Siemens. The Supervisory Board oversees and advises the Managing Board in its management of company business. It discusses business development, planning, strategy and implementation at regular intervals. It also reviews Siemens' quarterly reports and approves the annual, stand-alone financial statements of Siemens AG, as well as the Consolidated Financial Statements of Siemens, taking into account both the audit reports provided by the independent auditors and the results of the review conducted by the Audit Committee. In addition, the Supervisory Board appoints the members of the Managing Board and allocates members' individual duties.

Source: www.siemens.com, 2006

Strategic planning can be considered as being the opposite of financial management; strategic management as being an intermediate form.

The main internal and external circumstances that determine which method best suits a decentralised company can be divided into two groups.

1   *The degree of solidarity between the subsidiary companies*
- *The portfolio.*   If the portfolio is one-sided then strategic planning is ideal. If the portfolio is diverse, financial management is more appropriate.
- *The organisational structure.*   If the subsidiaries are relatively close, strategic planning is necessary. If the units are independent, financial management is the proper way to direct them.
- *Synergy.* If the subsidiaries are relatively close, strategic planning will be necessary to generate synergy.

2   *The extent of intervention by the parent company*
- *The preferred method of planning.*   When the goal of the main company is mainly to obtain long-term results then strategic planning is best. If short-term results are required, financial management is more suitable.
- *The level of risk of decisions.*   When decisions are high risk, strategic planning is the obvious choice. With less risky decisions, financial management should be used.
- *Stability of the business sector.*   With a stable business environment financial management is ideal; in a changeable environment strategic planning is better.
- *The maturity of the organisation.*   With organisations that are rapidly developing, strategic planning is desirable.
- *The performance.*   If company performance is uncertain, the parent organisation will be more involved in directing, so strategic planning will be necessary. When performance shows a high degree of certainty, financial management is ideal.

Figure 9.24 illustrates the choice of directive method diagrammatically.[7]

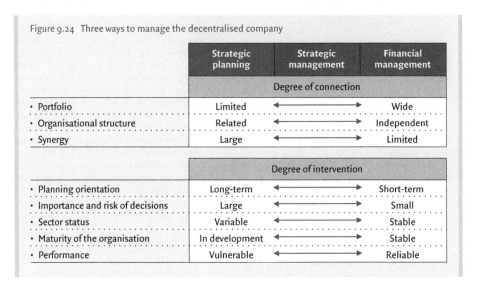

Figure 9.24 Three ways to manage the decentralised company

	Strategic planning	Strategic management	Financial management
	Degree of connection		
• Portfolio	Limited	←——————→	Wide
• Organisational structure	Related	←——————→	Independent
• Synergy	Large	←——————→	Limited
	Degree of intervention		
• Planning orientation	Long-term	←——————→	Short-term
• Importance and risk of decisions	Large	←——————→	Small
• Sector status	Variable	←——————→	Stable
• Maturity of the organisation	In development	←——————→	Stable
• Performance	Vulnerable	←——————→	Reliable

9.5 Mintzberg and organisational structures

Henry Mintzberg

As mentioned briefly in Chapter 1, Henry Mintzberg's book The structuring of organisations (1979) attempted to bring together the main theories concerning the structuring of organisations. In one of his later works, Mintzberg on Management (1991), he expands on and refines his theories.

9.5.1 Organisational properties

According to Mintzberg, the most appropriate organisational structure will become apparent by linking a number of the organisation's properties. Instead of organisa-
Configurations
tional structures, Mintzberg talks about organisational configurations. Figure 9.25 shows the properties that determine an organisational structure. They are:
- The organisational parts
- Coordination mechanisms
- Design parameters
- Contingency factors (situational factors).

The organisational part

The organisational part
The so-called primary processes – work that is directly related to the production of goods and services – form the basis of the organisation. Mintzberg calls them the
Operational core
operational core.
Every organisation needs to have at least one manager who is able to supervise all processes and manage the organisation. This individual is located within the strategic apex. In larger organisations, the Board of Directors and the Council of
Strategic apex
Commissioners form the strategic apex.
When an organisation increases in size there will be a need for more managers. They do not necessarily have to be managers who direct staff, but may include man-
Middle line
agers who direct other managers. An intermediate or middle line will thus arise. This layer of management was referred to in Chapter 6 as middle management. The more complex the organisation becomes, the more need there will be for staff who are able to analyse and support the primary processes. These staff will make

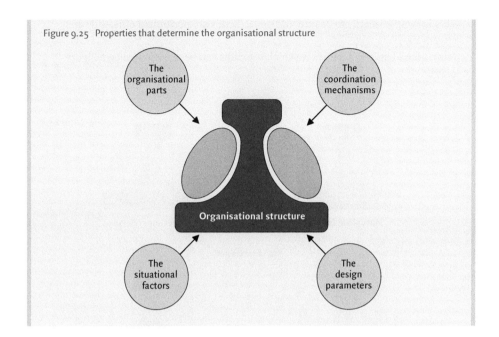

Figure 9.25 Properties that determine the organisational structure

The organisational parts

The coordination mechanisms

Organisational structure

The situational factors

The design parameters

plans and manage the work. This section of the organisation is known as the technical staff area. Supervisors, planners, and planning engineers fall under this category. Many organisations have support staff who supply services of one kind or another to the various departments. Salary administrators, public relations officers and Research & Development staff fall under the category of support staff.

Technical staff

Support staff

Figure 9.26 shows that the narrow strategic apex is connected to a broad operational core. This is a hierarchical structure. The support staff divisions fall outside the hierarchy and can only indirectly exercise influence over the operational core and the strategic apex.

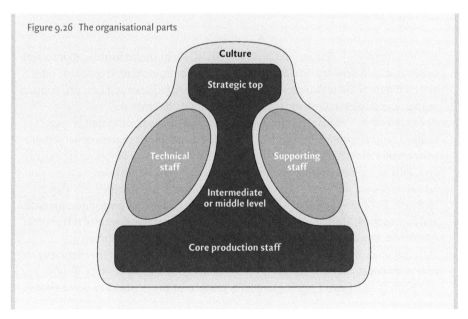

Figure 9.26 The organisational parts

Culture

Strategic top

Technical staff

Supporting staff

Intermediate or middle level

Core production staff

Coordination mechanisms

A characteristic feature of organisations is that current work must be divided amongst employees (task division) and that these activities have to be coordinated.

Coordination mechanisms

This is done primarily to ensure that the activities are performed efficiently and effectively.

Mintzberg identifies six ways in which activities can be coordinated (see Figure 9.27):

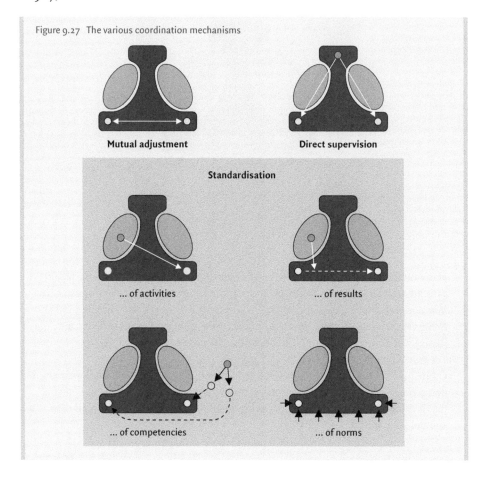

Figure 9.27 The various coordination mechanisms

Mutual adjustment

Direct supervision

Standardisation

... of activities

... of results

... of competencies

... of norms

1 *Mutual adjustment.* This method is characterised by significant formal and informal communication between workers. Regular consultation, evaluation sessions, speech and communication techniques, internships, meeting facilities and informal contact are some examples of the form that this communication may take.

2 *Direct supervision.* Managers issue assignments and instructions to staff in respect of tasks to be performed. This can happen during a review of progress or as part of a performance evaluation interview. The manager will make use of various techniques and skills as well as applying his / her own experience and knowledge.

3 *Standardisation of work processes.* In this method, tasks are specified and standardised (usually by technical staff). This is done on the basis of set procedures, manuals and instructions. Mechanisation and automation are essential aspects of this process (the production of standardised letters for making offers, for memos etc.).

4 *Standardisation of outputs.* In this method, a specification of results is drawn up. It may be related to financial targets for each company unit, to the content of contracts, to customer satisfaction norms, to quality criteria for the products to be developed, and so on.

5 *Standardisation of skills.* The activities to be performed are coordinated on the basis of the training and experience of the individuals. For example, a surgeon and an anaesthetist will be able to anticipate each other's standardised procedures virtually automatically.

6 *Standardisation of norms.*   In this method the staff within an organisation will behave similarly as they will share a similar set of opinions (a religious order, for example). Norms can also develop from a point of view shared by those in an organisation.

Research has shown that coordination mechanisms have a certain natural order. As the work becomes more complicated, the coordination mechanisms will shift from mutual adjustment to direct supervision. They will then shift to standardisation of work processes, output, skills, or norms then back again to mutual adjustment. This coordination mechanism also adapts well to complex processes.
All organisations make use of all of various different coordination mechanisms. However, they will normally have a preference for one.
Coordination mechanisms are arguably the most essential elements of an organisational structure.

Natural order

Design parameters
Design parameters are those parameters that determine the way tasks are divided in an organisation. The main design variables are:

Design parameters

a *Specialisation of tasks.*   This refers to the number of tasks per function and the way that responsibilities and authority are assigned.
b *Size of departments or groups.*   This is connected to the number of employees per unit or group.
c *Centralisation or decentralisation.*   This is the degree to which decision-making authority is assigned to staff lower down the hierarchy.
d *Formalisation of behaviour.*   The extent to which things such as rules, procedures and job descriptions standardise the duties.

Contingency factors (situational factors)
During the 1960s, a number of experts in organisational theory suggested that no one best organisational structure existed. Instead, it was claimed that the most appropriate form of organisational structure depends on the situation facing the organisation at that particular time. This approach is called the contingency approach.
Contingency or situational factors influence the way parts of the organisation are set up, the choice of coordination mechanism, and the most appropriate design parameters. Each of these aspects will also have an effect on the situational factors. According to Mintzberg the organisational structure is dependent on the following situational factors:

Contingency factors

1 *The technical system of an organisation:*   the level of automation that is used by the operational core (e.g. machines, automation). Organisations with complex technical systems generally have extensive professional support departments.
2 *The environmental characteristics of the organisation (dynamic, complex).*   Organisations with a dynamic environment have an organic organisational structure. With a complex environment, one will opt for decentralisation of responsibilities and authority.
3 *The age and size of the organisation.*   As an organisation ages or grows in size, it will also become more formal in nature.

The organisational properties previously mentioned (the organisation's parts, coordination mechanisms, design parameters and situational factors) must match each other in such a way as to create coherence. The configuration approach can be described as the 'mutual adjustment of the organisation's properties'.

9.5.2 Organisational forms

During his research involving hundreds of companies, Mintzberg isolated the following seven different organisational configurations:

1. The entrepreneurial organisation
2. The machine bureaucracy
3. The professional organisation
4. The diversified organisation
5. The innovative organisation
6. The missionary organisation
7. The political organisation

Figure 9.28 looks at the most important properties of each configuration.

Figure 9.28 Matrix of most important organisational properties per configuration

Name of configuration	Characteristic organisational part	Coordination mechanism	Design parameters	Situational factors
Entrepreneurial organisation	• strategic top	• direct supervision	• organic decentralised structure	• developed technical system • well-organised and dynamic environment • young and small organisation
Machine bureaucracy	• technical staff	• standardisation of activities	• formalised organisational behaviour • limited horizontal system • decentralisation	• rationalised oriented technical system • well-organised and stable environment • large and mature organisation
Professional organisation	• core production staff	• standardisation of knowledge and competencies	• horizontal decentralisation	• simple technical system • complex but stable system
Diversified organisation	• middle level	• standardisation of results	• limited vertical decentralisation	• considerable market diversity • largest and most mature organisations
Innovative organisation	• support staff	• mutual adjustment	• selective decentralisation	• high-quality and most automated technical system • complex and dynamic environment • usually a young organisation
Missionary organisation	• ideology	• standardisation of norms	• decentralisation	• differs
Political organisation	• none	• none	• differs	• differs

The next section briefly explains the above-mentioned configurations.

The entrepreneurial organisation

Entrepreneurial organisation

Figure 9.29 shows that the entrepreneurial organisation has a flat organisational structure, without staff departments. There is no space for middle management either. All activities revolve around the entrepreneur or manager, who has a charismatic and / or autocratic style of leadership. The strategy is somewhat visionary in nature. The entrepreneurial organisation is flexible, spontaneous in its actions and highly market-oriented.

Visionary in nature

Figure 9.29 The entrepreneurial organisation

This organisational form is encountered in small, new businesses. Communication is informal in character and the work is rarely, if ever, standardised.

The great advantage of this organisational form is that one can quickly anticipate changing market circumstances. The disadvantages of the form lie in its driving force: namely, dependence on the entrepreneur. The strategy pursued risks being unbalanced or unable to be implemented.

The machine bureaucracy

The machine bureaucracy contains formalised communication channels and decision-making processes. Technical and support staff play an important role. The technical staff are charged with the standardisation of duties such as the development of procedures, work instructions and plans. Figure 9.30 shows that both supporting units are separated from the 'trunk' of the organisation. These departments are independent.

Machine bureaucracy

The process of strategic management may look more like strategic programming, and in fact, a strategy is often formed with the help of various planning procedures.

Strategic programming

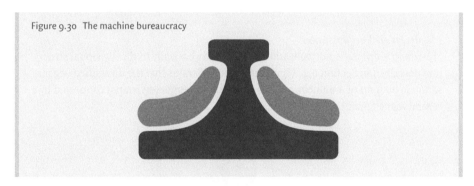

Figure 9.30 The machine bureaucracy

The machine organisational structure is typical of larger organisations with a relatively stable business environment. Typical businesses include mass production manufacturers, non-profit organisations, organisations with large-scale services, and organisations where the priority is the control of processes and safety. The advantage of this organisational form is that it is rational, reliable and consistent. However, it runs the risk of 'control obsession': of management trying to organise everything neatly and according to rules and procedures, sometimes at the cost of efficiency and effectiveness. Another disadvantage is that machine organisations are not really change-inclined. If and when changes take place they therefore can seem more like revolutions.

The professional organisation

This structure is found frequently in organisations with highly skilled or professional staff, in which activities are carried out in a fairly routine or professional manner. Intensive training programs can be developed to master difficult tasks.

Professional organisation

Coordination of the professional organisation is based on the standardisation of knowledge and skills. Universities and colleges, hospitals, accountant offices, and social aid agencies fall under this organisational form. Figure 9.31 shows that the operational core and support staff are of great importance. Support staff are very important because they assist the more expensive professionals at the operational core (specialists, professors etc.) to an extent that allows these professionals to concentrate on their primary tasks. Technical staff is limited as work at the operational core is influenced by the professional's autonomy.

Autonomy

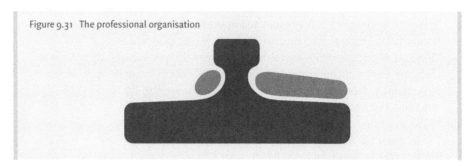

Figure 9.31 The professional organisation

In a professional organisation, the strategy pursued will be stable in character, although the minor details will change constantly. The advantages of this organisational form are the autonomy of the staff members and the democratic character of the organisation. The disadvantages are related to the existence of coordination problems between different functions or fields, the danger of professionals abusing their autonomy, and possible resistance to innovation.

The diversified organisation

Diversified organisation

Mintzberg's diversified organisation corresponds basically to the divisional structure described in Section 9.4. Figure 9.32 demonstrates that the diversified organisation is built up of a number of semi-independent units (divisions) connected by a central management or head office.

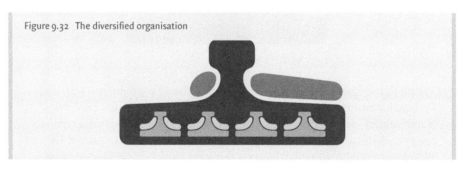

Figure 9.32 The diversified organisation

Product or market combinations

The divisions are active in different product or market combinations. There will only be a small central technical department because the divisions themselves manage their own support units. According to Mintzberg, the diversified form functions best with a machine organisation in its divisions. The head office formulates targets in terms of sales growth and output that the divisions have to reach. This organisational form can be found to a greater or lesser extent in the biggest 500 companies in the world (the so-called Fortune 500). The head office defines the group strategy. The separate divisions develop their own company strategies.

Spreading of risks

An important advantage of this organisational form is the spreading of group activ-

McKinsey: a successful partnership model for professionals

When James O. McKinsey founded McKinsey in 1926, he could not have imagined the reach his small firm would eventually have. More than 75 years later, the firm has grown into a global partnership serving three of the world's five largest companies and two-thirds of the Fortune 1000. McKinsey already had an established practice in budgeting and finance when he decided to test his theory that so-called 'management engineers' could go beyond rescuing sick companies to helping healthy companies thrive and grow. His vision opened the door to others who shaped a new profession as they built one of the world's best-known professional services firms. And through the years, his original mission has remained the same (with a little rewording from decade to decade): to help clients make distinctive, lasting, and substantial improvements in their performance and to build a great firm that is able to attract, develop, excite and retain exceptional people.

Source: www.McKinsey.com, 2006

ity risks. In addition, the delegation of responsibility and authority to the divisions, (which, after all, are closer to their market) allows faster reactions within the market place. One of the inherent dangers of this form is its potential to be very expensive because non-profitable divisions may be propped up with financial support from other divisions.

Delegation of responsibility

The innovative organisation

The innovative organisation (Mintzberg's ad-hocracy concept), features a highly organised structure. There is little standardisation. The organisation focusses on innovation and avoids getting into fixed patterns of behaviour. This organisational form is made up of multidisciplinary teams or project groups in which functional experts, managers or coaches, and support staff work together to bring about innovative processes. Two forms of innovative organisations can be identified, namely the operational innovative organisation and the managerial innovative organisation. The former refers to the fusion of managerial and operations actions into one single activity. For example, in some sorts of project work, the design, planning, and execution are indistinguishable. Figure 9.33 shows the broad 'trunk' of the operational innovative organisation. This trunk includes the strategic axis, the middle level, the technical and support staff, and the operational core.

Innovative organisation
Ad-hocracy

Operational innovative organisation

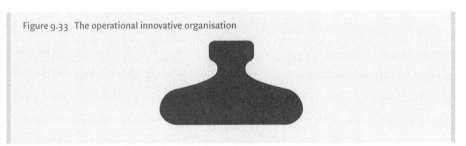

Figure 9.33 The operational innovative organisation

In a managerial innovative organisation, a distinction is made between managerial and operational activities. In this form the operational core is separated from the rest of the organisation. The dotted line in Figure 9.34 indicates the separated off operational core.

Managerial innovative organisation

The operational core will be separated off if its activities are similar to those characteristic of a machine organisation, thus preventing innovation on the part of management. This problem could be avoided in either of two ways:
· By setting up a separate company to carry out the operational activities
· By completely discarding or contracting out the operational activities.

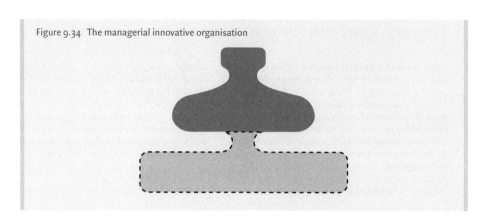

Figure 9.34 The managerial innovative organisation

As was indicated before, innovative organisations can be found in complex and dynamic environments. Their strategy is developed from the bottom up and management tends to form it itself rather than assigning it. The great advantage of the innovative organisation is that it is effective when innovation is required. A disadvantage is that this effectiveness may sometimes be at the expense of efficiency. Lack of clarity may also cause problems.

Despite these drawbacks, in Mintzberg's opinion, the innovative organisation was the organisational form of the second half of the 20th century. It has been widely adopted, especially in relatively young business sectors such as advertising, automation, the film industry, aviation and space travel, and research.

The missionary organisation

Missionary organisation
Ideology

A missionary organisation is based on a strong ideology and is found when an elaborate system of values and beliefs exists among the employees of an organisation. This sets this organisational apart from others. The values and beliefs are deeply anchored in the organisation. Leadership is charismatic and the aim of the organisation is clear and inspiring.

An ideology may be adopted by and added to any of the previously described configurations, particularly by an entrepreneurial or innovative organisation. When an ideology is the driving force, this will give rise to the missionary organisation.

Distinct form

The missionary organisation has no distinct form (see Figure 9.35). Staff work together in small units, all aligned in the same direction. There is little difference in status between employees.

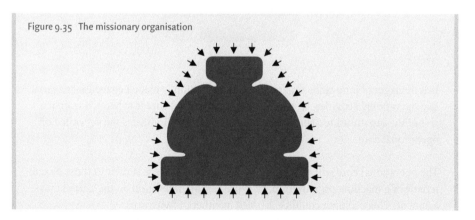

Figure 9.35 The missionary organisation

In its purest form, individuals will take it in turns to rotate their work tasks. The organisation is held together by standardisation of norms, with great importance being attached to the selection, indoctrination and socialisation of new colleagues. Missionary organisations are often very successful. Their success can be attributed to the fact that its members are not in conflict with each other. They identify completely with the organisation, and dedicate themselves fully to it. Missionary organisations do run the risk of becoming isolated. The traditional Israeli kibbutz is an example of a missionary organisation.

The political organisation

The way an organisation functions is determined by a number of influences. They include ideology, authority, expertise and politics. Of these, the only influence that is not recognised as legitimate is that of politics. Politics has to do with the use (or misuse) of power.

Political organisation

Individuals often use politics for their own personal ends, with as a consequence, conflicts or rifts between individuals or departments. In practically all of these configurations, politics plays a role to a lesser or greater extent. If to a greater extent, we describe it as a political organisation.

The arrows in Figure 9.36 show the different political influences within the organisation, all of which will have an effect on the strategy and the structure of the organisation. Political activities in organisations are often described in terms of political games.

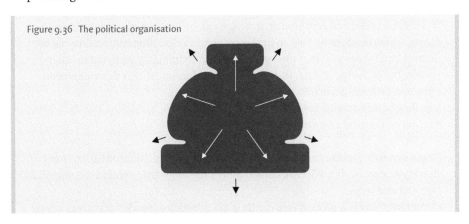

Figure 9.36   The political organisation

Political influences can be regarded as positive in some problem organisational situations. If legitimate influence systems fail to bring about necessary changes, political influences may provide a solution.

The danger of organisations under strong political influence is that most of the employees' energy will be directed internally and a chain of conspiracies and conflicts may arise.

9.6   Communication and consultation structures

The greater the complexity of an organisational structure, the greater the necessity for coordination between people, departments, divisions and locations in order to ensure that an organisation works effectively and efficiently. Managers have six different integration tools that may contribute to improvement of coordination and communication at their disposal. (See Figure 9.37.)

Figure 9.37 Types and examples of integration mechanisms

Simple

Direct contact A marketing manager and a research & development manager meet to 'brainstorm' new product development.

Liaison role A manager and a project manager identify the best product ideas to develop.

Task forces Various staff from Marketing, Research & Development and Production meet to talk about releasing a product on to the market.

Crossfunctional group A cross-functional group derived from various divisions is formed to supervise the product development process until the moment of product release.

Integration roles and divisions Senior management provides staff from cross-functional groups with important information from other groups and divisions.

Matrix structures Senior managers decide to adopt a matrix structure to ensure that a lot of new products can be developed simultaneously.

Complex

Communication and consultative structure

Designing a communication and consultative structure is one of the necessary aspects of creating an organisational structure. After all, company activities must be linked to each other. It is very easy for coherence to disappear during a division of tasks as some activities may be split and transferred to employees in various different departments. Coherence can be restored by providing a good communication and consultative structure.

Coordination facility
Communication

A communication and consultative structure can be thought of as a coordination facility which needs to be built in into every organisation. Communication can be defined as all those activities through which information is transferred to other people: the exchange of data, facts, thoughts, and feelings. This description contains two essential aspects:

1 The flow of information throughout the organisation
2 The interaction and cooperation between people.

These two core aspects need to remain in balance. After all, if information is not flowing smoothly, this will have consequences for cooperation within the organisation and vice versa.

Communication is a process (see Figure 9.38) in which a 'sender' transmits a message to a 'receiver'. This receiver interprets the message and sends a reaction to the sender, thereby enabling the sender to check whether the message sent has been understood correctly and that there have been no misunderstandings during the transmission.

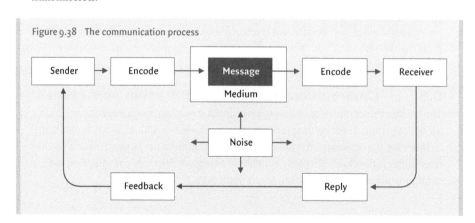

Figure 9.38 The communication process

Communication can take place in two ways within an organisation: via personal communication between two or more people and via impersonal communication using communicative means such as memos, e-mail and staff magazines. Personal information is, in general, the more effective, because of the possibility of obtaining direct feedback. Impersonal information has the advantage that the receiver can decide himself or herself when he / she will take in the information. The disadvantage is lack of certainty about the quality of reception: will the message be understood? Will it even be read?

Personal communication
Impersonal communication

A communication structure can be described in terms of the way and the direction in which the communication takes place. Communication can be either written or oral in nature, and follow one of three directions:

Communication structure

a *Horizontal communication*. This includes communication between divisions, departments or even individuals at the same hierarchical level of the organisation.

Horizontal communication

b *Vertical communication*. In contrast, this is communication between divisions, departments, or individuals at different hierarchical levels.

Vertical communication

c *Lateral communication*. This refers to relatively open communication that takes place between all individuals within the organisation, irrespective of their hierarchical level.

Lateral communication

A communication matrix is a good way of ensuring that everybody is kept sufficiently informed. Use of such a tool will ensure that no group is overlooked, the best means of communication is used, the messages are spread out, and the best times for optimal effect are determined. Table 9.2 shows an example of such a communication matrix.

Communication matrix

The ten most frequent mistakes involving internal communication

1 Communicating too soon. A message that is communicated too early will be forgotten by the time the contents of the message have become current. The staff will have had their expectations aroused, but when everything goes quiet after the meeting, the bubble of enthusiasm will simply burst.

2 Insufficient communication. If there is insufficient communication, the staff will get the impression that nothing good is going on. An absence of communication will therefore lead to distrust.

3 Unstructured communication. A lot of communication takes place in an ad hoc manner, with the risk of forgetting some groups of staff. A so-called communications matrix that sorts out every internal and external communication activity is a good way of preventing this from happening.

4 Badly adjusted contents. Be aware of your target group. Communicate with them in suitable ways.

5 One-sided communication. Many organisations only communicate from the top down. Proposals and ideas for improvement from the bottom rarely make it to the top. One will achieve better results with two-way communication.

6 Communicating in writing. If there is a lot of time pressure, you can easily find yourself communicating more in writing, thus paying little attention to the message and whether it has been satisfactorily received by the intended target group.

7 Always being the sender. Many top managers think that they have to send ('transmit') messages all the time. However, communication may be more effective if others are encouraged to transmit.

8 Unworkable working agreements. Research has shown that a work agreement is a strong aid to communication. This is because it is two-way communication and the barrier for participation is low.

9 Saying once is enough. Many think that if they say or write something once, then everybody will know about it. Research has shown this to be incorrect. Repeating the message enhances its chances of being remembered (as well as of being remembered accurately).

10 Communication about changes. In many companies, the communication is one-sided. Rather than merely communicating those things that are going to change, it is also nice to change the method of communication itself. It will provoke a response and go a long way to improving involvement, motivation and the atmosphere.

Table 9.2   Communication matrix

Target groups	Means of communication	Senders	Planning
Internal 1 Department heads	1.1 Staff meeting	1.1 General manager	1.1 Initial
2 Initiative takers	2.1 Extraordinary meetings	2.1 Project manager	2.1 Same day as department heads
3 Staff	3.1 General staff meeting	3.1 General manager	3.1 Day after department heads
	3.2 Speech on notice boards	3.2 Human resources posts	3.2 Right after the meeting
	3.3 Discussion of work progress	3.3 Department heads	3.3 Within two weeks of the meeting
	3.4 Interview in staff magazine	3.4 Project manager and two executives	3.4 Within a month of the meeting
4 Works council	4.1 Extraordinary works council meeting	4.1 General manager	4.1 On the same day as department heads
External 5 Shareholders	5.1 Extraordinary shareholders meeting	5.1 General manager	5.1 The week preceding the department heads
6 Customers	6.1 Informing big clients verbally	6.1 Head of sales/ account managers	6.1 Within two weeks of the staff meeting
	6.2 Informing small clients in writing	6.2 Inside service sales	6.2 Right after the staff meeting
7 Suppliers	7.1 Informing regular suppliers verbally	7.1 Buyers	7.1 Within two weeks of the staff meeting
	7.2 Informing remaining suppliers in writing	7.2 Purchase	7.2 Right after the staff meeting

Source: *Kwaliteit in bedrijf*, May 2001

Consultative body

Communication between staff in different departments or divisions and on different hierarchical levels of an organisation can take place via a suitable consultative body such as a consultative group or committee. These consultative bodies can be set up within the organisation on either a temporary or a permanent basis.

'Linking pin' structure

The so-called 'linking pin' structure (Figure 9.39), developed by Rensis Likert, depicts less standard consultative situations.

Figure 9.39   A few forms of Likert's pin-structure

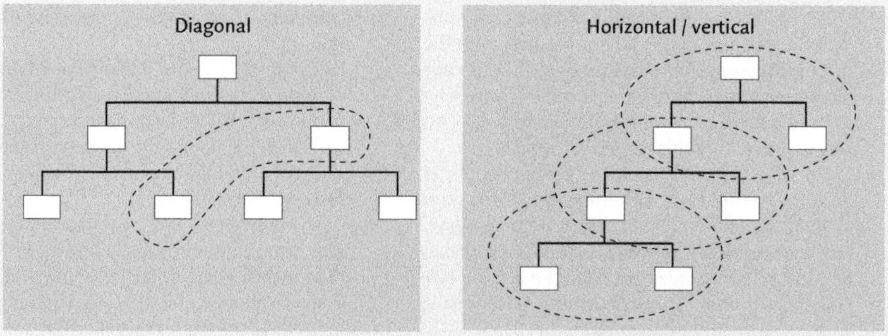

Likert described an organisational structure which features overlapping groups. The linking pin is the leader of a lower-level group. This person participates in and can influence decision-making within a higher level group. The link may be hori-

Structure and organisation

zontal, vertical, or diagonal. Likert also argued that workers would be more motivated if they participated as members of consultative groups rather than individually. Such a form of participation could deliver deliver better results for the organisation.

Organisations are in a constant state of development. In the next chapter, this issue will be looked at again.

9.7 Developments in the structuring of organisations

The business environment has changed more rapidly over the past fifteen years than at any other time. Such environmental events as the Internet revolution that started in the middle of the 1990s, increasing internationalisation, and the various social, political, and economical changes that were described in Chapter 2 have been of great significance for the commercial world and are implicated in the creation and disappearance of many businesses as well as in the changes experienced by many. Organisations that cannot adapt fast enough to new market circumstances are not likely to survive the coming years. Managers often describe traditional organisations as being too slow and bureaucratic, not being innovative enough, and being inadequately focussed on the needs of their customers. Their costs may be too high to be able to remain competitive. In other words, their efficiency and effectiveness may be inadequate for long-term achievement. It is thus important to identify what organisational characteristics are able that satisfy the demands of the 21st century customer.

In this section, a number of organisational structure trends already visible in a great many companies will be described. They are:
· Horizontal organisations
· Cluster organisations
· Virtual organisations
· Flat organisations

Horizontal organisations
Traditionally, organisations are structured according to functional divisions such as purchasing, production, marketing, sales, and distribution. As mentioned earlier in this chapter, these are known as functional organisations.

One of the disadvantages of such a form of structuring is that while the results achieved by the various divisions may be excellent, this will not necessarily lead to the best end result for the customer and therefore for the company. The problem may lie in insufficient interface between the activities of the divisions.

Organisations that are designed to optimise coordination between activities in the various divisions are known as horizontal or workflow organisations. The main reasons for transforming functional organisations into organisations that are more horizontal are:

Horizontal organisations

· Increased customer satisfaction
· Boosting of product and service quality
· Reduction in operating costs
· Increase in company process efficiency

Horizontal organisations have become a lot easier to set up with the arrival of modern information and communication technologies. (See Figure 9.40.)

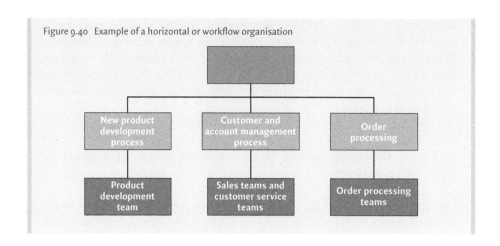
Figure 9.40 Example of a horizontal or workflow organisation

| New product development process | Customer and account management process | Order processing |
| Product development team | Sales teams and customer service teams | Order processing teams |

Cluster organisations

Organisations are making increasing use of people with large amounts of knowledge, skill, and experience. All organisational forms make use of teams: project teams, quality teams, cross-functional teams. Professional specialists may form part of one or more teams. Teams are disbanded once the goals have been reached. An organisational form in which a team structure is central is known as a cluster organisation (see Figure 9.41). According to the management guru, Peter Drucker (see also Chapter 1), most organisations will be structured around teams in the future.

Cluster organisation

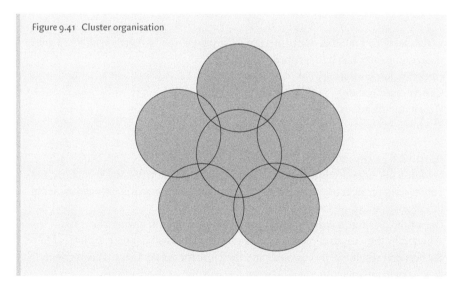
Figure 9.41 Cluster organisation

Virtual organisations

Up until the industrial revolution, employees worked at home under the instruction of employers. The industrial revolution saw to it that work moved from the home to large factories, and later to modern offices.

The arrival of the Internet and other technologies has made it possible for people to communicate with each other, to consult, to learn and to exchange information without actually having to come together in a physical location such as an office. They may e-mail each other or send text messages, use voicemail and hold virtual video conferences.

One consequence of this is that companies are no longer dependent for the execution of their activities upon people who are situated in a particular office. They can make use of people in geographically different parts of the world, and not only freelancers but also company employees. Companies that wish to enter a strategic alliance to jointly develop or sell new products and services have enhanced opportunities as a result.

Companies that rely heavily on such communicative situations are known as virtual or network organisations. Such a kind of organisation is also termed an 'unlimited company'. (See Figure 9.42.)

Virtual organisations

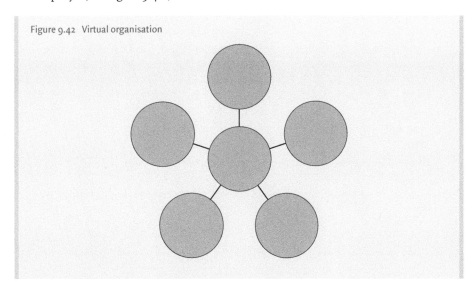

Figure 9.42 Virtual organisation

This organisational structure can deliver huge cost savings since there is no need to develop and to maintain a complex, international organisational structure. Many people in such organisations do not even have an employment contract but are bound to the virtual organisation via project work.

Flat organisations

The traditional organisation has a great number of management levels. The task of management has always been managing people and at the same time obtaining, processing, and distributing information. The Internet and other technologies have ensured that the latter aspect has been significantly simplified and consequently is less time-intensive. Managers are also delegating an increasing number of the tasks that they used to do, such as job planning, reporting, and administrative work.

Flat organisations

The above-mentioned developments plus the increasing pressure on organisations to work faster and cheaper have lead to a dramatic decrease in the number of management levels during the last decade. Many Fortune 500 companies have seen the number of management levels reduced from ten or more to four or five.

Another issue that is occupying managers (and scientists) is optimal organisation size. As an organisation grows, there is always a potential for loss of vitality. Managers have concluded that it is not so much the size of the organisation that counts, but how complex it is. Its complexity can be limited in various ways: for example, by creating small, more or less independent units in organisations, by decentralising decisions and authority, by streamlining company processes and by using modern information and communication technologies.

This chapter has aimed to show that there are various different ways of structuring organisations. There is no such thing as an ideal form. However, managers and experts do agree that an organisational structure must be consistent with the strategy of that organisation.

Doing business in Italy

How Italians organise and process information
In Italy, information is readily available and frequently discussed at great length. However, opinions rarely change. Information tends to be processed subjectively and associatively. Italians will look at each situation on its own merits. They will not expect laws or rules to provide solutions.

What Italians accept as evidence
Subjective feelings are more important than faith in an ideology or objective facts when deciding what is true. However, the ideologies of the church do permeate nearly all transactions. Italians who have a higher educational level tend to use facts to back their arguments.

The basis of behaviour
The ideologies of the Roman Catholic Church exert more influence than others. Value systems in the predominant culture – how right is distinguished from wrong, good from evil, and so on – are described under the next three headings.

The locus of decision-making
The individual is responsible for his or her decisions but is often expected to defer to the interests of the family or organisational unit. There is an admiration for urban life and an enduring loyalty to region and family.

Sources of anxiety reduction
While the extended family is getting smaller, it is still the major source of security and stability. Obtaining success in the eyes of the extended family and society is a major source of anxiety. While the strong Catholic and Communist elements would seem to oppose each other, in reality they are not seen as completely incompatible. For most, the church provides a sense of structure. Italians are remarkably diverse, though

they also have a strong capacity for social and cultural resilience and continuity.

Issues of equality/inequality
There are extreme contrasts between rich and poor. The population is stratified by income. Patron-client relationships provide a strong social and political base. Even though there is a large German-speaking group in the north and many mutually unintelligible dialects, there is one standard language that binds the country together. Women have made slow progress toward equality.

Ten Examples of Italian business practices
1 Italian business people prefer to deal with people they know, even if that acquaintance was limited to a perfunctory handshake at a trade fair. Before you invest in a trip to Italy, be sure to engage a representative to make appropriate introductions and appointments for you.
2 Be very aware of summer vacation periods. Most firms are closed in August. If you write asking for an appointment in mid-July, you may not get a satisfactory reply until September.
3 Italians like to become acquainted with each other and engage in small talk before getting down to business. They are hospitable and attentive. Expect to answer questions about your family.
4 The pace of negotiations is usually slower than in the US or the UK. The more important the contract, the more going on behind the scenes. Any obvious sense of urgency will be seen as weakening one's bargaining position.
5 A dramatic change in demands at the last minute is often a technique to unsettle the other side. Be patient and calm; just when it appears impossible, the contract may materialise.
6 Conversational subjects that are highly appreciated are Italian culture, art, food, wine, sports such as cycling and (in particular) soccer, family, Italian scenery, and films.
7 Italian hospitality plays an important role in business life, and most often means dining in a restaurant. No matter how you feel, refusing an invitation will offend.
8 Dining is a serious business, and real prestige can be gained or lost at the table. One may bring up business at a propitious moment.
9 Shake hands with everyone present when arriving and leaving. At a large gathering, if no one is providing formal introductions, it is regarded as proper to shake hands and introduce yourself.
10 Business gifts are sometimes given at a senior managerial level. They should be small and not obviously expensive, but made by craftsmen of prestige.

Source: Kiss, Bow, or Shake Hands: How to Do Business in Sixty Countries, by Terri Morrison, Wayne A. Conaway and George A. Borden, Adams Media, 2006

BUSINESS CULTURE ORIENTATION

Summary

Designing an organisational structure is a challenge: to reach the goals of the organisation people and resources must be utilised optimally. When designing an organisational structure, both the organic and the staff structures need to be taken into account.

Task division has both horizontal (functional or division formation) and vertical (vertical differentiation) aspects. Formal organisational structures can be represented using an organisational chart.

Organisational systems can be categorised according to a number of characteristics. These organisational forms include the following:

- Line organisation
- Line-staff organisation
- Funtional and line staff organisation
- Matrix organisation
- Project-based organisation
- Divisional organisation.

According to Mintzberg, organisational structures (or as he terms them, organisational configurations) can be determined by matching a number of organisational characteristics with each other. Their main determining properties are their individual parts, coordination activities, planning criteria, and contingency factors. Mintzberg identified the following configurations:

1 The entrepreneurial organisation
2 The machine bureaucracy
3 The professional organisation
4 The diversified organisation
5 The innovative organisation
6 The missionary organisation
7 The political organisation

One of the main aspects of organisational structure design is the design of a communication and consultative structure. Two important tools in this area are the so-called communication matrix and the linking pin-structure.

The business environment has changed faster in the past fifteen years than ever before. To be successful in this changing environment, organisations need to adapt their structures. Horizontal organisations, cluster organisations, virtual organisations and flat organisations all represent responses to the changing business environment.

While there is no one ideal way of structuring organisations, managers and experts in the field agree, however, that an organisational structure must be consistent with the strategy pursued by that organisation.

Definitions

§ 9.1 Structuring	The creation of an organisational structure in which people and resources are optimally utilised to reach the organisation's objectives. External and internal adjustments may be required before the ideal arrangement is found.
Organisational structure	The division of tasks, competencies and responsibilities and how they relate to each other.
§ 9.2 Task division	The division of activities into separate tasks which are assigned to team members or individuals in other departments.
§§ 9.2.1 Vertical differentiation	Organisational tasks grouped together and divided into levels. Cost considerations will mean that some activities will have to be transferred to a lower level.
Work structuring	The conscious consideration of the technical, economic, and social aspects of work within an organisation or a division.
Job enrichment	The addition of elements of a more meaningful and challenging nature to an individual's tasks.
Job enlargement	Increasing the range of duties by addition of tasks of a similar level.
Job rotation	Staff movement from one job to another via mutual exchange of jobs with colleagues.
§§ 9.2.2 Internal differentiation	An organisation's activities grouped by function into different divisions.
Internal specialisation	Activities divided into either product, market or geographical divisions with groupings based on the end result.
§§ 9.2.3 Authority	The right to make decisions necessary for the execution of a task.
Responsibility	Both the moral obligation to execute a task to the best of one's ability as well the duty to report back on the progress of that task.
Delegation	Tasks and responsibilities being handed over to someone else who has (or is able to obtain) the required skills and resources.
Centralisation	Decision-making power concentrated in one place, usually the senior level.
Decentralisation	Decision-making power spread out over more than one location, including the organisation's subsidiaries.

Span of control	The number of immediate subordinates who report directly to a given manager or supervisor.
Span depth	The number of levels directly or indirectly under a manager's control and in particular, the degree of influence that a manager exercises on the lowest levels of the organisation (also called 'depth of control').
§§ 9.2.5 Organisational chart	Gives a simplified visual display of formal organisational structures, command chains and relationships between individuals and / or departments.
§ 9.3 Mechanistic system	The functioning of the organisation in a rational, clear and practical manner. The organisation resembles a machine in its structure and functioning. Technical and financial efficiency are especially important.
Organic system	The functioning of the organisation in accordance with the social needs of its members. The organisation resembles a living organism in its structure and functioning. In this system, the functioning of the members is the key consideration.
§§ 9.3.1 Line organisation	Directives and instructions move exclusively along a vertical route from top to bottom and there is a strict hierarchical relationship between managers and subordinates.
§§ 9.3.2 Line and staff organisation	The same as a line organisation, but with the addition of support staff members with specialist knowledge and expertise who assist managers. Authority remains with the line manager, who is also responsible for decision-making.
§§ 9.3.5 Matrix organisation	The same as a line and staff organisation, but with the addition of project managers who are responsible for leading various projects, and have a horizontal relationship with the rest of the vertical organisation. This means that members of staff inside the organisation must report to two managers. A matrix organisation is always involved in issues of joint authority.
§§ 9.3.6 Project-based organisation (PBO)	In contrast to the line or the line-staff organisation, a PBO gives project managers control of all elements necessary to manage the projects. Project elements dominate the organisation. Another characteristic is the splitting up of the organisation into different divisions or 'pools'.
§ 9.4 Divisional organisation	An organisational form in which the company's activities are grouped into a number of related products or markets and allocated to divisions.

§§ 9.5.1 Operational core	The so-called primary processes that form the basis of the organisation. These processes involve work that is directly related to the production of goods and services. Mintzberg calls this the operational core.
Coordination activities	Ensure that the tasks allocated to employees are carried out efficiently and effectively.
Planning criteria	Determine the division of labour within an organisation based on variables including function specification, group size, centralisation or decentralisation, and degree of formality.
Contingency or situational factors	Factors that influence the choice of organisational elements, coordination activities and planning criteria. In turn, they are also influenced by these factors. The organisational structure is dependent on the level of technical involvement, environmental characteristics, and the size and expected life span of the organisation.
§ 9.6 Horizontal organisation	An organisational form also known as the workflow organisation, and designed to optimise links and activities between divisions.
Cluster organisation	An organisational form in which the team structure is central.
Virtual organisation	An organisational form in which the Internet and other technological tools are used to enable staff to communicate with and consult each other, to exchange information and to learn without having to physically be in the same location. This organisational form is also known as a networked organisation.
Flat organisation	An organisation in which a number of management levels have been reduced.
§ 9.7 Communication	All activities through which information is transferred to other people, including the exchange of data, facts, thoughts, and feelings.
Linking pin structure	A non-standard consultative structure with overlapping groups. The leader or connecting link of a group is the 'linking pin'. He / she can influence decision-making at a higher level. The link may be horizontal, vertical or diagonal.
Communication matrix	Indicates means of communication used, who the 'senders' are, and how each activity is planned. Internal and external target groups are included.

Statements

Which of the following statements are true and which false? Give reasons for your answers.

1 Organising involves adjusting to both external and internal factors.
2 The term 'task division' means transferring tasks to a lower level (vertical differentiation).
3 With internal differentiation, tasks are grouped together according to the desired end result.
4 Span of control means the number of staff a manager is either directly or indirectly in charge of.
5 An informal organisation is an organisation without rules or procedures.
6 Unity of command means that there is only one person in charge of the organisation.
7 The matrix organisation is a typical 'unity of command' organisation.
8 According to Mintzberg, an organisational structure is dependent on environmental features, the life span of the organisation, and its technical system.
9 The nucleus of the professional organisation (Mintzberg) is its operational core.
10 The linking pin structure developed by Likert is significant in that horizontal, vertical, and diagonal communication takes place within the organisation.

Theory questions

1 What do the terms 'job rotation', 'job enlargement', and 'job enrichment' mean?
2 When job descriptions are drawn up, the cost, management, social and societal motives are identified. Which of these motives may potentially clash with each other and why?
3 The textbook discusses the advantages and disadvantages of internal differentiation and internal specialisation. In what types of company will the advantages of each form outweigh the disadvantages?
4 How can the disadvantages of a matrix organisation be tackled?
5 In a diversified organisation, the advantages of a small organisation are combined with the advantages of a large organisation. Explain in what way.

Practical assignment

1 Mintzberg identifies seven configurations or organisational forms. Indicate which of Mintzberg's organisational forms dominate the following organisations. Justify your answers.
   · Carrefour
   · Amnesty International
   · Microsoft
   · Deloitte
   · Harvard Business School
2 Name the most important coordination mechanism.

 For answers see *www.marcusvandam.noordhoff.nl*.

Mini case study

Giorgetti

The Giorgetti Company produces exclusive office furniture which they usually design and construct according to the customer's wishes.

The senior management consists of Mr. Agapita Menarini and Miss Perlita Menarini, both children of the original founder. Agapita Menarini is in charge of purchase and production; Perlita Menarini is in charge of sales and administration.

Two supervisors work in the production department,

each supervising a team of six employees. Three people work in the purchasing department, one of whom supervises the section on a day-to-day basis.

Besides Perlita Menarini, the sales department also has another salesperson, an old hand who has been involved in the business from its foundation.

In addition, there is a technical developer and an adviser within the company.

Three part-time employees work in administration, and are supervised by a full-time member of staff.

Questions

1 Draw an organisation chart for this company.
2 Determine the organisational structure of this enterprise.
3 Which of Mintzberg's configurations does Giorgetti represent?
4 Mintzberg describes five important parts of organisations. Name these parts for Giorgetti.

E-mail case study

To:	Christopher Jensen
Cc:	
Bcc:	
Subject:	Deloitte: organisational structures and different management styles

Message:

Dear Christopher,

Last week the Swiss company UBS placed a valuable order with Deloitte. We have been expecting it for months, and now that it has arrived, we have to work on it straight away. The order is for the provision of information between the group headquarters and the various divisions of UBS. Senior management wants us to advise them about the best way to set up their information provision system.

We would like you to research the organisation. Your expertise is in that field and it would seem that you have staff who can be deployed to do the research.

We would like to know how UBS organises its activities, why they do it that way, and what management style they prefer. You'll need to focus on the structuring issues. Time is short, so I hope to receive a draft report from you in a week's time.

We could meet for lunch to talk about this. I'll call you towards the end of this week to make an appointment.

Regards,

Logan Gladwell

10

Managing organisational change and innovation

The issues that we will be dealing with in this chapter all relate to our main theme of the organisation and the changes that it is undergoing. Initially, we will pay attention to aspects of organisational culture and working in teams. Then we will examine the process of change within organisations, growth models, restructuring, and the 'learning organisation'. At the end of the chapter, attention will be paid to organisational consultation and research.

Contents

After studying this chapter:
- You will have an insight into how organisational effectiveness is achieved and other aspects of organisational culture and working in teams.
- You will have a knowledge of and insight into growth models pertaining to organisations, restructuring and aspects of the learning organisation.
- You will have a knowledge of and insight into organisational consultancy.
- You have a global understanding of organisational research.

10.1   Change

Because the organisation's environment is constantly subject to change, the organisation itself will have to change as well. As mentioned previously, the organisation needs to be attuned to its environment and to remain that way. The adaptation of the organisation to its environment can take many forms: for example, via the manufacture of other products, by adapting the organisational structure, by changing the payment or information system, or by aiming at different markets. Change may be an ongoing process: looking for new products with which to gain and retain a competitive advantage, for example. Change may also be an abrupt occurrence: a thorough restructuring, for example.

10.2   Effectiveness and successful organisations

Collaborations

Organisations are collaborations with a view to realising certain aims. All activities that take place within the organisation are directed towards achieving these set aims. The degree to which the set aims are achieved is what we describe as the organisation's effectiveness, goal-orientation, or efficiency. We can identify four areas of effectiveness and their corresponding criteria[1]:

Technical and economic effectiveness

1 *Technical and economic effectiveness.* This is the degree to which the organisation's resources are efficiently deployed. Efficient utilisation of resources is using the fewest possible means of production (input) to reach a certain output. One works purposefully.

Psychosocial effectiveness.

2 *Psychosocial effectiveness.* This is the degree to which one realises the needs of the organisational members: the satisfaction they experience in the execution of their job.

Social effectiveness

3 *Social effectiveness.* This is the degree to which one realises the needs of those parties within the external environment: are shareholders receiving sufficient dividends, is the organisation producing products for which there is sufficient demand and do exhaust fumes comply with environmental requirements? An organisation has a right to exist only when external parties such as consumers and financiers have their demands satisfied.

Managerial effectiveness

4 *Managerial effectiveness.* This is the degree to which the organisation can react to changed situations. Organisations must be able to anticipate changes quickly. This puts demands on the supply of information and the organisation's decision-making: they must be flexible and decisive. Flexibility is the organisation's ability to change and adapt itself. Decisive organisations have the ability to act rapidly and effectively.

Attaining a high rate of efficiency in economic and technical areas is usually where the emphasis lies. Organisations that place such an emphasis usually turn inwards, seeking the best possible way of organising the company's processes. However, organisations are only successful if they score well in all four areas of effectiveness.

Organisational balance

Such organisations can be described as having an organisational balance. To have an organisational balance entails rewarding the internal as well as the external shareholders in such a way that they remain motivated to participate within the organisation.

When confronted with changes within the business environment, one should look for new ways of achieving an organisational balance. The problem here lies in the difficulty of separating the various areas of effectiveness from each other since they may be highly interconnected.

How to deploy people in the most effective way will be a matter for consideration. If those people experience little satisfaction in their work, sickness will increase, and consequently the costs.

Name:	Rogier H.M. Rolink
Country of origin:	The Netherlands; currently lives and works in the US
International experience:	Has worked in the Netherlands, the United Kingdom and Switzerland
Job title:	Director of International Tax Operations
Website current company:	www.dupont.com

What important personal qualities must people have to be successful in international work?

To be successful in international work and to operate with people from different backgrounds and different habits, cultures and styles of communication, you need to recognise and appreciate these differences and to adapt to them. You need to be flexible enough to effectively communicate with the people involved and ultimately to earn their trust and respect. People from different cultures and background may have different preferences and feel more comfortable with other styles of communication and management (a less direct style, for example). Having the trust and respect of the people you are working with – people reporting to you directly or indirectly, your peers as well as those you are supervising – will enable you to operate more successfully.

What is the most important lesson that you have learned from working with people from different cultures?

The most important lesson I have learned from working with people from different cultures is that there are many angles to issues and there are many different ways of approaching them. I have learned to consider issues in a much broader context: there is often no one best answer or solution.

How important is the work / life balance in your country?

I believe that in the US there is an increasing amount of recognition and understanding that the work / life balance is important for both the employees and the companies and can add to productivity. I see more programs and opportunities for the employees to manage their work / life balance: working from home, flexible work hours, flexible work weeks such as four ten-hour days, the opportunity to acquire vacation days, flexible retirement arrangements and so on.

What is the most interesting aspect of your job?

The most interesting and challenging part of my job is striving to have the right people in place within the team globally, developing and challenging them, and ensuring that they are operating efficiently as a team. I enjoy working with the team and with people from different cultures and backgrounds, managing and dealing with a wide variety of constantly changing opportunities and challenges at the global level.

What is the best way to motivate people?

Although people are different and respond differently depending on their background, my experience is that as a general rule, people are best motivated by recognising them and their work that they are doing. The 'basics' need to be in place: having a assignments that are challenging and developmental, having appropriate and competitive financial rewards, having the opportunity to create a good balance between work and recreation, having a suitable work environment and so on. Once you have these basics the best way to motivate people is to tell them how much you appreciate their work and their achievements.

What kind of role does the Internet play in your job?

Internet plays a critical role in my job. Having the Internet and e-mail enables me to communicate quickly and efficiently with teams and people around the world, to access crucial information from various different sources, and to share information and experiences globally. The Internet also allows me to be flexible and operate efficiently, not only from the head office but also from remote office locations and from home. The Internet can also be helpful in managing your work / life balance.

Business culture key to success

In their bestseller *Built to last*, James Collins and Jerry Porras describe what makes organisations a success in the long term. They refer to a number of very successful organisations, including Walt Disney, Hewlett Packard, Sony and 3M. According to them, successful organisations often have cult-like cultures. The staff member who feels at home in such an organisation and makes the goals his or her own will be productive and feel extremely satisfied. Those who don't will be expelled. Cult-like cultures have four main characteristics. They have an ideology they adhere to firmly, there will be an element of indoctrination, one will need to adapt to the organisation, and there is a degree of elitism. Disney's ideology is to bring happiness to millions and to maintain and promote American values. Cynicism is not allowed. There is a fanatical attention to consistency and detail. Every new employee goes through the Disney University, where he or she learns the traditions, philosophy, organisation and way of doing business. The whole organisation directs itself towards creating a fairy tale. So as not to break the magic, the work behind the scenes remains a secret. Journalists hardly ever gain access. In this sense, Disney can be considered more a social or even a religious movement than a company: a movement that gave the world Snow White, Mickey Mouse and Peter Pan. Many in the organisation have the feeling that they belong to an elite. Collins and Porras' research demonstrates that a strong connection between the individual and the organisation leads to success for the organisation. People should be proud of their company and identify with it. Company culture can be a source of purpose and meaning for its employees, and provide them with a sense of structure. In traditional line and staff organisations, structures were the most significant binding force. Everybody knew to which compartment of the organisation he or she belonged, and who else belonged there. If such firm structures are exchanged for teams involved in various projects, one runs the risk of rocking the company's very foundations. The new binding elements are vision and culture. 'It is precisely now, when companies are increasingly taking on the character of networks and the percentage of flexible employees in the workforce is growing, that it is important to pay greater attention to social bonds, coherence and cohesion in companies', according to a recent working paper from the employers' federation VNO NCW.

Source: *Intermediary*, August 1998.

Continuity and changes in visionary companies

Preserve:
• values
• goal of the organisation

Change:
• mode of operation
• specific goals and strategies

Successful organisations

Research into successful organisations indicates that there is a relationship between success and an organisation's cultural characteristics. These cultural characteristics are its striving for quality, its customer orientation, its flexibility, the degree of internal entrepreneurship and innovative power, its teamwork, its management style, and the shared norms and values of the organisational members.

10.3   Organisational culture

Organisational culture

An organisational culture can be understood as being an assembly – sometimes captured in symbols and myths – of notions about work, each other, oneself and the organisation.[2] A culture is maintained by rules. These rules determine how one should behave, how one associates with the other, and how one should act. A culture provides guidelines on how individuals should function within an organisation and whether the expectations held in respect of individual organisational members are reasonable expectations.

There are various theories of or approaches to organisational culture. They include:
· Group processes and organisational culture
· Handy's typology
· The typology of G. Sanders and B. Neuijen
· The professional culture typology

Group processes and organisational culture

In this approach, the behaviour of individual organisational members is examined in terms of how to influence it from a group perspective. Every individual organisational member is part of one or more organisational group. The processes within this group or these groups exert an particular influence on the acts of individuals. The nature of the group process will depend on the following six aspects.[3]

Group perspective

1 *Affectivity.* Is the bond between the organisational members business-like or more like an emotional bond?
2 *Causality.* Are employees and / or systems liable to cause problems for the organisation's members?
3 *Hierarchy.* How do the organisation's members behave with respect to position, role, power and responsibility?
4 *Change.* How do the organisation's members react to threats or opportunities deriving from the environment?
5 *Cooperation.* Is there an atmosphere of 'we'll shoulder the burden together' or is it more like 'every man for himself'?
6 *Behaviour with respect to groups with other interests.* Are other groups in the organisation treated with particular antipathy or sympathy?

These aspects allow one to gain an insight into group process. The group culture holds the key to how employees will react to situations. One can change unwanted organisational behaviour on the part of individual members by prompting the development of a different culture within the group. For example, if openness to change is seen as being desirable, the various aspects of the group process must promote this rather than impede it. This is not to say that factors other than group process influence the acts of individual organisational members. Their task descriptions, the rules and so on also play a role.

Handy's typology

Handy's typology (1979) is a much-used method of typifying organisational culture. It has two aspects:

Handy

A cultural revolution at Nikko

Two American fund managers have shaken up the Japanese institution by challenging traditional work practices.

Nikko has been blighted by traditional Japanese work practices, including lifetime employment, seniority-based compensation and the belief that ordinary employees can be trained to do highly specialised jobs such as portfolio management. Unlike their Western rivals, Japanese funds have baulked at the idea of allowing their top fund managers to become super wealthy 'stars'. Nor have traditional fund managers been encouraged to take investment risks, reflecting a preference for committee-based decisions. Nikko fund managers were held back by a culture of shame, where you want to win by not losing. Listed below are the main changes and new measures taken by Nikko:

• A performance-related pay scheme, including a

share option plan for executives, fund managers and analysts, designed to encourage individual fund managers to take more risks in investment decisions
• A share savings plan to help retain and attract new talent
• Staff communication tools such as US-style 'town hall' meetings, suggestion boxes and employee surveys
• Refurbishment of offices in central Tokyo
• Underperforming bosses replaced by younger, highly motivated junior executives, bolstering staff morale across the company
• 'Mao-style' techniques to speed reforms, including taskforces led by sharp-minded junior employees in fund management and compliance

Source: *Financial Times*, March 2006

IN THE PRESS

1 *The degree of cooperation.* This is the extent to which people are prepared to work together.
2 *Power distribution.* This is the extent to which powers of decision are centralised or decentralised.

A high degree of cooperation assumes a relatively greater unity between the members of an organisation. A high degree of power distribution is a situation characterised by a high degree of delegation. Both of these aspects may vary according to the situation.

If we combine these two dimensions with each other, we will obtain an overview similar to that represented in Figure 10.1.

Figure 10.1 Four culture types

		Power distribution	
		Low	High
Degree of cooperation	Low	Role culture	Person culture
	High	Power culture	Task culture

The four culture typographies are as follows:

1 *Role culture.* The organisation revolves around rules and procedures. These give stability and security. Organisational functions set the tone, not the people who perform these functions. Bureaucratic organisations typify this type of organisation.

2 *Power culture.* The organisation revolves around the leading figure. The organisation is, as it were, an extension of that figure. The leading figure seeks out a circle of loyal staff members. This type of culture has few rules and procedures: decisions are made on an ad hoc basis. We frequently encounter power cultures within small and young organisations.

3 *Person culture.* A person culture is characterised by the priority given to the individual. The organisation is there to serve the human being. A manager within this type of organisation is on an equal level with other staff members. Management is regarded as a necessary evil: to keep the organisation going. A lawyer's or a solicitor's office is typical of a personality culture.

4 *Task culture.* The organisation is characterised by a task orientation and professionalism. The organisation consists of a network of loose / fixed task units, each of which is highly independent while at the same time carrying specific responsibilities within the whole. Such a culture is focussed on the achieving of results. A matrix organisation is a good example of a task culture.

Handy tried to relate the characteristics of the different culture types and the technological characteristics of organisations to each other. Which type of culture best matches each particular type of technology? Handy arrived at the following conclusions[4]:

- A role culture is suitable for routine technology.
- A role culture is suitable for costly technology.
- A role culture is suitable for mass production.
- A role culture is suitable for technology that demands a lot of coordination.

- A power or task culture is suitable for unit production.
- A power or task culture is suitable for technology that demands great flexibility.

The typology of G. Sanders and B. Neuijen

In their book Company culture, diagnosis and influencing, G. Sanders and B. Neuijen identify six company cultures and the attitudes that are typical of each. These are summarised in Figure 10.2.[5]

Figure 10.2 Summary of the six dimensions

① Process-oriented
Avoiding risks
As little exertion as possible
Every day about the same

Result-orientated
At ease in risky situations
Do their utmost
Every day represents a new challenge

② People-oriented
Take personal problems into consideration
Take responsibility for well-being of employees
Groups make decisions

Work-orientated
Exert strong pressure to complete work
Interested exclusively in the work that one delivers
Individuals make the decisions

③ Organisation-bound
Employees identify with their organisation
Attract staff from the right families,
social class and educational background
Work norms also apply at home
Do not think very far ahead

Professional
Employees identify with their profession
Attract those staff who are most suitable for the job
Private life is one's own business
Think years ahead

④ Open
Openness towards newcomers and outsiders
Nearly everyone fits into the organisation
New staff members quickly feel at home

Closed
Closed and secretive, even towards own staff members
You have to be unusual in some way to fit into the organisation
New staff members do not feel at home instantly

⑤ Tight control
Awareness of costs
Adhere strictly to meeting hours
Talk seriously about company and work

Loose control
Lack of awareness of costs
More or less adhere to meeting hours
Joke about the company and work

⑥ Pragmatic
The customer's wishes must be met
Results are more important than procedures
Pragmatic attitude towards ethics
Minimal contribution to societal goals

Normative
Procedures are adhered to
Procedures are more important than results
High ethical norms
Useful contribution to society

The professional culture typology

This typology describes four professional cultures by means of metaphors or myths. These metaphors arise because different professional groups strive for specific ideals. These ideals have consequences for the type of culture in which the organisational members can function best.

Bureaucratic culture

Bureaucratic culture / rationality

This culture is based on rational considerations. These allow the organisation's members to do their job purposefully. Such a culture is ideal for realising set organisational goals. A multitude of rules and procedures bind the organisation's members during the course of their daily work. Mutual tasks are precisely delineated. Every organisational member is a link within the larger whole. The organisation's members will automatically reach their goals by doing their job according to the way it has been designed. Bureaucratic cultures are not only to be found within government institutions.

The bureaucratic culture resembles Handy's role culture to a large extent.

Official culture

Official culture

Government institutions have specific characteristics associated with their societal function. They are responsible for organising and managing desired societal developments and processes. Doing so leads to an official culture with a strong internal orientation. This culture has its own myths, including the following[6]:

- The myth of society being controllable
- The myth of being superior to society
- The myth that the government aims for legal certainty and equality of rights
- The myth that the views, values and wishes of public servants do not influence their decisions

Professional culture

Professional culture / individual members of the organisation

In a professional culture, the individual members of the organisation occupy a central position. They also have control. The organisation can be seen as a collaboration between professionals who also form the organisation's management, and consequently their purposes are not at odds with each other: both consist of professionals. This culture also revolves around myths. They include the superiority of knowledge and autonomy. One consequence of this is that the team is subordinate to the individual professionals. The professional culture resembles Handy's personality culture to a considerable degree.

Commercial culture

In this culture, everything revolves around either the customer or the market. It is constructed around the myths that anything can be bought for money and that organisational members can achieve anything by working hard. This is a highly competitive culture and the individual is central.

Commercial culture / customer or the market

Competitive culture

The organisational culture must be attuned to the organisation's pursuit of effectiveness. However, neither this nor any other cultural type does this optimally, since constant changes within the organisation's environment mean that the culture can never be completely in harmony with the environment.

Moreover, organisations usually contain more than one type of culture. The marketing division will have one culture; the production division another. As such, orientation, aims, and power will differ. If the organisation contains a powerful division or group of individuals, that culture may be dominant.

Organisational culture affects the organisational culture to a greater or lesser degree, and consequently management has a vested interest in wanting to influence it. There are various ways in which it may do so. (See Figure 10.3.)

- *Via the person at the helm of the organisation.* We often see that the appointment of a new senior executive brings winds of change and new norms and values to the organisation. The new top executive will form a new group of people around him who will disseminate this new approach throughout the entire organisation.

- *Via ceremonies and rituals.* Initiating ceremonies and rituals is a way of formally recognising the norms and values and making them visible. The moment at which a person is taken on is an occasion which can be celebrated, as are periodical festivities, and special occasions such as annual prize-giving presentations.
- *Via stories and the language of communication.* An anecdote, stories about the past (heroes) and the language of communication reveal much about the culture of the organisation. They show the employees what behaviour is desirable and what is not, and how one should deal with certain matters.
- *Via socialisation.* Working with existing employees allows new employees to get to know the way the organisation expresses itself culturally. New employees learn how to deal with matters effectively and efficiently, and in accordance with the organisation's 'cultural rules'. Many organisations send new employees to courses in which the norms and values of the organisation are taught.

Socialisation

Figure 10.3   Possibilities for guiding / influencing the organisational culture

Symbolism

In the previous section, we mentioned the various approaches or typologies characteristic of the organisational culture. The social context was crucial to this.

Other aspects of organisational culture include the spatial dimensions (the organisation's buildings), the time dimension (how the organisation organises its time) and the linguistic dimension (how meaning is communicated). This is the realm of symbolism: the signs and symbols that reveal the organisation's degree of cohesion. We describe these dimension in greater detail below.

Symbolism

Spatial symbolism

Buildings tell a lot about the organisational culture. Spatial dimensions betray a lot about the organisation and how people function within it. The following are some aspects of this:

Spatial symbolism

- The architecture of the building itself and the environment in which the building is situated (the location)
- The interior, in which such things as the accessibility, size and furnishings of the offices all play a role.

Time symbolism

The way time is regulated within an organisation says a lot about the importance of the particular position and the kind of work that is done. These symbolic aspects include the following:

Time symbolism

Ikea: how to build a global cult brand

Perhaps more than any other company in the world, Ikea has become a curator of people's lifestyles, if not their lives. Ikea provides a one-stop sanctuary for coolness. It is a trusted safe zone that people can enter and immediately be part of a like-minded cost / design / environmentally-sensitive global tribe. Ikea sells a lifestyle that signifies hip design, thrift, and simplicity. For the aspiring global middle class, buying Ikea is a sign of success.

Here is how the Swedes do it:
- Create the story.   The retailer is a master at building buzz, which creates evangelists for its brand, who then spread the story by phone, word of mouth, and even blogs from Shanghai to Chicago. Essay contest winners get the chance to camp out in a store before it opens. That excites shoppers and generates huge publicity.
- Inspire the staff.   Employees won't get rich, but they do get to enjoy autonomy, very little hierarchy, and a family-friendly culture. In return they buy into the philosophy of frugality and style that drives the whole company.
- Seduce the shopper.   Customer focus is so intense that even top management must work

behind cash registers and in the warehouse for brief stints every year. The stores are laid out to promote fun: restaurants and play centres encourage shoppers to spend the day there. Simple touches from free pencils to paper measuring tapes make it easy to shop.

Source: *Business Week*, November 2005

- The time boundaries of the particular position (is there a clear distinction between work and non-work or is the work ongoing?)
- How flexible the working hours are
- How early one starts work

The symbolism of language

Symbolism of language

Language is the means par excellence for communicating with others. Language is also an instrument for sharing the meaning we give to things. Symbolism is a matter of how we deal with language. We can put the symbolic force of language to use in many ways. These include the following:

- *Influencing.*   The influence may be direct or indirect, subtle, flow from personal conviction or threat, and so on.
- *Identity.*   Language is a means for establishing group communality.

10.4   Organisational development

Organisational development

Organisations have to continually adapt to changes in their environment. One could regard them as living organisms trying to achieve an internal balance as it were. In doing so, the organisation itself will change, as will its members. Organisational development is a process of change during which its members and the organisation itself undergo development, and come out functioning better.[7] The organisation and its staff members will improve qualitatively, giving it a greater ability to resolve problems relating to changed circumstances within the business environment. Successful organisations are to some extent able to constructively handle and plan the developments that concern them. These developments are usually of an ongoing nature. Sometimes, however, a situation of change may arise abruptly, in the form of a restructuring.

Ongoing processes of development will now be treated, followed by restructuring processes.

Organisations may have any of the following characteristics:
- Customers in different countries
- Many alliances and forms of cooperation
- A focus on core activities
- Growth by takeovers and mergers
- High-quality technology supporting company processes
- A division of concerns into small, flexible, and market-oriented units
- Outsourcing of important parts of professional staff functions and a limited number of staff functions on both the permanent level and the contracting level
- Flexible and flat organisational structures
- 'Empowering' of staff members
- Control almost solely exercised by the subsidiary company, with central control restricted to financing, cash flow, and acquisitions policy
- Managers doing business as entrepreneurs, with at least part of their salary variable in nature and depending on the company's results.

An organisation's process of development can be indicated in various ways. Two development models will be treated here: *Development models*
1 Scott's growth model
2 Greiner's growth model

Global 20 largest Companies and Employers (2005)

Rank	By Revenue	By Number of employees	Number of Employees
1	EXXON Mobil	Wal-Mart Stores	1,800,000
2	Wal-Mart Stores	China National Petroleum	1,090,232
3	Royal Dutch Shell	State Grid	844,031
4	BP	U.S. Postal Offices	803,000
5	General Motors	Sinopec	730,800
6	Chevron	Deutsche Post	502,545
7	Daimlerchrysler	Agricultural Bank of China	478,895
8	Toyota	UES of Russia	461,200
9	Ford Motor	Siemens	461,000
10	Conocophilips	Mcdonald's	447,000
11	General Electric	Carrefour	440,479
12	Total	Compass Group	410,074
13	ING Group	China Telecommunications	407,982
14	CITYGROUP	United Parcel Service	407,000
15	Axa	Gazprom	396,571
16	Allianz	Daimlerchrysler	382,724
17	Volkswagen	Ind. & Comm. Bank of China	361,623
18	Fortis	Hitachi	355,879
19	Credit Agricole	Sears Holdings	355,000
20	American International Group	Volkswagen.	344,902

Source: *Fortune Magazine*, June 24, 2006

10.4.1   Scott's growth model

An organisation goes through three phases of development, each with their own specific characteristics.

Phase 1: The small organisation

The first phase is the small organisation. This organisation has only a limited number of functions, which the owner usually fills. As this organisation grows, the functions are divided up and other staff members are employed.

The characteristics of the small organisation are:
- *Structure.*   Functional division with little internal differentiation
- *Staff evaluation.*   According to non-formalised criteria
- *Management system.*   Personal management
- *Strategic planning.*   Dependent on the owner's personality.

Phase 2: The organisation comprised solely of departments

The second phase consists of an organisation comprised solely of departments. The functional departments of these organisations have been expanded to the fullest. The size of organisations of this kind makes it possible to develop specialised activities in various functional areas and to accommodate them within the organisation via staff or service duties. Organisational growth is sought in the form of increasing market share and expansion through product and market development.

The characteristics of an organisation made up solely of departments are:
- *Structure.*   Centralised functional division with a lot of internal differentiation
- *Staff evaluation.*   Based on technical and economical criteria (e.g. function classification)
- *Management system.*   Increasingly on an operational level based on delegation
- *Strategic planning.*   Personal decision-making
- *Research.*   Takes place systematically and with an emphasis on product improvement, product development and process innovation

Phase 3: The multidivisional organisation

The last phase is known as the multidivisional organisation. The level directly below the top management level is split up into product-market combinations or a geographical division. The growth of these organisations takes place particularly through diversification, and gives rise to independent business units (divisions). The top levels of the organisation have departments which are concerned with such things as strategy and legal and staff issues.

The characteristics of a multidivisional organisation are:
- *Structure.*   Decentralised division form with internal specialisation
- *Staff evaluation.*   A lot of emphasis on profit and other financial criteria
- *Management system.*   Strategic and operational decision-making decentralised with respect to product-market combinations
- *Strategic planning.*   Strong emphasis on processes with the top levels in particular aimed at division of resources within the concern, and entry to and exit from business sectors.

Fast growth at MTV

Launched in 1981 as a music video channel, MTV Networks today comprises a slew of channels, websites and wireless services to keep everyone from toddlers to boomers tuned in. All together, the $7 billion company reaches 440 million households in 169 countries.

CEO Judy McGrath had to remake her TV empire into a digital world. She hired a chief digital officer and adapted the company to the new media world. Some of the moves on the convergence front included:

- Online communities by acquiring such companies as Neopets, with its 25 million members
- Broadband

- A download service with the launch (with Microsoft) of music service URGE that will include exclusive MTV programs
- Wireless, with a worldwide reach of 750 million cell phone users
- Video on demand, to deliver on-demand programs from its channels
- Games via MTV Games, a division created to launch new video game titles

Source: *Business Week*, February 2006

The functionality of the MTV website drives hits and venues

10.4.2 Greiner's growth model

According to Greiner, the organisational growth process is a process of five phases. Keuning added two more phases to Greiner's five phases. These phases relate to ongoing developments (phases 6 and 7). Every phase is characterised by gradual development (evolution). These gradually developing phases are each characterised by a certain management style, typical for the phase in which the organisation finds itself.

Greiner

When a phase comes to an end, the organisation will find itself in a crisis (revolution) that cannot be resolved by gradual development. There will be a tendency for a new organisational management style to develop.

Crisis

Management style

In Greiner's view, as organisation's develop, the main issue is how to overcome internal crises rather than how to survive changes within the external environment. Figure 10.4 shows the phases of development of an organisation in diagram form.

Internal crises

The seven phases of the development of an organisation will now be discussed.

Phase 1: growth through creativity

This is the starting or pioneer phase of the organisation, in which creativity is the most important factor. The emphasis lies on development of the product and of the market. In this phase, there is hardly any question of a formal organisation and there is a lot of informal communication within the organisation. If the organisation grows substantially, a leadership crisis will arise. Organising and managing the activities will become more important. The time for different management will have arrived.

Leadership crisis

Figure 10.4 The growth phase and organisational crises

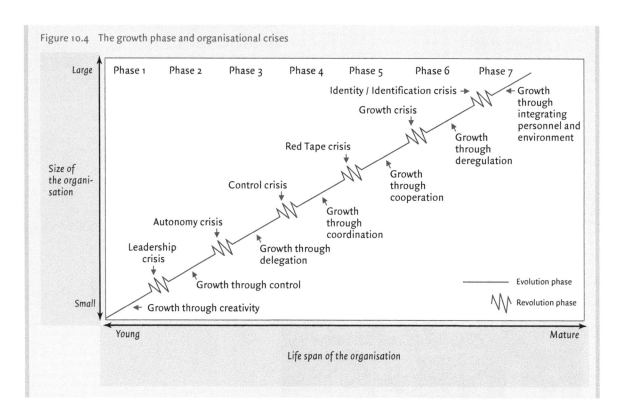

Life span of the organisation

Phase 2: growth through control

Control

The new management will either put emphasis on greater control or will occupy itself with guiding the organisation towards expansion.

The organisation's members will find their independence limited. If this continues for a long time, a situation will arise in which the individual members or departments will need greater responsibility. An autonomy crisis will arise.

Autonomy crisis

Phase 3: growth through delegation

Delegation

By creating more autonomy, the organisation will become more independent. This will take the form of delegating: transferring responsibilities and competencies to lower levels of the organisation. This carries the advantage of the organisation's members growing more motivated. Top management will feel it is no longer in control. The result will be a control crisis.

Control crisis

Phase 4: growth through coordination

Coordination

To regain the lost territory, extra coordination mechanisms must be built in. Consequently, there will be an increase in communication and information binding the organisation's members to rules and procedures. This outcome will be an inflexible organisation. A Red Tape crisis will arise.

Bureaucratic crisis

Phase 5: growth through cooperation

Cooperation

To increase the decisiveness and flexibility of the organisation, various forms of cooperation must arise between departments, committees and working groups. The purpose of these is to enhance work effectiveness. The consultation required to attune various activities to each other is time-consuming. If the result is a consultative culture, a consultation crisis will arise.

Consultation crisis

Why Youtube succeeded where so many others failed

YouTube, the online video-sharing site, has hit the sort of popular culture nerve that most people in that same branch can only dream about. Video has been a graveyard for Internet start-ups almost since the web browser first transformed the Internet into a mass-market medium. YouTube's early success reflects a formula that has been drawn partly from the experience of other web-based applications such as Google.

- Easy of use.   YouTube placed a high priority on making it simple for users to both upload their own videos and to watch other people's. No installing software, no encoding: YouTube does the work for you.

- Technology.   YouTube was one of the first video sites to put all of its videos into a format that can be played on Flash Player, found on virtually all PCs. So the viewer doesn't need up-to-date versions of the media players made by Microsoft, RealNetworks or Apple.
- Community.   YouTube lets users decide which videos are worth watching. In the past, other video sites made decisions about what was entertaining to the community.

Source: *Financial Times, October 2006*

Phase 6: growth by commercialisation and deregulation

During phase 5, the emphasis was on consultation aimed at attuning activities better. The drive to achieve results took backseat. To bring it again to the foreground, superfluous procedures and consultative structures will have to disappear. The organisation will deregulate itself. Internal entrepreneurship will also come to the fore. Business units that have a large degree of independence will arise. There will be a certain cooling off, with the pursuit of a higher degree of efficiency and a cutting into organisational structures predominating. Internally, a situation will arise that may be termed a social identity crisis. Externally, it will be seen as an identification crisis.

Commercialisation / deregulation

Social identity crisis
Identification crisis

Phase 7: growth by integrating human and environmental policy

During this phase, management will emphasise 'the public good'. A lot of time will be devoted to environmental issues, to an effective organisational culture, to the organisation's image and identity, and to finding how to satisfy staff members while enhancing the quality, efficiency and productivity of the organisation.

Human and environmental policy
The public good

Lewin's model

In Greiner's growth model, changes do not take place from one day to the next. Change is gradual, with uncertainties of one kind or another at every turn. A number of phases can be identified. Lewin's model consists of three phases. (See Figure 10.5.)

Lewin

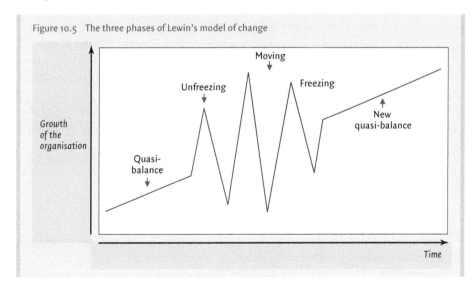

Figure 10.5   The three phases of Lewin's model of change

Unfreezing

Phase 1: unfreezing

During this phase, staff members are prepared for change. The consequences of the changes are clarified. The staff members have to distance themselves ('unfreezing') from the work methods that have been usual so far. This phase is very important because many people have a resistance to change. This resistance is a natural consequence of the insecurity that accompanies change. Staff members must also, of course, be motivated to get to work in the new situation. Acceptance of the changes is enhanced by involving those who are concerned at an early stage.

Moving

Phase 2: moving

As soon as the necessity for change has been accepted by the staff members, the process can get underway. Changes in such things as communication and data flows can be implemented. Staff members should be given the opportunity to prepare for the new situation through schooling and training.

Freezing

Phase 3: freezing

After the changes have been implemented, 'freezing' takes place: they become a fixed part of the standard organisation. During this phase, it is not unusual for staff members to slide back into their old habits. Extra attention should be paid to this if necessary.

Ezerman's strategies for change

Strategy for change

The purpose of a strategy for change is to increase acceptance of that change by the staff members involved. What is important here is to bring about an actual acceptation process instead of an apparent one. The purpose of the strategies shown below is to obtain as much cooperation as possible. Strategies for change are usually

Ezerman

applied simultaneously. Ezerman identifies seven strategies for change[8]:

- *Avoidance.*   It is important that people realise the need for change. Only then will they be prepared to accept it. Sometimes one needs to allow everything to fail and thereby demonstrate the necessity for change.
- *Facilitation.*   This is the creation of conditions or facilities to bring about the change. It may involve the physical realm (e.g., placing a personal computer in home situations) or the non-physical realm (e.g., initiating a common coffee break to stimulate informal contact).
- *Information.*   The staff members involved are updated about the coming changes. They can prepare for and / or get used to the idea.
- *Educational strategies.*   The staff members involved are educated, coached or guided in relation to the process of change. The accent can be put on the transfer of information, on acquiring skills, or on a change of attitude.
- *Negotiation.*   If people are not inclined to agree to change, negotiation is a possibility. As in most situations, a compromise will be necessary.
- *Convincing.*   With this strategy one aims to put a idea into someone's head with the help of arguments and logic. The advantages will be maximised and disadvantages minimised.
- *Power, force, and pressure strategy.*   The final strategy simply consists of enforcing the changes and thereafter applying rewards and punishments.

10.4.3   Restructuring

Restructuring

Restructuring can be defined as a non-recurrent and usually fundamental alteration of decision-making powers and the division of labour within the organisation. A restructuring is a once-only event and often brings about fundamental changes. The

How China will change your business

1 China's economy is much bigger than the official figures suggest

Local Chinese authorities underreport their growth rates since they are in competition for development funds. As well as this, the government only measures China's legal economy. China artificially depresses the value of its yuan against the dollar by as much as 40%.

2 The growth of China's economy has no equal in modern history

China is so committed to economic growth that its GDP is expanding at an annual rate of 9.5%. Neither Japan's nor South Korea's postwar boom comes anywhere close.

3 China is winning the global competition for investment capital

One reason China's economy is growing so fast is that the world keeps feeding it capital. Foreigners are investing more in building businesses in China than they are spending anywhere else in the world. With money comes knowledge. Foreign experts control China's trade: foreign companies operating in China have risen by over 40%.

4 China can be a bully

China can spend, and it can hire and dictate wages. It can throw old-line competitors out of work. Take the American wooden furniture companies, for example: the workforce has already dropped by one third and is sure to drop further.

5 China's economy is an entrepreneurial economy

For a world fretting over Chinese economic competition, the entities to fear are not government planners but enterprises that spring on the scene lean and mean, planned and financed by investors who want to make money quickly.

6 The most daunting thing about China is not its ability to make cheap consumer goods

A far bigger shift is occurring among the products that manufacturers and marketers trade with each other: the infinite number and variety of components that make up everything else that is made.

7 China is closing the research and development gap fast

When it comes to the more mainstream types of applied industrial development and innovation, the gap among Chinese, American, and other multinational firms is beginning to narrow.

8 China now sets the global benchmark for prices

'China price' has become interchangeable with the lowest price possible. The China price is part of the new conventional wisdom that companies can move nearly any kind of work to China and find huge savings.

9 China's growth is making raw materials more expensive

China's voracious demand for raw materials has caused prices to spike.

10 No company has embraced China's potential more vigorously than Wal-Mart

More than 80% of the 6,000 factories in Wal-Mart's worldwide database of suppliers are in China

Source: *INC Magazine*, March 2005

reasons for a restructuring may be many, and may include deteriorating results, changed situations in the external environment such as technological developments and consumer behaviour, changed management views, and organisational growth that is too rapid and has not included regular adaptation of the organisational structure. There are often clear signals that a restructuring is looming: there is a big staff turnover, the dividend is passed over, investment plans are postponed, government support is applied for, there is a gloomy outlook on the future, the recruitment of staff is frozen, there is an imminent merger or takeover and so on.

Purpose of restructuring

The purpose of a restructuring is to avert the threat of discontinuity and to promote the company's recovery. The restructuring must ensure that the strategic position of the organisation is reinforced, that the internal organisation functions optimally, and that the asset position and the profitability of the organisation improves.[9]

To achieve the purposes of the restructuring, changes may be necessary in many areas:
- Disposing of or closing down loss-making organisational units
- Achieving greater decisiveness and better decision-making
- Achieving a decrease in pressure on the organisation's management
- Achieving a decrease in overhead costs (a slim-down)
- Achieving better coordination
- Achieving a better distribution of responsibility
- Changing of the organisational culture

A restructuring is usually accompanied by a number of preconditions in various different areas, including the technical (production area), economical (cost area), staff (resistance), and legal preconditions (collective employment contract and employees council) areas.

The success or otherwise of a restructuring depends on many factors. In his book *Turnaround Management, reorganising companies in trouble* J.M.M. Sopers has described a model which incorporates a number of recommendations aimed at achieving a successful restructuring. In the model, he formulates three levels of objectives (see Figure 10.6).

Levels of objectives

a Level 1. The ultimate goal of the restructuring
b Level 2. Objectives relating to intrinsic and process-concerned aspects
c Level 3. Objectives aimed at creating conditions for achieving an intrinsically sound plan on the one hand, and initiating the process of change on the other.

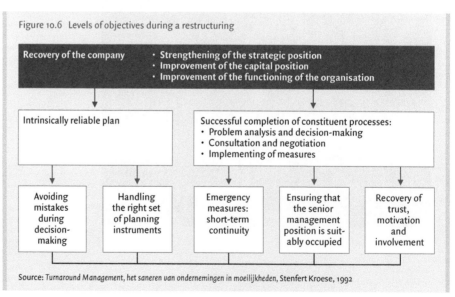

Figure 10.6 Levels of objectives during a restructuring

Source: *Turnaround Management, het saneren van ondernemingen in moeilijkheden*, Stenfert Kroese, 1992

World economy profits from stop on child labour

Banning child labour will yield the world economy well over 21% extra in the period up until 2020. The financial advantages of schooling and lower medical expenses will compensate for the educational costs and missed income from labour. This is demonstrated in a study by the ILO, the international labour market organisation of the United Nations. Although the social advantages are beyond dispute, the UN now has an economic argument in its fight against child labour. According to the UN, if child labour is banned now, the benefits will exceed the costs as from 2016. The costs will include education costs (building new schools, teachers' wages, the costs of teaching material), the missed profits from labour, and the compensation families ought to get for that. The profits will only follow in the long term. Providing schooling for children can only be regarded as fruitful if the work that they perform as an adult is more intelligent work than it would have been otherwise. A financial advantage which only appears later is the drop in medical expenses – these children often have complaints later in life. The profits are potentially greatest for the African countries south of the Sahara. In the coming twenty years, the economy would grow by well over 51% if child labour were abolished.

Source: *De Volkskrant*, February 4, 2004

It is usually advisable to replace the executive management because of its possible contribution to the current situation, in order to send clear signals to the organisation's stakeholders and in order to tackle the problems seriously. During a restructuring, restoring the trust of the main stakeholders of the organisation (internally as well as externally) is crucial. A large degree of involvement on the part of the stakeholders is usually necessary for the restructuring to be successful. A strong executive and control over a well-constructed restructuring plan is advisable. It is also advisable to enter into consultation with the various main parties early.

Stakeholders

A separate issue during restructurings is the setting up of a human resources policy. A restructuring usually involves a decrease in the work force. The human resources policy sets out how the employer intends to deal with staff during the restructuring. The parties who need to be involved in the drawing up of a human resources policy are management, the employees and the trades union.

Human resources policy

The human resources policy will replace the collective labour agreement and is a collective arrangement from which staff members extract individual rights. It not only deals with the arrangements but also the procedures to follow.

In theory, there are four options for dealing with personnel:
1 *Reemployment within the organisation.* Replacement on the same level is an important aspect of this.
2 *Reemployment by new employer.* Theoretically, the function offered should be at the same level as the previous employment.
3 *Voluntary ending of the work agreement.* With this option the goal is natural progress. The form this option is cast in can differ considerably: from a severance payment to a 'starter's premium'.

4 *Involuntary ending of the work agreement.* The employer can buy off his obligations via a one-off payment.

Beside these options, the employer can also use such instruments as outplacement and a job vacancy department.

10.4.4 The learning organisation

It will have become clear by now that organisations are faced with changes of many different kinds, whether technological, economical or social. To safeguard its continuity in the future, an organisation needs to respond adequately to these changes. The key question is how organisations can be set up so that they not keep up with, but more importantly, are ahead of changes in their environment.

Learning ability

The crucial matter is the ability of organisations to change permanently: the learning ability of organisations. Their ability to survive in the future depends on this factor. Learning organisations are organisations which are not only capable of learning, but also of learning to learn.[10] In other words, learning organisations not only have the capacity to become competent, but also to remain so. Because they can learn they can adapt their organisational behaviour, and in turn they can find the best way of attuning to a constantly changing environment and do this on an ongoing basis.

Collective learning process

The learning organisation also relates to a collective learning process and not only an individual one. Organisational behaviour can only be described as learning behaviour if individual behavioural changes affect the behaviour of other individuals.[11] Because there is a collective learning process, the collective capability of organisations and units within them will increase. A group of people or a division go through a process of change that has the effect of enhancing their capacity to change in the future. The ability of an organisation to learn has to do a lot with the organisational culture. The capacity to learn in an organisation is a shared opinion about the way in which one integrates experiences in order to find insights and skills useful for the future.[12]

How can we change an organisation into a learning organisation? What characteristics must an organisation possess to set a collective learning process in motion? Given that a collective learning process is involved, to answer this question we must examine the various aspects that determine how organisations function. The most important elements are[13]:

- *Strategy.* Continuous strategic development, with the organisation's mission at the forefront and the following focal points:
  - Attention to the short and the long term
  - Attention to both rational as well as intuitive behaviour
  - Attention to both active as well as proactive behaviour
  - Looking at all angles
- *Structure.* The structure should be constructed along organisational networks which have the following characteristics:
  - Loosely connected units and teams based around product-market combinations
  - Decentralisation
  - A mix of thinkers (staff) and doers (line)
  - Coordination by consultation
- *Culture.* There should be a task culture with the following characteristics:
  - Flexible
  - Problem-oriented
  - Creative

Twelve innovations that have shaped modern management

1. Scientific management (time and motion studies)
2. Cost accounting and variance analysis
3. The commercial research laboratory (the industrialisation of science)
4. ROI analysis and capital budgeting
5. Brand management
6. Large-scale project management
7. Divisionalisation
8. Leadership development
9. Industry consortia (multi-company collaborative structures)
10. Radical decentralisation (self-organisation)
11. Formalised strategic analysis
12. Employee-driven problem solving

Source: *Harvard Business Review*, February 2006

- *Systems.* The systems should have a supportive function and include the following:
  – Information to reflect upon
  – Information on which to act
  – Comprehensive information

How the organisation should be organised depends on the complexity of the environment. Only by including the environment in all its diversity can the learning ability of an organisation be effective. Learning organisations do not regard the contradictions that develop within the organisation as threats, but as a challenge to advance collectively.

To this point we have examined the topic of the learning organisation at the organisational level (strategy, structure, culture, and systems). What we will now consider is how can the learning ability of the organisation can be enhanced by a manager working concretely with his or her staff members. Peter Senge has drawn up five principles(Figure 10.7)

Peter Senge's principles

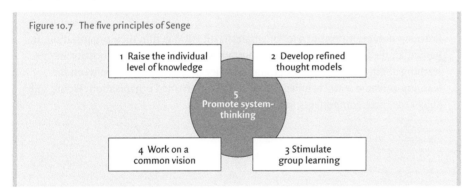

Figure 10.7 The five principles of Senge

1. *Raise the individual level of knowledge.* Staff members should be given the opportunity to experiment and to explore things. Managers should encourage this behaviour as much as possible and let it come from the staff members themselves. Staff members should have the feeling that they are expert in certain areas and be able to develop their expertise on an ongoing basis.
2. *Develop refined thought models.* Staff members should be encouraged to refine their thought patterns and work methods and thus execute their tasks more efficiently and effectively and contextualise them better.
3. *Stimulate group learning.* Learning in teams is more important than individual learning. Managers should emphasise this. The learning ability of organisations is particularly enhanced by group learning.
4. *Work on a common view.* Managers need to work on developing common norms and values, methods and thought models to serve as the basis for taking action, tackling problems, making use of opportunities and so on.

The most innovative companies

Getting inside the minds of customers is a crucial part of those 'aha!' moments that lead to innovation. With ethnographers and designers increasingly helping companies, true insight remains elusive: one quarter of our respondents still describe customer awareness as an obstacle to innovation.

While Apple and Google reign worldwide, local companies are often preferred in some regions.

Source: *Business Week*, April 2006

Asia-Pacific		Europe		North America	
1 Apple	9 Nokia	1 Apple	9 GE	1 Apple	9 IBM
2 Google	10 Infosys	2 Google	10 eBay	2 Google	10 Dell
3 3M	11 Virgin	3 Nokia	11 IKEA	3 P&G	11 Wal-Mart
4 Samsung	12 P&G	4 Microsoft	12 RyanAir	4 3M	12 IDEO
5 Microsoft	13 Dell	5 3M	13 Sony	5 Toyota	13 Target
6 IBM	14 Sony	6 Toyota	14 Intel	6 GE	14 Samsung
7 GE	15 Intel	7 Virgin	15 Porsche	7 Starbucks	15 Southwest
8 Toyota		8 BMW		8 Microsoft	

Source: *BusinessWeek*, April 24, 2006

5 *Promote systems thinking.* Managers should encourage staff members to consider the effects of their actions on other activities within the organisation, viewing their own activities as a link in a larger whole. Cause and effect relationships should inform the way tasks are executed.

HRM

Learning organisations put a lot of emphasis on HRM within their organisation. In particular, the training policy is an important way of increasing the organisation's learning ability. HRM (including training policy) forms the bridge between the learning-oriented staff member and the learning-oriented organisation. Figure 10.8 shows the three components in diagrammatic form.

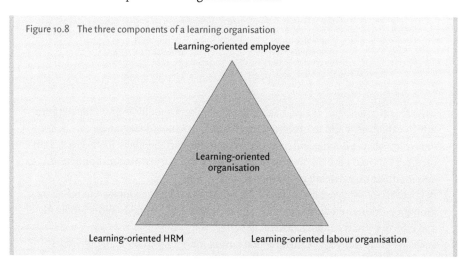

Figure 10.8   The three components of a learning organisation

Learning-oriented employee

Learning-oriented organisation

Learning-oriented HRM   Learning-oriented labour organisation

HRM should address learning in the fullest sense of the word. Learning is not only accumulating knowledge: it is more to do with personal development and that of other staff members. Classroom-style learning is only one aspect of learning. Research shows that adults learn particularly by performing many different kinds of functions during their careers, particularly when some of these connect to each other and constitute additional learning. Figure 10.9 shows various forms of learning.

It is important that organisations acknowledge these different forms of learning and give them a place within HRM.[14]

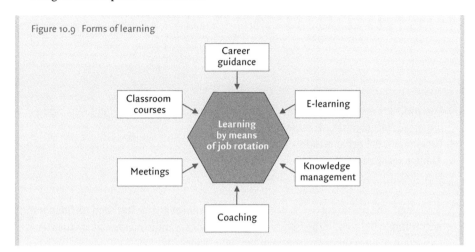

Figure 10.9 Forms of learning

10.4.5   Empowerment

The notion of empowerment is a current trend within the field of organisation and management. The guru in this field is James Belasco. His book *Teaching the Elephant to Dance: Empowering Change in your Organisation* is considered to be the quintessential text on the subject of processes of change. According to Belasco, organisations (especially large ones) are like elephants: acquired habits are hard to unlearn. Their behaviour is conditioned. Moreover, this behaviour is passed on from one generation to the next. Organisations are sometimes also victims of their own behaviour, particularly successful ones that find it hard to put their past behind them. In his book, Belasco has tried to formulate an answer to the question 'How do you teach an elephant to dance?' According to Belasco, the critical factor in processes of change is the organisational culture. As such, he also suggests which tools to use to change acquired habits into desired behaviour.

Rather than viewing change in organisations as a once-only event, he sees it as a process that can be pursued on the basis of following a model. Figure 10.10 shows the steps of the model diagrammatically.

Empowerment

Behaviour

Step 1:   preparation
When preparing for the process of change, two important issues must be considered from the outset: the urgency for it and the obstacles that may appear.
Everybody must be fired up to change. Top management plays an important role in this.
The obstacles lie in the field of behaviour: expectations that are too high, laxness, making mistakes, and so on.

Step 2:   designing the future
The organisation and its behaviour must change on an ongoing basis to survive.
The organisation as a whole should be constantly engaged in designing that future.

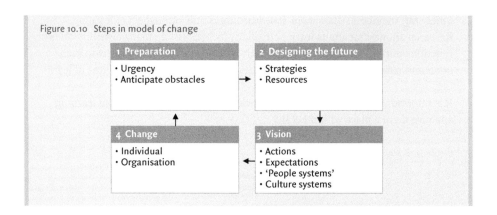

Figure 10.10 Steps in model of change

Two tools are available to it: strategy and the resources that can be deployed. Some important facets of the strategy are:
- Basing it on the organisation's strengths
- Aiming at core activities
- Not aiming at an extensive time horizon

In general, the resources at the organisation's disposal are its staff and its finances. According to Belasco, if the organisation really does want to change, it is crucially important to have the right people in the right places.

Step 3:   vision
During this step, the general strategy is formulated in terms of a vision that should give clarity about the way business is done in the organisation. It is vision that makes the difference between quickly scored short-term successes and the very long-term consequences of the change. A clearly formulated vision gives staff members the strength to change and the company the strength to retain staff members and keep them operational for years.[15] It is vision that finally gets the conditioned elephant dancing. Top management has an important directive role to play during this phase as well as an example to set.

Step 4:   change
During the actual process of change, the involvement of every staff member is important. If the latter fails to occur, the organisation runs the risk of the process of change becoming bogged down. The tools to bring about actual change and to keep it that way are putting 'agents for change' in key positions lower in the organisation and establishing a tangibly achievement-oriented culture. The vision of the agents for change and that of top management should not only be tightly linked but should also provide an univocal and clear-cut answer to 'what we will do and how we will do it'; it must be totally directed towards the daily tasks performed by staff
Achievement culture   members and towards their everyday realities.[16] Creating an achievement culture will cause the various activities of the organisation to mesh and to be measurable. However, it must be customer-oriented, both with regard to internal as well as external customers.

In practice, empowerment means placing responsibility, competencies and decision-making as low as possible within the organisation. Because staff members will
Self-operating teams   be working in self-operating teams and will themselves be responsible for the results there will be a high rate of change. Staff members will have a high rate of involvement in their results and will be prepared to work in a more customer-oriented way.

According to Belasco, such an approach to work has become necessary because the environment within which organisations operate demand it: a fiercely competitive climate and rapidly changing markets. In such an environment, organisational units must be flexible and able to manoeuvre quickly. Synonyms for empowerment are self-management, self-operation and entrepreneurship. Practice shows that applying the concept of empowerment increases the results of self-operating teams more than would have been the case with traditional organisational forms.

Self-management

10.4.6 Successful organisational change

The past years have witnessed an overwhelming degree of change in organisations. However, changes can be expected to take place even more rapidly and be even more dramatic in nature. Forces within the external environment will only increase, and organisations will have to make greater cost savings, develop more new products and markets, deliver higher quality, and increase productivity even more. The pace will also increase.

Succesful organisational change

To date, the effect of major processes of change has been that many organisations have become more competitive, have adapted appropriately and have anticipated new market opportunities. However, the changes have produced disappointing results in too many situations.

Harvard professor John Kotter has done extensive research on change processes in organisations. He has delineated eight causes of failure to implement organisational change. (See Figure 10.11.)

John Kotter

Figure 10.11 Mistakes made during processes of change

Common mistakes	Consequences
• Allowing a feeling of self-satisfaction • Failure to form a powerful coalition of leaders to guide the processes of change • Underestimating the power of vision • Insufficiently communicating the vision • Allowing all kinds of obstacles to block that vision • Failure to achieve short-term results • Insufficient anchoring of changes in the company culture	• Insufficient implementation of new strategies • Takeovers do not deliver the expected results • The re-engineering process takes too long and is too expensive • Downsizing does not deliver the expected cost advantages • Quality improvement programs do not deliver the expected results

Source: J. Kotter, *Leading Chance*, Harvard Business School Press, 1997

Making one or more of the abovementioned mistakes can be exceptionally costly and can have major consequences for the organisation. It may not succeed in putting new products or services on the market in time and against competitive prices and / or quality. This can lead to shrinking budgets, lay-offs and major uncertainty and stress for the remaining employees. However, many of the abovementioned mistakes can be avoided. Kotter has defined eight phases for successful implementation of major change:

1 *Explain that the situation is an urgent one.* Without a doomsday feeling it will be hard to mobilise management sufficiently to commit itself to putting enough time and energy into a process of change.

2 *Create a coalition of managers.* It is essential to create a team of managers who have enough power to direct the process of change. Those managers must work closely together. In no organisation can the general director successfully manage processes of change on his or her own.

3 *Develop a view and strategy.* See to it that you develop a vision that gives direction to

the process of change. There must also be strategies aimed at implementing this vision.

4 *Broadcast the 'vision of change'.*   It is highly important to continually broadcast the vision and for the coalition of managers to demonstrate exemplary behaviour.

5 *Ensure that the empowerment is broadly based.*   It is important that risks be taken and that there be room for non-conventional ideas, activities and actions. Those structures and systems that could undermine visions of change should be changed.

6 *Generate the short-term result.*   It is important to plan to achieve visible improvements in the organisation's results. Those individuals who have contributed to these results must be recognised and rewarded for them.

7 *Consolidate the results and generate more changes.*   It is essential that the results already achieved be consolidated and that the process of change be enhanced via new projects, themes and individuals who can guide the changes. Acquire, develop and encourage new staff who are capable of implementing change.

8 *Ensure that new approaches are anchored within the organisation's culture.*   Better results are achieved with customer and productivity-oriented behaviour as well as with better leadership and effective management. It is important to highlight the relationship between new behaviour and organisational success.

Managerial attitudes towards innovation

Many organisations find it hard to deal with innovation. The level of commitment that managers demonstrate may differ significantly. The illustration shows the level of commitment among different groups of managers.

Managerial attitudes to innovation

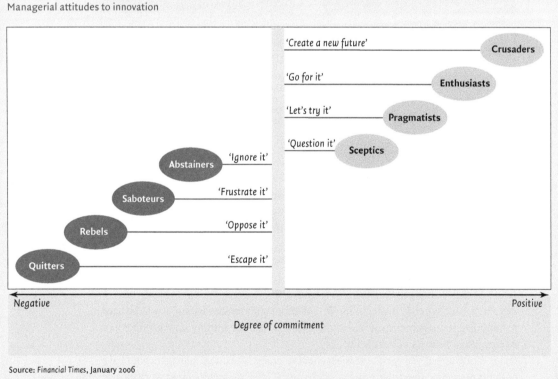

Source: Financial Times, January 2006

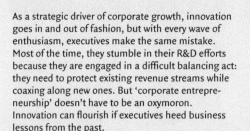

The lessons of innovation

As a strategic driver of corporate growth, innovation goes in and out of fashion, but with every wave of enthusiasm, executives make the same mistake. Most of the time, they stumble in their R&D efforts because they are engaged in a difficult balancing act: they need to protect existing revenue streams while coaxing along new ones. But 'corporate entrepreneurship' doesn't have to be an oxymoron. Innovation can flourish if executives heed business lessons from the past.

Strategy lessons
- Not every innovative idea has to be a blockbuster. Sufficient numbers of small or incremental innovations can lead to big profits.
- Don't just focus on new product development: transformative ideas can come from anywhere: for instance, from the marketing, production, finance or distribution departments.
- Successful innovators use an 'innovation pyramid', with several big bets at the top that most of the investment goes in to, a portfolio of promising midrange ideas at the test stage and a broad base of early stage ideas or incremental innovations.

Process lessons
- Tight controls strangle innovation. The planning, budgeting, and reviews that existing businesses are subject to will squeeze the life out of innovative effort.
- Companies should expect deviations from the plan. If employees are rewarded simply for doing what they committed to doing rather than acting as circumstances would suggest, their employers will stifle and drive out innovation.

Structural lessons
- A loosening of formal control should be accompanied by a tightening of the interpersonal connections between what is being done in terms of innovation and the rest of the business.
- 'Game-changing' innovations often cut across established channels or combine elements of existing capacity in new ways.
- If companies create two classes of corporate citizens and supply the innovators with more perks, privileges, and prestige, those in the existing business will make every effort to crush the innovation.

Skills Lessons
- Even the most technical of innovations requires strong leaders with great relationship and communication skills.
- Members of successful innovation teams stick together through the development of an idea, even if the company's approach to career timing requires faster job rotation.
- Because innovations need connectors – people who know how to find partners in the mainstream business or outside world – they flourish in cultures that encourage collaboration.

Source: *Harvard Business Review*, November 2006

Reitsma and Van Empel mention four kinds of approach to change in their book *Roads to change* (2004), namely:

1 *The direct approach.* With this approach, the content is fixed beforehand and there is a lot of direction based on exercising power. The emphasis here lies on planning and progress control.

2 *The tell and sell approach.* This approach is concerned with making the change attractive and selling it. Suggestions are appreciated, though not always accepted. Informal avenues are explored.

3 *The negotiating approach.* With this approach, the most suitable changes within certain frameworks are sought. Key figures are actively involved. The nature of the change is not predetermined.

4 *The developing approach.* This approach is concerned with management of the process and to a lesser degree, the content. Change comes from within. This approach is directed towards reinforcing competencies (skills, knowledge and attitudes).

The direct approach

The tell and sell approach

The negotiating approach

The developing approach

The success of a certain approach depends largely upon the purpose aimed for and the context in which the changes take place. It also depends to a large extent on the culture of the organisation and on the personal preferences of the agents of change and their competencies.

The authors developed a so-called key map for change processes. This map offers an orientation point to those involved in processes of change. (See Figure 10.12.)

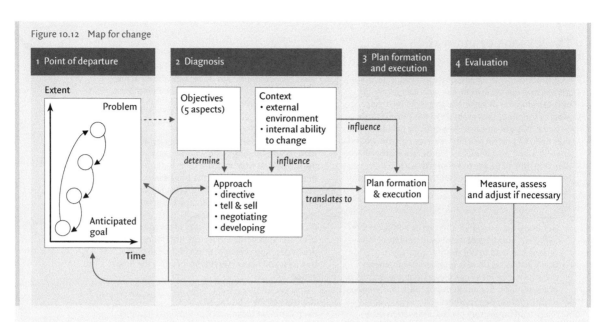

Figure 10.12 Map for change

| 1 Point of departure | 2 Diagnosis | 3 Plan formation and execution | 4 Evaluation |

Extent

Problem

Anticipated goal

Time

Objectives (5 aspects)

Context
• external environment
• internal ability to change

determine

influence

influence

Approach
• directive
• tell & sell
• negotiating
• developing

translates to

Plan formation & execution

Measure, assess and adjust if necessary

Source: Reitsma en Van Empel, *Wegen naar verandering*

The initial move is recognising the problem or delineating a task (e.g., integrating two organisations via a merger). It is essential to formulate a problem or set a task in such a way that a goal arises from it. If this can only be done with difficulty, it is advisable to do a so-called problem investigation.

It is advisable to describe the situation at the beginning of a process of change, including the view, mission, and core values of an organisation.

The second phase is a diagnosis that includes the purpose, the context, and the approach. It is advisable to stipulate the relationship between these three aspects. The purpose and the context may, for example, greatly influence the approach that one chooses.

During the third phase, a plan of approach is drawn up that aims towards systems or structures (hard factors) as well as people and culture (soft factors). Execution is also part of this phase and various instruments (tools / intervention) are deployed.

The last phase is the evaluation phase. Now is the time to consider whether the goal has been reached and whether anything needs to be adjusted. Sometimes this can lead to the choice of a new approach towards reaching the goal and going through the entire process again.

10.5 Organisational consultancy

Organisational consultancy

An organisational consultant often guides processes of change. The organisation in question (the client) will ask for specialist help (the consultant) with respect to certain aspects of the organisation. Organisational consultancy is the providing of independent and professional advice on determining and resolving organisational issues, and if necessary, assistance with implementing proposed solutions.[17] The purpose of consultancy is to improve the efficiency and / or the effectiveness of the organisation.

The role of management and leadership in changes

The successful implementing of changes in organisations is for 70% to 90% the result of good leadership, and for 10% to 30% the result of good management. In his book *Leading Change*, Kotter indicates the difference between management and leadership. The main tasks of management are:
- Planning and budgeting
- Organising and deploying of people
- Control and problem-solving

In particular, management has to take care that it achieves the anticipated short-term results.

The main leadership tasks are:
- The development of a vision of the future
- The communication of the vision
- The motivation and inspiring of people

According to Kotter, organisational change is largely a matter for leadership.
The following figure links quality of management and leadership and their influence on how change is implemented. It demonstrates that processes of change are only successful when both competent managers as well as leaders are involved, or leaders who have leadership as well as management skills.

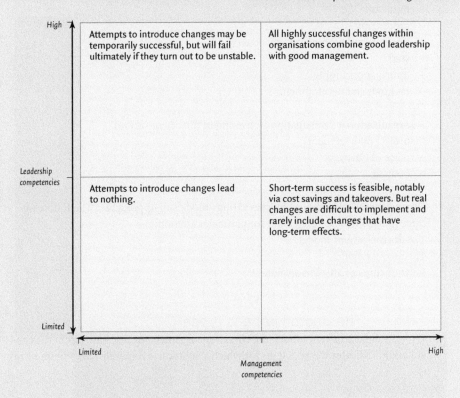

Attempts to introduce changes may be temporarily successful, but will fail ultimately if they turn out to be unstable.	All highly successful changes within organisations combine good leadership with good management.
Attempts to introduce changes lead to nothing.	Short-term success is feasible, notably via cost savings and takeovers. But real changes are difficult to implement and rarely include changes that have long-term effects.

Axes: Leadership competencies (High / Limited) on vertical; Management competencies (Limited / High) on horizontal.

Source: J. Kotter, *Leading Change*, Harvard Business School Press

In the Netherlands, most consultants are members of the Order of Organisational Experts and Advisors (OOA) or the Council of Organisational consultancies (ROA). The main aim of the OOA is to promote organisational skills in both a professional and a societal sense. The guarding of professional ethics and professional quality fall under this aim.[18] The aim of the ROA is twofold:

OOA

ROA

1 Protection of the collective interests of the affiliated agencies
2 Promotion of optimal conditions for the execution of consultancy assignments. This is done by, for example, keeping clients informed, employing admission norms, and monitoring of compliance with the rules of behaviour.[19]

The OOA and the ROA have a single system of handling complaints: the Committee of Supervision. If agreement cannot be reached by this committee than an appeal to the Council of Appeal is possible.

The areas of organisational consultancy are[20]:

a *General management issues*
- strategy and policy determination
- structure of the organisation
- organisational culture
- leadership styles
- public relations.

b *Functional management issues*
- sales
- purchase
- production
- finances and administration
- staff
- information supply
- research and development.

c *Exceptional issues*
- organisational investigation (screening of the organisation)
- project management
- place of business
- housing

Organisational consultancy follows various models or approaches. The following three models will be singled out for particular attention:

1 The doctor-patient model
2 The process model
3 Relationships of an advisory nature

10.5.1 The doctor-patient model

Doctor-patient model

With the doctor-patient model, the client (the organisation that has sought the consultation) indicates the problems for which a solution is required. (See Figure 10.13).

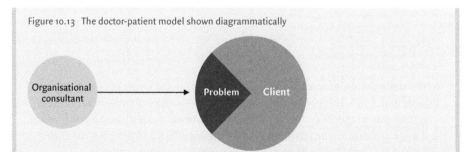

Figure 10.13 The doctor-patient model shown diagrammatically

The problem that has been presented to the consultant is examined in isolation from the existing organisation. After examining the problem, the consultant draws up a report containing a number of recommendations for resolving the problem. During the course of the consultative process, the consultant is mainly in contact with his direct client (usually senior management). The organisation's other members are involved in the process only to a limited extent.

This model gives rise to a number of issues:
- Has the client clearly defined the problem? Is the real problem perhaps elsewhere?
- Can the problem be seen separate from the rest of the organisation?
- Because the involvement of staff members is minimal, the proposed solutions may encounter some resistance.

10.5.2 The process model

The process model assumes that a problem cannot be viewed in isolation. (See Figure 10.14).

Process model

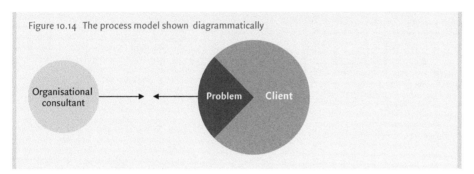

Figure 10.14 The process model shown diagrammatically

The staff members concerned also need to be involved in the consultancy process. In this model, the client presents the adviser with a problem of an indeterminate nature. The adviser, together with the staff members involved, then places the problem in its organisational context and a solution is sought jointly. This model is less structured, and this is its particular weakness. The adviser plays more of a supportive role, coaching the organisation to enhance its problem-solving capacity.

The factors that influence a choice between the two models are as follows[21]:
- The prestige enjoyed by top management
- The leadership style within the organisation
- The urgency of the problem
- The extent of the change
- Control systems within the organisation

A point that needs to be mentioned in relation to the two models is that the advisor's recommendations may focus on different areas. In one situation there may be a focus on content; in another, on guiding the process of change. Practice shows that the advisor fills the following three roles.

Advisor

1 *The role of expert.* The emphasis will lie on content in particular, with the adviser largely bringing his / her knowledge and experience to bear on a particular issue.

The role of expert

2 *The social-emotionally oriented role.* The adviser is mainly concerned with the human aspects of processes of change, showing how the organisation's members can take a different view of organisational problems and thereby enhance their capacity to deal with problems themselves. The adviser will act as a guide.

Social-emotionally oriented role

3 *The procedural oriented role.* The adviser puts the emphasis on designing guidelines and procedures to implement certain changes more efficiently and effectively.

Procedural oriented role.

Environmental Expert connects environmental advisors to companies

Environmental Expert connects over 400,000 environmental industry professionals from around the globe to over 10,000 companies, providing the products, services and information they need to do their job successfully.

Environmental Expert is more than just an online marketplace! Unlike other sites, the Environmental

Expert portal contains an unmatched wealth of industry-related information and resources, such as publications, events, articles, job postings, press releases & news, thus ensuring that professionals use Environmental Expert as a professional tool and keep coming back to stay in touch with what's happening in the industry.

10.5.3 Relationships of an advisory nature

Advisory relationships may take different forms. Two have already been mentioned: the doctor-patient model and the process model. How can such relationships be made more structured? When an advisory relationship is entered into, two factors largely determine the type of advisory relationship[22]: the expertise of the client and the kind of question about which advice is being sought. The expertise of the client may extend from not much to a lot, and the kind of advice sought from instrumental to strategic. Plotting these two factors against each other will produce a model for characterising advisory relationships. (Figure 10.15.)

Advisory relationship

Figure 10.15   Characterisation of relationships of an advisory nature

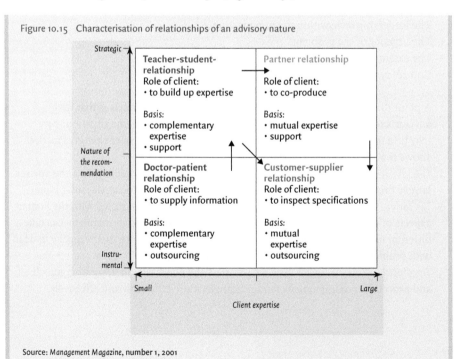

Source: *Management Magazine, number 1, 2001*

In conclusion, the remark should be made that during the life cycle of one particular consultative assignment, the advisory relationship can pass through all stages: for example, from a doctor-patient model to a teacher-student relationship to a partner relationship and finally to a customer-supplier relationship.

Four Scenario's for Google's future

The company that Sergey Brin and Larry Page founded a mere eight years ago is one of the new century's most cunning enterprises. Sales are still jumping, profits tripled to a projected $1.6 billion in 2006 and Wall Street answered with an unprecedented vote of confidence. That's a huge bet on future growth that seemed unthinkable during the post-bubble period. But in Google's case, the exuberance is well-founded. That's because Google has cornered online advertising: they have made it precision-targeted and dirt cheap.

Americans now spend more than 30% of their media-consuming time surfing the Web. When the ad dollars catch up to this trend, a mountain of cash awaits, and Google is positioned to scoop it up. Google is on track to spend more than $500 million on research and development in 2006, hires among the smartest people (mainly from Microsoft), and in 2005 it launched more free products in beta than in any previous year.

Which raises the most widely debated question in business: what kind of company will Google become in the coming decades? We asked scientists, consultants, former Google employees and tech visionaries. Here are four different scenarios for the company. Each details an extreme, but plausible, outcome.

Scenario 1 (circa 2025): Google is the media
Google TV, Google Mobile, and the rise of E-Paper create the perfect storm

Some say it began with the launch of Google News, the company's first media aggregation site. Others point to Google Book Search, completed in 2007. But those were just trial runs. Google's first media step was 2008, when it bought an obscure cable network and transformed it into Google TV. Since viewers had to enter their Google IDs, the company had already compiled a rich history of their searching and surfing habits. Google TV was an instant hit; advertisers, copyright owners, and cable customers all clamoured for more. Google Mobile followed in 2009, delivering the same service to cell phones for free. Then the dam broke in 2011, when E-ink and Siemens began mass-manufacturing electronic paper. By 2018 the cost of E-paper had fallen close to that of the real thing, and Google began delivering all forms of media wirelessly to our E-papers, sheets hung on living room walls, and thin phones. A new generation of content creators was growing up – one that did not see why a story should be printed in The New York Times or a movie distributed by Paramount if it was going to end up on Google anyway. So the company offered a guarantee to all writers and artists that their works would not be edited in any way by Google. In 2020, Google-based writers won the Pulitzer Prize, Google-sponsored bands won the Grammys, and a Google-director won the Oscar for the best picture.

Scenario 2 (circa 2015): Google is the Internet
Free Wi-Fi, a faster version of the Web, the G-browser, and the cube transform the technology landscape and our language.

During the past decade, especially among the generation born after the millennium, the word 'Google' has become interchangeable with 'Internet', 'computer', and 'phone call'. For most daily purposes, Google has become the technology platform, the communications network, and the Internet itself. The GoogleNet, which blankets every major urban centre in the world with free wireless access, cell phone service, and targeted local advertising (starting with the successful San Francisco experiment of 2007), is merely the most visible top of the iceberg. The GoogleNet became far faster and easier to use than the slowpoke Web itself. That's why G-browser, launched in 2008, took off: it had priority access to Google's version of the Web, unlike Microsoft's Internet Explorer. But the real genius of G-browser was to make the operating system irrelevant; since Google adopted the Linux-based OpenOffice software and bundled it. And 2010's Google Cube – a tiny server that was distributed as freely and as widely as those CDs that AOL used to give away – became the one indispensable item in every home, running the TV, stereo, thermostat, and, for less adventurous cooks, even the oven: have you googled dinner yet?

Scenario 3 (circa 2020): Google is dead
The once-mighty search engine falls prey to privacy intrusion, optimisers and Microsoft.

It was 15 years ago, when Google was in its ascendancy, that the seeds of its decline were sown. Not only did the company's deal with AOL introduce unpopular graphics-heavy banner ads onto what had formerly been a Spartan search site, but that was the year that search engine optimisers, or SEOs, became a nuisance. Optimisers could, for a fee, tweak how important your website appeared to Google's PageRank engine by, say, hijacking the homepage of a major university and adding a link to your site. When the quality of its searches slipped, so did Google's advertising business. The market for online ads turned out to be far softer than anyone – except Microsoft CEO Steve Ballmer – had predicted. Ballmer's smartest move – in 2008 – was to buy a company called Snap.com. On Google, an advertiser paid anytime a user clicked on its ad. With Snap, the advertiser paid only if the user did something useful after clicking, like buying a product or filling out a survey.

Google soldiered on. The strategy might have worked, if not for a psychotic former employee who hacked the company intranet and began stalking women in the San Francisco Bay Area using information about their habits gleaned from their Google IDs. After the stalker was convicted in 2017, his victims sued Google. A hearing in front of the Congress and Justice Department opened twin-track investigations: one into antitrust violations, the other into older allegations of click fraud (in which competitors create programs to click on ads repeatedly and cost an advertiser more money).

Overnight, Google's image had become tarnished. Microsoft, itself the reviled monopolist before Google's ascendancy, was now viewed as the more trustworthy company. MSN came to be seen as the better search engine, and Microsoft ads as the better bet for getting a message across.

In 2020, the search engine firm was acquired by Microsoft. Since most of the company's assets had already been auctioned off, many believe its Redmond rival was motivated by sheer historical schadenfreude.

Scenario 4 (circa 2105): Google is God
Human consciousness gets stored, upgraded, and net-worked.

In the last years of the 21st century, humanity finally grasped the importance of They-Who-Were-Google. Yet as early as 2005, Their destiny was clear to any semi-hyperintelligent being. Technologist suggested that Strong AI (an intelligent program capable of upgrading its own code) would emerge from Google-like data mining rather than a robotics lab. By 2020, They-Who-Were-Google had digitised and indexed every book, article, movie, TV show, and song ever created. By 2060, They could tell you the IP address and GPS location of every wireless smart chip. Their psychographic profiles of users' search needs bore little resemblance to the primitive cookies from which they descended. They had built a complete database of human desire, accurate in any given moment.

In 2072 StrongBot was born –humanity's first self-improving String AI software. Under StrongBot's guidance, death and want have been all but eradicated. Everyone has access to all knowledge. Human consciousness has been stored, upgraded, and networked. Bodies that wear out can be replaced. They-Who-Were-Google are not longer alone. Now we are all Google.

Source: Business 2.0, January / February 2006

10.6 Organisational research

Organisational research

Organisations change constantly. As has been stated before, organisations are living systems in a changing environment. To be able to evaluate whether changes are necessary to an organisation, organisational research is necessary. By organisational research we mean a systematic investigation and evaluation of any part of the organisation. Such research should not have a once-only character, but must take place periodically. Attuning to the internal and external environment is, after all, an ongoing developmental process.

The goals of organisational research and the research subjects do not necessarily correspond to each other.[33] The goal may be to remain ahead of possible future problems (preventive research) or to resolve existing problems (curative research). The subject of the research may relate to part of an organisation (partial research) or to the whole organisation (integral research). If only part of the organisation is being investigated, it is important not to lose sight of the other parts.

Preventive research

Curative research

Partial research

Integral research

The goals of organisational research and the various kinds of research subjects are shown diagrammatically in Figure 10.16.

Dutch consultancies make use of various research methods for organisational research. These methods differ in terms of the number and kind of indicators and mathematic / statistical techniques taken into consideration. A combination of automated checklists, analysis schemes, planning schemes and interviews are deployed.

Figure 10.16 Different kinds of organisational research

		Research subject	
		Partial	Integral
Goal	Preventative	*Example* • management audit • social audit • marketing audit	*Example* Company diagnoses
	Curative	*Example* Most organisational research addresses problem situations such as: • work climate research • conflict resolution • information research	*Example* A few common types of organisational research such as: • survival probability research • integral investigation

Doing business in China

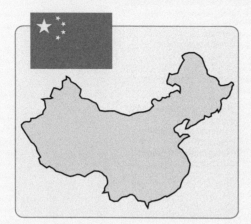

How Chinese citizens organise and process information

The Chinese are generally circumspect about outside sources of information. They usually process data through a subjective perspective, derived from experience – unless they have been educated at a Western university. Behaviour in conformity to Communist Party ideals is still required. There is still overt favouritism shown to members of the Communist Party.

What Chinese citizens accept as evidence

In general, truth is regarded as being subjective, and one's feelings, along with a modified belief in the Communist Party line, are primary sources of the truth. Facts are accepted by younger Chinese, particularly within the burgeoning entrepreneurial sector. However, they still take the other two resources into account and will not usually accept a proposal if it is in conflict with their personal feelings.

The basis of behaviour

China is still primarily a collectivistic culture dominated by the Communist Party. Value systems in the predominant culture – how right is distinguished from wrong, good from evil, and so on – are described under the next three headings.

The locus of decision-making

In a centrally controlled economy, responsibility rest with government planners, though individuals are held responsible for their decisions. Local decisions are made by the head of the collective, and members must behave accordingly. Collectives are insular, closed entities in which individual goals are subordinated to those of the collective. In the zones of free enterprise, businesses are experimenting with freedom from party rule but not from the collectivist way of thinking.

Sources of anxiety reduction

The family, school, work unit, and local community are the basic social structures that give stability to a person's life. There is a strong commitment to the extended family. The state, rather than religion, has traditionally dictated the standards of wisdom, morality, and the common good. Obedience to parents is integral to

a sense of security and stability. Maintaining harmony is vital.

Issues of equality / inequality

Relative to the general population (over 1 billion), the number of people who are powerful members of the Communist Party is small. There has always been some concern about inequality in a system in which equality is the purpose, but being a member of the party is the only avenue available for obtaining a position of authority. Free enterprise is purported to breed inequality and uncertainty, but there are rapidly increasing areas where it is allowed to flourish. Age is a source of inequality because old age is still revered. Woman are purported to be equal to men, though economic and social inequalities continue.

Ten examples of Chinese business practices

1 Punctuality is very important in China, and not only for business meetings but for social occasions as well. Lateness or a cancellation constitutes a serious affront.

2 Be sure to establish contacts in China before you invest in a trip. Your government's Department of Trade or Commerce can usually assist in arranging appointments with local Chinese business and government officials and can identify importers, buyers, agents, distributors, and joint venture partners.

3 Expect to make presentations to many different groups and at different levels. Unless you understand the significance of different colours in China, use black and white for your collateral materials.

4 Foreign executives have a reputation for impatience, and the Chinese will drag out negotiations well beyond your deadlines just to gain an advantage. They may try to renegotiate everything on the final day of your visit, and they may continue to try for a better deal even after the contract is signed.

5 Bring business cards with a translated printed (in Mandarin Chinese) on the reverse side. Never place a person's card in your wallet and then put it in your back pocket.

6 When entering a business meeting, the highest-ranking member of your group should lead the way.

7 Be patient, expect delays, show little emotion, and do not talk about your deadlines.

8 Good topics of conversation include Chinese sights, art, calligraphy, and inquiries about the health of the other's family. Generally, conversation during a meal focusses on the meal itself and is full of compliments for the cook.

9 Never take the last bit of food from a serving dish: this can signify that you are still hungry.

10 The Chinese are very sensitive to status and titles, so you should use official titles such as 'General', 'Committee Member', or 'Bureau Chief' when possible. Most people you meet should be addressed with a title and their name. If a person does not have a professional title (President, Engineer, Doctor), simply use 'Mr', 'Madam' or 'Miss', plus the person's name.

Source: *Kiss, Bow, or Shake Hands: How to Do Business in Sixty Countries*, by Terri Morrison, Wayne A. Conaway and George A. Borden, Adams Media, 2006

Summary

The organisation and its development are central to this chapter. The degree to which the set aims are reached is what we term the organisation's effectiveness. An organisation should be effective in four different areas: technical, economic, psychosocial and managerial.

Research into successful organisations has shown that there is a relationship between success and an organisation's cultural characteristics. We looked briefly at the following approaches or typologies which describe the organisational culture or aspects of it: group processes and organisational culture, Handy's typology, the typology of G. Sanders and B. Neuijen, and the professional culture typology. Organisational development was firstly described at the hand of two growth models: Scott's growth model and Greiner's growth model. If a change process is a once-only event and has fundamental changes as its result, it is termed a restructuring. The conditions necessary for success and its goals were examined. One speaks of a learning organisation if the organisation possesses the ability to change on an ongoing basis and collectively. According to Belasco, to be successful, processes of organisational change need to follow a model to be successful. We looked at the various steps of a model.

Processes of change are often under the guidance of an organisational consultant. We looked at three models: the doctor / patient model, the process model and the advisory relationship model. To be able to evaluate whether the organisation needs to implement change, organisational research is necessary.

Definitions

§ 10.2 Effectiveness — The degree to which the set aims are achieved.

Technical and economic effectiveness — The degree to which the resources of an organisation are effectively deployed. Efficient utilisation of resources is using the fewest possible means of production (input) to reach a certain output.

Psychosocial effectiveness — The degree to which the needs of the employees are recognised.

Social effectiveness — The degree to which the needs of external parties are recognised.

Managerial effectiveness — The degree to which the organisation can react to changing situations with flexibility and decisiveness.

§ 10.3 Organisational culture — A collection of opinions about work, each other, oneself, and the organisation.

Power distribution — The degree to which decision-making power is centralised or decentralised.

Role culture — The organisation is based on rules and procedures. Functions in the organisation determine the tone, not the people who carry out the tasks.

Power culture — The organisation revolves around a leading figure. The organisation is more or less an extension of that figure.

Person culture — The individual is important. The organisation exists to serve people, and the manager is on the same level as his / her staff.

Task culture — The organisation can be characterised in terms of its focus on tasks and its professionalism. It is made up of a network of loose and fixed task units, with each unit possessing a lot of independence and bearing responsibility for part of the overall operation.

§10.4 Organisational development — A process of change in which the staff and the organisation itself develop so that their performance improves.

§§10.4.1 Small organisation — An organisation which only has a limited number of functions, usually filled by the owner.

Complete departmental organisation — An organisation in which the functional departments have been fully set up.

Multidivisional organisation — An organisation that is divided into product-market combinations or geographical divisions at the level immediately below the top management level.

§§ 10.4.2 Crisis	Occurs when the organisation has a problem that cannot be resolved by gradual development. A significant change in management style will be required.
§§ 10.4.3 Restructuring	Significant and unique changes are made to the decision-making process and the way that tasks are divided. It is a one-off occurrence and often results in fundamental alterations to the way the organisation is run.
§§ 10.4.4 Learning organisation	Organisations which are not only able to learn, but also to learn to learn. They have the capacity to become competent and the potential to remain so.
§§ 10.4.5 Empowerment	Organisations can be compared to elephants: i.e. old habits die hard. Empowerment is the power an organisation has to change. It is a tool that can be deployed to change old habits into desired behaviour. Change is never a one-off incident, but a process that should be adopted on an ongoing basis.
§ 10.5 Organisational consultancy	The providing of independent and professional advice with lems, and the necessary support or assistance while introducing the proposed solutions.
§§ 10.5.1 The doctor-patient model	The client company identifies a problem that the consultant is asked to solve. The problem is isolated and investigated by the adviser who will eventually deliver a report with solutions. The organisation's staff are rarely included with this method.
§§ 10.5.2 The process model	Rather than isolating the problem, this model attempts to link it to other factors. In addition, those staff who are involved in the area under investigation are encouraged to be involved. The client initially comes up with a undefined problem. In cooperation with the relevant staff, the consultant places the problem inside the organisational context, with all parties working together towards a solution. The consultant plays more of a facilitating role during the process.
§ 10.6 Organisational research	A methodical investigation and evaluation of a part or all of an organisation.

Statements

Indicate whether the following statements are correct or incorrect, giving reasons for your choice.

1 The degree to which a company achieves the set aims is what is known as the company's economic efficiency.
2 Societal efficiency is the degree to which the needs of parties within the external environment are realised.
3 Achieving an organisational balance implies rewarding the external participants in such a way that they continue to want to remain part of the organisation.
4 The individual members of the organisation and their interests lie at the core of a bureaucratic culture, as does the power culture.
5 Organisational culture has a powerful effect on the organisation's results.
6 According to Greiner, as organisations develop, overcoming internal crises is more important than surviving changes within the external environment.
7 Change can be regarded as a restructuring if a once-off and usually fundamental change in decision-making powers and in the division of labour within the organisation takes place.
8 In a learning organisation, it is the learning experiences of the individual members of the organisation that are particularly important.
9 Organisational consultancy is the providing of independent and professional advice on organisational problems and the resolving thereof.
10 Curative integral research is organisational research that relates to incidental problems within a functional area.

Theory questions

1 a Which four areas of effectiveness and their corresponding criteria can be identified?
  b The various areas cannot be viewed separately from each other. Think of an example.
2 Indicate the danger of regarding a team solely as the sum of its individual parts.
3 What is the difference between organisational development and a restructuring?
4 Indicate why 'the learning organisation' must be an important cultural characteristic in the future.
5 Peter Senge has formulated five principles that a manager and his staff members can use to enhance learning ability. Give a short description of these five principles.

Practical assignment

Section 10.3 described the six dimensions of the company culture of G. Sanders and B. Neuijen. One can adopt a position in relation to any of the six dimensions and use it to obtain a useful view of the present culture.
1 Choose an organisation (it does not matter what sort: whether one from the business world, a government organisation, a non-profit organisation, a production company, a service provider etc).
2 Arrange an interview with a representative from the organisation. Prepare well for the interview. During your preparation consult sources such as the Internet, annual reports and newspaper articles. During the interview, discuss the six dimensions and indicate the position of the organisation in relation to each. During the interview, discuss the reasons for the choices made.

3 Present the findings to each other.
4 Discuss whether the findings have anything in common.

 For answers see www.marcusvandam.noordhoff.nl.

Outsourcing to India

Research carried out by the American company NASSCOM (The National Association of Software and Service Companies) and consulting firm McKinsey and Co indicates that outsourcing to India in 2010 of software and helpdesk services (of which Indian companies account for more than half of the global services) can produce a turnover of sixty billion dollars. By the end of this decade, the total world market for outsourcing is expected to amount to 110 billion dollars.
The current situation is that India provides 65 percent of offshore software development and 46 per-

cent in the area of software services worldwide. In total this provides a turnover of seventeen billion dollars and offers employment to well over 700 thousand people. To increase the turnover to 60 billion would require considerable investment in the infrastructure. This is because a minimum of ten to twelve 'knowledge cities' are requires to accommodate employees, offices and airports. These knowledge cities need to provide accommodation for at least 1.6 million employees and their families.

Source: Tweakers.net

Questions:
1 Could outsourcing increase the effectiveness of an organisation? Give reasons for your answer.
2 Describe three advantages and disadvantages to a company associated with the outsourcing of services abroad.
3 What challenges are faced by a company that has decided to perform a part of certain activities in India?
4 Indicate the differences between company culture in India and that in the Netherlands.

E-mail case study

To:	Isadora Palmela,
Cc:	
Bcc:	
Subject:	Cultural differences within banks in the European Union

Message:

Dear Isadora,

It's a pity we didn't see each other during college last week. I heard from your friends that you've been ill. Are you getting better now?

Our project group on Europe got together a week ago to divide tasks. Because you weren't there, we had to decide on your behalf what your tasks are, especially since this week promises to be a busy one for our project.

The idea is that we look for the cultural characteristics and differences that exist between the various sectors of the member countries of the European Union. It is certainly not the intention to involve all countries of the European Union; per sector, we may make a selection of three member countries. Our project group has chosen the sectors of small and medium-sized businesses, and the financial sector.

We have reserved the financial sector for you. The idea is that you choose three member countries and within these three countries look at what professional culture is dominant within the financial sector. You have to indicate on what basis you've reached your conclusions. You might like to pick out a country from three different zones: say, North, Middle, or South Europe. An Eastern European country is, of course, always a possibility.

Isadora, this isn't an easy assignment, but it's probably fun and certainly interesting! At the end of the week, we expect half a page per country.

Greetings,

Bernardo Alentejo.

Chapter 8

1 Schieman, C.J. (e.a.), *Management – Beheersing van bedrijfsprocessen*, EPN, Houten, 1997.

2 Johansson, H., McHugh, P., Pendlebury, A.J., Wheeler III, W., John Wiley & Sons, Chichester, 'Business Proces Re-engineering. Breakpoint Strategies for Market Dominance' in: *Management Selectuur*, No. 5, October 1993.

3 *Computerworld*: 12-1992.

4 Tideman, ir. B., *Prestatieverbetering door Business Process Design*, Lansa Publishing BV, 1993.

5 Gale, B.T., Buzell, R.D., in: *Planning Review*, March / April 1989.

6 *Bedrijfskunde*, 1, 1989.

7 Bij, J.D. de, 'Certificering en de structuur van kwaliteitssystemen', from: *Bedrijfskunde*, No. 2, 1990.

8 *www.aimingbetter.nl*

9 Bakker, C.G., Goor, A.R. van, Houten, J.W.M. van, *Logistiek / Goederenstroombesturing*, Stenfert Kroese, 1989.

10 *Rendement*, November 1992.

11 • *www.logicaomg.com*,
   • *www.modifiedcontent.com*,
   • *www.emerce.nl* and *www.aim-ned.nl*

12 *www.icsb.nl*

13 *Sales Management*, October 1999.

14 *www.icsb.nl*

15 *www.icsb.nl*

16 Heijnsdijk, J., *Besturen van het bedrijf*, Wolters-Noordhoff, Groningen, 1988.

17 Reddin, W.J., *Effectief MBO*, Samsom/NIVE, Alphen aan den Rijn, 1977.

18 Reddin, W.J., *Effectief MBO*, Samsom/NIVE, Alphen aan den Rijn, 1977.

19 Lap, Drs. H.H.M., *Resultaatgericht management*, Human Resources Management, 1988.

20 T&S, *Opleidingsadviezen en trainingen*, 's-Hertogenbosch.

21 T&S, *Opleidingsadviezen en trainingen*, 's-Hertogenbosch.

22 T&S, *Opleidingsadviezen en trainingen*, 's-Hertogenbosch.

23 Claes, P.F., Meerman, H.J.J.M., *Risk management, inleiding tot het risicobeheersproces*, Stenfert Kroese, Leiden, 1991.

24 Claes, P.F., Meerman, H.J.J.M., *Risk management, inleiding tot het risicobeheersproces*, Stenfert Kroese, Leiden, 1991.

25 Wissema, J.G., *Unit-management, het decentraliseren van ondernemerschap*, Van
   Gorcum/Stichting Management Studies, Assen, 1987.
26 Wissema, J.G., *Unit-management, het decentraliseren van ondernemerschap*, Van
   Gorcum/Stichting Management Studies, Assen, 1987.
27 Wissema, J.G., *Unit-management, het decentraliseren van ondernemerschap*, Van
   Gorcum/Stichting Management Studies, Assen, 1987.
28 Groot, B., in: *Harvard Holland Review*, nr. 14, Spring 1988.
29 Schieman, C.J., Huyen, RA and J.H., *Bedrijfsbestuur en -organisatie*, Stenfert Kroese,
   Leiden, 1981.

Chapter 9
1 Keuning, D., and Eppink, D.J., *Management & Organisatie, Theorie en Praktijk*, Stenfert
   Kroese, Houten, 1996.
2 Heijnsdijk, J., *Besturen van het bedrijf*, Wolters-Noordhoff, Groningen, 1988.
3 Keuning, D., *Organiseren en leiding geven*, Stenfert Kroese, Houten, 1996.
4 *Leidinggeven en organiseren*, 40, 1990, 2.
5 Wijk, J. van, *Bedrijfsorganisatie*, Thieme, Zutphen, 1989.
6 *Jaarverslag Coopers & Lybrand*, 1997.
7 *Rendement*, July-August 1993.

Chapter 10
1 Keuning, D., and Eppink, D.J., *Management & Organisatie*, Theorie en Praktijk,
   Stenfert Kroese, Houten, 1996.
2 Grumbkow, J. von (red.), *Cultuur in organisaties*, Van Gorcum, Assen / Maastricht and
   Open Universiteit, Heerlen, 1991.
3 Grumbkow, J. von (red.), *Cultuur in organisaties*, Van Gorcum, Assen / Maastricht and
   Open Universiteit, Heerlen, 1991.
4 Grumbkow, J. von (red.), *Cultuur in organisaties*, Van Gorcum, Assen / Maastricht and
   Open Universiteit, Heerlen, 1991.
5 Sanders, G., and Neuijen, B., *Bedrijfscultuur, diagnose en beïnvloeding*, Van Gorcum /
   Stichting Management Studies, 1992.
6 Grumbkow, J. von (red.), *Cultuur in organisaties*, Van Gorcum, Assen / Maastricht and
   Open Universiteit, Heerlen, 1991.
7 Wijk, J. van, *Bedrijfsorganisatie*, 1989, Thieme, Zutphen, 1989.
8 Nathans, J.M.C., 'Invoeren van veranderingen', in: *Personeelsbeleid*, 23 nr. 10, 1987.
9 Sopers, J.M.M., *Turnaround Management, het saneren van ondernemingen in moeilijkheden*,
   Stenfert Kroese, Leiden, 1992.
10 Swieringa, J, and Wierdsma, A.F.M., *Op weg naar een lerende organisatie*, Wolters-
   Noordhoff Management, Groningen, 2001.
11 Swieringa, J, and Wierdsma, A.F.M., *Op weg naar een lerende organisatie*, Wolters-
   Noordhoff Management, Groningen, 2001.
12 Grumbkow, J. von (red.), *Cultuur in organisaties*, Van Gorcum, Assen / Maastricht,
   Open Universiteit, Heerlen, 1991.
13 Swieringa, J., and Wierdsma, A.F.M., *Op weg naar een lerende organisatie*, Wolters-
   Noordhoff Management, Groningen, 2001.
14 Nick van Dam, Deloitte Consulting.
15 *Selectuur*, No. 6, December 1991.
16 Swieringa, J., and Wierdsma, A.F.M., *Op weg naar een lerende organisatie*, Wolters-
   Noordhoff Management, Groningen, 2001.
17 Twijnstra, A., and Keuning, D., *Organisatie Advieswerk*, Stenfert Kroese, Leiden, 1988.
18 Orde van Organisatiedeskundigen en -Adviseurs, Yearbook 1988–1989, VUGA,
   's-Gravenhage.

19 Swieringa, J., and Wierdsma, A.F.M., *Op weg naar een lerende organisatie*, Wolters-Noordhoff Management, Groningen, 2001.
20 Swieringa, J., and Wierdsma, A.F.M., *Op weg naar een lerende organisatie*, Wolters-Noordhoff Management, Groningen, 2001.
21 Ruijter, H. de, and Wiersema, J.H.D., 'Typering van adviesprocessen', in: J.J.J. van Dijck and J.A.P. van Hoof, *Organisaties in ontwikkeling*, NIVE-UPR, 's-Gravenhage, 1976.
22 *Management consultants Magazine*, nummer 1, 2001.
23 Kempen, P.M., *Bedrijfsdiagnose alias Management Audit*, Samsom, Alphen aan den Rijn, 1980.

Illustrations

Index

For Product Safety Concerns and Information please contact our EU representative GPSR@taylorandfrancis.com Taylor & Francis Verlag GmbH, Kaufingerstraße 24, 80331 München, Germany

T - #0111 - 230425 - C0 - 280/210/27 - PB - 9789001577049 - Gloss Lamination